DERBYSHIRE

FOUNDATION TRUST

MENTAL CAPACITY

Other available titles from Law Society Publishing:

Pensions and Family Breakdown (2nd edn)
David Davidson
978 1 85328 669 8

Trust Practitioner's Handbook (2nd edn)
Gill Steel
978 1 85328 648 3

Inheritance Act Claims
A Practical Guide
Tracey Angus, Anna Clarke, Paul Hewitt and Penelope Reed
978 1 85328 553 0

Lasting Powers of Attorney
Craig Ward
978 1 85328 503 5

Probate Practitioner's Handbook (5th edn)
General Editor: Lesley King
978 1 85328 934 7

Will Draftsman's Handbook (8th edn)
Robin Riddett
978 1 85328 826 5

All books from Law Society Publishing can be ordered from all good bookshops or direct (telephone 0870 850 1422, email **lawsociety@prolog.uk.com** or visit our online shop at **www.lawsociety.org.uk/bookshop**).

MENTAL CAPACITY

A Guide to the New Law

SECOND EDITION

Nicola Greaney, Fenella Morris and Beverley Taylor

The Law Society

ISBN 978–1–85328–679–7

First edition published 2005
This second edition published in 2008 by the Law Society
113 Chancery Lane, London WC2A 1PL

Typeset by J&L Composition Ltd, Filey, North Yorkshire

Printed by MPG Books Ltd, Bodmin, Cornwall

PEFC

PEFC/16-33-111
CATG-PEFC-052
www.pefc.org

The paper used for the text pages of this book is PEFC certified.
PEFC (the Programme for the Endorsement of Forest Certification schemes)
is an independent organisation promoting sustainable
management of the world's forests.

CONTENTS

Appendices   185

FOREWORD

The title of the revised second edition of *Mental Capacity: A Guide to the New Law* remains apt. The measures introduced in October 2007 are still new, and further provisions brought about by the Mental Health Act 2007 do not come into force until April 2009.

The guide has an important new section on the protective jurisdiction of the Court of Protection in respect of the deprivation of liberty of patients in hospitals and care homes. This safeguarding jurisdiction has now been given statutory footing to fill the existing 'Bournewood' Gap'. The authors look carefully at the relationship between the statutory regimes of the Mental Capacity Act 2005 and the Mental Health Act 1983 and anticipate that, following commencement of the provisions inserted by the Mental Health Act 2007, many of the difficulties they discuss will fall away.

The authors have taken the opportunity to include the final version of the Code of Practice, which was still in draft form in the first edition. The book is also substantially expanded through the useful inclusion of the Law Society's Practice Note and the Statutory Instrument governing Lasting Powers of Attorney, Enduring Powers of Attorney and the Public Guardian.

In short, this revised Guide is a comprehensive 'vade mecum' for practitioners in the field and the authors are to be congratulated on its production.

Sir Mark Potter
President of the Family Division and Head of Family Justice
July 2008

PREFACE

This has been and continues to be a period of rapid and continuous change in the law of capacity. The law is stated here as at 1 July 2008, although the changes anticipated into 2009 are also discussed.

Since the first edition of the book there have been a number of significant cases developing the law in this area, and they are all considered in this second edition.

The Appendix to the second edition includes the full text of the Mental Capacity Act 2005 as in force on 18 April 2008 and also shows the amendments made by the Mental Health Act 2007 which are expected to come into force in April 2009.

The Mental Capacity Act Code of Practice, which is proving important to the interpretation and implementation of the Act itself, and the Deprivation of Liberty Safeguards Code of Practice, which provides important guidance in particular on the definition of deprivation of liberty are also included.

Nicola Greaney, Fenella Morris, and Beverley Taylor
July 2008

ABBREVIATIONS

2007 Regulations	Lasting Powers of Attorney, Enduring Powers of Attorney and Public Guardian Regulations 2007
the Act	Mental Capacity Act 2005
ADR	alternative dispute resolution
ANH	artificial nutrition and hydration
CLS	Community Legal Service
the Code	Mental Capacity Act 2005 Code of Practice
CPR	Civil Procedure Rules 1998
ECHR	European Convention on Human Rights
EPA	Enduring Power of Attorney
EPAA 1985	Enduring Powers of Attorney Act 1985
FPR	Family Proceedings Rules 1991
HRA 1998	Human Rights Act 1998
IMCA	Independent Mental Capacity Advocate
IMCA General Regulations	Mental Capacity Act 2005 (Independent Mental Capacity Advocates) (General) Regulations 2006
LPA	Lasting Power of Attorney
MCA 2005	Mental Capacity Act 2005
MHA 1983	Mental Health Act 1983
MHA 2007	Mental Health Act 2007
OPG	Office of the Public Guardian
PAA 1971	Powers of Attorney Act 1971
PCT	Primary Care Trust
PD	Practice Direction
PVS	persistent vegetative state
the Rules	Court of Protection Rules
the Scottish Act	Adults with Incapacity (Scotland) Act 2000

TABLE OF CASES

TABLE OF STATUTES

TABLE OF STATUTORY INSTRUMENTS

TABLE OF EUROPEAN LEGISLATION

1 INTRODUCTION

1.1 BACKGROUND TO THE MENTAL CAPACITY ACT 2005

The Act is the culmination of a 15-year-long consultation process. In 1989 the Law Commission started a six-year consultation period on all aspects of mental incapacity. In 1995 it published its Report and Draft Bill *Mental Incapacity*[1] which set out detailed recommendations for the introduction of comprehensive legislation for making decisions on behalf of people who lack capacity. The Report recognised that:

> . . . in this area, the law as it now stands is unsystematic and full of glaring gaps. It does not rest on clear or modern foundations of principle. It has failed to keep up with social and demographic changes. It has also failed to keep up with developments in our understanding of the rights and needs of those with mental disability.[2]

The government responded in 1997 with a Green Paper, *Who Decides?*,[3] seeking views on the Commission's proposals for reform. The government published the Policy Statement *Making Decisions*[4] in 1999. *Making Decisions* confirmed the government's commitment to legislation on issues relating to mental incapacity and set out the areas intended to be covered in future legislation.

The government published a Draft Mental Incapacity Bill in June 2003. The Bill was subject to pre-legislative scrutiny by a Committee of both Houses.[5] The Committee concluded:

> On the whole, we endorse the principles and general direction of the draft Bill . . . We believe that there is a clear need for the Bill and our report, whilst critical, should be read accordingly . . . Those it is intended to help have waited long enough.

It made substantial recommendations for improving the Draft Bill. The government published its response in February 2004 which included a commitment to rename the bill the Mental Capacity Bill, to 'emphasise its focus on enablement'.[6]

The Mental Capacity Bill was published on 17 June 2004. In accordance with the Joint Committee's recommendations the Bill now included a set of key principles to frame the Bill (at 43–4), the removal of the power for deputies to refuse consent to life-sustaining treatment (at 184), clearer safeguards regarding advance decisions to refuse treatment (at 205–9), provisions on research (at 288–91) with strict safeguards, and additional reassurance regarding euthanasia (at 204).

The Act received Royal Assent on 7 April 2005 and finally came into force on 1 October 2007. The Act has since been amended by the Mental Health Act 2007; the relevant amendments are due to come into force in April 2009.

---

1   Law Com No. 231, 1995.
2   Ibid., p.1.
3   *Who Decides? Making Decisions on behalf of Mentally Incapacitated Adults*, Cm. 3903, 1997.
4   *Making Decisions*, Cm. 4465, 1999.
5   Report of the Joint Committee on the Draft Mental Incapacity Bill, vol.1 HL Paper 189-1, HC 1083-1.
6   Parliamentary Under-Secretary of State for Constitutional Affairs, Mr David Lammy MP. House of Commons Hansard Debate, 11 October 2004: col.22.

1.2   AIM AND PURPOSE OF THE ACT

Lord Filkin in a letter to the Joint Committee stated that the aim of the Bill was to:

> maximise the capacity of those who lack or may lack capacity to make certain decisions for themselves, protect vulnerable adults with mental incapacity issues from abuse and neglect, and, provide clarity to families, informal carers and professionals as to when they may act or make decisions themselves.[1]

In order to achieve this aim the Act provides a comprehensive statutory framework for assisting those lacking capacity to make decisions for themselves, wherever possible, and allows for decisions to be taken properly on their behalf and in their best interests when they lack capacity. It rests on well-established common law principles of 'best interests' and the presumption of capacity. The Act seeks to strike a delicate balance between respect for individual autonomy and the need to protect the vulnerable.[2]

The Act affects a large range of people. It is estimated that over 700,000 people in the UK currently suffer from dementia, and this is projected to rise to around 840,000 by 2010. Around 145,000 adults in England have severe and profound learning disabilities and at least 1.2 million have a mild to moderate disability. In Wales more than 12,000 people were registered as having a learning disability in 2001. It is estimated that at some point in their lives approximately 1 per cent of the UK population will suffer from schizophrenia, 1 per cent will be subject to manic depression and 5 per cent will have serious or clinical depression.[3] In addition, many people suffer serious brain injury. Many of these people are likely to lack capacity to make some or all decisions for themselves and decisions will have to be made for them.

The main purpose of the Act is stated to be to:

> clarify and reform obscure common law provisions which govern the ways in which people can and should deal with people who lack decision-making capacity, supplemented by new and reformed statutory schemes for advance decision making and court-based resolution of disputes or difficulties.[4]

The Act is in three parts. Part 1 sets out a number of key principles, contains provisions defining 'persons who lack capacity', sets out a statutory checklist to be used in ascertaining their best interests and establishes statutory protection for 'acts done in connection with the care or treatment' of persons who lack capacity. Part 1 also establishes a new statutory scheme for powers of attorney which can extend to personal welfare and health care matters and which survive the incapacity of the donor, known as 'lasting powers of attorney' (LPAs). Part 1 sets out the jurisdiction of the Court of Protection to make declarations, orders and directions in relation to persons who lack capacity, and provides that the court may also appoint substitute decision makers, 'deputies' for them. It also sets out rules about making an advance decision to refuse medical treatment and for participation in research, and sets up a new independent mental capacity advocacy (IMCA) service for particularly vulnerable people. It provides for Codes of Practice to give guidance about the legislation and creates a new offence of neglect or ill-treatment.

Part 2 of the Act deals with the setting up of the Court of Protection, establishes a new statutory official – the Public Guardian – and provides for Court of Protection Visitors.

Part 3 of the Act contains technical and consequential provisions.

The Mental Capacity Act Code of Practice ('the Code') is available from the Ministry of Justice's website (**www.justice.gov.uk/guidance/mca-code-of-practice. htm**) and is set out in **Appendix D** of this book. The Mental Capacity Act 2005: Deprivation of Liberty Safeguards – Codes of Practice to supplement the main Code is available on the Department of Health website (**www.dh.gov.uk**) and is set out at Appendix E.

---

1 Report of the Joint Committee on the Draft Mental Incapacity Bill, vol.1 HL Paper 189-1, HC 1083-1, at 34.
2 Ibid.
3 News Release, DCA 22 April 2004.
4 Draft Mental Capacity Bill Commentary and Explanatory Notes.

1.3   DECISIONS EXCLUDED FROM THE OPERATION OF THE ACT

The Act expressly does not govern 'family relationship decisions' (s.27(1)) taken on behalf of 'P' and questions about the voting rights of incapable persons (s.29) whether taken by the court, a deputy or an attorney under an LPA.

The excluded 'family relationship decisions' laid down by s.27(1) are:

(a) consent to marriage or civil partnership;
(b) consent to sexual relations;
(c) consent to divorce on the grounds of two years' separation;
(d) consent to dissolution of marriage on the grounds of two years' separation;
(e) consent to a child being placed for adoption;
(f) consent to the making of an adoption order;[1]
(g) discharging parental responsibilities in relation to matters not concerning the child's property; and
(h) giving consent under the Human Fertilisation and Embryology Act 1990.

The approach to the question of whether a person has capacity to marry was considered by the court in the case of *Sheffield City Council* v. *E and S* [2004] EWHC 2808 (Fam), [2005] Fam 326. Munby J held that the test was capacity to understand the nature of the marriage contract and not the implications of a particular marriage or the identity of a particular partner. Marriage lawfulness depended entirely on consent and, if a person lacked capacity, no one could consent on that person's behalf. Nor could the doctrine of necessity apply. Capacity to marry would necessarily involve capacity to consent to sexual intercourse. The test has been upheld by the Court of Appeal in *Westminster City Council* v. *C* [2008] EWCA Civ 198.

The approach to the question of whether a person has capacity to consent to sexual intercourse has been given close consideration in *X City Council* v. *MB* [2006] EWHC 168 (Fam), [2006] 2 FLR 968, Munby J, and *London Borough of Ealing* v. *KS & Ors* [2008] EWHC 636 (Fam), Roderic Wood J. On both occasions the court held that the test of capacity to consent to sexual intercourse should not be the situation-specific test laid down in the Act but a much narrower test derived from the criminal law, i.e. whether a person understands the nature and character of sexual intercourse and the reasonably foreseeable consequences of sexual intercourse. The desirability of the civil and criminal law tests 'matching' has been emphasised (*R* v. *C* [2008] EWCA Crim 1155).

However, as noted in **Chapter 10**, the test of capacity to be applied in respect of the criminal offences of ill-treatment and neglect under this Act does adopt the wider, situation-specific test of capacity derived from the common law and now enshrined in this legislation. This might cast doubt on whether it is appropriate to retain a narrow view of the test of capacity in the criminal realm, and by extension whether any related civil test should be cast in the narrow rather than the situation-specific sense. The adoption of a situation-specific test of capacity to consent to sexual intercourse would be consistent with the joint BMA/Law Society publication, *Assessment of Mental Capacity, Guidance for Doctors and Lawyers* (chap.10).

---

1   The Explanatory Notes provide that the rules as to dispensing of consent under the adoption legislation will apply (para.93).

1.4   CHILDREN AND YOUNG PEOPLE

1.4.1   Children under 16

The Act does not generally apply to people under 16 except that:

- the Court of Protection can make decisions about a child's property or finances (or appoint a deputy to do so) if the child lacks capacity to make such decisions and is likely to still lack capacity to make financial decisions when he or she reaches 18 (s.18(3));
- offences of ill-treatment or wilful neglect of a person who lacks capacity can also apply to those under 16 (s.44);
- medical care and treatment of children under the age of 16 is generally governed by common law principles.

Although generally the powers under the Act may not be exercised until the person concerned has reached the age of 16 (s.2(5)), powers in relation to that person's property and affairs may be exercised if the Court considers it likely that the person will still lack capacity to make decisions in respect of that matter when he or she reaches the age of 18 (s.18(3)). This allows the Court to become involved in long-term planning without artificial cut-off points which would not be in a person's best interests. For example, it is easy to imagine how this power might be exercised in relation to an award of damages made consequent upon a brain injury to a teenager.

1.4.2   Young people aged 16–17 years

Most of the Act applies to young people aged 16–17 years, who may lack capacity to make specific decisions. There are three exceptions:

- only people aged 18 and over can make a Lasting Power of Attorney (LPA), (s.9(2)(c));
- only people aged 18 and over can make an advance decision to refuse medical treatment (s.24(1));
- the Court of Protection may only make a statutory will for a person aged 18 or over (s.18(2)).

There is an overlap with the Children Act 1989 and with the High Court's inherent powers to deal with cases involving young people.[1]

1.4.3   Capacity for 16–17 year olds to make treatment decisions

The Family Law Reform Act 1969 presumes that young people have the legal capacity to agree to surgical, medical or dental treatment.[2] This does not apply to some types of procedures (organ donation, non-therapeutic procedures or research). The test is whether the person is 'Gillick competent'.[3]

When there is a disagreement between a young person who has capacity to make a treatment decision and a person with parental responsibility, then it is appropriate to make an application to the Family Division of the High Court for an order.

If a young person lacks capacity within the meaning of the Act and there is a disagreement as to his or her capacity or best interests, then the Act will apply, and if the disagreement cannot be resolved it is appropriate to make an application to the Court of Protection for a declaration or order.

Depending on the circumstances a case may be heard in the Family Courts or the Court of Protection, as appropriate. For example, if the parents of a 17-year-old with profound learning difficulties are in dispute about residence or contact then it may be more appropriate for the Court of Protection to deal with the case since an order made under the Children Act 1989 would expire on the child's eighteenth birthday (Code, para.79).

There are currently no rules or Practice Directions for deciding when to use the Children Act 1989, the MCA 2005 or the inherent jurisdiction of the High Court (see Code, chapter 12). The remit of the Children and Family Court Advisory and Support Service (Cafcass) does not appear to extend to the Court of Protection.

---

1   See Code, chapter 12.
2   Family Law Reform Act 1969, s 8(1).
3   *Gillick* v. *West Norfolk and Wisbech Area Health Authority* [1986] 1 AC 112.

1.5   TRANSFER OF PROCEEDINGS

The difficulties in deciding upon the appropriate forum for disputes concerning 16- and 17-year-olds who may also be incapable once they become adults at the age of 18 is anticipated by s.21 of the Act. The section provides that the Lord Chancellor may make provision for the transfer of proceedings relating to a person aged under 18 from the Court of Protection to a court having jurisdiction under the Children Act 1989 or vice versa. See Mental Capacity Act 2005 (Transfer of Proceedings) Order 2007, SI 2007/1899.

1.6   DATA PROTECTION AND CONFIDENTIALITY

Difficulties frequently arise over the access to personal data of incapable persons, particularly when it is sought by persons seeking to make a decision on their behalf. Access to personal data is regulated by the Data Protection Act 1998, the common law duty of confidence, the professional codes of conduct on confidentiality, and the Human Rights Act 1998 and the European Convention on Human Rights (ECHR) (see Code, para.16.3).

Both the common law and the professional codes are based on the common law requirement for consent to be given to disclosure of personal information by the person to whom it relates. It follows that if a person is able to give his or her consent to disclosure of personal information then the person should be asked to do so.

Attorneys and deputies are entitled to request such information to which their authority extends.

A person making a decision on behalf of someone who lacks capacity to make that decision and to consent to disclosure of personal information, will need to have access to personal information and may be required to disclose personal information about that person. Medical professionals, financial institutions and various public authorities are sometimes reluctant to disclose information about a patient to a third party who is not acting under formal powers without the person's consent. Before the Act came into force, if such difficulties persisted the Court of Protection would issue a limited authority for the purposes of obtaining information. The Court may continue this practice (see Code, para.16.26) by issuing a single order; however it will now be necessary to make a formal application to the court in accordance with the Court of Protection Rules and pay an application fee. If it is apparent at the start of or during the course of proceedings that disclosure or such information will be required then an appropriate direction can be sought from the court.

Guidance on this complex area is contained in chapter 16 of the Code of Practice which can be found in **Appendix D** of this book.

Further information can be obtained from the website of the Information Commissioner's Office (**www.ico.gov.uk**).

1.7 SCOTLAND

The Adults with Incapacity (Scotland) Act 2000 ('the Scottish Act') was one of the first Acts of the Scottish Parliament. The Scottish Act to some extent mirrors the provisions of the England and Wales Act, but it also has important differences. A detailed examination of the Scottish Act is outside the scope of this book.

1.8 INTERNATIONAL PROTECTION OF ADULTS

The provisions for the international protection of adults in the private international law of England and Wales are contained in Sched.3 to the Act. The Act gives effect in England and Wales to the Convention on the International Protection of Adults.[1] The aims of the Convention are to:

- provide for the protection in international situations of adults, who by reason of impairment or insufficiency of their personal faculties, are not in a position to defend their interests;
- establish rules on jurisdiction, applicable law, and international recognition and enforcement of protective measures which are to be respected by all states.

Schedule 3 is divided into six parts. Part 1 deals with definitions and other preliminary matters. Part 2 sets out the jurisdiction of the 'competent authority'; the competent authority for England and Wales is the Court of Protection. Part 3 makes provision as to which law applies in various situations. Part 4 provides for the recognition and enforcement of protective measures taken in other countries. Part 5 deals with co-operation between the appropriate authorities in England and Wales and authorities in other Convention countries. Part 6 deals with general matters. For a fuller overview of the provisions of the Schedule, see paras.169–84 of the Explanatory Notes to the Act.

Scotland and Germany[2] are the only countries that have ratified the Convention, which must be ratified by three countries before it will come into force. The provisions of Sched.3 are compatible with the provisions contained in the Scottish Act. Once the Act is in force, Sched.3 will provide private international law rules to govern jurisdictional issues between England and Wales, and Scotland *irrespective of whether the Convention is in force.*

---

1   The Convention was signed in the Hague on 13 January 2000, Cm. 5881. The text of the Convention is available from the Hague Conference website (**http://hcch.e-vision. nl/index_en.php?act=text.display&tid=1**).
2   Germany ratified the Convention on 3 April 2007.

1.9   MENTAL HEALTH ACT 1983 AND MENTAL HEALTH ACT 2007

The Mental Health Act (MHA) 1983 currently governs the detention, care and treatment of those with a mental disorder. The Mental Capacity Act 2005 provides that if a person is detained under the MHA 1983, the person's treatment for that mental disorder, or the persons giving consent for that treatment, must be dealt with under the MHA 1983 and not the MCA 2005 (s.28). This is intended to ensure that there may be no conflict in relation to treatment of incapable patients who are also detained under the MHA 1983, and the provisions of MCA 2005: all the safeguards under the MHA 1983 are retained.[1]

The Mental Health Act (MHA) 2007 significantly amends the MHA 1983, while retaining the position that there is still no single, harmonised legislation that deals with both mental disorder and lack of capacity.

One of the principal changes effected by the MHA 2007 is a statutory scheme for the authorisation of deprivation of liberty for persons who lack capacity and an attempt to define when a person should be detained under the MHA 2003 and when under the Act (see **Chapter 5** at 5.3.3).

In addition, the following key issues arise when considering the relationship between the two legislative schemes:

- patients who are subject to the MHA 1983 may still have capacity to make decisions about their health, welfare and finances;
- the Act applies, including its provisions as to advance decisions, in respect of all decision-making in respect of persons subject to the MHA 1983 save in relation to treatment for their disorder given under the MHA 1983.

---

1   Explanatory Notes at para.94.

1.10   THE CODE OF PRACTICE

The Code can be found at **Appendix D** of this book. The Code plays a key role in the interpretation of the Act and its implementation, and very often, as this text demonstrates, the Code is the principal guide to the legislation. The Joint Committee specifically recommended that the Act should not be introduced to Parliament until it could be considered alongside a Draft Code.[1] Its importance to the Committee was reinforced by the fact that many of its recommendations related to matters which it considered should be covered in the Code such as the duty of care of attorneys and deputies,[2] the standards of conduct of decision-makers[3] and the requirements to be fulfilled upon an assessment of capacity.[4]

It had been anticipated that the Code would be reviewed after the first year and revised regularly, 'perhaps several times a year'[5] thereafter. The Ministry of Justice has confirmed that a review of the workings of the Act and the Code is to be carried out, starting in October 2008.[6]

1.10.1   The duty to have regard to the Code

Section 42(4) of the Act imposes a duty on a person to 'have regard to any relevant code if he is acting in relation to a person who lacks capacity' and is doing so in one of the ways listed. Section 12(5) provides that a court or tribunal conducting any criminal or civil proceedings may find the Code or a failure to comply with it a relevant matter to be taken into account in its adjudication. The Code itself provides that persons who are under a duty to 'have regard to' it must be able to demonstrate that they are familiar with the relevant part of it, and if they depart from it they will be expected to give reasons why (para.1.9).

The website of the Public Guardian suggests that the following have a legal duty to have regard to the Code:

- professionals and anyone who is paid for the work they do in relation to people who lack capacity, e.g. doctors, nurses, social workers, care managers, solicitors, police officers, ambulance crew and paid carers;

- attorneys appointed under a Lasting Power of Attorney (LPA), or Enduring Power of Attorney (EPA); and
- deputies appointed by the Court of Protection (the Court).

Family, friends and unpaid carers do not have a legal obligation to 'have regard' to the Code but will still find the guidance helpful, and should follow it where they are aware of it.

---

1 Preface to the Draft Code of Practice.
2 Paragraph 154.
3 Paragraph 98.
4 Paragraph 245.
5 David Lammy MP, Hansard, HC Committee Stage, 4 November 2004, col.378.
6 Bridget Prentice in Written Answers, Hansard, 23 June 2008, Column 58W.

1.11   EUTHANASIA AND ASSISTED SUICIDE

Throughout the passage of the Bill and during debates, a great deal of parliamentary time and column inches in the press were taken up discussing whether key clauses in the Bill would authorise 'euthanasia by omission', 'suicidally motivated advance directives' and 'euthanasia by the back door'.

Concerns were expressed that:

- allowing people to make advance decisions to refuse life-sustaining treatments, in particular the refusal of artificial nutrition and hydration (ANH), would legalise euthanasia by omission;
- a doctor who complies with a patient's contemporaneous or advance refusal of treatment by withholding or withdrawing treatment, may be committing euthanasia or a mercy killing or assisting a suicide;
- attorneys, deputies or those providing care and treatment for a person may seek to harm that person at the end of his or her life.

The common law is clear that the refusal of medical treatment by a competent adult that results in death is not suicide. A competent adult is entitled to refuse any medical treatment even if the treatment is life-sustaining.[1] In *Airedale NHS Trust v. Bland*,[2] Lord Goff stated:

> I wish to add that in cases of this kind, there is no question of the patient having committed suicide, nor therefore of the doctor having aided or abetted him in doing so. It is simply that the patient has, as he is entitled to do so, declined to consent to treatment which might or would have the effect of prolonging his life, and the doctor in accordance with his duty, complied with the patient's wishes.

The law is also clear that a doctor who complies with a patient's contemporaneous or advance refusal of treatment, by withholding or withdrawing treatment, is not committing euthanasia or mercy killing or assisting a suicide.

. . . the law draws a crucial distinction between cases in which doctors decide not to provide, or to continue to provide, for his patient treatment or care which could or might prolong his life and those which he decides, for example by administering a lethal drug, actively to bring his patient's life to an end.[3]

The government resisted all attempts to include a clause in the Bill stating that the Bill did not permit euthanasia. Instead s.62 (then cl.58) was added which provides:

> For the avoidance of doubt, it is hereby declared that nothing in this Act is to be taken to affect the law relating to murder or manslaughter of the operation of section 2 of the Suicide Act 1961.

The final debates on the Lords' amendments to the Bill have made it clear that this provision is unlikely to resolve the ethical arguments surrounding the issue.

Specific safeguards have been included in the Act concerning the withdrawal or withholding of life-sustaining treatment:

- *Advance decisions:* Provision for a patient to make an advance decision regarding treatment in ss.24–26 of the Act (see **Chapter 7**) will not apply to life-sustaining treatment unless the person has specified that it should (s.25(5)) and that it complies with the additional formalities set out in s.25(6).
- *Lasting Powers of Attorney (LPA):* The donee of an LPA cannot make a healthcare decision relating to life-sustaining treatment unless he or she is expressly authorised to do so (s.11(8)(a)) (see **Chapter 4**).
- *Acts in connection with care or treatment:* If there is any doubt whether the life-sustaining treatment is in the best interests of the patient, s.6(7) allows treatment to be given whilst a decision is sought from the Court (see **Chapter 5**).
- *Independent Mental Capacity Advocate (IMCA):* The Act creates a new service, to help particularly vulnerable people who lack capacity and have no family or friends when decisions are being made by NHS bodies or local authorities about serious medical treatment or where they should live (see **Chapter 9**).
- *Best interests:* Section 4(5) sets out in statutory form the current common law position that the person making a decision on behalf of another person about treatment that is necessary to sustain life must not be motivated by a desire to bring about that person's death.
- Deputies may not refuse consent to the carrying out or continuation of life-sustaining treatment (s.20(5)).

The Code of Practice provides at paras.6.18–6.19 and paras.8.18–8.24 instances when serious healthcare and treatment decisions must be or are likely to be referred to the Court of Protection for a decision.

---

1 *St George's Healthcare NHS Trust v. S* [1998] 3 All ER 673 (CA); *Re B (Adult: Refusal of Medical Treatment)* [2002] EWHC 429 (Fam); (2002) BMLR 149 (Butler-Sloss P).
2 [1993] 1 All ER 821, at 869.
3 Ibid., at 869.

1.12   COMPATIBILITY WITH THE ECHR

Although the Act has been certified by Parliament as compatible with the ECHR, it is likely that human rights issues will arise in its implementation and in litigation.

The following Articles are potentially engaged by issues arising under the Act:

- 2 (the right to life);
- 3 (prohibition of torture);
- 5 (right to liberty and security);
- 6 (right to a fair trial);
- 8 (right to respect for private and family life and home);
- 9 (freedom of thought, conscience and religion);
- 14 (prohibition on discrimination); and
- Article 1 of the First Protocol (protection of property).

Inevitably, these Articles will be invoked in decision-making and litigation under the Act. Certainly, the case law which developed the common law which the Act is intended to enshrine frequently considered the impact of the ECHR, for example, *Local Authority* X v. *MM* [2007] EWHC 2003 (Fam). However, no case in this area apart from *HL* v. *United Kingdom* (Appn. No.45598/99) (2005), 81 BMLR 131 has had a different conclusion because of the impact of the ECHR. For its impact, see **Chapter 5** at **5.3.3**.

Careful consideration to the human rights consequences of the Act was given by the Joint Parliamentary Select Committee on Human Rights 23rd Report 2003–2004, and 15th Report 2004–2005. The Explanatory Notes set out the way in which the Act is considered to fulfil the requirements of the ECHR (paras.10–16). There is no specific discussion, however, of the impact of the ECHR in the Code of Practice.

1.13   THE REMAINS OF THE INHERENT JURISDICTION

Although cases that have been brought in the Family Division under the inherent jurisdiction will generally speaking continue to be resolved under that regime, even after the coming into force of the Act, the continuing role of the inherent jurisdiction is uncertain.

Where decisions, such as those set out at **1.3** above, are excluded from the operation of the Act, any disputes will still fall to be determined within it.

However, the judgment in the case *Re SA (Vulnerable Adult with Capacity: Marriage)* [2005] EWHC 2942, [2006] 1 FLR 867 seemed to leave open the possibility of a continuing flexible jurisdiction that might be applied to protect the vulnerable even though they would not be found to lack capacity under the Act. The existence of this jurisdiction might be doubted on the grounds that the new statutory scheme excludes the possibility of residual common law powers. The issues still fall to be resolved.

1.14   REPRESENTATION OF P IN PROCEEDINGS BEFORE THE COURT OF PROTECTION

The Court of Protection Rules 2007 ('the Rules') define 'P' as:

> any person (other than a protected party) who lacks or, so far as consistent with the context, is alleged to lack capacity to make a decision or decisions in relation to any matter that is the subject of an application to the court and references to a person who lacks capacity are to be construed in accordance with the Act.

Rule 73(4) of the Rules provides that P is not to be named as a party to the proceedings unless the court directs. The court may direct that P be made a party to the proceedings 'if it considers it desirable to do so for the purpose of the application'. If P is made a party to proceedings, the court must appoint a litigation friend to conduct proceedings on behalf of P and Part 17 of the Rules and Practice Direction A apply. The Official Solicitor, who is the litigation friend of last resort, may be invited to act as litigation friend of P subject to his consent.

It is the experience of the authors that where there is an application for serious medical treatment before the Court, the usual practice is for the Court to join P as a party to the proceedings and invite the Official Solicitor to act as P's litigation friend. In other welfare cases where P is joined as a party to proceedings, the Official Solicitor is generally invited to act as litigation friend of P.

1.14.1   The Role of the Official Solicitor in healthcare and welfare cases

Official solicitor bringing proceeding as litigation friend

The Official Solicitor may consider bringing proceedings as litigation friend of P if he is satisfied that:

- the action complained of is not susceptible to any other remedy;
- there is no other person who is willing and able bring proceedings to protect P's interests, or on P's behalf;
- P lacks capacity to conduct proceedings within the meaning of MCA 2005, s.2;
- the proposed applicant fulfils the definition of 'P' within the meaning of rule 6 of the Rules,
- there is a serious justiciable issue and it is in P's best interests for proceedings to be brought on P's behalf; and
- his costs of so doing will be met either from public funds or from P's estate.

The Official Solicitor does not need the court's permission to make a healthcare or welfare application on behalf of P.

When P is a respondent to an application and the Official Solicitor has been invited to act as litigation friend.

Cases conducted 'in house'

The Official Solicitor conducts serious medical treatment cases in house. The Official Solicitor will usually instruct counsel to represent P and will carry out his enquiries if time and circumstances permit by visiting P to investigate P's circumstances and wishes and feelings (if P is able to express them) on the decision(s) in issue. The Official Solicitor may also ascertain the views of P's family and friends and those treating P if they are not parties to the proceedings. He will also commission such expert reports as are necessary to assist in representing P and establishing P's capacity and best interests.

Other cases

In other cases where P is eligible for public funding the Official Solicitor will instruct solicitors to act for P taking their instructions from the Official Solicitor as litigation friend. In the event that P is ineligible for public funding, the Official Solicitor will usually instruct solicitors to act for P but will require provision to be made for his costs to be met by the applicant, or from P's estate. Again, depending on time and the circumstances of the case the Official Solicitor will usually require the solicitors he instructs to visit P to ascertain P's circumstances, wishes and feeling and those of any family and friends. The solicitors may be required to instruct experts to report on capacity and best interests and to instruct counsel to represent P at court.

Advocate to the court

The official solicitor may be invited by the court to act as advocate to the court in order to assist the court.

1.14.2   Costs in healthcare and welfare cases

Rule 157 provides:

> Where the proceedings concern P's personal welfare the general rule is that there will be no order as to the costs of the proceedings . . .

Generally when P is eligible for public funding the costs incurred by solicitors representing P and instructed by the Official Solicitor will be met from public funds. Where P is ineligible for public funding the Rules make special provision for the Official Solicitor to be able to recover his or her costs from P's funds.

However, in medical cases, the Official Solicitor will seek to recover a proportion of his or her costs of acting as litigation friend from those seeking the protection of a declaration or order. For a fuller discussion see **para 11.5.19** 'Departing from the general rule'.

1.15   PUBLIC FUNDING IN THE COURT OF PROTECTION

Where legal services are required for eligible clients in relation to issues under the Act, Legal Help will be the normal vehicle for funding such advice and assistance as the client requires.

The Court of Protection is a superior court of record but is not part of the High Court. Therefore advocacy brought before the Court of Protection is not within the scope of Sched.2 to the Access to Justice Act 1999. The Lord Chancellor has issued an authorisation under s.6(8) of that Act bringing certain cases before the Court of Protection within the scope of CLS funding.[1]

The wording of the authorisation makes it clear that funding can extend not just to P himself but sometimes to other parties such as P's immediate family.

The authorisation is intended to capture the serious health and welfare cases which would previously have been considered by the High Court under its inherent jurisdiction. It also includes applications to the Court in respect of deprivation of liberty.

All applications for legal representation before the Court should be made to the Legal Services Commission's Mental Health Unit, which is based in the Nottingham and Liverpool offices. Cases before the Court are subject to the usual financial eligibility rules for CLS funding.

---

1   Available from the Legal Services Commission's website (**www.legalservices.gov.uk/ civil/guidance/guidance_funding_decisions.asp#mentalhealth**).

2 THE PRINCIPLES

2.1 BACKGROUND TO REFORM

The Joint Committee in its Report of 28 November 2003 recommended that in order to achieve the Bill's stated aim it was essential that a statement of fundamental principles on which the Bill is based be inserted as an initial point of reference; this would give invaluable guidance to the courts, as well as helping non-lawyers to weigh up difficult decisions.

The Joint Committee[1] suggested five principles similar to those set out in s.1 of the Scottish Act. It was noted by the Joint Committee, however, that the Scottish Act was designed to run in conjunction with the common law, whereas the Draft Bill was designed to codify existing common law practice in statute.

The government ultimately accepted the recommendation and inserted a new cl.1 in the Bill, now s.1 of the Act.

---

1 Recommendations 4 and 5 of Joint Committee on the Draft Mental Incapacity Bill, HL Paper 189–1.

2.2 KEY PRINCIPLES

Section 1 of the Act sets out the key principles that underpin the Act. The Act is designed to codify the existing common law practice in statute. It is here that the existing case law may most assist the court in interpreting the Act.

2.2.1 Section 1(1)

Applies the key principles to the Act.

2.2.2 Section 1(2)

The presumption of capacity:

> A person must be assumed to have capacity unless it is established that he lacks capacity.

The ethical principle that every person has a right to self-determination and to have their autonomy respected is reflected in the common law presumption that every adult is competent to make his or her own decisions[1] – unless it can be shown that the person lacks capacity to make that particular decision. Section 3 of the Act (see **3.3** and **3.4**), sets out the test for assessing whether a person is able to make a particular decision. The test is issue specific,[2] i.e. can this person, make this decision, now?

Section 2(3) of the Act (see **3.3.3**) introduces what the Explanatory Notes call 'a principle of equal consideration' in relation to determining a person's capacity. It ensures that those assessing a person's capacity do not make unjustified assumptions about their capacity based on prejudices and preconceptions relating to a person's age, condition, appearance or behaviour.

However, consideration ought also to be given to the conclusion reached by Dame Elizabeth Butler-Sloss (Butler-Sloss LJ as she then was) in the seminal case of *Re MB (Medical Treatment)*[3] that:

> . . . the graver the consequences of the decision, the commensurately greater the level of competence is required to take the decision.

This view can be balanced against the view expressed by Munby J in the recent cases of *X City Council* v. *MB* [2006] EWHC 168 (Fam), [2006] 2 FLR 968:

> We must be careful not to set the test of capacity to marry too high, lest it operate as an unfair, unnecessary and indeed discriminatory bar against the mentally disabled.

2.2.3   Section 1(3)

Maximising decision-making capacity:

> A person is not to be treated as unable to make a decision unless all practicable steps to help him to do so have been taken without success.

Again, in order to assist a person to make autonomous decisions, the Act requires all practical steps be taken to support a person in arriving at his or her own decision. A person should be supported and enabled to make as many decisions for him or herself as possible. The stated aim of this provision is to ensure that 'people who make decisions for themselves, but may need help and support to do so, are not automatically labelled as incapable of making these decisions and therefore subjected to unnecessary interventions'.[4] The Code of Practice suggests that such help and support may include using specific communication strategies such as involving an expert to help that person to express his or her views, and choosing the best time and location.

2.2.4   Section 1(4)

Unwise decisions:

> A person is not to be treated as unable to make a decision merely because he makes
> an unwise decision.

Again, in *Re MB*, Butler-Sloss LJ made it clear that:

> A competent woman, who has capacity to decide, may, for religious reasons, other
> reasons, for rational or irrational reasons or for no reason at all, choose not to have
> medical intervention . . .

The Act makes it clear that in determining the criteria of competence the guiding principle is respect for autonomy: the Act should be enabling rather than restricting. Each person has his or her own values, beliefs, preferences and attitudes to risk, which ought to be respected. However, those assessing capacity must be aware of circumstances when a person may have a misconception of reality such as to render that person unable to make that decision.

A key concern of stakeholders was whether the functional approach, which deals only with specific-issue incapacity, would sufficiently protect those with general incapacity. The Master of the Court of Protection, Master Lush, giving evidence to the Joint Committee, gave examples of the potential for people with on-going incapacity to make a series of judgments or decisions that may have disastrous consequences. In those circumstances, under the current law the Court of Protection may appoint a receiver. The Joint Committee recommended that consideration be given to recognising the issue of 'general incapacity' in the Draft Bill in a way that would not 'undermine the primacy of the functional approach'.

In response the government stated that it was committed to the functional approach, but agreed to provide guidance as to how this might work in order to provide people with adequate protection. Some professional financial deputies and banks are finding the change from the receivership approach (general financial incapacity) to the functional approach a challenge.

2.2.5   Section 1(5)

Best interests:

> An act done, or decision made, under this Act for or on behalf of a person who lacks
> capacity must be done, or made, in his best interests.

Since the decision of the House of Lords in the leading case of *Re F (Mental Patient: Sterilisation)* [1990] 2 AC 1, HL, the courts have recognised the necessity to act and make decisions for another person when the person lacks capacity to make decisions for him or herself and that such decisions and acts should be in that person's 'best interests'.

At common law, a best interests determination can only be made once it has been shown that a person lacks capacity to make the decision him or herself. The Family Division of the High Court, exercising its inherent jurisdiction has developed the concept of best interests, to include not only 'medical best interests' but also a wide range of ethical, social, moral, emotional and welfare considerations.[5]

> In deciding what is best for the disabled patient the judge must have regard to the patient's welfare as the paramount consideration. That embraces issues far wider than the medical. Indeed it would be undesirable and probably impossible to set bounds to what is relevant to a welfare determination.[6]

The court has extended the jurisdiction to making decisions in relation to an incompetent adult's welfare as well as medical treatment.

> The court has jurisdiction to grant whatever relief in declaratory form is necessary to safeguard and promote the incapable adult's welfare and interests.[7]

Thorpe LJ in *Re A Male Sterilisation*[8] suggested that an evaluation of best interests could be facilitated by the use of a balance sheet:

> there can be no doubt in my mind that the evaluation of best interests is akin to a welfare appraisal . . . it seems to me that the first instance judge with the responsibility to make an evaluation of the best interests of a claimant lacking capacity should draw up a balance sheet. The first entry should be of any factor or factors of actual benefit . . . Then on the other sheet the judge should write any counterbalancing dis-benefits to the applicant. . . . Then the judge should enter on each sheet the potential gains and losses in each instance making some estimate of the extent of the possibility that the gain or loss might accrue. At the end of that exercise the judge should be better placed to strike a balance between the sum of the certain and possible gains against the sum of the certain and possible losses. Obviously, only if the account is in relatively significant credit will the judge conclude that the application is likely to advance the best interests of the claimant.

The Court of Appeal in *Burke* v. *General Medical Council*[9] rejected Munby J's suggestion at first instance that in the context of life-prolonging treatment the touchstone of 'best interests' is the 'intolerability' of continued life and stated that:

> We do not think it is possible to attempt to define what is in the best interests of a patient by a single test, applicable in all circumstances.

Section 1(5) now enshrines the best interests principle in statute as the principle that must guide all actions done for, or decisions made on behalf of, someone lacking capacity. Section 4 of the Act sets out statutory guidance and a checklist of factors that must be taken into account when assessing a person's best interests (see **Chapter 3** for a more detailed consideration).

Section 4(5) makes it clear that where the best interests determination relates to life-sustaining treatment, the person considering whether the treatment is in the best interests of the person concerned must not be motivated by a desire to bring about his death. (For a full discussion see **Chapter 3**.)

In any case where there is a doubt or dispute about whether a particular act or decision is in the patient's best interests, the Court of Protection will have jurisdiction to resolve the doubt or dispute.

2.2.6   Section 1(6)

Least restrictive alternative:

> Before the act is done, or the decision is made, regard must be had to whether the purpose for which it is needed can be as effectively achieved in a way that is less restrictive of the person's rights and freedom of action.

In order to safeguard and protect the rights and freedoms of people lacking capacity it is necessary to consider first, whether the act or decision needs to be done or taken at all, and then if the act or decision is necessary, the least restrictive way of carrying out the action or decision in their best interests.

Again, the decision-maker must achieve a delicate balance between respecting a person's autonomy (e.g. allowing them to experience day-to-day risks without placing them in danger) and providing that person with adequate protection. This places a considerable burden on those owing a duty of care to the incapacitated person, who may find themselves liable in negligence, or the tort of conversion or subject to the criminal law if their judgment proves wrong (see s.5(3) and later at **Chapter 5**).

---

1 *Re T (Adult: Refusal of Treatment)* [1992] 3 WLR 782; *Re B (Adult: Refusal of Medical Treatment)* [2002] 2 All ER 449.
2 *Masterman-Lister* v. *Jewell Joined Cases: Masterman-Lister* v. *Brutton & Co* [2002] EWCA Civ 1889.
3 [1997] 2 FLR 426, CA.
4 Paragraph 2.6–2.9 of the Draft Code of Practice.
5 *Re A Male Sterilisation* [2001] FLR 549 per Thorpe LJ.
6 *Re S (Adult Patient: Sterilisation: Patient's Best Interests)* [2001] Fam 15 per Thorpe LJ, at p.30E.
7 *Re S (Adult Patient) (Inherent Jurisdiction: Family Life)* [2002] EWHC 2278 (Fam), [2003] 1 FLR 292. See also *Sheffield City Council* v. *E* [2004] EWHC 2808 (Fam); [2005] Fam 326; *Local Authority X* v. *MM & Anor* [2007] EWHC 2003 (Fam).
8 Supra at p.560E.
9 [2005] EWCA Civ 1003 per Lord Phillips MR at p.63. See also *Portsmouth NHS Trust* v. *Wyatt* sub nom: *Wyatt (A Child) (Medical Treatment: Continuation of Order)*, Re [2005] EWCA Civ 1181 per Wall LJ at p.84.

3 MENTAL CAPACITY AND BEST INTERESTS

3.1 BACKGROUND

Having established the 'principles' which are to govern the operation of the Act in s.1, this part of the Act lays down the statutory definitions or tests to be applied in relation to the key concepts of the Act: incapacity and best interests. The provisions follow closely the original recommendations of the Law Commission, which in turn reflected to a great extent the then common law.[1] First, the test of capacity has both a diagnostic and a functional element. Secondly, a further provision is added to cover persons who are unable to communicate the decisions they might otherwise be found capable of making. Thirdly, the test to be adopted when making decisions on behalf of those persons found to be incapable – the best interests test – builds upon and develops the common law original.

Underpinning the whole of this part of the statutory scheme is a commitment to involving the person in the decision-making process as much as possible. First, before being found to be incapable, all efforts must be made to 'enhance' the person's capacity. Second, if the person is found to be incapable, the person's wishes and feelings should nevertheless be taken into account in making the decision, even though they cannot be determinative of it.

Although the Act emphasises the importance of an assessment of capacity, it does not require that an assessment is carried out by a doctor or other professional before each decision that is taken upon a person's behalf. The Code provides that usually the assessor will be whoever is concerned with the person and the relevant decision at the time (para.4.37), but complex or disputed decisions or those where assessment is a legal requirement do indicate a need for formal assessment by a professional (paras.4.42 and 4.52). This approach to the making of assessments to capacity seems to be taking some time to bed down in practice, with considerable confusion amongst health and social care professionals as to when each type of assessment – informal or professional – is required, and who is responsible for arranging it.

---

1 Mental Incapacity Law Com. No. 231, February 1995.

3.2   'DIAGNOSTIC TEST' OF CAPACITY

Section 2(1) provides that, for the purposes of the Act:

> . . . a person lacks capacity in relation to a matter if at the material time he is unable to make a decision for himself in relation to the matter because of an impairment of, or a disturbance in the functioning of, the mind or brain.

The 'diagnostic test' under s.2(1) has the following two elements:

(a) Capacity is to be assessed in relation to a particular decision at a particular time.

This part of the test emphasises the principle that there must be a 'time-specific and decision-specific approach to determining capacity'.[1] It derives directly from the common law principle expressed most clearly in *Masterman-Lister* v. *Brutton and Co* [2002] EWCA Civ 1889, [2003] 3 All ER 167. In that case the court held that a lack of capacity in respect of one matter did not automatically mean a lack of capacity in relation to another, and in particular the fact that the claimant required a litigation friend did not automatically mean he was under a disability for the purposes of limitation periods in litigation. It is particularly important to note the change in approach from the former Court of Protection which operated a general test of incapacity to manage property and affairs. The Court's approach now will be to look at the specific decision or decisions in question.

(b) Incapacity must derive from an impairment or disturbance of the person's mind or brain.

This 'diagnostic' element is designed to cover a wide range of conditions including 'psychiatric illness, learning disability, dementia, brain damage or even a toxic confusional state'[2] and 'physical or medical conditions that cause confusion, drowsiness or loss of consciousness, delirium, concussion and the symptoms of alcohol or drug use'.[3] The test reflects the common law position that incapacity may derive from an 'impairment or disturbance of mental functioning' of an organic cause, e.g. brain injury or non-organic cause, e.g. personality disorder (*R (Brady)* v. *Collins and Ashworth Hospital Authority* [2000] Lloyd's Rep Med 355[4]) or phobia (*Re MB (Medical Treatment)* [1997] 2 FLR 426). The Code also gives the example of anorexia nervosa as a condition that affects a person's ability to weigh information, and therefore that person's capacity (para.4.22).

It should be borne in mind that the requirement for 'an impairment or disturbance of the person's mind or brain' under the Act is distinct from the definitions of 'mental disorder', 'mental illness' and 'mental impairment' under MHA 1983, although in many cases there will be an overlap between the groups of persons falling within the two sets of definitions. These narrower definitions will, however, be replaced with a broad definition of 'mental disorder' when MHA 2007 comes into force.

It should also be noted that the incapacity must 'derive from' the impairment or disturbance. This echoes the need to avoid automatically assuming incapacity because of a person's condition (see **3.3.3**).

The Act specifically provides that the impairment or disturbance which causes the incapacity may be permanent or temporary (s.2(2)). Again this reflects the common law position, typically arising in cases where loss of capacity is temporary, e.g. caused by the effects of a particular short-lived illness or medical procedure (*Re T (Adult: Refusal of Treatment)* [1993] Fam 95).

The question of whether an impairment or disturbance is temporary or permanent will often be vitally relevant to decisions whether or not to act in a person's best interests. For example, if a person is temporarily incapable and requires non-urgent treatment, it will not be appropriate to give the treatment during that temporary period of incapacity rather than wait for his capacity to be 'enhanced' and allow him to make the choice himself. However, where urgent treatment is required, the fact that incapacity is temporary will make the incapacity no less significant, and it will be necessary and appropriate to make decisions on the basis of the incapacity.

The Code addresses the related and difficult situation of fluctuating capacity (paras.4.26–4.27). For example, the fact that a person is able to retain the information relevant to the decision for a short period only does not necessarily prevent him from being regarded as able to make the decision (Code, para.4.20). Thus in some cases the person may be able to make the necessary decision during a period in which he is capable. This approach should be used with caution, however, where serious decisions are being made, and steps should be put in place to ensure that there is the necessary level of capacity at the relevant time.

---

1 David Lammy MP, Hansard, HC Committee Stage, 19 October 2004.
2 Explanatory Notes at para.22.
3 Code of Practice at para.4.12.
4 It should be noted that this was a controversial decision, Maurice Kay J being satisfied that 'whilst Mr Brady had the intellectual capacity to appreciate the risks of his food refusal and the possible consequences, his ability to "weigh the information" was impaired by the emotions and perceptions he had at the time, these being engendered by the move and his reaction to it   Although he weighs facts, his set of scales are not calibrated properly in a whole range of things'.

3.3 'FUNCTIONAL TEST' OF CAPACITY

Section 3 of the Act lays down the 'functional test' for determining capacity. It provides as follows:

a person is unable to make a decision for himself if he is unable –

(a) to understand the information relevant to the decision,
(b) to retain that information,
(c) to use or weigh that information as part of the process of making the decisions, or

(d) to communicate his decision (whether by talking, using sign language or any other means).

The Code provides that the first three parts of the test should be 'applied together' (para.4.15).

The test follows very closely, on the recommendation of the Law Commission,[1] the common law test of capacity laid down by the Court of Appeal in *Re MB (Medical Treatment)* above. Butler-Sloss LJ, as she then was, in giving the judgment of the court held at 553–4:

> A person lacks capacity if some impairment or disturbance of mental functioning renders the person unable to make a decision whether to consent to or to refuse treatment. That inability to make a decision will occur when:
>
> (a) the patient is unable to comprehend and retain the information which is material to the decision, especially as to the likely consequences of having or not having the treatment in question; or
> (b) the patient is unable to use the information and weigh it in the balance as part of the process of arriving at a decision.[2]

The Act adds a further element at s.3(1)(d) to cover the residual class of persons who cannot communicate their decisions, such as those who are unconscious or in a coma, or suffering from 'locked-in syndrome'. If such a person cannot communicate at all, e.g. not even by blinking, then he or she may be treated as incapable under the Act (Explanatory Notes, para.27). The Code provides that careful assessment must be undertaken before deciding that a person lacks capacity on this ground (paras.4.24 and 4.25).

3.3.1   The enhancement of capacity

A person is not to be regarded as unable to understand the information relevant to a decision if he is able to understand an explanation of it given to him in a way that is appropriate to his circumstances (simple language, visual aids or any other means) (s.3(2)). This provision focuses on a key recommendation of the Law Commission: that a person's capacity should be enhanced as far as possible. This particular amendment was added at the House of Commons' Committee Stage in order that 'no one should be labelled incapable merely because insufficient efforts have been made to help him understand and communicate'.[3] It reflects an issue that arose in cases under the common law inherent jurisdiction where it was sometimes said on behalf of apparently incapable individuals that insufficient efforts appropriate to their understanding had been made to enable them to acquire the necessary capacity to make a particular decision, and therefore they should not yet be declared as lacking capacity, e.g. *E (by her litigation friend the Official Solicitor) v. Channel Four* [2005] EWHC 1144 (Fam).

The Code of Practice makes extensive suggestions as to the steps that might be taken to enhance a person's capacity in Chapter 3: 'How should people be helped to make their own decisions?' including in summary:

- providing all the relevant information, e.g. all the detail that a person needs, but not so much that the person becomes confused;[4]
- communicating in an appropriate way, e.g. using simple language or visual aids or in consultation with a Speech and Language Therapist;
- making the person feel at ease, e.g. discussing the issue at a particular location or time of day;
- supporting the person, e.g. using advocacy or other individuals who are close to the person or professionals who are familiar to the person, such as a GP.[5]

These suggestions should be considered alongside those given to doctors in the joint publication of the British Medical Association and the Law Society, *Assessment of Mental Capacity: Guidance for Doctors and Lawyers* (2nd edn, 2004) (3rd edn forthcoming) at paras.2.3 and 14.7.

3.3.2   The significance of the consequences of the decision under consideration

The information relevant to a decision includes information about the reasonably foreseeable consequences of:

(a) deciding one way or another;
(b) failing to make the decision (s.3(4)).

Again, this provision in the Act derives from the common law *Re MB* test set out above – the key information upon which the person must decide relates to the consequences of his decision.

This provision has particular significance for the assessment of capacity since in grave, controversial or borderline cases it will be important to identify carefully what information is relevant, and to what degree it must be understood, retained and weighed in the balance (Code, para.4.19). For example, decisions about moving from one care home to another, or choosing between surgery or more conservative medical treatment may be made upon different levels of information. An assessment of capacity in such circumstances may only be meaningful where the assessor has identified what information is relevant in that case, and then considered the person's understanding, retention and weighing in the balance of those particular pieces of information.

3.3.3   The need to avoid assumptions and discrimination

A lack of capacity may not be established merely by reference to:

- a person's age or appearance; or
- a condition of his or an aspect of his behaviour which lead others to make unjustified assumptions about his capacity (s.2(3)).

This provision was added at the third reading in the House of Lords.[6] It was intended to 'reinforce the belief . . . that no-one should be assumed to lack capacity, excluded from decision-making, or discriminated against or given substandard care and treatment simply, for example, as a result of disability'. A key principle is that no fact about a person, e.g. his mental disorder, should automatically imply incapacity.

The Code provides that 'appearance' is intended to be construed broadly to include all aspects of appearance from physical characteristics of conditions such as Down's syndrome, to other aspects of appearance such as skin colour, religious dress, tattoos or body piercings (para.4.8).

Similarly, the words 'condition' and 'behaviour' in the Act are intended to be construed broadly (para.4.9).

3.3.4   Lack of capacity decided on the balance of probabilities

The question of whether a person lacks capacity within the meaning of the Act must be decided on the balance of probabilities (s.2(4)).

3.3.5   Refusal of assessment of capacity

Before starting to assess a person's capacity, a professional should check whether the person can consent to the assessment and if he is consenting. If the person is capable and refuses consent or is incapable and resistant, he cannot be forced to participate in the assessment (Code, para.4.59). It may be possible to persuade an individual to co-operate, or to carry out an assessment to the necessary standard without direct contact with the person (Code, para.4.58). If not, however, there may only be further intervention in the life of the person if the use of compulsory powers, for example under MHA 1983 or the National Assistance Act 1948, is justified. Simply refusing an assessment of capacity is not of itself grounds for the use of MHA 1983 (Code, para.4.59).

---

1   Law Com. 231, para.3.23.
2   This formulation built upon that adopted in the case of *Re C (Adult: Refusal of Medical Treatment)* [1994] 1 All ER 819 which emphasised the need for a link between the impairment or disturbance of functioning and the inability to take the decision concerned.
3   Hansard, HC, 14 December 2004, col.1632.
4   Often the giving of concrete information, such as visiting a proposed placement, rather than discussing it in the abstract will significantly enhance capacity.
5   The Code states that providing appropriate help with decision-making should form part of care planning processes for persons receiving health or social care services.
6   Hansard, 15 March 2005, col.1318.

3.4   THE APPLICATION OF THE TEST OF CAPACITY IN THE ACT

The test under the Act has been applied now on a number of occasions by the courts, thus far without argument as to its interpretation. In *Local Authority X* v. *MM and KM* [2007] EWHC 2003 (Fam), a case decided under the inherent jurisdiction, the court considered the development of the law leading to the test as it is currently framed under the Act and applied it in that case (paras.62–82). It held that the case law concerning the definition and application of the old common law test should be relied upon when considering the new statutory test of incapacity. In *Saulle* v. *Nouvet* [2007] EWHC 2902, QB, a claim for damages for personal injury, the court was asked to decide whether a person lacked capacity where the issue was disputed. The court approached the task by considering not only expert evidence, but also the person's medical records and the evidence of lay witnesses including members of the person's family.

3.5   INCAPABLE PERSON'S BEST INTERESTS

3.5.1   Background to this section

The Law Commission in its report was in no doubt that this principle, long-established in the common law (see **2.2.5**), should govern decision-making on behalf of incapable persons. The issue was what criteria should be devised for the assessing of best interests. The Law Commission's initial proposed list of four factors[1] has grown into the 11 subsections of s.4 of the Act.

The best interests test laid down by s.4 'underpins the [Act] and expands on the principle set out in [s.1(5) of the Act] . . . It is the fundamental principle that governs everything that is done for a person who lacks capacity'.[2] The best interests test was preferred over an assessment of 'benefit' to P for the following reasons:

> . . . although the concept of benefit would place the focus firmly on the person concerned, it might not allow for a consideration of other relevant factors, such as those affecting carers. Let me give an example. Someone caring for their mother or young child might want to arrange for them to go into a care home for a few weeks in order to give the carer a rest, and they might want the care home to provide the respite care that all of us have heard carers in our community talking about. There is a hospice not far from any constituency where people experience that. That situation would be to the benefit of the carer and the mother or partner. It might not be to the direct benefit of the person who lacks capacity, but it would certainly be in their best interest, as it would better for the carer to have had that respite care. That encapsulates why 'best interests' is an all-embracing concept. 'Benefit' is narrower and more prescriptive. That is why the Joint Committee ruled out that test.[3]

The test has both objective and subjective elements. Clause 4 of the Bill was amended at the House of Commons Committee Stage in order 'to make clear that the test of best interests should be objective' as well as taking into account subjective considerations such as the individual's wishes and feelings and 'all the factors that a reasonable person would consider relevant'.[4]

3.5.2   The need to avoid assumptions or discrimination

In a provision mirroring s.2(3) (see 3.3.3), s.4(1) provides that:

> In determining for the purposes of this Act what is in a person's best interests, the person making the determination must not take it merely on the basis of –
>
> (a) the person's age or appearance, or
> (b) a condition of his, or an aspect of his behaviour, which might lead others to make unjustified assumptions about what might be in his best interests.

The best interests test is intended to protect against any kind of discrimination, including disability discrimination.[5]

3.5.3   The method of determining best interests

The method of decision making as to best interests laid down by the Act applies to the court, a deputy, the donee of a Lasting Power of Attorney (LPA), or an informal decision-maker (s.4(8) and (9)). It is also extended to decisions made by an attorney, deputy or any person exercising powers under the Act when he reasonably believes a person to lack capacity although in fact the person does not (s.4(8) and Explanatory Notes, para.34). Where the decision is taken by an informal decision-maker, he will have complied sufficiently with the requirements of the section if, having gone through the specified steps, he 'reasonably believes that what he does or decides is in the best interests of the person concerned' (s.4(9)). The test of 'reasonable belief' is objective (Explanatory Notes, at para.35). Health and social care workers are expected carefully to determine and record their best interests decisions (Code, paras.5.15 and 5.52).

The Act requires that best interests are determined by:

(a) considering all the relevant circumstances, which are defined as those of which the decision-maker is aware, and which it would be reasonable to regard as relevant (s.4(11)); and
(b) taking the steps set out in the succeeding subsections (s.4(2)).

The steps are intended as a checklist not a definition nor an exhaustive list of factors: the assessment of best interests always depends on the facts of the case (Code, para.5.13). The question of what is a 'relevant circumstance' is addressed in the Code, giving useful examples in both the health and financial sphere (paras.5.19–5.20).

The best interests checklist

First, the decision-maker must consider whether it is likely that P will at some time have capacity in relation to the matter and, if so, when (s.4(3)). This provision allows for the possibility that the decision may be put off until the person has capacity to take it.[6] The Code gives useful guidance on this issue at paras.5.25–5.28. In an emergency it may not be possible to wait until P regains capacity, but in other cases it may be possible to work on the development of understanding to enable P to make the decision in the future. Alternatively, a short-term decision may be taken on behalf of P with a view to enabling him to take other decisions himself in the future.

Secondly, the decision-maker must, so far as reasonably practicable, permit and encourage P to participate, or to improve P's ability to participate, as fully as possible in any act done for P and any decision affecting P (s.4(4)). This provision embodies one of the fundamental purposes of the Act, i.e. the enhancement and improvement of individual's involvement in such decision making: a finding of incapacity does not completely disempower P. The decision-maker should 'do whatever is possible to permit and encourage the person to take part, or to improve their ability to take part, in making the decision' (Code, para.5 summary). It suggests using the same or similar practical steps to those proposed in relation to the enhancement of capacity (see **3.3.1**) including the use of simple language or visual aids, asking questions at the right time and location, breaking the information down, and using familiar or trusted individuals to aid communication (Code, para.5.24).

Regard should also be had to the guidance issued jointly by the Law Society and BMA on the assessment of capacity, *op. cit.*, at pp.17 and 159.

The purpose of the inclusion of the words 'so far as reasonably practicable' in the section is to allow for situations, either urgent or not, in which it would not be appropriate or in a person's best interests to delay acting, for those steps to be taken.[7]

Thirdly, the decision-maker must consider, so far as is reasonably ascertainable:

(a) P's past and present wishes and feelings (including any written statement made by him when he had capacity);
(b) the beliefs and values that would be likely to influence his decision if he had capacity; and
(c) the other factors that he would be likely to consider if he were able to do so (s.4(6)).

The first of these factors may require particular work. The Code provides that evidence may be found in verbal or written expression, behaviour or habits. In practice, it may be useful to keep a note of spontaneous expressions of wishes and feelings, or instruct day-to-day carers to do this, rather than relying only upon formal assessments and interviews which are often artificial. It is important, however, that this material does not lead decision-makers into confusing P's wishes, feelings or past values with what is in P's best interests given P's lack of capacity (Code, para.5.38).

The court has expressly held that P's religious beliefs, in that case Islam, may be relevant to the assessment of P's best interests (*Ahsan* v. *University Hospital Leicester NHS Trust* [2006] EWHC 2624, QB, [2007] PIQR P19). Although, see also the observations of the Court of Appeal in *City of Westminster* v. *KC, NNC and IC* [2008] EWCA Civ 198.

Further, the guidance offered by the Code is that decision-makers should consider previous written statements carefully and if they do not act in accordance with them they should record the reasons why, so that they are able to justify their decision (paras 5.42–5.43).

Fourthly, the decision-maker must, if it is practicable and appropriate to consult them, take into account the views of:

(a) anyone named by P as someone to be consulted on the matter in question or on matters of that kind;
(b) anyone engaged in caring for P or interested in P's welfare;
(c) any donee of an LPA granted by P;
(d) any deputy appointed by the court for P;

as to what would be in the person's best interests (s.4(7)).

An IMCA must be consulted in certain circumstances, including where major medical treatment or a change in where P should live is proposed and there is no one who fits into the above categories available for consultation (see **Chapter 9**).

When consulting with others, the decision-maker should take care not to interfere disproportionately with P's confidentiality or interest in his privacy. The Code reminds us that it might not be appropriate to share every piece of information with everyone (para.5.56) and that professionals must comply with their own guidance in relation to confidentiality (para.5.57).

It is worth noting that this subsection does not expressly refer to P's relatives rather than a 'carer' or 'person interested in his welfare'. The Code, however, states that it is 'good practice' to give careful consideration to the views of family carers, if it is possible to do so (Code, para.5.51).

Although relatives are likely to have a significant role in some cases, there is no guarantee that they are the best arbiters of P's best interests. Moreover, there is no common law presumption in favour of an adult child's residence or contact with his parents either at common law (*Re D-R (Adult: Contact)* [1999] 1 FLR 1161, CA) or under Art.8 of the ECHR. This approach was adopted and expanded by Munby J in *Re S (Adult Patient) (Inherent Jurisdiction: Family Life)* [2002] EWHC 2278 (Fam), [2003] 1 FLR 292. His Lordship held that an individual's right to private life under Art.8 may in some cases require his or her separation from members of the individual's family. However, where P has resided with P's family all his or her life, then there is an evidential burden on those who wish to accommodate P elsewhere.

3.5.4   Difficult cases

Where there is conflicting evidence or disagreement as to best interests, the Code provides that the following methods of resolution should be tried (paras.5.62–5.69):

- the statutory checklist should be reviewed;
- there should be a meeting with all concerned;
- the balance sheet approach (see **2.2.5**) should be applied;
- an advocate may be involved;
- a second opinion may be obtained;
- mediation may be attempted;
- ultimately responsibility for determining best interests rests with the decision-maker; but if all else fails, the Court of Protection might need to decide what is in P's best interests (see **Chapter 6**).

3.5.5   The application of the best interests test under the Act

Since the Act was passed but before it came into force, the court considered again the application of the best interests test in a case of conflicting views between a family and health and social services as to the best interests of P (*Westminster City Council v. IC and others* [2007] EWHC 3096 (Fam) at 125–134, upheld in the Court of Appeal (above)). The court upheld the view that there are no threshold criteria to be met for the intervention by health and social services in the life of P as there would be for intervention in the life of a child under the Children Act 1989. However, it is necessary for those who propose the intervention in P's life to demonstrate that the alternative they propose is better for P than the status quo, whether in the immediate or longer term. For example, it may be better for a young P to move from the family home to another setting arranged by social services in a gradual and planned way, to avoid the possibility that if P's parents suffer failing health or worse this could precipitate an urgent and potentially traumatic move.

3.5.6   The interests of third parties

At common law, considerable difficulty arose in cases where powerful interests of third parties were engaged by the decision in issue. For example, in *Re Y (Mental Patient) (Bone Marrow Donation)* [1997] 2 WLR 556 the court was asked to declare that it was lawful to harvest bone marrow from an incapable person in order to treat her sister's lymphoma. Connell J held that it was lawful because:

> it is to the benefit of the [incapable person] that she should act as donor to her sister, because in this way her positive relationship with her sister is most likely to be prolonged. Further, if the transplant occurs, this is likely to improve the [incapable person's] relationship with her mother who in her heart clearly wishes it to take place and also to improve her relationship with [her sister] who will be eternally grateful to her.

Whether this was the correct approach or not, when the court next considered a similar matter, it 'left open' the question of whether a third party's interests should also be considered (*R-B (A Patient)* v. *The Official Solicitor* sub nom *Re A (Mental Patient: Sterilisation)* (2000) Lloyd's Rep Med 87).

It should be noted that the foetus of a pregnant, incapable woman does not have an independent set of interests to be weighed against the woman's (*St. George's Healthcare NHS Trust* v. *S* [1998] 3 All ER 673).

The Code now gives guidance in relation to the interests of third parties, in summary that any act which may benefit another must still be in P's best interests, although those interests may include a wide range of benefits (paras.5.47–5.48).

3.5.7   Life-sustaining treatment

Where the determination relates to life-sustaining treatment, the decision-maker must not, in considering whether the treatment is in the best interests of P, be motivated by a desire to bring about his death (s.4(5)). 'Life-sustaining treatment' is defined as 'treatment which in the view of a person providing health care for P is necessary to sustain life' (s.4(10)). The Explanatory Notes explain this part of the Act as follows (para.31):

> This means that whatever a decision-maker personally feels about, or wants for, the person concerned this must not affect his assessment of whether a particular treatment is in the person's best interests . . . It does not mean that doctors are under an obligation to provide, or to continue to provide, life-sustaining treatment where that treatment is not in the bests interests of the person.

Thus the protracted ethical debates which accompanied the passage of the Bill through Parliament are dealt with in a few words.

The Code provides that decisions about life-sustaining treatment should not be made on the basis of assumptions about the person's quality of life. It deals in detail with such decisions (paras.5.29–5.36).

For cases that must be decided by the Court (see **Chapter 6**).

---

1   The ascertainable past and present wishes and feelings of the person concerned and the factors the person would consider if able to do so; the need to permit and encourage the person to participate or improve his ability to participate as fully as possible in anything done for and any decision making affecting him; the views of other people whom it is appropriate and practical to consult about the person's wishes and feelings and what would be in his best interests; and whether the purpose for which any action or decision is required can be as effectively achieved in a manner less restrictive of the person's freedom of action.
2   David Lammy MP, Hansard, HC Committee Stage, 19 October 2004.
3   Ibid.
4   Hansard, HC, 14 December 2004, col.1631 and David Lammy MP, HC Committee Stage, 21 October 2004.
5   David Lammy MP, Hansard, HC Committee Stage, 19 October 2004.
6   Explanatory Notes at para.28.
7   David Lammy MP, Hansard, HC Committee Stage, 21 October 2004, col.092.

4 LASTING POWERS OF ATTORNEY

4.1 BACKGROUND

4.1.1 EPAs

A power of attorney involves the grant of a legal power by the donor to another person, the donee or attorney, to act on the donor's behalf. Prior to the introduction of enduring powers of attorney by the Enduring Powers of Attorney Act (EPAA) 1985, powers of attorney only had effect while the donor had capacity and were automatically revoked upon incapacity of the donor. The EPAA 1985 introduced a particular type of power of attorney, the Enduring Power of Attorney (EPA) which permitted the attorney to continue to act on the donor's behalf in relation to property and financial affairs after the donor lacked capacity to act on his or her own behalf.

4.1.2 Differences between EPAs and LPAs

The Act introduces a new type of power of attorney, the Lasting Power of Attorney (LPA). LPAs replace EPAs as the type of power of attorney which can operate after a person ceases to have capacity. An important difference between LPAs and EPAs is that LPAs can authorise the attorney to make decisions on the donor's behalf in respect of welfare matters as well as matters related to property and financial affairs. Accordingly, the power to make decisions about medical treatment, residence and contact with other persons can be given to an attorney.

Welfare LPAs can only be used once a donor has lost capacity. The test of incapacity under the Act is a functional and time-specific test (s. 2, see **Chapter 3**). Accordingly, capacity will vary according to the particular decision to be taken at the particular time. A property and affairs LPA can be used even if the person has capacity to make the decision, unless the person has stated in the LPA that they will make their own decisions while they have capacity to do so.

The Code of Practice contains a comparison between LPAs and EPAs (para.7.5).

It is important to note that an LPA must be registered before it is valid and, therefore, before any powers conferred by it can be exercised. It can, however, be registered at any time before it is used. This contrasts with the situation in respect of EPAs which do not require registration until the donee believes the donor is or is becoming mentally incapable (EPAA 1985, s.4(1) and (2)). The LPA must be registered with the Public Guardian. The practical effect will be that the Public Guardian will know about all LPAs in use. This is not the situation with EPAs because many have not been registered (either because the donor has capacity or there has been a failure to comply with the registration requirements by the donee).

4.1.3   Abuse

There was much debate in both Houses of Parliament in relation to concerns about abuse of LPAs by donees and conflicts of interest. Evidence presented to the Joint Committee indicated that financial abuse occurred in approximately 10–20 per cent of cases involving EPAs (para.138 of the Joint Committee report on the Draft Mental Capacity Bill). But all proposals for more rigorous controls (in addition to the requirement to register, which is discussed below) to prevent abuse such as routine monitoring of LPAs by the Public Guardian were resisted on the basis that respect has to be accorded to the individual's autonomy to choose the person whom he or she wishes to act and for the state to respect that choice and place the responsibility on the donor to make a good choice. The appointment must after all be made when the donor has capacity (see in particular the debates in the House of Lords at the Committee Stage on 8 February 2005 at col.761).

The Code contains a section on what a person can do if he or she thinks that an attorney is abusing his or her position, and sets out a list of signs that an attorney may be exploiting a donor (or failing to act in the donor's best interests) including stopping relatives or friends from contacting the donor, sudden unexplained changes in living arrangements, not allowing health or social care staff to see the donor, unpaid bills and spending money on things obviously not related to the donor or spending money in an unusual or extravagant way (para.7.70). If a person suspects abuse, he or she should contact the Office of the Public Guardian (OPG) immediately. The OPG can direct a Court of Protection Visitor to visit an attorney and investigate. If there is a suspicion of physical or sexual abuse, theft or serious fraud, then the police should be contacted. A referral might also be made to local authority adult protection procedures. In serious cases the OPG will refer the matter to the Court of Protection which may revoke the LPA or through the Public Guardian prevent the LPA from being registered (Code, paras.7.71–7.72).

An attorney who thinks that someone else is abusing the donor, should refer the matter to the OPG and seek advice on what action to take or refer the matter to the police if they suspect physical or sexual abuse, theft or serious fraud. A referral might also be made to local authority adult protection procedures (Code, para.7.73).

4.2   DEFINITION OF LPAS

Section 9(1) of the Act defines an LPA as a power of attorney under which the donor (P) confers on the donee(s) authority to make decisions about all or any of the following matters:

- P's personal welfare or specified matters concerning P's personal welfare;
- P's property and affairs or specified matters concerning P's property and affairs.

This also includes authority to make decisions in circumstances where P no longer has capacity.

The following points should be noted:

- P can confer power on more than one attorney. This could involve P choosing to have separate attorneys for welfare and property matters. P could also choose to have different attorneys in respect of specific financial or property matters.
- P can confer general powers on an attorney to make welfare and/or financial and property decisions or specify specific matters in respect of which an attorney has powers.
- In order to be a valid LPA, the instrument must include authority to make decisions once P loses capacity. Otherwise, it is simply an ordinary power of attorney. Further, no authority can be conferred to make welfare decisions prior to P losing capacity in respect of this matter (see discussion of s.11(7) at 4.4.1).

The OPG has issued various guidance about LPAs (for people wanting to make an LPA, for people taking on the role of attorney and for certificate providers) which explain the application and registration process and can be found on the OPG's website (**www.publicguardian.gov.uk**). The various LPA forms can also be downloaded from this website. The Law Society has also issued some helpful guidance about LPAs: see the LPA Practice Note dated 24 September 2007.

4.2.1   Different attorneys

P might choose different individuals to act as attorneys in respect of welfare and property and financial matters so as to avoid any conflicts arising (e.g. whether P should go into an expensive residential home when this would have a substantial impact on the size of P's savings and investments).

However, there is no obligation under the Act to choose separate persons. It is a matter for each donor to decide which powers should be conferred on which individual(s).

4.3   VALIDITY REQUIREMENTS OF AN LPA

Sections 9 and 10 contain the requirements for the creation of a valid LPA. Unless these requirements are complied with, the LPA confers no authority (s.9(3)).

The validity requirements can be divided into three categories:

- the use of a particular form and registration;
- appointment of the donees in compliance with s.10;
- that the donor has reached the age of 18 at the time of execution of the instrument and has capacity to execute the instrument.

Each of these validity requirements are considered in turn.

4.3.1   Form and registration

The instrument must be in the prescribed form and be registered in accordance with Sched.1 to the Act (s.9(2)(b)). Further, it must confer authority to make general or specific decisions about welfare and/or property and financial affairs and include authority to make decisions when P no longer has capacity (s.9(1)).

The requirements set down in Sched.1 have been supplemented by regulations: the Lasting Powers of Attorney, Enduring Powers of Attorney and Public Guardian Regulations 2007, SI 2007/1253 ('the 2007 Regulations'), which have been amended by the Lasting Powers of Attorney, Enduring Powers of Attorney and Public Guardian (Amendment) Regulations 2007, SI 2007/2161. These regulations contain further details about the particular requirements of the prescribed forms and other matters. Where the word 'prescribed' is used below, it relates to matters which are prescribed by regulations. The current regulations are the 2007 Regulations (as amended), although new regulations may be issued in the future and LPAs will need to be in the form prescribed by the regulations in force at the time of execution by the donor. The requirements of Sched.1 as supplemented by the 2007 Regulations are set out below.

There is further guidance on the registration process in the Code (paras.7.14–7.17). This suggests that an LPA should be registered soon after it has been made by the donor, in order to avoid delay when the LPA needs to be used. The Code also states that if an LPA has been registered but not used for some time, the attorney should inform the OPG when he or she begins to act under it so that the attorney can be sent relevant and up-to-date information.

Requirements of the instrument (Part 1 of Schedule 1)

An instrument creating an LPA must be in a prescribed form and have a specific content. Regulation 5 of the 2007 Regulations provides that particular forms are to be used to create an LPA. These forms are supposed to be set out in Sched.1 to the Regulations; however at the time of writing the forms are not found in that Schedule, although they can be downloaded from the website of the Office of the

Public Guardian (**www.publicguardian.gov.uk**). There are separate forms for creating a welfare LPA (LPA PW) and a property and affairs LPA (LPA PA). The forms set out the prescribed information and the statements that have to be made by the donor/donee. The prescribed LPA forms are significantly longer than the previous EPA forms and will take some time to complete. There are notes which accompany both LPA forms.

The LPA must include:

- '[P]rescribed information about the purpose of the instrument and the effect of a lasting power of attorney' (MCA 2005, Sched.1, para.2(1)(a)). The LPA forms contain the prescribed information (set out under the heading 'prescribed information',) which includes a summary of the principles of the Act and the powers of an attorney.
- A statement by the donor stating that he has read the prescribed information and intends the instrument to confer power to make decisions when he no longer has capacity (MCA 2005, Sched.1, para.2(1)(b)).
- A statement by the donor naming persons whom the donor wishes to be notified of any application to register (who cannot be donees under the instrument) known as 'named persons', or stating that he or she does not wish any persons to be notified (MCA 2005, Sched.1, para.2(1)(c)). Regulation 6 of the 2007 Regulations states that the maximum number of named persons is five. There is a requirement for two LPA certificates if no one is to be notified of an application to register (see below).
- A statement by the donee that he has read the prescribed information and understands the duties imposed on an LPA under s.1 (the principles) and s.4 (best interests) (MCA 2005, Sched.1, para.2(1)(d)).
- An LPA certificate, i.e. a certificate (in the prescribed form containing the prescribed information) by a person of a prescribed description (who cannot be a donee under the instrument) that in his opinion at the time when the donor executes the instrument the donor understands the purpose and scope of the instrument, no fraud or undue pressure is being used and there is nothing else to prevent an LPA being created (MCA 2005, Sched.1, para.2(1)(e)).

LPA CERTIFICATE

The LPA certificate forms part of the LPA forms. The certificate provider needs to complete Part B of the LPA form which sets out the information and matters that the provider needs to certify, including that he is acting independently and that he is aged 18 or over.

The persons who can give an LPA certificate are described in reg.8 of the 2007 Regulations. They fall into two categories: (i) a person chosen by the donor who has known the donor personally for at least two years at the point when the LPA certificate is signed; or (ii) a professional person chosen by the donor on the basis that the donor reasonably considers that the person is competent to make the judgments required (i.e. whether the donor understands the purpose and scope of the instrument). Examples of such professional persons are set out in reg.8 and include registered healthcare professionals, solicitors and barristers. There are also categories of persons who are disqualified, such as family members of the donor, the donee of the power, a business partner/employee of the donor or donee, and personnel at any care home where the donor is living when the instrument is executed (see further reg.8(3)). The requirement of two years' personal knowledge or the use of a professional person is a change from the system for EPAs, and is intended to reduce the instances of litigation arising from disputes regarding the capacity of the donor at the time of execution of the LPA instrument.

There is a requirement for two LPA certificates when there are no named persons (i.e. persons to be notified of any application to register the LPA instrument). The two LPA certificates must be completed and signed by different people (2007 Regulations, reg.7). This is an additional safeguard to prevent fraud. It was stated in the House of Lords on behalf of the government that it was considered that this provided sufficient additional protection against fraud and that specific provisions for monitoring by the Public Guardian on LPAs where no named persons are notified were neither necessary nor justified (see Committee debates on 8 February 2005 at col.761).

FAILURE TO COMPLY WITH PRESCRIBED FORM

If an instrument fails to comply with the prescribed form, the Public Guardian is to treat it as sufficient to create an LPA if it differs in an immaterial respect. Otherwise, the Court of Protection may declare that an instrument is to be treated as a valid LPA if satisfied that the person executing the instrument intended to create an LPA (MCA 2005, Sched.1, para.3).

EXECUTION OF THE INSTRUMENT

Regulation 9 of the 2007 Regulations sets out the way in which the LPA instrument must be executed. It is a step-by-step guide to execution. In summary, it requires that the following sequence is followed:

- the donor must read (or have read to him or her) the prescribed information (which is contained in the instrument);
- as soon as reasonably practicable thereafter, the donor needs to complete Part A of the instrument and sign it in the presence of a witness;
- as soon as reasonably practicable thereafter, the person (or persons if there is a need for two certificates) must complete the LPA certificate in Part B of the instrument;
- as soon as reasonably practicable thereafter, the donee or donees must read (or have read to them) the prescribed information in the instrument, complete Part C of the instrument and sign the instrument in the presence of a witness.

This sequence is necessary because the certificate provider must confirm that he or she has read Part A and because the donee(s) cannot accept a power that has not yet been conferred.

The witness needs to be at least 18. Neither the donor nor donee can witness each other's signature. It would not be advisable for the donor's spouse or civil partner to witness the donor's signature due to the rules of evidence about compellability.

If the donor or donee is unable to sign, he or she may leave a mark. Alternatively, a person can sign at the direction of the donor or donee, in which case it will have to be signed in the presence of the donor or donee and two witnesses.

Registration requirements (Part 2 of Schedule 1)

No powers in an LPA can be exercised until the instrument is registered. This is a key difference between the LPAs and the old EPA procedure. The application for registration is made to the Public Guardian.

The OPG has issued guidance on the registration of an LPA (LPA108), which is available from the OPG's website.

The procedure and requirements can be summarised as follows.

THE APPLICATION TO REGISTER

- The application to register an instrument intended to be an LPA must be in the prescribed form and contain prescribed information (MCA 2005, Sched.1, para.4(1)). The form to be used is LPA002. This form and the accompanying guidance notes can be downloaded from the OPG's website.
- The application must attach the instrument (MCA 2005, Sched.1, para.4(3)). Where the instrument sent with the application is neither the original instrument creating the power nor a certified copy of it, the Public Guardian must not register unless directed by the Court to do so (2007 Regulations, reg.11(2)).
- The application must be accompanied by the fee for registration. The fee has been prescribed by the Public Guardian (Fees etc.) Regulations 2007, SI 2007/2051 and is £150 (Public Guardian (Fees etc.) Regulations, reg.5 and Schedule).
- The application to register may be made by the donor or donees or by any of the donees if two or more are appointed to act jointly or severally in respect of any matter to the Public Guardian (MCA 2005, Sched.1, para.4(2)).
- There is criminal liability for false statements in applications to register (MCA 2005, Sched.1, para.4(4)).

NOTIFICATION OF AN APPLICATION TO REGISTER

- The donor or the donee (or donees) about to make an application for registration of an instrument must notify any named persons in the instrument to inform them that he or she is about to do so (MCA 2005, Sched.1, para.6). Notice must be given to the named persons using form LPA001. The Law Society's LPA Practice Note (24 September 2007) suggests sending the notice with an accompanying letter explaining the circumstances so as to avoid concerns being raised unnecessarily (para.11.3). There is no statutory requirement to do so, but a copy of the instrument could also be sent to the named persons given that one of the grounds of objection to registration is that the instrument is not valid as an LPA.

■ The Public Guardian must notify the donor or donee(s) (depending upon who makes the application) of the fact that an application to register has been received as soon as practicable after receiving it (MCA 2005, Sched.1, para.6(7), (8)). If only one of the donees has made the application, the Public Guardian must notify the other donee(s) as well as the donor. The forms to be used for giving notice are referred to in Sched.4 to the 2007 Regulations (forms LPA003A and LPA003B). There are separate forms for giving notice to the donor and to the donees. In respect of the donor, there is a duty on the Public Guardian, where it appears to him or her that there is good reason to so do, to provide or make provision for explaining the notice and its effect to the donor personally and in a way appropriate to his or her circumstances (2007 Regulations, reg.13(3)).

■ The court has the power to dispense with notification requirements upon application by the donor or donee(s) if satisfied they will serve no useful purpose (MCA 2005, Sched.1, para.10).

REGISTRATION BY THE PUBLIC GUARDIAN

■ Subject to there being problems with the instrument or objections being raised to registration, the Public Guardian must register the instrument as a LPA at the end of a period of six weeks beginning with the date when the Public Guardian gave notice to the donor and/or donee(s) that an application had been received (MCA 2005, Sched.1, para.4(5); 2007 Regulations, reg.12).

■ If it appears to the Public Guardian that the instrument accompanying an application was not made in accordance with Sched.1, he must not register the instrument unless the Court directs him to do so (MCA 2005, Sched.1, para.11(1)). The Public Guardian is not, however, required to make an application to the Court him or herself in these circumstances.

■ If it appears to the Public Guardian that the instrument contains a provision which would be ineffective as part of an LPA or would prevent the instrument from operating as a valid LPA, he must not register it at that time but refer the matter to the Court of Protection for a determination under s.23(1) of the Act (powers of the Court to determine any matters as to the meaning or effect of an LPA) (MCA 2005, Sched.1, para.11(2), (3)).

■ If the Court determines under s.23(1) that the LPA contains a provision which would be ineffective as part of an LPA or would prevent the instrument from operating as a valid LPA, the Court must notify the Public Guardian that it has severed the offending provision (so that it can be registered) or direct the Public Guardian not to register it. If the Court has severed a provision, the Public Guardian must register the instrument with a note to that effect (MCA 2005, Sched.1, para.11(4), (5)).

- The Public Guardian must not register an instrument if there is a deputy appointed by the Court whose powers would conflict with the attorney under the LPA unless directed to do so by the Court. (There is no obligation on the Public Guardian himself to refer the matter to the Court in these circumstances (MCA 2005, Sched.1, para.12).)
- Where the instrument to be registered which is sent with the application is neither the original instrument nor a certified copy of it, the Public Guardian must not register the instrument unless the Court directs him or her to do so (2007 Regulations, reg.11(2)).

OBJECTIONS TO REGISTRATION

Objections by the donee or named person to the Public Guardian

- A donee or named person who receives notice that an application for registration is about to be made or that an application has been received by the Public Guardian, can give notice to the Public Guardian of an objection to registration on certain factual grounds, namely that an event described in s.13(3) or (6)(a)–(d) has occurred within a period of five weeks beginning with the date when notice was given (MCA 2005, Sched.1, para.13(1); 2007 Regulations, reg.14 (as amended)). These grounds (s.13(3) or (6)(a)–(d)) are that the LPA has already been revoked by: P's bankruptcy (in respect of a property and affairs LPA); a disclaimer of the appointment by the donee; the death of the donee; the bankruptcy of the donee (in respect of property and affairs, note also particular provisions for interim bankruptcy orders); or the dissolution or annulment of a marriage or civil partnership between the donor and donee.

It is also clear that a factual ground of objection to registration is that the donor is dead. Curiously, this is not referred to in s.13 (which does list all of the other factual grounds of objection) and must be an omission. However, the prescribed forms provide for objection being made on this ground.

- The objection must be made in writing and contain certain information (2007 Regulations, reg.14(3)). There is also a particular form that can be used for this purpose (LPA007 available from the OPG website), although the 2007 Regulations do not require that this form is used.
- The Public Guardian must notify the objector as to whether he is satisfied that the ground of objection is established (2007 Regulations, reg.14(4)). The Public Guardian also has the power to require the objector to provide further information or to produce documents (reg.14(4), (5)).
- If the Public Guardian is satisfied that the ground is made out, he must not register the instrument unless the Court on an application of the person applying for registration is satisfied that the ground is not established and directs the Public Guardian to register the instrument (MCA 2005, Sched.1, para.13(2)).
- There is a requirement for the Public Guardian to include a note explaining if the ground of objection is made out but the instrument is not revoked on

the basis of s.13(7) of the Act which provides for circumstances where a donee's appointment is terminated but the instrument is not revoked (e.g. the donee is replaced under the terms of the instrument (2007 Regulations, reg.14(6)).

■ A donee or named person can make a further objection to the Public Guardian (provided that the five week time limit has not expired) in circumstances where the Public Guardian is not satisfied that the particular ground of objection is made out (2007 Regulations, reg.14(7)).

Objections by the donee or named person to the Court

■ The donee or named person who receives notice that an application for registration is about to be made or that an application has been received by the Public Guardian can make an application to the Court objecting to registration within a period of five weeks beginning on the date when notice was given (2007 Regulations, reg.15(3)). The grounds for making an objection application to the Court are wider than the grounds of objection to the Public Guardian but specifically exclude those categories of objection that can (and, therefore, must) be made to the Public Guardian (2007 Regulations, reg.15(2)):

(a) that one or more of the requirements for creation of an LPA have not been met;

(b) that the power has been revoked, or has otherwise come to an end, on a ground other than the grounds set out in paragraph 13(1) of Schedule 1 to the Act [the events referred to in section 13(3) and (6)(a)–(d) of the Act, described above];

(c) any of the grounds set out in paragraph (a) or (b) of section 22(3) of the Act [use of fraud or undue pressure on P to execute an LPA or create an LPA or the donee(s) behaves (or proposes to behave) in a way to contravene his authority or contrary to P's best interests].

There is a specific application form for making such an objection (COP 7, available from the OPG's website).

The donee or named person must notify the Public Guardian in writing of the application to the Court and the Public Guardian must not register the instrument unless the Court directs him to do so (MCA 2005, Sched.1, para.13(3), (4); 2007 Regulations, reg.15(4)). Form LPA008 can be used for notifying the Public Guardian, and this can be downloaded from the OPG's website.

Objections by the donor to the Public Guardian

■ When a donor receives notice from the Public Guardian that an application to register an instrument by a donee (or donees) has been received (pursuant to para.8 of Sched.1 to the Act), the donor can give notice of objection to the Public Guardian within five weeks of the date when he received notice from the Public Guardian (2007 Regulations, reg.14A, inserted by the amendment regulations). Unlike the situation for donees or named persons, a donor is not restricted to objections that the instrument has been revoked when giving notice to the Public Guardian (s.13) and can object generally or on any ground whatsoever, which would include that the donor no longer wants to confer powers on the donee. The notice of objection must be in writing and contain certain information (e.g. the ground of objection) (2007 Regulations, reg.14A(3)). Form LPA006 can be used to give notice (available from the OPG's website), but the 2007 Regulations do not require that this form is used. The donor does not have to make an application to the Court to object and can simply give notice of objection to the Public Guardian.

■ The effect of such notice of objection being given by the donor is that the Public Guardian must not register the instrument unless the Court, on the application of a donee, is satisfied that the donor lacks capacity to object to the registration and directs the Public Guardian to register the instrument (MCA 2005, Sched.1, para.14). These provisions protect a donor's decision-making autonomy and reflect the donor's power to revoke a power at any time (s.13(2)). Upon any such application by the donee, the Court would, in the event that the donor was found to lack capacity to object, have power to determine whether the requirements for creation of a LPA have been met, whether the power has been revoked or otherwise have come to an end and to revoke the power in cases of fraud etc. (s.22) and would direct the Public Guardian to cancel the registration of the instrument in certain circumstances (MCA 2005, Sched.1, para.18).

NOTIFICATION OF REGISTRATION

The Public Guardian must give notice of registration to the donor and donee(s) (MCA 2005, Sched.1, para.15; 2007 Regulations, reg.17). The form to be used is LPA 004. The Public Guardian must also arrange for further explanation of these matters to the donor if it appears to him that there is good reason to do so (2007 Regulations, reg.17).

The Public Guardian must retain a copy of the instrument registered as an LPA and return to the person(s) who applied for registration, the original instrument or certified copy which was sent for registration (2007 Regulations, reg.17).

NOTIFICATION OF NON-REGISTRATION

The Public Guardian must notify the person(s) who applied for registration of the fact of non-registration (2007 Regulations, reg.16).

EVIDENCE OF REGISTRATION

Following registration, the existence of an LPA can be proved by the original stamped instrument, an office copy or a certified copy (MCA 2005, Sched.1, para.16). In case of doubt, a third party could search the register of LPAs maintained by the Public Guardian (see **12.3.1**).

4.3.2   Appointment of donees

A donee must be an individual who has reached the age of 18 or in respect of property and affairs, a trust corporation. A trust corporation is defined in s.68(1) of the Trustee Act 1925 as the Public Trustee or a corporation either appointed by the court in a particular case to be a trustee or entitled by rules made under s.4(3) of the Public Trustee Act 1906 to act as a custodian trustee. An individual is therefore required to make welfare decisions (s.10(1)).

A person who is bankrupt may not act as a donee in respect of property and affairs (s.10(2)). But such a person is not prevented from being a donee in respect of welfare.

These provisions mirror those in respect of deputies (see **6.6**).

More than one donee

When there is more than one donee, the instrument creating the LPA can appoint them to act jointly or severally or jointly in respect of some matters and severally in respect of others (s.10(4)). Jointly means that both attorneys must act together in any act carried out under the LPA (e.g. both must sign cheques). Jointly and severally means that the attorneys can act separately from one another (e.g. the signature of one attorney on the cheque is enough). The LPA forms do not use these legal terms but refer to attorneys 'working together', 'together and independently' or 'together in respect of some matters and together and independently in respect of others'. One of these alternatives should be ticked by the donor in the LPA form.

In the absence of specification in the instrument about this, donees are assumed to be appointed to act jointly (s.10(5)). However, care needs to be taken when specifying how attorneys are to act. The Court of Appeal has held in a case about an EPA that where three attorneys were appointed to act jointly 'save that any two of the attorneys may sign', that the instrument could not operate as an EPA (*Re E* [2000] 3 WLR 1974). It is likely that the same approach would be adopted in respect of an LPA because the fall-back provision in s.10(5) only applies when no specification has been made. However, this error should be avoided by the fact that the LPA form provides tick boxes for specifying how attorney(s) are to act.

If they are appointed to act jointly or severally, a failure by one donee to satisfy the formality requirements as regards execution of the instrument or failure to meet the requirements about age or non-bankruptcy does not prevent the instrument having effect in respect of other donees (s.10(7)).

Successive donees

An instrument creating an LPA cannot give the donee the power to appoint his own successor. The power to appoint a donee is personal to the donor and any instrument conferring a power of substitution on the donee will not be a valid LPA (ss.10(8), 9(3)). But the instrument can itself appoint a person to replace a donee (or, if there is more than one, any donee) in the event that a donee's power is automatically revoked in accordance with s.13(6). Section 13(6) provides that the power will be revoked upon the occurrence of: disclaimer of the appointment by the donee; death, bankruptcy or winding up of the donee (for a property and financial affairs LPA); dissolution or annulment of a marriage or civil partnership between the donor and donee; or the lack of capacity of the donee (discussed further at 4.8).

4.3.3   Age and capacity of donor

Under s.9(2)(c) of the Act, the donor must have reached the age of 18 at the time of execution of the instrument.

The donor must have capacity to execute the instrument. However, there is no specific test of what level of capacity is required to make an LPA, and the Code of Practice does not contain any guidance on the assessment of capacity of a person to execute an LPA. The presumption of capacity will apply so that the burden will be on a person objecting to registration to establish lack of capacity.

It is likely that the courts will consider established case law on capacity to make an EPA. The leading case is the Court of Appeal's decision in *Re W (Enduring Power of Attorney)* [2001] 2 WLR 957 which endorsed a four-stage test – that the donor should understand:

(1) the scope of the authority;
(2) the terms of the power (i.e. to do anything which the donor could have done);
(3) that the authority will continue upon incapacity of the donor;
(4) that when a person becomes incapable the power will be irrevocable without the intervention of the Court.

(It should be noted that the particular phrasing of the test in *Re W* reflected the fact that the EPA related only to financial matters, but it can be summarised as stated here so as to make it of general application.)

It is to be noted that Sched.1 to the Act requires certification to the effect that the donor understands the purpose of the instrument and the scope of the authority conferred under it (para.2(1)(e), which sets out the test of capacity in a simpler form than in *Re W*). In addition, the certificate provider must certify that no fraud or undue pressure is being used to induce the donor to create the LPA and that there is nothing else which would prevent the LPA being created.

4.4   CONTENT OF LPAS

As stated above, LPAs can cover property and financial affairs and welfare matters. There are separate forms for property and affairs LPAs and welfare LPAs. A personal welfare attorney has no authority to make financial decisions and vice versa, although the same person could be appointed in separate LPAs to carry out both these roles.

Property and financial affairs LPAs (financial LPAs) can be used both before and after the donor loses capacity. Welfare LPAs can only be used when the person lacks capacity. It is important to note that the incapacity test under the Act is a functional and time-specific test (s.2, see **Chapter 3**). This means that there will not generally be one point in time when a donor stops acting and a donee takes over all decision-making.

The donor must be clear whether the LPA is to be a general power, giving the attorney(s) authority to manage all the donor's property and affairs or to make all personal welfare decisions, or whether any restrictions and/or conditions are to be placed on their power. All powers are subject to any conditions or restrictions specified in the instrument granting the LPA (s.9(4)(b)). In this way the donor is able to regulate exactly what powers are to be granted to the donee.

As well as imposing restrictions/conditions on the attorney(s), the prescribed LPA forms (for both property and affairs LPAs and personal welfare LPAs) make provision for guidance to be provided to the attorney when making decisions in the donor's best interests. Unlike restrictions or conditions, this guidance is not binding but will be something to be taken into account by the attorney(s) when making decisions about best interests.

Donees of LPAs must act within the scope of their powers and must also comply with all the provisions in the Act and, in particular, the principles set out in s.1 and they must always act in the best interests of the donor who lacks capacity (in accordance with s.4) (s.9(4)) (see **4.7.2**). (The express reference to the general principles in Part 1 was added to the Bill at the report stage in the House of Lords (HL Bill 48).) The Code also refers attorneys to chapters 3, 4 and 5 of the Code when assessing the donor's capacity and best interests (paras.7.18–7.20).

4.4.1   Welfare LPAs

Donors are able to make a general welfare LPA which permits a donee to act in respect of all matters concerning welfare, or an LPA which lists specific matters in respect of which the donee has authority. For example, a donor may only want a donee to make decisions about social care but not health care matters.

Welfare LPAs can only be used once the donor has lost capacity or the donee reasonably believes that he has lost capacity (s.11(7)(a)).

There is no list in the Act of the types of decisions which welfare donees can be authorised to take, although the list in s.17 of powers which the Court has in respect of welfare matters is instructive, even though it is only a sample list of those powers. The Code of Practice also provides a sample list of powers which a welfare donee could be authorised to take by an LPA (at para.7.21). Welfare powers include:

- deciding where the donor should live;
- deciding about day-to-day care, including diet and dress;
- deciding what contact, if any, the donor is to have with specified persons;
- giving or refusing consent to medical examination and/or treatment (including the continuation of treatment);
- arranging for the donor to access medical, dental or optical treatment;
- applying for and having access to confidential documents and personal information relating to the donor held by any organisation, such as medical records or personal files held by social services authorities.

A general LPA will permit a donee to make all of the sorts of decisions listed above. However, it is open to the donor to specify or exclude specific powers. Certain powers have to be specified in the instrument in order for the donee to be able to exercise them (see 4.5.3).

The Code states that an attorney must before making a decision under a personal welfare LPA make sure that (para.7.24):

- the LPA has been registered with the OPG;
- the donor lacks capacity to make the particular decision or the attorney reasonably believes that the donor lacks capacity to make the decision covered by the LPA (having applied the Act's principles); and
- the attorney is making the decision in the donor's best interests.

Where professionals are preparing a care plan for a person who has appointed a personal welfare attorney, if the donor lacks capacity to agree to the care plan or parts of it, professionals must consult the attorney and obtain his or her agreement to the care plan, and consult the attorney when considering what action is in the person's best interests (Code, para.7.25).

4.4.2   Financial LPAs

Financial LPAs can include powers to be exercised:

- while a donor retains capacity and to continue after the donor loses capacity;
- only once a donor loses capacity.

The Code of Practice states that while the donor retains capacity or has fluctuating or partial capacity, the attorney should allow and encourage the donor to do as much as possible and should only act when the donor asks them to or to make those decisions that the donor lacks capacity to make. Although, the Code acknowledges that in some cases the donor may wish to hand over all decisions to the attorney, even those which he or she has capacity to make (para.7.34).

Donors can make a general financial LPA covering all matters relating to their property and affairs or grant powers in specific areas to the donee. There is no list in the Act of powers included in financial LPAs. However, the list provided in respect of the Court of Protection's powers in respect of financial matters is a useful guide, save that certain restrictions are placed on the powers that can be exercised by donees of financial LPAs (s.18). Further, there is a list of the types of powers that can be granted and exercised in the Code of Practice (at para.7.36).

The Code of Practice lists the types of powers that can be granted under a financial LPA as including:

- buying or selling property;
- opening, closing or operating any bank, building society or other account containing the donor's funds;
- giving access to financial information to others concerning the donor;
- claiming, receiving and using on the donor's behalf all benefits, pensions, allowances, rebates etc. to which the donor may be entitled (unless another person has already been appointed to do this by the Department for Work and Pensions and all want this arrangement to continue);
- receiving any income, inheritance or other entitlement of the donor;
- dealing with the donor's tax affairs;
- paying the donor's mortgage, rent and/or household expenses;
- making appropriate arrangements to insure, maintain and repair the donor's property;
- investing the donor's savings;
- making gifts on behalf of the donor (but subject to restrictions – see 4.6);
- paying for private medical care and/or residential care or nursing home fees;
- applying for any entitlement to funding for NHS care, social care or adaptations;
- using the donor's income or capital to purchase a vehicle or any aids, adaptations or equipment required by the donor where these are not provided free of charge;
- repaying interest and capital on any loan taken out by the donor or donee on the donor's behalf.

The Code suggests that the donor might want to appoint somone (a family member or professsional) to go through the accounts with the attorney from time to time. Any such arrangements should be included in the LPA (para.7.39).

Access to personal information

Welfare and financial and affairs attorneys may need access to personal information about the donor. Chapter 16 of the Code discusses the donee's rights to access personal information.

4.5   RESTRICTIONS ON LPAS

4.5.1   Restraint

The restrictions on LPAs are contained mainly in s.11 of the Act. This restriction applies to financial LPAs and welfare LPAs.

The principal restriction upon donees of LPAs relates to the use of restraint. This is discussed in more detail at **5.3** and those paragraphs should be referred to for more detailed analysis of the use of restraint.

An attorney may restrain the donee of a power only if three conditions are satisfied (s.11(1)):

- P lacks or the donee reasonably believes that P lacks capacity in relation to the matter (s.11(2));
- the donee reasonably believes that it is necessary to do the act to prevent harm to P (s.11(3));
- the act is a proportionate response to the likelihood of P suffering harm and the seriousness of that harm (s.11(4)).

Further, the donee must be satisfied that it is in P's best interests to restrain P. This requirement arises from the fact that a donee's authority is subject to the provisions of the Act generally and, in particular, the best interests provisions in s.4 (s.9(4)(a)).

Restraint is defined as (s.11(5)):

- the use or threat of use of force to secure the doing of an act which P resists;
- the restriction of P's liberty of movement whether or not P resists.

A donee is not authorised to deprive P of his liberty within the meaning of Art.5(1) of the ECHR (s.11(6)). See further discussion of deprivation of liberty in **Chapter 5**.

4.5.2   Restrictions imposed by the instrument

A donee will be subject to any restrictions and conditions which are contained in the instrument (s.9(4)(b)).

4.5.3   Specific restrictions on welfare LPAs

The specific restrictions on welfare LPAs are as follows:

- The powers cannot be exercised except where P lacks capacity or the donee reasonably believes P lacks capacity (s.11(7)). Reasonable belief is an objective test and the donee will need to show reasonable grounds for believing that P lacks capacity. This particular restriction ensures that P's autonomy to make decisions about matters most personal to him or her is preserved.

- The welfare powers are subject to advance decisions about treatment made by P (s.11(7)(b)). Advance decisions are discussed in **Chapter** 7. This restriction ensures proper respect for the wishes of P. If P has made an advance decision about a particular medical treatment, that decision usually takes priority. An attorney cannot consent if the donor has made a valid and applicable advance decision to refuse specific treatment. But if the donor made an LPA after the advance decision, and gave the attorney the right to consent to or refuse the treatment, the attorney can choose not to follow the advance decision (Code, para.7.27).

- There is no general power to give or refuse consent to the carrying out or continuation of life-sustaining treatment unless the instrument contains express provision to that effect and that power will be subject to any conditions or restrictions laid down by the instrument (although there is a general power to give or refuse consent to the carrying out or continuation of other types of medical treatment) (s.11(7)(c) and (8)). The need for an express grant of a power in respect of decisions concerning life-sustaining treatment reflects the fundamental importance of such a power. While the donor may be happy for a donee to make all other types of welfare decisions, the donor may not be content for the donee to have authority to decide matters of life and death. A donor may choose instead to make an advance directive or prefer to leave this type of decision to medical professionals. The welfare LPA form (at question 6) requires the donor to choose either option A (grant of power to give or refuse consent to life-sustaining treatment) or option B (no authority to give or refuse consent to life-sustaining treatment).

LPAs cannot give attorneys the power to demand specific forms of medical treatment that staff do not believe are necessary or appropriate (Code, para.7.28).

In the event of a disagreement between health professionals about a donor's best interests, the Code suggests that the healthcare staff should discuss the case with other medical experts and/or get a second opinion and then discuss the matter further with the attorney. If agreement cannot be reached, they can apply to the Court of Protection. While the court is coming to a decision, healthcare staff can give life-sustaining treatment to prolong the donor's life or stop the donor's condition getting worse (Code, para.7.29).

4.6   SCOPE OF FINANCIAL LPAS: GIFTS

4.6.1   Background

Restrictions on gifts that could be made by a donee of an EPA were imposed by EPAA 1985. Section 3(5) provided that an attorney could make gifts on behalf of charities or persons 'related to or connected with the donor'. In respect of gifts, they had to be of 'a seasonal nature or at a time, or on an anniversary, of a birth or marriage' implying that it applied to a gift given on a regular basis as opposed to one-off gifts on customary occasions (save for the specific occasions of weddings and births which were expressly mentioned).

There was also a provision that the size of the gift should not be unreasonable having regard to all the circumstances and, in particular, the size of the donor's estate.

4.6.2   Position under the Mental Capacity Act

Although the provisions relating to gifts in the Act are largely the same as those in EPAA 1985, the wording has been changed to permit gifts being made on customary but one-off occasions such as baptism or graduation.

A donee may make gifts (s.12(2)):

■   on customary occasions to persons (including him or herself) who are related to or connected with the donor if the value of the gift is not unreasonable having regard to all the circumstances and, in particular, the size of the donor's estate;

■   to any charity to whom the donor made or might have been expected to make gifts if the value of the gift is not unreasonable having regard to all the circumstances and, in particular, the size of the donor's estate.

4.6.3   Customary occasion

This is defined as:

■   the occasion or anniversary of a birth, a marriage or formation of a civil partnership; or

■   any other occasion on which presents are customarily given within families or among friends or associates.

This definition, therefore, includes the occasion and anniversary of a civil partnership as well as marriage.

Further, in contrast with the definition in the EPAA 1985, there is a broader definition of other occasions when gifts may be made. The requirement is that gifts must be given customarily on that occasion but it does not need to be a regularly occurring event (e.g. a graduation, retirement, housewarming).

The customary occasion requirement does not apply to charitable gifts, which can be made at any time of the year.

4.6.4   Reasonableness of size

The test is the same as that under EPAA 1985. It will depend on all the circumstances, and the donee has to apply his own judgment. In general, it can be said that gifts ought to be made from surplus income or should not be significant with respect to the size of the donor's estate. The Code states that it would not be reasonable to buy expensive gifts at Christmas if the donor was living on modest means and had to do without essential items in order to pay for them (para.7.41).

4.6.5   Other restrictions in the instrument

The donor cannot use the LPA to make more extensive gifts than are allowed by s.12. However, the donor can impose stricter conditions or requirements on gifting. The donor may also include specific restrictions and conditions on the donee's powers to make a gift which must be adhered to by the donee (s.12(4)). The Law Society's LPA Practice Note (24 September 2007, at para.7.2) suggests that this should be considered by the donor, because improper gifting in relation to EPAs was a widespread form of abuse in attorneyship. For example, the donor could specify in the power the circumstances in which the attorney(s) may make gifts of money or property.

4.6.6   Application to the Court of Protection

If the proposed gift is not covered by s.12(2) or if the donee is in doubt, the donee can apply to the Court of Protection which has the power to authorise the making of gifts which are not within s.12(2) (s.23(4)).

4.7   DUTIES ON ATTORNEYS

4.7.1   Background

The Act does not materially alter the general duties imposed on attorneys of LPAs from the duties that are imposed on attorneys of EPAs.

An authority conferred by an LPA does not oblige a donee to act, but it authorises a donee to act if he or she wishes to do so. Once a donee starts to act, the donee will assume a number of duties and responsibilities which are imposed by the Act and the common law, including a duty of care and fiduciary duties. The attorney acts as the donor's agent and has all the duties and obligations of an agent.[1] As an agent, an attorney owes the same duties to his principal as does a Deputy (who also acts as an agent: see s.19(6) and discussion at 6.6.1). If the donee fails to comply, this could result in his or her removal as attorney; alternatively, the donee could be liable for civil or criminal offences.

Donees are in a position of trust so there is always the potential for abuse. The main protection against abuse is the donor selecting a suitable donee. However, that will not always be an adequate safeguard against abuse. One change from the EPA scheme is that LPAs must be registered before they can be used, and it is envisaged that the new registration requirements will assist in combating abuse. The notification to named persons of an application to register should also help to reduce abuse. Concerns about abuse of powers by donees can be reported to the OPG, which can direct a Court of Protection Visitor to visit a donee or donor to investigate and report to the Public Guardian (s.58(1)(d)). The Public Guardian could then report to the Court and the Court of Protection could decide to revoke the LPA or instrument (s.22(3), which is discussed further below) or (through the Public Guardian) prevent the instrument from being registered.

4.7.2   Duties on the attorney of an LPA

Duty to act within the scope of the LPA

A donee must act within the actual scope of the powers set out in the LPA including any specific conditions and restrictions laid down by the donor (s.9(4)(b)). If the donee considers that additional powers are needed to act, he or she must make an application to the Court of Protection (see **Chapters 6** and **11**).

However, as an agent an attorney will have implied authority to do what is necessary for or incidental to the effective execution of express authority. This is not a matter addressed in the Code of Practice or the Explanatory Notes.

The Code states that it is good practice for decision-makers to consult attorneys about any decision or action, whether or not it is covered by the LPA. This is because an attorney is likely to have important information about the wishes and feelings of the donor (para.7.57).

Duty to act in accordance with the principles of the Act and in the donor's best interests

When donees of LPAs exercise their powers, they must comply with all the provisions in the Act and, in particular, the principles set out in s.1, and they must always act in the best interests of the donor (in accordance with s.4) (s.9(4)). This means, for example, that the donee must (see **Chapter 3** for detailed discussion of ss.1 and 4):

■   consider whether the donor has capacity to make the decision for himself (ss.2, 3) and if not, should consider whether the donor is likely to regain capacity (s.4(3));

■   not treat the donor as unable to make a decision unless all practicable steps have been taken to help him to do so without success (s.1(3));

■   not treat the donor as incapable merely because he makes an unwise decision (s.1(4));

■   make decisions or take actions in accordance with the best interests of a person who lacks capacity (s.1(5));

■   in coming to a view as to the donor's best interests, consider whether the donor is likely to obtain capacity in the future, permit and encourage the donor to participate as fully as possible in the decision, consider the donor's past and present wishes and feelings and beliefs, and consult where appropriate with friends and relatives with an interest in P's welfare (s.4).

An attorney is also under a specific obligation imposed by the Act to have regard to the Code of Practice when acting in relation to a person who lacks capacity as the donee of an LPA (s.42(4) of the Act). The Code states that attorneys ought to pay special attention to chapters 2–5 inclusive (para.7.54) and might find it useful to refer to guidance in other chapters (para.7.55).

Duty to comply with directions of the Court of Protection

The Court of Protection has wide powers under ss.22 and 23 of the Act to determine questions and give directions as to the meaning and effect of an LPA. The Court can also require donees to provide accounts, reports or records, require the donee to supply information or produce documents or things in the possession of the donee, give directions for remuneration of the donee and relieve the donee wholly or partly from any liability incurred for breach of his or her duties as donee. Donees must comply with any orders or directions of the Court.

Not to disclaim without notifying the donor and the Court

A person cannot give up the role of attorney without notifying the donor and the Court. Schedule 6 to the 2007 Regulations sets out the prescribed form that must be used by a donee to disclaim his or her appointment as donee. The completed form must be sent to the donor and a copy must be sent to the Public Guardian and any other donee who is appointed under the power.

Duty to keep accounts

A financial donee must keep up-to-date accounts of his or her dealings and transactions on the donor's behalf. The Code of Practice states that where a lay person, such as a family member, is acting as donee, and the donor's affairs are fairly straightforward, a record of the donor's income and expenditure (for example, through bank statements) may be enough (para.7.67). However, more will be required when the attorney is acting as a professional attorney or the donor's financial affairs are complicated.

Duty to preserve the separate character of the donor's property

The donee should keep the donor's money separate from his or her own. A possible exception stated in the Code is where the donee is a husband or wife and the couple have agreed in the past to have a joint bank account. But in most circumstances, finances should be kept separate.

Duty of care

A donee owes the donor a duty of care in carrying out his or her functions as attorney, commensurate with any skills the donee has or holds him or herself out as having. A higher standard of care will be expected of a professional attorney who receives remuneration for acting (Code, para.7.59).

Duty not to delegate

It is a principle of the law of agency that an agent cannot delegate his or her authority. The donee is the agent of the donor. It is only in respect of tasks which the donor would not expect the donee to carry out personally which can be delegated. Any wider powers of delegation will need to be expressly set out in the instrument.

Duty not to take advantage of his position

The donee is a fiduciary and must not profit from his or her position. Donees must avoid any conflicts between their responsibilities towards the donor and their own interests. They must be guided by the principles of the Act and the duty to act in the donor's best interests. If a donee is concerned about a conflict of interest, he or she can apply to the Court for directions as to how to operate the LPA or for approval of a gift (s.23(2) and (4)).

Duty of good faith

A donee must act honestly and in good faith.

Duty of confidentiality

A donee has a duty to keep the donor's affairs confidential unless the donor has consented to disclosure or there is some other good reason for disclosing personal or financial information which overrides the duty such as the public interest.

---

1 See *Bowstead on Agency* 18th edn (Sweet & Maxwell) for more detailed discussions of the duty of an agent.

4.8 REVOCATION OF AN LPA

4.8.1 Background

The revocation provisions in EPAA 1985 are broadly similar to those in the Act, although it is no longer necessary for the court to confirm revocation by the donor, as was necessary under EPAA 1985 (in respect of instruments which had been registered) (EPAA 1985, ss.7(1)(a), 8(3)). The court previously had to confirm that the donor had done what was necessary to effect an express revocation and that the donor had capacity to revoke. However, with an EPA the donor would already be incapable or becoming incapable, otherwise the instrument would not be registered at all. Confirmation by the court is no longer required

(MCA 2005, s.13(2)). However, the court has the power to declare whether the instrument has in fact been revoked by the donor if an application to it is made (s.22(2)(b)). Under EPAA 1985, it was the court which had the responsibility for cancelling the registration of an instrument in circumstances where it had been revoked (EPAA 1985, s.8(4)). That is now the remit of the Public Guardian (see MCA 2005, Sched.1, Part 3).

4.8.2   Position under the Act

The revocation provisions apply when the donor has executed an instrument with a view to creating an LPA or when an LPA has been registered. The term 're-voking the power' is used in the Act to include revoking the instrument. It should also be noted that the Court of Protection has additional powers of revocation in situations of fraud, undue pressure, contravention of authority or acts contrary to a donor's best interests (see 6.8).

The situations where the appointment power will be revoked under s.13 are as follows.

Matters affecting the donor:

- The donor revokes the power when he or she has capacity to do so (s.13(2)). Regulation 21 of the 2007 Regulations provides that the donor who has revoked an LPA must notify the Public Guardian and donee(s) of the revocation. The Public Guardian must then cancel the registration of the LPA if he is satisfied that the donor has taken the necessary legal steps to revoke the LPA. The Public Guardian must give notice of cancellation of registration to the donor and donee(s).
- The donor's bankruptcy revokes the power in respect of property and affairs (s.13(3)); however, the power is merely suspended if an interim bankruptcy order is made for the duration of the order (s.13(4)).
- The death of the donor is not listed as one of the events revoking the power in s.13; however, revocation of the LPA must follow from death of the donor (as is the case for EPAs).

Matters affecting the donee:

- The disclaimer by the donee of his power (s.13(5), (6)(a)). Schedule 6 to the 2007 Regulations sets out the form which the donee must use to disclaim (form LPA005). The completed form must be sent to the donor and a copy of it to the Public Guardian and any other donee (2007 Regulations, reg.20);
- The death of a donee (s.13(5), (6)(b)).
- The bankruptcy of a donee in respect of financial powers but not welfare powers (save that if an interim bankruptcy restrictions order is made, the financial powers will only be suspended for the duration of that order) (s.13(5), (6)(b), (8), (9)).
- The dissolution or annulment of a marriage or civil partnership between the donor or donee unless the instrument expressly provides that it does not have that effect (s.13(6)(c), (11)).

■   The lack of capacity of the donee (s.13(6)(d)).

If the donee has been replaced under the instrument or there remain other donee(s) appointed to act jointly and severally, the effect of these events will be only to terminate the appointment of the donee but not to revoke the power itself (s.13(6), (7)).

Following revocation of the instrument, the Public Guardian must cancel the registration of an instrument as an LPA on being satisfied that it has been revoked as a result of the donor's bankruptcy, the donor's death or on the occurrence of an event affecting the donee as provided for in s.13(6)(a)–(d) (listed above) or when directed by the Court of Protection to cancel the instrument (MCA 2005, Sched.1, Part 3; 2007 Regulations, reg.22). If the Public Guardian cancels the registration of the instrument, he must notify the donor and donee(s).

4.8.3   Concerns

Save for the duty on the donor to notify the Public Guardian when he revokes the power, there is no mechanism in the Act for the Public Guardian being informed of acts or circumstances giving rise to revocation of the LPA (except when the Court of Protection directs him to cancel registration). Unless the Public Guardian is made so aware, he or she will not be in a position to cancel the registration of the instrument and the register will include LPAs that have in fact been revoked pursuant to the provisions of s.13 of the Act.

4.9   PROTECTION IF NO POWER CREATED OR REVOKED

4.9.1   Background

Protection is afforded by the EPAA 1985 to provide protection to the attorney under an EPA and any person dealing with him in good faith (EPAA 1985, s.9). These provisions are broadly mirrored in the Act (s.14).

4.9.2   No power created

The protection provided by the Act applies in circumstances where the LPA instrument was registered under MCA 2005, Sched.1 (see registration provisions discussed above) but an LPA was not created, regardless of whether or not the registration has been cancelled at the time of the act or transaction in question.

Protection for donees (s.14(2))

A donee exercising powers when a LPA was registered but not created, does not incur liability to the donor or others because of the non-existence of the power unless:

- he knows an LPA was not created; or
- he is aware of circumstances which would have terminated his authority to act even if an LPA had been created.

The test is one of actual knowledge or awareness and not an objective test as to whether the donee ought reasonably to have known.

Protection for other persons (s.14(3))

Transactions between a donee and other person (in circumstances where an LPA was registered but was not created) which are in favour of that person (and not the donee) are valid unless that person, at the time of the transaction:

- knew an LPA was not created; or
- was aware of circumstances which would have terminated the donee's authority to act even if an LPA had been created.

Further, s.14(4) of the Act provides that there is a presumption of validity in a transaction between a donee and another person where the interest of the purchaser (i.e. a third party) depends on the transaction being valid under s.14(3), if the transaction was completed within 12 months of the instrument being registered or the third party makes a statutory declaration within three months after completion of the purchase stating that he had no reason to doubt the donee's authority to dispose of the property at the time of purchase.

4.9.3   Power revoked

Section 5 of the Powers of Attorney Act (PAA) 1971 applies to provide protection to the donee and third parties where the LPA is revoked. The donee is protected if at the time he did not know of the revocation (or of an event which has the effect of revoking the power, e.g. death of the donor) (PAA 1971, s.5(1), (5)). A transaction between the donee and a third party is valid in favour of the third party if the third party did not know of the revocation (or of an event which has the effect of revoking the power) (PAA 1971, s.5(2), (5)). The same presumption of validity in respect of disposals of property applies (PAA 1971, s.5(4)).

Section 14(5) provides that the protection afforded by PAA 1971, s.5 also applies in situations where an LPA covers welfare as well as property and affairs and it is only the donee's powers in respect of property and affairs which have come to an end, e.g. as a result of bankruptcy of the donee.

4.10   POWERS OF THE COURT IN RESPECT OF LPAS

The Court has powers in relation to the validity and operation of LPAs (MCA 2005, ss.22 and 23) (see further discussion in **Chapter 11**).

4.11   RECORDS OF ALTERATIONS

Part 4 of Sched.1 to the Act sets out the circumstances in which the Public Guardian must make notes on the instrument about alterations affecting the power, e.g. partial revocation or suspension of a power as a result of bankcruptcy, severance of ineffective provisions, replacement of a donee, termination of an appointment of the donee which does not revoke the power.

If such a note has to be attached to the instrument, notice must be given by the Public Guardian to the donor and the donee(s) requiring them to deliver to the Public Guardian the original instrument, any office copy and any certified copy. After the notes have been attached, the documents will be returned (2007 Regulations, reg.18). If any such document has been lost or destroyed, there is a requirement that information be provided to the Public Guardian in writing as the date of loss or destruction (2007 Regulations, reg.19).

4.12   ROLE OF THE PUBLIC GUARDIAN IN RESPECT OF LPAS

The Public Guardian has a number of functions in respect of LPAs which include:

- establishing and maintaining a register of all LPAs (s.58);
- visiting, or directing a Court of Protection Visitor to visit, a donor or donee (s.58);
- exercising his power to require information from donees of LPAs where there are circumstances suggesting that the attorney may be contravening his authority or acting contrary to the best interests of the donor (or proposing to so behave) or the attorney has failed to comply with an order or directions of the Court (2007 Regulations, reg.46).

The role of the Public Guardian is discussed in further detail in **Chapter 12**.

4.13   ARRANGEMENTS FOR EPAS

4.13.1   Background

The Act repeals EPAA 1985 (s.66), and therefore it will not be possible to execute an EPA once the Act is in force. However, many EPAs will have been executed prior to the coming into force of the Act. It was expressly stated in Parliament that it would be unfair to deprive those who had executed EPAs of the ability to use them once the Act comes into force. Further, given that registration of EPAs occurs only when the donor loses or is believed to be losing capacity, in practice it would not be possible to contact all those who have executed EPAs in order to arrange for an LPA to be executed instead (if the donor still had capacity) (see Hansard in the Committee Stage in the House of Lords at col.783). Of course, the donor may decide to destroy the EPA and create an LPA instead.

If a donor still has capacity after the Act comes into force, he can cancel the EPA and make an LPA covering his property and affairs.

4.13.2   Arrangements for EPAs

Schedule 4 to the Act reproduces EPAA 1985 almost in its entirety, save that minor amendments are made to take account of changes in the Court of Protection and the role of the new Public Guardian in the registration process (see in particular paras.13–17).

Schedule 4, para.1(1) specifically excludes the principles of the Act applying to the EPA attorney. However, the EPA attorney owes duties to the donor under the law of agency (which are referred to at 4.7.1 when discussing the duties of attorneys under LPAs) and has a common law duty to act in the best interests of a donor who lacks capacity.

EPA attorneys do not have a legal duty to have regard to the Code of Practice (Code, para.7.5), although the guidance in the Code will be of some assistance to them and the Code suggests that they may find it helpful (para.7.79). However, a solicitor acting as a EPA attorney may be under a duty to have regard to the Code because he will be acting in a professional capacity in relation to a person who lacks capacity (MCA 2005, s.42(4)(e)). It is important to note that Sched.4 does not introduce for EPAs the functional and time-specific test of capacity which applies to LPAs. Schedule 4 preserves the situation for EPAs whereby the application to register must be made when the attorney 'has reason to believe that the donor is or is becoming mentally incapable'. After registration, the EPA attorney has the responsibility and authority to exercise the financial decision-making functions conferred on him or her by the EPA.

Part 3 of the 2007 Regulations are concerned with EPAs. These regulations supplement Sched.4 and the amendments made to the EPA regime to take account of the changes to the Court of Protection and the role of the Public Guardian and registration. New EPA forms are introduced including:

- a notice of intention to apply for registration of an EPA (form EP1PG, set out at Sched.7 to the 2007 Regulations);
- a notice for making an application to the Public Guardian for the registration of an instrument creating an EPA (form EP2PG, set out at Sched.8 to the 2007 Regulations).

The 2007 Regulations also deal with objections made to the Public Guardian to registration of an instrument creating an EPA (reg.25), the requirement on the Public Guardian to give notice of non-registration of an EPA (reg.26), the process of registration by the Public Guardian (regs.27–28) and loss or destruction of the instrument registered as an EPA (reg.29).

The 2007 Regulations give the Public Guardian certain functions in respect of EPAs which are similar to his functions in respect of LPAs, such as: the power to require information from EPA attorneys in circumstances where there are circumstances suggesting that the attorney may be unsuitable to be the donor's attorney (reg.47); the power to direct a Court of Protection Visitor to visit an attorney or donor of an EPA and report back to the Public Guardian (reg.48; for further information about Court of Protection Visitors see 11.6); and the power to deal with representations about the way in which an EPA attorney is exercising his powers (reg.48) (see further discussion of the role of the Public Guardian in **Chapter 12**).

There are some new Court of Protection forms which relate to EPAs. Form COP8 is to be used by intended attorneys or relatives entitled to be notified by Sched.4 to the Act of an application to register the EPA who want to object to registration or seek registration of the EPA. There is a Practice Direction addressing such applications (PD09H). Form COP17 is to be used by the Public Guardian when applying to the Court of Protection for directions relating to an objection to the registration of an EPA, and rule 201 of the Court of Protection Rules 2007 makes further provisions in relation to a Public Guardian's application for directions in these circumstances. It is to be noted that the Public Guardian, having received notice of an objection to the registration of an instrument creating an EPA, is prevented from registering the instrument except in accordance with the Court's directions (MCA 2005, Sched.4, para.13(5)).

EPA attorneys can be found liable under s.44 of the Act, which sets out the criminal offence of ill-treatment and wilful neglect.

4.13.3   Transitional and saving provisions

Part 2 of Sched.5 also contains transitional and saving provisions relating to EPAs which arise as a result of the repeal of the EPAA 1985. Provision is made for pending applications and appeals under the EPAA 1985 to be treated as proceedings brought under Sched.4 to the Act, insofar as that is possible. Provision is also made in respect of the exercise of powers of donor as trustee.

5 SECTION 5 ACTS AND LIMITATIONS

5.1 BACKGROUND

5.1.1 The problem

Many everyday actions involve touching another person or their property. At common law, touching someone without their consent can amount to the tort of battery or the crime of assault. Interfering with someone's property without their consent may amount to the crime of theft or the tort of conversion. The need for consent is the legal reflection of the ethical principle of respect for autonomy.

Carers of people lacking capacity, whether they are family members or professionals, are faced every day with having to carry out tasks for people who are unable to do them for themselves and who are unable to consent to others doing those tasks for them. These actions may range from simple acts like washing and dressing, buying food or paying gas or electricity bills, to more major matters such as moving a person from his or her own home to a care home, or performing surgery to preserve or enhance a person's life.

The courts have long accepted that any physically invasive medical treatment or procedure, however trivial, is unlawful unless authorised by consent or other lawful authority.[1] When a person lacked capacity to give consent the common law doctrine of necessity was relied upon to provide lawful authority for the action:

> ... not only (1) must there be a necessity to act when it is not practicable to communicate with the assisted person, but also (2) the action taken must be such as a reasonable person would in all the circumstances take, acting in the best interests of the assisted person.[2]

5.1.2 The common law solution

The uncertainty surrounding which actions are lawful without a valid consent, particularly when there have been doubts or disputes about a person's best interests, led to a number of high profile and costly cases. These cases were heard in the Family Division of the High Court and determined under the Court's inherent jurisdiction. The use of this jurisdiction for granting declaratory relief in respect of incapacitated adults was relatively new, starting with the case of *Re F*[3] in 1990 and continued to be developed by the High Court to cover new situations. By the time of the coming into force of the Act there was a wealth of decisions covering a range of issues, with multiple dicta supporting the flexible use of the jurisdiction.[4]

The claimant in such a case was usually the relevant local authority or NHS Trust or primary care trust (PCT), which sought declarations as to the incapacity of the person concerned and the lawfulness of the proposed action.[5] The purpose of bringing proceedings for a declaration was to protect both the patient and the doctors and to reassure the patient's family and the public that what was proposed to be done was lawful.

Was there a legal requirement to bring cases to court?

Certain acts were considered to be so serious that each case ought to be brought before the court. They were the proposed withdrawal of artificial nutrition and hydration (ANH) from a person in a permanent vegetative state (PVS) and the non-therapeutic sterilisation of a person lacking capacity to consent. In all other cases of doubt or dispute over capacity and/or best interests the approach was as follows:

> Good practice may require medical practitioners to seek such a declaration where the legality of the proposed treatment is in doubt. This is not, however, something that they are required to do as a matter of law.[6]

Munby J at first instance in *Burke*, when considering the decision of the European Court in *Glass* v. *UK* [2004] 1 FLR 1019, held that the advent of the Human Rights Act (HRA) 1998 converted what had previously only been a 'matter of good practice' in this regard into a 'matter of legal requirement'. The Court of Appeal rejected this suggestion.[7] However, the court cited without comment at para.74 the observations of Coleridge J in *D* v. *NHS Trust (Medical Treatment: Consent: Termination)* [2003] EWHC 2793, [2004] 1 FLR 1110 at p.31:

> The advent of the Human Rights Act 1998 has enhanced the responsibility of the court to protect the welfare of these patients and, in particular, to protect the patient's right to respect for her private and family life under Art 8(1) of the European Convention for the Protection of Human Rights and Fundamental Freedoms 1950.

Procedure under the common law

The claimant issued an application under Part 8 of the Civil Procedure Rules 1998 in the Family Division of the High Court.[8] The Official Solicitor was usually appointed by the court to act as litigation friend of the person under a disability. The court had power to make interim and final declarations and injunctions. In an appropriate case the court could make a prospective declaration to cover the happening of a future event.[9] The court also had power to declare that some specified person, in relation to specified matters, was effectively a surrogate decision-maker for the incapable adult.[10]

Declarations were generally only a 'snapshot in time' and did not provide continuing authority to act in a particular way if new circumstances arose. A declaration could not make lawful that which without a declaration would have been unlawful or make unlawful that which without a declaration would have been lawful. The limitations on the jurisdiction were sometimes perceived as leaving both the incapacitated person and those caring for the person in a vulnerable position.

5.1.3   The solution under the Mental Incapacity Bill

The Draft Bill of June 2003 provided for a 'general authority' to act on behalf of a person who lacked capacity. The provision had been intended to clarify the common law principle of necessity and to make lawful many day-to-day decisions made on behalf of people without capacity. There was, however, widespread misunderstanding of the concept and purpose of the 'general authority' and it was criticised in the report of the Joint Committee. The government agreed that 'the term "general authority" created false and unhelpful impressions'[11] and it agreed to change it.

As a result, the Mental Capacity Bill of 17 June 2005 contained a new cl.5, entitled 'acts in connection with care or treatment'. This clause survived without amendment to become s.5 of the Act.

5.1.4   The solution under the Act

The purpose of s.5 of the Act is to 'allow carers, healthcare and social care staff to carry out certain tasks without fear of liability'.[12] While some serious healthcare and treatment, and other decisions will still have to come before the Court of Protection (see **Chapter 11** for a discussion of what cases must or may be brought before the Court of Protection) for a determination, the vast majority of decision-making in respect of persons who lack capacity will be carried out under s.5.

Much of the detail of the operation of s.5 powers has been left to the Code of Practice and Practice Directions. The government also acknowledged that it would be important for the Act to be accompanied by appropriate training for professionals, and for substantial information to be provided for informal carers who will be affected by the Act's provisions. Only then would the law, as implemented, properly safeguard the interests of informal and professional carers as well as some of the most vulnerable members of society.

---

1   *Re F (Mental Patient: Sterilisation)* [1990] 2 AC 1; *Re T (Adult: Refusal of Treatment)* [1993] Fam 95; *Re MB* [1997] 8 Med LR 217, CA.

2   *In re F (Mental Patient: Sterilisation)* [1990] 2 AC 1, 75–76 per Lord Goff of Chieveley.

3   Ibid.
4   See, for example, *Re Local Authority (Inquiry: Restraint on Publication)* [2003] EWHC
     2746 (Fam), [2004] 1 FLR 541 and *Re SA (Vulnerable Adult with Capacity: Marriage)*
     [2005] EWHC 2942 (Fam), [2006] 1 FLR 867.
5   *St George's Healthcare NHS Trust v. S* [1999] Fam 26.
6   *Burke v. GMC and Others* [2005] EWCA 1003 (Fam) per Lord Phillips MR, at para 80;
     [2005] All ER (D) 445. See also, Coleridge J at paras.32, 34 and 36 of *D v. NHS Trust
     (Medical Treatment: Consent: Termination)* [2003] EWHC 2793 (Fam), [2004] 1 FLR
     1110 for a full discussion regarding termination of pregnancy.
7   Ibid., at para 74.
8   See *Practice Note (Official Solicitor Declaratory Proceedings: Medical and Welfare
     Decisions for Adults who Lack Capacity)* [2001] 2 FLR 158.
9   *Re S (Adult Patient) (Inherent Jurisdiction: Family Life)* [2002] EWHC 2278 (Fam),
     [2003] 1 FLR 292. See also *Wyatt & Anor v. Portsmouth Hospital NHS & Anor* [2005]
     EWCA Civ 1181 per Wall LJ at paras.117 and 118.
10   Ibid.
11   *Government Response to Recommendation 30 of the Scrutiny Committee's Report on the
     Draft Mental Incapacity Bill*, February 2004.
12   Chapter 6 of the Code.

5.2   SECTION 5 ACTS

5.2.1   'Acts in connection with care or treatment'

Section 5 applies to provide protection from liability to a person who does an act
in connection with the care or treatment of another person.

'A person'

The Act does not define 'a person'. The section therefore refers to any person
carrying out such an act and may relate to a number of people at any given time.
The Code makes it clear that:

■   there is no question of one person having a statutory power which excludes
     all others;
■   the provisions do not confer any special powers on anyone to make substitute
     decisions or to give substitute consent (paras.6.3 and 6.21).

The Code also provides that the drawing up of care plans, whether for health or
social care, for persons who lack capacity should always include an assessment of
capacity to consent to the actions covered by the plan, and confirm that the
actions are in the person's best interests (para.6.25). All staff acting in accordance
with the plan may then be protected by s.5, provided that capacity and best
interests are reviewed regularly (para.6.25).

Care or treatment

The Act does not define 'care' or 'treatment', other than to state at s.64(1) that
'"treatment" includes a diagnostic or other procedure'. The category is therefore

left intentionally wide and the words should be given their ordinary meaning. The Code at para.6.5 gives a large number of examples of the matters that may be covered by s.5.

As a rule of thumb, it is necessary to comply with s.5 requirements if consent would normally be required from a person of full capacity to the carrying out of a particular act (s.5(2)).

The Code makes clear, however, that major decisions that may have significant consequences, even if made pursuant to s.5, do require particularly careful consideration (para.6.7). The two sets of examples of such major decisions that the Code gives are in relation to a change of residence, and medical treatment decisions. In relation to decisions about a change of residence, the Code includes the following:

- before making a decision about a move of home the decision-maker must consider whether the move is in the person's best interests using the best interests checklist and in particular checking the person's past and present wishes and feelings (para.6.8);
- before making a decision about a move of home the decision-maker must consider whether there is a less restrictive option particularly where the person does not want the move (paras.6.8 and 6.10);
- consideration should be given to the appointment of an Independent Mental Capacity Advocate (IMCA) (para.6.9) (see **Chapter 9**);
- even where the person continues to object to the move, s.5 may be relied upon to authorise it, although not to the extent that it requires restraint or deprivation of liberty in excess of that permitted under the Act (see **5.3**), nor where there is a 'serious disagreement' about the need to move the person (paras.6.11–14).

In relation to decisions about medical treatment, the Code includes the following:

- even where an incapable person is objecting to treatment, s.5 may be relied upon to authorise that treatment provided that it does not require restraint or deprivation of liberty in excess of that permitted under the Act (see **5.3**) (para.6.15);
- before making a decision about treatment the decision-maker should consider whether it is in the person's best interests using the best interests checklist and in particular checking the past and present wishes and feelings of the incapable person, his beliefs and values and any advance statements (see **5.3**) (para.6.16);
- multi-disciplinary meetings are often the best way to decide on a person's best interests (para.6.17);
- the member of the healthcare staff responsible for the incapable person's treatment is responsible for the decision and should record it, how they reached it and the reasons in the clinical notes (para.6.18);
- the Court of Protection must be asked to make certain serious treatment decisions (see **Chapter 7**).

5.2.2   Conditions the person doing the act must fulfil

Take reasonable steps to establish whether P lacks capacity in relation to the matter in question: s.5(1)(a)

Reasonable steps must be taken to ascertain whether a person has capacity in relation to the particular decision (see **Chapter 3**). The principles relating to assessment of capacity are set out in ss.2 and 3 of the Act. The key principles apply and all practical steps must be taken to assist the person to make his own decision.

Reasonably believe that the person lacks capacity, and that it is in the best interests of that person for the act to be done: s.5(1)(b)

Provided that the person who intends to do the act has reasonable grounds of believing that the person lacks capacity, the person must then consider whether there are reasonable grounds for believing that it is in the incapacitated person's best interests for the act to be done (see **Chapter 3**), taking into account all the circumstances, the best interests checklist and the key principles.

The Code provides guidance as to how decisions about lack of capacity should be made by those relying upon s.5 (paras.6.30–6.35).

5.2.3   No protection from civil or criminal liability resulting from negligent acts

The Act makes it clear that s.5 does not provide a defence to negligent acts. This is consistent with the common law principle that consent does not provide a defence to the tort of negligence. A surgeon may obtain a patient's consent to an operation but if he then performs that operation negligently he can still be sued in the tort of negligence. If the patient then dies as a result of the surgeon's gross negligence the surgeon may then be charged with the manslaughter of the patient.

5.2.4   Effect of an advance decision to refuse treatment

An advance decision effectively exercises a person's autonomy after he has lost capacity to make a decision him or herself. If a person has made a valid and applicable advance decision then this takes priority over s.5 (see ss.24–26 of the Act and **Chapter 7** for further details about advance decisions).

Provided the healthcare professional is satisfied that the advance decision exists, is valid and applicable to the circumstances, he must act in accordance with the advance decision even if he believes that in doing so he will not be acting in the patient's best interests. If a healthcare professional does not act in accordance with the advance decision in these circumstances then he will not be protected from liability (Code, para.6.38). However, if the professional did not know of the advance decision or was not satisfied that it was valid or applied in the circumstances, then he will be protected from liability under s.5 if he does not act in accordance with the advance decision (Code, para.6.38).

5.3   LIMITATION ON S.5 ACTS

5.3.1   Background

The limitations provided for in s.6 of the Act expressly restrict the immunity from liability granted by s.5 in respect of acts carried out by persons in connection with care and treatment of an incapable person. In essence, s.5 may not be relied upon to authorise the use or threat of force, save in some limited circumstances, or the deprivation of liberty at all.

Both Houses of Parliament were concerned by this issue. Given that the purpose of s.5 was to reduce the number of occasions when carers or other people would not feel it necessary to go to court in order to obtain a declaration that a particular act is in a person's best interests, it was obviously of importance to make it as clear as possible when the use or threat of force would be sanctioned under the Act, and the point at which actions would amount to a deprivation of liberty that could not be sanctioned under the Act without the authority of the court.

There was debate in both Houses of Parliament about a potential conflict between s.5 and Art.5 of the ECHR if the effect of s.5 was that a person who lacks capacity could be deprived of his or her liberty in breach of Art. 5, in particular by the Joint Committee of Human Rights (see 4th Report and 23rd Report of the Joint Committee of Human Rights). It was for that reason that an amendment was introduced at the Report Stage in the House of Lords to include the provision in s.6(5) that restraint does not include a deprivation of liberty within the meaning of Art.5(1) of the Convention (see Hansard 17 March 2005, col.1468 and HL Bill 48). Although this amendment made it clear that deprivations of liberty are not sanctioned under s.5, identifying what amounts to a deprivation of liberty within the meaning of the Act has not proved to be straightforward (see below).

At the time of writing the law relating to deprivation of liberty and its authorisation under the Act is still in a state of development. There are a number of sources that seek to inform decisions as to what amounts to a deprivation of liberty, and efforts are being made to identify the correct process by which a deprivation may be authorised by the Court of Protection relying upon its powers under the Act, and by which such authorisation may be continued under a process of review. This will be of particular significance once the authorisation of deprivation of liberty scheme introduced by the Mental Health Act 2007 by way of amendment to this Act comes into force, probably in April 2009.

5.3.2   Restraint

There is no general protection from liability under s.5 in respect of acts intended to restrain a person lacking capacity, but those restraining P may be protected in certain defined circumstances.

The Code draws attention to the need for all health and social care staff to refer to their own professional guidance on the use of restraint, and any national regulations or guidance that controls its use (para.6.42).[1] It also reminds readers of the continuing common law power to restrain a person where his acts may cause harm to others, even if taking such action is not covered by the express protection from liability conferred by s.5 of the Act (para.6.43).

Definition of restraint

Section 6(4) provides that someone restrains a person (P) if he or she: (1) uses or threatens to use force to secure the doing of an act which P resists; or (2) restricts P's liberty of movement, whether or not P resists.

It is important to note that it is the threat of force as well as the use of actual force which is covered. Also, compliance by P is irrelevant if the act involves a restriction of P's liberty of movement. Holding a person down or locking a person in a room would both involve restrictions of liberty of movement and potentially a full deprivation of liberty.

Although the Draft Code of Practice expressly referred to chemical restraint (e.g. a person being given sleeping pills in order to sedate him or her and restrict a person's liberty of movement (at para.5.28)) as falling within the definition under the Act, this provision does not appear in the final Code. It is difficult to understand the omission, but in the view of the authors there is no reason to discount this type of restraint as not falling within the provisions of Act. Certainly, there is a respectable body of professional opinion that considers that the giving of a general anaesthetic, for clinical purposes other than restriction of movement, would amount to a restraint within the meaning of the Act. The Deprivation of Liberty Safeguards Code does include sedation as a form of restraint (para.2.5)

The restrictions in the Act on the protections afforded those who use restraint apply to financial decisions as well as welfare decisions. While it seems generally less likely that an act of restraint would be justified in the context of a financial decision, the Code does give the example of financial harm resulting from excessive spending as something that might justify the use of restraint for which there is protection under the Act (para.6.45). Apart from emergencies, however, it may be that remedies targeted at an individual's finances rather than his physical liberty will be more effective and proportionate in such situations.

Conditions justifying the use of restraint

In order for there to be protection from liability for an individual using restraint, the first two requirements of reliance upon s.5 set out above at **5.2.2** must first be fulfilled, i.e. the individual has taken reasonable steps to establish that P does indeed lack capacity and also reasonably believes that P lacks capacity in relation to the matter, and that it is in P's best interests for the act to be done.

In addition to these requirements, two further conditions must both be satisfied:

■   the person acting must reasonably believe that it is necessary to do the act in order to prevent harm to P (s.6(2)); and
■   the act is a proportionate response to the likelihood of P suffering harm and the seriousness of the harm (s.6(3)).

Necessity

The Act requires reasonable belief in the necessity of acting. This is an objective test. The onus is on the decision-maker to identify reasons which provide objective justification for the belief that the act is necessary in order to avert harm.

The purpose of the act must be to avert harm. The Act does not sanction restraint when the purpose is simply to enable a carer or someone else to do something more quickly or easily (Code, para.6.44). The reference is simply to 'harm'. There is no requirement of a risk of serious harm (although the degree of harm is relevant to the proportionality of the response – see below).

There is no definition in the Act of what constitutes 'harm'. The difficulties of defining what constitutes harm in a particular situation meant that no such definition was considered suitable. The obvious types of harm covered would be mental or physical injury, but there is no reason why the definition of harm should be so restricted. The Code gives guidance as to what 'harm' might be (para.6.45).

Clearly the type of harm is relevant to the issues of necessity and proportionality. In many cases it will be possible to avert some or all of the risk by taking measures which do not amount to the use or threat of force or restraint of liberty. If not, a proportionate response will be required (Code, para.6.36).

Proportionality

The concept of proportionality is now fairly familiar following the coming into force of HRA 1998. Section 6(3) of the Act requires that an act of restraint is proportionate to the likelihood of P suffering harm and the seriousness of that harm. The effect of this in practice is that the means of restraint should be commensurate with the desired outcome, e.g. the minimum degree of force for the shortest time possible should be used (Code, para.6.46). The more likely and more serious the risk of harm, the greater the degree of force that will be justified.

An example that was initially provided in the Draft Code of Practice (at para.5.33) was significantly modified in the final Code. The example given is of a man with learning difficulties who gets distressed in his college class and sometimes hits the wall in frustration. Staff do not want to stop him attending the class because he enjoys it and do not want to sit a support worker next to him in class because he gets upset and they regard it as inappropriately invasive for the support worker actively to restrain him. In the Draft Code the suggestion was that he could be provided with a restrictive hand cuff for a few weeks while the staff worked with him to find other ways to manage his emotions. The final Code instead suggests seeking expert advice from members of the community team, including observation and the development of a support strategy (Code, para.6.48).

Restraint may trigger assessment under the Mental Health Act 1983

The Code of Practice to the MHA 1983 provides that when restraint is used on a person (whether in an emergency or as part of a treatment plan) consideration should be given as to whether formal detention under the MHA 1983 is appropriate, particularly if the restraint occurred on a repeated basis (para.19.8). The provisions on restraint in the Act and Code do not refer to this issue but carers and others ought to be aware that if restraint is being used on a repeated basis, consideration should be given by the appropriate professionals as to whether formal detention under the MHA 1983 is required.

5.3.3 Deprivation of liberty

Section 6(5) expressly provides that the definition of restraint in the Act, for which in limited circumstances protection from liability is afforded, does not cover restraint that amounts to a deprivation of liberty for the purpose of Art.5(1) of the ECHR. This subsection was included in the Mental Capacity Bill at the Report Stage (HL Bill 48), the Joint Parliamentary Select Committee on Human Rights in its 15th report 2004–2005 being concerned that the proposed Bill might lead to deprivations of liberty which were not compatible with Art.5 of the ECHR, or involuntary placement of an incapable person in a psychiatric hospital (paras.4.6–4.9).

Definition of deprivation of liberty

'Deprivation of liberty' in the context of incapable persons and the Act still lacks a clear and precise definition. Attempts at a definition have been made by a number of sources, but none has prevailed over the others. At this stage in the development of the law therefore, it is wise to test a situation against all the various sets of criteria that are put forward in order to determine whether or not it amounts to deprivation of liberty for the purposes of the Act. It needs to be borne in mind that determining whether or not something amounts to a deprivation of liberty is not just an academic exercise, since it engages a fundamental human right, has vitally important consequences for a person's care both in imposition and omission, and errors carry a risk of awards of damages under HRA 1998 against public authorities.

Bournewood and the European case law

The leading case concerning the deprivation of liberty of a person who lacks capacity is the *Bournewood* case (*HL* v. *United Kingdom* Case No. 45508/99, 81 BMLR 131). The relevant circumstances of HL, the applicant, who was incapable of making the relevant decisions, were as follows:

- he was admitted to hospital for in-patient investigation and treatment;
- contact between him and his carers was initially prohibited and then subsequently restricted to once a week;
- he was sedated while in hospital, although he had not been while in the community;
- he was kept under continuous supervision by nursing staff; and
- those responsible for his care indicated that if he tried to leave he would be assessed with a view to detaining him under the MHA 1983.

The European Court found that HL had been deprived of his liberty in breach of the requirements of Art.5. The court's reasoning (paras.89–93) is set out below:

> . . . in order to determine whether there has been a deprivation of liberty, the starting point must be the specific situation of the individual concerned and account must be taken of a whole range of factors arising in a particular case such as the type, duration, effects and manner of implementation of the measure in question. The distinction between a deprivation of, and restriction upon, liberty is merely one of degree or intensity and not one of nature or substance . . . the Court considers the key factor in the present case to be that the health care professionals treating and managing the applicant exercised complete and effective control over his care and movements . . . strict control over his assessment, treatment, contacts, and, notably, movement and residence . . . the concrete situation was the applicant was under continuous supervision and control and was not free to leave . . . it is not determinative whether the ward was 'locked' or 'lockable'.

The court distinguished the earlier case of *HM* v. *Switzerland* (2004) 38 EHRR 17, where HM's compulsory admission to a residential care home in her best interests had been held not to amount to a breach of Art.5, on the grounds that the home in her case was an 'open' institution which allowed freedom of movement and encouraged contacts with the outside world.

The judgment in *HL* was followed in *Storck* v. *Germany* (2006) 43 EHRR 6, which also sought to distinguish the decision in *HM*.

The Department of Health's Bournewood guidance

The Department of Health issued this interim guidance[2] in December 2004 to advise on the domestic implications of the decision in *Bournewood*. It adopted the reasoning of the European Court in identifying the factors that might lead to a finding of deprivation of liberty in a particular case but said expressly that not every incapacitated patient admitted to a hospital or care home would be deprived of his liberty just because he was prevented from leaving unescorted for his own safety (*Bournewood* guidance, para.14).

The Code under the Act

The Code's guidance on identifying or defining a deprivation of liberty, at para.6.52, follows the Department of Health *Bournewood* guidance quite closely.

The domestic case law

The first case that considered the application of the European Court's criteria was *JE v. DE* [2006] EWHC 3459 (Fam), [2007] 2 FLR 1150. The judgment in that case took a strong line on what amounted to deprivation of liberty in the domestic context, before the coming into force of the Act, and appears potentially to have lowered the threshold for a finding of deprivation of liberty from that set out in the case law and guidance above.

The relevant circumstances of DE, who was incapable of making the relevant decisions, were as follows:

- DE's wife (JE) had allegedly abused and neglected DE while they resided together, and she had terminated contact between DE and his daughter;
- JE put DE on the street and asked the council to take him away;
- the council accommodated DE in a care home where he repeatedly asked to return to live with JE;
- the council did not allow DE to return to live with JE in his own best interests, although it was happy to facilitate his residence anywhere else;
- DE's contacts with JE were only briefly restricted when she was abusive;
- DE was not permitted to leave the home spontaneously with JE alone;
- DE's life was otherwise unrestricted and uncontrolled in terms of his movements and contacts.

The court held that DE was deprived of his liberty at the home because he was not 'free to leave' (paras.77 and 114–15). It was accepted that DE was not subject to the same degree of 'invasive control' as HL in *Bournewood*, but it was held that he was nevertheless deprived of his liberty.

The difficulty with the approach taken in DE's case is that it appears to reduce the multi-factorial approach adopted in all the sources above to one feature – whether the person who lacks capacity is free to leave. Moreover, it does not seem to address one of the central features of the case, i.e. DE was free to go anywhere save one place (namely, to live with JE at their home). This is markedly different from the situation of a person who is required to remain in a hospital or a residential care home, and not return to the community at all even though he may have contact with it.

Very shortly after judgment in DE's case, the Joint Committee on Human Rights in its Fourth Report dated 4 February 2007, stated that difficulties with the definition of deprivation of liberty meant that it should be defined in the then Mental Health Bill.[3] It suggested the following approach at para.89:

if it is known that a person will be taken from their home to a place where they will be prevented from leaving, and complete and effective control will be exercised over their movements, that person is deprived of their liberty from the point of removal from their home.

However, this definition did not find its way into the MHA 2007 and the Deprivation of Liberty Safeguards Code of Practice appears to involve a return to the multi-factorial criteria contained in the earlier guidance rather than a complete adoption of the decision in *DE*.

The Deprivation of Liberty Safeguards Code accompanying the Bournewood *proposals in the Mental Health Act 2007*

A scheme, not yet in force, that is intended to fill the *Bournewood* gap and provide a mechanism for lawful authorisation of such deprivations of liberty is introduced by MHA 2007. Obviously, it is important that this scheme is able to define what is and is not to be authorised. Its Code, in respect of which consultation concluded in January 2008, gives detailed guidance in chapter 2 for the identification of a deprivation of liberty.

It includes a checklist of relevant factors and a review of the European and domestic case law. It does not offer a single test and emphasises the importance of making decisions on a case by case basis.

Recent cases

Since the judgment in DE's case at the end of 2006 there have been surprisingly few cases concerned with deprivation of liberty, whether under the inherent jurisdiction or under the Act since it came into force in October 2007. It is particularly odd when one considers how many incapable people might be said to be not 'free to leave' in the sense of DE's case, and the numbers of persons who were said by the Secretary of State to be potentially affected by the judgment when the case of *Bournewood* was before the domestic courts. The two reported cases are *City of Sunderland* v. *PS and others* [2007] EWHC 623 (Fam), [2007] 2 FLR 1083, where a deprivation of liberty was found, and *LLBC* v. *TG and others* [2007] EWHC 2640 (Fam) where the court held that TG was not deprived of his liberty, although it was 'near the borderline', on the following grounds (paras.104–8):

■ he was in an 'ordinary' care home with 'ordinary' restrictions;
■ his contacts were largely unrestricted;
■ he was compliant and happy at the home;
■ he was not objectively deprived of his liberty; and
■ the fact that some members of his family opposed the placement was not sufficient to render it a breach of Art. 5.

It is the present experience of the authors that the court and parties are beginning to shy away from prolonged litigation over whether a particular arrangement amounts to a deprivation of liberty or not, in favour of the court authorising a particular arrangement on alternative bases, i.e. whether or not it amounts to a deprivation of liberty. This saves lengthy and costly argument on issues that may ultimately prove academic, and preserves the focus on the central issues of capacity and best interests.

It should be noted that the court has during the same period considered the definition and interpretation of the concept of deprivation in other contexts, particularly those subject to control orders (*Secretary of State for the Home Department v. JJ* [2007] UKHL 45, [2007] 3 WLR 642 and *Secretary of State for the Home Department v. E and S* [2007] UKHL 47, [2007] 1 WLR 720).

The authorisation of deprivation of liberty

While the coming into force of the authorisation scheme under the MHA 2007 is awaited (currently expected to be April 2009), some public bodies and others have been turning to the court, initially under the inherent jurisdiction, and now under the Act, to authorise (or refuse) the deprivation. This is despite the fact that the Department of Health *Bournewood* guidance (see above) gave no indication that such applications would be required while the coming into force of MHA 2007 was awaited. Given the very limited number of applications, commented upon above, it is clear that public authorities are preferring to wait and see, rather than embark on potentially costly litigation to ensure that their arrangements do not amount to a breach of Art.5 in each case. It may be a sound appreciation of the fact that in HL's case the European Court did not decide what might be done to authorise such a deprivation of liberty, whether under the inherent jurisdiction or the Act, pending the coming into force of the MHA 2007. The risk remains, therefore, that none of the steps taken or the steps available would be enough to avoid a finding of a breach of Art.5 before the European Court on the grounds that it was not 'in accordance with a procedure prescribed by law' within the meaning of Art.5(1) because neither the inherent jurisdiction nor the Act may offer a sufficient degree of certainty. However, the Code does seem to envisage that the Act gives the court the power to authorise restraint and deprivation of liberty (para.6.51), as do the Practice Directions (Practice Direction E – Applications relating to Serious Medical Treatment, para.6). Certainly, the Act as amended by the MHA 2007 provides that deprivation of liberty may be authorised either under the statutory scheme or by the court (s.4A(3)). In *A Primary Care Trust v. P, AH and A Local Authority*, Sir Mark Potter QC, the President, held that the Court of Protection might authorise a deprivation of liberty under its s.15 powers.

The first case in which a deprivation of liberty was found and then authorised by the court was *City of Sunderland v. PS and others* (above), under the inherent jurisdiction. The court held that requirements for authorisation were as follows:

- The deprivation of liberty must be authorised by the court by the making of an application by the public authority before the deprivation commences.

This is because Art.5(1) requires that any deprivation must be 'in accordance with a procedure prescribed by law'.

- There must be evidence of 'unsound mind' of a kind or degree that warrants compulsory confinement. This is to fulfil the requirement of Art.5(1)(e) as explained in the case of *Winterwerp v. The Netherlands* [1979] 2 EHRR 387. It is envisaged that this will usually be medical evidence, except in the most urgent cases.

- There must be provision for adequate review at reasonable intervals, in particular with a view to ascertaining whether there still persists unsoundness of mind of a kind or degree warranting compulsory confinement. This is because Art.5(4) requires that a person who is deprived of his liberty must have the right to take proceedings by which the lawfulness of his detention shall be decided speedily by a court, and his release ordered if detention is not lawful, but also because any unsoundness of mind relied upon to justify deprivation of liberty must be found to be persisting. The court needs to take responsibility for arranging the review since the person of unsound mind cannot be expected themselves to take the initiative in seeking a review (*Winterwerp* (above)). Guidelines for the review process are set out at *In the matter of GJ, NJ and BJ (Incapacitated Adults)* [2008] EWHC 1097 (Fam).

The relationship between deprivation of liberty and the Mental Health Acts 1983 and 2007

The Act as it is currently in force does not expressly contemplate the authorisation of deprivation of liberty by the Court of Protection, and so does not impose any restrictions on its functions in this regard. The Code does touch upon the topic, although its guidance is not absolutely conclusive (para.6.50). The Code does not say whether or not an application to the Court could lead to 'formal authorisation'.

A question arises as to which statutory regime should take precedence when seeking authorisation – the Act or the MHA 1983. The new MHA Code of Practice gives comprehensive guidance on this question (paras.4.13–4.22). In summary, where P may be safely and effectively managed under the MCA that scheme should be used in preference to the MHA.

Mental Health Act 2007

Upon coming into force, the MHA 2007 will amend the Act to introduce a scheme for the authorisation of the deprivation of liberty of persons lacking capacity. Currently the MHA 2007 is not expected to come into force before April 2009. Before the MHA 2007 does come into force, the Code suggests that its provisions should not influence decision-making under the Act (para.13.55). Once it is in force, however, it seems that many of the difficulties set out above arising out the use of the powers of the Court of Protection to authorise deprivation of liberty will fall away. What will remain, however, is the problem of the definition of, and/or threshold for, a deprivation of liberty, which it appears still awaits a complete resolution.

The statutory scheme for the authorisation of deprivation of liberty

The MHA 2007 amends the Act to introduce a new scheme for the authorisation of the deprivation of liberty in order to close the *Bournewood* gap (MHA 2007, s.50 and Sched.7, inserting ss.4A and 4B and Scheds.A1 and 1A into the Act). The Deprivation of Liberty Safeguards Code gives guidance as to the operation of the scheme.

When deprivation of liberty may be authorised

Deprivation of liberty, when the amendments to the Act come into force, may be authorised in three ways:

- the Court of Protection exercising its powers to make personal welfare decisions under s.15(1)(c) of the Act;
- in accordance with the new authorisation scheme set out in MCA 2005, Sched.A1 (inserted by MHA 2007, Sched.7);
- where it is necessary in order to give life-sustaining treatment or do any 'vital act'[4] while a decision is sought from the court (MHA 2007, s.4B).

The bodies that will authorise deprivation of liberty under Schedule A1

There are two classes of supervisory body that may authorise deprivation of liberty: PCTs (or the National Assembly for Wales in Wales) and local authorities.

PCTs are responsible for authorisation in respect of persons in hospital (MCA 2005, Sched.A1, para.180). The relevant PCT will usually be the one that commissions the treatment, or otherwise the PCT for the area in which the hospital is situated.

Local authorities are responsible for authorisation in respect of persons in care homes (MCA 2005, Sched.A1, para.182). The relevant local authority will be the one for the area in which the person lacking capacity is ordinarily resident (see the Ordinary Residence guidance, LAC(93)7). If a person has no ordinary residence, then the responsible local authority will be the one for the area in which the care home is situated.

The requirements for standard authorisation

The hospital or home, where it appears to them that it is likely that, either currently or at some time in the next 28 days, a person lacking capacity accommodated by them will be deprived of his liberty, must apply to the supervisory body for authorisation of that deprivation of liberty (MCA 2005, Sched.A1, para.44).

Within 21 days of the application being made the supervisory body must arrange assessments of whether the six statutory criteria for authorisation of deprivation of liberty, set out below, are fulfilled.

The age requirement

The person must be 18 or over (MCA 2005, Sched.A1, para.13).

The mental health requirement

The person must be suffering from a mental disorder within the meaning of MHA 1983 (except that a person suffering from a mental impairment need not have the impairment associated with abnormally aggressive or seriously irresponsible conduct as required under MHA 1983) (MCA 2005, Sched.1A, para.14). It should be noted that this is distinct from, and significantly narrower than, the broad 'diagnostic' element of the test of incapacity applied in the main part of the Act (see **Chapter 3**).

The assessment of this requirement must be carried out by a doctor approved under MHA 1983, s.12 or one whom the supervisory body has decided has special experience in the diagnosis and treatment of mental disorder (Draft Mental Capacity (Deprivation of Liberty: Eligibility and Selection of Assessors) Regulations 2008).

The mental capacity requirement

Applying the general principles laid down in ss.1–3 of the Act, the person must lack capacity to decide whether or not he should be accommodated in the relevant hospital or home for the purposes of being given the relevant care or treatment (MCA 2005, Sched.A1, para.15).

This assessment need not be carried out by a doctor, although in practice it seems more likely than not that it will be (Draft Mental Capacity (Deprivation of Liberty: Eligibility and Selection of Assessors) Regulations 2008).

The best interests requirement

This requirement has four parts:

- the person is or will be a detained resident;
- it is in the person's best interests to be a detained resident;
- it is necessary for the person to be detained to prevent harm to him or herself; and
- deprivation of liberty is a proportionate response to the likelihood of the person suffering harm and the seriousness of that harm (MCA 2005, Sched.A1, para.16).

The best interests assessment may be carried out by a range of individuals, not just approved mental health professionals, as long as they have the appropriate skills and experience (Draft Mental Capacity (Deprivation of Liberty: Eligibility and Selection of Assessors) Regulations 2008).

The best interests assessor must carry out a number of tasks in the course of his or her assessment – the assessor must:

- consult with the managing authority of the hospital or home and have regard to needs assessments and care plans produced by them;
- record in writing the name and address of every person with whom he or she consults;
- state the maximum period of authorisation (MCA 2005, Sched.A1, paras.39–43 and 51–3).

The 'eligibility' requirement

A person is 'ineligible' if:

- the person is subject to the hospital treatment regime under the MHA 1983;
- the authorisation of deprivation of liberty would be inconsistent with a requirement imposed under the MHA 1983 to reside somewhere else, e.g. pursuant to guardianship, or a community treatment order (under MHA 2007);
- the person may be detained under the MHA 1983 but is not in fact (MCA 2005, Scheds.A1 and 1A).

This last ground of ineligibility is difficult to interpret. Paragraph 12 of Sched.1A provides as follows:

(1) P is within the scope of the Mental Health Act if –

    (a) an application in respect of P could be made under section 2 or 3 of the Mental Health Act, and
    (b) P could be detained in a hospital in pursuance of such an application, were one made.

. . .

(3) If the grounds in section 2(2) of the Mental Health Act are met in P's case, it is to be assumed that the recommendations referred to in section 2(3) of that Act have been given.

(4) If the grounds in section 3(2) of the Mental Health Act are met in P's case, it is to be assumed that the recommendations referred to in section 3(3) of that Act have been given.

(5) In determining whether the ground in section 3(2)(c) of the Mental Health Act is met in P's case, it is to be assumed that the treatment referred to in section 3(2)(c) cannot be provided under this Act.

This seems to suggest that where P is found to be ineligible under the Act but in need of care and treatment in detention, then he will somehow automatically be detained under the MHA 1983. The Deprivation of Liberty Safeguards Code certainly appears to envisage that steps will be taken to effect an admission under the MHA 1983 (para.3.66). What neither the Act nor the Code consider is the situation where the assessor under the Act considers that P is ineligible because he should be dealt with under the MHA 1983, but those responsible for making the necessary application and recommendations under the MHA 1983 consider that he should be deprived of his liberty under the MCA 2005. This is not a fanciful issue, since it has already arisen in practice.

One possible resolution of the problem would involve the interpretation of the word 'could' in para.12(1)(a) above, as 'could in fact' so that where applications and recommendations under the MHA 1983 are not forthcoming from those responsible, the hypothetical possibility of detention under the MHA 1983 does not inhibit the authorisation of deprivation of liberty under the Act.

The absence of 'refusals' requirement

P may not be made subject to an authorisation of deprivation of liberty if:

- he made a valid advance decision refusing some of the treatment that would be provided were he made subject to an authorisation of deprivation of liberty;
- his attorney or deputy has made a decision, e.g. with respect to his treatment with which deprivation of liberty would be inconsistent (MCA 2005, Sched.A1, para.18–20).

The issuing of standard authorisation

If, after receipt of written assessments, the supervisory body is satisfied that the six requirements are met then it must issue the authorisation (MCA 2005, Sched.A1, para.50). If it is not so satisfied, then it may not issue the authorisation (MCA 2005, Sched.1A, para.50). The authorisation should be granted for the shortest time possible (Deprivation of Liberty Safeguards Code, Chapter 3).

A standard authorisation must include the following:

- name of P;
- name of the hospital or home;
- period during which authorisation is to be in force;
- purpose for which authorisation given;
- conditions subject to which the authorisation is given; and
- reason why each requirement is met (MCA 2005, Sched.A1, paras.54–5).

Patient representatives and IMCAs

If P is believed potentially to come within the authorisation of deprivation of liberty scheme then the hospital or home where P is residing must establish whether there is an independent person who is available to advocate on P's behalf. If they believe that there is no one, then the supervisory body must appoint an IMCA (ss.39A, 39C and 39D) (see **Chapter 9**). The role of the IMCA will be to take such steps as are practicable to help the person under the effect of the authorisation, the purpose of the authorisation, the duration of the authorisation and any conditions to which it is subject, and the person's rights under the Act and how to exercise them including the person's right to apply for a review to the supervisory body or to the court (s.39D). The Deprivation of Liberty Safeguards Code provides further guidance at paras.3.25–3.30.

Once P has been made subject to an authorisation of deprivation of liberty the supervisory body must appoint a patient representative for P (MCA 2005, Sch.A1, para.139). The role of the representative will be to maintain contact with P, support and represent P in relation to the deprivation of liberty (Mental Capacity (Deprivation of Liberty: Appointment of Relevant Person's Representative) Regulations 2008, SI 2008/1315).

Urgent authorisation

Obviously, there will be many cases where the need to authorise deprivation of liberty arises long before the 21-day period envisaged for the standard authorisation process is completed. These cases may be dealt with under the urgent authorisation process.

Urgent authorisation may be granted in two circumstances:

- the hospital or home is required by the Act to make a request for standard authorisation but believes that the need for P to be deprived of his liberty is so urgent that it is appropriate to begin the deprivation of liberty before the request for authorisation is made; or
- the hospital or home has already made a request for standard authorisation but believes that the need for P to be deprived of his liberty has in the meantime become so urgent that it is appropriate to begin the deprivation of liberty before the standard authorisation has been issued (MCA 2005, Sched.A1, paras.74–79).

An urgent authorisation may not exceed seven days (MCA 2005, Sched.A1, para.78).

An urgent authorisation may be extended by the supervisory body on one occasion after an application has been made for standard authorisation provided that:

- there are exceptional reasons why the request for standard authorisation has not yet been determined, and
- it is essential for the existing detention to continue until the request has been determined (MCA 2005, Sched.A1, para.84).

Review of authorisation

A standard authorisation of deprivation of liberty will usually be for 12 months. If P moves during that period, the new hospital or home must make a fresh request for authorisation (MCA 2005, Sched.A1, paras.25–6).

The hospital or home where P is deprived of his or her liberty is under an obligation to monitor P and consider whether any of the requirements set out above appears to require review (MCA 2005, Sched.A1, para.103). The P who is deprived of his or her liberty may request a review, as may his or her representative (MCA 2005, Sched.A1, para.102). The supervisory body may review a case at any time (MCA 2005, Sched.A1, para.102).

A requirement may be reviewable on one of these grounds:

- P no longer meets all the requirements;
- the reason why P now meets the requirements is not the reason given in the authorisation issued in his case;
- there has been a change in P's case and, because of the change, it would be appropriate to vary the conditions to which the authorisation is subject (MCA 2005, Sched.A1, paras.104–7).

The Court of Protection has the power to review a standard authorisation of deprivation of liberty on any of the following grounds:

- P is said not to meet the requirements;
- the period of the authorisation is too long;
- the purpose of the authorisation is incorrect;
- the conditions are wrongly imposed.

The court has the power to vary or terminate the authorisation or to order the supervisory body to vary or terminate it (s.21A).

The Court of Protection has the power to review an urgent authorisation of deprivation of liberty on any of the following grounds:

- the urgent authorisation should not have been given;
- the period of the authorisation is too long;
- the purpose of the authorisation is incorrect (s.21A).

The court has similar powers to vary or terminate the authorisation or to order the hospital or home to vary or terminate it (s.21A).

Even if the court does vary or terminate an authorisation or order another body to do so, it has the power to make any order maintaining a person's exclusion from liability under the Act despite its decision (s.21A).

Where a third party believes that P is deprived of his or her liberty and such deprivation is not authorised, the third party may ask the supervisory body to decide whether there is an unauthorised deprivation of liberty (MCA 2005, Sched.A1, paras.67–9). This may be the point at which many of the arguments about the definition of deprivation of liberty outlined above will arise.

The Draft Addendum Code provides further guidance on the making of such an application to the supervisory body.

5.3.4   Effect on formal decision-making powers

Where formal powers already exist for making decisions on P's behalf under an existing LPA (see **Chapter 4**) or by a deputy appointed by the Court (see **Chapter 6**), these decision-making powers take priority over the general s.5 power (s.6(6)). However, it is only if a donee of an LPA or a deputy has authority to make decisions in respect of the particular matter in question. An LPA, the deputy or the Court of Protection is able to provide consent on behalf of P so it is not necessary for a carer or other person to act without consent in reliance on the s.5 immunity. This avoids acts being done which conflict with the decision of an LPA (who has been chosen by P to make decisions on his behalf) or that of the deputy appointed by the Court to make this decision.

However, in cases of conflict or uncertainty, there is a fall-back provision which permits healthcare or other care staff to take action to provide life-sustaining treatment or acts reasonably necessary to prevent a serious deterioration in the condition of the person lacking capacity while the Court is approached for a decision to be made (s.6(7)). This addresses the situation where care staff are of the view than an LPA or deputy is not acting outside the scope of their authority or not in the best interests of the patient, or where the existence or validity of the relevant documents are in doubt, and they want to seek guidance from the Court about this but cannot wait to do this before taking immediate action in the best interests of the incapable person (Code, paras.6.54 and 6.55).

A deputy or a donee is similarly restricted in the use or authorisation of restraint as a person acting under s.5 (see **Chapter 4**).

1   See, for example, the NICE Guidelines for the management of disturbed/violent behaviour in psychiatric settings.
2   Available to download from the Department of Health's website (see **www.dh.gov.uk/en/ Policyandguidance/Healthandsocialcaretopics/Mentalhealth/DH_4077674**).
3   The Mental Health Bill was intended to, and now as the Mental Health Act 2007 has, laid down a scheme for the authorisation of the deprivation of liberty of incapable adults with a view to remedying the failings of the domestic law identified by the European Court in *Bournewood*.
4   A vital act is defined as 'any act which the person doing it reasonably believes to be necessary to prevent a serious deterioration in P's condition'.

5.4   PAYMENT FOR NECESSARY GOODS AND SERVICES

5.4.1   Background

The general position at common law is that a contract is voidable if entered into by a person who lacks capacity and the other contracting party knows or ought to have known (i.e. constructive knowledge) of the other's incapacity. The Sale of

Goods Act 1979, s.3 created an exception to this rule in respect of 'necessaries', i.e. goods which are necessary in a person's life. The effect of s.7 of the Act is to consolidate the law in this area and to provide a comprehensive definition of 'necessaries'.

An amendment proposed to this provision at the Committee Stage in the House of Lords was to change the underlying common law position that contracts are voidable if it is established that the other contracting party knew or ought to have known of the other person's incapacity. It was proposed (by Lord Goodhart (see Hansard 27 January 2005, at col.1396)) that an amendment should be introduced to bring the law in England and Wales into line with that in Scotland where there is no requirement that the other contracting party knew or ought to have known of the incapacity. The proposal was stated to address the situation where unfair advantage is taken of persons who lack capacity. The proposed amendment was resisted on the basis that the current law enables persons who lack capacity to ensure that they can obtain the goods and services to enable them to live independently. Traders can supply necessaries in the knowledge that they will be able to recoup a reasonable price. There was concern that businesses would be reluctant to do business with incapacitated persons if all contracts could be set aside. Further, it was considered that other legislative initiatives such as the Consumer Credit Bill and the Unfair Commercial Practices Directive will address the position of unfairness in commercial relationships as they affect incapacitated persons (see Baroness Ashton of Upholland, Hansard 27 January 2005, at cols.1388–1410). Baroness Ashton committed the government at the Committee Stage in the House of Lords to carrying out further research into the current law and the nature of the problems facing persons who lack capacity in commercial transactions (see Hansard 27 January 2005, at col.1471).

5.4.2   The definition of necessary

The definition in s.7(2) of the Act is that 'necessary' means suitable to a person's condition in life and to his actual requirements at the time when the goods or services are supplied.

5.4.3   Condition in life

The Code indicates that the purpose of this part of the provision is to ensure that P is able to maintain a similar standard of living and way of life to that experienced prior to losing capacity (para.6.58). If a uniform definition of 'necessary' in respect of goods and services were adopted, this would have the effect of introducing a lowest common denominator. So if P has always bought expensive clothes and food, P ought to be able to continue to buy these as necessary goods.

5.4.4   Actual requirements at the time of supply

This requires that there is an actual need for the goods or services at the time of supply. There will be no actual requirement at the time of supply if P already has an existing stock which is sufficient or has no need for the goods or services at all. The example given by the Code (para.6.59) is that while buying one or two pairs of shoes may be necessary, buying a dozen pairs would probably not be.

In extreme cases, it will not be difficult to ascertain whether something is or is not necessary goods or services (e.g. supplying gardening tools to a person without a garden). In more subtle situations, there is unlikely to be a clear line defining whether goods or services are necessary because the test necessarily involves a considerable subjective element when deciding whether something is necessary with regard to P's condition in life.

5.4.5   The obligation to pay a reasonable price

Section 7(1) of the Act imposes an obligation on P to pay a reasonable price in respect of necessary goods or services. The legal responsibility for making payment rests on P even if he or she lacks capacity to contract for the goods or services. Insofar as a dispute arose about what constitutes a reasonable price which could not be resolved between the parties, it would ultimately be a matter which the county court or High Court (depending on the value of the claim) would have to adjudicate upon. The ascertainment of a reasonable price would not be for the Court of Protection whose jurisdiction is concerned with making decisions on behalf of or appointing deputies to make decisions on behalf of P.

5.5   EXPENDITURE

5.5.1   Background

Section 8 of the Act operates with s.5 to enable a carer or other person who arranges for goods or services to be supplied to P also to make arrangements for payment in respect of those goods or services.

Expenditure is made lawful under s.8 in respect of acts to which s.5 applies, so this requires that the goods or services are supplied in connection with care and treatment and ordered by the decision maker with the reasonable belief that P does indeed lack capacity and the supply of the goods or services is in the best interests of P.

Section 8 permits a carer to use P's money to pay directly for the goods or services, or to pay on P's behalf and to be reimbursed by P. The Code emphasises the need for those handling P's money to keep bills, receipts and other proof of payment (para.6.62).

5.5.2   Use of the person lacking capacity's money

Section 8(1) permits a carer or other person to pledge credit to P and use money in that person's possession to pay for goods or services contracted for by the carer or other person on P's behalf. The money has to be in that person's possession. Hence, this provision does not authorise a carer to access P's bank account or other investments to obtain the necessary money. The specific authority of an LPA, a deputyship or a single order of the Court of Protection would usually be required to access a bank account or other savings.

As for the 'pledging of credit', the Code notes that a supplier may not be happy with this, or that the decision-maker may be concerned that he or she will be held liable for the debt (para.6.61)

5.5.3   Reimbursement

Section 8(2) authorises the decision-maker to reimburse him or herself from money in the possession of P if the decision-maker has paid for the goods or services supplied on behalf of P. This provision also permits the decision-maker to be 'otherwise indemnified by [P]'. It is not clear what is thereby permitted. The only example provided in the Code was that P could give an 'IOU' to the decision-maker pending specific authority being obtained to access a bank account (at para.6.61). It seems unlikely that the provision would be given a wide interpretation by the courts so as to allow, for example, P to give the decision-maker an item of property so as to compensate the decision-maker for his expenditure. The Code states that this section does not authorise the decision-maker to sell property belonging to P in order to secure funds (para.6.63). Unless P has money in his possession sufficient to meet the debt, carers and others persons should apply to the Court or to request the sum from an LPA or deputy (when one is appointed to deal with property and affairs). Otherwise the carer or other person puts him or herself at risk of not complying with ss.5 and 8 and acting unlawfully.

5.5.4   Formal powers

Section 8(3) provides that the provisions in s.8 do not affect any formal powers held by others to control P's money or spend money on P's behalf. Formal powers in this respect could be held by an LPA or by a deputy appointed by the Court of Protection, or be effected by a single order of the Court of Protection. Informal powers under ss.5 and 8 in respect of P's money or property cannot, therefore, be used by carers or others to conflict with formal powers held by attorneys or deputies (Code, para.6.66).

Also, P may receive his or her State benefits through an appointee. The appointee still does not have the power to deal with assets from other sources (Code, para.6.65).

6 POWERS OF THE COURT OF PROTECTION

6.1 BACKGROUND

This part of the Act contains the core jurisdiction of the Court.[1] It is intended to provide a forum for resolution of difficult cases or complex decisions (Code, para.8.25). It empowers the Court to make decisions on behalf of incapable persons, or to confer (or remove) a power to make those decisions upon a new statutory creature – the Deputy. It also provides for decision-making about LPAs, including determining their validity, giving directions to an attorney and cancelling the power altogether.

In relation to declarations, the Act frames within a statutory structure the existing common law powers exercised under the inherent jurisdiction of the court and extends them to include the making of declarations about general 'matters' rather than only specific decisions, and the conferring (or removal) of authority on a Deputy to make a specific decision or decisions about certain matters on behalf of the person lacking capacity.

There is a presumption in favour of the court making specific orders and declarations in respect of decisions rather than the appointment of a Deputy, which is intended to be a 'de minimis' power.[2] Further, there are a number of substantial restrictions on a Deputy's functions, and his or her powers may be varied or revoked by the court.

The amendments to the Act by MHA 2007 also include powers of the court to review and authorise deprivation of liberty (see **Chapter 5**).

These narrowly circumscribed powers may be contrasted with the broad ones granted under the Scottish Act when issues of statutory interpretation arise.

---

1 Explanatory Notes at para.65.
2 Hansard, HC, 11 October 2004, col.29.

6.2   COURT'S POWER TO MAKE DECLARATIONS

The Court may, by s.15(1) of the Act, make three types of declaration:

(a) whether a person has or lacks capacity to make a decision specified in the declaration;[1]
(b) whether a person has or lacks capacity to make decisions on such matters as are described in the declaration;
(c) the lawfulness or otherwise of any act done or yet to be done in relation to the person.

6.2.1   Declarations as to capacity or incapacity

It is anticipated that the need for a declaration as to capacity will be relatively rare, but the Code gives examples of cases such as a person who wants to challenge a decision that he lacks capacity, professionals disagreeing about an individual's capacity to make a specific, important decision or a dispute between family members about whether a person has capacity (para.8.16). Proceedings might also be brought in order that health and social care services may establish that a person lacks capacity, in order then to be enabled to make decisions about that person's future. It should be borne in mind, however, that the Code indicates that a person cannot be forced to undergo an assessment of capacity (see **Chapter 3**), and the powers of the Court in this regard may be somewhat limited in their effect.

The Act retains the common law distinction between declarations as to capacity to make specific decisions[2] and declarations as to what is lawful, being in the best interests of a patient.[3] This reflects the common law practice which preceded the Act of making separate declarations as to lack of capacity in respect of the decision concerned and as to the lawfulness of the act proposed. The making of a declaration of lack of capacity to make decisions about 'matters' more generally was not usually exercised under the common law. It emerges in the Act in the guise of the entirely new power to appoint a Deputy to take over the decision-making function in relation to 'matters' generally rather than just a specific decision (see below).

6.2.2   Declarations as to the lawfulness of an act

The power in s.15(1)(c) of the Act engages all types of health and welfare decisions, including residence, care and contact (previously dealt with under the common law inherent jurisdiction of the Family Division of the High Court), deprivation of liberty (*A PCT* v. *P & AH & A Local Authority*, 25 June 2008, President of the Family Division, Sir Mark Potter QC) and those concerning property and affairs (previously dealt with under Part VII of the MHA 1983 by the Court of Protection and the Public Guardianship Office by the appointment of a receiver or the making of a short order).

In particular, it is expected that the court's declaratory power will be invoked in relation to serious medical treatment cases, including those which were previously referred to the Family Division's inherent jurisdiction. The Code provides that the following types of case should be brought before the court:

- decisions about the withholding or withdrawal of artificial nutrition and hydration (ANH) from patients in a persistent vegetative state (PVS);
- those involving bone marrow donation by P;
- those involving non-therapeutic sterilisation of P;
- all other cases where there is a doubt or dispute about whether a particular treatment will be in P's best interests, e.g. ethical dilemmas, or uncertainty as to whether treatment would be in P's best interests (paras.8.18–8.24).

More detailed guidance as to which cases must be referred to the Court is contained in the relevant Practice Direction (see Practice Direction 12).

6.2.3   Acts and omissions

As well as allowing the Court to make declarations as to both the present and future (s.15(1)(c)), it is expressly provided that an 'act' in the context of s.15(1)(c) of the Act includes both an omission and a course of conduct (s.15(2)).

---

1   For the definition of capacity and the methods to be adopted when assessing capacity, see **Chapter 3**.
2   For the grounds upon which such a declaration may be made, see ss.1, 2 and 3 of the Act.
3   For the grounds upon which such a declaration may be made, see ss.1 and 4 of the Act.

6.3   COURT'S POWER TO MAKE DECISIONS AND APPOINT DEPUTIES

The Court may, by s.16(2) of the Act, either make a decision or decisions on behalf of an incapable person or appoint a Deputy to make a specific decision or one about 'matters' identified by the Court.

The Code gives examples of specific decisions that the court might be asked to make, including:

- making or amending a will;
- making a major decision, e.g. about where P should live or to terminate a tenancy agreement;
- resolving doubt or disagreement about the existence, validity or applicability of an advance decision (see **Chapter 7**);
- obtaining personal information, such as health or social services records, about P; and
- seeking to prevent abuse of P, in proceedings brought both by individuals or public authorities (paras.8.27–8.28).

The Code gives examples of when a Deputy might be appointed, including:

■   in circumstances where the old Court of Protection would have appointed a receiver to manage P's property and affairs (Code, para.8.35);
■   where someone needs to make series of linked welfare decisions over time and it would not be beneficial or appropriate to require all of those decisions to be made by the court;
■   where there is a history of serious family disputes that could have a detrimental effect on P unless a Deputy is appointed (Code, para.8.39).

At the time of writing there have been very few welfare Deputies appointed, as against financial Deputies.

6.3.1   The principles to be applied by the Court

When making decisions or appointing a Deputy, the Court must act in accordance with the other provisions of the Act, and in particular the principles of s.1 of the Act and the method of determining P's best interests laid down by s.4 (s.16(3)) – see 3.5.

The Court must also, however, when exercising its powers under this Part of the Act, have regard to the following key principles:

(a)   a decision by the Court is to be preferred to the appointment of a Deputy to make a decision; and
(b)   the powers conferred on a Deputy should be as limited in scope and duration as is reasonably practicable in the circumstances (s.16(4)).

The application of the first of these principles suggests that there is little scope for the appointment of Deputies on a general basis effectively to act as if they were donees of a general power under an LPA.

6.3.2   The other powers of the Court

If the Court decides to make an order making a decision upon P's behalf it may:

(a)   make further orders or directions as it considers necessary or expedient for giving effect to or otherwise in connection with the order or appointment (s.16(5));
(b)   vary or discharge the order (s.16(7)).

This provision acknowledges the difficulty faced by courts making orders under the common law where they only have a 'snapshot' of the individual's capacity and interests at the time of the order (see 3.5). It ameliorates the problem by expressly allowing for the matter to return to court on a wide range of grounds.

If the Court does decide to appoint a Deputy it may:

(a)   make further orders or directions, or confer on the Deputy such powers or impose on the Deputy such duties as it considers necessary or expedient for giving effect to or otherwise in connection with the order or appointment (s.16(5));

(b) revoke the Deputy's appointment or vary the powers conferred on the Deputy if it is satisfied that the Deputy:

    (i) has behaved or is behaving in a way that contravenes the authority conferred on him or her or is not in P's best interests; or

    (ii) proposes to behave in a way that would contravene that authority or would not be in P's best interests (s.16(8)).

This provision was added in order to bring the Court's powers in relation to Deputies and attorneys into line (see **4.8**).

The Court has a general 'own motion' power to make orders or give directions in a person's best interests even though no application is before it (s.16(6), and rules 25(2) and (5) and 27 of the Court of Protection Rules) (see **Chapter 11**).

6.4   COURT POWERS: PERSONAL WELFARE

Section 17 of the Act sets out a list of personal welfare issues which the jurisdiction, whether in relation to the making of declarations or orders or the appointment of Deputies, is intended to cover. It includes where P is to live, what contact, if any, he is to have with specific persons, the prohibition of contact with specific persons, giving or refusing consent for treatment and giving a direction that responsibility for health care is transferred to another person. The list of issues reflects those which have typically been decided under the common law, although not all of them, given the wide range of the common law jurisdiction which covers all 'serious justiciable issues'.[1] The list, however, is intended to be indicative rather than exhaustive,[2] and the court's jurisdiction may even go beyond the old common law parameters.

The extent of a Deputy's decision-making powers in relation to personal welfare is not extended by this section past the limits laid down in s.20 of the Act (s.17(2)). It is expected that a Deputy will be appointed to take personal welfare decisions in only the most extreme cases, and the Court will usually seek to make an order in respect of a decision rather than confer an on going power on a Deputy (s.17(2)).

---

1   In *Re S (Hospital Patient: Court's Jurisdiction) (No.1)* [1996] Fam 1 at 18.
2   Explanatory Notes at paras.70 and 71.

6.5   COURT POWERS: PROPERTY AND AFFAIRS

The aspects of P's property and affairs upon which the Court or a Deputy may decide are listed at s.18(1) of and Sched.2 to the Act. They include the acquisition, control and management of property, gifts or other dispositions, carrying on of professions, trades or business, carrying out of contracts, discharge of debts, executions of wills, exercise of the powers under trusts and the conduct of legal proceedings. In essence, they are the old Court of Protection powers.

The extent of a Deputy's decision-making powers in relation to property and affairs is not extended by this section past the limits laid down in s.20 of the Act (s.18(6)).

6.6   WHO MAY BE APPOINTED A DEPUTY BY THE COURT

A person may be appointed a Deputy if he or she:

(a) is aged 18 or over, or, in relation to a person's property and affairs, a trust corporation (s.19(1));
(b) consents to the appointment (s.19(3)).

In deciding whether to appoint a Deputy, and who, the Court will consider whether the proposed Deputy is reliable and trustworthy and has an appropriate level of skill and competence to carry out the necessary tasks. The decision about the identity of the Deputy will be influenced by the type of issue to be decided by him or her (Code, para.8.32).

It is intended that a Deputy will be someone known to P;[1] but the Court may appoint an independent or professional Deputy, e.g. where P's needs are complicated. The OPG has a panel of professional Deputies who may be appointed to deal with property or affairs (Code, para.8.33). The Code provides that paid care workers should not be appointed Deputies because of the potential conflict of interest (para.8.41).

The Court may appoint two or more Deputies to act jointly, jointly and severally or jointly in respect of some matters and jointly and severally in respect of others (s.19(4)). The Code explains how these arrangements might operate (paras.8.42–8.43).

The Court may also appoint a successor to a Deputy, for example, when a person who is involved in the life of P is likely to become ill or die within a short time.[2]

These provisions mirror those made in respect of attorneys appointed under an LPA (see 4.3.2).

6.6.1   Agency

Crucially, s.19(6) of the Act provides that a Deputy will be treated as an agent of the person who lacks capacity. The Explanatory Notes state that the law of agency is specifically engaged here (para.73). For a more detailed treatment of the law see *Bowstead and Reynolds on Agency* 18th edn. (Sweet & Maxwell, 2006), but the following issues should be borne in mind:

- an agent has an implied authority to do what is necessary for or incidental to effective execution of express authority; so it appears that a Deputy will have such implied authority in respect of those powers expressly conferred on him by the Court, although this issue does not appear to have been addressed in the Code or the Explanatory Notes;
- an agent is under a fiduciary duty to his principal and should not take advantage of his position;
- an agent is under a duty to use due care and skill in performing his duties;
- an agent may not delegate his authority.

(See also 4.7.2.)

The Code also sets out a list of the duties on Deputies and explains their content and practical implications (para.8.56).

Once a Deputy is appointed:

(a) the Deputy is entitled to be reimbursed out of P's property for his or her reasonable expenses in discharging his functions and, if the Court so directs, for remuneration for discharge of his functions (s.19(7));

(b) the Court may confer on the Deputy a power to take possession or control of any part of P's property or to exercise a range of powers in respect of it including investment (s.19(8));

(c) the Deputy may be required to give the Public Guardian security for the discharge of his or her functions and to submit reports to him or her (s.19(9)).[3]

---

1   David Lammy MP, Hansard, HC Committee Stage, 26 October 2004, col.195.
2   Section 19(6) of the Act and Code, para.8.44.
3   It is intended that the Court should decide upon what matters a Deputy should report in each case (David Lammy MP, HC Committee Stage, 26 October 2004, col.189).

6.7   RESTRICTIONS ON DEPUTIES

A Deputy's powers are significantly limited by the Act, which by implication makes clear that he or she does not assume a complete or general decision-making power in respect of a person.

First, a Deputy does not have power to make a decision on behalf of a person if he or she knows or has reasonable grounds to believe that the person has capacity (s.20(1)). This provision covers the situation of fluctuating capacity, where a person may sometimes have capacity to make decisions and sometimes not. It serves to emphasise that the appointment of a Deputy is not a final act.

If the person has capacity in relation to a particular issue, including one in respect of which the Deputy has been given a particular power because of the person's incapacity at the relevant time, the Deputy may not make a decision in relation to that issue if the person regains capacity, even on a temporary basis. While the intention of the provision is clear, and the motive laudable, it may be a brave

Deputy who declines to exercise his power on the grounds that he or she has formed the view that the person has capacity when a court has declared that the person lacks it in order to appoint the Deputy in the first place. A prudent Deputy may wish to confirm his or her view with a professional assessment.

Secondly, although a Deputy may be given a power to make decisions about 'matters' generally identified by the Court in a declaration or order, the Deputy's powers cannot extend to prohibiting a named individual from having contact or allowing a different person to take over responsibility for P's healthcare (s.20(2)). It remains the case that the most important decisions, such as termination of contact and big healthcare decisions, will be decided by the Court and not hived off to Deputies.

Thirdly, a Deputy may not be given powers with respect to the execution of the person's will, the settlement of his property or the exercise of any power vested in the person under a trust (s.20(3)).

Fourthly, a Deputy may not be given power to make a decision inconsistent with a decision made by the donee of an LPA (s.20(4)). The Explanatory Notes emphasise that a Deputy may not 'trump' an attorney chosen by the donor at a time when he or she had capacity (para.77). If there is concern about an attorney the Court must use its statutory powers under ss.22 and 23 rather than appoint a Deputy. It is easy to imagine circumstances in which the views of attorneys and Deputies divide.

Fifthly, a Deputy may not refuse consent to the carrying out of continuation of life-saving treatment in relation to the person (s.20(5)). The original clause in the Bill provided that a Deputy might not refuse consent 'unless the court has conferred on the Deputy express authority to that effect . . . in exceptional circumstances'. The provision was removed in the light of widespread anxieties and consequent Parliamentary debate about the unintended introduction of euthanasia and assisted suicide by the Act.

Sixthly, a Deputy must exercise powers in accordance with the guiding principles of the Act contained in s.1 and the method of determining best interests in s.4 (see **3.5**) (Code para.8.51). The Deputy should have particular regard for the provisions of the Code (para.8.52).

These restrictions also mirror those imposed on an attorney appointed under an LPA (see **4.5**).

6.7.1   A Deputy may not 'restrain' a person

A Deputy may not do an act that is intended to restrain P unless four conditions are satisfied (s.20(7)):

(a) in doing the act, the Deputy is acting within the scope of an authority expressly conferred on him or her by the Court (s.20(8));

(b) P lacks, or the Deputy reasonably believes that P lacks, capacity in relation to the matter in question (s.20(9));

(c) the Deputy reasonably believes that it is necessary to do the act in order to prevent harm to P (s.20(1));

(d) the act is a proportionate response to:

    (i) the likelihood of the person suffering harm; or

    (ii) the seriousness of that harm (s.20(11)).

The meaning and effect of these requirements is considered under the heading of the parallel prohibitions on attorneys or any other person restraining incapable persons (see **4.5.2** and **5.3.2**).

The concept of 'restraint' is defined by s.20(12) of the Act. A Deputy restrains P if he:

(a) uses, or threatens to use, force to secure the doing of an act which P resists; or

(b) restricts P's liberty of movement whether or not P resists.

This also mirrors the definition contained in s.6(4) of the Act in relation to restraint by attorneys or others. The meaning and effect of this is discussed at **5.3.2**.

The Act further provides, at s.20(13), that a Deputy does more than merely restrain P if he deprives P of his or her liberty within the meaning of Art.5(1) of the ECHR (see **Chapter 5**).

6.8   POWERS OF THE COURT: LPAS

6.8.1   Background

The powers of the Court in respect of LPAs are broadly similar to the powers contained in the EPAA 1985.

6.8.2   Powers in relation to validity of LPA

The Court can determine any question relating to whether the requirements for the creation of an LPA have been met or whether the power has been revoked or come to an end (s.22(2)).

Further, the Court can direct that an instrument is not registered or revoke the instrument or LPA (where the donor does not have capacity to do so) where it is satisfied:

■   that fraud or undue pressure was put on the donor to create an LPA; or

■   that the donee is behaving or proposing to behave so as to contravene his or her authority or contrary to the donor's best interests (s.14(3), (4)).

6.8.3   Powers in relation to the operation of LPAs

This provision allows the Court to decide questions about the meaning or effect of LPAs (s.23(1)). Further, the Court has power to give directions to donees or give consent or authorisation on behalf of the donor where the donor lacks capacity to do so (s.23(2), (3)). The directions that the Court may give when the donor lacks capacity include directions in respect of:

■   rendering accounts and reports and associated records;
■   requiring the provision of information by the donee or produce documents or other things in his possession as donee;
■   remuneration or expenses of the donee;
■   relieving the donee wholly or partly from any liability which he or she has incurred in breach of his or her duties as donee.

The Court can also authorise the making of gifts which are not covered by s.12(2) (s.23(4)).

7 ADVANCE DECISIONS TO REFUSE TREATMENT

7.1 BACKGROUND

At common law, advance directives, known as 'living wills', are given legal effect provided that they meet the elements necessary for validity as set out in *Re T*[1] and *HE v. NHS Trust A and AE* [2003] EWHC 1017 (Fam), [2003] 2 FLR 408. The constituent elements of a valid advance refusal of treatment at common law are that the patient:

- is competent at the time the decision was made;
- is free from undue influence;
- is sufficiently informed; and
- intends the refusal to apply to the circumstances that subsequently arise.

However, an advance directive requiring a certain specific form of treatment or treatments (as opposed to refusing treatment) which the doctor considers to be clinically unnecessary, futile or inappropriate, is not binding on the doctor. This was confirmed by the Court of Appeal in *R (on the application of Burke) v. GMC* [2005] EWCA 1003 Civ at 55.

The common law, however, was felt to be unclear and poorly understood. The Law Commission's Report No.231 *Mental Incapacity*, February 1995, recommended the need for specific statutory provision for those cases where the patient has decided in advance to refuse some particular form of treatment.

The Report also noted that 'there is a clear distinction to be drawn between the legal effect of an *advance expression of views and preferences* on the one hand and an *advance decision* on the other'. The Report similarly made a distinction between an Advance Decision *in favour* of a particular treatment and a decision *against* such treatment.

The Report went on further to propose that the court should not have power to override a valid and applicable anticipatory decision in the exercise of its 'best interests' jurisdiction. Resort should only be had to the court where a decision is required over the validity of the refusal or its applicability. The Report recommended that if such a decision was required from the courts, the refusal should not preclude those treating the patient from taking any steps necessary to prevent the death or a serious deterioration of the maker of the advance refusal. This has found statutory expression in s.26(5) of the Act.

The government accepted the need to place advance directives within a statutory framework so that their legal status and the safeguards governing them would be clearly stated. The Draft Mental Incapacity Bill followed the recommendations of the Law Commission's Report. The pre-legislative Joint Committee supported the need for the Bill to make provision for the making of Advance Decisions to refuse treatment. The provisions relating to advance directives are now contained in ss.24–6 of the Act.

However, the Joint Committee expressed great concern about the possible connections between the Draft Bill and euthanasia and it suggested that an additional clause be added to the Bill to provide additional assurance. The government responded by inserting a new cl.58 into the Bill, which made it clear that 'nothing in this Act is to be taken to affect the law relating to murder or manslaughter or the operation of section 2 of the Suicide Act 1961'.

Despite the addition of cl.58, the debates in both Houses and in the press during the passage of the Bill were dominated by discussions of 'euthanasia by omission' and 'suicidally motivated advance directives'. In the event the clause survived without change as s.62 of the Act.

---

1   *Re T (Adult: Refusal of Medical Treatment)* [2004] EWHC 1279 (Fam).

7.2   ADVANCE DECISIONS TO REFUSE TREATMENT: GENERAL

In accordance with the decision in *Burke* (above) an Advance Decision cannot be used to require the provision of treatment. An Advance Decision as defined in s.25(1) of the Act is a special type of advance statement that represents an actual decision to refuse treatment, even though it was made at an earlier date. The effect of a valid Advance Decision will be to enable that decision to be carried out even though at a point in the future that person no longer has the capacity to give or refuse consent to that treatment. The terms 'advance directive' and 'living wills' are now subsumed into the new statutory term 'Advance Decision'.

7.2.1   Characteristics of an Advance Decision to refuse treatment for the purposes of the Act

- The decision must be made by a person who is aged 18 or over.
- At the time it was made, the person had capacity to make the decision (see **Chapter 3**).
- It must specify the treatment that is to be refused (s.24(1)(a)). It can be expressed in medical language or lay person's terms, as long as it is clear what is meant (s.24(2)).

■   It may set out the circumstances in which the refusal will apply (s.24(1)(a)).

It will only apply when the person lacks capacity to consent to the specified treatment (s.24(1)(b)).

7.2.2   Withdrawal or alteration of an Advance Decision to refuse treatment

■   A person may withdraw or change an Advance Decision if he or she has the capacity to do so (s.24(3)).
■   A withdrawal, or partial withdrawal, need not be in writing, and can be by any means (s.24(4)).
■   An alteration to an Advance Decision need not be in writing unless it applies to an Advance Decision refusing life-sustaining treatment, in which case s.25(5) applies (see below).

7.3   VALIDITY AND APPLICABILITY OF ADVANCE DECISIONS

The consequences of complying with an Advance Decision to refuse treatment for both the person making the Advance Decision and the person's family and the professionals involved are serious. Section 25 provides two important safeguards in relation to an Advance Decision to refuse treatment, i.e. that at the material time the decision is both *valid* and *applicable*.

7.3.1   Validity

A valid Advance Decision must comply with the requirements of s.24.

In addition, an Advance Decision would be invalid if:

■   the maker has withdrawn the decision while he still has capacity to do so (s.25(2)(a));
■   the maker subsequently made an LPA giving a donee the authority to consent or refuse consent to the treatment specified in the Advance Decision (s.25(2)(b));
■   the person has acted in a way that is clearly inconsistent with the Advance Decision remaining his or her fixed decision (s.25(2)(c)).

7.3.2   Applicability

The Advance Decision will not apply if:

■   the maker still has capacity to make his own decisions at the time of the proposed treatment (s.24(3));

- the proposed treatment is not treatment specified in the Advance Decision (s.25(4)(a));
- the circumstances are different from those set out in the Advance Decision (s.25(4)(b)); or
- there are reasonable grounds for believing that circumstances have now arisen which were not anticipated by the person when making the Advance Decision and which would have affected their Advance Decision had the maker anticipated them at the time (s.25(4)(c)).

In relation to the last three bullet points, consideration will have to be given to the length of time that has passed since the Advance Decision was made, the change in the maker's personal circumstances and any developments in treatment or therapies for the maker's medical condition.

7.3.3   Advance decisions relating to life-sustaining treatment

Additional safeguards have been added where the person intends the Advance Decision to apply to the refusal of life-sustaining treatment:[1]

- the Advance Decision must contain a statement by the maker confirming that the decision is to apply to that treatment even if life is at risk (s.25(5)(a)); and
- it must be in writing (s.25(6)(a)); and
- it must be signed by the maker or by another person in the maker's presence and by the maker's direction (s.25(6)(b)); and
- the signature must be properly witnessed (s.25(6)(c)–(d)).

The Mental Capacity Act 2005 (Transitional and Consequential Provisions) Order 2007, SI 2007/1898, gives effect to an advance directive made before the coming into force of the Act in October 2007, even though it does not comply with s.25(5)(a) and (6)(b)–(d) of the Act, provided that the advance directive meets with the conditions set out in art.5 of the Order.

---

1   See paras.9.24–9.28 of the Code of Practice.

7.4   FORMALITIES

Apart from the above requirements relating to Advance Decisions regarding life-sustaining treatment, there are no specified formats for Advance Decisions. To meet the statutory requirements, they must exist, be valid and apply to the treatment under consideration.

Advance Decisions can be made orally or in writing. The Draft Code of Practice contains helpful suggestions about what may be included in a written Advance Decision and how both written and oral Advance Decisions should be recorded (Code, paras.9.18–9.23).

7.5   EFFECT OF A VALID AND APPLICABLE ADVANCE DECISION

A valid and applicable Advance Decision will be as effective as a contemporaneous refusal of consent by a person with capacity to make the decision.[1] The treatment provider is obliged to carry out the maker's Advance Decision (s.26(1)). The treatment cannot lawfully then be given. If treatment is given, nonetheless, those treating the maker may face both civil and criminal liability.

Section 26(2) and (3) clarify the position for the treatment provider. The treatment provider may continue or start treating without incurring liability, provided that he or she is satisfied at that time that the patient has not made a valid and applicable advance refusal of treatment. Conversely, the treatment provider may withhold or withdraw treatment from the patient without incurring liability if he or she has reasonable grounds for believing that there exists a valid and applicable advance directive.

A valid and applicable Advance Decision takes precedence over a consent made by a donee acting under a welfare LPA made before the Advance Decision was made, or a consent given by a court-appointed deputy.

Once the treatment providers are satisfied that an Advance Decision is effective, the provisions of s.5 (consideration of the incapacitated person's best interests) do not apply.

---

1   See *Re T* and *HE* v. *NHS Trust* (above).

7.6   ROLE OF THE COURT OF PROTECTION IN RELATION TO AN ADVANCE DECISION

The Court of Protection only has power to make declarations as to the existence, validity and applicability of the Advance Decision in relation to the treatment under consideration (s.26(4)). The Court has no power to override an effective Advance Decision.

If, however, there is a doubt as to the existence, or a dispute as to the validity or applicability, of an Advance Decision, the doctors may take action to prevent the death of or deterioration in the condition of the person concerned while the matter is resolved by the Court (s.26(5)).

7.7   STEPS THAT CAN BE TAKEN BY HEALTHCARE PROFESSIONALS TO COMPLY WITH THE ACT

7.7.1   Ascertain if an Advance Decision exists

If a health professional has reasonable grounds to believe that an Advance Decision may exist, then he should, if possible, make reasonable efforts to find out what that decision was. It is suggested in the Code (at para.9.49) that reasonable efforts might include discussions with the patient's relatives, contacting the patient's GP and looking through the patient's clinical or nursing records.

7.7.2   Validity and applicability

Once the health professional is satisfied that the Advance Decision exists, then consideration needs to be given to whether it complies with s.21 of the Act, and whether it is valid and applicable to the treatment proposed.

Again, the Code suggests (at para.9.41) that particular care needs to be given to whether the Advance Decision is applicable in the circumstances which have now arisen. Particular care should be given to considering how long ago the Advance Decision was made, and any change of circumstances.

7.7.3   Emergencies

Unless a doctor is satisfied that a valid and applicable Advance Decision exists, he or she may legally treat the patient relying on s.26(2):

> A person does not incur liability for carrying out or continuing the treatment unless, at the time, he is satisfied that an advance decision exists which is valid and applicable to the treatment.

Treatment should not be delayed in order to search for an Advance Decision if there is no clear indication that one exists.

Equally a doctor will not incur liability for the consequences of withholding or withdrawing a treatment from P, if at the time, he reasonably believes that an Advance Decision exists which is valid and applicable to the treatment (s.26(3)).

If a doubt arises as to the existence of an Advance Decision, the matter may be referred to the court for a decision and s.26(4)(a) applies.

7.8   ADVANCE DECISIONS AND ADVANCE STATEMENTS

There is a clear legal distinction between an Advance Decision which complies with s.24 (i.e. it exists, is valid and applicable and is binding on those treating the patient), and a more general advance statement dealing with a person's wishes and feelings about how he or she wishes to be cared for and treated in the future.

A general advance statement will be taken into account by those determining a person's best interests in accordance with s.4(6)(a) of the Act, as an expression of past wishes and feelings once that person has lost capacity to make a particular decision. An advance statement will, however, be one of only a number of considerations to be taken into account when assessing a person's best interests (see for example, the case of W Healthcare NHS Trust v. H and Others [2004] EWCA Civ 1324, [2005] 1 WLR 834).[1] The Court of Appeal held that H's statement, remembered by her family, that she 'wouldn't want to be kept alive by machines', was not a valid advance directive because she could not at the time of making the statement have anticipated that if the statement was complied with, her death would be as a result of dehydration and starvation. The court concluded that it was in her best interests for the PEG feeding tube to be reinserted.[2]

---

1 H suffered from the end stages of multiple sclerosis, she was sensate, but totally dependent on others. Her PEG feeding tube had become dislodged and the family did not wish it to be replaced. Those treating H applied for a declaration that it was lawful for the PEG tube to be reinserted.

2 See also HE v. NHS Trust A and AE [2003] EWHC 1017 (Fam), [2003] 2 FLR 408.

7.9   ADVANCE DECISIONS AND LASTING POWERS OF ATTORNEY

Often advice is sought on whether someone should give a Lasting Power of Attorney (LPA) to a person or persons of his choosing, or make an Advance Decision with regards to refusing treatment.

LPAs are discussed in **Chapter 4**, and 4.5.4 sets out a number of specific restrictions on welfare LPAs, in particular, welfare powers are subject to Advance Decisions about treatment made by P (s.11(7)(b)). If P has made an Advance Decision about a particular medical treatment, that decision takes precedence. If however the donor made an LPA after the Advance Decision, and gave the attorney the right to consent to or refuse the treatment, the attorney can choose not to follow the Advance Decision.

An Advance Decision can (as set out at 7.3.3 above) apply to the refusal of life-sustaining treatment provided it meets the requirements with regards to formalities set out in s.25(5) and (6). An LPA does not grant power to the donee to give or refuse consent to the carrying out or continuation of life-sustaining treatment unless the LPA contains an express provision to that effect and is subject to any conditions or restriction in the LPA (s.11(8)).

It is worth noting that once the donor of an LPA loses capacity his attorney is able to exercise his or her powers even if circumstances change. An Advance Decision is only binding if it is valid and applicable to the decision at the material time (s.25).

8 RESEARCH

8.1 BACKGROUND

Since 1991, research has been carried out under the Medical Research Council's guidelines. The Law Commission in its Report *Mental Incapacity* in 1995 complained about and called for improvements to the 'lack of clarity around research'. It also considered that non-therapeutic research on mentally incapacitated adults was unlawful.[1] Nevertheless, the Law Commission supported the use of mentally incapacitated adults in clinical trials and proposed the introduction of safeguards.

The Draft Mental Incapacity Bill did not make provision for incapacitated adults to take part in research. The Royal College of Psychiatrists gave evidence to the Joint Committee considering the Mental Incapacity Bill that legislation was needed because 'the common law does not strictly provide such authority, as it cannot be argued that research is necessarily in the incapacitated person's best interests'.

Evidence to the Joint Committee included that the Bill would deny patients without capacity the possibility of benefit if they were unable to participate in research. At the same time, concerns were expressed that unregulated research could well lead to opportunities for abuse. The Joint Committee concluded that 'a clause should be included in the Bill to enable strictly controlled medical research to explore the causes and consequences of mental incapacity and to develop effective treatment for such conditions'. The Joint Committee then suggested that key principles governing research should be added to the Bill and covered in the Code of Practice.

The recommendations were largely accepted by the government and became ss.30–4 of the Act.

The law in the United Kingdom makes a distinction between two types of research involving people. These are: (1) clinical trials for medical products; and (2) other research involving people. Regulatory provision has already been made for some clinical trials under the Medicines for Human Use (Clinical Trials) Regulations 2004, SI 2004/1031.[2] Trials which are governed by the clinical trials regulations are excluded from the Act because protection is already provided by those regulations (s.30(3) and (5)). In contrast, the Act introduces a legal framework for research in general.

1 Paragraph 6.29.
2 This gave effect to Directive 2001/20/EC. The Directive provides: 'Persons who are incapable of giving legal consent should be given special protection . . . in cases such as persons with dementia, psychiatric patients, etc . . . the written consent of the person's legal representative, given in cooperation with the treating doctor, is necessary before participation in any such trial.'

8.2 RESEARCH

The stated aim of the Act and the Code of Practice in relation to research is 'to establish the right balance between the need for research to bring benefit or information and the need for protection against exploitation and abuse'.

The Act applies to intrusive research which would require consent as a matter of law if the person involved was capable of giving consent (s.30(2)). A researcher who complies with all the requirements of ss.30–4 will have lawful authority for his or her actions.

The research is not limited to research in a healthcare setting but includes social care research and any other intrusive research.

Under s.42(4) of the Act researchers carrying out research approved under the Act are required to have regard to the Code.

8.2.1 Hierarchy of safeguards

Baroness Andrews during the second day of the Report Stage of the Bill in the House of Lords set out a hierarchy of safeguards that are contained in the Act:

- research must entail negligible risk;
- anything done must not interfere with the person's freedom and privacy;
- it must not be unduly invasive or restrictive;
- consultation must take place with the person's carers or a consultee;
- there must be an assessment of whether the research itself is burdensome;
- the people concerned must be listened to and respected if they show any distress or objection; and
- the whole process must be validated and reviewed by a research ethics committee (REC).

Sections 30–3 therefore allow 'intrusive research' to be lawfully carried out on a person who lacks capacity provided that the research project is carried out by:

- an appropriate body; and
- in accordance with the requirements set out in ss.32 and 33 of the Act.

8.2.2   'Appropriate body' and 'appropriate authority'

Section 30(4) defines an 'appropriate body'. The appropriate authority, defined in s.30(6) as the Secretary of State in relation to research in England and the National Assembly for Wales in relation to research in Wales, must specify an appropriate body for approving research projects. In England the 'appropriate body' must be a research ethics committee recognised by the Secretary of State.[1] In Wales the 'appropriate body' must be a research ethics committee recognised by the National Assembly for Wales.[2]

Ethics committees are already established in England and Wales under the standards framework governance arrangements for NHS research ethics committees. In reviewing a proposed study the committee's task is to protect the dignity, rights and well-being of actual or potential research participants.

---

1   Mental Capacity Act 2005 (Appropriate Body) (England) Regulations 2006, SI 2006/2810.
2   Mental Capacity Act 2005 (Appropriate Body) (Wales) Regulations 2007, SI 2007/833.

8.2.3   Requirements for approval

Section 31 defines the bounds of what kind of research can be approved involving people who lack capacity to consent.

Section 31(1) provides that the research must be connected with an impairing condition which affects the person participating in the research or with the treatment of the condition.

'Impairing condition' is defined in s.31(3) and means one that is, or may be, attributable to or causes or contributes to the impairment of or disturbance in the functioning of the person's mind or brain.

Section 31(4) requires that there are reasonable grounds for believing that there is no alternative to the involvement of the person in the research, and it could not be carried out as effectively if only people who have capacity to consent take part.

Section 31(5) states that the research must meet one of two requirements:

- it must have potential to benefit the subject of the research without imposing a burden that is disproportionate to the benefit (s.31(5)(a)); or
- it must intend to provide knowledge relevant to the causes, treatment or care of people affected by the same or similar conditions (s.31(5)(b)).

If researchers rely on s.31(5)(b), then the Act sets out further requirements that must be met:

- the risk to the person lacking capacity must be negligible (s.31(6)(a)); and
- the research must not interfere with the person's freedom of action or privacy in a significant way or be unduly invasive or restrictive (s.31(6)(b)).

Risk must be negligible

The Code at para.11.18 states that:

> This means that a person should suffer no harm or distress by taking part. Researchers must consider risks to psychological wellbeing as well as physical wellbeing.

Unduly invasive

The Code at para.11.19 states that:

> Actions will not usually be classed as unduly invasive if they do not go beyond the experience of daily life, a routine medical examination or a psychological examination.

8.3   ADDITIONAL SAFEGUARDS

8.3.1   Consultees

The person conducting the research, before taking any steps to involve a person in approved research, must take all reasonable steps to identify someone (a personal consultee) who is close to the person and who is prepared to be consulted about the person's involvement in research (s.32(2)). This other person must *not* be someone acting in a professional capacity or for payment, such as a carer. A donee under an LPA or a Deputy can be a person consulted under s.32 (s.32(7)).

If the researcher cannot find such a person, then the researcher must nominate a person independent of the research (a nominated consultee) in accordance with guidance issued by the appropriate authority, the Secretary of State for Health in England or the National Assembly for Wales (s.32(3)).[1]

Section 32(4) requires the researcher to provide the person consulted with information about the research and asks that person to:

- provide advice as to whether the incapable person should take part in the research; and
- indicate what in his or her opinion the incapable person's wishes and feelings about taking part in the project would be likely to be if the person had capacity in relation to the matter.

The Act's core principles emphasise the importance of respecting the wishes of P, both before and at the time that the research is undertaken. Researchers need to plan in advance and be able to satisfy the REC that the arrangements they propose for consultation address this core duty.[2]

Section 32(5) further provides that if the person consulted advises the researcher that in his opinion the person's wishes and feelings would be likely to lead him to decline to take part in the project then the researcher must ensure that the person does not take part in the project, or if already under way, is withdrawn from the research.

Section 32(6) requires treatment to be continued even if the person is withdrawn from research if there is a significant health risk to the person if the treatment was discontinued.

Section 32(8)–(10) provides additional safeguards in an emergency when it is not practical to consult within the meaning of the Act (for example, severe head injuries, cardiac arrest, septic shock or accidental injuries to people with dementia). If the emergency care must take place before it is possible to consult in the usual way, then P can be enrolled in an approved project with either:

- the agreement of a doctor who is not connected to the project; or
- in accordance with a procedure previously agreed with the REC where it is not reasonably practicable to obtain agreement from a doctor who has no connection with the project.

Any such decision should take into account the views of the person being treated or those of their family or friends who are with them.

8.3.2   Additional safeguards once research has begun

The researcher is asked to respect any signs of resistance from the person where the person 'appears to object (whether by showing signs of resistance or otherwise)', and not to involve the person in any research that would be contrary to any valid and applicable advance decision or any other form of statement made and not subsequently withdrawn (s.33(2)).

Although it is not clear from the subsection, one assumes that the Act refers to a statement that was made when the person still had capacity to make his or her own decisions. It is not clear why here such a statement is binding on the researchers and not merely a matter to be taken into account (in accordance with s.4(6)(a)) in a best interest assessment (see **Chapter 3**).

It is, however, clearly stated in s.33(3) that the interests of the person must be assumed to outweigh those of science and society.

The person must be withdrawn from the project without delay if the person indicates that he or she wishes to be withdrawn from it or if the researcher has reasonable ground for believing that any of the requirements for approval of the project as set out in s.31(2)–(7) are no longer met.

8.3.3   Loss of capacity during the research project and transitional provisions

Section 34 was a late government amendment to the Act. It provides for a transitional regulation-making power to cover research that starts before s.30 comes into force and which involves people who had capacity when the research project started, but lose capacity before the end of the project. It enables ongoing and essential research to continue and is particularly important for long-term projects.

Researchers will be able to continue research as long as they comply with the conditions set out in the Mental Capacity Act 2005 (Loss of Capacity During Research Project) (England) Regulations 2007[3] or similar Welsh regulations.[4] The regulations apply only where the research started before October 2007 and the person concerned initially consents before 30 March 2008. They do not cover research involving direct intervention after loss of capacity. Any such research must comply with ss.30–3 to be lawful.

The Regulations require a researcher to seek out a project that is approved by the REC. Schedule 2 of the Regulations sets out requirements to identify or nominate a consultee which are similar to those in s.32 of the Act.

---

1 Guidance on nominating a consultee for research involving adults who lack capacity to consent (Department of Health, 22 February 2008).
2 Ibid, p.16.
3 SI 2007/679.
4 Mental Capacity Act 2005 (Loss of Capacity during Research Project) (Wales) Regulations 2007, SI 2007/837.

9 INDEPENDENT MENTAL CAPACITY ADVOCATE SERVICE

9.1 BACKGROUND

Access to advocacy services was one of the more problematic issues throughout the passage of the Act. The government, while recognising the value of independent advocacy services to people with capacity problems, made it clear from the outset that it did not wish to provide for general advocacy. The Draft Mental Incapacity Bill therefore contained no provision for independent advocacy.

Subsequently, very real concerns were expressed in relation to the 'unbefriended'. These are particularly vulnerable adults without capacity who have lost contact with family or friends, or whose relatives have passed away and have no one to represent and support them when decisions are being taken about serious medical treatment or significant changes of residence. The government responded by introducing into the Mental Capacity Bill the 'independent consultee' who was to advise NHS bodies and local authorities on a person's best interests.

Further concern was expressed during the deliberations of the House of Commons Standing Committee by Mr Paul Burstow (Liberal Democrat MP for Sutton and Cheam), about the confusion surrounding the role of the independent consultee. He noted a 'conflation between advocacy and the independent appointee type of function' in the provisions of the Bill.

The government was well aware of the difficulties and made it clear that the provisions relating to the independent consultee were a 'work in progress' and that the government needed time to develop its thinking and to consult widely.

Baroness Ashton of Upholland on the second day of the Report Stage of the Bill in the House of Lords,[1] when moving amendments to the Bill stated that:

> it was always our intention that the role of the IMCA is to support the individual by making representations about their wishes, feelings, beliefs and values, at the same time as bringing to the attention of the decision maker all factors that are relevant to the decision. The IMCA can also challenge the decision maker on behalf of the person if appropriate.

The amendments removed references contained in the Draft Bill to 'independent consultees' giving advice about the person's 'best interests', and changed the name from independent consultee to 'independent mental capacity advocate (IMCA)' to reflect the new thinking that the role of the IMCA was to support and represent the person. The provisions are contained in ss.35–41 of the Act. Much of the detail about how the IMCA service operates is not contained in the Act but can be found in regulations made and guidance issued under the Act.

Before the implementation of the Act the government consulted widely on the role of the IMCA and in particular whether the IMCA should be involved in situations beyond the two specified in the Act: serious medical treatment and accommodation moves. The responses supported the adding of two further situations:

- where an adult protection allegation had been made; and
- in care reviews.

The government responded by extending the Act through regulations in England[2] and Wales[3] to include these two further situations.

In addition, as part of the development work associated with implementing the IMCA service, seven IMCA pilot schemes were set up in January 2006 to help identify the practical issues involved in implementing the service. In December 2006 the Department of Health published an independent evaluation of the IMCA pilots which had been carried out by a team of researchers at the University of Cambridge. A copy of the report can be found on the Department of Health's website (**www.dh.gov.uk/imca**).

The service started in England on 1 April 2007 and in Wales on 1 October 2007. The Department of Health maintains a list of organisations which have been appointed to provide IMCA services, in July 2007 there were 173 such organisations listed on the IMCA website. There is some concern that whilst local authorities do appear to be appointing IMCAs in appropriate cases, NHS bodies are not appointing IMCAs to the same extent. It is therefore important that advisors ensure that IMCAs are appointed in good time in all appropriate cases.

---

1   At col.1524.
2   Mental Capacity Act 2005 (Independent Mental Capacity Advocate) (Expansion of Role) Regulations 2006, SI 2006/2883.
3   Mental Capacity Act 2005 (Independent Mental Capacity Advocate) (Wales) Regulations 2007, SI 2007/852.

9.2   APPOINTMENT OF IMCA

Section 35(1) places a duty upon the 'appropriate authority' to make 'such arrangements as it considers reasonable' for the provision of a new IMCA Service. The 'appropriate authority' for England is the Secretary of State and, in relation to Wales, the National Assembly for Wales (s.35(7)). Regulations adjust the obligation to make arrangements imposed by s.35 of the Act to include making provision for IMCAs to carry out representation and support of eligible persons in accommodation reviews and in adult protection cases.

Section 35(2) and (3) provide for the appropriate authority to make regulations as to the appointment and conditions of appointment of IMCAs. The Explanatory Notes to the Act comment that this provision will ensure that an individual will need to meet common standards in order to be approved as an IMCA. The Mental Capacity Act 2005 (Independent Mental Capacity Advocates) (General) Regulations 2006[1] (the 'IMCA General Regulations') contain provisions as to who can be appointed to act as an IMCA and as to the functions of an IMCA when he has been instructed to represent a person in a particular case.

Regulation 5 of the IMCA General Regulations provides that a person can only act as an IMCA if he has been approved by a local authority or is a member of a class which had been so approved. For an IMCA to be appointed, he or she must satisfy certain requirements as to experience, training, good character and independence.

Section 35(4) importantly provides that the IMCA should be as far as possible independent of the person making the decision concerned. Subsection 35(5) provides for payment of the IMCA.

In order properly to represent and support the person concerned, s.35(6) provides that the IMCA may:

- interview the person concerned in private (s.35(6)(a)); and
- examine and take copies of health records, social services records and care homes' records (s.35(6)(b)(i)–(iii)).

9.2.1   Duty or power to appoint an IMCA

NHS bodies and local authorities *have a duty* under s.37 (serious medical treatment decisions) and s.38 (changes in accommodation) of the Act to instruct an IMCA where the eligibility criteria are met.

For care reviews and adult protection procedures, local authorities and NHS bodies in England *may* appoint an IMCA where they consider it would be of particular benefit to the person concerned.[2]

---

1   SI 2006/1832.
2   Mental Capacity Act 2005 (Independent Mental Capacity Advocate) (Expansion of Role) Regulations 2006, SI 2006/2883.

9.3   FUNCTIONS OF IMCA

Section 36(1) provides for the appropriate authority to make regulations setting out the functions of the IMCAs.

Section 36(2) provides for the regulations to set out the steps that the IMCA is required to take in order to carry out these functions. These steps should ensure that the IMCA:

- provides support to enable the person to participate as fully as possible in the decision (s.36(2)(a));
- obtains and evaluates the relevant information (s.36(2)(b));
- ascertains and represents the person's wishes, feelings, beliefs and values (s.36(2)(c)). It is worth noting that the curious wording of the subsection introduces the possibility of the IMCA substituting his or her own judgment for that of the person, particularly if that person has always lacked capacity and has never been able to express his or her own wishes and feelings;
- finds out about available options (s.36(2)(d)); and
- seeks further medical opinions if necessary (s.36(2)(e));

The IMCA General Regulations referred to above have been made in exercise of the powers conferred on the secretary of state by s.36 and set out the functions of an IMCA.

In addition to determining 'in all the circumstances how best to represent and support P' (reg.6(3)). The IMCA must prepare a report for the authorised person who instructs him or her (reg.6(6)) and may include in the report such submissions as the IMCA considers appropriate in relation to P and the act or decision which is proposed in relation to P (reg.6(7)).

9.3.1   Challenging decisions

Section 36(3) provides that the regulations may also set out the circumstances in which the IMCA may challenge the decision maker or provide assistance for the purpose of challenging any relevant decision.

The government noted in its consultation document at paras.19 and 20 that:

> the government does not regard the new IMCA Service as a replacement or substitute for independent advocacy as it is commonly understood . . . Many people take the view that the conventional independent advocacy role is to represent the person's wishes and feelings, but not to influence the decision itself. The role of the IMCA goes further than this, it includes not only representing and supporting the person but also bringing to the attention of the decision maker all factors that are relevant to the person's best interests; and challenging the decision, where necessary.

As a result the IMCA General Regulations provides that (reg.7(2)):

> The IMCA has the same rights to challenge the decision as he would have if he were a person (other than an IMCA) engaged in caring for P or interested in his welfare.

The explanatory note accompanying the regulations explains that this includes challenging any decision as to whether P is a person who lacks capacity.

The Department of Health booklet 'Making decisions: the Independent Mental Capacity Advocate (IMCA) Service', which can be downloaded from the Department of Health's website, suggests that the IMCA may initially use informal methods of challenge. Where the IMCA has serious concerns about the decision made, it suggests that formal methods may be used such as:

- using the relevant complaints procedure;
- referring to the Independent Complaints Advocacy Service;
- consulting the Patient Advice and Liaison Service in England or Community Health Councils in Wales;
- referring the case to the Court of Protection; and
- approaching the Official Solicitor.

The Code of Practice at para.10.38 states that:

> The first step in making a formal challenge is to approach the Official Solicitor (OS) with the facts of the cases. The OS can decide to apply to the court as litigation friend (acting on behalf of the person the IMCA is representing). If the OS decides not to apply himself, the IMCA can ask permission to apply to the Court of Protection. The OS can still be asked to act as litigation friend for the person who lacks capacity.

The Code continues at para.10.39:

> In extremely serious cases, the IMCA might want to consider an application for judicial review in the High Court. This might happen if the IMCA thinks there are very serious consequences to a decision that has been made by a public authority. There are time limits for making an application and the IMCA would have to instruct solicitors – and may be liable for the costs of the case going to court. So IMCAs should get legal advice before choosing this approach. The IMCA can also ask the OS to consider making the claim.

The fact that no provision has been made for the costs of the IMCA in the event that he instructs solicitors to advise with a view to making an application to court is a serious obstacle to the ability of IMCAs to obtain proper advice at an early stage. Although there have been a number of approaches to the Official Solicitor for advice, at the time of writing none of these approaches have thus far resulted in an application to the Court of Protection or the Administrative Court by the Official Solicitor.

It is the view of the authors that in the event that the public authority does not accept the IMCA's submissions and an area of doubt or dispute remains that cannot be resolved through the appropriate dispute procedures, the matter should be brought before the Court of Protection by the public authority for resolution at the earliest opportunity. An order can be sought by the applicant that the person concerned (P) be made a party to the proceedings and be represented by a litigation friend (or by his or her own legal representative if capacity is in issue) (rule 73(4)).[1] In the event that the public authority does not bring the matter before the Court the Official Solicitor may make an application to the Court of Protection (or Administrative Court if appropriate) as litigation friend. It may be necessary for combined judicial review and Court of Protection proceedings to be brought on P's behalf[2] particularly where the public body's decision is based on a disputed view of what is in P's best interest.[3] An application will have to be made to both the Administrative Court and the Court of Protection and directions sought that the cases be: (1) transferred to be heard by a nominated High Court judge of the Court of Protection (in the case of the application to the Court of Protection); and (2) heard together by a High Court judge who is both a judge of the Court of Protection and a judge of the Administrative Court.

In a number of cases currently before the Court of Protection an IMCA has been appointed by the public authority concerned and has provided a report to the authority. This report may form part of the evidence within the proceedings and the IMCA may be called upon to give evidence during the course of the proceedings.

1 Court of Protection Rules 2007, SI 2007/1744.
2 *A (A Patient) v. A Health Authority Joined Cases: J (A Child) (Choice of Forum), Re; R. (on the application of S) v. Secretary of State for the Home Department* [2002] EWHC 18, [2002] Fam 213, [2003] 3 WLR 24.
3 *CH and others v. Merton and Sutton Primary Care Trust* [2005] ACD 40, [2004] EWHC 2984 (Admin).

9.4   PROVISION OF SERIOUS MEDICAL TREATMENT BY NHS BODY

Section 37(1) applies where 'serious medical treatment' is to be provided or arranged by the NHS for a person who lacks capacity, and there is no one with whom the decision-maker can consult in determining what would be in the person's best interests. An IMCA is to be instructed if there is no one from the list in s.40 (i.e. a person nominated by the person, an attorney under an LPA (but not a financial LPA only), or a deputy or a donee of an EPA) or a non-professional carer or friend whom it is appropriate to consult.

9.4.1   'Serious medical treatment'

Section 37(6) provides a general definition of what constitutes 'serious medical treatment'. It means:

> . . . treatment which involves providing, withholding or withdrawing treatment of a kind prescribed by regulations made by the appropriate authority.

Regulation 4(2) of the IMCA General Regulations[1] defines serious medical treatment for the purposes of s.37 as:

> . . . treatment which involves providing, withdrawing or withholding treatment in circumstances where –
>
> (a) in a cases where a single treatment is being proposed there is a fine balance between its benefits to the patient and the burdens and risks it is likely to entail for him,
>
> (b) in a cases where there is a choice of treatments, a decision as to which one to use is finely balanced, or

(c)   what is proposed would be likely to involve serious consequences for the patient.

Para 10.44 of the Code states that 'serious consequences' are 'those which could have a serious impact on the patient, either from the effects of the treatment itself or its wider implications' and may include treatments which cause serious and prolonged pain, distress or side effects; have potentially major consequences for the patient; or have a serious impact on the patient's future life choices.

Para.10.46 of the Code provides that the duty on the NHS body to instruct an IMCA need not be followed when an urgent decision is needed.

The definitions of 'serious medical treatment' and 'serious consequences' contained in reg.4 and in the Code are the same as those definitions contained in Practice Direction 9E (which supplements Part 9 of the Court of Protection Rules 2007) 'Applications Relating to Serious Medical Treatment' (PD9E).

The following decisions are considered so serious for the purpose of the Rules and the Practice Direction that they must be brought to court for the Court of Protection to make the decision (PD9E, para.5):

(a)   decision about the proposed withholding or withdrawal of artificial nutrition and hydration from a person in a permanent vegetative state or a minimally conscious state;
(b)   cases involving organ or bone marrow donation by a person who lacks capacity to consent; and
(c)   cases involving non-therapeutic sterilisation of a person who lacks capacity to consent.

The Code states at para.10.48 that 'responsible bodies should still instruct an IMCA in these cases' if presumably the person meets the criteria.

The IMCA will represent and support the person in accordance with the regulations made under s.36. Section 37(5) provides that the NHS body must take into account any submissions made or information given by the IMCA when arriving at its decision.

Subsection (2) provides that where the person's treatment is regulated by Part 4 of MHA 1983, then the IMCA need not be instructed under s.37(3). Provision is made in s.37(4) for urgent treatment and s.37(7) makes provision for regulations which will define the particular 'NHS bodies' which will become subject to the duties.[2]

---

1   SI 2006/1832.
2   Ibid, reg.3(1).

9.5   PROVISION OF ACCOMMODATION BY NHS BODY

Section 38 applies if an NHS body proposes to provide or arrange long-stay accommodation in a hospital or care home, or to move a person between such accommodations. Subsections (6) and (7) define the types of care homes and hospitals which are covered by this section. For the purposes of ss.37 and 38 'NHS body' means a Strategic Health Authority, an NHS foundation trust, a Primary Care Trust, an NHS Trust, or a Care Trust.[1]

An IMCA must be instructed where such accommodation is proposed and the person concerned lacks capacity to agree to the arrangements and there is no one with whom the decision-maker can consult in determining what would be in that person's best interests. Any information or submissions from the IMCA must be taken into account by the NHS body.

Section 38(9) provides that this section only applies if such accommodation is provided for more than 28 days in hospital or more than eight weeks in a care home; or where a shorter term is later extended into the applicable period (s.38(4)).

Section 38 does not apply where the person concerned is to be accommodated as a result of an obligation imposed on him or her under MHA 1983 (s.38(2)). Subsection (3) makes provision in relation to urgent placements.

Subsection (8) provides that regulations will also define which particular NHS bodies will become subject to the duties under this section.

The NHS responsibilities for community care services are complex and the IMCA may need specialist advice to represent the incapable person and to challenge decisions on the person's behalf. Ultimately, if a decision is taken by the NHS authority that is contrary to the IMCA's submissions, then judicial review proceedings may need to be brought on behalf of the incapable person. In these circumstances the IMCA should refer the matter to a solicitor for consideration. The solicitor may then approach the Official Solicitor, who may, if he considers it appropriate, bring proceedings in the Administrative Court on behalf of the incapable person.

---

1   SI 2006/1832, reg.3.

9.6   PROVISION OF ACCOMMODATION BY LOCAL AUTHORITY

Section 39 applies to long-stay (eight weeks or more) accommodation arranged by the local authority or a change in such accommodation. It applies to residential accommodation provided in accordance with s.21 or s.29 of the National Assistance Act 1948, or MHA 1983, s.117, as a result of a decision taken by the local authority under s.47 of the National Health Service and Care in the Community Act 1990 (s.39(2)).

'Residential accommodation' can mean accommodation in a care home, a nursing home, ordinary and sheltered housing, housing association or other registered housing, or in private sector housing provided by a local authority or in hostel accommodation (see Explanatory Notes, para.121).

The provisions mirror the provisions made in relation to accommodation by an NHS body. The IMCA is to be instructed where a person lacks capacity to make decisions about where he or she should live and there is no one with whom the decision-maker can consult when determining what would be in that person's best interests. Any information or submissions from the IMCA must be taken into account by the local authority (s.39(6)).

It is interesting to consider what role the IMCA may have once a social services authority has assessed an incapable person as eligible for accommodation under the National Assistance Act 1948, s.21. The local authority is then obliged to make arrangements for accommodation in a care home for that person in a place of his or her choice provided certain conditions are satisfied.[1] If the person is incapable of making the choice the guidance provides that the local authority should act on the preferences and wishes of the person's carers unless exceptionally that would be against the best interests of the resident. It seems that an IMCA should be treated as a 'carer' for the purposes of this provision.

Section 39(3) provides that the section does not apply where the person concerned is accommodated as a result of an obligation imposed on him under MHA 1983. Subsection (4) makes provision for urgent accommodation.

Subsection (5) ensures that an IMCA is provided for a person whose residence was initially intended to be less than eight weeks, but is then extended.

Again, if a decision is taken by the local authority which does not accord with the IMCA's submissions the IMCA may wish to refer the matter to a solicitor to consider challenging the decision by way of judicial review in the Administrative Court on the person's behalf. In such a case, it may be appropriate for the Official Solicitor to be asked to consider representing the person as his or her litigation friend in the absence of another suitable individual.

---

1   National Assistance Act 1948 (Choice of Accommodation) Directions 1992 (as amended).

9.7   REVIEW OF ARRANGEMENTS AS TO ACCOMMODATION

The responsible body *may* instruct an IMCA to support and represent a person who lacks capacity when:

- it has arranged accommodation for that person;
- it aims to review the arrangements (as part of a care plan or otherwise); and
- there are no family or friends whom it would be appropriate to consult.[1]

Such reviews should relate to decision about accommodation:

- for someone who lacks capacity to make a decision about accommodation;
- that will be provided for a continuous period of more than 12 weeks;
- that are not the result of an obligation under the 1983 Act, and
- that do not relate to circumstances where ss.37 and 39 of the Act would apply.[2]

1   SI 2006/2883, reg.3.
2   Code, para.10.64.

9.8   ADULT PROTECTION CASES

The responsible body *may* instruct an IMCA to support and represent a person who lacks capacity where:

- it is alleged that the person is or has been abused or neglected by another person;
- it is alleged that the person is abusing or has abused another person.[1]

Local authorities and NHS bodies can only instruct an IMCA if they propose to take or have already taken protective measures.[2]

In these cases access to IMCAs is not restricted to people who have no one else to support or represent them. People who lack capacity who do have family and friends are still entitled to have an IMCA to support them in adult protection procedures. The responsible body must be satisfied that having an IMCA will benefit the person.

1   Mental Capacity Act 2005 (Independent Mental Capacity Advocate) (Expansion of Role) Regulations 2006, SI 2006/2883, regs.4 and 5.
2   See for England *No secrets: Guidance on developing and implementing multi-agency policies and procedures to protect vulnerable adults from abuse* (available from **www.dh.gov.uk**); for Wales *In safe hands* (available from **www.ssiacymru.org.uk**).

9.9   EXCEPTIONS

Section 40 provides that the NHS body or local authority concerned does not have to instruct an IMCA for a person who lacks capacity in accordance with ss.37(3), 38(3) and (4) and 39(4) and (5) if there is:

- a person chosen in advance; or
- an attorney under an LPA or EPA; or
- a Deputy (s.40(a)–(d)).

The exceptions contained in s.40(b)–(d) may undermine the purpose of the IMCA Service, which is to safeguard vulnerable people who are facing important decisions about treatment and residence. Section 40 removes the duty on the appropriate authorities to appoint an IMCA for an incapacitated person even if the attorney under an LPA has only been given authority to make financial decisions on behalf of a person, or the Court has only authorised the deputy to deal with a person's property and business affairs. The Court-appointed deputy may have been appointed from a list of panel Deputies and he or she may have no personal knowledge of the person concerned.

It will be open to the appropriate authorities to appoint an IMCA even if a person set out in s.40(b)–(d) has been appointed or chosen on behalf of the person, although there will be no duty upon the appropriate authority to do so.

9.10   POWER TO ADJUST THE ROLE OF THE IMCA

Both the scope of the IMCA Service and the obligations to make arrangements imposed by s.35 may be extended or altered by regulations made by the Secretary of State in England or, in Wales, the National Assembly for Wales.[1]

---

1   Further information on the IMCA service can be obtained from **www.dh.gov.uk/imca** or by emailing **imca@dh.gsi.gov.uk**.

10 ILL-TREATMENT OR NEGLECT

10.1 BACKGROUND

The current law criminalises certain conduct against mentally disordered persons. The Sexual Offences Act 2003 created a number of offences 'against persons with a mental disorder impeding choice' which prohibits sexual activity with or in the presence of those with a mental disorder impeding choice as well as the incitement, procuring, threatening or use of deception to bring about such acts (Sexual Offences Act 2003, ss.30–37). Under the MHA 1983 there are three offences of ill-treatment or neglect of mentally disordered persons by:

(1) employees or managers of hospitals and care homes in respect of mentally disordered persons who are in-patients or out-patients;
(2) a guardian or some other person with care and custody of a mentally disordered person in the community; and
(3) any person in respect of a patient who is subject to supervised discharge (s.127).

It is a prerequisite of all the offences under the MHA 1983 that the person has a 'mental disorder' within the meaning of s.1 of that Act.

Further, there is guidance from the Department of Health and the Home Office about the procedures that local authorities should adopt to monitor and respond to adult abuse.[1] This does not contain any new powers but is concerned with the process local authorities should follow and also provides clarification of the roles of different agencies, i.e. the police and NHS bodies.

The Mental Capacity Bill contained a new criminal offence of ill-treatment or neglect by an attorney, deputy or carer of a person who lacks capacity. This broadens the current protection against ill-treatment and neglect contained in the MHA 1983 because it is not necessary to show that the person has a mental disorder as defined by the MHA 1983, but only that the person lacks capacity.

The Joint Committee on the Draft Mental Incapacity Bill recommended that the Bill should go further by granting statutory authorities greater powers of investigation and intervention in cases of alleged physical, sexual or financial abuse of persons lacking capacity.[2] That recommendation was rejected by the government on the basis that the *No Secrets*[3] and *In Safe Hands*[4] adult protection guidance requires councils to liaise with other public bodies and agencies to adopt a joint strategy and procedure for handling incidents. Also, the government relied on the fact that the Public Guardian has powers to cooperate with other agencies (see Cm. 6121).

It is indeed the case, in the view of the authors, that, given the difficulties in succeeding in criminal prosecutions where the victim lacks capacity, most instances of abuse or neglect of incapable adults will be dealt with under *No Secrets*, and, where it concerns professional care, under the Protection of Vulnerable Adults List scheme set up under Part 7 of the Care Standards Act 2000. This scheme came into force in 2004 and requires the listing of names of individuals who have been found to have abused, neglected or otherwise harmed vulnerable adults in their care, or placed vulnerable adults in their care at risk of harm.

The Joint Committee also recommended in its Report (at para.272) that the new criminal offence be extended to include the misappropriation of property and financial assets of the person lacking capacity, but this was rejected by the government on the basis that it is already covered by the current law of theft (Cm.6121). However, the Fraud Act 2006 now creates an offence of fraud by abuse of position, which will apply to attorneys and deputies under the Act.

The Code gives detailed guidance as to the steps to be taken where there are concerns that a person lacking capacity is being abused or neglected, and sets out the agencies responsible for preventing such abuse and neglect (Code, chapter 12).

---

1 *No Secrets: Guidance on Developing and Implementing Multi-agency Policies and Procedures to Protect Vulnerable Adults from Abuse* (March 2000).
2 *Joint Committee on the Draft Mental Incapacity Bill Report*, para.73.
3 See fn.1. Many local authorities have now set up Adult Protection Committees in response to this guidance.
4 The parallel guidance issued by the National Assembly for Wales.

10.2 POSITION UNDER THE MENTAL CAPACITY ACT 2005

10.2.1 Persons liable

The offence of ill-treatment or neglect applies to three categories of person (all referred to here as 'D'):

- a person who has the care of a person (P) who lacks capacity or whom D reasonably believes lacks capacity (this includes professional carers as well as non-professionals such as relatives);
- the donee of an LPA or an EPA created by P;
- a deputy appointed by the court for P.

10.2.2   A person who lacks capacity or whom D reasonably believes lacks capacity

Lack of capacity is defined carefully in the Act (see **Chapter 3**). It therefore appears that the intention of Parliament was to adopt this situation-specific test in respect of the constituent parts of the criminal offence created under the Act.

This contrasts with the approach taken by the courts in cases concerning capacity to consent to sexual intercourse (see **Chapter 1**) where the court has been at pains to emphasise that the test of capacity to consent to sexual intercourse, to be applied under the Sexual Offences Act 2003, is different from the more complex, situation-specific, test to be applied in all other civil contexts, and in particular in proceedings in the inherent jurisdiction that preceded the Act. It is submitted that the fact that Parliament has expressly adopted the situation-specific test of capacity in respect of this criminal offence under the Act, indicates that there is no inherent difficulty in bringing the two tests of capacity into line, and that there is no reason for keeping the narrow test of incapacity to consent to sexual intercourse adopted recently by the courts in the context of proceedings concerning welfare under the Act, since neither the Sexual Offences Act 2003 nor the criminal parts of this Act appear to require such an approach in any event.

10.2.3   D is guilty of an offence if he or she ill-treats or wilfully neglects P

There is no definition of ill-treatment or wilful neglect in the Act, although the Code now provides guidance (paras.14.25–14.26).

However, there is case law in respect of the MHA 1983 offences of ill-treatment or neglect of mentally disordered persons which provides guidance.[1] The Court of Appeal has held that ill-treatment and wilful neglect under the MHA 1983 ought not to be equated and that they should appear as separate counts in an indictment (*R v. Newington* (1990) 91 Cr App R 247). This applies equally to the offence of ill-treatment or wilful neglect under the Act.

Ill-treatment

In *R v. Newington*, the Court of Appeal gave guidance on the requirements of the offence of ill-treatment in the context of the offence of ill-treatment of a mentally disordered person under MHA 1983, s.127. It is necessary for the prosecution to prove:

(1) deliberate conduct by the accused which can properly be described as ill-treatment irrespective of whether or not it damaged or threatened to damage the victim's health; and

(2) a guilty mind: either an appreciation by the accused that he or she was inexcusably ill-treating a person or recklessness as to whether he or she was inexcusably acting in this way.

The Court did not accept that violence would always amount to ill-treatment because violence necessarily used for the control of a patient would not amount to ill-treatment.

Wilful neglect

The leading case on wilful neglect is *R v. Sheppard* [1981] AC 394, HL. The primary meaning of the word 'wilful' is deliberate. As a matter of general principle, recklessness is also covered (see Lord Keith, at 418). Neglect is an objective state which is not defined by the Act. Neglect could consist of an omission.

10.2.4   Penalties

The offence is triable either way and the penalties are:

- on summary conviction, a maximum prison term of 12 months and/or a fine not exceeding the statutory maximum;
- on conviction on indictment, a maximum prison term of five years and/or a fine.

The penalties are, following the amendment of the MHA 1983 by the MHA 2007, the same as those for the offences of ill-treatment and wilful neglect under that Act.

1   For more detailed discussion, refer to Richard Jones *Mental Health Act Manual* 10th edn (Sweet & Maxwell, 2007) and *Blackstone's Criminal Practice* (OUP, 2008).

11 THE COURT OF PROTECTION

11.1 BACKGROUND

The jurisdiction of the previous Court of Protection was entirely statutory and derived from Part VII of the MHA 1983 and the EPAA 1985.[1] It was an office of the Supreme Court. Its jurisdiction was restricted to matters relating to the property and affairs of a patient within its jurisdiction, and it had no jurisdiction over matters relating to the patient's welfare such as residence, medical treatment or contact between the patient and other persons.

---

1 Both are repealed by the Act (s.66).

11.2 POSITION UNDER THE MENTAL CAPACITY ACT 2005

11.2.1 Changes introduced

The Act introduces important changes in respect of the Court of Protection, affecting its jurisdiction and powers. First, it is made a superior court of record with all the powers of the High Court. Secondly, its jurisdiction is no longer restricted to matters concerning the property and affairs of a person who lacks capacity but also covers the person's personal welfare. Thirdly, there is no longer any provision for the appointment of receivers. Receivers have been replaced by Deputies under the Act. The Court is responsible for the appointment of Deputies.

The particular powers of the Court of Protection are explained in other chapters of this book (see **Chapters 4, 6** and **7**).

11.2.2 When to apply to the Court?

Welfare cases

The Code of Practice states that in cases concerning personal welfare matters, the core principles of the Act, the best interests checklist and s.5 of the Act will be sufficient to help people take action or make decisions in the best interests of someone who lacks capacity to make decisions about care or treatment or find ways of settling disagreements about such actions or decisions. However, the Code acknowledges that an application to the Court may be necessary for:

- particularly difficult decisions;
- disagreements that cannot be resolved in any other way;
- situations where ongoing decisions may need to be made about the personal welfare of a person who lacks capacity to make decisions for him or herself (Code, para.8.3).

In certain situations, such as cases concerning serious medical treatment, it is necessary to make an application to the Court (see PD9E, para.5).

Chapter 15 of the Code places a strong emphasis on use being made of alternative dispute resolution (ADR) mechanisms such as mediation, complaints procedures or referral of a complaint to the relevant Ombudsman. It states that it is in everyone's interests that disputes should be settled quickly and effectively with minimal stress and costs. This chapter of the Code contains detailed guidance about using alternative dispute resolution mechanisms. However, in the view of the authors it is likely that many medical (which do not involve serious medical treatment) and welfare cases will continue to be brought to Court where the dispute, commonly between family members and professionals, is intractable and cannot be resolved other than through court proceedings. Further, where there is a dispute over capacity, it is difficult to see how that could be resolved informally. In practice, it seems unlikely that there will be far fewer welfare applications made to the Court of Protection under the Act than were previously brought in the Family Division of the High Court.

Property and affairs cases

Chapter 8 of the Code recognises that an order of the Court will usually be necessary for matters relating to the property and affairs of persons who lack capacity to make specific financial decisions for themselves unless the only income is state benefits (in which case the benefits can be managed by an appointee appointed by the Department for Work and Pensions) or they have previously made an EPA or an LPA to give someone authority to manage their property and affairs (Code, para.8.4).

11.2.3   Repeals

Part VII of the MHA 1983 and the EPAA 1985 are repealed by the Act, although transitional provisions are in place for existing receivers and the EPAA 1985 is re-enacted in Sched.4 to the Act with amendments (see discussion at **4.13.2**).

11.3   THE COURT: JURISDICTION AND POWERS

11.3.1   The Court of Protection

The Court of Protection previously existed only as an office of the Supreme Court and not as a separate court. The Court of Protection is now made a court of record (s.45(1)) which means that records of its proceedings which are preserved in its archives are called records and will be conclusive evidence of that recorded in them (*R v. Tyrone Justices* [1917] 2 IR 437). It is able to establish precedent.

Further, it is made a superior court, which means that no matter is deemed to be beyond its jurisdiction unless expressly shown to be so. An objection to the jurisdiction of a superior court must show that another court has jurisdiction so as to show that the exercise of the general jurisdiction of a superior court is unnecessary.

The office of the Supreme Court called the Court of Protection has ceased to exist.

The Court of Protection has its own official seal. This is consistent with it being a separate court.

The Court of Protection may sit anywhere in England or Wales (s.45(3)). It has a central office and registry in Archway, London. This is the only registry of the Court at present and hence all applications must be issued and processed in Archway. There are several regional hearing venues across England and Wales. The Court can allocate cases to these regional centres but applications cannot be issued or processed at any of these centres.

The regional centres are :

- Birmingham;
- Bristol;
- Cardiff;
- Manchester;
- Newcastle;
- Preston.

Some cases are also heard in the Royal Courts of Justice. It was intended that Brent Magistrates' Court would be used when a larger court room is required in London but, at the time of writing, that court is yet to be used although Gee Street Magistrates' Court in London has been.

11.3.2   Judges of the Court of Protection

Judges in the Court of Protection must be nominated by the Lord Chief Justice or the President of the Court of Protection or a judicial office holder nominated on behalf of the Lord Chief Justice (s.46(1), (2)). Those who can be nominated are listed in s.46(2) and are the President of the Family Division, the Vice-Chancellor, a puisne judge of the High Court, a circuit judge or a district judge. There is no statutory provision for Deputy district judges of the Court of Protection to be appointed.

Sir Mark Potter, the President of the Family Division has been appointed as President of the Court of Protection and Sir Andrew Morritt, the Chancellor of the Chancery Division as Vice President.

The day-to-day running of the court is the responsibility of the Senior Judge. Denzil Lush (formerly Master of the Court of Protection) has been appointed as Senior Judge.

The President has nominated a number of additional High Court, Circuit and District Judges to hear Court of Protection cases. At the Court's central registry in Archway, Senior Judge Denzil Lush and District Judges are currently hearing cases. Other judges are hearing cases part time in the courts where they are based across England and Wales.

11.3.3   General powers and effect of orders

Same powers, rights, privileges and authority of the High Court

The new Court of Protection's jurisdiction is expanded so that it is has the same powers, rights, privileges and authority of the High Court (s.47(1)). The High Court's powers derive from the Supreme Court Act 1981 as well as a variety of other statutes and the common law. The Court of Protection has, therefore, powers to fine or imprison for contempt of court (but no bailiffs or anywhere to hold anyone at Archway), to grant injunctions, to summons witnesses and order the production of documents, to secure and preserve evidence and has enforcement powers.

The Act specifically provides that the Court has power to make interim orders and directions (s.48) and has the power to call for reports on the incapable person, P (s.49). Both of these powers are discussed in more detail below (p.152 and pp.160–162).

Section 204 of the Law of Property Act 1925 (s.47(2)) which makes orders conclusive in favour of purchasers applies to the Court of Protection.

Office copies of orders or directions issued by the Court and sealed with the official seal are admissible in legal proceeding without further proof (s.47(3)).

The Court's powers to make declarations and orders and powers in respect of EPAs, LPAs and Deputies are discussed in other chapters of this book (**Chapters 4 and 6**).

11.4   COURT OF PROTECTION FEES

The Court of Protection Fees Order 2007, SI 2007/1745 (made pursuant to ss.54 and 65) sets the fees to be paid for applications to the Court. The current fee levels are:

(a) application fee for bringing proceedings: £400 (this is paid on making an application for permission if permission is required (see art.4));
(b) appeal fee: £400;
(c) hearing fee: £500 (this is payable when a hearing has been held to determine a case or appeal and a final order, declaration or decision has been made (see art.6);
(d) copy of court document fee, non-certified or certified: £5/£25.

This order sets out various circumstances in which the above fees are not payable, exemptions from fees and reduction or remission of fees in exceptional circumstances.

Fees payable can be recovered as civil debt (s.54(5)).

11.5   COURT OF PROTECTION: PRACTICE AND PROCEDURE

11.5.1   Court of Protection Rules 2007

The procedure of the Court of Protection is set out in the Court of Protection Rules 2007, SI 2007/1744 ('the Rules') and the various Practice Directions which accompany it. (The Rules are made in exercise of powers conferred by ss.49(5), 50(2), 51, 53(2) and (4), 55, 56 and 65(1) and in accordance with Part 1 of Sched.1 to the Constitutional Reform Act 2005.) The Rules and Practice Directions are made pursuant to ss.51 and 52 of the Act. The Rules revoke the Court of Protection Rules 2001 and the Court of Protection (Enduring Powers of Attorney) Rules 2001 (rule 2).

The Court of Protection Rules are closely modelled on the Civil Procedure Rules 1998 (CPR). The Rules state that the CPR may be applied with necessary modifications in any case not expressly provided for under the Rules and Practice Directions insofar as is necessary to further the overriding objective (rule 9).

In a book of this length, it is not possible to set out an exhaustive guide to the Rules, nor was that considered necessary given the similarity of the Rules to the CPR in many respects. The various Parts of the Rules are discussed below. For ease of reference, this discussion adopts the same order as the Rules and refers where appropriate to the relevant Practice Directions (PDs).

11.5.2   Part 2: The overriding objective

Rule 3 provides that the Rules have the overriding objective of dealing with a case justly having regard to the principles in the Act and that the Court will seek to give effect to the overriding objective when exercising any power under the Rules and when interpreting any rule or practice direction. The examples of dealing with a case justly include the familiar CPR concepts of expedition, fairness, proportionality and the saving of expense. Particular reference is also made to ensuring that P's interests and position are properly considered which is of particular importance, given that P will not always be a party to the proceedings (see below at p.146) (rule 3(2)(b)).

As is the case in the CPR, the parties have a duty to help the Court to further the overriding objective (rule 4).

The Court is required to further the overriding objective by actively managing cases (rule 5). Active case management has been an important feature of post-CPR proceedings in the High Court and County Courts. The Court will similarly take a hands-on approach to management to ensure efficiency and save costs. Rule 5 sets out various features of active case management which include encouraging the parties to co-operate, identifying at an early stage the issues in the case and who should be a party to the proceedings, deciding promptly which issues require full investigation and hearing and those which do not and encouraging ADR. It can be expected that the Court will be very proactive in encouraging ADR given the focus in the Code of Practice on ADR (Code, chapter 15).

11.5.3   Part 3: Interpretation provisions

It is important to understand the difference between 'P' and 'protected party'. 'P' is any person (other than a protected party) who lacks or is alleged to lack capacity to make a decision or decisions in relation to a matter which is the subject of an application to the Court. 'Lacks capacity' is construed in accordance with the Act.

'Protected party' means a party or an intended party (other than P or a child) who lacks capacity to conduct the proceedings. In other words, the application before the Court is not to do with a protected party's lack or alleged lack of capacity to make decisions. If a person's decision-making capacity is the subject of the application before the Court, then he is referred to as P and not as a protected party. It is to be noted that there is the potential for confusion because the definition of 'protected party' in the CPR and the Family Proceedings Rules 1991 (FPR) differs from the definition in the Rules because any party or intended party (including P) who lacks capacity within the meaning of the Act is known as a 'protected party' in the CPR and FPR (CPR, rule 21.1; FPR 1991, rule 9.1).

There is also a distinction between application forms and application notices. An application form is the document used to bring proceedings in accordance with Part 9 or other provisions which require the use of an application form. An application notice is a document used to make an application in accordance with Part 10 of the Rules or other provisions.

11.5.4   Part 4: Court documents

Form of documents

PD4A supplements this part of the Rules.

Rule 10 sets out those documents which will be stamped by the Court including permission forms, applications forms and notices and court orders. PD4A states that documents signed electronically or mechanically must also bear the printed name of the person (para.1).

There are specific provisions about the form of documents to be used at Court (PD4A, paras.2–4) which include requirements that A4 paper should be used with a margin of at least 3.5 cm, that documents should normally be typed, that paragraphs and pages should be numbered, and that all numbers, including dates, are to be expressed as figures.

There are detailed requirements about filing documents by fax (PD4A, para.7). If a document is filed by fax, no hard copy should be sent in addition.

Statement of truth

Rule 11 and PD4B deal with documents which are required to be verified by a statement of truth. The following must be so verified (rule 11(1)):

(a) permission forms, application forms or notices where the applicant relies on matters set out in the document as evidence;
(b) a witness statement;
(c) certificates of service/non-service, notification or non-notification;
(d) a Deputy's declaration; and
(e) any other document required to be so verified by a rule or practice direction.

Rule 11 and PD4B set out requirements as to who must sign the statement of truth. If a statement of truth is to be signed by a person who is unable to read or sign the document, an authorised person must sign a certificate in a particular form (PD4B, paras.17–20).

If a document is not verified with a statement of truth when required, court permission is required to rely on it (rule 12).

Proceedings for contempt of court may be brought in respect of false statement in documents verified by a statement of truth without an honest belief in its truth (rule 14).

Withholding information

When a party does not wish to reveal personal details such as the home address or telephone number of him or herself, or of P, or of the person with whom P is living, those particulars must be provided to the Court. Those details will not be revealed unless directed by the Court (rule 15).

A party can also apply to the Court for an order that part of a document is to be edited before its service or disclosure (rule 19). Any such application must be made in accordance with Part 10, using a COP9 application notice and must provide the Court with the document with the parts sought to be deleted clearly marked (PD4A, paras.8–9).

Public Guardian

When a Deputy is appointed by the Court or an order is made varying the Deputy's appointment, the Public Guardian is entitled to be provided with copies of relevant documents filed at court if he or she reasonably considers it necessary to have them in connection with the discharge of his supervisory functions under s.58 of the Act over the Deputy (rule 20).

Court orders requiring action or inaction on the part of the Public Guardian must be served on him or her no later than seven days after the order was made (rule 21).

Slip rule

There is a slip rule allowing the Court to correct clerical mistakes or slips (rule 23).

11.5.5   Part 5: General case management powers

The Court has a wide range of general case management powers (rule 25). These include the power to require P, a party or his or her legal representative or litigation friend to attend Court.

Some of the security for costs provisions in the CPR apply (rule 25(7)).

The Court can dispense with the requirement of any rule (rule 26).

The Court may exercise its powers on its own initiative and may do so without hearing the parties or giving them an opportunity to make representations (rule 27).

The Court has a general power to rectify errors of procedure and a failure to comply with a rule or Practice Direction does not invalidate any step in the proceedings unless the court so orders (rule 28).

11.5.6   Part 6: Service of documents

The rules as to service of documents are similar to the CPR and are not, therefore, considered in detail. The rules as to service of documents apply also to the requirement under rule 20 for a person to be notified of the issue of an application form (rule 29(1)). PD6A deals with service of documents and makes provisions about different methods of service and applications to the Court for alternative service or to dispense with service. PD6A also provides that form

COP20 is to be used where a certificate of service or non-service is required (para.16).

There are some specific rules dealing with service on protected parties and on P, if P becomes a party.

Rule 32 sets out the person on whom documents must be served in respect of children and protected parties (e.g. a person authorised to conduct the proceedings on the protected party's behalf or a person appointed as attorney, donee or Deputy of the protected party).

Rule 33 deals with service on P if P becomes a party and provides that all documents must be served on P's litigation friend or the person duly authorised to conduct proceedings on P's behalf, although the Court may order documents to be served on some other person.

11.5.7   Part 7: Notifying P

This part of the Rules deal with the important issue of notifying P of matters in respect of proceedings which relate to P but in respect of which P is not a party. As is discussed further below (at p.146), P does not automatically become a party to proceedings, even though the subject of the proceedings are matters which concern P (namely, decision in respect of which P lacks capacity or is alleged to lack capacity). These notification requirements are intended to provide some protection to P's interest by providing P with some information about the proceedings.

Part 7 is supplemented by a Practice Direction which deals with notification of P (PD7A).

If P is a party, the Part 7 notification provisions do not apply and P must be served with documents in the ordinary way under Part 6 (see above).

When must P be notified

It is mandatory to notify P of the following matters, unless the Court orders otherwise (rules 42–45, rule 40(3)).

(a) that an application form (which means a document used to bring proceedings (rule 6)) has been issued by the Court or withdrawn;
(b) of the date on which a hearing is to be held for disposing of the application;
(c) that an appellant's notice has been issued by the Court or withdrawn;
(d) that a final order has been made; and
(e) of any other matter as the Court may direct.

It follows that there is no requirement to notify P of an application notice issued in accordance with Part 10 (i.e. an application issued during proceedings). However, PD7A states that an applicant may notify P of such an application if the applicant considers it appropriate to do so, and must do so if the Court makes a direction to that effect (para.3).

Who is to notify P

Notification of P must be effected by the applicant or the appellant (if the matter is an appeal) or an agent appointed by the applicant or appellant or such other person as the court may direct (rule 41).

Of what P is to be notified

Rules 42 and 43 set out the specific matters which P must be notified of by the person effecting notification:

(a) who the applicant/appellant is;
(b) that the application raises the question of whether P lacks capacity in relation to matter/matters and what that means or what the issues in the appeal are, or that the application form has been withdrawn;
(c) what will happen if the court makes the order or direction that has been applied for, or the consequences of the withdrawal;
(d) if there is an application for a person to be appointed to make decisions on behalf of P in relation to the matters which are the subject of the application to the Court, who that person is;
(e) that P may seek advice or assistance in relation to any matter of which P is notified.

P must also be provided with a COP5 form for acknowledging notification (rule 47) and a COP14 form which explains the matter for which notification is being provided.

How P is to be notified

Rule 46 sets out the manner in which P is to be notified. The information must be provided to P personally and in a way which is appropriate to P's circumstances (e.g. using sign language). In general, notification must be effected within 21 days of the event triggering the requirement to notify (e.g. the issue of the application notice or the making of an order).

Certifications of notification and non-notification

Certificates of notification must be filed within seven days of effecting notification (rule 48). This part of the Rules does not refer to a certificate of non-notification but PD7A (para.7) states that a non-notification certificate must be filed (by reference to rule 37 which in fact deals with certificates of non-service under Part 6). The certificate must be filed using the COP20 form.

Dispensing with notification

A person required to notify can apply to the Court for an order dispensing with the requirement to notify P or requiring some other person to effect notification. A COP9 application notice must be used in accordance with Part 10 (rule 49). PD7A states that such an application would be appropriate where, for example, P is in a persistent vegetative state (PVS) or where notification is likely to cause significant and disproportionate stress to P.

11.5.8   Part 8: Permission

An applicant must apply for permission to start proceedings under the Act, unless s.50 of the Act or para.20(2) of Sched.3 to the Act (an application for declarations relating to private international law) or rule 51 applies. If permission is required, the application form will not be issued by the Court until permission is granted (rule 61(3)).

There is a Practice Direction dealing with permission (PD8A).

Permission not required

Section 50 of the Act provides that the following applicants do not require permission from the Court to start proceedings:

- a person who lacks or is alleged to lack capacity (or if that person is not yet 18, anyone with parental responsibility for the person);
- the donor or donee of an LPA to which the application relates (the application to the Court must, therefore, relate to the LPA);
- a Deputy for a person to whom the application relates;
- a person named in an existing order of the Court, if the application relates to the order.

Further, rule 51 provides that permission is not required when:

(a) an application is made by either the Official Solicitor or the Public Guardian;
(b) where the application concerns –

   (i) P's property and affairs save for certain applications listed in rule 52 (which do require permission);
   (ii) an LPA which is, or purports to be created, under the Act (in other words it is not only donors or donees of an LPA who do not need permission); or
   (iii) an instrument which is, or purports to be, an EPA;

(c) where an application is made in accordance with Part 10 (applications within proceedings);
(d) where a person files an acknowledgement of service or notification in accordance with Part 8 or Part 9 for any order proposed that is different from that sought by the appellant.

Permission required

Apart from the exceptions listed above, permission from the Court will be required to bring an application. In deciding whether to grant permission, the Court must have regard to the following factors (s.50(3)):

■   the applicant's connection with the person to whom the application relates;
■   the reasons for the application;
■   the benefit to the person to whom the application relates of a proposed order or directions; and
■   whether the benefit can be achieved in any other way.

If part of the application is a matter for which permission is required, then permission must be sought for that part of the application (rule 53(2)). PD8A (paras.3–4) states that a person can file a single application form seeking both orders or separate application forms (and pay two application fees). If the former, the application form will not be issued until permission has been granted in respect of the part of the application which requires it.

Application for permission (rule 54)

The applicant must file the permission form (COP2) and must file with it the following documents:

(a) a draft of the application form using form COP1;
(b) an assessment of capacity form using form COP3.

If the applicant is unable to complete an assessment of capacity form (e.g. P refuses to undergo the assessment), the applicant should file a witness statement with the permission form stating:

(a) why the applicant has not been able to obtain an assessment of capacity;
(b) what attempts (if any) have been made to obtain the said assessment;
(c) why the applicant knows or believes that P lacks capacity to make a decision or decisions in relation to any matter that is the subject of the proposed application to the Court (PD8A, para.7).

The applicant is not required to file any of the annexes to the application form (i.e. supporting information or any other documents required by rule 64 (see below)), but may do so if he or she wishes (PD8A, para.7).

A person may file expert evidence with the permission form without permission from the Court if it is evidence:

(a) that a person lacks capacity to make the decision/decisions in question in the proceedings;
(b) as to P's best interests; or
(c) that is required to be filed by any rule or Practice Direction with the permission form or application form (which would include the COP3 assessment of

capacity form which has to be completed by a medical practitioner) (rule 120, discussed further below at pp.139–140, 163).

Permission decision (rule 55)

Within 14 days, the Court will either:

(a) grant the application without a hearing, in whole or in part, or subject to conditions and may give directions in connection with the issue of the application form;

(b) refuse the application without a hearing; or

(c) fix a date for a hearing of the permission application.

When the Court fixes a date for the permission hearing, it will notify the applicant and other person as it thinks fit and provide them with a copy of the documents mentioned in rule 54 (i.e. those which the applicant was required to lodge with the permission form). It would, therefore, seem that copies of additional documents such as annexes which the applicant choose voluntarily to lodge will not be copied. The Court can also direct that any document is to be provided on an edited basis (rule 54(2)). The Court will also provide a form for acknowledging notification (COP5) which must be filed by any person wanting to take part in the permission hearing in accordance with rule 57.

The COP5 acknowledgement of notification must be filed not more than 21 days after notice of the application was given by the Court (rule 57(2)) and must state (rule 57(4)):

(a) whether he or she consents to the application;

(b) whether he or she opposes it and if so, on what grounds;

(c) whether he or she proposes that permission should be granted to make an application for a different order and if so, what that order is;

(d) provide an address for service within the jurisdiction; and

(e) be signed by him or her, or his or her legal representative.

If permission is opposed or it is proposed that permission should be given for an application for a different order, the person must file a witness statement setting out the evidence he or she relies upon (subject to the restrictions on expert evidence in rules 120 and 123 discussed at p.163) (rule 57(6)).

If a person notified of an application for permission fails to serve an acknowledgement of notification in accordance with rule 57, the person cannot take part in the permission hearing unless the court permits him or her to do so (rule 58).

Grant or refusal of permission

The Court serves the order refusing or granting permission on the applicant and any other person notified of the application who acknowledged service (rule 59).

When permission is granted, the Court may give directions in connection with the issue of the application form. The applicant will need to lodge a final version of the application form and in many cases additional documents (e.g. the annexes to the application form, if not previously provided). Rule 65 provides that the Court will issue an application form once permission has been granted.

Where the Court grants or refuses permission following a hearing, an appeal can be brought in accordance with Part 20 (see below).

11.5.9   Part 9: How to start proceedings

The application form

In order to begin proceedings, the applicant must file an application form (COP1). Proceedings begin once an application form is issued by the Court (rule 62(1)). As stated above, an application form will not be issued in cases where permission is required, until permission has been granted (rule 61(3)).

The application form must contain certain information which is set out in rule 63. The form COP1 asks for all this information, e.g. the matter which the applicant wants the court to decide and the order sought. It is necessary to name the applicant, P, the respondents to the application and any person who is to be notified under rule 70.

There is an important distinction between respondents and persons to be notified (rule 63):

(a) a respondent is a person other than P whom the applicant reasonably believes to have an interest which means that he ought to be heard in relation to the application (as opposed to simply being notified);

(b) a person who is notified about the application will not be heard by the Court but is considered to have an interest in knowing about the proceedings in relation to P.

PD9B (discussed further below) contains some helpful guidance as to those sorts of persons who are likely (and indeed are to be presumed) to have an interest in being notified of an application. However, in practice applicants are likely to struggle with the distinction between the circumstances in which a person should be made a respondent to the proceedings (and hence a party as per rule 73 if he or she serves an acknowledgement of service) and when it suffices simply to notify a person. Clearly each case will need to be looked at on its own facts, but it is suggested that if a person has a direct interest in the proceedings, i.e. is P's carer and the proceedings relate to an issue concerning P's care and welfare, then that person ought properly to be a respondent, as opposed to being merely notified of the proceedings.

It is important to note that an applicant must *reasonably believe* a person to have an interest in being heard before making him or her a respondent to the proceedings, a requirement which is obviously designed to avoid persons becoming parties without good reason. However, there is no Practice Direction dealing with the particular issue of deciding whether to make a person or a body a respondent or simply to notify them or how applicants are to judge whether a person has an interest in being heard.

Further, as discussed below, PD9B which deals with notification, describes some situations when a person or body should be notified (e.g. the NHS body responsible for P's care, where there is an application by another person to provide or withdraw medical treatment: it seems extraordinary that in such circumstances the NHS body providing care would not have an interest in being heard as to whether or not its patient should receive or cease to receive particular medical treatment). Of course, persons who are notified can serve an acknowledgement of notification indicating that they wished to be joined as a party to the proceedings and the Court has powers to order a person be joined as a party, if for example, he or she has only been notified of the proceedings. It would appear that the Court is keen to keep tight control over which persons/bodies become parties by encouraging notification of other persons as opposed to naming them as respondents (which automatically makes them parties).

PD9A also sets out requirements about information to be included in the application form (e.g. the addresses which must be included).

There are specific requirements about documents which must be filed with an application form (rule 64 and PD9A, paras.9–14). In PD9A, there is a very helpful table setting out which documents are required for which types of application. The documents which may need to be filed include:

(a) any order granting permission;
(b) assessment of capacity form (COP3) (unless already filed with the permission application);
(c) Annex A (COP1A) for property and affairs applications or Annex B (COP1B) for personal welfare applications;
(d) COP 4 if an application is being made to appoint a Deputy;
(e) the LPA or EPA where the application is concerned with the court's power under ss.22 or 23 of, or Sched.4 to, the Act; and
(g) an order appointing a litigation friend.

The application must also be supported by evidence in the form of a witness statement or in the application form (provided that it is verified by a statement of truth). The evidence must set out the facts on which the applicant relies and all material facts known to the applicant of which the Court should be made aware (PD9A, paras.9–11). Applicants have, therefore, an obligation of candour to the Court.

A person may file expert evidence with the application form (and with the permission form) without permission from the Court if it is evidence:

(a) that a person lacks capacity to make the decision/decisions in question in the proceedings;
(b) as to P's best interests; or

(c) that is required to be filed by any rule or Practice Direction with the permission form or application form (which would include the COP3 assessment of capacity form which has to be completed by a medical practitioner) (rule 120, discussed further below at p.163).

The Court will issue the application form as soon as practicable after it is filed in any case where permission is not required or has been granted (rule 65).

Steps following issue of an application form

SERVICE ON THE RESPONDENTS

The applicant must serve a copy of the application form and copy documents filed with it on all of those persons named as respondents in the application form as soon as reasonably practicable and in any event within 21 days of issue (rule 66).

The applicant must also serve on the respondent a form for acknowledging service (COP5).

The applicant must file a certificate of service within seven days of serving the documents (COP20).

NOTIFY P

The applicant must notify P in accordance with Part 7 (see above) that an application form has been issued, unless the requirement to do so has been dispensed with under rule 49 (rule 69).

NOTIFICATION OF OTHER PERSONS

The applicant must notify those persons who are specified in PD9B of:

(a) the fact that an application notice has been issued;
(b) whether it relates to the exercise of the court's jurisdiction in respect of P's property and affairs or his personal welfare or both; and
(c) of the order or orders sought (rule 70).

The applicant must also provide to those notified a form for acknowledging notification (COP5).

PD9B gives some detailed guidance of the sorts of persons who should be so notified. Members of P's close family are, by virtue of their relationship with P, likely to have an interest in being notified that an application to the Court has been made concerning P. It is further submitted that in many cases, a close relative will also on any reasonable view have an interest in being heard and hence ought to be made a respondent, particularly if that relative is caring for P and the application relates to a matter connected with P's care. It is to be presumed that a spouse or civil partner, any other partner, parents and children are likely to have an interest in the application. That presumption can be displaced, e.g. if the applicant knows that the relative has little or no involvement in P's life and has shown no inclination to do so (PD9B, para.6). There is a list of people according to presumed closeness who should be notified in descending order as appropriate to P's circumstances (PD9B, para.7).

As a safeguard, PD9B requires the evidence to address why the presumption of notification has been displaced in respect of any person listed in para.7.

There is also a supplementary list of persons (PD9A, para.10) who must be notified where appropriate of the application including:

(a) any legal or natural person who is likely to be affected by the outcome of any application. PD9B states that where an organisation including an NHS body responsible for P's care (and the application is made by another person) the organisation should be notified where the application relates to the provision to or withdrawal from P of medical or other treatment or accommodation. As stated above, it seems strange that in such circumstances the NHS body concerned should in fact not be named a respondent so that it can be heard on this issue;

(b) any Deputy or attorney under an EPA or LPA where that person has power to make decisions on behalf of P in regard to the matter to which the application relates. Given that this person has either been appointed by the Court or chosen by P to make the decision in question, it is suggested that in many cases such a person should be a respondent to the proceedings and not merely notified.

Notification is to be made using the COP15 form. The rules about service and PD6A dealing with service apply similarly to notification (rule 29(1)).

Applications relating to LPAs (rule 67) and EPAs (rule 68)

Where the application concerns the Court's powers in respect of LPAs or EPAs, there are additional rules which require service of the application form and accompanying documents on additional persons (so as to ensure that the donor and all donees of the power are served), unless they have already been served or notified (rules 67(1), 68(1)).

Furthermore, if the application relates solely to an objection to a registration of a power, the service and notification requirements in rules 66 and 70 do not apply and alternative rules apply (rules 67(2), 68(2)).

There are also provisions requiring the applicant to notify the donor in accordance with Part 7 (procedure for notifying P) if the applicant has reasonable grounds to believe that the donor of the power lacks capacity to make a decision in relation to any matter which is the subject of the application (rules 67(5), 68(5)).

Requirements for certain applications

Rule 71 provides that Practice Directions may make additional or different provisions in relation to specified applications. There are Practice Directions dealing specifically with the following applications.

PD9E – APPLICATIONS RELATING TO SERIOUS MEDICAL TREATMENT

Serious medical treatment is defined for the purpose of the Rules and PD9E as follows:

> Treatment involving providing, withdrawing or withholding treatment in circumstances where:
>
> > single treatment – fine balance between benefits to P and burdens and risks it is likely to entail;
> > choice of treatments – decision is finely balanced; or
> > treatment, procedure or investigation proposed would be likely to involve serious consequences for P.
>
> Serious consequences are those which could have a serious impact on P, either from the effects of treatment, procedure or investigation or its wider implications. May include those which:
>
> > cause, or may cause, serious and prolonged pain, distress or side effects;
> > have potentially major consequences for P; or
> > have a serious impact on P's future life choices.

Matters which should be brought to court

The Practice Direction provides examples of those types of cases which should be regarded as serious medical treatment and should be brought to Court (para.5). These include:

(1) decisions about the proposed withdrawal of artificial nutrition and hydration from a person in a persistent vegetative state or minimally conscious state;
(2) cases involving organ or bone marrow donation by a person who lacks capacity to consent; and
(3) cases involving non-therapeutic sterilisation of a person who lacks capacity to consent.

There are also examples of cases which *might* constitute serious medical treatment and hence *might* need to be brought to Court:

(a) certain terminations of pregnancy in relation to a person who lacks capacity to consent;
(b) a medical procedure performed on a person who lacks capacity to consent when the procedure is for the purpose of donation to another;
(c) a medical procedure or treatment to be carried out on a person who lacks capacity to consent where a degree of force to restrain a person is required;

(d) an experimental or innovative treatment for the benefit of a person who lacks capacity to consent; and

(e) a case involving an ethical dilemma in an untested area.

Other procedures or treatments might be regarded as serious medical treatment depending upon the circumstances and consequences for the patient.

Parties

PD9E states that the organisation responsible for care and treatment should usually be named as respondent to the proceedings (para.9). The Court will consider at the first directions hearing whether to make P a party to the proceedings and will consider whether anyone else should be joined as a party (paras.9, 14).

Consultation with official solicitor

PD9E records that members of the Official Solicitor's staff are willing to discuss serious medical treatment applications in advance of such an application being made (tel: 020 7911 7127, fax: 020 7911 7105 and e-mail: **enquiries@offsol.gsi. gov.uk**).

It is suggested by the authors that consultation with the Official Solicitor is generally advisable and will be particularly important in cases where an urgent application is to be made. This is because the Official Solicitor will need to be on notice in the event that P is to be made a party and the Official Solicitor is being invited to act as litigation friend.

Allocation of serious medical treatment cases

The proceedings in a serious medical treatment case (including permission, directions and any hearing) must be heard in the High Court by a judge nominated by virtue of s.46(2)(a)–(c) (i.e. the President of the Family Division, the Chancellor of a puisne judge of the High Court) (see PD12A). If the case involves the lawfulness of withholding or withdrawing of artificial nutrition and hydration from a person in persistent vegetative state or minimally conscious state or involves an ethical dilemma in an untested area, the case must be heard by the President or a judge nominated by the President.

The judge to whom a serious medical treatment case is allocated in accordance with PD12A may determine that the matter is one which can be dealt with by a judge other than a designated High Court judge (para.5, PD12A).

Procedure if urgent application

If the case is urgent, the urgent applications procedure should be followed (see further below at **11.14.5**). The urgent applications procedure provides that if the case is 'exceptionally urgent' it is acceptable to apply for an order at Court without filing an application form first. The claimant will be required to issue an application form at the Court of Protection as soon as possible thereafter (PD10B, para.9). If an application form has already been issued at the Court of Protection but an exceptionally urgent application needs to be made, an application can be made to the Court without filing a application notice in advance (PD10, para.8).

If making an urgent application, it is important to note that PD10B states that the applicant should take steps to advise the respondent by telephone or in writing of an urgent application unless justice would be defeated by so doing (para.5).

Matters to be considered at the first directions hearing

It is to be noted that this hearing must be heard by a High Court judge (see PD12A).

If the matter does not need to be disposed of urgently, the Court will list a serious medical treatment case for a first directions hearing. The matters to be considered at such a hearing include (see PD9E, para.14):

(a) whether to join P as a party;
(b) if P is to be joined as a party, whether the Official Solicitor should be appointed to act as litigation friend or whether someone else should be so appointed;
(c) any applications by persons seeking to be joined as parties; and
(d) setting a timetable for the proceedings.

Declarations

PD9E sets out the proposed form of the declaration sought in serious medical treatment cases:

(a) that P lacks capacity to make a decision in relation to the (proposed medical treatment/procedure);
(b) that, having regard to the best interests of P, it is lawful for the (proposed medical treatment/procedure) to be carried out by (proposed healthcare provider).

In relation to the withdrawal of life-sustaining treatment, the order sought should be in the following or similar terms:

(a) that P lacks capacity to consent to continued life-sustaining treatment measures (and specify what these are); and
(b) that, having regard to the best interests of P, it is lawful for (name of healthcare provider) to withdraw the life-sustaining treatment from P.

OTHER PART 9 PRACTICE DIRECTIONS

The other Part 9 Practice Directions are:

(a) PD9D: Applications by currently appointed Deputies, attorneys and donees in relation to P's property and affairs. This makes provision for a simplified application procedure in relation to decisions that the Deputy, attorney or donee does not have authority to make but which are likely to be uncontested and do not involve large sums of money.
(b) PD9F: Applications relating to statutory wills, codicils, settlements and other dealings with P's property.
(c) PD9G: Applications to appoint or discharge a trustee.
(d) PD9H: Applications relating to the registration of EPAs.

The reader is referred to those documents for the details of the specific procedures which apply in each case.

Responding to an application (rule 72)

A person who is served with or notified of an application form and wants to take part in the proceedings must file an acknowledgement of service (if served as a respondent) or notification (if only notified) within 21 days of service or notification (rule 72(1), (2)).

The following information must be included in an acknowledgement of service or notification:

(a) whether the person consents to the application;
(b) whether the person opposes the application and, if so, the grounds for doing so;
(c) whether the person seeks a different order from that set out in the application form and, if so, what that order is;
(d) an address for service within the jurisdiction; and
(e) the signature of the person or the person's legal representative (rule 72(4)).

A person who has been served with the application (i.e. as a respondent or pursuant to the additional service provisions in rules 67 and 68) and opposes the application or seeks a different order, must file a witness statement with the acknowledgement of service containing any evidence which the person seeks to rely on (rule 72(5)). The restrictions on expert evidence apply and expert evidence cannot be filed without the permission of the Court (rules 120 and 123).

A person who has been notified pursuant to rules 69 (notification to P of the issue of an application form), 70 (notification to other interested persons of the issue of an application form) or 67(5) or 68(5) (notification to the donor of an LPA or an EPA of the applicant's belief that he lacks capacity), the acknowledgement of notification must be accompanied by a witness statement containing evidence of his interest in the proceedings and if he opposes the application or seeks a different order, any evidence which the person intends to rely (rule 72(7). The restrictions on expert evidence apply and expert evidence cannot be filed without the permission of the Court (rules 120 and 123).

There is a Practice Direction which deals with responding to an application (PD9C). This explains the procedures for becoming a party (discussed below) and also sets out provisions about signing the acknowledgement (e.g. who must sign: in relation to an individual, the person acknowledging or his litigation friend or legal representative), the address for service and making corrections or amendments to the acknowledgement.

Parties

Unless otherwise directed by the Court, the parties to the proceedings are:

(a) the applicant;
(b) a person named as a respondent who has filed an acknowledgement of service in respect of the application form (rule 73(1)).

As is generally the case, the Rules provide that parties are bound by any order or direction of the Court made in the course of the proceedings to which he is a party (rule 73(5)).

P

There is a specific rule that P is not to be named as a respondent unless the Court directs (rule 73(4)). It follows that P cannot become a party to the proceedings except by order of the Court.

The Court has power to order a person to be joined as a party if it considers that 'it is desirable to do so for the purpose of dealing with the application' (rule 73(2)).

It is, therefore, envisaged that there will be persons interested in the proceedings who will not become parties, including P himself. The Rules deal with the difficulty of binding non-parties by orders made by the Court by stating that P and any person who had been served with or notified of an application form in accordance with the Rules are bound by an order or direction of the Court, as though they were parties (rule 74). The fact that non-parties such as P will be so bound by the orders of the Court is, of course, necessary to avoid the Court's orders being unenforceable against all those persons affected by them. However, this consequence will raise important issues about fairness and the ECHR Art.6 rights of P and other interested persons who will not be parties to proceedings which determine important issues affecting their lives. The Court has power to hear P on the question of whether or not an order should be made, whether or not he or she is party (rule 88(1)) and has power to allow other non-parties to take part in the hearing (rule 88(3)(b)). However, it is anticipated that there will be litigation about the circumstances in which P ought to be made a party on fairness/Art.6 grounds and arguments about the extent to which hearing P on the question of whether or not an order should be made will suffice in terms of ensuring a fair hearing.

The Court has a duty to identify at as early a stage as is possible who the parties to the proceeding should be (rule 5(2)(b)(ii)) and so will seek to determine applications to be joined as parties and any disputes about who should be joined as a party as soon as possible.

The Court may also order at any time that a person is to be removed as a party (rule 73(3)). A person who wishes to be removed as a party must apply to the Court in accordance with Part 10 of the Rules (using a COP9 application notice) (rule 76).

Becoming a party

PERSONS SERVED WITH AN APPLICATION FORM

If a person has been served with an application form (as a respondent pursuant to rule 66 or served under the additional service provisions in rules 67 and 68 (dealing with LPAs and EPAs), he must file an acknowledgement of service form (COP5) in order to be joined as a party (rules 72(1), 73(1)).

A person must still acknowledge service or notification of the issue of an application form even if the person already filed an acknowledgement of notification of a permission application (in accordance with rule 57) (rule 72(10)).

PERSONS NOTIFIED OF AN APPLICATION

Where a person has been notified of an application pursuant to rules 69 (notification to P of the issue of an application form), 70 (notification to other interested persons of the issue of an application form) or 67(5) or 68(5) (notification to the donor of an LPA or an EPA of the applicant's belief that he or she lacks capacity), the person must indicate in the acknowledgment of notification (COP 5) if the person wishes to be joined as a party to the proceedings and state his or her interest in the proceedings (rule 72(6)). The Court will then decide whether or not to join the person as a party (rule 72(8)). It is not necessary for such a person to make a separate application to be joined as a party pursuant to rule 75 if the person files an acknowledgement of notification in accordance with rule 72 (rule 72(9)). The rule 75 procedure applies to persons who have not been notified or have been notified but did not file an acknowledgement of notification in accordance with rule 72.

A person so notified could file an acknowledgement of notification which sets out his or her position in respect of the application (i.e. whether he or she consents or objects) but indicates that he or she does not wish to be joined as a party. Such a person's role would be limited to informing the Court of his or her position in the acknowledgement form but not being a party, would not heard at the hearing and would have no right to attend a private hearing (rule 90(2)).

The Court will consider whether to join a person who files an acknowledgement of notification as a party and will make an order to that effect, if it chooses to do so (rule 72(8)). The Court is not restricted to making someone a party only if that person wishes to become a party. The Court could choose to make someone a party against the person's wish if the Court considers that the person should be a party given his or her interest and/or the position he or she has taken in response to the application.

PERSONS NOT SERVED WITH OR NOTIFIED OF AN APPLICATION

When a person is not served with or notified of an application form, the person must apply to the Court to become a party by filing an application notice to be joined as a party (COP10) in accordance with rule 75.

Rule 75 provides that anyone with sufficient interest can apply to be joined as a party. The COP10 form is a specific application notice to be joined as a party. The general procedures for making an application within proceedings under Part 10 of the Rules must be complied with. The COP10 form asks for all the information required by rule 75. As is the case with persons acknowledging notification, the person must (in addition to basic information such as name, address, address for service etc.) state:

(a) the person's interest in the proceedings;
(b) whether the person consents to the application;
(c) whether the person opposes the application and, if so, the grounds for doing so;
(d) whether the person seeks a different order from that set out in the application form and, if so, what that order is (rule 75(2)).

As with persons acknowledging notification, an application to be joined must be accompanied by a witness statement containing evidence of the person's interest in the proceedings and, if the person opposes the application or seeks a different order, any evidence on which the person intends to rely (rule 75(3)). The restrictions on expert evidence apply and expert evidence cannot be filed without the permission of the Court (rules 120 and 123).

Additionally, the applicant must provide a sufficient number of copies of the application to enable service on every other party to the proceedings (rule 75(3)(b)). The Court will serve the application on all the parties (rule 75(4)).

The Court will decide whether or not to join the person as a party and will make an order accordingly (rule 75(5)).

11.5.10   Part 10: Applications within proceedings

There are two Practice Directions which supplement this Part:

(a) PD10A on applications; and
(b) PD10B on urgent and interim applications.

Filing an application notice

The Part 10 application procedure is to be used for applications:

(a) in the course of existing proceedings; or
(b) as provided for in a rule or Practice Direction (rule 77).

An application under Part 10 must be made using the COP9 form, although, in certain circumstances (e.g. exceptional urgency) the Court may permit an application to be made without filing an application notice (rule 78(5), PD10B, para.9).

The applicant must include the following in the application notice (rule 79 and PD10A, para.3):

(a) what order or direction the applicant is seeking;
(b) briefly, the grounds on which the applicant is seeking the order or direction;
(c) the name of P (the person to whom the application relates);
(d) the case number (if available);
(e) the full name of the applicant;
(f) where the applicant is not already a party, the applicant's address; and
(g) a draft of the order sought.

The applicant can indicate in the application notice if it is urgent and/or should be dealt with by a particular judge or level of judge and/or requires a hearing and/or that a direction is sought for a telephone hearing (PD10A, paras.17–19). The court will not normally direct a telephone hearing unless every party entitled to notice of the application has consented to such a direction (PD10A, para.20).

If the order sought is long or complex, the applicant should make available to the Court a disk containing the draft order (in a format compatible with the software used by the Court).

The application notice must be supported by evidence set out either:

(a) in a witness statement; or
(b) the application notice if it is verified by a statement of truth.

The evidence needs to set out the facts that the applicant relies upon and any material facts known to the applicant which the Court should be made aware of (PD10A, para.7).

If the application is for a consent order, the parties must ensure that they provide the Court with sufficient material so that it can be satisfied that it is appropriate to make the order and a letter signed by the parties will generally be acceptable for this purpose (subject to any rule or Practice Direction). The parties must inform the Court immediately when a consent order is agreed in relation to a matter for which a hearing date is fixed (PD10A, paras.22–3).

Issue of the application and notice

The Court will issue the application notice and if there is to be a hearing, give notice of the hearing date (rule 78(3)). Notice of the hearing date will be given to the applicant, all parties, any named respondent (who has not become a party) and any other person directed by the Court (which could include those notified of the issue of the application form).

The applicant must serve a copy of the application notice and evidence within 21 days of issue on:

(a) every party;
(b) anyone named as a respondent in the application notice (if not otherwise a party);
(c) any other person as directed by the Court (rule 80(1)).

The applicant must serve a certificate of service within seven days beginning with the date of service of the documents (rule 80(3)).

There is no need to serve the evidence on a person on whom it has already been served but notice must be given to that person of the evidence which the applicant intends to rely on (rule 80(4)).

Application without service of an application notice

An application may be made without service of an application notice only (PD10A, para.9):

(a) where there is exceptional urgency (PD10B deals with urgent applications and is discussed further below);
(b) where the overriding objective is best furthered by doing so;
(c) by consent of all the parties;
(d) with the permission of the court; or
(e) where a rule or other practice direction permits.

The evidence in support of the application should state why service was not effected on a respondent (PD10A, para.10).

The Court can order that other persons ought to be served or notified of it (PD10A, para.11).

Without notice applications

The applicant should take steps to advise the respondent by telephone or in writing of the application, unless justice would be defeated by so doing (PD10B, para.5). If an applicant is making a without notice application, the evidence in support of an application must state why notice has not been given (rule 78(6)).

Where the Court deals with an application which was made without notice having been given to any person, the applicant must as soon as practicable or as directed by the Court serve copies of the application notice, evidence and the Court's order on every party, anyone named as a respondent in the application notice (but not otherwise a party to the proceedings) and any other person as directed by the Court (rule 81). An order made without notice will ordinarily contain an undertaking about service of these documents on the respondent and other persons as directed by the Court and a return date for a further hearing (PD10B, para.6).

Orders made without notice to any person can be the subject of reconsideration by the Court (rule 89).

Urgent applications

PD10B states that urgent applications should generally be made within Court hours. Such applications will generally be dealt with at Court but in cases of extreme urgency may be dealt with by telephone (tel: 0845 3302900). Where an application has to be made out of hours, the security officer at the Royal Courts of Justice should be contacted (tel: 020 79476000) and informed of the nature of the case. The Practice Direction states that it is undesirable that urgent applications arise because applications to the Court have not been pursued sufficiently promptly (paras.1–4).

It is important to note that it is not intended that urgent applications be dealt with only by High Court judges in the High Court (although urgent applications in serious medical treatment cases and cases where declaration of incompatibility under the Human Rights Act 1998 is sought are required to be dealt with by a High Court Judge by virtue of PD12A). However, the authors are aware that at the time of writing many of the urgent applications are being heard in the High Court. This appears to be due to the greater availability of High Court Judges to hear urgent business.

If a hearing is dealt with by telephone it should be conducted by tape-recorded conference call and arranged and paid for in the first instance by the applicant (PD10B, para.12).

If an urgent application is being made without notice, the provisions for without notice applications will apply (see above)

It is to be noted that the procedure to be followed in urgent medical cases is dealt with in PD9E (see p.142).

Applications for interim injunctions need to set out clearly what the respondent or other person must or must not do (PD10B, para.17).

Where application form has already been issued

If the urgent application is made after the issue of an application form (the document used to begin proceedings), the COP9 form, evidence in support and draft order should be filed with the Court in advance of the hearing whenever possible. If the application is heard before the filing of these documents, a draft order should be provided at the hearing and the other documents filed on the next working day or as ordered by the Court (PD10B, paras.7–8).

Applications made before issue

In cases of exceptional urgency, the Court may allow an application to be made without an application form (the document used to begin proceedings) having been filed at Court. Although, such an application should be made in writing, if time permits (presumably, this means that the official application form or application notice need not necessarily be used). If the application is made orally, the Court will require an undertaking that an application form (the document used to bring proceedings) drafted to reflect the terms of the oral application is filed on the next working day or as required by the Court (para.9).

An order made before issue of the application form should state in the title after the names 'the Applicant and the Respondent in an Intended Application'.

Interim remedies

The Court will make an interim orders or directions in respect of a matter if it is satisfied that (MHA 2005, s.48):

(a) There is reason to believe that a person lacks capacity in relation to the matter (s.48(a)). The Explanatory Notes to the Act state that this allows the Court to make interim orders even if evidence as to lack of capacity is not yet available. However, clearly some evidence from carers or others concerned with a person's care will have to be presented to the Court setting out the facts and matters relied upon as the basis for the belief that a person lacks capacity.

(b) The matter is one to which its powers extend. The powers of the Court of Protection are discussed in **Chapters 4, 6** and **7**.

(c) It is in the incapable person's best interests to make the order, or give the directions without delay. This incorporates the best interests test at the interim stage. For discussion of the principle of best interests, see **Chapter 3**.

The Court has power to grant interim injunctions, interim declarations and any other interim order it considers appropriate (rule 82).

A person on whom an application form has been served under Part 9 or has been given notice of proceedings cannot apply for an interim remedy before he has filed an acknowledgement of service or notification under Part 9, unless the Court orders otherwise (rule 82(2)).

11.5.11   Part 11: Human rights

A person who seeks to rely on a provision of the Human Rights Act 1998 or claim any remedy under that Act, must specify which right under the European Convention on Human Rights he alleges had been infringed with details and the remedy sought including whether a declaration of incompatibility is sought. A Human Rights Act claim must be included in the application form (COP1) or the acknowledgement of service (COP5). If the claim is made during proceedings, the COP9 form should be completed.

PD11A also provides details about giving notice to the Crown in the event that a declaration of incompatibility is sought and joining of the Crown as a party.

Where a Human Rights Act claim is made, the proceedings must be conducted before a judge nominated under s.46(2)(a) of the Act, namely the President of the Family Division, the Chancellor or a puisne judge of the High Court (PD11A, para.9).

11.5.12   Part 12: Dealing with applications

The Court will decide how to deal with an application as soon as practicable after it has been issued. The Court will decide whether or not to deal with any application or any part of an application at a hearing or without a hearing. Rule 84(3) sets out the factors which the Court will have regard to in deciding whether it is necessary to hold a hearing. These are:

(a) the nature of the proceedings and the orders sought;
(b) whether the application is opposed by a person who appears to the court to have an interest in matters relating to P's best interests;
(c) whether the application involves a substantial dispute of fact;
(d) the complexity of the facts and the law;
(e) any wider public interest in the proceedings;
(f) the circumstances of P and of any party, in particular as to whether their rights would be adequately protected if a hearing were not held;
(g) whether the parties agree that the court should dispose of the application without a hearing; and
(h) any other relevant matter in a Practice Direction.

If the Court decides to hold a hearing, it will give notice of the hearing to the parties and any other person, stating whether the hearing is for disposal or directions. If the Court decides to deal with the matter without holding a hearing, it will do so and serve a copy of the order on the parties and any other person it directs (rule 84(4), (5)).

The Court has general powers to make directions which include adding and removing parties (including joining P as a party and if joined, giving directions for the appointment of a litigation friend) and requiring a report to be made to it by the Public Guardian or a Court of Protection Visitor pursuant to s.49 of the Act (rule 85). The Court may give directions at any time on its own initiative or on the application of a party (rule 85(3)). The parties can agree in writing to vary the time specified by a rule or by the Court to do something unless prohibited from doing so by the Rules or a Practice Direction. The Rules expressly prohibit the parties agreeing to vary the date fixed for a final hearing or the period during which the final hearing is to take place or agreeing a variation which would make it necessary to vary the date which the Court has fixed for any hearing or the period during which the final hearing is to take place (rule 85(4)–(6)).

As regards the sort of directions that may be made by the Court in welfare cases, it is to be noted that in the case of *A Local Authority* v. *NA & MU & A PCT* (unreported, 5 June 2007). Charles J gave some guidance as to the sort of directions that a judge could consider making in welfare cases. That case involved a dispute between the family of two incapable and severely disabled adults with diagnoses of cerebral palsy (NA and MU) and health and social care bodies about the best interests of those incapable adults in relation to medical treatment and residence. There was an important issue as to whether or not the incapable adults could be safely cared for at home and whether the family would co-operate with a care package. Charles J held that the ambit of the factual and legal disputes in the case should have been defined at an earlier stage and advised that in other proceedings of this type, he invited other judges, the Official Solicitor, the local authority and the PCT to consider making or seeking a direction at an early stage in the proceedings that each of the parties do prepare a statement of: (a) the approach in law to be taken; (b) the relevant issues and thus the relevant risks, and how they maintain they could and should be dealt with; and (c) the factual issues they maintain should be determined and the witnesses who should be called as to them. He also commented that it would be probably helpful if in such cases each of the parties would individually consider what the details of the care plans to identify risks should be, rather than waiting for such plans to be produced by the local authority (see in particular paras.66 and 70 of the judgment).

It is also observed that no general provision is made in the Rules or Practice Directions about the requirements for case summaries, lists of issues and position statements being served by the parties prior to hearings (which differs from the approach taken in the High Court under the inherent jurisdiction where the President issued a detailed Practice Direction in relation to family proceedings about such matters: see [2006] 2 FLR 199). It is anticipated that judges in the Court will include such directions in individual orders.

Allocation to specific judges (rule 86)

PD12A specifies those types of cases which may only be dealt with by the President, the Vice-President or a puisne judge of the High Court.

The cases which must be heard in their entirety (including permission and directions) by the President of the Family Division or another judge nominated by the President are:

(a) applications relating to the lawfulness of withholding or withdrawing artificial nutrition and hydration from a person in a persistent vegetative state, or a minimally conscious state; or
(b) a case involving an ethical dilemma in an untested area.

The cases which must be heard in their entirety (including permission and directions) by a Judge nominated under s.46(2)(a)–(c) of the Act (i.e. the President, the Chancellor or a puisne judge of the High Court) are:

(a) an application in relation to serious medical treatment (other than those cases referred to above which must be heard by the President or his nominee) or;
(b) an application which involve a Human Rights Act claim where a declaration of incompatibility is sought.

The Court will decide whether the matter is one to which PD12A applies. However, the judge to whom a matter has been allocated pursuant to PD12A has a general discretion as to allocation and may determine that the matter may properly heard by a judge of the Court other than one nominated by s.46(2)(a)–(c) of the Act and may reallocate the matter accordingly (PD12A, para.5).

Applications which are not specified in PD12A may be dealt with by any judge (rule 86(3)).

Applications for disputing the Court's jurisdiction (rule 87)

PD12B deals with disputing jurisdiction.

A person who wishes to dispute the Court's jurisdiction to hear an application or argue that the Court should not exercise such jurisdiction as it has must make an application (rule 87(1)). The application must be made in the acknowledgement of service or notification form (COP5) when a person has been given notice of a permission application or has been served with or notified of an application form. In any other case, a person must file an application notice using COP9.

The application must be supported by evidence (rule 87(2)).

An order declaring that the Court has no jurisdiction or will not exercise jurisdiction can also make orders setting aside the application, discharging any orders made or staying the proceedings (rule 87(3)).

P ceases to lack capacity

If P ceases to lack capacity, an application may be made to bring the proceedings to an end (rule 148). An application may be made by P, P's litigation friend or any other person who is a party to the proceedings. The application must be made using a COP9 and all parties to the proceedings must be served (rule 148(4)). The application should be supported by evidence that P has capacity to make decisions. Further information about procedure is provided in PD23B.

Participation in hearings

P

The Court may hear P on the question of whether or not an order should be made whether or not P is party to the proceedings (rule 88(1)). In practice, this gives the Court a discretion to hear P at any hearing because a Court will invariably be deciding whether to make an order of some sort. However, P has no right to be heard, unless he or she is a party. Even if P is a party, the Court has a discretion to proceed in P's absence if it considers it appropriate to do so (rule 88(2)).

OTHER PERSONS

A person other than P who is served with or notified of an application may only take part in a hearing if the person files an acknowledgement in accordance with the Rules and is made a party to the proceedings or the Court otherwise permits (rule 88(3)).

Reconsideration of Court orders made without a hearing or without notice (rule 89)

There is a procedure for an order of the Court to be reconsidered if the order was made without a hearing or without notice to any person who is affected by it. Orders made without a hearing or without notice must contain a statement of the right to apply for reconsideration (rule 89(9)).

An application form (COP9) must be filed within 21 days of the order (or such other period determined by the Court) (rule 89(3)). An application may be made by P, any party to the proceedings or any other person affected by the order (rule 89(2)).

The Court will either reconsider the order without directing a hearing or fix a date for the matter to be heard and notify all parties. The applicant can request that the reconsideration application is dealt with at a hearing (rule 89(10)).

The Court's powers on reconsideration are to affirm, set aside or vary the order made (rule 89(5)). It is not possible to apply for reconsideration of a reconsideration decision (rule 89(7)). Instead, a reconsideration decision must be appealed (rule 89(8)).

Reconsideration can be carried out by the judge who made the initial decision. If another judge is carrying out the reconsideration, he must be a prescribed higher judge (as defined by s.53(3)) i.e. if the decision was made by a district judge, the reconsideration needs to be by a circuit judge or higher judge (rule 89(6)).

11.5.13   Part 13: Hearings

PD13A supplements this part of the Rules.

Private hearings

The general rule is that a hearing will be held in private (rule 90(1)). A private hearing is one where only the following people are entitled to attend (rule 90(2)):

(a) the parties;
(b) P (whether or not P is a party);
(c) any person acting in the proceedings as a litigation friend;
(d) any legal representative of a person specified in any of (a)–(c) above;
(e) any court officer.

At private hearings the Court may make an order authorising any person or class of person to attend the hearing or part of it; or excluding any person, or class of person, from attending the hearing or a part of it (rule 90(3)). Such an order should be made only where it appears to the Court that there is good reason for making the order (rule 93(1)(a)).

Publication of information about the proceedings of the Court when sitting in private will generally be contempt of court (Administration of Justice Act 1960, s.12(1)). But there will be no contempt where the Court has authorised publication of the information under rule 91 (see below).

The Court has a general power to authorise the publication of information relating to a private hearing (rule 91). The Court can authorise the publication of such information as it may specify or the publication of the text or summary of the whole or part of any judgment or order made by the court. Where the Court makes such an order for publication in relation to a private hearing, it may do so on such terms as it thinks fit and may, in particular, impose restrictions on the publication of the identity of any person or information which might lead to the identification of any person if it appears to the Court that there is good reason to do so (rules 91(3), 93(1)(a)). Such restrictions on publication may be imposed on the Court's own initiative or on the application of any person (usually a party) (rule 93(1)(c)).

Part 2 of PD13A sets out notice requirements in relation to reporting restrictions but these do not apply when restrictions are imposed as part of the order authorising publication. The notice requirements in Part 2 of PD13A will, however, apply if reporting restrictions are imposed subsequent to the order authorising publication (PD13A, para.8). This is discussed further below.

Public hearings

The Court may make an order for a hearing to be held in public (or part of it) or excluding any person, or class of persons from attending a public hearing or part of it (rule 92(1)). Where such an order is made, the Court may at the same time or by a subsequent order:

(a) impose restrictions on the publication of the identity of any person or of any information that may lead to any such person being identified;

(b) prohibit the further publication of any information relating to the proceedings from such date as the court may specify; and

(c) impose such other restrictions on the publication of information relating to the proceedings as the court may specify (rule 92(2)).

If restrictions are imposed as part of the order for the hearing to be held in public, there is no need to comply with the notification requirements in Part 2 of PD13A. However, Part 2 will need to be complied with if the Court has already made an order for a hearing to be held in public and the Court is subsequently deciding whether to impose restrictions (or further restrictions) or vary restrictions which have already been imposed (see PD13A, para.12).

Restrictions on a public hearing may be imposed on an application made by any person or on the Court's own initiative (rule 93(1)(c)).

Procedure for applications under rules 90, 91 or 92

Any person applying for an order under rules 90 (attendance at a private hearing), 91 (publication of information about proceedings in private) or 92 (powers to order hearing to be in public and restrictions on publication) must commence an application by filing an application notice (COP9) in accordance with part 10 (PD13A, para.4)

The Court should consider whether to direct that the application should be dealt with as a discrete issue (PD13A, para.6).

PD13A, Part 2 – notification to the press in relation to reporting restrictions

The requirements to notify in accordance with Part 2 of PD13A will apply in any case where:

(a) The court has made an order for publication of information about proceedings which are conducted in private and, *after* the order has been made:

   (i) an application founded on P's Convention rights is made to the court for an order under rule 91(3) which would impose restrictions (or further restrictions) on the information which may be published; or

   (ii) of its own initiative, the Court is considering whether to impose such restrictions on the basis of P's Convention rights; or

(b) the Court has already made an order for a hearing to be held in public and:

   (i) an application founded on Convention rights is made to the court for an order under rule 92(2) which would impose restrictions (or further restrictions) on the information that may be published, or

   (ii) of its own initiative, the court is considering whether to vary or impose further such restrictions (para.12). (Note para.11 of PD13A appears to suggest that notification should be given in any case where the Court is making an order under rule 92(2) of its own initiative even when it is made at the same time as making the order that the hearing is to be in public. However, it is not understood that this is the position, and the position is correctly stated in PD13A, para.12.)

Part 2 of PD13A sets out the way in which notice is to be given to the press of an application to impose reporting restrictions. It also gives guidance as to the issues to be considered at the hearing of such an application and the nature of the orders that can be made.

11.5.14   Part 14: Admissions, evidence and depositions

This part of the Rules follows the approach in the CPR to evidence.

Admissions

In relation to admissions, a party may admit the truth or the whole or part of an allegation by giving notice in writing (without prejudice to the ability to make an admission in another way). The Court has a discretion to allow a party to amend or withdraw an admission (rule 94).

Evidence

As is the case under the CPR, it is the Court which has a general and wide-ranging power to control evidence including the issues on which evidence is required, the nature of the evidence required and the way in which evidence is to be placed before the Court (see rule 95).

The general rule is that any fact which needs to be proved by evidence of a witness is to be proved at a final hearing, by that person's oral evidence and at any other hearing, by the person's evidence in writing (rule 96(1)). A witness statement will stand as evidence in chief unless the Court directs otherwise and the Court's permission is required to amplify the statement and update the Court as to events since the filing of the statement. The Rules provide that such permission will only be given if there is good reason not to confine the evidence of the witness to the contents of the statement (rules 96(3) and (4)). The Rules further state that a witness statement for use at the final hearing is a statement of the evidence which that person will be allowed to give orally (rule 99(1)). Taken together these rules suggest the Court of Protection may adopt a less flexible approach to examination-in-chief than has been the general practice in declaratory relief proceedings in the High Court.

In the case of *A Local Authority v. NA & MU & A PCT* (unreported, 5 June 2007, see discussion above at **11.5.12**), Charles J emphasised the need in cases where there are factual disputes which the Court is being asked to adjudicate upon, of direct evidence being called from the relevant witnesses to any disputed factual incidents. It was not sufficient in these circumstances for health or social care bodies to rely on hearsay evidence from the manager of the relevant health or social care professionals.

Written evidence needs to be filed in accordance with the Rules and Practice Directions in order to be relied upon, unless the Court gives permission (rule 97). PD14A provides detailed guidance on the required form of witness statements and affidavits.

There is provision in the Rules for evidence to be given by video link and Annex 2 to PD14A gives guidance about this.

The Rules also make provision for:

(a) the filing of witness summaries (rule 101);
(b) affidavits (if so required: rules 102–104 and see PD14A on the required form of affidavits); and
(c) the summoning of witnesses (rule 106, see also PD14D (rules 101–106)).

The Court has an express power to require a party to prepare and file a document recording information when it has access to information which is not reasonably available to the other party (Rule 107).

There are also detailed rules about evidence by deposition (and taking evidence outside the jurisdiction (rules 108–116 and PD14B)).

Power to call for reports: s.49 and rules 117–118

The Court has the power to call for reports where in proceedings relating to an incapable person, the Court is considering a question relating to the incapable person (s.49(1)). Further, the Court when giving directions may require a s.49 report to be made (rule 85(2)(a)). The annex to PD14E sets out the proposed form of order and directions for requiring a report under s.49 of the Act.

The Court can require the Public Guardian (see discussion of the Public Guardian and his role in **Chapter 12**), a Court of Protection Visitor (see further discussion on the role and functions of Visitors at **11.2.8**), a local authority or NHS body to report to it (s.49(2), (3))

Where a report is to be made by either the Public Guardian or a Court of Protection Visitor, a copy of the order and directions will be sent to the Public Guardian. In the case of a report by a Court of Protection Visitor, the Public Guardian has to ensure that a person is nominated from the Panel of General or Special Visitors as appropriate (which should be done within seven days of the Public Guardian receiving a copy of the order) and must notify the Court of the name and contact details of the said Visitor as soon as practicable (PD14E, paras.3–5). Regulation 44 of the Lasting Power of Attorney, Enduring Power of Attorney and Public Guardian Regulations 2007, SI 2007/1253 ('the 2007 Regulations') makes further provisions in relation to visits by the Public Guardian or visits by Court of Protection Visitors directed by the Public Guardian.

Where a report is to be made by a local authority or an NHS body, a copy of the order will be sent to a senior officer of that authority or body. That person must ensure that an appropriate person is nominated (which should be within seven days of the said senior officer receiving a copy of the order) and the Court notified of the name and contact details as soon as practicable (PD14E, paras.6–7).

Content of the report (s.49(4), (5), rule 117)

The Court may direct that the report deals with specific matters. Further, the Rules specify that unless the Court otherwise directs, the person making the report must:

(a) contact or seek to interview such persons as he thinks appropriate or as the Court directs;
(b) to the extent that it is practicable and appropriate to do so, ascertain what P's wishes and feelings are and the beliefs and values that would be likely to influence P if he had capacity to make the decision in question
(c) describe P's circumstances; and
(d) address such other matters as required by a Practice Direction or by the Court. PD14E contains detailed requirements about the content and layout of s.49 reports (paras.11–16).

The Public Guardian and a Court of Protection Visitor may interview the incapable person in private for the purpose of reporting to the court when a report has been ordered by the court (s.49(8))

A Court of Protection Visitor who is a Special Visitor (i.e. medical professional appointed by the Lord Chancellor) ordered by the court to report on the incapable person, may carry out a medical, psychiatric or psychological examination of the incapable person in private, if the Court directs that he may do so (s.49(9)).

The Court may direct that the report be in writing or be given orally. This provides the Court the greatest flexibility. In cases of urgency, an oral report will have the advantage of speed (s.49(6)).

Duty of the maker of the report

The person required by the Court to report under s.49 of the Act is under a duty to help the court on matters within his expertise (rule 117(2)).

Disclosure of reports

The Court will send a copy of the report to the parties and to such persons as the court may direct (rule 117(4)).

Access to information

The Public Guardian and a Court of Protection Visitor may examine and take copies at all reasonable times of any health records, social services records or registered care home records so far as those records relate to the incapable person (s.49(7)).

Further, the person required to make the report may examine and take copies of any document in court records, although the Court may direct that particular documents are not to be inspected or that information is to be provided to the maker of the report on an edited basis (rule 117(5), (6), (7)). The Court will generally provide to the person required to report a copy of the application form (and annexes), the name and contact details of P and the parties and their respective legal representatives (PD14E, para.8).

Written questions (rule 118)

A party may apply to the Court to put written questions to the maker of a s.49 report. The questions must be submitted to the Court, which may put them to the maker of the report (with such amendments as it thinks fit) and the maker of the report will reply in writing. The Court will send a copy of the replies to the parties and any other persons as directed by the Court.

11.5.15   Part 15: Experts

A reference to an expert in the Rules does not include a person instructed to prepare a report under s.49 (rule 119(2)).

The Rules states that expert evidence must be limited to that which is reasonably required to resolve the proceedings (rule 121) and hence mirrors closely the CPR's fairly restrictive approach to the use of expert evidence.

Further, as is the case under the CPR, the expert's overriding duty is to the Court (rule 122). The expert is under a duty to be independent and to help the court on matters within the expert's expertise (see further paras.2–7 of PD15A).

In the spirit of limiting expert evidence, the Court may direct that evidence is to be given by a single joint expert (rule 130). The practice in High Court in inherent jurisdiction proceedings involving incapable adults was invariably to appoint single joint experts to report on capacity and best interests. It is anticipated by the authors that this general approach to expert evidence will continue in the Court. In the event of a single joint instruction, the Rules provide that each party may give instructions to the expert (rule 131(1)). The Court may also limit the amount of fees or expenses to be paid to a single joint expert (rule 131(4)). Unless otherwise ordered, the instructing parties are jointly and severally liable for the payment of the fees and expenses of a single joint expert (rule 131(5)).

Expert evidence is to be given in writing unless otherwise directed by the Court (rule 124).

PD15A deals with expert evidence.

It is for the party instructing the expert, or in the case of single joint expert, the applicant, to serve on the expert a copy of a Court order which requires him or her to act or affects him or her (PD15A, para.15).

Restriction on filing an expert's report (rule 120)

No person may file expert evidence unless the Court or a Practice Direction permits save that there is general permission for a person to file with the permission form or application form expert evidence:

(a) that a person lacks capacity to make the decision/decisions in question in the proceedings;
(b) as to P's best interests; or
(c) that is required to be filed by any rule or Practice Direction with the permission form or application form (which would include the COP3 assessment of capacity form which has to be completed by a medical practitioner).

The Court will determine the extent and for what purposes a person may rely on any expert evidence filed in support of the permission or application form.

Application to rely on expert evidence (rule 123)

The Rules require a person seeking permission from the Court to rely on expert evidence to provide information about the field in respect of which he or she seeks to rely on expert evidence and where practicable, identify the expert, provide material information about the expert and a draft letter of instruction. In giving permission for the expert, the Court may specify the field/fields in respect of which expert evidence can be provided, may specify the person to provide the evidence, give directions about service and limit the amount of the expert's fees and expenses that may be recovered from any other party.

Content of expert reports (rule 126)

Rule 126 and PD15A set out the requirements for the content of an expert's report which includes particular statements/declarations, including the required statement of truth, that must be included in the report.

Use of reports (rule 127)

Any party may use an expert's report disclosed by another party as evidence at any hearing in the proceedings.

Written questions to experts (rule 125)

The general rule is that written questions to experts must be put within 28 days of service of the report and must be for the purpose of clarification only (rule 125(2)). Cross-examination of experts via written questions is not permitted. The Court has power to impose sanctions in the event of an expert failing to answer written questions put in accordance with rule 125 which are precluding reliance on the expert or precluding recovery of fees of the expert from any other party (rule 115(5), (6)).

Discussions between experts (rule 128)

The Court may order there to be discussions between experts for the purpose of identifying the issues and areas of agreement and producing a joint statement of areas of agreement/disagreement and reasons for disagreeing.

Expert's request for directions (rule 129)

An expert may file a written request for directions to assist the expert in carrying out his or her function as an expert.

11.5.16   Part 16: Disclosure (rules 132–139)

This part of the Rules applies the familiar CPR provisions relating to disclosure. The Court may make orders for general or specific disclosure. There is an on-going duty of disclosure. The procedure is that disclosure is made by list and there is a right to inspect (subject to the document no longer being in control of the disclosing party or there being a right or duty to withhold inspection). A party may not rely upon any document which the party fails to disclose or in respect of which the party fails to permit inspection unless the Court permits.

The incorporation in the Rules of the general CPR disclosure rules signals a more formal approach to disclosure than has hitherto tended to be adopted in inherent jurisdiction proceedings in the High Court, where generally the only orders made about disclosure were in respect of disclosure of documents to experts instructed in the case.

Unlike the CPR, there is no provision made in the Rules for pre-action disclosure.

The Code in chapter 16 summarises the different ways in which information may be obtained in relation to persons who lack capacity, including applications under the Data Protection Act 1998 (discussed further at 1.6). Carers need to have relevant information in order to make a decision in the best interests of P. The Code indicates that in situations where there is a dispute between health and social care staff (the information holders) and carers as to whether disclosure of information to the carer is in the best interests of P taking account of P's right to confidentiality and such dispute cannot be resolved through other means (namely, alternative dispute resolution mechanisms outlined in chapter 15 of the Code), the carer can apply to the Court for the right to access specific information (para.16.32). In other words, proceedings could be commenced in the Court specifically to obtain access to information. The Court will have to balance P's right to privacy and confidentiality against the carer's interests in having sufficient information to act in P's interest. Similar issues were considered by the Court of Appeal in the context of an incapable patient subject to guardianship under the MHA 1983 in *R (on the application of S)* v. *Plymouth City Council* [2002] EWCA Civ 388, [2002] 1 WLR 2583.

11.5.17   Part 17: Litigation friend

A litigation friend is required to act on behalf of the following persons in the following circumstances (rule 141):

(a) P if a party to the proceedings (unless the appointment is brought to an end by court order pursuant to rule 147);
(b) a protected party if party to the proceedings;
(c) a child if party to the proceedings unless the Court makes an order permitting the child to conduct proceedings without a litigation friend.

A person may act as litigation friend if he or she can fairly and competently conduct proceedings on behalf of the person and has no interests adverse to those of the person (rule 140).

A litigation friend can be appointed in certain circumstances without a court order (see rule 142). However, a Court order appointing a litigation friend is required in relation to P and where the Official Solicitor is to act as litigation friend (rules 142(1), 143).

The Court has power to direct that a person cannot act as litigation friend, to terminate the appointment of a litigation friend and to appoint a replacement litigation friend (rule 144).

The Rules make provision for the procedure for the appointment of a litigation friend coming to an end. In relation to P and to protected parties who cease to lack capacity to conduct proceedings (or if P ceases both to lack capacity to conduct proceedings and in relation to the subject matter of the proceedings), a court order is required to bring the appointment of a litigation friend to an end (rules 146, 147, 148; see also PD23B in relation to P).

PD17A provides more detail about the procedures to be followed in relation to appointments of litigation friends.

11.5.18   Part 18: Change of solicitor

Rules 150–154 and PD18A set out the procedure for parties to follow who have a solicitor and want to change that solicitor or act in person or who have acted in person and want to appoint a solicitor. The relevant forms are COP30 and COP9, and PD18A explains when each form is to be used.

11.5.19   Part 19: Costs

The Act seeks to put the Court of Protection in the same position as other civil courts in respect of its costs rules (see Explanatory Notes at para.141). The general approach in the Rules is to apply Parts 44, 47 and 48 of the CPR in relation to costs but subject to modifications (rule 160). PD19A in respect of costs also applies the Practice Directions supplementing Parts 43–8 of the CPR subject to modifications.

The general rule

The Court has a general discretion in relation to costs (s.55).

The Rules set out general costs rules that are to apply in, respectively, property and affairs and welfare cases.

In property and affairs cases, the general rule is that costs of the proceedings or of that part of the proceedings which concern P's property and affairs, will be paid by P or charged to his estate (rule 156).

In welfare cases, the general rule is that there will be no order as to costs of the proceedings or that part of the proceedings that concern P's property and affairs (rule 157).

The Court will insofar as practicable, apportion costs between the respective issues when a case concerns both property and affairs and welfare (rule 158).

Departing from the general rule

Under rule 159, the Court has a discretion to depart from the general rules as to costs if justified and in deciding whether so to depart will have regard to all the circumstances including:

(a) the conduct of the parties;
(b) whether a party has succeeded on part of his case, even if he has not been wholly successful; and
(c) the role of any public body involved in the proceedings.

The conduct of the parties and whether the party has been successful in the proceedings are factors which are commonly taken account of by the High Court when making costs orders.

The reference to the role of any public body involved in the proceedings, in particular, gives the Official Solicitor the opportunity to make an application for general rule to be departed from and for his or her costs (or a proportion of them) to be paid by one or more of the parties, which has been his practice particularly in medical treatment cases where he deals with the cases 'in house'. Rule 163 also provides that any costs incurred by the Official Solicitor in relation to proceedings under the Rules or directions given by the Court (and not remunerated under rule 167 – remuneration of a Deputy, donee or attorney) will be paid out of such funds or by such persons as the court may direct.

There have been several cases in which the High Court has considered in what circumstances it is appropriate for an NHS Trust to make a contribution towards the costs of the Official Solicitor in acting as litigation friend in a medical treatment case and different views have been expressed by different judges (see *Tameside and Glossop Acute Services Trust* v. *CH* [1996] 1 FLR 72 (per Wall J); *Hospital NHS Trust, A* v. *S* [2003] EWHC 365 (per Dame Butler-Sloss); *X NHS Trust* v. *J* [2006] Lloyd's Med Reports 180 (per Munby J); *NHS Trust* v. *D* [2006] Lloyd's Med Reports 193 (per Coleridge J); and most recently the President in *A Hospital* v. *SW and A PCT* [2007] EWHC 425 (Fam) who gave careful consideration to the earlier authorities on this issue). There is a tension between placing additional financial constraints on the public body concerned by making an order for costs against it and the importance of recognising the vital work carried out by the Official Solicitor and the financial constraints that the Official Solicitor operates under.

The President in *A Hospital* v. *SW* (above), held that Munby J (in *X NHS Trust* v. *J* (above)) was correct in his analysis of the cases that by analogy with the historic position of local authorities in relation to public law children cases, the court has approached the question of costs in medical treatment cases (and particularly in Persistent Vegetative State (PVS) cases) involving the Official Solicitor on the basis of a rule of thumb that, subject to particular circumstances, a 'half costs order' in favour of the Official Solicitor (paid for by the NHS Trust concerned) is generally appropriate. It is for the judge in any individual case to make such order as he or she thinks appropriate. The President was not of the view that pragmatism had no place in the approach of the Court in these types of cases (disagreeing with Coleridge J's view expressed in *NHS Trust* v. *D* (above)). He commented that the necessity for the Official Solicitor to be involved in the proceedings is one that springs from the functions and obligations of the NHS Trust to provide proper and lawful treatment and so, the burden of costs can in a broad sense be regarded as an incident of the overall costs of the administration (or withdrawal in a PVS case) of such treatment. He took the view that as the Official Solicitor generally acts not as an adversary but a facilitator, and that the part played in the proceedings is helpful and not obstructive, 'the half-costs solution' (whereby the Official Solicitor is awarded half of his costs to be paid by the NHS Trust) 'is, in principle, a reasonable starting point in cases of this kind' (see paras.61–7 of the judgment).

It is interesting to note that although the 'usual practice' in the case law is recognised as generally emanating from medical cases involving PVS patients, the President refers in some passages to medical cases generally (albeit that the *SW* case was a PVS case). It remains to be seen whether judges will adopt the half-costs solution as a reasonable starting point in medical cases generally or restrict it to PVS cases.

In non-medical welfare cases, the costs of the solicitors instructed by the Official Solicitor are generally met from public funds (where P is in receipt of Community Legal Service funding) or special provision is made (pursuant to rule 163) to recover costs from P's funds.

There is further discussion of the role of the Official Solicitor in health and welfare cases at **1.14.1**.

Costs paid out of P's estate – fixed costs

PD19B sets out the rates of fixed costs that applies to claims by solicitors or public authorities acting in Court of Protection proceedings and the fixed costs that may be claimed by solicitors and office holders in public authorities appointed to act as a Deputy for P. PD19B applies where the solicitor or Deputy is entitled to be paid out of P's estate but does not apply where the court orders that one party is to receive costs from another party. PD19B applies to fixed costs where the period covered by the fixed costs or remuneration ends on or after 1 April 2008.

Wasted costs (s.55(4), (5), (6))

The Court has power to disallow wasted costs or to order legal or other representatives to meet such wasted costs.

This provision provides the Court with more draconian powers in respect of costs than were previously available. For further guidance on the principles applicable in wasted costs applications, see *Civil Procedure* vol.1 (Sweet & Maxwell, 2007 at para.48.7).

'Wasted costs' are defined in s.55(6) as costs incurred as the result of improper, unreasonable or negligent acts or omissions of a party's representative (legal or other) or any employee of a representative or which in light of such an act or omission, it considers it unreasonable to expect the party to pay.

Costs following P's death

The Court can order a payment of costs out of or charged on P's estate within six years of P's death (rule 165)

Assessment of costs

Costs can be assessed by way of summary or detailed assessment. Detailed assessment proceedings in the High Court (rules 161, 164).

Costs against non-parties

The Court has power to make costs orders for or against non-parties (rule 166). Such persons must be made a party to the proceedings for the purpose of costs only.

Remuneration of Deputy, donee or attorney

Where the court makes an order that a Deputy, donee or attorney is entitled to remuneration out of P's estate for discharging his or her functions, the Court has a discretion to determine the amount of any such remuneration. PD19B (see above) sets out the fixed rates of remuneration for Deputies when such costs are paid out of P's estate from 1 April 2008 onwards.

Public funding

This is discussed at 1.15.

11.5.20   Part 20: Appeals

It is to be noted that rule 89 (in Part 12) provides for a reconsideration procedure for court orders made without a hearing or without notice to any person affected by it (see p.156 above).

Appeal to a higher judge of the Court of Protection (s.53(2), (3))

As permitted by the Act, the Rules make provision for appeals from certain judges in the Court to be heard by higher judges in the Court. Rule 180 provides that except in accordance with the relevant Practice Direction (PD20A on appeals does not make any different provision):

(a) an appeal from a first instance decision of a circuit judge shall be heard by a judge nominated by virtue of s.46(2)(a)–(c) of the Act (namely, the President, Vice-Chancellor or puisne judge of the High Court);

(b) an appeal from a decision of a district judge shall be heard by a circuit judge.

Appeal to the Court of Appeal (s.53(1))

Where the decision appealed is that of the President, Vice-Chancellor or puisne judge of the High Court (i.e. a judge nominated by virtue of s.46(2)(a)–(c) of the Act), an appeal will lie only to the Court of Appeal (rule 181). The judge nominated pursuant to s.46(2)(a)–(c) of the Act may grant permission to appeal to the Court of Appeal in accordance with Part 20 of the Rules where the judge made the decision sought to be appealed as a first instance judge. Otherwise, Part 20 of the Rules and PD20A do not apply to appeals to the Court of Appeal and the CPR apply to such an appeal.

Further, second appeals must be made to the Court of Appeal (i.e. an appeal against a decision of a judge which was itself made on appeal from a judge of the Court) (rule 182). Permission is required from the Court of Appeal for such an appeal and permission will only be granted if the appeal would raise an important point of principle or practice or there is some other compelling reason for the Court of Appeal to hear it. This incorporates the second appeal test from the CPR.

Appeals to a higher judge of the Court of Protection

PERMISSION

Permission is required to appeal, save for an appeal against an order for committal to prison (for which permission is not required) (rule 172). An application for permission may be made to the first instance judge or to the appeal judge (rule 172(4)). If permission is refused by the first instance judge, a further application for permission may be made to a higher judge in the Court of Protection (rule 172(5), (6), (7)).

The test for permission is identical to that applied under the CPR. Permission will be granted only where:

(a) the court considers that the appeal would have a real prospect of success; or
(b) there is some other compelling reason why the appeal should be heard (rule 173).

PROCEDURE FOR APPEALING

The procedure for appeals is set out in detail in rules 175–177 and PD20A.

An appellant must file an appellant's notice which unless otherwise ordered/directed, must be filed within 21 days of the date of the decision being appealed.

A respondent who seeks permission to appeal or to uphold the order of the first instance judge for reasons different from or additional to those given by the first instance judge must serve a respondent's notice which must be served within 21 days of the relevant date (as specified in rule 176(4)) unless otherwise ordered/directed.

PD20A sets out the documents that must be filed with the appeal and contains provisions in relation to skeleton arguments.

THE APPEAL HEARING

An appeal is limited to a review of the decision of the first instance judge unless a Practice Direction provides otherwise or an appeal judge considers that it would be in the interests of justice to hold a re-hearing (rule 179).

The appeal judge has all the powers of the first instance judge whose decision is being appealed (rule 178).

11.5.21   Part 21: Enforcement

Rule 184 applies the following enforcement provisions (with such modifications as may be necessary) to orders made by the Court under these Rules:

(a) of the CPR:

   (i)   Part 70 (General Rules about Enforcement of Judgments and Orders);
   (ii) Part 71 (Orders to Obtain Information from Judgment Debtors);
   (iii) Part 72 (Third Party Debt Orders);
   (iv) Part 73 (Charging Orders, Stop Orders and Stop Notices).

(b) of the Rules of the Supreme Court:

   (i)   Order 45 (Enforcement of Judgments and Orders: General);
   (ii) Order 46 (Writs of Execution: General);
   (iii) Order 47 (Writs of Fieri Facias).

Contempt of Court

The Court has power to commit a person to prison for contempt of court. Rules 185–194 set out the procedure for applications for committal and the Court's powers. PD21A contains further information about the procedure including the requirements of the affidavit in support of an application for committal. An application for an order for committal must be commenced by filing a COP9 application notice in accordance with Part 21.

11.5.22   Part 22: Transitory and transitional provisions

The Mental Capacity Act 2005 (Transitional and Consequential Provisions) Order 2007, SI 2007/1898, makes provision in respect of proceedings about P's personal welfare begun in the High Court before 1 October 2007. There is a discretion to continue to deal with the proceedings under the inherent jurisdiction until they are finally decided (art.2). However, the judge may choose to apply the Act when making decisions in the case as opposed to the common law principles applied in the inherent jurisdiction.

PD22A makes provision in relation to applications under the old Rules received prior to commencement of the Act on 1 October 2007. It is unlikely that there will be further cases to which this Practice Direction applies.

Rules 195–196 and PD19B make provision for applications by a receiver appointed under MHA 1983 who became a Deputy pursuant to Sched.5 of the Act to be dealt with by a nominated officer in certain circumstances. This is a simplified procedure to obtain approval for actions not covered in the original order. No fee is required and the COP9 form can be used. PD22B states that rules 195 and 196 and PD22B will cease to have effect on 30 June 2008 after which a Deputy who wishes to apply to the court for an order must use the procedure under either Parts 9 or 10 of the Rules (i.e. a COP1 will need to be used unless there are existing proceedings).

PD22C makes provision in relation to appeals against decision made under MHA 1983, Part 7 (receivers) or under the EPAA 1985.

11.5.23   Part 23: Miscellaneous

P ceases to lack capacity or dies

Where P ceases to lack capacity, the Court may make an order for any relevant property to be transferred to P or at P's direction if satisfied that P has the capacity to make decision in relation to that property (rule 202).

PD23B sets out the steps to be taken and procedure to be followed in relation to proceedings or orders of the Court where P ceases to lack capacity or dies. Rule 148 (see **11.5.17**) about the procedure where P ceases to lack capacity also needs to be considered.

Other matters

Provision is also made for the following matters:

(a) rule 200: the court can order or give a direction requiring a Deputy or other person to give security for the discharge of his functions; the Lasting Power of Attorney, Enduring Power of Attorney and Public Guardian Regulations 2007 also deal with security for discharge of functions (regs.33–7);

(b) rule 201 and PD23A: the Public Guardian may request the court's directions where a notice of objection prevents him from registering an instrument certain an enduring power of attorney.

11.6   COURT OF PROTECTION VISITORS

The role of Court of Protection Visitors is to provide independent advice to the Court and to the Public Guardian to assist in decision-making and case management. In particular, Court of Protection Visitors can be asked to report on how persons such as Deputies or attorneys are carrying out their functions in relation to persons who lack capacity. However, their role is not limited to investigating potential abuse and the Code emphasises that they have a wider role to play in checking on the general well-being of a person who lacks capacity and providing support to Deputies and attorneys in carrying out their roles (para.14.11).

In 2007 the Office of the Public Guardian carried out a review of the Visitors service. It was decided that the Visitors service will have a central role to play in supervising and supporting court-appointed Deputies to ensure that they are carrying out the terms of the court order and acting in the best interests of the client. It was decided that there will be fewer routine visits than in the past. In the past Visitors have been self-employed contractors. It is intended to change this with a mix of regionally-based employed Visitors who will carry out general regulatory visits and a bank of self-employed contractors with specialist medical, legal, financial or welfare skills who will provide specialist reports to the Court or Public Guardian. The new service is expected to be operational by the summer of 2008 (see Mental Capacity Update edition 17, March 2008).

There are two types of visitor: General Visitors and Special Visitors. Special Visitors are registered medical practitioners with relevant expertise. Visitors are appointed to a panel by the Lord Chancellor who also determines the terms and conditions of their appointment and their remuneration and allowances (s.61(1), (4)).

11.6.1   Special Visitors (s.61(2))

The necessary qualifications to be a Special Visitor are that a person:

■ is a registered medical practitioner or appears to the Lord Chancellor to have other suitable qualifications and training; and
■ appears to the Lord Chancellor to have a special knowledge and experience in cases of impairment of or disturbance in the functioning of the mind and brain. This requirement refers to the definition of incapacity in s.2 of the Act.

11.6.2   General Visitors (s.61(3))

No qualifications are specified in respect of General Visitors, although the Act specifies that a General Visitor does not require medical qualifications.

The Court or Public Guardian can send whichever type of Visitor is most appropriate to visit and interview a person who may lack capacity. Visitors can also interview attorneys or Deputies or P in private and inspect any relevant healthcare or social care records.

Attorneys and Deputies are required to co-operate with Visitors and if they do not, the Court can cancel their appointment, where it thinks that they have not acted in the person's best interests (ss.22(3), (4) and 16(8) of the Act).

11.6.3   Functions of Court of Protection Visitors

Court of Protection Visitors are appointed to carry out visits and produce reports as directed by the Court of Protection (s.49(2)) or the Public Guardian (s.58(1)(d)) in respect of persons who lack capacity (see further commentary on these sections at p.160 and 12.3.6).

Regulation 44 of the Lasting Power of Attorney, Enduring Power of Attorney and Public Guardian Regulations 2007 (SI 2007/1253) makes further provisions in relation to visits by Court of Protection Visitors directed by the Public Guardian.

11.6.4   Access to records and interview (s.61(5), (6))

A Court of Protection Visitor has power to examine and take copies of relevant health, social services or care records which relate to a person who lacks capacity. A Court of Protection Visitor can also interview the person who lacks capacity in private.

These powers are the same as those held by the Public Guardian (s.58(5), (6)).

11.7   EXISTING RECEIVERS

Schedule 5 of the Act sets out transitional arrangements arising from the repeal of Part VII of the MHA 1983. Part 1 of Sched.5 sets out provisions applying to receivers appointed under Part VII of the MHA 1983.

Persons appointed as receivers under the MHA 1983 will be treated under the Act as though they are Deputies appointed by the Court of Protection and hence will be supervised by the Public Guardian. They will retain the functions given to them as receivers.

The Court of Protection has powers to end their appointment as Deputies (Sched.5, para.1(3), (5)).

Rules 195–6 and PD19B make provision for a simplified procedure for applications by a receiver appointed under the MHA 1983 who became a Deputy pursuant to Sched.5 to the Act to obtain approval for actions not covered by the original order (see **11.5.22**). However, this procedure will come to an end on 30 June 2008.

12 THE PUBLIC GUARDIAN

12.1 BACKGROUND

The Public Guardian is a new statutory office-holder created by the Act with specific powers and duties to supervise and regulate those appointed to make decisions on behalf of those who cannot do so themselves. Previously, there was a Public Guardianship Office but it carried out only the administrative functions arising from the Court of Protection's jurisdiction, including overseeing and supporting the activities of receivers and managing the financial affairs of patients when no one else was willing to act as receiver. It has been stated by the Mental Capacity Implementation Programme that:

> A significant difference between the Public Guardianship office and the Office of the Public Guardian will be the emphasis placed on promoting the concept of an assumption of capacity of the clients of the Court of Protection and the understanding that every client has differing levels of capacity.

> (Mental Capacity Update, Edition 16[1])

The Public Guardian has an expanded remit and a greater regulatory role. Furthermore, there is a new Office of the Public Guardian (OPG) which was introduced at the time of the Act and this assists the Public Guardian in carrying out his duties. The OPG is an agency of the Ministry of Justice. Concerns had been expressed about the amount of abuse by attorneys and others which had gone unchecked, as well as the quality of the work carried out by the Public Guardianship Office.[2] The creation of the OPG with an expanded remit was one of the methods adopted to combat these problems.

---

1 Available from the OPG's website: **www.publicguardian.gov.uk**.
2 See Hansard, Lord Kingsland at Committee Stage in the Lords 8 February 2005, at col.765.

12.2   THE POSITION UNDER THE MENTAL CAPACITY ACT 2005

This Act provides for the appointment of a new public official, the Public Guardian (s.57(1)), who has a range of functions contributing to the protection of persons who lack capacity.

The Public Guardian has been appointed by the Lord Chancellor. The Lord Chancellor provides officers, staff and services to the Public Guardian (s.58(4)) and the Public Guardian can authorise his or her officers to perform functions on his or her behalf (s.58(5)).

Baroness Andrews on behalf of the government in the House of Lords at the Committee Stage stated that the Public Guardian has regulatory functions which fall into three main areas: (1) the registration body for LPAs; (2) the supervision of Deputies appointed by the Court; and (3) investigative functions.[1]

1   See Hansard, 8 February 2005, at col.770.

12.3   FUNCTIONS OF THE PUBLIC GUARDIAN

The Act provides that the Public Guardian has the following functions.

12.3.1   Establishing and maintaining a register of LPAs (s.58(1)(a))

The application and procedure for registration and the role of the Public Guardian is discussed in **Chapter 4**. The Public Guardian has to ensure that the application complies with the statutory requirements.

LPAs cannot be used until they have been registered, which means that the Public Guardian will have a comprehensive register of all LPAs in operation. This differs from the current position in respect of EPAs. Before registering an LPA, the Public Guardian will ensure that it meets the requirements of the Act and will check the documentation. (See **Chapter 4** for further discussion.)

The Public Guardian is also responsible for cancelling the registration of an instrument as an LPA (see MCA 2005, Sched.1, Part 3) and for making notes of alterations to registered LPAs (e.g. that the power has been revoked or suspended – see Sched.1, Part 4).

The government resisted proposed amendments to the Mental Capacity Bill which would have required the Public Guardian to be responsible for the regular supervision of attorneys of LPAs, primarily on the basis that this would under-mine respect for the autonomy of the individual who chose that particular attor-ney to act on his or her behalf. However, the Public Guardian can investigate cases of suspected abuse upon the issue being brought to his or her attention (see further below).

The Code emphasises that an LPA is a private arrangement between the donor and the attorney and donors should only choose attorneys whom they can trust. The OPG produces information to help donors understand LPAs and what to consider when choosing an attorney. The Code also provides that the Public Guardian will not usually get involved once somebody has registered an LPA, unless somebody has concerns about how an attorney is carrying out his or her duties (Code, paras.14.12–14.14 and see further below dealing with complaints or concerns about attorneys). The Public Guardian has powers to require donees of LPAs to provide him with information or produce documents in circumstances where it appears to the Public Guardian that there is cause for concern about the conduct of the donee (Lasting Powers of Attorney, Enduring Powers of Attorney and Public Guardian Regulations 2007 ('the 2007 Regulations'), reg.46, discussed in further detail below at **12.3.10**).

The registration fee for an LPA is currently £150 (Public Guardian (Fees etc.) Regulations 2007, SI 2007/2051).

12.3.2   Establishing and maintaining a register of EPAs

The Public Guardian is also charged with establishing and maintaining a register of EPAs (MCA 2005, Sched.4, Part 4, para.14). The Public Guardian is also responsible for cancelling the registration of an instrument as an EPA (Sched.4, Part 4, para.17).

The registration fee for an EPA is currently £120 (Public Guardian (Fees etc.) Regulations 2007, SI 2007/2051).

12.3.3   Establishing and maintaining a register of orders appointing Deputies (s.58(1)(b))

The Public Guardian has a full list of all those appointed by the Court to act as Deputies. This is necessary for the Public Guardian to carry out supervisory functions in respect of Deputies (see below).

The fee charged for placing a Deputy's name on the register and carrying out a risk assessment to determine the supervision regime (see further below) is currently £125 (Public Guardian (Fees etc.) Regulations 2007, SI 2007/2051).

12.3.4   Functions and powers in relation to registers

The 2007 Regulations contain further provision in relation to Public Guardian's functions in respect of the registers (i.e. the register of LPAs, EPAs or court orders appointing Deputies).

Content of the registers

The Public Guardian has a discretion to include in the register:

(a) such descriptions of information about a registered instrument or registered order as he considers appropriate, and
(b) entries which relate to an instrument or order for which registration has been cancelled (reg.30(2)).

Searches of the registers

In particular, any person may make an application (in the manner specified) to the Public Guardian to search one or more of the registers, and the Public Guardian must disclose to the applicant the information appearing on the register (if there is such an entry on the register) (reg.31). The form used is OPG100. A fee is payable, which is currently £25 (Public Guardian (Fees etc.) Regulations 2007, SI 2007/2051).

The Public Guardian has a discretion to disclose additional information to a person who has made an application to search the register(s) and has obtained information about an LPA, EPA or court order appointing a Deputy which confers authority to make decisions about matters concerning P (reg.32). The additional information includes any information which the Public Guardian has obtained in exercising his functions but which does not appear on the register. An application must be made to the Public Guardian for disclosure of the additional information (in the form required by reg.32(4)) and the application triggers the power to disclose (reg.32(2)). The Public Guardian must have regard to a list of factors before deciding whether or not to disclose any additional information (reg.32(6)).

12.3.5   Supervising Deputies appointed by the Court (s.58(1)(c))

Appointment of a Deputy is by the Court and is made at the time when a person lacks capacity. There are more stringent safeguards in place for supervision of Deputies than for attorneys of LPAs to protect persons who lack capacity from abuse.

The particular procedure and methods that will be adopted by the Public Guardian in order to supervise Deputies are not set out in the Act. However, this is dealt with in the Code of Practice and in the 2007 Regulations.

Chapter 6 deals with the Court's powers in relation to Deputies. There are measures to make sure that the Court appoints an appropriate Deputy. The OPG may run checks on potential Deputies if requested to do so by the Court or carry out a risk assessment to determine what kind of supervision a Deputy will need once appointed.

Deputies are accountable to the Court and the Court can cancel a Deputy's appointment at any time.

The OPG supervises the Deputy's actions on behalf of the Court. The Court may want the Deputy to provide financial accounts or other reports to the OPG. The Office of the Public Guardian has produced guidance about the supervision of Deputies (OPG507). This states that when a Deputy is appointed, the OPG carries out an assessment to determine the appropriate level of supervision and support. Deputies are allocated either Type I, II or III level of supervision. Type I is the highest level of supervision. This guidance gives examples of the situations where a particular level of supervision would be appropriate. In practice, supervision by the Public Guardian might involve any of the following:

- ensuring compliance by the Deputy with requirements of the Court order e.g. providing an annual report to the Public Guardian;
- sending a Court of Protection Visitor to visit the Deputy and P;
- regular contact with the Deputy and others with an interest in the welfare of P.

It is envisaged that there will be a less intrusive approach to supervision than applied to the supervision of receivers (see Mental Capacity Update edition 16 from the Mental Capacity Implementation Programme, available from the OPG's website).

Section 58(2) provides that the supervisory function in relation to Deputies can be carried out in cooperation with other persons who have functions in relation to the care and treatment of P (e.g. health bodies or local authorities).

An annual supervision fee is charged for Types I and II supervision (Public Guardian (Fees etc.) Regulations 2007, reg.8). The current annual fees, which are payable annually in arrears on 31 March, are:

- £800 p.a. – Type I (highest);
- £175 p.a. – Type II (lower).

When a Deputy is appointed by the Court or an order is made varying the Deputy's appointment, the Public Guardian is entitled to be provided with copies of relevant documents filed at court if he reasonably considers it necessary to have them in connection with the discharge of his supervisory functions under s.58 of the Act over the Deputy (Court of Protection Rules 2007, rule 20).

12.3.6 Directing visits by Court of Protection Visitors (s.58(1)(d))

The Public Guardian has power to direct Court of Protection Visitors (see definition and discussion at 11.5) to visit:

- a donee of an LPA;
- a Deputy appointed by the court;

- P (the donor of the LPA or for whom the Deputy is appointed),

and report to the Public Guardian on such matters as directed.

The Public Guardian also has powers to direct a Court of Protection Visitor to visit an attorney under an EPA or a donor under an EPA (2007 Regulations, reg.48).

The power to direct such visits previously only lay with the Court of Protection itself (MHA 1983, s.103). However, the Court of Protection has wider powers to call for reports (from persons other than Court of Protection Visitors, including from the Public Guardian) than the Public Guardian.

Regulation 44 of the 2007 Regulations makes further provision in relation to visits by the Public Guardian and visits by Court of Protection Visitors directed by the Public Guardian.

12.3.7   Receiving security which the court requires a person to give for the discharge of his functions (s.59(1)(e))

The Court can require a person (including a Deputy) to give security for the discharge of his or her functions to the Public Guardian. Rule 200 of the Court of Protection Rules 2007 and regs.33–7 of the 2007 Regulations make further provision in relation to the giving of security which is done by means of a bond.

12.3.8   Receiving reports from donees of LPAs and Deputies appointed by the court (s.58(1)(f))

A donor of an LPA or the Court of Protection in respect of Deputies can require that reports are provided to the Public Guardian by the donee of the LPA or the Deputy respectively. Form OPG102 is to be used by a Deputy when reporting to the Public Guardian.

There are provisions in the 2007 Regulations regarding orders by the Court for Deputies to report to the Public Guardian. The Deputy can apply to the Public Guardian for additional time to submit a report (reg.38) and there are mandatory requirements in relation to the content of the report (reg.39). The Public Guardian has power to require a Deputy to submit a final report on termination of his appointment (reg.40).

12.3.9   Reporting to the court on such matters relating to these proceedings as the court requires (s.59(1)(g))

The Court of Protection has power to call for a report from the Public Guardian (s.49(2)). (See further discussion of this power of the Court at pp.160–162.)

12.3.10   Dealing with representations including complaints about the way in which a donee or a Deputy is exercising his powers (s.58(1)(h))

Any person may make representations or complaints to the Public Guardian about the way in which a donee of an LPA or a Deputy is exercising his functions, and the Public Guardian can carry out investigations. Section 58(2) provides that this function can be carried out in co-operation with other persons/agencies who have functions in relation to P's care and treatment.

The Code states that anyone who is worried about how attorneys or Deputies carry out their duties should contact the Public Guardian (para.14.19). The OPG will not always be the most appropriate organisation to investigate all complaints and it may investigate a case jointly with health or social care bodies or in some cases the police.

The OPG will usually refer concerns about personal welfare LPAs or personal welfare Deputies to the relevant agency and in certain circumstances will alert the police. The OPG will make sure that the relevant agency keeps it informed of any action taken and will provide the Court with the information it needs to take possible action against the attorney or the Deputy (paras.14.20–14.21). Two examples are given in the Code: if there was a complaint that a welfare attorney was physically abusing a donor, the OPG would refer this case to the relevant local authority adult protection procedures and possibly the police; and if the OPG found that a solicitor appointed as a financial Deputy for an elderly woman had defrauded her estate, the case would be referred to the police and to the Law Society Consumer Complaints Service (para.14.22).

The Public Guardian has wide powers to require Deputies or donees of LPAs to provide him with information or documents in circumstances where there are concerns about their conduct.

When the Public Guardian has received representations including complaints about the way in which a Deputy is exercising his powers or failing to exercise them, or it appears to the Public Guardian that there are circumstances which give rise to concern about the conduct of the Deputy, or there is otherwise good reason to seek information, the Public Guardian has powers to require Deputies to provide information and/or produce documents to him (2007 Regulations, reg.41).

The Public Guardian also has powers to require donees of LPAs to provide him or her with information or documents when it appears to the Public Guardian that the donee has behaved, may be behaving, or proposes to behave in a way that contravenes his or her authority or is not in the best interests of the donor, or has failed to comply with an order or directions made (2007 Regulations, reg.46). The Public Guardian has similar powers in relation to EPAs when it appears to him or her that the attorney may be unsuitable to be the donor's attorney (2007 Regulations, reg.47).

12.3.11   Publishing in any manner the Public Guardian thinks appropriate, any information he thinks appropriate about the discharge of his functions (s.58(1)(i))

The Public Guardian has a wide discretion as to how and what information to make available about the discharge of his or her functions.

12.3.12   Co-operating with others (s.58(2))

The Public Guardian may discharge his functions in respect of supervision of Deputies and dealing with representations and complaints by co-operating with other persons concerned with P's care and treatment. It is intended that the Public Guardian will work closely with organisations such as local authorities and NHS bodies (see Explanatory Notes at para.146 and the Code at paras.14.19–14.22). This is discussed further above.

12.3.13   Accessing records and interviewing P (s.58(5), (6))

The Public Guardian has power to examine and take copies of relevant health, social services or care records in so far as they relate to P and to interview P (i.e. the donor of an LPA or person in respect of whom a Deputy is appointed) in private. This is to enable the Public Guardian to carry out his functions.

The Public Guardian has similar rights when reporting to the Court of Protection (s.49(7), (8)). Court of Protection Visitors have the same rights (s.61(5) and (6) – see discussion at 11.6.4).

12.3.14   Functions in relation to persons carrying out specific transactions (reg.45)

If a person (T) has been authorised to carry out a specific transaction in relation to P by an order of the Court pursuant to s.16(2)(a) of the Act, the Public Guardian has the functions of receiving any reports from T as are required by the Court and dealing with any representations including complaints about the way in which T carries out or fails to carry out the transaction (2007 Regulations, reg.45). Hence, if a Court authorised by way of an order a large gift to be paid out by a donee under an LPA, it might require the donee to report to the Public Guardian about this transaction and persons could make representations to the Public Guardian about the donee's conduct in relation to this transaction – for example, if the money was not gifted as authorised by the Court.

The Public Guardian's additional powers in relation to Deputies in reg.38–41 (reports and power to require information) also apply to T in these circumstances (reg.45(3)).

12.3.15 Making applications to the Court of Protection (reg.43)

The Public Guardian can make applications to the Court in connection with his or her functions under the Act as he or she considers it necessary or appropriate to do so (2007 Regulations, reg.43).

12.3.16 Review of decisions made in respect of Deputies (reg.42)

A Deputy may require the Public Guardian to reconsider any decision he has made in relation to a Deputy (2007 Regulations, reg. 42). The Public Guardian must give written notice and a statement of reasons if he or she upholds the previous decision on reconsideration.

12.4 FEES

The fees charged by the Public Guardian are contained in the Public Guardian (Fees, etc.) Regulations 2007 (as amended by the Public Guardian (Fees etc.) (Amendment) Regulations 2007, SI 2007/2616) (and see also the OPG's website **www.publicguardian.gov.uk** for further information in relation to fees). An application can be made for an exemption or remission of fees (OPG506A form and guidance OPG506).

12.5 PUBLIC GUARDIAN BOARD

Section 59 provides for a body, the Public Guardian Board, which supervises the work of the Public Guardian.

The functions of the Public Guardian Board are to:

- scrutinise and review the way in which the Public Guardian discharges his or her functions; and
- make such recommendations to the Lord Chancellor as it thinks appropriate (s.59(2)).

12.5.1 Consideration of recommendations by the Lord Chancellor

The Lord Chancellor must give due consideration to recommendations of the Public Guardian Board when discharging his or her functions in respect of the Public Guardian, e.g. in providing officers and staff to the Public Guardian or making regulations in respect of the Public Guardian's functions (s.59(3)).

12.5.2   Membership of the Public Guardian Board

The Lord Chancellor is responsible for the appointment of members to the Board (s.59(4)). There must be at least one member who is a judge of the Court of Protection and at least four members who appear to the Lord Chancellor to have appropriate knowledge or experience of the Public Guardian's work (s.59(5)).

The Public Guardian Board Regulations 2007, SI 2007/1770 have been made by the Lord Chancellor (pursuant to s.59(6) of the Act) and provides for the appointment of a Chairman of the Board, the terms of office of members of the Board, the procedure of the Board and requires that the Board holds at least one public meeting per year.

12.5.3   Annual report of the Public Guardian Board

The Public Guardian Board must report annually to the Lord Chancellor about the discharge of its functions (s.59(9)) and the Lord Chancellor must lay a copy of that report before Parliament within one month of receiving it.

This is the mechanism for ensuring that the work of the Public Guardian Board is subject to scrutiny.

Appendix A
MENTAL CAPACITY ACT 2005

The Mental Capacity Act 2005 is shown as amended until 18 April 2008. See the Mental Capacity Act 2005 (Commencement No.2) Order 2007 in Appendix B of this book for the dates on which the sections came into force in England and Wales.

The prospective amendments not yet in force made by the Mental Health Act 2007 are also shown in this reproduction of the Mental Capacity Act 2005.

MENTAL CAPACITY ACT 2005

CONTENTS

PART 1   PERSONS WHO LACK CAPACITY

PART 2   THE COURT OF PROTECTION AND THE PUBLIC GUARDIAN

PART 3   MISCELLANEOUS AND GENERAL

SCHEDULES

SCHEDULE 1 – LASTING POWERS OF ATTORNEY: FORMALITIES
Part 1 – Making instruments
Part 2 – Registration
Part 3 – Cancellation of registration and notification of severance
Part 4 – Records of alterations in registered powers

[*SCHEDULE 1A – PERSONS INELIGIBLE TO BE DEPRIVED OF LIBERTY BY THIS ACT*
Part 1 – Ineligible persons
Part 2 – Interpretation]

SCHEDULE 2 – PROPERTY AND AFFAIRS: SUPPLEMENTARY PROVISIONS

SCHEDULE 3 – INTERNATIONAL PROTECTION OF ADULTS
Part 1 – Preliminary
Part 2 – Jurisdiction of competent authority
Part 3 – Applicable law
Part 4 – Recognition and enforcement
Part 5 – Co-operation
Part 6 – General

SCHEDULE 4 – PROVISIONS APPLYING TO EXISTING ENDURING POWERS OF ATTORNEY
Part 1 – Enduring powers of attorney
Part 2 – Action on actual or impending incapacity of donor
Part 3 – Notification prior to registration
Part 4 – Registration
Part 5 – Legal position after registration
Part 6 – Protection of attorney and third parties
Part 7 – Joint and joint and several attorneys
Part 8 – Interpretation

SCHEDULE 5 – TRANSITIONAL PROVISIONS AND SAVINGS
Part 1 – Repeal of Part 7 of the Mental Health Act 1983
Part 2 – Repeal of the Enduring Powers of Attorney Act 1985

SCHEDULE 6 – MINOR AND CONSEQUENTIAL AMENDMENTS

SCHEDULE 7 – REPEALS

An Act to make new provision relating to persons who lack capacity; to establish a superior court of record called the Court of Protection in place of the office of the Supreme Court called by that name; to make provision in connection with the Convention on the International Protection of Adults signed at the Hague on 13th January 2000; and for connected purposes.

[7th April 2005]

BE IT ENACTED by the Queen's most Excellent Majesty, by and with the advice and consent of the Lords Spiritual and Temporal, and Commons, in this present Parliament assembled, and by the authority of the same, as follows: –

PART 1   PERSONS WHO LACK CAPACITY

The principles

1 The principles

(1) The following principles apply for the purposes of this Act.

(2) A person must be assumed to have capacity unless it is established that he lacks capacity.

(3) A person is not to be treated as unable to make a decision unless all practicable steps to help him to do so have been taken without success.

(4) A person is not to be treated as unable to make a decision merely because he makes an unwise decision.

(5) An act done, or decision made, under this Act for or on behalf of a person who lacks capacity must be done, or made, in his best interests.

(6) Before the act is done, or the decision is made, regard must be had to whether the purpose for which it is needed can be as effectively achieved in a way that is less restrictive of the person's rights and freedom of action.

Preliminary

2 People who lack capacity

(1) For the purposes of this Act, a person lacks capacity in relation to a matter if at the material time he is unable to make a decision for himself in relation to the matter because of an impairment of, or a disturbance in the functioning of, the mind or brain.

(2) It does not matter whether the impairment or disturbance is permanent or temporary.

(3) A lack of capacity cannot be established merely by reference to –

(a) a person's age or appearance, or

(b) a condition of his, or an aspect of his behaviour, which might lead others to make unjustified assumptions about his capacity.

(4) In proceedings under this Act or any other enactment, any question whether a person lacks capacity within the meaning of this Act must be decided on the balance of probabilities.

(5) No power which a person ('D') may exercise under this Act –

(a) in relation to a person who lacks capacity, or

(b) where D reasonably thinks that a person lacks capacity,

is exercisable in relation to a person under 16.

(6) Subsection (5) is subject to section 18(3).

3 Inability to make decisions

(1) For the purposes of section 2, a person is unable to make a decision for himself if he is unable –

(a) to understand the information relevant to the decision,

(b) to retain that information,

(c) to use or weigh that information as part of the process of making the decision, or

(d) to communicate his decision (whether by talking, using sign language or any other means).

(2) A person is not to be regarded as unable to understand the information relevant to a decision if he is able to understand an explanation of it given to him in a way that is appropriate to his circumstances (using simple language, visual aids or any other means).

(3) The fact that a person is able to retain the information relevant to a decision for a short period only does not prevent him from being regarded as able to make the decision.

(4) The information relevant to a decision includes information about the reasonably foreseeable consequences of –

  (a) deciding one way or another, or

  (b) failing to make the decision.

4 Best interests

(1) In determining for the purposes of this Act what is in a person's best interests, the person making the determination must not make it merely on the basis of –

  (a) the person's age or appearance, or

  (b) a condition of his, or an aspect of his behaviour, which might lead others to make unjustified assumptions about what might be in his best interests.

(2) The person making the determination must consider all the relevant circumstances and, in particular, take the following steps.

(3) He must consider –

  (a) whether it is likely that the person will at some time have capacity in relation to the matter in question, and

  (b) if it appears likely that he will, when that is likely to be.

(4) He must, so far as reasonably practicable, permit and encourage the person to part-icipate, or to improve his ability to participate, as fully as possible in any act done for him and any decision affecting him.

(5) Where the determination relates to life-sustaining treatment he must not, in considering whether the treatment is in the best interests of the person concerned, be motivated by a desire to bring about his death.

(6) He must consider, so far as is reasonably ascertainable –

  (a) the person's past and present wishes and feelings (and, in particular, any relevant written statement made by him when he had capacity),

  (b) the beliefs and values that would be likely to influence his decision if he had capacity, and

  (c) the other factors that he would be likely to consider if he were able to do so.

(7) He must take into account, if it is practicable and appropriate to consult them, the views of –

  (a) anyone named by the person as someone to be consulted on the matter in question or on matters of that kind,

  (b) anyone engaged in caring for the person or interested in his welfare,

  (c) any donee of a lasting power of attorney granted by the person, and

  (d) any deputy appointed for the person by the court,

as to what would be in the person's best interests and, in particular, as to the matters mentioned in subsection (6).

(8) The duties imposed by subsections (1) to (7) also apply in relation to the exercise of any powers which –

  (a) are exercisable under a lasting power of attorney, or

  (b) are exercisable by a person under this Act where he reasonably believes that another person lacks capacity.

(9) In the case of an act done, or a decision made, by a person other than the court, there is sufficient compliance with this section if (having complied with the requirements of subsections (1) to (7)) he reasonably believes that what he does or decides is in the best interests of the person concerned.

(10) 'Life-sustaining treatment' means treatment which in the view of a person providing health care for the person concerned is necessary to sustain life.

(11) 'Relevant circumstances' are those –

    (a) of which the person making the determination is aware, and

    (b) which it would be reasonable to regard as relevant.

[4A Restriction on deprivation of liberty

(1) *This Act does not authorise any person ('D') to deprive any other person ('P') of his liberty.*

(2) *But that is subject to –*

    (a) *the following provisions of this section, and*

    (b) *section 4B.*

(3) *D may deprive P of his liberty if, by doing so, D is giving effect to a relevant decision of the court.*

(4) *A relevant decision of the court is a decision made by an order under section 16(2)(a) in relation to a matter concerning P's personal welfare.*

(5) *D may deprive P of his liberty if the deprivation is authorised by Schedule A1 (hospital and care home residents: deprivation of liberty).]*

Note:
Section 4A is inserted by Mental Health Act 2007, s.50(2) to come into force at a time appointed by the Secretary of State in a statutory instrument.

[4B Deprivation of liberty necessary for life-sustaining treatment etc

(1) *If the following conditions are met, D is authorised to deprive P of his liberty while a decision as respects any relevant issue is sought from the court.*

(2) *The first condition is that there is a question about whether D is authorised to deprive P of his liberty under section 4A.*

(3) *The second condition is that the deprivation of liberty –*

    (a) *is wholly or partly for the purpose of –*

        (i) *giving P life-sustaining treatment, or*

        (ii) *doing any vital act, or*

    (b) *consists wholly or partly of –*

        (i) *giving P life-sustaining treatment, or*

        (ii) *doing any vital act.*

(4) *The third condition is that the deprivation of liberty is necessary in order to –*

    (a) *give the life-sustaining treatment, or*

    (b) *do the vital act.*

(5) *A vital act is any act which the person doing it reasonably believes to be necessary to prevent a serious deterioration in P's condition.]*

Note:
Section 4B is inserted by Mental Health Act 2007, s.50(2) to come into force at a time appointed by the Secretary of State in a statutory instrument.

5 Acts in connection with care or treatment

(1) If a person ('D') does an act in connection with the care or treatment of another person ('P'), the act is one to which this section applies if –

    (a) before doing the act, D takes reasonable steps to establish whether P lacks capacity in relation to the matter in question, and

    (b) when doing the act, D reasonably believes –

        (i) that P lacks capacity in relation to the matter, and

        (ii) that it will be in P's best interests for the act to be done.

(2) D does not incur any liability in relation to the act that he would not have incurred if P –

    (a) had had capacity to consent in relation to the matter, and
    (b) had consented to D's doing the act.

(3) Nothing in this section excludes a person's civil liability for loss or damage, or his criminal liability, resulting from his negligence in doing the act.

(4) Nothing in this section affects the operation of sections 24 to 26 (advance decisions to refuse treatment).

6 Section 5 acts: limitations

(1) If D does an act that is intended to restrain P, it is not an act to which section 5 applies unless two further conditions are satisfied.

(2) The first condition is that D reasonably believes that it is necessary to do the act in order to prevent harm to P.

(3) The second is that the act is a proportionate response to –

    (a) the likelihood of P's suffering harm, and
    (b) the seriousness of that harm.

(4) For the purposes of this section D restrains P if he –

    (a) uses, or threatens to use, force to secure the doing of an act which P resists, or
    (b) restricts P's liberty of movement, whether or not P resists.

(5) [*But D does more than merely restrain P if he deprives P of his liberty within the meaning of Article 5(1) of the Human Rights Convention (whether or not D is a public authority).*]

(6) Section 5 does not authorise a person to do an act which conflicts with a decision made, within the scope of his authority and in accordance with this Part, by –

    (a) a donee of a lasting power of attorney granted by P, or
    (b) a deputy appointed for P by the court.

(7) But nothing in subsection (6) stops a person –

    (a) providing life-sustaining treatment, or
    (b) doing any act which he reasonably believes to be necessary to prevent a serious deterioration in P's condition,

while a decision as respects any relevant issue is sought from the court.

Note:
Section 6(5) is omitted by Mental Health Act 2007, s.50(4)(a) at a time to be appointed by the Secretary of State in a statutory instrument.

7 Payment for necessary goods and services

(1) If necessary goods or services are supplied to a person who lacks capacity to contract for the supply, he must pay a reasonable price for them.

(2) 'Necessary' means suitable to a person's condition in life and to his actual requirements at the time when the goods or services are supplied.

8 Expenditure

(1) If an act to which section 5 applies involves expenditure, it is lawful for D –

    (a) to pledge P's credit for the purpose of the expenditure, and
    (b) to apply money in P's possession for meeting the expenditure.

(2) If the expenditure is borne for P by D, it is lawful for D –

    (a) to reimburse himself out of money in P's possession, or
    (b) to be otherwise indemnified by P.

(3) Subsections (1) and (2) do not affect any power under which (apart from those subsections) a person –

   (a)   has lawful control of P's money or other property, and

   (b)   has power to spend money for P's benefit.

Lasting powers of attorney

9 Lasting powers of attorney

(1) A lasting power of attorney is a power of attorney under which the donor ('P') confers on the donee (or donees) authority to make decisions about all or any of the following –

   (a)   P's personal welfare or specified matters concerning P's personal welfare, and

   (b)   P's property and affairs or specified matters concerning P's property and affairs, and which includes authority to make such decisions in circumstances where P no longer has capacity.

(2) A lasting power of attorney is not created unless –

   (a)   section 10 is complied with,

   (b)   an instrument conferring authority of the kind mentioned in subsection (1) is made and registered in accordance with Schedule 1, and

   (c)   at the time when P executes the instrument, P has reached 18 and has capacity to execute it.

(3) An instrument which –

   (a)   purports to create a lasting power of attorney, but

   (b)   does not comply with this section, section 10 or Schedule 1, confers no authority.

(4) The authority conferred by a lasting power of attorney is subject to –

   (a)   the provisions of this Act and, in particular, sections 1 (the principles) and 4 (best interests), and

   (b)   any conditions or restrictions specified in the instrument.

10 Appointment of donees

(1) A donee of a lasting power of attorney must be –

   (a)   an individual who has reached 18, or

   (b)   if the power relates only to P's property and affairs, either such an individual or a trust corporation.

(2) An individual who is bankrupt may not be appointed as donee of a lasting power of attorney in relation to P's property and affairs.

(3) Subsections (4) to (7) apply in relation to an instrument under which two or more persons are to act as donees of a lasting power of attorney.

(4) The instrument may appoint them to act –

   (a)   jointly,

   (b)   jointly and severally, or

   (c)   jointly in respect of some matters and jointly and severally in respect of others.

(5) To the extent to which it does not specify whether they are to act jointly or jointly and severally, the instrument is to be assumed to appoint them to act jointly.

(6) If they are to act jointly, a failure, as respects one of them, to comply with the requirements of subsection (1) or (2) or Part 1 or 2 of Schedule 1 prevents a lasting power of attorney from being created.

(7) If they are to act jointly and severally, a failure, as respects one of them, to comply with the requirements of subsection (1) or (2) or Part 1 or 2 of Schedule 1 –

   (a)   prevents the appointment taking effect in his case, but

   (b)   does not prevent a lasting power of attorney from being created in the case of the other or others.

(8) An instrument used to create a lasting power of attorney –

    (a) cannot give the donee (or, if more than one, any of them) power to appoint a substitute or successor, but

    (b) may itself appoint a person to replace the donee (or, if more than one, any of them) on the occurrence of an event mentioned in section 13(6)(a) to (d) which has the effect of terminating the donee's appointment.

11 Lasting powers of attorney: restrictions

(1) A lasting power of attorney does not authorise the donee (or, if more than one, any of them) to do an act that is intended to restrain P, unless three conditions are satisfied.

(2) The first condition is that P lacks, or the donee reasonably believes that P lacks, capacity in relation to the matter in question.

(3) The second is that the donee reasonably believes that it is necessary to do the act in order to prevent harm to P.

(4) The third is that the act is a proportionate response to –

    (a) the likelihood of P's suffering harm, and

    (b) the seriousness of that harm.

(5) For the purposes of this section, the donee restrains P if he –

    (a) uses, or threatens to use, force to secure the doing of an act which P resists, or

    (b) restricts P's liberty of movement, whether or not P resists, or if he authorises another person to do any of those things.

(6) [*But the donee does more than merely restrain P if he deprives P of his liberty within the meaning of Article 5(1) of the Human Rights Convention.*]

(7) Where a lasting power of attorney authorises the donee (or, if more than one, any of them) to make decisions about P's personal welfare, the authority –

    (a) does not extend to making such decisions in circumstances other than those where P lacks, or the donee reasonably believes that P lacks, capacity,

    (b) is subject to sections 24 to 26 (advance decisions to refuse treatment), and

    (c) extends to giving or refusing consent to the carrying out or continuation of a treatment by a person providing health care for P.

Note:
Section 11(6) is omitted by Mental Health Act 2007, s.50(4)(b) at a time to be appointed by the Secretary of State in a statutory instrument.

(8) But subsection (7)(c) –

    (a) does not authorise the giving or refusing of consent to the carrying out or continuation of life-sustaining treatment, unless the instrument contains express provision to that effect, and

    (b) is subject to any conditions or restrictions in the instrument.

12 Scope of lasting powers of attorney: gifts

(1) Where a lasting power of attorney confers authority to make decisions about P's property and affairs, it does not authorise a donee (or, if more than one, any of them) to dispose of the donor's property by making gifts except to the extent permitted by subsection (2).

(2) The donee may make gifts –

    (a) on customary occasions to persons (including himself) who are related to or connected with the donor, or

    (b) to any charity to whom the donor made or might have been expected to make gifts, if the value of each such gift is not unreasonable having regard to all the circumstances and, in particular, the size of the donor's estate.

(3) 'Customary occasion' means –

    (a) the occasion or anniversary of a birth, a marriage or the formation of a civil partnership, or

    (b) any other occasion on which presents are customarily given within families or among friends or associates.

(4) Subsection (2) is subject to any conditions or restrictions in the instrument.

13 Revocation of lasting powers of attorney etc.

(1) This section applies if –

    (a) P has executed an instrument with a view to creating a lasting power of attorney, or

    (b) a lasting power of attorney is registered as having been conferred by P,

and in this section references to revoking the power include revoking the instrument.

(2) P may, at any time when he has capacity to do so, revoke the power.

(3) P's bankruptcy revokes the power so far as it relates to P's property and affairs.

(4) But where P is bankrupt merely because an interim bankruptcy restrictions order has effect in respect of him, the power is suspended, so far as it relates to P's property and affairs, for so long as the order has effect.

(5) The occurrence in relation to a donee of an event mentioned in subsection (6) –

    (a) terminates his appointment, and

    (b) except in the cases given in subsection (7), revokes the power.

(6) The events are –

    (a) the disclaimer of the appointment by the donee in accordance with such require-ments as may be prescribed for the purposes of this section in regulations made by the Lord Chancellor,

    (b) subject to subsections (8) and (9), the death or bankruptcy of the donee or, if the donee is a trust corporation, its winding-up or dissolution,

    (c) subject to subsection (11), the dissolution or annulment of a marriage or civil partnership between the donor and the donee,

    (d) the lack of capacity of the donee.

(7) The cases are –

    (a) the donee is replaced under the terms of the instrument,

    (b) he is one of two or more persons appointed to act as donees jointly and severally in respect of any matter and, after the event, there is at least one remaining donee.

(8) The bankruptcy of a donee does not terminate his appointment, or revoke the power, in so far as his authority relates to P's personal welfare.

(9) Where the donee is bankrupt merely because an interim bankruptcy restrictions order has effect in respect of him, his appointment and the power are suspended, so far as they relate to P's property and affairs, for so long as the order has effect.

(10) Where the donee is one of two or more appointed to act jointly and severally under the power in respect of any matter, the reference in subsection (9) to the suspension of the power is to its suspension in so far as it relates to that donee.

(11) The dissolution or annulment of a marriage or civil partnership does not terminate the appointment of a donee, or revoke the power, if the instrument provided that it was not to do so.

14 Protection of donee and others if no power created or power revoked

(1) Subsections (2) and (3) apply if –

(a) an instrument has been registered under Schedule 1 as a lasting power of attorney, but

(b) a lasting power of attorney was not created,

whether or not the registration has been cancelled at the time of the act or transaction in question.

(2) A donee who acts in purported exercise of the power does not incur any liability (to P or any other person) because of the non-existence of the power unless at the time of acting he –

(a) knows that a lasting power of attorney was not created, or

(b) is aware of circumstances which, if a lasting power of attorney had been created, would have terminated his authority to act as a donee.

(3) Any transaction between the donee and another person is, in favour of that person, as valid as if the power had been in existence, unless at the time of the transaction that person has knowledge of a matter referred to in subsection (2).

(4) If the interest of a purchaser depends on whether a transaction between the donee and the other person was valid by virtue of subsection (3), it is conclusively presumed in favour of the purchaser that the transaction was valid if –

(a) the transaction was completed within 12 months of the date on which the instrument was registered, or

(b) the other person makes a statutory declaration, before or within 3 months after the completion of the purchase, that he had no reason at the time of the transaction to doubt that the donee had authority to dispose of the property which was the subject of the transaction.

(5) In its application to a lasting power of attorney which relates to matters in addition to P's property and affairs, section 5 of the Powers of Attorney Act 1971 (c. 27) (protection where power is revoked) has effect as if references to revocation included the cessation of the power in relation to P's property and affairs.

(6) Where two or more donees are appointed under a lasting power of attorney, this section applies as if references to the donee were to all or any of them.

General powers of the court and appointment of deputies

15 Power to make declarations

(1) The court may make declarations as to –

(a) whether a person has or lacks capacity to make a decision specified in the declaration;

(b) whether a person has or lacks capacity to make decisions on such matters as are described in the declaration;

(c) the lawfulness or otherwise of any act done, or yet to be done, in relation to that person.

(2) 'Act' includes an omission and a course of conduct.

16 Powers to make decisions and appoint deputies: general

(1) This section applies if a person ('P') lacks capacity in relation to a matter or matters concerning –

(a) P's personal welfare, or

(b) P's property and affairs.

(2) The court may –

(a) by making an order, make the decision or decisions on P's behalf in relation to the matter or matters, or

(b) appoint a person (a 'deputy') to make decisions on P's behalf in relation to the matter or matters.

(3) The powers of the court under this section are subject to the provisions of this Act and, in particular, to sections 1 (the principles) and 4 (best interests).

(4) When deciding whether it is in P's best interests to appoint a deputy, the court must have regard (in addition to the matters mentioned in section 4) to the principles that –

(a) a decision by the court is to be preferred to the appointment of a deputy to make a decision, and

(b) the powers conferred on a deputy should be as limited in scope and duration as is reasonably practicable in the circumstances.

(5) The court may make such further orders or give such directions, and confer on a deputy such powers or impose on him such duties, as it thinks necessary or expedient for giving effect to, or otherwise in connection with, an order or appointment made by it under subsection (2).

(6) Without prejudice to section 4, the court may make the order, give the directions or make the appointment on such terms as it considers are in P's best interests, even though no application is before the court for an order, directions or an appointment on those terms.

(7) An order of the court may be varied or discharged by a subsequent order.

(8) The court may, in particular, revoke the appointment of a deputy or vary the powers conferred on him if it is satisfied that the deputy –

(a) has behaved, or is behaving, in a way that contravenes the authority conferred on him by the court or is not in P's best interests, or

(b) proposes to behave in a way that would contravene that authority or would not be in P's best interests.

[16A Section 16 powers: Mental Health Act patients etc

(1) If a person is ineligible to be deprived of liberty by this Act, the court may not include in a welfare order provision which authorises the person to be deprived of his liberty.

(2) If –

(a) a welfare order includes provision which authorises a person to be deprived of his liberty, and

(b) that person becomes ineligible to be deprived of liberty by this Act,

the provision ceases to have effect for as long as the person remains ineligible.

(3) Nothing in subsection (2) affects the power of the court under section 16(7) to vary or discharge the welfare order.

(4) For the purposes of this section –

(a) Schedule 1A applies for determining whether or not P is ineligible to be deprived of liberty by this Act;

(b) 'welfare order' means an order under section 16(2)(a).]

Note:
Section 16A is inserted by Mental Health Act 2007, s.50(3) to come into force at a time appointed by the Secretary of State in a statutory instrument.

17 Section 16 powers: personal welfare

(1) The powers under section 16 as respects P's personal welfare extend in particular to –

(a) deciding where P is to live;

(b) deciding what contact, if any, P is to have with any specified persons;

(c) making an order prohibiting a named person from having contact with P;

(d) giving or refusing consent to the carrying out or continuation of a treatment by a person providing health care for P;

(e) giving a direction that a person responsible for P's health care allow a different person to take over that responsibility.

(2) Subsection (1) is subject to section 20 (restrictions on deputies).

18 Section 16 powers: property and affairs

(1) The powers under section 16 as respects P's property and affairs extend in particular to –

(a) the control and management of P's property;
(b) the sale, exchange, charging, gift or other disposition of P's property;
(c) the acquisition of property in P's name or on P's behalf;
(d) the carrying on, on P's behalf, of any profession, trade or business;
(e) the taking of a decision which will have the effect of dissolving a partnership of which P is a member;
(f) the carrying out of any contract entered into by P;
(g) the discharge of P's debts and of any of P's obligations, whether legally enforceable or not;
(h) the settlement of any of P's property, whether for P's benefit or for the benefit of others;
(i) the execution for P of a will;
(j) the exercise of any power (including a power to consent) vested in P whether beneficially or as trustee or otherwise;
(k) the conduct of legal proceedings in P's name or on P's behalf.

(2) No will may be made under subsection (1)(i) at a time when P has not reached 18.

(3) The powers under section 16 as respects any other matter relating to P's property and affairs may be exercised even though P has not reached 16, if the court considers it likely that P will still lack capacity to make decisions in respect of that matter when he reaches 18.

(4) Schedule 2 supplements the provisions of this section.

(5) Section 16(7) (variation and discharge of court orders) is subject to paragraph 6 of Schedule 2.

(6) Subsection (1) is subject to section 20 (restrictions on deputies).

19 Appointment of deputies

(1) A deputy appointed by the court must be –

(a) an individual who has reached 18, or
(b) as respects powers in relation to property and affairs, an individual who has reached 18 or a trust corporation.

(2) The court may appoint an individual by appointing the holder for the time being of a specified office or position.

(3) A person may not be appointed as a deputy without his consent.

(4) The court may appoint two or more deputies to act –

(a) jointly,
(b) jointly and severally, or
(c) jointly in respect of some matters and jointly and severally in respect of others.

(5) When appointing a deputy or deputies, the court may at the same time appoint one or more other persons to succeed the existing deputy or those deputies –

(a) in such circumstances, or on the happening of such events, as may be specified by the court;
(b) for such period as may be so specified.

(6) A deputy is to be treated as P's agent in relation to anything done or decided by him within the scope of his appointment and in accordance with this Part.

(7) The deputy is entitled –

(a) to be reimbursed out of P's property for his reasonable expenses in discharging his functions, and

(b) if the court so directs when appointing him, to remuneration out of P's property for discharging them.

(8) The court may confer on a deputy powers to –

(a) take possession or control of all or any specified part of P's property;

(b) exercise all or any specified powers in respect of it, including such powers of investment as the court may determine.

(9) The court may require a deputy –

(a) to give to the Public Guardian such security as the court thinks fit for the due discharge of his functions, and

(b) to submit to the Public Guardian such reports at such times or at such intervals as the court may direct.

20 Restrictions on deputies

(1) A deputy does not have power to make a decision on behalf of P in relation to a matter if he knows or has reasonable grounds for believing that P has capacity in relation to the matter.

(2) Nothing in section 16(5) or 17 permits a deputy to be given power –

(a) to prohibit a named person from having contact with P;

(b) to direct a person responsible for P's health care to allow a different person to take over that responsibility.

(3) A deputy may not be given powers with respect to –

(a) the settlement of any of P's property, whether for P's benefit or for the benefit of others,

(b) the execution for P of a will, or

(c) the exercise of any power (including a power to consent) vested in P whether beneficially or as trustee or otherwise.

(4) A deputy may not be given power to make a decision on behalf of P which is inconsistent with a decision made, within the scope of his authority and in accordance with this Act, by the donee of a lasting power of attorney granted by P (or, if there is more than one donee, by any of them).

(5) A deputy may not refuse consent to the carrying out or continuation of life-sustaining treatment in relation to P.

(6) The authority conferred on a deputy is subject to the provisions of this Act and, in particular, sections 1 (the principles) and 4 (best interests).

(7) A deputy may not do an act that is intended to restrain P unless four conditions are satisfied.

(8) The first condition is that, in doing the act, the deputy is acting within the scope of an authority expressly conferred on him by the court.

(9) The second is that P lacks, or the deputy reasonably believes that P lacks, capacity in relation to the matter in question.

(10) The third is that the deputy reasonably believes that it is necessary to do the act in order to prevent harm to P.

(11) The fourth is that the act is a proportionate response to –

(a) the likelihood of P's suffering harm, ~~or~~ and

(b) the seriousness of that harm.

(12) For the purposes of this section, a deputy restrains P if he –

(a) uses, or threatens to use, force to secure the doing of an act which P resists, or

(b) restricts P's liberty of movement, whether or not P resists,

or if he authorises another person to do any of those things.

(13) [*But a deputy does more than merely restrain P if he deprives P of his liberty within the meaning of Article 5(1) of the Human Rights Convention (whether or not the deputy is a public authority).*]

Notes:
In s.20(11)(a) 'or' is replaced with 'and' by Mental Health Act 2007, s.51 with effect on 1 October 2007 by the Mental Health Act (Commencement No.2) Order 2007, SI 2007/2635.
Section 20(13) is omitted by Mental Health Act 2007, s.50(4)(c) at a time to be appointed by the Secretary of State in a statutory instrument.

21 Transfer of proceedings relating to people under 18

[(1)] The [Lord Chief Justice, with the concurrence of the Lord Chancellor,] [~~Lord Chancellor~~] may by order make provision as to the transfer of proceedings relating to a person under 18, in such circumstances as are specified in the order –

(a)   from the Court of Protection to a court having jurisdiction under the Children Act 1989 (c. 41), or

(b)   from a court having jurisdiction under that Act to the Court of Protection.

[(2) The Lord Chief Justice may nominate any of the following to exercise his functions under this section –

(a)   the President of the Court of Protection;

(b)   a judicial office holder (as defined in section 109(4) of the Constitutional Reform Act 2005).]

Note:
Section 21 is amended by The Lord Chancellor (Transfer of Functions and Supplmentary Provisions) (No.2) Order 2006, SI 2006/1016, Sched.1, para.31 which came into force on 3 April 2006.

[*Powers of the court in relation to Schedule A1*

21A *Powers of court in relation to Schedule A1*

(1)   *This section applies if either of the following has been given under Schedule A1 –*

(a)   *a standard authorisation;*

(b)   *an urgent authorisation.*

(2)   *Where a standard authorisation has been given, the court may determine any question relating to any of the following matters –*

(a)   *whether the relevant person meets one or more of the qualifying requirements;*

(b)   *the period during which the standard authorisation is to be in force;*

(c)   *the purpose for which the standard authorisation is given;*

(d)   *the conditions subject to which the standard authorisation is given.*

(3)   *If the court determines any question under subsection (2), the court may make an order –*

(a)   *varying or terminating the standard authorisation, or*

(b)   *directing the supervisory body to vary or terminate the standard authorisation.*

(4)   *Where an urgent authorisation has been given, the court may determine any question relating to any of the following matters –*

(a)   *whether the urgent authorisation should have been given;*

(b)   *the period during which the urgent authorisation is to be in force;*

(c)   *the purpose for which the urgent authorisation is given.*

(5)   *Where the court determines any question under subsection (4), the court may make an order –*

(a) *varying or terminating the urgent authorisation, or*

(b) *directing the managing authority of the relevant hospital or care home to vary or terminate the urgent authorisation.*

(6) *Where the court makes an order under subsection (3) or (5), the court may make an order about a person's liability for any act done in connection with the standard or urgent authorisation before its variation or termination.*

(7) *An order under subsection (6) may, in particular, exclude a person from liability.*]

Note:
Section 21A is inserted by Mental Health Act 2007, Sched.9, para.2 which is brought into effect by Mental Health Act 2007, s.50(7) at a time appointed by the Secretary of State in a statutory instrument.

Powers of the court in relation to lasting powers of attorney

22 Powers of court in relation to validity of lasting powers of attorney

(1) This section and section 23 apply if –

(a) a person ('P') has executed or purported to execute an instrument with a view to creating a lasting power of attorney, or

(b) an instrument has been registered as a lasting power of attorney conferred by P.

(2) The court may determine any question relating to –

(a) whether one or more of the requirements for the creation of a lasting power of attorney have been met;

(b) whether the power has been revoked or has otherwise come to an end.

(3) Subsection (4) applies if the court is satisfied –

(a) that fraud or undue pressure was used to induce P –

(i)   to execute an instrument for the purpose of creating a lasting power of attorney, or

(ii) to create a lasting power of attorney, or

(b) that the donee (or, if more than one, any of them) of a lasting power of attorney –

(i)   has behaved, or is behaving, in a way that contravenes his authority or is not in P's best interests, or

(ii) proposes to behave in a way that would contravene his authority or would not be in P's best interests.

(4) The court may –

(a) direct that an instrument purporting to create the lasting power of attorney is not to be registered, or

(b) if P lacks capacity to do so, revoke the instrument or the lasting power of attorney.

(5) If there is more than one donee, the court may under subsection (4)(b) revoke the instrument or the lasting power of attorney so far as it relates to any of them.

(6) 'Donee' includes an intended donee.

23 Powers of court in relation to operation of lasting powers of attorney

(1) The court may determine any question as to the meaning or effect of a lasting power of attorney or an instrument purporting to create one.

(2) The court may –

(a) give directions with respect to decisions –

(i)   which the donee of a lasting power of attorney has authority to make, and
(ii)   which P lacks capacity to make;

(b) give any consent or authorisation to act which the donee would have to obtain from P if P had capacity to give it.

(3) The court may, if P lacks capacity to do so –

(a) give directions to the donee with respect to the rendering by him of reports or accounts and the production of records kept by him for that purpose;
(b) require the donee to supply information or produce documents or things in his possession as donee;
(c) give directions with respect to the remuneration or expenses of the donee;
(d) relieve the donee wholly or partly from any liability which he has or may have incurred on account of a breach of his duties as donee.

(4) The court may authorise the making of gifts which are not within section 12(2) (permitted gifts).

(5) Where two or more donees are appointed under a lasting power of attorney, this section applies as if references to the donee were to all or any of them.

Advance decisions to refuse treatment

24 Advance decisions to refuse treatment: general

(1) 'Advance decision' means a decision made by a person ('P'), after he has reached 18 and when he has capacity to do so, that if –

(a) at a later time and in such circumstances as he may specify, a specified treatment is proposed to be carried out or continued by a person providing health care for him, and
(b) at that time he lacks capacity to consent to the carrying out or continuation of the treatment,

the specified treatment is not to be carried out or continued.

(2) For the purposes of subsection (1)(a), a decision may be regarded as specifying a treatment or circumstances even though expressed in layman's terms.

(3) P may withdraw or alter an advance decision at any time when he has capacity to do so.

(4) A withdrawal (including a partial withdrawal) need not be in writing.

(5) An alteration of an advance decision need not be in writing (unless section 25(5) applies in relation to the decision resulting from the alteration).

25 Validity and applicability of advance decisions

(1) An advance decision does not affect the liability which a person may incur for carrying out or continuing a treatment in relation to P unless the decision is at the material time –

(a) valid, and
(b) applicable to the treatment.

(2) An advance decision is not valid if P –

(a) has withdrawn the decision at a time when he had capacity to do so,
(b) has, under a lasting power of attorney created after the advance decision was made, conferred authority on the donee (or, if more than one, any of them) to give or refuse consent to the treatment to which the advance decision relates, or
(c) has done anything else clearly inconsistent with the advance decision remaining his fixed decision.

(3) An advance decision is not applicable to the treatment in question if at the material time P has capacity to give or refuse consent to it.

(4) An advance decision is not applicable to the treatment in question if –

    (a) that treatment is not the treatment specified in the advance decision,

    (b) any circumstances specified in the advance decision are absent, or

    (c) there are reasonable grounds for believing that circumstances exist which P did not anticipate at the time of the advance decision and which would have affected his decision had he anticipated them.

(5) An advance decision is not applicable to life-sustaining treatment unless –

    (a) the decision is verified by a statement by P to the effect that it is to apply to that treatment even if life is at risk, and

    (b) the decision and statement comply with subsection (6).

(6) A decision or statement complies with this subsection only if –

    (a) it is in writing,

    (b) it is signed by P or by another person in P's presence and by P's direction,

    (c) the signature is made or acknowledged by P in the presence of a witness, and

    (d) the witness signs it, or acknowledges his signature, in P's presence.

(7) The existence of any lasting power of attorney other than one of a description mentioned in subsection (2)(b) does not prevent the advance decision from being regarded as valid and applicable.

26 Effect of advance decisions

(1) If P has made an advance decision which is –

    (a) valid, and

    (b) applicable to a treatment,

the decision has effect as if he had made it, and had had capacity to make it, at the time when the question arises whether the treatment should be carried out or continued.

(2) A person does not incur liability for carrying out or continuing the treatment unless, at the time, he is satisfied that an advance decision exists which is valid and applicable to the treatment.

(3) A person does not incur liability for the consequences of withholding or withdrawing a treatment from P if, at the time, he reasonably believes that an advance decision exists which is valid and applicable to the treatment.

(4) The court may make a declaration as to whether an advance decision –

    (a) exists;

    (b) is valid;

    (c) is applicable to a treatment.

(5) Nothing in an apparent advance decision stops a person –

    (a) providing life-sustaining treatment, or

    (b) doing any act he reasonably believes to be necessary to prevent a serious deterioration in P's condition,

while a decision as respects any relevant issue is sought from the court.

Excluded decisions

27 Family relationships etc.

(1) Nothing in this Act permits a decision on any of the following matters to be made on behalf of a person –

    (a) consenting to marriage or a civil partnership,

    (b) consenting to have sexual relations,

(c)   consenting to a decree of divorce being granted on the basis of two years' separation,

(d)   consenting to a dissolution order being made in relation to a civil partnership on the basis of two years' separation,

(e)   consenting to a child's being placed for adoption by an adoption agency,

(f)   consenting to the making of an adoption order,

(g)   discharging parental responsibilities in matters not relating to a child's property,

(h)   giving a consent under the Human Fertilisation and Embryology Act 1990 (c. 37).

(2)   'Adoption order' means –

(a)   an adoption order within the meaning of the Adoption and Children Act 2002 (c. 38) (including a future adoption order), and

(b)   an order under section 84 of that Act (parental responsibility prior to adoption abroad).

28 Mental Health Act matters

(1)   Nothing in this Act authorises anyone –

(a)   to give a patient medical treatment for mental disorder, or

(b)   to consent to a patient's being given medical treatment for mental disorder,

if, at the time when it is proposed to treat the patient, his treatment is regulated by Part 4 of the Mental Health Act.

[(1A) *Subsection (1) does not apply in relation to any form of treatment to which section 58A of that Act (electro-convulsive therapy, etc.) applies if the patient comes within subsection (7) of that section (informal patient under 18 who cannot give consent).*]

[(1B) *Section 5 does not apply to an act to which section 64B of the Mental Health Act applies (treatment of community patients not recalled to hospital).*]

Notes:
Section 28(1A) is inserted by Mental Health Act 2007, s.28(10) to come into effect at a time appointed by the Secretary of State in a statutory instrument.
Section 28(1B) is inserted by Mental Health Act 2007, s.35(5) to come into effect at a time appointed by the Secretary of State in a statutory instrument.

(2)   'Medical treatment', 'mental disorder' and 'patient' have the same meaning as in that Act.

29 Voting rights

(1)   Nothing in this Act permits a decision on voting at an election for any public office, or at a referendum, to be made on behalf of a person.

(2)   'Referendum' has the same meaning as in section 101 of the Political Parties, Elections and Referendums Act 2000 (c. 41).

Research

30 Research

(1)   Intrusive research carried out on, or in relation to, a person who lacks capacity to consent to it is unlawful unless it is carried out –

(a)   as part of a research project which is for the time being approved by the appropriate body for the purposes of this Act in accordance with section 31, and

(b)   in accordance with sections 32 and 33.

(2)   Research is intrusive if it is of a kind that would be unlawful if it was carried out –

(a)   on or in relation to a person who had capacity to consent to it, but

(b)   without his consent.

(3) A clinical trial which is subject to the provisions of clinical trials regulations is not to be treated as research for the purposes of this section.

(4) 'Appropriate body', in relation to a research project, means the person, committee or other body specified in regulations made by the appropriate authority as the appropriate body in relation to a project of the kind in question.

(5) 'Clinical trials regulations' means –

(a) the Medicines for Human Use (Clinical Trials) Regulations 2004 (SI 2004/1031) and any other regulations replacing those regulations or amending them, and

(b) any other regulations relating to clinical trials and designated by the Secretary of State as clinical trials regulations for the purposes of this section.

(6) In this section, section 32 and section 34, 'appropriate authority' means –

(a) in relation to the carrying out of research in England, the Secretary of State, and

(b) in relation to the carrying out of research in Wales, the National Assembly for Wales.

31 Requirements for approval

(1) The appropriate body may not approve a research project for the purposes of this Act unless satisfied that the following requirements will be met in relation to research carried out as part of the project on, or in relation to, a person who lacks capacity to consent to taking part in the project ('P').

(2) The research must be connected with –

(a) an impairing condition affecting P, or

(b) its treatment.

(3) 'Impairing condition' means a condition which is (or may be) attributable to, or which causes or contributes to (or may cause or contribute to), the impairment of, or disturbance in the functioning of, the mind or brain.

(4) There must be reasonable grounds for believing that research of comparable effectiveness cannot be carried out if the project has to be confined to, or relate only to, persons who have capacity to consent to taking part in it.

(5) The research must –

(a) have the potential to benefit P without imposing on P a burden that is disproportionate to the potential benefit to P, or

(b) be intended to provide knowledge of the causes or treatment of, or of the care of persons affected by, the same or a similar condition.

(6) If the research falls within paragraph (b) of subsection (5) but not within paragraph (a), there must be reasonable grounds for believing –

(a) that the risk to P from taking part in the project is likely to be negligible, and

(b) that anything done to, or in relation to, P will not –

(i) interfere with P's freedom of action or privacy in a significant way, or

(ii) be unduly invasive or restrictive.

(7) There must be reasonable arrangements in place for ensuring that the requirements of sections 32 and 33 will be met.

32 Consulting carers etc.

(1) This section applies if a person ('R') –

(a) is conducting an approved research project, and

(b) wishes to carry out research, as part of the project, on or in relation to a person ('P') who lacks capacity to consent to taking part in the project.

(2) R must take reasonable steps to identify a person who –

(a) otherwise than in a professional capacity or for remuneration, is engaged in caring for P or is interested in P's welfare, and

(b) is prepared to be consulted by R under this section.

(3) If R is unable to identify such a person he must, in accordance with guidance issued by the appropriate authority, nominate a person who –

(a) is prepared to be consulted by R under this section, but
(b) has no connection with the project.

(4) R must provide the person identified under subsection (2), or nominated under subsection (3), with information about the project and ask him –

(a) for advice as to whether P should take part in the project, and
(b) what, in his opinion, P's wishes and feelings about taking part in the project would be likely to be if P had capacity in relation to the matter.

(5) If, at any time, the person consulted advises R that in his opinion P's wishes and feelings would be likely to lead him to decline to take part in the project (or to wish to withdraw from it) if he had capacity in relation to the matter, R must ensure –

(a) if P is not already taking part in the project, that he does not take part in it;
(b) if P is taking part in the project, that he is withdrawn from it.

(6) But subsection (5)(b) does not require treatment that P has been receiving as part of the project to be discontinued if R has reasonable grounds for believing that there would be a significant risk to P's health if it were discontinued.

(7) The fact that a person is the donee of a lasting power of attorney given by P, or is P's deputy, does not prevent him from being the person consulted under this section.

(8) Subsection (9) applies if treatment is being, or is about to be, provided for P as a matter of urgency and R considers that, having regard to the nature of the research and of the particular circumstances of the case –

(a) it is also necessary to take action for the purposes of the research as a matter of urgency, but
(b) it is not reasonably practicable to consult under the previous provisions of this section.

(9) R may take the action if –

(a) he has the agreement of a registered medical practitioner who is not involved in the organisation or conduct of the research project, or
(b) where it is not reasonably practicable in the time available to obtain that agreement, he acts in accordance with a procedure approved by the appropriate body at the time when the research project was approved under section 31.

(10) But R may not continue to act in reliance on subsection (9) if he has reasonable grounds for believing that it is no longer necessary to take the action as a matter of urgency.

33 Additional safeguards

(1) This section applies in relation to a person who is taking part in an approved research project even though he lacks capacity to consent to taking part.

(2) Nothing may be done to, or in relation to, him in the course of the research –

(a) to which he appears to object (whether by showing signs of resistance or otherwise) except where what is being done is intended to protect him from harm or to reduce or prevent pain or discomfort, or
(b) which would be contrary to –

(i)   an advance decision of his which has effect, or
(ii) any other form of statement made by him and not subsequently withdrawn,

of which R is aware.

(3) The interests of the person must be assumed to outweigh those of science and society.

(4) If he indicates (in any way) that he wishes to be withdrawn from the project he must be withdrawn without delay.

(5) P must be withdrawn from the project, without delay, if at any time the person conducting the research has reasonable grounds for believing that one or more of the requirements set out in section 31(2) to (7) is no longer met in relation to research being carried out on, or in relation to, P.

(6) But neither subsection (4) nor subsection (5) requires treatment that P has been receiving as part of the project to be discontinued if R has reasonable grounds for believing that there would be a significant risk to P's health if it were discontinued.

34 Loss of capacity during research project

(1) This section applies where a person ('P') –

(a) has consented to take part in a research project begun before the commencement of section 30, but

(b) before the conclusion of the project, loses capacity to consent to continue to take part in it.

(2) The appropriate authority may by regulations provide that, despite P's loss of capacity, research of a prescribed kind may be carried out on, or in relation to, P if –

(a) the project satisfies prescribed requirements,

(b) any information or material relating to P which is used in the research is of a prescribed description and was obtained before P's loss of capacity, and

(c) the person conducting the project takes in relation to P such steps as may be prescribed for the purpose of protecting him.

(3) The regulations may, in particular, –

(a) make provision about when, for the purposes of the regulations, a project is to be treated as having begun;

(b) include provision similar to any made by section 31, 32 or 33.

Independent mental capacity advocate service

35 Appointment of independent mental capacity advocates

(1) The appropriate authority must make such arrangements as it considers reasonable to enable persons ('independent mental capacity advocates') to be available to represent and support persons to whom acts or decisions proposed under sections 37, 38 and 39 relate [*or persons who fall within section 39A, 39C or 39D*].

(2) The appropriate authority may make regulations as to the appointment of independent mental capacity advocates.

(3) The regulations may, in particular, provide –

(a) that a person may act as an independent mental capacity advocate only in such circumstances, or only subject to such conditions, as may be prescribed;

(b) for the appointment of a person as an independent mental capacity advocate to be subject to approval in accordance with the regulations.

(4) In making arrangements under subsection (1), the appropriate authority must have regard to the principle that a person to whom a proposed act or decision relates should, so far as practicable, be represented and supported by a person who is independent of any person who will be responsible for the act or decision.

(5) The arrangements may include provision for payments to be made to, or in relation to, persons carrying out functions in accordance with the arrangements.

(6) For the purpose of enabling him to carry out his functions, an independent mental capacity advocate –

(a) may interview in private the person whom he has been instructed to represent, and

(b) may, at all reasonable times, examine and take copies of –

   (i)   any health record,
   (ii) any record of, or held by, a local authority and compiled in connection with
         a social services function, and
   (iii) any record held by a person registered under Part 2 of the Care Standards
         Act 2000 (c. 14),

which the person holding the record considers may be relevant to the independent
mental capacity advocate's investigation.

(7) In this section, section 36 and section 37, 'the appropriate authority' means –

   (a) in relation to the provision of the services of independent mental capacity
        advocates in England, the Secretary of State, and
   (b) in relation to the provision of the services of independent mental capacity
        advocates in Wales, the National Assembly for Wales.

Note:
Section 35(1) is amended by Mental Health Act 2007, Sched.9, para.3 to come into effect
at a time appointed by the Secretary of State in a statutory instrument.

36 Functions of independent mental capacity advocates

(1) The appropriate authority may make regulations as to the functions of independent
     mental capacity advocates.
(2) The regulations may, in particular, make provision requiring an advocate to take such
     steps as may be prescribed for the purpose of –

   (a) providing support to the person whom he has been instructed to represent ('P')
        so that P may participate as fully as possible in any relevant decision;
   (b) obtaining and evaluating relevant information;
   (c) ascertaining what P's wishes and feelings would be likely to be, and the beliefs
        and values that would be likely to influence P, if he had capacity;
   (d) ascertaining what alternative courses of action are available in relation to P;
   (e) obtaining a further medical opinion where treatment is proposed and the
        advocate thinks that one should be obtained.

(3) The regulations may also make provision as to circumstances in which the advocate
     may challenge, or provide assistance for the purpose of challenging, any relevant
     decision.

37 Provision of serious medical treatment by NHS body

(1) This section applies if an NHS body –

   (a) is proposing to provide, or secure the provision of, serious medical treatment for
        a person ('P') who lacks capacity to consent to the treatment, and
   (b) is satisfied that there is no person, other than one engaged in providing care or
        treatment for P in a professional capacity or for remuneration, whom it would be
        appropriate to consult in determining what would be in P's best interests.

(2) But this section does not apply if P's treatment is regulated by Part 4 [or 4A] of the
     Mental Health Act.
(3) Before the treatment is provided, the NHS body must instruct an independent mental
     capacity advocate to represent P.
(4) If the treatment needs to be provided as a matter of urgency, it may be provided even
     though the NHS body has not been able to comply with subsection (3).
(5) The NHS body must, in providing or securing the provision of treatment for P, take
     into account any information given, or submissions made, by the independent men-
     tal capacity advocate.
(6) 'Serious medical treatment' means treatment which involves providing, withholding or
     withdrawing treatment of a kind prescribed by regulations made by the appropriate
     authority.

(7) 'NHS body' has such meaning as may be prescribed by regulations made for the purposes of this section by –

    (a) the Secretary of State, in relation to bodies in England, or

    (b) the National Assembly for Wales, in relation to bodies in Wales.

Note:
Section 37(2) is amended by Mental Health Act 2007, s.35(6) to come into effect at a time appointed by the Secretary of State in a statutory instrument.

38 Provision of accommodation by NHS body

(1) This section applies if an NHS body proposes to make arrangements –

    (a) for the provision of accommodation in a hospital or care home for a person ('P') who lacks capacity to agree to the arrangements, or

    (b) for a change in P's accommodation to another hospital or care home,

and is satisfied that there is no person, other than one engaged in providing care or treatment for P in a professional capacity or for remuneration, whom it would be appropriate for it to consult in determining what would be in P's best interests.

(2) But this section does not apply if P is accommodated as a result of an obligation imposed on him under the Mental Health Act.

[(2A) *And this section does not apply if –*

    (a) *an independent mental capacity advocate must be appointed under section 39A or 39C (whether or not by the NHS body) to represent P, and*

    (b) *the hospital or care home in which P is to be accommodated under the arrangements referred to in this section is the relevant hospital or care home under the authorisation referred to in that section.*]

(3) Before making the arrangements, the NHS body must instruct an independent mental capacity advocate to represent P unless it is satisfied that –

    (a) the accommodation is likely to be provided for a continuous period which is less than the applicable period, or

    (b) the arrangements need to be made as a matter of urgency.

(4) If the NHS body –

    (a) did not instruct an independent mental capacity advocate to represent P before making the arrangements because it was satisfied that subsection (3)(a) or (b) applied, but

    (b) subsequently has reason to believe that the accommodation is likely to be provided for a continuous period –

        (i) beginning with the day on which accommodation was first provided in accordance with the arrangements, and

        (ii) ending on or after the expiry of the applicable period,

it must instruct an independent mental capacity advocate to represent P.

(5) The NHS body must, in deciding what arrangements to make for P, take into account any information given, or submissions made, by the independent mental capacity advocate.

(6) 'Care home' has the meaning given in section 3 of the Care Standards Act 2000 (c. 14).

(7) 'Hospital' means –

    (a) a health service hospital as defined by [section 275 of the National Health Service Act 2006 or section 206 of the National Health Service (Wales) Act 2006], or

    (b) an independent hospital as defined by section 2 of the Care Standards Act 2000.

(8) 'NHS body' has such meaning as may be prescribed by regulations made for the purposes of this section by –

(a)   the Secretary of State, in relation to bodies in England, or

(b)   the National Assembly for Wales, in relation to bodies in Wales.

(9) 'Applicable period' means –

(a)   in relation to accommodation in a hospital, 28 days, and

(b)   in relation to accommodation in a care home, 8 weeks.

[(10)   For the purposes of subsection (1), a person appointed under Part 10 of Schedule A1 to be P's representative is not, by virtue of that appointment, engaged in providing care or treatment for P in a professional capacity or for remuneration.]

Notes:
Section 38(2A) is inserted by Mental Health Act 2007, Sched.9, para.4(2) to come into effect at a time appointed by the Secretary of State in a statutory instrument.
Section 38(7) is amended by the National Health Service (Consequential Provisions) Act 2006, Sched.1, para.278 on 1 March 2007.
Section 38(10) is inserted by Mental Health Act 2007, Sched.9, para.4(3) to come into effect at a time appointed by the Secretary of State in a statutory instrument.

39 Provision of accommodation by local authority

(1) This section applies if a local authority propose to make arrangements –

(a)   for the provision of residential accommodation for a person ('P') who lacks capacity to agree to the arrangements, or

(b)   for a change in P's residential accommodation,

and are satisfied that there is no person, other than one engaged in providing care or treatment for P in a professional capacity or for remuneration, whom it would be appropriate for them to consult in determining what would be in P's best interests.

(2) But this section applies only if the accommodation is to be provided in accordance with –

(a)   section 21 or 29 of the National Assistance Act 1948 (c. 29), or

(b)   section 117 of the Mental Health Act,

as the result of a decision taken by the local authority under section 47 of the National Health Service and Community Care Act 1990 (c. 19).

(3) This section does not apply if P is accommodated as a result of an obligation imposed on him under the Mental Health Act.

[(3A)   And this section does not apply if –

(a)   an independent mental capacity advocate must be appointed under section 39A or 39C (whether or not by the local authority) to represent P, and

(b)   the place in which P is to be accommodated under the arrangements referred to in this section is the relevant hospital or care home under the authorisation referred to in that section.]

(4) Before making the arrangements, the local authority must instruct an independent mental capacity advocate to represent P unless they are satisfied that –

(a)   the accommodation is likely to be provided for a continuous period of less than 8 weeks, or

(b)   the arrangements need to be made as a matter of urgency.

(5) If the local authority –

(a)   did not instruct an independent mental capacity advocate to represent P before making the arrangements because they were satisfied that subsection (4)(a) or (b) applied, but

(b)   subsequently have reason to believe that the accommodation is likely to be provided for a continuous period that will end 8 weeks or more after the day on which accommodation was first provided in accordance with the arrangements,

they must instruct an independent mental capacity advocate to represent P.

(6) The local authority must, in deciding what arrangements to make for P, take into account any information given, or submissions made, by the independent mental capacity advocate.

[(7) *For the purposes of subsection (1), a person appointed under Part 10 of Schedule A1 to be P's representative is not, by virtue of that appointment, engaged in providing care or treatment for P in a professional capacity or for remuneration.*]

Notes:
Section 39(3A) is inserted by Mental Health Act 2007, Sched.9, para.5(2) to come into effect at a time appointed by the Secretary of State in a statutory instrument.
Section 39(7) is inserted by Mental Health Act 2007, Sched.9, para.5(3) to come into effect at a time appointed by the Secretary of State in a statutory instrument.

[*39A Person becomes subject to Schedule A1*

(1) *This section applies if –*
   (a) *a person ('P') becomes subject to Schedule A1, and*
   (b) *the managing authority of the relevant hospital or care home are satisfied that there is no person, other than one engaged in providing care or treatment for P in a professional capacity or for remuneration, whom it would be appropriate to consult in determining what would be in P's best interests.*

(2) *The managing authority must notify the supervisory body that this section applies.*
(3) *The supervisory body must instruct an independent mental capacity advocate to represent P.*
(4) *Schedule A1 makes provision about the role of an independent mental capacity advocate appointed under this section.*
(5) *This section is subject to paragraph 161 of Schedule A1.*
(6) *For the purposes of subsection (1), a person appointed under Part 10 of Schedule A1 to be P's representative is not, by virtue of that appointment, engaged in providing care or treatment for P in a professional capacity or for remuneration.*]

Note:
Section 39A is inserted by Mental Health Act 2007, Sched.9, para.6 to come into effect at a time appointed by the Secretary of State in a statutory instrument.

[*39B Section 39A: supplementary provision*

(1) *This section applies for the purposes of section 39A.*
(2) *P becomes subject to Schedule A1 in any of the following cases.*
(3) *The first case is where an urgent authorisation is given in relation to P under paragraph 76(2) of Schedule A1 (urgent authorisation given before request made for standard authorisation).*
(4) *The second case is where the following conditions are met.*
(5) *The first condition is that a request is made under Schedule A1 for a standard authorisation to be given in relation to P ('the requested authorisation').*
(6) *The second condition is that no urgent authorisation was given under paragraph 76(2) of Schedule A1 before that request was made.*
(7) *The third condition is that the requested authorisation will not be in force on or before, or immediately after, the expiry of an existing standard authorisation.*
(8) *The expiry of a standard authorisation is the date when the authorisation is expected to cease to be in force.*
(9) *The third case is where, under paragraph 69 of Schedule A1, the supervisory body select a person to carry out an assessment of whether or not the relevant person is a detained resident.*]

Note:
Section 39B is inserted by Mental Health Act 2007, Sched.9, para.6 to come into effect at a time appointed by the Secretary of State in a statutory instrument.

[*39C Person unrepresented whilst subject to Schedule A1*

(1) *This section applies if –*

    (a) *an authorisation under Schedule A1 is in force in relation to a person ('P'),*

    (b) *the appointment of a person as P's representative ends in accordance with regulations made under Part 10 of Schedule A1, and*

    (c) *the managing authority of the relevant hospital or care home are satisfied that there is no person, other than one engaged in providing care or treatment for P in a professional capacity or for remuneration, whom it would be appropriate to consult in determining what would be in P's best interests.*

(2) *The managing authority must notify the supervisory body that this section applies.*

(3) *The supervisory body must instruct an independent mental capacity advocate to represent P.*

(4) *Paragraph 159 of Schedule A1 makes provision about the role of an independent mental capacity advocate appointed under this section.*

(5) *The appointment of an independent mental capacity advocate under this section ends when a new appointment of a person as P's representative is made in accordance with Part 10 of Schedule A1.*

(6) *For the purposes of subsection (1), a person appointed under Part 10 of Schedule A1 to be P's representative is not, by virtue of that appointment, engaged in providing care or treatment for P in a professional capacity or for remuneration.*]

Note:
Section 39C is inserted by Mental Health Act 2007, Sched.9, para.6 to come into effect at a time appointed by the Secretary of State in a statutory instrument.

[*39D Person subject to Schedule A1 without paid representative*

(1) *This section applies if –*

    (a) *an authorisation under Schedule A1 is in force in relation to a person ('P'),*

    (b) *P has a representative ('R') appointed under Part 10 of Schedule A1, and*

    (c) *R is not being paid under regulations under Part 10 of Schedule A1 for acting as P's representative.*

(2) *The supervisory body must instruct an independent mental capacity advocate to represent P in any of the following cases.*

(3) *The first case is where P makes a request to the supervisory body to instruct an advocate.*

(4) *The second case is where R makes a request to the supervisory body to instruct an advocate.*

(5) *The third case is where the supervisory body have reason to believe one or more of the following –*

    (a) *that, without the help of an advocate, P and R would be unable to exercise one or both of the relevant rights;*

    (b) *that P and R have each failed to exercise a relevant right when it would have been reasonable to exercise it;*

    (c) *that P and R are each unlikely to exercise a relevant right when it would be reasonable to exercise it.*

(6) *The duty in subsection (2) is subject to section 39E.*

(7) *If an advocate is appointed under this section, the advocate is, in particular, to take such steps as are practicable to help P and R to understand the following matters –*

    (a) *the effect of the authorisation;*

    (b) *the purpose of the authorisation;*

(c) the duration of the authorisation;

(d) any conditions to which the authorisation is subject;

(e) the reasons why each assessor who carried out an assessment in connection with the request for the authorisation, or in connection with a review of the authorisation, decided that P met the qualifying requirement in question;

(f) the relevant rights;

(g) how to exercise the relevant rights.

(8) The advocate is, in particular, to take such steps as are practicable to help P or R –

(a) to exercise the right to apply to court, if it appears to the advocate that P or R wishes to exercise that right, or

(b) to exercise the right of review, if it appears to the advocate that P or R wishes to exercise that right.

(9) If the advocate helps P or R to exercise the right of review –

(a) the advocate may make submissions to the supervisory body on the question of whether a qualifying requirement is reviewable;

(b) the advocate may give information, or make submissions, to any assessor carrying out a review assessment.

(10) In this section –

'relevant rights' means –

(a) the right to apply to court, and

(b) the right of review;

'right to apply to court' means the right to make an application to the court to exercise its jurisdiction under section 21A;

'right of review' means the right under Part 8 of Schedule A1 to request a review.]

Note:
Section 39D is inserted by Mental Health Act 2007, Sched.9, para.6 to come into effect at a time appointed by the Secretary of State in a statutory instrument.

[39E Limitation on duty to instruct advocate under section 39D

(1) This section applies if an advocate is already representing P in accordance with an instruction under section 39D.

(2) Section 39D(2) does not require another advocate to be instructed, unless the following conditions are met.

(3) The first condition is that the existing advocate was instructed –

(a) because of a request by R, or

(b) because the supervisory body had reason to believe one or more of the things in section 39D(5).

(4) The second condition is that the other advocate would be instructed because of a request by P.]

Note:
Section 39E is inserted by Mental Health Act 2007, Sched.9, para.6 to come into effect at a time appointed by the Secretary of State in a statutory instrument.

[40 Exceptions

[(1)]   The duty imposed by section 37(3), 38(3) or (4) or [39(4) or (5)] [39(4) or (5), 39A(3), 39C(3) or 39D(2)] does not apply where there is –

(a) a person nominated by P (in whatever manner) as a person to be consulted on matters to which that duty relates,

(b) a donee of a lasting power of attorney created by P who is authorised to make decisions in relation to those matters, or

(c) a deputy appointed by the court for P with power to make decisions in relation to those matters.]

[(2) *A person appointed under Part 10 of Schedule A1 to be P's representative is not, by virtue of that appointment, a person nominated by P as a person to be consulted in matters to which a duty mentioned in subsection (1) relates.*]

Notes:
Section 40 is substituted by Mental Health Act 2007, s.49 and brought into effect by the Mental Health Act 2007 (Commencement No.3) Order 2007, SI 2007/2798, para.2(h).
Section 40 is renumbered 40(1) by Mental Health Act 2007, Sched.9, para.7(2) to come into effect at a time appointed by the Secretary of State in a statutory instrument.
The words '39(4) or (5)' are substituted by Mental Health Act 2007, Sched.9, para.7(3) to come into effect at a time appointed by the Secretary of State in a statutory instrument.
Subsection 40(2) is inserted by Mental Health Act 2007, Sched.9, para.7(4) to come into effect at a time appointed by the Secretary of State in a statutory instrument.

41 Power to adjust role of independent mental capacity advocate

(1) The appropriate authority may make regulations –

(a) expanding the role of independent mental capacity advocates in relation to persons who lack capacity, and

(b) adjusting the obligation to make arrangements imposed by section 35.

(2) The regulations may, in particular –

(a) prescribe circumstances (different to those set out in sections 37, 38 and 39) in which an independent mental capacity advocate must, or circumstances in which one may, be instructed by a person of a prescribed description to represent a person who lacks capacity, and

(b) include provision similar to any made by section 37, 38, 39 or 40.

(3) 'Appropriate authority' has the same meaning as in section 35.

Miscellaneous and supplementary

42 Codes of practice

(1) The Lord Chancellor must prepare and issue one or more codes of practice –

(a) for the guidance of persons assessing whether a person has capacity in relation to any matter,

(b) for the guidance of persons acting in connection with the care or treatment of another person (see section 5),

(c) for the guidance of donees of lasting powers of attorney,

(d) for the guidance of deputies appointed by the court,

(e) for the guidance of persons carrying out research in reliance on any provision made by or under this Act (and otherwise with respect to sections 30 to 34),

(f) for the guidance of independent mental capacity advocates,

[(fa) for the guidance of persons exercising functions under Schedule A1,

(fb) for the guidance of representatives appointed under Part 10 of Schedule A1,]

(g) with respect to the provisions of sections 24 to 26 (advance decisions and apparent advance decisions), and

(h) with respect to such other matters concerned with this Act as he thinks fit.

(2) The Lord Chancellor may from time to time revise a code.

(3) The Lord Chancellor may delegate the preparation or revision of the whole or any part of a code so far as he considers expedient.

(4) It is the duty of a person to have regard to any relevant code if he is acting in relation to a person who lacks capacity and is doing so in one or more of the following ways –

(a) as the donee of a lasting power of attorney,

(b) as a deputy appointed by the court,

(c) as a person carrying out research in reliance on any provision made by or under this Act (see sections 30 to 34),

(d) as an independent mental capacity advocate,

[(da) in the exercise of functions under Schedule A1,

(db)   as a representative appointed under Part 10 of Schedule A1,]

(e) in a professional capacity,

(f) for remuneration.

(5) If it appears to a court or tribunal conducting any criminal or civil proceedings that –

(a) a provision of a code, or

(b) a failure to comply with a code,

is relevant to a question arising in the proceedings, the provision or failure must be taken into account in deciding the question.

(6) A code under subsection (1)(d) may contain separate guidance for deputies appointed by virtue of paragraph 1(2) of Schedule 5 (functions of deputy conferred on receiver appointed under the Mental Health Act).

(7) In this section and in section 43, 'code' means a code prepared or revised under this section.

Notes:
Subsections 42(1)(fa) and (fb) are inserted by Mental Health Act 2007, Sched.9, para.8(2) which came into effect on 1 April 2008 by the Mental Health Act 2007 (Commencement No.4) Order 2008.
Subsections 42(4)(da) and (db) are inserted by Mental Health Act 2007, Sched.9, para.8(3) which came into effect on 1 April 2008 by the Mental Health Act 2007 (Commencement No.4) Order 2008.

43 Codes of practice: procedure

(1) Before preparing or revising a code, the Lord Chancellor must consult –

(a) the National Assembly for Wales, and

(b) such other persons as he considers appropriate.

(2) The Lord Chancellor may not issue a code unless –

(a) a draft of the code has been laid by him before both Houses of Parliament, and

(b) the 40 day period has elapsed without either House resolving not to approve the draft.

(3) The Lord Chancellor must arrange for any code that he has issued to be published in such a way as he considers appropriate for bringing it to the attention of persons likely to be concerned with its provisions.

(4) '40 day period', in relation to the draft of a proposed code, means –

(a) if the draft is laid before one House on a day later than the day on which it is laid before the other House, the period of 40 days beginning with the later of the two days;

(b) in any other case, the period of 40 days beginning with the day on which it is laid before each House.

(5) In calculating the period of 40 days, no account is to be taken of any period during which Parliament is dissolved or prorogued or during which both Houses are adjourned for more than 4 days.

44 Ill-treatment or neglect

(1) Subsection (2) applies if a person ('D') –

(a) has the care of a person ('P') who lacks, or whom D reasonably believes to lack, capacity,

(b) is the donee of a lasting power of attorney, or an enduring power of attorney (within the meaning of Schedule 4), created by P, or

(c) is a deputy appointed by the court for P.

(2) D is guilty of an offence if he ill-treats or wilfully neglects P.

(3) A person guilty of an offence under this section is liable –

(a) on summary conviction, to imprisonment for a term not exceeding 12 months or a fine not exceeding the statutory maximum or both;

(b) on conviction on indictment, to imprisonment for a term not exceeding 5 years or a fine or both.

PART 2   THE COURT OF PROTECTION AND THE PUBLIC GUARDIAN

The Court of Protection

45 The Court of Protection

(1) There is to be a superior court of record known as the Court of Protection.

(2) The court is to have an official seal.

(3) The court may sit at any place in England and Wales, on any day and at any time.

(4) The court is to have a central office and registry at a place appointed by the Lord Chancellor [after consulting the Lord Chief Justice].

(5) The Lord Chancellor may[, after consulting the Lord Chief Justice,] designate as additional registries of the court any district registry of the High Court and any county court office.

[(5A)   The Lord Chief Justice may nominate any of the following to exercise his functions under this section –

(a) the President of the Court of Protection;

(b) a judicial office holder (as defined in section 109(4) of the Constitutional Reform Act 2005).]

(6) The office of the Supreme Court called the Court of Protection ceases to exist.

Note:
Section 45(4) is amended by Lord Chancellor (Transfer of Functions and Supplementary Provisions) (No.2) Order 2006, SI 2006/1016, Sched.1, para.32(2) with effect on 3 April 2006.
Section 45(5) is amended by Lord Chancellor (Transfer of Functions and Supplementary Provisions) (No.2) Order 2006, SI 2006/1016, Sched.1, para.32(3) with effect on 3 April 2006.
Section 45(5A) is inserted by Lord Chancellor (Transfer of Functions and Supplementary Provisions) (No.2) Order 2006, SI 2006/1016, Sched.1, para.32(4) with effect on 3 April 2006.

46 The judges of the Court of Protection

(1) Subject to Court of Protection Rules under section 51(2)(d), the jurisdiction of the court is exercisable by a judge nominated for that purpose by –

(a) the [Lord Chief Justice], or

[(b) where nominated by the Lord Chief Justice to act on his behalf under this subsection –

(i) the President of the Court of Protection; or

(ii) a judicial office holder (as defined in section 109(4) of the Constitutional Reform Act 2005)].

(2) To be nominated, a judge must be –

    (a) the President of the Family Division,

    (b) the Vice-Chancellor,

    (c) a puisne judge of the High Court,

    (d) a circuit judge, or

    (e) a district judge.

(3) The [Lord Chief Justice, after consulting the Lord Chancellor,] must –

    (a) appoint one of the judges nominated by virtue of subsection (2)(a) to (c) to be President of the Court of Protection, and

    (b) appoint another of those judges to be Vice-President of the Court of Protection.

(4) The [Lord Chief Justice, after consulting the Lord Chancellor,] must appoint one of the judges nominated by virtue of subsection (2)(d) or (e) to be Senior Judge of the Court of Protection, having such administrative functions in relation to the court as the Lord Chancellor[, after consulting the Lord Chief Justice,] may direct.

Notes:
Section 46 (1)(a) is amended by Lord Chancellor (Transfer of Functions and Supplementary Provisions) (No.2) Order 2006, SI 2006/1016, Sched.1, para.33(2) with effect on 3 April 2006.
Section 46 (1)(b) is inserted by Lord Chancellor (Transfer of Functions and Supplementary Provisions) (No.2) Order 2006, SI 2006/1016, Sched.1, para.33(3) with effect on 3 April 2006.
Section 46(3) is amended by Lord Chancellor (Transfer of Functions and Supplementary Provisions) (No.2) Order 2006, SI 2006/1016, Sched.1, para.33(4) with effect on 3 April 2006.
Section 46(4) is amended by Lord Chancellor (Transfer of Functions and Supplementary Provisions) (No.2) Order 2006, SI 2006/1016, Sched.1, para.33(5) with effect on 3 April 2006.

Supplementary powers

47 General powers and effect of orders etc.

(1) The court has in connection with its jurisdiction the same powers, rights, privileges and authority as the High Court.

(2) Section 204 of the Law of Property Act 1925 (c. 20) (orders of High Court conclusive in favour of purchasers) applies in relation to orders and directions of the court as it applies to orders of the High Court.

(3) Office copies of orders made, directions given or other instruments issued by the court and sealed with its official seal are admissible in all legal proceedings as evidence of the originals without any further proof.

48 Interim orders and directions

The court may, pending the determination of an application to it in relation to a person ('P'), make an order or give directions in respect of any matter if –

    (a) there is reason to believe that P lacks capacity in relation to the matter,

    (b) the matter is one to which its powers under this Act extend, and

    (c) it is in P's best interests to make the order, or give the directions, without delay.

49 Power to call for reports

(1) This section applies where, in proceedings brought in respect of a person ('P') under Part 1, the court is considering a question relating to P.

(2) The court may require a report to be made to it by the Public Guardian or by a Court of Protection Visitor.

(3) The court may require a local authority, or an NHS body, to arrange for a report to be made –

(a) by one of its officers or employees, or

(b) by such other person (other than the Public Guardian or a Court of Protection Visitor) as the authority, or the NHS body, considers appropriate.

(4) The report must deal with such matters relating to P as the court may direct.

(5) Court of Protection Rules may specify matters which, unless the court directs otherwise, must also be dealt with in the report.

(6) The report may be made in writing or orally, as the court may direct.

(7) In complying with a requirement, the Public Guardian or a Court of Protection Visitor may, at all reasonable times, examine and take copies of –

(a) any health record,

(b) any record of, or held by, a local authority and compiled in connection with a social services function, and

(c) any record held by a person registered under Part 2 of the Care Standards Act 2000 (c. 14),

so far as the record relates to P.

(8) If the Public Guardian or a Court of Protection Visitor is making a visit in the course of complying with a requirement, he may interview P in private.

(9) If a Court of Protection Visitor who is a Special Visitor is making a visit in the course of complying with a requirement, he may if the court so directs carry out in private a medical, psychiatric or psychological examination of P's capacity and condition.

(10) 'NHS body' has the meaning given in section 148 of the Health and Social Care (Community Health and Standards) Act 2003 (c. 43).

(11) 'Requirement' means a requirement imposed under subsection (2) or (3).

Practice and procedure

50 Applications to the Court of Protection

(1) No permission is required for an application to the court for the exercise of any of its powers under this Act –

(a) by a person who lacks, or is alleged to lack, capacity,

(b) if such a person has not reached 18, by anyone with parental responsibility for him,

(c) by the donor or a donee of a lasting power of attorney to which the application relates,

(d) by a deputy appointed by the court for a person to whom the application relates, or

(e) by a person named in an existing order of the court, if the application relates to the order.

[(1A) *Nor is permission required for an application to the court under section 21A by the relevant person's representative.*]

(2) But, subject to Court of Protection Rules and to paragraph 20(2) of Schedule 3 (declarations relating to private international law), permission is required for any other application to the court.

(3) In deciding whether to grant permission the court must, in particular, have regard to –

(a) the applicant's connection with the person to whom the application relates,

(b) the reasons for the application,

(c) the benefit to the person to whom the application relates of a proposed order or directions, and

(d) whether the benefit can be achieved in any other way.

(4) 'Parental responsibility' has the same meaning as in the Children Act 1989 (c. 41).

Note:
Subsection 50(1A) is inserted by Mental Health Act 2007, Sched.9, para.9 to come into effect at a time appointed by the Secretary of State in a statutory instrument.

51 Court of Protection Rules

[(1) Rules of court with respect to the practice and procedure of the court (to be called 'Court of Protection Rules') may be made in accordance with Part 1 of Schedule 1 to the Constitutional Reform Act 2005.]

(2) Court of Protection Rules may, in particular, make provision –

(a) as to the manner and form in which proceedings are to be commenced;

(b) as to the persons entitled to be notified of, and be made parties to, the proceedings;

(c) for the allocation, in such circumstances as may be specified, of any specified description of proceedings to a specified judge or to specified descriptions of judges;

(d) for the exercise of the jurisdiction of the court, in such circumstances as may be specified, by its officers or other staff;

(e) for enabling the court to appoint a suitable person (who may, with his consent, be the Official Solicitor) to act in the name of, or on behalf of, or to represent the person to whom the proceedings relate;

(f) for enabling an application to the court to be disposed of without a hearing;

(g) for enabling the court to proceed with, or with any part of, a hearing in the absence of the person to whom the proceedings relate;

(h) for enabling or requiring the proceedings or any part of them to be conducted in private and for enabling the court to determine who is to be admitted when the court sits in private and to exclude specified persons when it sits in public;

(i) as to what may be received as evidence (whether or not admissible apart from the rules) and the manner in which it is to be presented;

(j) for the enforcement of orders made and directions given in the proceedings.

(3) Court of Protection Rules may, instead of providing for any matter, refer to provision made or to be made about that matter by directions.

(4) Court of Protection Rules may make different provision for different areas.

Note:
Section 51(1) is substituted by Lord Chancellor (Transfer of Functions and Supplementary Provisions) (No.2) Order 2006, SI 2006/1016, Sched.1, para.34 with effect on 3 April 2006.

[52 Practice directions

(1) Directions as to the practice and procedure of the court may be given in accordance with Part 1 of Schedule 2 to the Constitutional Reform Act 2005.

(2) Practice directions given otherwise than under subsection (1) may not be given without the approval of –

(a) the Lord Chancellor, and

(b) the Lord Chief Justice.

(3) The Lord Chief Justice may nominate any of the following to exercise his functions under this section –

(a) the President of the Court of Protection;

(b) a judicial office holder (as defined in section 109(4) of the Constitutional Reform Act 2005).]

Note:
Section 52 is substituted by Lord Chancellor (Transfer of Functions and Supplementary Provisions) (No.2) Order 2006, SI 2006/1016, Sched.1, para.35 with effect on 3 April 2006.

53 Rights of appeal

(1) Subject to the provisions of this section, an appeal lies to the Court of Appeal from any decision of the court.

(2) Court of Protection Rules may provide that where a decision of the court is made by –

    (a) a person exercising the jurisdiction of the court by virtue of rules made under section 51(2)(d),

    (b) a district judge, or

    (c) a circuit judge,

an appeal from that decision lies to a prescribed higher judge of the court and not to the Court of Appeal.

(3) For the purposes of this section the higher judges of the court are –

    (a) in relation to a person mentioned in subsection (2)(a), a circuit judge or a district judge;

    (b) in relation to a person mentioned in subsection (2)(b), a circuit judge;

    (c) in relation to any person mentioned in subsection (2), one of the judges nominated by virtue of section 46(2)(a) to (c).

(4) Court of Protection Rules may make provision –

    (a) that, in such cases as may be specified, an appeal from a decision of the court may not be made without permission;

    (b) as to the person or persons entitled to grant permission to appeal;

    (c) as to any requirements to be satisfied before permission is granted;

    (d) that where a higher judge of the court makes a decision on an appeal, no appeal may be made to the Court of Appeal from that decision unless the Court of Appeal considers that –

        (i) the appeal would raise an important point of principle or practice, or

        (ii) there is some other compelling reason for the Court of Appeal to hear it;

    (e) as to any considerations to be taken into account in relation to granting or refusing permission to appeal.

Fees and costs

54 Fees

(1) The Lord Chancellor may with the consent of the Treasury by order prescribe fees payable in respect of anything dealt with by the court.

(2) An order under this section may in particular contain provision as to –

    (a) scales or rates of fees;

    (b) exemptions from and reductions in fees;

    (c) remission of fees in whole or in part.

(3) Before making an order under this section, the Lord Chancellor must consult –

    (a) the President of the Court of Protection,

    (b) the Vice-President of the Court of Protection, and

    (c) the Senior Judge of the Court of Protection.

(4) The Lord Chancellor must take such steps as are reasonably practicable to bring information about fees to the attention of persons likely to have to pay them.

(5) Fees payable under this section are recoverable summarily as a civil debt.

55 Costs

(1) Subject to Court of Protection Rules, the costs of and incidental to all proceedings in the court are in its discretion.

(2) The rules may in particular make provision for regulating matters relating to the costs of those proceedings, including prescribing scales of costs to be paid to legal or other representatives.

(3) The court has full power to determine by whom and to what extent the costs are to be paid.

(4) The court may, in any proceedings –

  (a) disallow, or
  (b) order the legal or other representatives concerned to meet,

  the whole of any wasted costs or such part of them as may be determined in accordance with the rules.

(5) 'Legal or other representative', in relation to a party to proceedings, means any person exercising a right of audience or right to conduct litigation on his behalf.

(6) 'Wasted costs' means any costs incurred by a party –

  (a) as a result of any improper, unreasonable or negligent act or omission on the part of any legal or other representative or any employee of such a representative, or
  (b) which, in the light of any such act or omission occurring after they were incurred, the court considers it is unreasonable to expect that party to pay.

56 Fees and costs: supplementary

(1) Court of Protection Rules may make provision –

  (a) as to the way in which, and funds from which, fees and costs are to be paid;
  (b) for charging fees and costs upon the estate of the person to whom the proceedings relate;
  (c) for the payment of fees and costs within a specified time of the death of the person to whom the proceedings relate or the conclusion of the proceedings.

(2) A charge on the estate of a person created by virtue of subsection (1)(b) does not cause any interest of the person in any property to fail or determine or to be prevented from recommencing.

The Public Guardian

57 The Public Guardian

(1) For the purposes of this Act, there is to be an officer, to be known as the Public Guardian.

(2) The Public Guardian is to be appointed by the Lord Chancellor.

(3) There is to be paid to the Public Guardian out of money provided by Parliament such salary as the Lord Chancellor may determine.

(4) The Lord Chancellor may, after consulting the Public Guardian –

  (a) provide him with such officers and staff, or
  (b) enter into such contracts with other persons for the provision (by them or their sub-contractors) of officers, staff or services,

  as the Lord Chancellor thinks necessary for the proper discharge of the Public Guardian's functions.

(5) Any functions of the Public Guardian may, to the extent authorised by him, be performed by any of his officers.

58 Functions of the Public Guardian

(1) The Public Guardian has the following functions –

(a)   establishing and maintaining a register of lasting powers of attorney,
(b)   establishing and maintaining a register of orders appointing deputies,
(c)   supervising deputies appointed by the court,
(d)   directing a Court of Protection Visitor to visit –

  (i)   a donee of a lasting power of attorney,
  (ii)   a deputy appointed by the court, or
  (iii) the person granting the power of attorney or for whom the deputy is appointed ('P'),

  and to make a report to the Public Guardian on such matters as he may direct,
(e)   receiving security which the court requires a person to give for the discharge of his functions,
(f)   receiving reports from donees of lasting powers of attorney and deputies appointed by the court,
(g)   reporting to the court on such matters relating to proceedings under this Act as the court requires,
(h)   dealing with representations (including complaints) about the way in which a donee of a lasting power of attorney or a deputy appointed by the court is exercising his powers,
(i)   publishing, in any manner the Public Guardian thinks appropriate, any information he thinks appropriate about the discharge of his functions.

(2)   The functions conferred by subsection (1)(c) and (h) may be discharged in co-operation with any other person who has functions in relation to the care or treatment of P.

(3)   The Lord Chancellor may by regulations make provision –

(a)   conferring on the Public Guardian other functions in connection with this Act;
(b)   in connection with the discharge by the Public Guardian of his functions.

(4)   Regulations made under subsection (3)(b) may in particular make provision as to –

(a)   the giving of security by deputies appointed by the court and the enforcement and discharge of security so given;
(b)   the fees which may be charged by the Public Guardian;
(c)   the way in which, and funds from which, such fees are to be paid;
(d)   exemptions from and reductions in such fees;
(e)   remission of such fees in whole or in part;
(f)   the making of reports to the Public Guardian by deputies appointed by the court and others who are directed by the court to carry out any transaction for a person who lacks capacity.

(5)   For the purpose of enabling him to carry out his functions, the Public Guardian may, at all reasonable times, examine and take copies of –

(a)   any health record,
(b)   any record of, or held by, a local authority and compiled in connection with a social services function, and
(c)   any record held by a person registered under Part 2 of the Care Standards Act 2000 (c. 14),

so far as the record relates to P.

(6)   The Public Guardian may also for that purpose interview P in private.

59 Public Guardian Board

(1)   There is to be a body, to be known as the Public Guardian Board.
(2)   The Board's duty is to scrutinise and review the way in which the Public Guardian discharges his functions and to make such recommendations to the Lord Chancellor about that matter as it thinks appropriate.

(3) The Lord Chancellor must, in discharging his functions under sections 57 and 58, give due consideration to recommendations made by the Board.

(4) [. . .]

(5) The Board must have –

(a) at least one member who is a judge of the court, and

(b) at least four members who are persons appearing to the Lord Chancellor to have appropriate knowledge or experience of the work of the Public Guardian.

[(5A)   Where a person to be appointed as a member of the Board is a judge of the court, the appointment is to be made by the Lord Chief Justice after consulting the Lord Chancellor.]

[(5B)   In any other case, the appointment of a person as a member of the Board is to be made by the Lord Chancellor.]

(6) The Lord Chancellor may by regulations make provision as to –

(a) the appointment of members of the Board (and, in particular, the procedures to be followed in connection with appointments);

(b) the selection of one of the members to be the chairman;

(c) the term of office of the chairman and members;

(d) their resignation, suspension or removal;

(e) the procedure of the Board (including quorum);

(f) the validation of proceedings in the event of a vacancy among the members or a defect in the appointment of a member.

(7) Subject to any provision made in reliance on subsection (6)(c) or (d), a person is to hold and vacate office as a member of the Board in accordance with the terms of the instrument appointing him.

(8) The Lord Chancellor may make such payments to or in respect of members of the Board by way of reimbursement of expenses, allowances and remuneration as he may determine.

(9) The Board must make an annual report to the Lord Chancellor about the discharge of its functions.

[(10)   The Lord Chief Justice may nominate any of the following to exercise his functions under this section –

(a) the President of the Court of Protection;

(b) a judicial office holder (as defined in section 109(4) of the Constitutional Reform Act 2005).]

Notes:
Section 59(4) is omitted by Lord Chancellor (Transfer of Functions and Supplementary Provisions) (No.2) Order 2006, SI 2006/1016, Sched.1, para.36(2) with effect on 3 April 2006.
Subsections 59(5A) and (5B) are inserted by Lord Chancellor (Transfer of Functions and Supplementary Provisions) (No.2) Order 2006, SI 2006/1016, Sched.1, para.36(3) with effect on 3 April 2006.
Subsection 59(10) is inserted by Lord Chancellor (Transfer of Functions and Supplementary Provisions) (No.2) Order 2006, SI 2006/1016, Sched.1, para.36(4) with effect on 3 April 2006.

60 Annual report

(1) The Public Guardian must make an annual report to the Lord Chancellor about the discharge of his functions.

(2) The Lord Chancellor must, within one month of receiving the report, lay a copy of it before Parliament.

Court of Protection Visitors

61 Court of Protection Visitors

(1) A Court of Protection Visitor is a person who is appointed by the Lord Chancellor to –

    (a) a panel of Special Visitors, or

    (b) a panel of General Visitors.

(2) A person is not qualified to be a Special Visitor unless he –

    (a) is a registered medical practitioner or appears to the Lord Chancellor to have other suitable qualifications or training, and

    (b) appears to the Lord Chancellor to have special knowledge of and experience in cases of impairment of or disturbance in the functioning of the mind or brain.

(3) A General Visitor need not have a medical qualification.

(4) A Court of Protection Visitor –

    (a) may be appointed for such term and subject to such conditions, and

    (b) may be paid such remuneration and allowances,

    as the Lord Chancellor may determine.

(5) For the purpose of carrying out his functions under this Act in relation to a person who lacks capacity ('P'), a Court of Protection Visitor may, at all reasonable times, examine and take copies of –

    (a) any health record,

    (b) any record of, or held by, a local authority and compiled in connection with a social services function, and

    (c) any record held by a person registered under Part 2 of the Care Standards Act 2000 (c. 14),

    so far as the record relates to P.

(6) A Court of Protection Visitor may also for that purpose interview P in private.

PART 3   MISCELLANEOUS AND GENERAL

Declaratory provision

62 Scope of the Act

For the avoidance of doubt, it is hereby declared that nothing in this Act is to be taken to affect the law relating to murder or manslaughter or the operation of section 2 of the Suicide Act 1961 (c. 60) (assisting suicide).

Private international law

63 International protection of adults

Schedule 3 –

    (a) gives effect in England and Wales to the Convention on the International Protection of Adults signed at the Hague on 13th January 2000 (Cm. 5881) (in so far as this Act does not otherwise do so), and

    (b) makes related provision as to the private international law of England and Wales.

General

64 Interpretation

(1) In this Act –

'the 1985 Act' means the Enduring Powers of Attorney Act 1985 (c. 29),
'advance decision' has the meaning given in section 24(1),
['authorisation under Schedule A1' means either –

  (a) a standard authorisation under that Schedule, or
  (b) an urgent authorisation under that Schedule;]

'the court' means the Court of Protection established by section 45,
'Court of Protection Rules' has the meaning given in section 51(1),
'Court of Protection Visitor' has the meaning given in section 61,
'deputy' has the meaning given in section 16(2)(b),
'enactment' includes a provision of subordinate legislation (within the meaning of the Interpretation Act 1978 (c. 30)),
'health record' has the meaning given in section 68 of the Data Protection Act 1998 (c. 29) (as read with section 69 of that Act),
'the Human Rights Convention' has the same meaning as 'the Convention' in the Human Rights Act 1998 (c. 42),
'independent mental capacity advocate' has the meaning given in section 35(1),
'lasting power of attorney' has the meaning given in section 9,
'life-sustaining treatment' has the meaning given in section 4(10),
'local authority'[, except in Schedule A1,] means –

  (a) the council of a county in England in which there are no district councils,
  (b) the council of a district in England,
  (c) the council of a county or county borough in Wales,
  (d) the council of a London borough,
  (e) the Common Council of the City of London, or
  (f) the Council of the Isles of Scilly,

'Mental Health Act' means the Mental Health Act 1983 (c. 20),
'prescribed', in relation to regulations made under this Act, means prescribed by those regulations,
'property' includes any thing in action and any interest in real or personal property,
'public authority' has the same meaning as in the Human Rights Act 1998,
'Public Guardian' has the meaning given in section 57,
'purchaser' and 'purchase' have the meaning given in section 205(1) of the Law of Property Act 1925 (c. 20),
'social services function' has the meaning given in section 1A of the Local Authority Social Services Act 1970 (c. 42),
'treatment' includes a diagnostic or other procedure,
'trust corporation' has the meaning given in section 68(1) of the Trustee Act 1925 (c. 19), and
'will' includes codicil.

(2) In this Act, references to making decisions, in relation to a donee of a lasting power of attorney or a deputy appointed by the court, include, where appropriate, acting on decisions made.

(3) In this Act, references to the bankruptcy of an individual include a case where a bankruptcy restrictions order under the Insolvency Act 1986 (c. 45) has effect in respect of him.

(4) 'Bankruptcy restrictions order' includes an interim bankruptcy restrictions order.

[(5) In this Act, references to deprivation of a person's liberty have the same meaning as in Article 5(1) of the Human Rights Convention.]

[(6) For the purposes of such references, it does not matter whether a person is deprived of his liberty by a public authority or not.]

Notes:
A definition of 'authorisation under Schedule A1' is inserted in subsection 64(1) by Mental Health Act 2007, Sched.9, para.10(2) brought into force on 1 April 2008 by Mental Health Act 2007 (Commencement No.4) Order 2008, SI 2008/745, para.4(b).
The definition of 'local authority' is amended by Mental Health Act 2007, Sched.9, para.10(3) brought into force on 1 April 2008 by Mental Health Act 2007 (Commencement No.4) Order 2008, SI 2008/745, para.4(b).
Subsections 1(5) and (6) are inserted by Mental Health Act 2007, Sched.9, para.10(4) brought into force on 1 April 2008 by Mental Health 2007 (Commenencement No.4) Order 2008, SI 2008/745, para.4(b).

65 Rules, regulations and orders

(1) Any power to make rules, regulations or orders under this Act[, other than the power in section 21] –

   (a) is exercisable by statutory instrument;
   (b) includes power to make supplementary, incidental, consequential, transitional or saving provision;
   (c) includes power to make different provision for different cases.

(2) Any statutory instrument containing rules, regulations or orders made by the Lord Chancellor or the Secretary of State under this Act, other than –

   (a) regulations under section 34 (loss of capacity during research project),
   (b) regulations under section 41 (adjusting role of independent mental capacity advocacy service),
   (c) regulations under paragraph 32(1)(b) of Schedule 3 (private international law relating to the protection of adults),
   (d) an order of the kind mentioned in section 67(6) (consequential amendments of primary legislation), or
   (e) an order under section 68 (commencement),

   is subject to annulment in pursuance of a resolution of either House of Parliament.
(3) A statutory instrument containing an Order in Council under paragraph 31 of Schedule 3 (provision to give further effect to Hague Convention) is subject to annulment in pursuance of a resolution of either House of Parliament.
(4) A statutory instrument containing regulations made by the Secretary of State under section 34 or 41 or by the Lord Chancellor under paragraph 32(1)(b) of Schedule 3 may not be made unless a draft has been laid before and approved by resolution of each House of Parliament.
[(4A) Subsection (2) does not apply to a statutory instrument containing regulations made by the Secretary of State under Schedule A1.]
[(4B) If such a statutory instrument contains regulations under paragraph 42(2)(b), 129, 162 or 164 of Schedule A1 (whether or not it also contains other regulations), the instrument may not be made unless a draft has been laid before and approved by resolution of each House of Parliament.]
[(4C) Subject to that, such a statutory instrument is subject to annulment in pursuance of a resolution of either House of Parliament.]
[(5) An order under section 21 –

   (a) may include supplementary, incidental, consequential, transitional or saving provision;
   (b) may make different provision for different cases;
   (c) is to be made in the form of a statutory instrument to which the Statutory Instruments Act 1946 applies as if the order were made by a Minister of the Crown; and

(d) is subject to annulment in pursuance of a resolution of either House of Parliament.]

Notes:
Section 65(1) is amended by Lord Chancellor (Transfer of Functions and Supplementary Provisions) (No.2) Order 2006, Sched.1, para.37(2) in force on 3 April 2008.
Sections 65(4A), (4B) and (4C) are inserted by Mental Health Act 2007, Sched.9, para.11(2) brought into force by Mental Health Act 2007 (Commencement No.4) Order 2008, SI 2008/745, para.4(b) on 1 April 2008.
Section 65(5) is inserted by Lord Chancellor (Transfer of Functions and Supplementary Provisions) (No.2) Order 2006, Sched.1, para.37(3) in force on 3 April 2008.

66 Existing receivers and enduring powers of attorney etc.

(1) The following provisions cease to have effect –

(a) Part 7 of the Mental Health Act,
(b) the Enduring Powers of Attorney Act 1985 (c. 29).

(2) No enduring power of attorney within the meaning of the 1985 Act is to be created after the commencement of subsection (1)(b).

(3) Schedule 4 has effect in place of the 1985 Act in relation to any enduring power of attorney created before the commencement of subsection (1)(b).

(4) Schedule 5 contains transitional provisions and savings in relation to Part 7 of the Mental Health Act and the 1985 Act.

67 Minor and consequential amendments and repeals

(1) Schedule 6 contains minor and consequential amendments.

(2) Schedule 7 contains repeals.

(3) The Lord Chancellor may by order make supplementary, incidental, consequential, transitional or saving provision for the purposes of, in consequence of, or for giving full effect to a provision of this Act.

(4) An order under subsection (3) may, in particular –

(a) provide for a provision of this Act which comes into force before another provision of this Act has come into force to have effect, until the other provision has come into force, with specified modifications;
(b) amend, repeal or revoke an enactment, other than one contained in an Act or Measure passed in a Session after the one in which this Act is passed.

(5) The amendments that may be made under subsection (4)(b) are in addition to those made by or under any other provision of this Act.

(6) An order under subsection (3) which amends or repeals a provision of an Act or Measure may not be made unless a draft has been laid before and approved by resolution of each House of Parliament.

68 Commencement and extent

(1) This Act, other than sections 30 to 41, comes into force in accordance with provision made by order by the Lord Chancellor.

(2) Sections 30 to 41 come into force in accordance with provision made by order by –

(a) the Secretary of State, in relation to England, and
(b) the National Assembly for Wales, in relation to Wales.

(3) An order under this section may appoint different days for different provisions and different purposes.

(4) Subject to subsections (5) and (6), this Act extends to England and Wales only.

(5) The following provisions extend to the United Kingdom –

(a) paragraph 16(1) of Schedule 1 (evidence of instruments and of registration of lasting powers of attorney),

(b) paragraph 15(3) of Schedule 4 (evidence of instruments and of registration of enduring powers of attorney).

(6) Subject to any provision made in Schedule 6, the amendments and repeals made by Schedules 6 and 7 have the same extent as the enactments to which they relate.

69 Short title

This Act may be cited as the Mental Capacity Act 2005.

SCHEDULES

[SCHEDULE A1   HOSPITAL AND CARE HOME RESIDENTS: DEPRIVATION OF LIBERTY

PART 1   AUTHORISATION TO DEPRIVE RESIDENTS OF LIBERTY ETC

Application of Part

1   (1)   This Part applies if the following conditions are met.

(2)   The first condition is that a person ('P') is detained in a hospital or care home – for the purpose of being given care or treatment – in circumstances which amount to deprivation of the person's liberty.

(3)   The second condition is that a standard or urgent authorisation is in force.

(4)   The third condition is that the standard or urgent authorisation relates –

(a)   to P, and

(b)   to the hospital or care home in which P is detained.

Authorisation to deprive P of liberty

2   The managing authority of the hospital or care home may deprive P of his liberty by detaining him as mentioned in paragraph 1(2).

No liability for acts done for purpose of depriving P of liberty

3   (1)   This paragraph applies to any act which a person ('D') does for the purpose of detaining P as mentioned in paragraph 1(2).

(2)   D does not incur any liability in relation to the act that he would not have incurred if P –

(a)   had had capacity to consent in relation to D's doing the act, and

(b)   had consented to D's doing the act.

No protection for negligent acts etc

4   (1)   Paragraphs 2 and 3 do not exclude a person's civil liability for loss or damage, or his criminal liability, resulting from his negligence in doing any thing.

(2)   Paragraphs 2 and 3 do not authorise a person to do anything otherwise than for the purpose of the standard or urgent authorisation that is in force.

(3)   In a case where a standard authorisation is in force, paragraphs 2 and 3 do not authorise a person to do anything which does not comply with the conditions (if any) included in the authorisation.

PART 2   INTERPRETATION: MAIN TERMS

Introduction

5   This Part applies for the purposes of this Schedule.

Detained resident

6   'Detained resident' means a person detained in a hospital or care home – for the purpose of being given care or treatment – in circumstances which amount to deprivation of the person's liberty.

Relevant person etc

7   In relation to a person who is, or is to be, a detained resident –
     'relevant person' means the person in question;
     'relevant hospital or care home' means the hospital or care home in question;
     'relevant care or treatment' means the care or treatment in question.

Authorisations

8   'Standard authorisation' means an authorisation given under Part 4.
9   'Urgent authorisation' means an authorisation given under Part 5.
10   'Authorisation under this Schedule' means either of the following –

     (a)   a standard authorisation;
     (b)   an urgent authorisation.

11   (1)   The purpose of a standard authorisation is the purpose which is stated in the authorisation in accordance with paragraph 55(1)(d).
     (2)   The purpose of an urgent authorisation is the purpose which is stated in the authorisation in accordance with paragraph 80(d).

PART 3   THE QUALIFYING REQUIREMENTS

The qualifying requirements

12   (1)   These are the qualifying requirements referred to in this Schedule –

           (a)   the age requirement;
           (b)   the mental health requirement;
           (c)   the mental capacity requirement;
           (d)   the best interests requirement;
           (e)   the eligibility requirement;
           (f)   the no refusals requirement.

     (2)   Any question of whether a person who is, or is to be, a detained resident meets the qualifying requirements is to be determined in accordance with this Part.
     (3)   In a case where –

           (a)   the question of whether a person meets a particular qualifying requirement arises in relation to the giving of a standard authorisation, and
           (b)   any circumstances relevant to determining that question are expected to change between the time when the determination is made and the time when the authorisation is expected to come into force, those circumstances are to be taken into account as they are expected to be at the later time.

The age requirement

13   The relevant person meets the age requirement if he has reached 18.

The mental health requirement

14 (1) The relevant person meets the mental health requirement if he is suffering from mental disorder (within the meaning of the Mental Health Act, but disregarding any exclusion for persons with learning disability).

(2) An exclusion for persons with learning disability is any provision of the Mental Health Act which provides for a person with learning disability not to be regarded as suffering from mental disorder for one or more purposes of that Act.

The mental capacity requirement

15 The relevant person meets the mental capacity requirement if he lacks capacity in relation to the question whether or not he should be accommodated in the relevant hospital or care home for the purpose of being given the relevant care or treatment.

The best interests requirement

16 (1) The relevant person meets the best interests requirement if all of the following conditions are met.

(2) The first condition is that the relevant person is, or is to be, a detained resident.

(3) The second condition is that it is in the best interests of the relevant person for him to be a detained resident.

(4) The third condition is that, in order to prevent harm to the relevant person, it is necessary for him to be a detained resident.

(5) The fourth condition is that it is a proportionate response to –

(a) the likelihood of the relevant person suffering harm, and

(b) the seriousness of that harm,

for him to be a detained resident.

The eligibility requirement

17 (1) The relevant person meets the eligibility requirement unless he is ineligible to be deprived of liberty by this Act.

(2) Schedule 1A applies for the purpose of determining whether or not P is ineligible to be deprived of liberty by this Act.

The no refusals requirement

18 The relevant person meets the no refusals requirement unless there is a refusal within the meaning of paragraph 19 or 20.

19 (1) There is a refusal if these conditions are met –

(a) the relevant person has made an advance decision;

(b) the advance decision is valid;

(c) the advance decision is applicable to some or all of the relevant treatment.

(2) Expressions used in this paragraph and any of sections 24, 25 or 26 have the same meaning in this paragraph as in that section.

20 (1) There is a refusal if it would be in conflict with a valid decision of a donee or deputy for the relevant person to be accommodated in the relevant hospital or care home for the purpose of receiving some or all of the relevant care or treatment –

(a) in circumstances which amount to deprivation of the person's liberty, or

(b) at all.

(2)   A donee is a donee of a lasting power of attorney granted by the relevant person.

(3)   A decision of a donee or deputy is valid if it is made –

(a)   within the scope of his authority as donee or deputy, and

(b)   in accordance with Part 1 of this Act.

PART 4   STANDARD AUTHORISATIONS

Supervisory body to give authorisation

21   Only the supervisory body may give a standard authorisation.

22   The supervisory body may not give a standard authorisation unless –

(a)   the managing authority of the relevant hospital or care home have requested it, or

(b)   paragraph 71 applies (right of third party to require consideration of whether authorisation needed).

23   The managing authority may not make a request for a standard authorisation unless –

(a)   they are required to do so by paragraph 24 (as read with paragraphs 27 to 29),

(b)   they are required to do so by paragraph 25 (as read with paragraph 28), or

(c)   they are permitted to do so by paragraph 30.

Duty to request authorisation: basic cases

24   (1)   The managing authority must request a standard authorisation in any of the following cases.

(2)   The first case is where it appears to the managing authority that the relevant person –

(a)   is not yet accommodated in the relevant hospital or care home,

(b)   is likely – at some time within the next 28 days – to be a detained resident in the relevant hospital or care home, and

(c)   is likely –

(i)   at that time, or

(ii)   at some later time within the next 28 days,

to meet all of the qualifying requirements.

(3)   The second case is where it appears to the managing authority that the relevant person –

(a)   is already accommodated in the relevant hospital or care home,

(b)   is likely – at some time within the next 28 days – to be a detained resident in the relevant hospital or care home, and

(c)   is likely –

(i)   at that time, or

(ii)   at some later time within the next 28 days,

to meet all of the qualifying requirements.

(4)   The third case is where it appears to the managing authority that the relevant person –

(a)   is a detained resident in the relevant hospital or care home, and

(b)   meets all of the qualifying requirements, or is likely to do so at some time within the next 28 days.

(5)   This paragraph is subject to paragraphs 27 to 29.

Duty to request authorisation: change in place of detention

25   (1)   The relevant managing authority must request a standard authorisation if it appears to them that these conditions are met.

(2)   The first condition is that a standard authorisation –

(a)   has been given, and

(b)   has not ceased to be in force.

(3)   The second condition is that there is, or is to be, a change in the place of detention.

(4)   This paragraph is subject to paragraph 28.

26   (1)   This paragraph applies for the purposes of paragraph 25.

(2)   There is a change in the place of detention if the relevant person –

(a)   ceases to be a detained resident in the stated hospital or care home, and

(b)   becomes a detained resident in a different hospital or care home ('the new hospital or care home').

(3)   The stated hospital or care home is the hospital or care home to which the standard authorisation relates.

(4)   The relevant managing authority are the managing authority of the new hospital or care home.

Other authority for detention: request for authorisation

27   (1)   This paragraph applies if, by virtue of section 4A(3), a decision of the court authorises the relevant person to be a detained resident.

(2)   Paragraph 24 does not require a request for a standard authorisation to be made in relation to that detention unless these conditions are met.

(3)   The first condition is that the standard authorisation would be in force at a time immediately after the expiry of the other authority.

(4)   The second condition is that the standard authorisation would not be in force at any time on or before the expiry of the other authority.

(5)   The third condition is that it would, in the managing authority's view, be unreasonable to delay making the request until a time nearer the expiry of the other authority.

(6)   In this paragraph –

(a)   the other authority is –

(i)   the decision mentioned in sub-paragraph (1), or

(ii)   any further decision of the court which, by virtue of section 4A(3), authorises, or is expected to authorise, the relevant person to be a detained resident;

(b)   the expiry of the other authority is the time when the other authority is expected to cease to authorise the relevant person to be a detained resident.

Request refused: no further request unless change of circumstances

28   (1)   This paragraph applies if –

(a)   a managing authority request a standard authorisation under paragraph 24 or 25, and

(b)   the supervisory body are prohibited by paragraph 50(2) from giving the authorisation.

(2)   Paragraph 24 or 25 does not require that managing authority to make a new request for a standard authorisation unless it appears to the managing authority that –

(a)   there has been a change in the relevant person's case, and

(b)   because of that change, the supervisory body are likely to give a standard authorisation if requested.

Authorisation given: request for further authorisation

29   (1)   This paragraph applies if a standard authorisation –

(a)   has been given in relation to the detention of the relevant person, and

(b)   that authorisation ('the existing authorisation') has not ceased to be in force.

(2)   Paragraph 24 does not require a new request for a standard authorisation ('the new authorisation') to be made unless these conditions are met.

(3)   The first condition is that the new authorisation would be in force at a time immediately after the expiry of the existing authorisation.

(4)   The second condition is that the new authorisation would not be in force at any time on or before the expiry of the existing authorisation.

(5)   The third condition is that it would, in the managing authority's view, be unreasonable to delay making the request until a time nearer the expiry of the existing authorisation.

(6)   The expiry of the existing authorisation is the time when it is expected to cease to be in force.

Power to request authorisation

30   (1)   This paragraph applies if –

(a)   a standard authorisation has been given in relation to the detention of the relevant person,

(b)   that authorisation ('the existing authorisation') has not ceased to be in force,

(c)   the requirement under paragraph 24 to make a request for a new standard authorisation does not apply, because of paragraph 29, and

(d)   a review of the existing authorisation has been requested, or is being carried out, in accordance with Part 8.

(2)   The managing authority may request a new standard authorisation which would be in force on or before the expiry of the existing authorisation; but only if it would also be in force immediately after that expiry.

(3)   The expiry of the existing authorisation is the time when it is expected to cease to be in force.

(4)   Further provision relating to cases where a request is made under this paragraph can be found in –

(a)   paragraph 62 (effect of decision about request), and

(b)   paragraph 124 (effect of request on Part 8 review).

Information included in request

31   A request for a standard authorisation must include the information (if any) required by regulations.

Records of requests

32   (1)   The managing authority of a hospital or care home must keep a written record of –

(a)   each request that they make for a standard authorisation, and

(b)   the reasons for making each request.

(2) A supervisory body must keep a written record of each request for a standard authorisation that is made to them.

Relevant person must be assessed

33 (1) This paragraph applies if the supervisory body are requested to give a standard authorisation.
(2) The supervisory body must secure that all of these assessments are carried out in relation to the relevant person –

  (a) an age assessment;
  (b) a mental health assessment;
  (c) a mental capacity assessment;
  (d) a best interests assessment;
  (e) an eligibility assessment;
  (f) a no refusals assessment.

(3) The person who carries out any such assessment is referred to as the assessor.
(4) Regulations may be made about the period (or periods) within which assessors must carry out assessments.
(5) This paragraph is subject to paragraphs 49 and 133.

Age assessment

34 An age assessment is an assessment of whether the relevant person meets the age requirement.

Mental health assessment

35 A mental health assessment is an assessment of whether the relevant person meets the mental health requirement.
36 When carrying out a mental health assessment, the assessor must also –

  (a) consider how (if at all) the relevant person's mental health is likely to be affected by his being a detained resident, and
  (b) notify the best interests assessor of his conclusions.

Mental capacity assessment

37 A mental capacity assessment is an assessment of whether the relevant person meets the mental capacity requirement.

Best interests assessment

38 A best interests assessment is an assessment of whether the relevant person meets the best interests requirement.
39 (1) In carrying out a best interests assessment, the assessor must comply with the duties in sub-paragraphs (2) and (3).
(2) The assessor must consult the managing authority of the relevant hospital or care home.
(3) The assessor must have regard to all of the following –

  (a) the conclusions which the mental health assessor has notified to the best interests assessor in accordance with paragraph 36(b);

      (b)   any relevant needs assessment;

      (c)   any relevant care plan.

(4) A relevant needs assessment is an assessment of the relevant person's needs which –

      (a)   was carried out in connection with the relevant person being accommodated in the relevant hospital or care home, and

      (b)   was carried out by or on behalf of –

          (i)   the managing authority of the relevant hospital or care home, or

          (ii) the supervisory body.

(5) A relevant care plan is a care plan which –

      (a)   sets out how the relevant person's needs are to be met whilst he is accommodated in the relevant hospital or care home, and

      (b)   was drawn up by or on behalf of –

          (i)   the managing authority of the relevant hospital or care home, or

          (ii) the supervisory body.

(6) The managing authority must give the assessor a copy of –

      (a)   any relevant needs assessment carried out by them or on their behalf, or

      (b)   any relevant care plan drawn up by them or on their behalf.

(7) The supervisory body must give the assessor a copy of –

      (a)   any relevant needs assessment carried out by them or on their behalf, or

      (b)   any relevant care plan drawn up by them or on their behalf.

(8) The duties in sub-paragraphs (2) and (3) do not affect any other duty to consult or to take the views of others into account.

40   (1) This paragraph applies whatever conclusion the best interests assessment comes to.

     (2) The assessor must state in the best interests assessment the name and address of every interested person whom he has consulted in carrying out the assessment.

41   Paragraphs 42 and 43 apply if the best interests assessment comes to the conclusion that the relevant person meets the best interests requirement.

42   (1) The assessor must state in the assessment the maximum authorisation period.

     (2) The maximum authorisation period is the shorter of these periods –

      (a)   the period which, in the assessor's opinion, would be the appropriate maximum period for the relevant person to be a detained resident under the standard authorisation that has been requested;

      (b)   1 year, or such shorter period as may be prescribed in regulations.

     (3) Regulations under sub-paragraph (2)(b) –

      (a)   need not provide for a shorter period to apply in relation to all standard authorisations;

      (b)   may provide for different periods to apply in relation to different kinds of standard authorisations.

     (4) Before making regulations under sub-paragraph (2)(b) the Secretary of State must consult all of the following –

      (a)   each body required by regulations under paragraph 162 to monitor and report on the operation of this Schedule in relation to England;

      (b)   such other persons as the Secretary of State considers it appropriate to consult.

     (5) Before making regulations under sub-paragraph (2)(b) the National Assembly for Wales must consult all of the following –

      (a)   each person or body directed under paragraph 163(2) to carry out any function of the Assembly of monitoring and reporting on the operation of this Schedule in relation to Wales;

      (b)   such other persons as the Assembly considers it appropriate to consult.

43   The assessor may include in the assessment recommendations about conditions to which the standard authorisation is, or is not, to be subject in accordance with paragraph 53.

44   (1)   This paragraph applies if the best interests assessment comes to the conclusion that the relevant person does not meet the best interests requirement.

      (2)   If, on the basis of the information taken into account in carrying out the assessment, it appears to the assessor that there is an unauthorised deprivation of liberty, he must include a statement to that effect in the assessment.

      (3)   There is an unauthorised deprivation of liberty if the managing authority of the relevant hospital or care home are already depriving the relevant person of his liberty without authority of the kind mentioned in section 4A.

45   The duties with which the best interests assessor must comply are subject to the provision included in appointment regulations under Part 10 (in particular, provision made under paragraph 146).

Eligibility assessment

46   An eligibility assessment is an assessment of whether the relevant person meets the eligibility requirement.

47   (1)   Regulations may –

      (a)   require an eligibility assessor to request a best interests assessor to provide relevant eligibility information, and

      (b)   require the best interests assessor, if such a request is made, to provide such relevant eligibility information as he may have.

      (2)   In this paragraph –

      'best interests assessor' means any person who is carrying out, or has carried out, a best interests assessment in relation to the relevant person;

      'eligibility assessor' means a person carrying out an eligibility assessment in relation to the relevant person;

      'relevant eligibility information' is information relevant to assessing whether or not the relevant person is ineligible by virtue of paragraph 5 of Schedule 1A.

No refusals assessment

48   A no refusals assessment is an assessment of whether the relevant person meets the no refusals requirement.

Equivalent assessment already carried out

49   (1)   The supervisory body are not required by paragraph 33 to secure that a particular kind of assessment ('the required assessment') is carried out in relation to the relevant person if the following conditions are met.

      (2)   The first condition is that the supervisory body have a written copy of an assessment of the relevant person ('the existing assessment') that has already been carried out.

      (3)   The second condition is that the existing assessment complies with all requirements under this Schedule with which the required assessment would have to comply (if it were carried out).

      (4)   The third condition is that the existing assessment was carried out within the previous 12 months; but this condition need not be met if the required assessment is an age assessment.

      (5)   The fourth condition is that the supervisory body are satisfied that there is no reason why the existing assessment may no longer be accurate.

(6) If the required assessment is a best interests assessment, in satisfying themselves as mentioned in sub-paragraph (5), the supervisory body must take into account any information given, or submissions made, by –

    (a)   the relevant person's representative,

    (b)   any section 39C IMCA, or

    (c)   any section 39D IMCA.

(7) It does not matter whether the existing assessment was carried out in connection with a request for a standard authorisation or for some other purpose.

(8) If, because of this paragraph, the supervisory body are not required by paragraph 33 to secure that the required assessment is carried out, the existing assessment is to be treated for the purposes of this Schedule –

    (a)   as an assessment of the same kind as the required assessment, and

    (b)   as having been carried out under paragraph 33 in connection with the request for the standard authorisation.

Duty to give authorisation

50 (1) The supervisory body must give a standard authorisation if –

    (a)   all assessments are positive, and

    (b)   the supervisory body have written copies of all those assessments.

(2) The supervisory body must not give a standard authorisation except in accordance with sub-paragraph (1).

(3) All assessments are positive if each assessment carried out under paragraph 33 has come to the conclusion that the relevant person meets the qualifying requirement to which the assessment relates.

Terms of authorisation

51 (1) If the supervisory body are required to give a standard authorisation, they must decide the period during which the authorisation is to be in force.

(2) That period must not exceed the maximum authorisation period stated in the best interests assessment.

52 A standard authorisation may provide for the authorisation to come into force at a time after it is given.

53 (1) A standard authorisation may be given subject to conditions.

(2) Before deciding whether to give the authorisation subject to conditions, the supervisory body must have regard to any recommendations in the best interests assessment about such conditions.

(3) The managing authority of the relevant hospital or care home must ensure that any conditions are complied with.

Form of authorisation

54 A standard authorisation must be in writing.

55 (1) A standard authorisation must state the following things –

    (a)   the name of the relevant person;

    (b)   the name of the relevant hospital or care home;

    (c)   the period during which the authorisation is to be in force;

    (d)   the purpose for which the authorisation is given;

    (e)   any conditions subject to which the authorisation is given;

    (f)   the reason why each qualifying requirement is met.

(2) The statement of the reason why the eligibility requirement is met must be framed by reference to the cases in the table in paragraph 2 of Schedule 1A.

56 (1) If the name of the relevant hospital or care home changes, the standard authorisation is to be read as if it stated the current name of the hospital or care home.

(2) But sub-paragraph (1) is subject to any provision relating to the change of name which is made in any enactment or in any instrument made under an enactment.

Duty to give information about decision

57 (1) This paragraph applies if –

(a) a request is made for a standard authorisation, and

(b) the supervisory body are required by paragraph 50(1) to give the standard authorisation.

(2) The supervisory body must give a copy of the authorisation to each of the following –

(a) the relevant person's representative;

(b) the managing authority of the relevant hospital or care home;

(c) the relevant person;

(d) any section 39A IMCA;

(e) every interested person consulted by the best interests assessor.

(3) The supervisory body must comply with this paragraph as soon as practicable after they give the standard authorisation.

58 (1) This paragraph applies if –

(a) a request is made for a standard authorisation, and

(b) the supervisory body are prohibited by paragraph 50(2) from giving the standard authorisation.

(2) The supervisory body must give notice, stating that they are prohibited from giving the authorisation, to each of the following –

(a) the managing authority of the relevant hospital or care home;

(b) the relevant person;

(c) any section 39A IMCA;

(d) every interested person consulted by the best interests assessor.

(3) The supervisory body must comply with this paragraph as soon as practicable after it becomes apparent to them that they are prohibited from giving the authorisation.

Duty to give information about effect of authorisation

59 (1) This paragraph applies if a standard authorisation is given.

(2) The managing authority of the relevant hospital or care home must take such steps as are practicable to ensure that the relevant person understands all of the following –

(a) the effect of the authorisation;

(b) the right to make an application to the court to exercise its jurisdiction under section 21A;

(c) the right under Part 8 to request a review;

(d) the right to have a section 39D IMCA appointed;

(e) how to have a section 39D IMCA appointed.

(3) Those steps must be taken as soon as is practicable after the authorisation is given.

(4) Those steps must include the giving of appropriate information both orally and in writing.

(5) Any written information given to the relevant person must also be given by the managing authority to the relevant person's representative.

(6) They must give the information to the representative as soon as is practicable after it is given to the relevant person.

(7) Sub-paragraph (8) applies if the managing authority is notified that a section 39D IMCA has been appointed.

(8) As soon as is practicable after being notified, the managing authority must give the section 39D IMCA a copy of the written information given in accordance with sub-paragraph (4).

Records of authorisations

60   A supervisory body must keep a written record of all of the following information –

(a) the standard authorisations that they have given;

(b) the requests for standard authorisations in response to which they have not given an authorisation;

(c) in relation to each standard authorisation given: the matters stated in the authorisation in accordance with paragraph 55.

Variation of an authorisation

61   (1) A standard authorisation may not be varied except in accordance with Part 7 or 8.

(2) This paragraph does not affect the powers of the Court of Protection or of any other court.

Effect of decision about request made under paragraph 25 or 30

62   (1) This paragraph applies where the managing authority request a new standard authorisation under either of the following –

(a) paragraph 25 (change in place of detention);

(b) paragraph 30 (existing authorisation subject to review).

(2) If the supervisory body are required by paragraph 50(1) to give the new authorisation, the existing authorisation terminates at the time when the new authorisation comes into force.

(3) If the supervisory body are prohibited by paragraph 50(2) from giving the new authorisation, there is no effect on the existing authorisation's continuation in force.

When an authorisation is in force

63   (1) A standard authorisation comes into force when it is given.

(2) But if the authorisation provides for it to come into force at a later time, it comes into force at that time.

64   (1) A standard authorisation ceases to be in force at the end of the period stated in the authorisation in accordance with paragraph 55(1)(c).

(2) But if the authorisation terminates before then in accordance with paragraph 62(2) or any other provision of this Schedule, it ceases to be in force when the termination takes effect.

(3) This paragraph does not affect the powers of the Court of Protection or of any other court.

65   (1) This paragraph applies if a standard authorisation ceases to be in force.

(2) The supervisory body must give notice that the authorisation has ceased to be in force.

(3) The supervisory body must give that notice to all of the following –

(a)   the managing authority of the relevant hospital or care home;

(b)   the relevant person;

(c)   the relevant person's representative;

(d)   every interested person consulted by the best interests assessor.

(4)   The supervisory body must give that notice as soon as practicable after the authorisation ceases to be in force.

When a request for a standard authorisation is 'disposed of'

66   A request for a standard authorisation is to be regarded for the purposes of this Schedule as disposed of if the supervisory body have given –

(a)   a copy of the authorisation in accordance with paragraph 57, or

(b)   notice in accordance with paragraph 58.

Right of third party to require consideration of whether authorisation needed

67   For the purposes of paragraphs 68 to 73 there is an unauthorised deprivation of liberty if –

(a)   a person is already a detained resident in a hospital or care home, and

(b)   the detention of the person is not authorised as mentioned in section 4A.

68   (1)   If the following conditions are met, an eligible person may request the supervisory body to decide whether or not there is an unauthorised deprivation of liberty.

(2)   The first condition is that the eligible person has notified the managing authority of the relevant hospital or care home that it appears to the eligible person that there is an unauthorised deprivation of liberty.

(3)   The second condition is that the eligible person has asked the managing authority to request a standard authorisation in relation to the detention of the relevant person.

(4)   The third condition is that the managing authority has not requested a standard authorisation within a reasonable period after the eligible person asks it to do so.

(5)   In this paragraph 'eligible person' means any person other than the managing authority of the relevant hospital or care home.

69   (1)   This paragraph applies if an eligible person requests the supervisory body to decide whether or not there is an unauthorised deprivation of liberty.

(2)   The supervisory body must select and appoint a person to carry out an assessment of whether or not the relevant person is a detained resident.

(3)   But the supervisory body need not select and appoint a person to carry out such an assessment in either of these cases.

(4)   The first case is where it appears to the supervisory body that the request by the eligible person is frivolous or vexatious.

(5)   The second case is where it appears to the supervisory body that –

(a)   the question of whether or not there is an unauthorised deprivation of liberty has already been decided, and

(b)   since that decision, there has been no change of circumstances which would merit the question being decided again.

(6)   The supervisory body must not select and appoint a person to carry out an assessment under this paragraph unless it appears to the supervisory body that the person would be –

(a)   suitable to carry out a best interests assessment (if one were obtained in connection with a request for a standard authorisation relating to the relevant person), and

(b)   eligible to carry out such a best interests assessment.

(7) The supervisory body must notify the persons specified in subparagraph (8) –

   (a)   that the supervisory body have been requested to decide whether or not there is
         an unauthorised deprivation of liberty;
   (b)   of their decision whether or not to select and appoint a person to carry out an
         assessment under this paragraph;
   (c)   if their decision is to select and appoint a person, of the person appointed.

(8) The persons referred to in sub-paragraph (7) are –

   (a)   the eligible person who made the request under paragraph 68;
   (b)   the person to whom the request relates;
   (c)   the managing authority of the relevant hospital or care home;
   (d)   any section 39A IMCA.

70 (1) Regulations may be made about the period within which an assessment under
         paragraph 69 must be carried out.

   (2) Regulations made under paragraph 129(3) apply in relation to the selection and
        appointment of a person under paragraph 69 as they apply to the selection of a per-
        son under paragraph 129 to carry out a best interests assessment.

   (3) The following provisions apply to an assessment under paragraph 69 as they
        apply to an assessment carried out in connection with a request for a standard
        authorisation –

      (a)   paragraph 131 (examination and copying of records);
      (b)   paragraph 132 (representations);
      (c)   paragraphs 134 and 135(1) and (2) (duty to keep records and give copies).

   (4) The copies of the assessment which the supervisory body are required to give under
        paragraph 135(2) must be given as soon as practicable after the supervisory body are
        themselves given a copy of the assessment.

71 (1) This paragraph applies if –

      (a)   the supervisory body obtain an assessment under paragraph 69,
      (b)   the assessment comes to the conclusion that the relevant person is a detained
            resident, and
      (c)   it appears to the supervisory body that the detention of the person is not
            authorised as mentioned in section 4A.

   (2) This Schedule (including Part 5) applies as if the managing authority of the relevant
        hospital or care home had, in accordance with Part 4, requested the supervisory body
        to give a standard authorisation in relation to the relevant person.

   (3) The managing authority of the relevant hospital or care home must supply the super-
        visory body with the information (if any) which the managing authority would, by
        virtue of paragraph 31, have had to include in a request for a standard authorisation.

   (4) The supervisory body must notify the persons specified in paragraph 69(8) –

      (a)   of the outcome of the assessment obtained under paragraph 69, and
      (b)   that this Schedule applies as mentioned in sub-paragraph (2).

72 (1) This paragraph applies if –

      (a)   the supervisory body obtain an assessment under paragraph 69, and
      (b)   the assessment comes to the conclusion that the relevant person is not a
            detained resident.

   (2) The supervisory body must notify the persons specified in paragraph 69(8) of the
        outcome of the assessment.

73 (1) This paragraph applies if –

      (a)   the supervisory body obtain an assessment under paragraph 69,
      (b)   the assessment comes to the conclusion that the relevant person is a detained
            resident, and

(c)   it appears to the supervisory body that the detention of the person is authorised as mentioned in section 4A.

(2)   The supervisory body must notify the persons specified in paragraph 69(8) –

(a)   of the outcome of the assessment, and

(b)   that it appears to the supervisory body that the detention is authorised.

PART 5   URGENT AUTHORISATIONS

Managing authority to give authorisation

74   Only the managing authority of the relevant hospital or care home may give an urgent authorisation.

75   The managing authority may give an urgent authorisation only if they are required to do so by paragraph 76 (as read with paragraph 77).

Duty to give authorisation

76   (1)   The managing authority must give an urgent authorisation in either of the following cases.

(2)   The first case is where –

(a)   the managing authority are required to make a request under paragraph 24 or 25 for a standard authorisation, and

(b)   they believe that the need for the relevant person to be a detained resident is so urgent that it is appropriate for the detention to begin before they make the request.

(3)   The second case is where –

(a)   the managing authority have made a request under paragraph 24 or 25 for a standard authorisation, and

(b)   they believe that the need for the relevant person to be a detained resident is so urgent that it is appropriate for the detention to begin before the request is disposed of.

(4)   References in this paragraph to the detention of the relevant person are references to the detention to which paragraph 24 or 25 relates.

(5)   This paragraph is subject to paragraph 77.

77   (1)   This paragraph applies where the managing authority have given an urgent authorisation ('the original authorisation') in connection with a case where a person is, or is to be, a detained resident ('the existing detention').

(2)   No new urgent authorisation is to be given under paragraph 76 in connection with the existing detention.

(3)   But the managing authority may request the supervisory body to extend the duration of the original authorisation.

(4)   Only one request under sub-paragraph (3) may be made in relation to the original authorisation.

(5)   Paragraphs 84 to 86 apply to any request made under subparagraph (3).

Terms of authorisation

78   (1)   If the managing authority decide to give an urgent authorisation, they must decide the period during which the authorisation is to be in force.

(2)   That period must not exceed 7 days.

Form of authorisation

79   An urgent authorisation must be in writing.

80   An urgent authorisation must state the following things –

    (a)   the name of the relevant person;

    (b)   the name of the relevant hospital or care home;

    (c)   the period during which the authorisation is to be in force;

    (d)   the purpose for which the authorisation is given.

81   (1)   If the name of the relevant hospital or care home changes, the urgent authorisation is to be read as if it stated the current name of the hospital or care home.

    (2)   But sub-paragraph (1) is subject to any provision relating to the change of name which is made in any enactment or in any instrument made under an enactment.

Duty to keep records and give copies

82   (1)   This paragraph applies if an urgent authorisation is given.

    (2)   The managing authority must keep a written record of why they have given the urgent authorisation.

    (3)   As soon as practicable after giving the authorisation, the managing authority must give a copy of the authorisation to all of the following –

        (a)   the relevant person;

        (b)   any section 39A IMCA.

Duty to give information about authorisation

83   (1)   This paragraph applies if an urgent authorisation is given.

    (2)   The managing authority of the relevant hospital or care home must take such steps as are practicable to ensure that the relevant person understands all of the following –

        (a)   the effect of the authorisation;

        (b)   the right to make an application to the court to exercise its jurisdiction under section 21A.

    (3)   Those steps must be taken as soon as is practicable after the authorisation is given.

    (4)   Those steps must include the giving of appropriate information both orally and in writing.

Request for extension of duration

84   (1)   This paragraph applies if the managing authority make a request under paragraph 77 for the supervisory body to extend the duration of the original authorisation.

    (2)   The managing authority must keep a written record of why they have made the request.

    (3)   The managing authority must give the relevant person notice that they have made the request.

    (4)   The supervisory body may extend the duration of the original authorisation if it appears to them that –

        (a)   the managing authority have made the required request for a standard authorisation,

        (b)   there are exceptional reasons why it has not yet been possible for that request to be disposed of, and

        (c)   it is essential for the existing detention to continue until the request is disposed of.

(5) The supervisory body must keep a written record that the request has been made to them.

(6) In this paragraph and paragraphs 85 and 86 –

    (a) 'original authorisation' and 'existing detention' have the same meaning as in paragraph 77;

    (b) the required request for a standard authorisation is the request that is referred to in paragraph 76(2) or (3).

85 (1) This paragraph applies if, under paragraph 84, the supervisory body decide to extend the duration of the original authorisation.

    (2) The supervisory body must decide the period of the extension.

    (3) That period must not exceed 7 days.

    (4) The supervisory body must give the managing authority notice stating the period of the extension.

    (5) The managing authority must then vary the original authorisation so that it states the extended duration.

    (6) Paragraphs 82(3) and 83 apply (with the necessary modifications) to the variation of the original authorisation as they apply to the giving of an urgent authorisation.

    (7) The supervisory body must keep a written record of –

        (a) the outcome of the request, and

        (b) the period of the extension.

86 (1) This paragraph applies if, under paragraph 84, the supervisory body decide not to extend the duration of the original authorisation.

    (2) The supervisory body must give the managing authority notice stating –

        (a) the decision, and

        (b) their reasons for making it.

    (3) The managing authority must give a copy of that notice to all of the following –

        (a) the relevant person;

        (b) any section 39A IMCA.

    (4) The supervisory body must keep a written record of the outcome of the request.

No variation

87 (1) An urgent authorisation may not be varied except in accordance with paragraph 85.

    (2) This paragraph does not affect the powers of the Court of Protection or of any other court.

When an authorisation is in force

88 An urgent authorisation comes into force when it is given.

89 (1) An urgent authorisation ceases to be in force at the end of the period stated in the authorisation in accordance with paragraph 80(c) (subject to any variation in accordance with paragraph 85).

    (2) But if the required request is disposed of before the end of that period, the urgent authorisation ceases to be in force as follows.

    (3) If the supervisory body are required by paragraph 50(1) to give the requested authorisation, the urgent authorisation ceases to be in force when the requested authorisation comes into force.

    (4) If the supervisory body are prohibited by paragraph 50(2) from giving the requested authorisation, the urgent authorisation ceases to be in force when the managing authority receive notice under paragraph 58.

    (5) In this paragraph –

'required request' means the request referred to in paragraph 76(2) or (3);

'requested authorisation' means the standard authorisation to which the required request relates.

(6) This paragraph does not affect the powers of the Court of Protection or of any other court.

90 (1) This paragraph applies if an urgent authorisation ceases to be in force.

(2) The supervisory body must give notice that the authorisation has ceased to be in force.

(3) The supervisory body must give that notice to all of the following –

(a) the relevant person;

(b) any section 39A IMCA.

(4) The supervisory body must give that notice as soon as practicable after the authorisation ceases to be in force.

PART 6   ELIGIBILITY REQUIREMENT NOT MET: SUSPENSION OF STANDARD AUTHORISATION

91 (1) This Part applies if the following conditions are met.

(2) The first condition is that a standard authorisation –

(a) has been given, and

(b) has not ceased to be in force.

(3) The second condition is that the managing authority of the relevant hospital or care home are satisfied that the relevant person has ceased to meet the eligibility requirement.

(4) But this Part does not apply if the relevant person is ineligible by virtue of paragraph 5 of Schedule 1A (in which case see Part 8).

92 The managing authority of the relevant hospital or care home must give the supervisory body notice that the relevant person has ceased to meet the eligibility requirement.

93 (1) This paragraph applies if the managing authority give the supervisory body notice under paragraph 92.

(2) The standard authorisation is suspended from the time when the notice is given.

(3) The supervisory body must give notice that the standard authorisation has been suspended to the following persons –

(a) the relevant person;

(b) the relevant person's representative;

(c) the managing authority of the relevant hospital or care home.

94 (1) This paragraph applies if, whilst the standard authorisation is suspended, the managing authority are satisfied that the relevant person meets the eligibility requirement again.

(2) The managing authority must give the supervisory body notice that the relevant person meets the eligibility requirement again.

95 (1) This paragraph applies if the managing authority give the supervisory body notice under paragraph 94.

(2) The standard authorisation ceases to be suspended from the time when the notice is given.

(3) The supervisory body must give notice that the standard authorisation has ceased to be suspended to the following persons –

(a) the relevant person;

(b) the relevant person's representative;

(c) any section 39D IMCA;

(d) the managing authority of the relevant hospital or care home.

(4) The supervisory body must give notice under this paragraph as soon as practicable after they are given notice under paragraph 94.

96 (1) This paragraph applies if no notice is given under paragraph 94 before the end of the relevant 28 day period.

(2) The standard authorisation ceases to have effect at the end of the relevant 28 day period.

(3) The relevant 28 day period is the period of 28 days beginning with the day on which the standard authorisation is suspended under paragraph 93.

97 The effect of suspending the standard authorisation is that Part 1 ceases to apply for as long as the authorisation is suspended.

PART 7   STANDARD AUTHORISATIONS: CHANGE IN SUPERVISORY RESPONSIBILITY

Application of this Part

98 (1) This Part applies if these conditions are met.

(2) The first condition is that a standard authorisation –

(a) has been given, and

(b) has not ceased to be in force.

(3) The second condition is that there is a change in supervisory responsibility.

(4) The third condition is that there is not a change in the place of detention (within the meaning of paragraph 25).

99 For the purposes of this Part there is a change in supervisory responsibility if –

(a) one body ('the old supervisory body') have ceased to be supervisory body in relation to the standard authorisation, and

(b) a different body ('the new supervisory body') have become supervisory body in relation to the standard authorisation.

Effect of change in supervisory responsibility

100 (1) The new supervisory body becomes the supervisory body in relation to the authorisation.

(2) Anything done by or in relation to the old supervisory body in connection with the authorisation has effect, so far as is necessary for continuing its effect after the change, as if done by or in relation to the new supervisory body.

(3) Anything which relates to the authorisation and which is in the process of being done by or in relation to the old supervisory body at the time of the change may be continued by or in relation to the new supervisory body.

(4) But –

(a) the old supervisory body do not, by virtue of this paragraph, cease to be liable for anything done by them in connection with the authorisation before the change; and

(b) the new supervisory body do not, by virtue of this paragraph, become liable for any such thing.

PART 8   STANDARD AUTHORISATIONS: REVIEW

Application of this Part

101 (1)   This Part applies if a standard authorisation –

  (a)   has been given, and
  (b)   has not ceased to be in force.

  (2)   Paragraphs 102 to 122 are subject to paragraphs 123 to 125.

Review by supervisory body

102 (1)   The supervisory body may at any time carry out a review of the standard authorisation in accordance with this Part.

  (2)   The supervisory body must carry out such a review if they are requested to do so by an eligible person.

  (3)   Each of the following is an eligible person –

  (a)   the relevant person;
  (b)   the relevant person's representative;
  (c)   the managing authority of the relevant hospital or care home.

Request for review

103 (1)   An eligible person may, at any time, request the supervisory body to carry out a review of the standard authorisation in accordance with this Part.

  (2)   The managing authority of the relevant hospital or care home must make such a request if one or more of the qualifying requirements appear to them to be reviewable.

Grounds for review

104 (1)   Paragraphs 105 to 107 set out the grounds on which the qualifying requirements are reviewable.

  (2)   A qualifying requirement is not reviewable on any other ground.

Non-qualification ground

105 (1)   Any of the following qualifying requirements is reviewable on the ground that the relevant person does not meet the requirement –

  (a)   the age requirement;
  (b)   the mental health requirement;
  (c)   the mental capacity requirement;
  (d)   the best interests requirement;
  (e)   the no refusals requirement.

  (2)   The eligibility requirement is reviewable on the ground that the relevant person is ineligible by virtue of paragraph 5 of Schedule 1A.

  (3)   The ground in sub-paragraph (1) and the ground in subparagraph (2) are referred to as the non-qualification ground.

Change of reason ground

106 (1) Any of the following qualifying requirements is reviewable on the ground set out in sub-paragraph (2) –

(a)   the mental health requirement;
(b)   the mental capacity requirement;
(c)   the best interests requirement;
(d)   the eligibility requirement;
(e)   the no refusals requirement.

(2) The ground is that the reason why the relevant person meets the requirement is not the reason stated in the standard authorisation.

(3) This ground is referred to as the change of reason ground.

Variation of conditions ground

107 (1) The best interests requirement is reviewable on the ground that –

(a)   there has been a change in the relevant person's case, and
(b)   because of that change, it would be appropriate to vary the conditions to which the standard authorisation is subject.

(2) This ground is referred to as the variation of conditions ground.

(3) A reference to varying the conditions to which the standard authorisation is subject is a reference to –

(a)   amendment of an existing condition,
(b)   omission of an existing condition, or
(c)   inclusion of a new condition (whether or not there are already any existing conditions).

Notice that review to be carried out

108 (1) If the supervisory body are to carry out a review of the standard authorisation, they must give notice of the review to the following persons –

(a)   the relevant person;
(b)   the relevant person's representative;
(c)   the managing authority of the relevant hospital or care home.

(2) The supervisory body must give the notice –

(a)   before they begin the review, or
(b)   if that is not practicable, as soon as practicable after they have begun it.

(3) This paragraph does not require the supervisory body to give notice to any person who has requested the review.

Starting a review

109 To start a review of the standard authorisation, the supervisory body must decide which, if any, of the qualifying requirements appear to be reviewable.

No reviewable qualifying requirements

110 (1) This paragraph applies if no qualifying requirements appear to be reviewable.

(2) This Part does not require the supervisory body to take any action in respect of the standard authorisation.

One or more reviewable qualifying requirements

111 (1) This paragraph applies if one or more qualifying requirements appear to be reviewable.

(2) The supervisory body must secure that a separate review assessment is carried out in
relation to each qualifying requirement which appears to be reviewable.

(3) But sub-paragraph (2) does not require the supervisory body to secure that a best
interests review assessment is carried out in a case where the best interests
requirement appears to the supervisory body to be non-assessable.

(4) The best interests requirement is non-assessable if –

(a) the requirement is reviewable only on the variation of conditions ground, and
(b) the change in the relevant person's case is not significant.

(5) In making any decision whether the change in the relevant person's case is significant,
regard must be had to –

(a) the nature of the change, and
(b) the period that the change is likely to last for.

Review assessments

112 (1) A review assessment is an assessment of whether the relevant person meets a
qualifying requirement.

(2) In relation to a review assessment –

(a) a negative conclusion is a conclusion that the relevant person does not meet the
qualifying requirement to which the assessment relates;
(b) a positive conclusion is a conclusion that the relevant person meets the
qualifying requirement to which the assessment relates.

(3) An age review assessment is a review assessment carried out in relation to the age
requirement.

(4) A mental health review assessment is a review assessment carried out in relation to
the mental health requirement.

(5) A mental capacity review assessment is a review assessment carried out in relation to
the mental capacity requirement.

(6) A best interests review assessment is a review assessment carried out in relation to
the best interests requirement.

(7) An eligibility review assessment is a review assessment carried out in relation to the
eligibility requirement.

(8) A no refusals review assessment is a review assessment carried out in relation to the
no refusals requirement.

113 (1) In carrying out a review assessment, the assessor must comply with any duties which
would be imposed upon him under Part 4 if the assessment were being carried out in
connection with a request for a standard authorisation.

(2) But in the case of a best interests review assessment, paragraphs 43 and 44 do not
apply.

(3) Instead of what is required by paragraph 43, the best interests review assessment must
include recommendations about whether – and, if so, how – it would be appropriate
to vary the conditions to which the standard authorisation is subject.

Best interests requirement reviewable but non-assessable

114 (1) This paragraph applies in a case where –

(a) the best interests requirement appears to be reviewable, but

(b)   in accordance with paragraph 111(3), the supervisory body are not required to secure that a best interests review assessment is carried out.

(2)   The supervisory body may vary the conditions to which the standard authorisation is subject in such ways (if any) as the supervisory body think are appropriate in the circumstances.

Best interests review assessment positive

115 (1)   This paragraph applies in a case where –

   (a)   a best interests review assessment is carried out, and

   (b)   the assessment comes to a positive conclusion.

(2)   The supervisory body must decide the following questions –

   (a)   whether or not the best interests requirement is reviewable on the change of reason ground;

   (b)   whether or not the best interests requirement is reviewable on the variation of conditions ground;

   (c)   if so, whether or not the change in the person's case is significant.

(3)   If the supervisory body decide that the best interests requirement is reviewable on the change of reason ground, they must vary the standard authorisation so that it states the reason why the relevant person now meets that requirement.

(4)   If the supervisory body decide that –

   (a)   the best interests requirement is reviewable on the variation of conditions ground, and

   (b)   the change in the relevant person's case is not significant, they may vary the conditions to which the standard authorisation is subject in such ways (if any) as they think are appropriate in the circumstances.

(5)   If the supervisory body decide that –

   (a)   the best interests requirement is reviewable on the variation of conditions ground, and

   (b)   the change in the relevant person's case is significant, they must vary the conditions to which the standard authorisation is subject in such ways as they think are appropriate in the circumstances.

(6)   If the supervisory body decide that the best interests requirement is not reviewable on –

   (a)   the change of reason ground, or

   (b)   the variation of conditions ground,

this Part does not require the supervisory body to take any action in respect of the standard authorisation so far as the best interests requirement relates to it.

Mental health, mental capacity, eligibility or no refusals review assessment positive

116 (1)   This paragraph applies if the following conditions are met.

(2)   The first condition is that one or more of the following are carried out –

   (a)   a mental health review assessment;

   (b)   a mental capacity review assessment;

   (c)   an eligibility review assessment;

   (d)   a no refusals review assessment.

(3)   The second condition is that each assessment carried out comes to a positive conclusion.

(4)   The supervisory body must decide whether or not each of the assessed qualifying requirements is reviewable on the change of reason ground.

(5)   If the supervisory body decide that any of the assessed qualifying requirements is reviewable on the change of reason ground, they must vary the standard authorisation so that it states the reason why the relevant person now meets the requirement or requirements in question.

(6)   If the supervisory body decide that none of the assessed qualifying requirements are reviewable on the change of reason ground, this Part does not require the supervisory body to take any action in respect of the standard authorisation so far as those requirements relate to it.

(7)   An assessed qualifying requirement is a qualifying requirement in relation to which a review assessment is carried out.

One or more review assessments negative

117 (1)   This paragraph applies if one or more of the review assessments carried out comes to a negative conclusion.

(2)   The supervisory body must terminate the standard authorisation with immediate effect.

Completion of a review

118 (1)   The review of the standard authorisation is complete in any of the following cases.

(2)   The first case is where paragraph 110 applies.

(3)   The second case is where –

(a)   paragraph 111 applies, and

(b)   paragraph 117 requires the supervisory body to terminate the standard authorisation.

(4)   In such a case, the supervisory body need not comply with any of the other provisions of paragraphs 114 to 116 which would be applicable to the review (were it not for this sub-paragraph).

(5)   The third case is where –

(a)   paragraph 111 applies,

(b)   paragraph 117 does not require the supervisory body to terminate the standard authorisation, and

(c)   the supervisory body comply with all of the provisions of paragraphs 114 to 116 (so far as they are applicable to the review).

Variations under this Part

119 Any variation of the standard authorisation made under this Part must be in writing.

Notice of outcome of review

120 (1)   When the review of the standard authorisation is complete, the supervisory body must give notice to all of the following –

(a)   the managing authority of the relevant hospital or care home;

(b)   the relevant person;

(c)   the relevant person's representative;

(d)   any section 39D IMCA.

(2)   That notice must state –

(a)   the outcome of the review, and

(b)   what variation (if any) has been made to the authorisation under this Part.

Records

121 A supervisory body must keep a written record of the following information –

(a)   each request for a review that is made to them;

(b)   the outcome of each request;

(c)   each review which they carry out;

(d)   the outcome of each review which they carry out;

(e)   any variation of an authorisation made in consequence of a review.

Relationship between review and suspension under Part 6

122 (1) This paragraph applies if a standard authorisation is suspended in accordance with Part 6.

(2) No review may be requested under this Part whilst the standard authorisation is suspended.

(3) If a review has already been requested, or is being carried out, when the standard authorisation is suspended, no steps are to be taken in connection with that review whilst the authorisation is suspended.

Relationship between review and request for new authorisation

123 (1) This paragraph applies if, in accordance with paragraph 24 (as read with paragraph 29), the managing authority of the relevant hospital or care home make a request for a new standard authorisation which would be in force after the expiry of the existing authorisation.

(2) No review may be requested under this Part until the request for the new standard authorisation has been disposed of.

(3) If a review has already been requested, or is being carried out, when the new standard authorisation is requested, no steps are to be taken in connection with that review until the request for the new standard authorisation has been disposed of.

124 (1) This paragraph applies if –

(a)   a review under this Part has been requested, or is being carried out, and

(b)   the managing authority of the relevant hospital or care home make a request under paragraph 30 for a new standard authorisation which would be in force on or before, and after, the expiry of the existing authorisation.

(2) No steps are to be taken in connection with the review under this Part until the request for the new standard authorisation has been disposed of.

125 In paragraphs 123 and 124 –

(a)   the existing authorisation is the authorisation referred to in paragraph 101;

(b)   the expiry of the existing authorisation is the time when it is expected to cease to be in force.

PART 9   ASSESSMENTS UNDER THIS SCHEDULE

Introduction

126 This Part contains provision about assessments under this Schedule.

127 An assessment under this Schedule is either of the following –

    (a)   an assessment carried out in connection with a request for a standard authorisation under Part 4;

    (b)   a review assessment carried out in connection with a review of a standard authorisation under Part 8.

128 In this Part, in relation to an assessment under this Schedule –

'assessor' means the person carrying out the assessment;
'relevant procedure' means –

    (a)   the request for the standard authorisation, or
    (b)   the review of the standard authorisation;

'supervisory body' means the supervisory body responsible for securing that the assessment is carried out.

Supervisory body to select assessor

129 (1) It is for the supervisory body to select a person to carry out an assessment under this Schedule.

    (2) The supervisory body must not select a person to carry out an assessment unless the person –

        (a)   appears to the supervisory body to be suitable to carry out the assessment (having regard, in particular, to the type of assessment and the person to be assessed), and
        (b)   is eligible to carry out the assessment.

    (3) Regulations may make provision about the selection, and eligibility, of persons to carry out assessments under this Schedule.

    (4) Sub-paragraphs (5) and (6) apply if two or more assessments are to be obtained for the purposes of the relevant procedure.

    (5) In a case where the assessments to be obtained include a mental health assessment and a best interests assessment, the supervisory body must not select the same person to carry out both assessments.

    (6) Except as prohibited by sub-paragraph (5), the supervisory body may select the same person to carry out any number of the assessments which the person appears to be suitable, and is eligible, to carry out.

130 (1) This paragraph applies to regulations under paragraph 129(3).

    (2) The regulations may make provision relating to a person's –

        (a)   qualifications,
        (b)   skills,
        (c)   training,
        (d)   experience,
        (e)   relationship to, or connection with, the relevant person or any other person,
        (f)   involvement in the care or treatment of the relevant person,
        (g)   connection with the supervisory body, or
        (h)   connection with the relevant hospital or care home, or with any other establishment or undertaking.

    (3) The provision that the regulations may make in relation to a person's training may provide for particular training to be specified by the appropriate authority otherwise than in the regulations.

    (4) In sub-paragraph (3) the 'appropriate authority' means –

        (a)   in relation to England: the Secretary of State;
        (b)   in relation to Wales: the National Assembly for Wales.

    (5) The regulations may make provision requiring a person to be insured in respect of liabilities that may arise in connection with the carrying out of an assessment.

(6) In relation to cases where two or more assessments are to be obtained for the purposes of the relevant procedure, the regulations may limit the number, kind or combination of assessments which a particular person is eligible to carry out.

(7) Sub-paragraphs (2) to (6) do not limit the generality of the provision that may be made in the regulations.

Examination and copying of records

131 An assessor may, at all reasonable times, examine and take copies of –

(a) any health record,

(b) any record of, or held by, a local authority and compiled in accordance with a social services function, and

(c) any record held by a person registered under Part 2 of the Care Standards Act 2000,

which the assessor considers may be relevant to the assessment which is being carried out.

Representations

132 In carrying out an assessment under this Schedule, the assessor must take into account any information given, or submissions made, by any of the following –

(a) the relevant person's representative;

(b) any section 39A IMCA;

(c) any section 39C IMCA;

(d) any section 39D IMCA.

Assessments to stop if any comes to negative conclusion

133 (1) This paragraph applies if an assessment under this Schedule comes to the conclusion that the relevant person does not meet one of the qualifying requirements.

(2) This Schedule does not require the supervisory body to secure that any other assessments under this Schedule are carried out in relation to the relevant procedure.

(3) The supervisory body must give notice to any assessor who is carrying out another assessment in connection with the relevant procedure that they are to cease carrying out that assessment.

(4) If an assessor receives such notice, this Schedule does not require the assessor to continue carrying out that assessment.

Duty to keep records and give copies

134 (1) This paragraph applies if an assessor has carried out an assessment under this Schedule (whatever conclusions the assessment has come to).

(2) The assessor must keep a written record of the assessment.

(3) As soon as practicable after carrying out the assessment, the assessor must give copies of the assessment to the supervisory body.

135 (1) This paragraph applies to the supervisory body if they are given a copy of an assessment under this Schedule.

(2) The supervisory body must give copies of the assessment to all of the following –

(a) the managing authority of the relevant hospital or care home;

(b) the relevant person;

(c) any section 39A IMCA;

(d) the relevant person's representative.

(3) If –

    (a)   the assessment is obtained in relation to a request for a standard authorisation, and

    (b)   the supervisory body are required by paragraph 50(1) to give the standard authorisation,

the supervisory body must give the copies of the assessment when they give copies of the authorisation in accordance with paragraph 57.

(4) If –

    (a)   the assessment is obtained in relation to a request for a standard authorisation, and

    (b)   the supervisory body are prohibited by paragraph 50(2) from giving the standard authorisation,

the supervisory body must give the copies of the assessment when they give notice in accordance with paragraph 58.

(5) If the assessment is obtained in connection with the review of a standard authorisation, the supervisory body must give the copies of the assessment when they give notice in accordance with paragraph 120.

136 (1) This paragraph applies to the supervisory body if –

    (a)   they are given a copy of a best interests assessment, and

    (b)   the assessment includes, in accordance with paragraph 44(2), a statement that it appears to the assessor that there is an unauthorised deprivation of liberty.

(2) The supervisory body must notify all of the persons listed in subparagraph (3) that the assessment includes such a statement.

(3) Those persons are –

    (a)   the managing authority of the relevant hospital or care home;

    (b)   the relevant person;

    (c)   any section 39A IMCA;

    (d)   any interested person consulted by the best interests assessor.

(4) The supervisory body must comply with this paragraph when (or at some time before) they comply with paragraph 135.

PART 10   RELEVANT PERSON'S REPRESENTATIVE

The representative

137 In this Schedule the relevant person's representative is the person appointed as such in accordance with this Part.

138 (1) Regulations may make provision about the selection and appointment of representatives.

(2) In this Part such regulations are referred to as 'appointment regulations'.

Supervisory body to appoint representative

139 (1) The supervisory body must appoint a person to be the relevant person's representative as soon as practicable after a standard authorisation is given.

(2) The supervisory body must appoint a person to be the relevant person's representative if a vacancy arises whilst a standard authorisation is in force.

(3) Where a vacancy arises, the appointment under sub-paragraph (2) is to be made as soon as practicable after the supervisory body becomes aware of the vacancy.

140 (1) The selection of a person for appointment under paragraph 139 must not be made unless it appears to the person making the selection that the prospective representative would, if appointed –

(a) maintain contact with the relevant person,

(b) represent the relevant person in matters relating to or connected with this Schedule, and

(c) support the relevant person in matters relating to or connected with this Schedule.

141 (1) Any appointment of a representative for a relevant person is in addition to, and does not affect, any appointment of a donee or deputy.

(2) The functions of any representative are in addition to, and do not affect –

(a) the authority of any donee,

(b) the powers of any deputy, or

(c) any powers of the court.

Appointment regulations

142 Appointment regulations may provide that the procedure for appointing a representative may begin at any time after a request for a standard authorisation is made (including a time before the request has been disposed of).

143 (1) Appointment regulations may make provision about who is to select a person for appointment as a representative.

(2) But regulations under this paragraph may only provide for the following to make a selection –

(a) the relevant person, if he has capacity in relation to the question of which person should be his representative;

(b) a donee of a lasting power of attorney granted by the relevant person, if it is within the scope of his authority to select a person;

(c) a deputy, if it is within the scope of his authority to select a person;

(d) a best interests assessor;

(e) the supervisory body.

(3) Regulations under this paragraph may provide that a selection by the relevant person, a donee or a deputy is subject to approval by a best interests assessor or the supervisory body.

(4) Regulations under this paragraph may provide that, if more than one selection is necessary in connection with the appointment of a particular representative –

(a) the same person may make more than one selection;

(b) different persons may make different selections.

(5) For the purposes of this paragraph a best interests assessor is a person carrying out a best interests assessment in connection with the standard authorisation in question (including the giving of that authorisation).

144 (1) Appointment regulations may make provision about who may, or may not, be –

(a) selected for appointment as a representative, or

(b) appointed as a representative.

(2) Regulations under this paragraph may relate to any of the following matters –

(a) a person's age;

(b) a person's suitability;

(c) a person's independence;

(d) a person's willingness;

(e) a person's qualifications.

145 *Appointment regulations may make provision about the formalities of appointing a person as a representative.*

146 *In a case where a best interests assessor is to select a person to be appointed as a representative, appointment regulations may provide for the variation of the assessor's duties in relation to the assessment which he is carrying out.*

Monitoring of representatives

147 *Regulations may make provision requiring the managing authority of the relevant hospital or care home to –*

(a) *monitor, and*

(b) *report to the supervisory body on,*

the extent to which a representative is maintaining contact with the relevant person.

Termination

148 *Regulations may make provision about the circumstances in which the appointment of a person as the relevant person's representative ends or may be ended.*

149 *Regulations may make provision about the formalities of ending the appointment of a person as a representative.*

Suspension of representative's functions

150 (1) *Regulations may make provision about the circumstances in which functions exercisable by, or in relation to, the relevant person's representative (whether under this Schedule or not) may be –*

(a) *suspended, and*

(b) *if suspended, revived.*

(2) *The regulations may make provision about the formalities for giving effect to the suspension or revival of a function.*

(3) *The regulations may make provision about the effect of the suspension or revival of a function.*

Payment of representative

151 *Regulations may make provision for payments to be made to, or in relation to, persons exercising functions as the relevant person's representative.*

Regulations under this Part

152 *The provisions of this Part which specify provision that may be made in regulations under this Part do not affect the generality of the power to make such regulations.*

Effect of appointment of section 39C IMCA

153 *Paragraphs 159 and 160 make provision about the exercise of functions by, or towards, the relevant person's representative during periods when –*

(a) *no person is appointed as the relevant person's representative, but*

(b) *a person is appointed as a section 39C IMCA.*

PART 11   IMCAS

Application of Part

154 This Part applies for the purposes of this Schedule.

The IMCAs

155 A section 39A IMCA is an independent mental capacity advocate appointed under section 39A.

156 A section 39C IMCA is an independent mental capacity advocate appointed under section 39C.

157 A section 39D IMCA is an independent mental capacity advocate appointed under section 39D.

158 An IMCA is a section 39A IMCA or a section 39C IMCA or a section 39D IMCA.

Section 39C IMCA: functions

159 (1) This paragraph applies if, and for as long as, there is a section 39C IMCA.

(2) In the application of the relevant provisions, references to the relevant person's representative are to be read as references to the section 39C IMCA.

(3) But sub-paragraph (2) does not apply to any function under the relevant provisions for as long as the function is suspended in accordance with provision made under Part 10.

(4) In this paragraph and paragraph 160 the relevant provisions are –

(a) paragraph 102(3)(b) (request for review under Part 8);

(b) paragraph 108(1)(b) (notice of review under Part 8);

(c) paragraph 120(1)(c) (notice of outcome of review under Part 8).

160 (1) This paragraph applies if –

(a) a person is appointed as the relevant person's representative, and

(b) a person accordingly ceases to hold an appointment as a section 39C IMCA.

(2) Where a function under a relevant provision has been exercised by, or towards, the section 39C IMCA, there is no requirement for that function to be exercised again by, or towards, the relevant person's representative.

Section 39A IMCA: restriction of functions

161 (1) This paragraph applies if –

(a) there is a section 39A IMCA, and

(b) a person is appointed under Part 10 to be the relevant person's representative (whether or not that person, or any person subsequently appointed, is currently the relevant person's representative).

(2) The duties imposed on, and the powers exercisable by, the section 39A IMCA do not apply.

(3) The duties imposed on, and the powers exercisable by, any other person do not apply, so far as they fall to be performed or exercised towards the section 39A IMCA.

(4) But sub-paragraph (2) does not apply to any power of challenge exercisable by the section 39A IMCA.

(5) And sub-paragraph (3) does not apply to any duty or power of any other person so far as it relates to any power of challenge exercisable by the section 39A IMCA.

(6) Before exercising any power of challenge, the section 39A IMCA must take the views of the relevant person's representative into account.

(7) A power of challenge is a power to make an application to the court to exercise its jurisdiction under section 21A in connection with the giving of the standard authorisation.

PART 12   MISCELLANEOUS

Monitoring of operation of Schedule

162 (1) Regulations may make provision for, and in connection with, requiring one or more prescribed bodies to monitor, and report on, the operation of this Schedule in relation to England.

(2) The regulations may, in particular, give a prescribed body authority to do one or more of the following things –

(a)   to visit hospitals and care homes;

(b)   to visit and interview persons accommodated in hospitals and care homes;

(c)   to require the production of, and to inspect, records relating to the care or treatment of persons.

(3) 'Prescribed' means prescribed in regulations under this paragraph.

163 (1) Regulations may make provision for, and in connection with, enabling the National Assembly for Wales to monitor, and report on, the operation of this Schedule in relation to Wales.

(2) The National Assembly may direct one or more persons or bodies to carry out the Assembly's functions under regulations under this paragraph.

Disclosure of information

164 (1) Regulations may require either or both of the following to disclose prescribed information to prescribed bodies –

(a)   supervisory bodies;

(b)   managing authorities of hospitals or care homes.

(2) 'Prescribed' means prescribed in regulations under this paragraph.

(3) Regulations under this paragraph may only prescribe information relating to matters with which this Schedule is concerned.

Directions by National Assembly in relation to supervisory functions

165 (1) The National Assembly for Wales may direct a Local Health Board to exercise in relation to its area any supervisory functions which are specified in the direction.

(2) Directions under this paragraph must not preclude the National Assembly from exercising the functions specified in the directions.

(3) In this paragraph 'supervisory functions' means functions which the National Assembly have as supervisory body, so far as they are exercisable in relation to hospitals (whether NHS or independent hospitals, and whether in Wales or England).

166 (1) This paragraph applies where, under paragraph 165, a Local Health Board ('the specified LHB') is directed to exercise supervisory functions ('delegated functions').

(2) The National Assembly for Wales may give directions to the specified LHB about the Board's exercise of delegated functions.

(3) The National Assembly may give directions for any delegated functions to be exercised, on behalf of the specified LHB, by a committee, sub-committee or officer of that Board.

(4)   The National Assembly may give directions providing for any delegated functions to be exercised by the specified LHB jointly with one or more other Local Health Boards.

(5)   Where, under sub-paragraph (4), delegated functions are exercisable jointly, the National Assembly may give directions providing for the functions to be exercised, on behalf of the Local Health Boards in question, by a joint committee or joint subcommittee.

167 (1)   Directions under paragraph 165 must be given in regulations.

(2)   Directions under paragraph 166 may be given –

(a)   in regulations, or

(b)   by instrument in writing.

168 The power under paragraph 165 or paragraph 166 to give directions includes power to vary or revoke directions given under that paragraph.

Notices

169 Any notice under this Schedule must be in writing.

Regulations

170 (1)   This paragraph applies to all regulations under this Schedule, except regulations under paragraph 162, 163, 167 or 183.

(2)   It is for the Secretary of State to make such regulations in relation to authorisations under this Schedule which relate to hospitals and care homes situated in England.

(3)   It is for the National Assembly for Wales to make such regulations in relation to authorisations under this Schedule which relate to hospitals and care homes situated in Wales.

171 It is for the Secretary of State to make regulations under paragraph 162.

172 It is for the National Assembly for Wales to make regulations under paragraph 163 or 167.

173 (1)   This paragraph applies to regulations under paragraph 183.

(2)   It is for the Secretary of State to make such regulations in relation to cases where a question as to the ordinary residence of a person is to be determined by the Secretary of State.

(3)   It is for the National Assembly for Wales to make such regulations in relation to cases where a question as to the ordinary residence of a person is to be determined by the National Assembly.

PART 13   INTERPRETATION

Introduction

174 This Part applies for the purposes of this Schedule.

Hospitals and their managing authorities

175 (1)   'Hospital' means –

(a)   an NHS hospital, or

(b)   an independent hospital.

(2)   'NHS hospital' means –

(a)   a health service hospital as defined by section 275 of the National Health Service Act 2006 or section 206 of the National Health Service (Wales) Act 2006, or

(b)   a hospital as defined by section 206 of the National Health Service (Wales) Act 2006 vested in a Local Health Board.

(3) 'Independent hospital' means a hospital as defined by section 2 of the Care Standards Act 2000 which is not an NHS hospital.

176 (1) 'Managing authority', in relation to an NHS hospital, means –

(a)   if the hospital –

(i)   is vested in the appropriate national authority for the purposes of its functions under the National Health Service Act 2006 or of the National Health Service (Wales) Act 2006, or

(ii)   consists of any accommodation provided by a local authority and used as a hospital by or on behalf of the appropriate national authority under either of those Acts,

the Primary Care Trust, Strategic Health Authority, Local Health Board or Special Health Authority responsible for the administration of the hospital;

(b)   if the hospital is vested in a Primary Care Trust, National Health Service trust or NHS foundation trust, that trust;

(c)   if the hospital is vested in a Local Health Board, that Board.

(2) For this purpose the appropriate national authority is –

(a)   in relation to England: the Secretary of State;

(b)   in relation to Wales: the National Assembly for Wales;

(c)   in relation to England and Wales: the Secretary of State and the National Assembly acting jointly.

177 'Managing authority', in relation to an independent hospital, means the person registered, or required to be registered, under Part 2 of the Care Standards Act 2000 in respect of the hospital.

Care homes and their managing authorities

178 'Care home' has the meaning given by section 3 of the Care Standards Act 2000.

179 'Managing authority', in relation to a care home, means the person registered, or required to be registered, under Part 2 of the Care Standards Act 2000 in respect of the care home.

Supervisory bodies: hospitals

180 (1) The identity of the supervisory body is determined under this paragraph in cases where the relevant hospital is situated in England.

(2) If a Primary Care Trust commissions the relevant care or treatment, that Trust is the supervisory body.

(3) If the National Assembly for Wales or a Local Health Board commission the relevant care or treatment, the National Assembly are the supervisory body.

(4) In any other case, the supervisory body are the Primary Care Trust for the area in which the relevant hospital is situated.

(5) If a hospital is situated in the areas of two (or more) Primary Care Trusts, it is to be regarded for the purposes of sub-paragraph (4) as situated in whichever of the areas the greater (or greatest) part of the hospital is situated.

181 (1) The identity of the supervisory body is determined under this paragraph in cases where the relevant hospital is situated in Wales.

(2) The National Assembly for Wales are the supervisory body.

(3) But if a Primary Care Trust commissions the relevant care or treatment, that Trust is the supervisory body.

Supervisory bodies: care homes

182 (1) The identity of the supervisory body is determined under this paragraph in cases where the relevant care home is situated in England or in Wales.

(2) The supervisory body are the local authority for the area in which the relevant person is ordinarily resident.

(3) But if the relevant person is not ordinarily resident in the area of a local authority, the supervisory body are the local authority for the area in which the care home is situated.

(4) In relation to England 'local authority' means –

(a) the council of a county;

(b) the council of a district for which there is no county council;

(c) the council of a London borough;

(d) the Common Council of the City of London;

(e) the Council of the Isles of Scilly.

(5) In relation to Wales 'local authority' means the council of a county or county borough.

(6) If a care home is situated in the areas of two (or more) local authorities, it is to be regarded for the purposes of sub-paragraph (3) as situated in whichever of the areas the greater (or greatest) part of the care home is situated.

183 (1) Subsections (5) and (6) of section 24 of the National Assistance Act 1948 (deemed place of ordinary residence) apply to any determination of where a person is ordinarily resident for the purposes of paragraph 182 as those subsections apply to such a determination for the purposes specified in those subsections.

(2) In the application of section 24(6) of the 1948 Act by virtue of subsection (1), section 24(6) is to be read as if it referred to a hospital vested in a Local Health Board as well as to hospitals vested in the Secretary of State and the other bodies mentioned in section 24(6).

(3) Any question arising as to the ordinary residence of a person is to be determined by the Secretary of State or by the National Assembly for Wales.

(4) The Secretary of State and the National Assembly must make and publish arrangements for determining which cases are to be dealt with by the Secretary of State and which are to be dealt with by the National Assembly.

(5) Those arrangements may include provision for the Secretary of State and the National Assembly to agree, in relation to any question that has arisen, which of them is to deal with the case.

(6) Regulations may make provision about arrangements that are to have effect before, upon, or after the determination of any question as to the ordinary residence of a person.

(7) The regulations may, in particular, authorise or require a local authority to do any or all of the following things –

(a) to act as supervisory body even though it may wish to dispute that it is the supervisory body;

(b) to become the supervisory body in place of another local authority;

(c) to recover from another local authority expenditure incurred in exercising functions as the supervisory body.

Same body managing authority and supervisory body

184 (1) This paragraph applies if, in connection with a particular person's detention as a resident in a hospital or care home, the same body are both –

(a) the managing authority of the relevant hospital or care home, and

(b) the supervisory body.

(2)   The fact that a single body are acting in both capacities does not prevent the body from carrying out functions under this Schedule in each capacity.

(3)   But, in such a case, this Schedule has effect subject to any modifications contained in regulations that may be made for this purpose.

Interested persons

185   Each of the following is an interested person –

(a)   the relevant person's spouse or civil partner;

(b)   where the relevant person and another person of the opposite sex are not married to each other but are living together as husband and wife: the other person;

(c)   where the relevant person and another person of the same sex are not civil partners of each other but are living together as if they were civil partners: the other person;

(d)   the relevant person's children and step-children;

(e)   the relevant person's parents and step-parents;

(f)   the relevant person's brothers and sisters, half-brothers and half-sisters, and stepbrothers and stepsisters;

(g)   the relevant person's grandparents;

(h)   a deputy appointed for the relevant person by the court;

(i)   a donee of a lasting power of attorney granted by the relevant person.

186   (1)   An interested person consulted by the best interests assessor is any person whose name is stated in the relevant best interests assessment in accordance with paragraph 40 (interested persons whom the assessor consulted in carrying out the assessment).

(2)   The relevant best interests assessment is the most recent best interests assessment carried out in connection with the standard authorisation in question (whether the assessment was carried out under Part 4 or Part 8).

187   Where this Schedule imposes on a person a duty towards an interested person, the duty does not apply if the person on whom the duty is imposed –

(a)   is not aware of the interested person's identity or of a way of contacting him, and

(b)   cannot reasonably ascertain it.

188   The following table contains an index of provisions defining or otherwise explaining expressions used in this Schedule –

age assessment	paragraph 34
age requirement	paragraph 13
age review assessment	paragraph 112(3)
appointment regulations	paragraph 138
assessment under this Schedule	paragraph 127
assessor (except in Part 8)	paragraph 33
assessor (in Part 8)	paragraphs 33 and 128
authorisation under this Schedule	paragraph 10
best interests (determination of)	section 4
best interests assessment	paragraph 38
best interests requirement	paragraph 16
best interests review assessment	paragraph 112(6)
care home	paragraph 178
change of reason ground	paragraph 106
complete (in relation to a review of a standard authorisation)	paragraph 118
deprivation of a person's liberty	section 64(5) and (6)
care home	paragraph 178
change of reason ground	paragraph 106
complete (in relation to a review of a standard authorisation)	paragraph 118

deprivation of a person's liberty	section 64(5) and (6)
deputy	section 16(2)(b)
detained resident	paragraph 6
disposed of (in relation to a request for a standard authorisation)	paragraph 66
eligibility assessment	paragraph 46
eligibility requirement	paragraph 17
eligibility review assessment	paragraph 112(7)
eligible person (in relation to paragraphs 68 to 73)	paragraph 68
eligible person (in relation to Part 8)	paragraph 102(3)
expiry (in relation to an existing authorisation)	paragraph 125(b)
existing authorisation (in Part 8)	paragraph 125(a)
hospital	paragraph 175
IMCA	paragraph 158
in force (in relation to a standard authorisation)	paragraphs 63 and 64
in force (in relation to an urgent authorisation)	paragraphs 88 and 89
ineligible (in relation to the eligibility requirement)	Schedule 1A
interested person	paragraph 185
interested person consulted by the best interests assessor	paragraph 186
lack of capacity	section 2
lasting power of attorney	section 9
managing authority (in relation to a care home)	paragraph 179
managing authority (in relation to a hospital)	paragraph 176 or 177
maximum authorisation period	paragraph 42
mental capacity assessment	paragraph 37
mental capacity requirement	paragraph 15
mental capacity review assessment	paragraph 112(5)
mental health assessment	paragraph 35
mental health requirement	paragraph 14
mental health review assessment	paragraph 112(4)
negative conclusion	paragraph 112(2)(a)
new supervisory body	paragraph 99(b)
no refusals assessment	paragraph 48
no refusals requirement	paragraph 18
no refusals review assessment	paragraph 112(8)
non-qualification ground	paragraph 105
old supervisory body	paragraph 99(a)
positive conclusion	paragraph 112(2)(b)
purpose of a standard authorisation	paragraph 11(1)
purpose of an urgent authorisation	paragraph 11(2)
qualifying requirements	paragraph 12
refusal (for the purposes of the no refusals requirement)	paragraphs 19 and 20
relevant care or treatment	paragraph 7
relevant hospital or care home	paragraph 7
relevant managing authority	paragraph 26(4)
relevant person	paragraph 7

relevant person's representative	*paragraph 137*
relevant procedure	*paragraph 128*
review assessment	*paragraph 112(1)*
reviewable	*paragraph 104*
section 39A IMCA	*paragraph 155*
section 39C IMCA	*paragraph 156*
section 39D IMCA	*paragraph 157*
standard authorisation	*paragraph 8*
supervisory body (except in Part 8)	*paragraph 180, 181 or 182*
supervisory body (in Part 8)	*paragraph 128 and paragraph 180, 181 or 182*
unauthorised deprivation of liberty	*paragraph 67*
(in relation to paragraphs 68 to 73)	
urgent authorisation	*paragraph 9*
variation of conditions ground	*paragraph 107*

Note:
Schedule A1 is inserted by Mental Health Act 2007, Sched.7 and will be brought into force by s.50(5) of that Act at a time to be appointed by Secretary of State in a statutory instrument. Schedule A1 is brought into effect, but only for purposes limited to making regulations and directions and inserting any definition relevant to those regulations and directions, by Mental Health Act 2007 (Commencement No.4) Order 2008, SI 2008/745, para.4(a) on 1 April 2008.]

SCHEDULE 1   LASTING POWERS OF ATTORNEY: FORMALITIES

Section 9

PART 1   MAKING INSTRUMENTS

General requirements as to making instruments

1   (1)   An instrument is not made in accordance with this Schedule unless –

    (a)   it is in the prescribed form,

    (b)   it complies with paragraph 2, and

    (c)   any prescribed requirements in connection with its execution are satisfied.

  (2)   Regulations may make different provision according to whether –

    (a)   the instrument relates to personal welfare or to property and affairs (or to both);

    (b)   only one or more than one donee is to be appointed (and if more than one, whether jointly or jointly and severally).

  (3)   In this Schedule –

    (a)   'prescribed' means prescribed by regulations, and

    (b)   'regulations' means regulations made for the purposes of this Schedule by the Lord Chancellor.

Requirements as to content of instruments

2   (1)   The instrument must include –

    (a)   the prescribed information about the purpose of the instrument and the effect of a lasting power of attorney,

    (b)   a statement by the donor to the effect that he –

      (i)   has read the prescribed information or a prescribed part of it (or has had it read to him), and

      (ii)   intends the authority conferred under the instrument to include authority to make decisions on his behalf in circumstances where he no longer has capacity,

    (c)   a statement by the donor –

      (i)   naming a person or persons whom the donor wishes to be notified of any application for the registration of the instrument, or

      (ii)   stating that there are no persons whom he wishes to be notified of any such application,

    (d)   a statement by the donee (or, if more than one, each of them) to the effect that he –

      (i)   has read the prescribed information or a prescribed part of it (or has had it read to him), and

      (ii)   understands the duties imposed on a donee of a lasting power of attorney under sections 1 (the principles) and 4 (best interests), and

    (e)   a certificate by a person of a prescribed description that, in his opinion, at the time when the donor executes the instrument –

      (i)   the donor understands the purpose of the instrument and the scope of the authority conferred under it,

      (ii)   no fraud or undue pressure is being used to induce the donor to create a lasting power of attorney, and

      (iii)   there is nothing else which would prevent a lasting power of attorney from being created by the instrument.

(2) Regulations may –

    (a) prescribe a maximum number of named persons;

    (b) provide that, where the instrument includes a statement under sub-paragraph (1)(c)(ii), two persons of a prescribed description must each give a certificate under sub-paragraph (1)(e).

(3) The persons who may be named persons do not include a person who is appointed as donee under the instrument.

(4) In this Schedule, 'named person' means a person named under sub-paragraph (1)(c).

(5) A certificate under sub-paragraph (1)(e) –

    (a)   must be made in the prescribed form, and

    (b)   must include any prescribed information.

(6) The certificate may not be given by a person appointed as donee under the instrument.

Failure to comply with prescribed form

3   (1) If an instrument differs in an immaterial respect in form or mode of expression from the prescribed form, it is to be treated by the Public Guardian as sufficient in point of form and expression.

    (2) The court may declare that an instrument which is not in the prescribed form is to be treated as if it were, if it is satisfied that the persons executing the instrument intended it to create a lasting power of attorney.

PART 2   REGISTRATION

Applications and procedure for registration

4   (1) An application to the Public Guardian for the registration of an instrument intended to create a lasting power of attorney –

    (a)   must be made in the prescribed form, and

    (b)   must include any prescribed information.

    (2) The application may be made –

    (a)   by the donor,

    (b)   by the donee or donees, or

    (c)   if the instrument appoints two or more donees to act jointly and severally in respect of any matter, by any of the donees.

    (3) The application must be accompanied by –

    (a)   the instrument, and

    (b)   any fee provided for under section 58(4)(b).

    (4) A person who, in an application for registration, makes a statement which he knows to be false in a material particular is guilty of an offence and is liable –

    (a)   on summary conviction, to imprisonment for a term not exceeding 12 months or a fine not exceeding the statutory maximum or both;

    (b)   on conviction on indictment, to imprisonment for a term not exceeding 2 years or a fine or both.

5   Subject to paragraphs 11 to 14, the Public Guardian must register the instrument as a lasting power of attorney at the end of the prescribed period.

Notification requirements

6   (1)   A donor about to make an application under paragraph 4(2)(a) must notify any named persons that he is about to do so.

     (2)   The donee (or donees) about to make an application under paragraph 4(2)(b) or (c) must notify any named persons that he is (or they are) about to do so.

7   As soon as is practicable after receiving an application by the donor under paragraph 4(2)(a), the Public Guardian must notify the donee (or donees) that the application has been received.

8   (1)   As soon as is practicable after receiving an application by a donee (or donees) under paragraph 4(2)(b), the Public Guardian must notify the donor that the application has been received.

     (2)   As soon as is practicable after receiving an application by a donee under paragraph 4(2)(c), the Public Guardian must notify –

            (a)   the donor, and
            (b)   the donee or donees who did not join in making the application,

            that the application has been received.

9   (1)   A notice under paragraph 6 must be made in the prescribed form.

     (2)   A notice under paragraph 6, 7 or 8 must include such information, if any, as may be prescribed.

Power to dispense with notification requirements

10   The court may –

      (a)   on the application of the donor, dispense with the requirement to notify under paragraph 6(1), or
      (b)   on the application of the donee or donees concerned, dispense with the requirement to notify under paragraph 6(2),

      if satisfied that no useful purpose would be served by giving the notice.

Instrument not made properly or containing ineffective provision

11   (1)   If it appears to the Public Guardian that an instrument accompanying an application under paragraph 4 is not made in accordance with this Schedule, he must not register the instrument unless the court directs him to do so.

      (2)   Sub-paragraph (3) applies if it appears to the Public Guardian that the instrument contains a provision which –

             (a)   would be ineffective as part of a lasting power of attorney, or
             (b)   would prevent the instrument from operating as a valid lasting power of attorney.

      (3)   The Public Guardian –

             (a)   must apply to the court for it to determine the matter under section 23(1), and
             (b)   pending the determination by the court, must not register the instrument.

      (4)   Sub-paragraph (5) applies if the court determines under section 23(1) (whether or not on an application by the Public Guardian) that the instrument contains a provision which –

             (a)   would be ineffective as part of a lasting power of attorney, or
             (b)   would prevent the instrument from operating as a valid lasting power of attorney.

      (5)   The court must –

(a)   notify the Public Guardian that it has severed the provision, or

(b)   direct him not to register the instrument.

(6) Where the court notifies the Public Guardian that it has severed a provision, he must register the instrument with a note to that effect attached to it.

Deputy already appointed

12 (1) Sub-paragraph (2) applies if it appears to the Public Guardian that –

(a)   there is a deputy appointed by the court for the donor, and

(b)   the powers conferred on the deputy would, if the instrument were registered, to any extent conflict with the powers conferred on the attorney.

(2) The Public Guardian must not register the instrument unless the court directs him to do so.

Objection by donee or named person

13 (1) Sub-paragraph (2) applies if a donee or a named person –

(a)   receives a notice under paragraph 6, 7 or 8 of an application for the registration of an instrument, and

(b)   before the end of the prescribed period, gives notice to the Public Guardian of an objection to the registration on the ground that an event mentioned in section 13(3) or (6)(a) to (d) has occurred which has revoked the instrument.

(2) If the Public Guardian is satisfied that the ground for making the objection is established, he must not register the instrument unless the court, on the application of the person applying for the registration –

(a)   is satisfied that the ground is not established, and

(b)   directs the Public Guardian to register the instrument.

(3) Sub-paragraph (4) applies if a donee or a named person –

(a)   receives a notice under paragraph 6, 7 or 8 of an application for the registration of an instrument, and

(b)   before the end of the prescribed period –

(i)   makes an application to the court objecting to the registration on a prescribed ground, and

(ii)   notifies the Public Guardian of the application.

(4) The Public Guardian must not register the instrument unless the court directs him to do so.

Objection by donor

14 (1) This paragraph applies if the donor –

(a)   receives a notice under paragraph 8 of an application for the registration of an instrument, and

(b)   before the end of the prescribed period, gives notice to the Public Guardian of an objection to the registration.

(2) The Public Guardian must not register the instrument unless the court, on the application of the donee or, if more than one, any of them –

(a)   is satisfied that the donor lacks capacity to object to the registration, and

(b)   directs the Public Guardian to register the instrument.

Notification of registration

15   Where an instrument is registered under this Schedule, the Public Guardian must give
notice of the fact in the prescribed form to –

(a)   the donor, and

(b)   the donee or, if more than one, each of them.

Evidence of registration

16   (1)   A document purporting to be an office copy of an instrument registered under
this Schedule is, in any part of the United Kingdom, evidence of –

(a)   the contents of the instrument, and

(b)   the fact that it has been registered.

(2)   Sub-paragraph (1) is without prejudice to –

(a)   section 3 of the Powers of Attorney Act 1971 (c. 27) (proof by certified
copy), and

(b)   any other method of proof authorised by law.

PART 3   CANCELLATION OF REGISTRATION AND NOTIFICATION OF SEVERANCE

17   (1)   The Public Guardian must cancel the registration of an instrument as a lasting
power of attorney on being satisfied that the power has been revoked –

(a)   as a result of the donor's bankruptcy, or

(b)   on the occurrence of an event mentioned in section 13(6)(a) to (d).

(2)   If the Public Guardian cancels the registration of an instrument he must notify –

(a)   the donor, and

(b)   the donee or, if more than one, each of them.

18   The court must direct the Public Guardian to cancel the registration of an instrument
as a lasting power of attorney if it –

(a)   determines under section 22(2)(a) that a requirement for creating the power was
not met,

(b)   determines under section 22(2)(b) that the power has been revoked or has
otherwise come to an end, or

(c)   revokes the power under section 22(4)(b) (fraud etc.).

19   (1)   Sub-paragraph (2) applies if the court determines under section 23(1) that a
lasting power of attorney contains a provision which –

(a)   is ineffective as part of a lasting power of attorney, or

(b)   prevents the instrument from operating as a valid lasting power of attorney.

(2)   The court must –

(a)   notify the Public Guardian that it has severed the provision, or

(b)   direct him to cancel the registration of the instrument as a lasting power of
attorney.

20   On the cancellation of the registration of an instrument, the instrument and any office
copies of it must be delivered up to the Public Guardian to be cancelled.

PART 4   RECORDS OF ALTERATIONS IN REGISTERED POWERS

Partial revocation or suspension of power as a result of bankruptcy

21   If in the case of a registered instrument it appears to the Public Guardian that under section 13 a lasting power of attorney is revoked, or suspended, in relation to the donor's property and affairs (but not in relation to other matters), the Public Guardian must attach to the instrument a note to that effect.

Termination of appointment of donee which does not revoke power

22   If in the case of a registered instrument it appears to the Public Guardian that an event has occurred –

(a)   which has terminated the appointment of the donee, but

(b)   which has not revoked the instrument,

the Public Guardian must attach to the instrument a note to that effect.

Replacement of donee

23   If in the case of a registered instrument it appears to the Public Guardian that the donee has been replaced under the terms of the instrument the Public Guardian must attach to the instrument a note to that effect.

Severance of ineffective provisions

24   If in the case of a registered instrument the court notifies the Public Guardian under paragraph 19(2)(a) that it has severed a provision of the instrument, the Public Guardian must attach to it a note to that effect.

Notification of alterations

25   If the Public Guardian attaches a note to an instrument under paragraph 21, 22, 23 or 24 he must give notice of the note to the donee or donees of the power (or, as the case may be, to the other donee or donees of the power).

[SCHEDULE 1A   PERSONS INELIGIBLE TO BE DEPRIVED OF LIBERTY BY THIS ACT

PART 1   INELIGIBLE PERSONS

Application

1   This Schedule applies for the purposes of –

(a)   section 16A, and

(b)   paragraph 17 of Schedule A1.

Determining ineligibility

2   *A person ('P') is ineligible to be deprived of liberty by this Act ('ineligible') if –*

    (a) P falls within one of the cases set out in the second column of the following table, and

    (b) the corresponding entry in the third column of the table – or the provision, or one of the provisions, referred to in that entry – provides that he is ineligible.

	Status of P	*Determination of ineligibility*

Case A	P is –
	  (a) subject to the hospital treatment regime, and
	  (b) detained in a hospital under that regime.
		P is ineligible.

Case B	P is –
	  (a) subject to the hospital treatment regime, but
	  (b) not detained in a hospital under that regime.
		See paragraphs 3 and 4.

Case C	P is subject to the community treatment regime.	See paragraphs 3 and 4.
Case D	P is subject to the guardianship regime.	See paragraphs 3 and 5.

Case E	P is –
	  (a) within the scope of the Mental Health Act, but
	  (b) not subject to any of the mental health regimes.
		See paragraph 5.

Authorised course of action not in accordance with regime

3   (1) *This paragraph applies in cases B, C and D in the table in paragraph 2.*

    (2) *P is ineligible if the authorised course of action is not in accordance with a requirement which the relevant regime imposes.*

    (3) *That includes any requirement as to where P is, or is not, to reside.*

    (4) *The relevant regime is the mental health regime to which P is subject.*

Treatment for mental disorder in a hospital

4   (1) *This paragraph applies in cases B and C in the table in paragraph 2.*

    (2) *P is ineligible if the relevant care or treatment consists in whole or in part of medical treatment for mental disorder in a hospital.*

P objects to being a mental health patient etc

5   (1) *This paragraph applies in cases D and E in the table in paragraph 2.*

    (2) *P is ineligible if the following conditions are met.*

    (3) *The first condition is that the relevant instrument authorises P to be a mental health patient.*

    (4) *The second condition is that P objects –*

    (a)   to being a mental health patient, or

    (b)   to being given some or all of the mental health treatment.

(5)   The third condition is that a donee or deputy has not made a valid decision to consent to each matter to which P objects.

(6)   In determining whether or not P objects to something, regard must be had to all the circumstances (so far as they are reasonably ascertainable), including the following –

    (a)   P's behaviour;

    (b)   P's wishes and feelings;

    (c)   P's views, beliefs and values.

(7)   But regard is to be had to circumstances from the past only so far as it is still appropriate to have regard to them.

PART 2   INTERPRETATION

Application

6   This Part applies for the purposes of this Schedule.

Mental health regimes

7   The mental health regimes are –

    (a)   the hospital treatment regime,

    (b)   the community treatment regime, and

    (c)   the guardianship regime.

Hospital treatment regime

8   (1)   P is subject to the hospital treatment regime if he is subject to –

    (a)   a hospital treatment obligation under the relevant enactment, or

    (b)   an obligation under another England and Wales enactment which has the same effect as a hospital treatment obligation.

(2)   But where P is subject to any such obligation, he is to be regarded as not subject to the hospital treatment regime during any period when he is subject to the community treatment regime.

(3)   A hospital treatment obligation is an application, order or direction of a kind listed in the first column of the following table.

(4)   In relation to a hospital treatment obligation, the relevant enactment is the enactment in the Mental Health Act which is referred to in the corresponding entry in the second column of the following table.

Hospital treatment obligation	Relevant enactment
Application for admission for assessment	Section 2
Application for admission for assessment	Section 4
Application for admission for treatment	Section 3
Order for remand to hospital	Section 35
Order for remand to hospital	Section 36
Hospital order	Section 37
Interim hospital order	Section 38
Order for detention in hospital	Section 44

Hospital direction	Section 45A
Transfer direction	Section 47
Transfer direction	Section 48
Hospital order	Section 51

Community treatment regime

9   P is subject to the community treatment regime if he is subject to –

(a)   a community treatment order under section 17A of the Mental Health Act, or

(b)   an obligation under another England and Wales enactment which has the same effect as a community treatment order.

Guardianship regime

10   P is subject to the guardianship regime if he is subject to –

(a)   a guardianship application under section 7 of the Mental Health Act,

(b)   a guardianship order under section 37 of the Mental Health Act, or

(c)   an obligation under another England and Wales enactment which has the same effect as a guardianship application or guardianship order.

England and Wales enactments

11   (1)   An England and Wales enactment is an enactment which extends to England and Wales (whether or not it also extends elsewhere).

(2)   It does not matter if the enactment is in the Mental Health Act or not.

P within scope of Mental Health Act

12   (1)   P is within the scope of the Mental Health Act if –

(a)   an application in respect of P could be made under section 2 or 3 of the Mental Health Act, and

(b)   P could be detained in a hospital in pursuance of such an application, were one made.

(2)   The following provisions of this paragraph apply when determining whether an application in respect of P could be made under section 2 or 3 of the Mental Health Act.

(3)   If the grounds in section 2(2) of the Mental Health Act are met in P's case, it is to be assumed that the recommendations referred to in section 2(3) of that Act have been given.

(4)   If the grounds in section 3(2) of the Mental Health Act are met in P's case, it is to be assumed that the recommendations referred to in section 3(3) of that Act have been given.

(5)   In determining whether the ground in section 3(2)(c) of the Mental Health Act is met in P's case, it is to be assumed that the treatment referred to in section 3(2)(c) cannot be provided under this Act.

Authorised course of action, relevant care or treatment & relevant instrument

13   In a case where this Schedule applies for the purposes of section 16A –

'authorised course of action' means any course of action amounting to deprivation of liberty which the order under section 16(2)(a) authorises;

'relevant care or treatment' means any care or treatment which –

   (a)   comprises, or forms part of, the authorised course of action, or
   (b)   is to be given in connection with the authorised course of action;

'relevant instrument' means the order under section 16(2)(a).

14   In a case where this Schedule applies for the purposes of paragraph 17 of Schedule A1 –

'authorised course of action' means the accommodation of the relevant person in the relevant hospital or care home for the purpose of being given the relevant care or treatment;

'relevant care or treatment' has the same meaning as in Schedule A1;

'relevant instrument' means the standard authorisation under Schedule A1.

15   (1)   This paragraph applies where the question whether a person is ineligible to be deprived of liberty by this Act is relevant to either of these decisions –

      (a)   whether or not to include particular provision ('the proposed provision') in an order under section 16(2)(a);
      (b)   whether or not to give a standard authorisation under Schedule A1.

(2)   A reference in this Schedule to the authorised course of action or the relevant care or treatment is to be read as a reference to that thing as it would be if –

   (a)   the proposed provision were included in the order, or
   (b)   the standard authorisation were given.

(3)   A reference in this Schedule to the relevant instrument is to be read as follows –

   (a)   where the relevant instrument is an order under section 16(2)(a): as a reference to the order as it would be if the proposed provision were included in it;
   (b)   where the relevant instrument is a standard authorisation: as a reference to the standard authorisation as it would be if it were given.

Expressions used in paragraph 5

16   (1)   These expressions have the meanings given –

'donee' means a donee of a lasting power of attorney granted by P;

'mental health patient' means a person accommodated in a hospital for the purpose of being given medical treatment for mental disorder;

'mental health treatment' means the medical treatment for mental disorder referred to in the definition of 'mental health patient'.

(2)   A decision of a donee or deputy is valid if it is made –

   (a)   within the scope of his authority as donee or deputy, and
   (b)   in accordance with Part 1 of this Act.

Expressions with same meaning as in Mental Health Act

17   (1)   'Hospital' has the same meaning as in Part 2 of the Mental Health Act.
     (2)   'Medical treatment' has the same meaning as in the Mental Health Act.
     (3)   'Mental disorder' has the same meaning as in Schedule A1 (see paragraph 14).]

Note:
Schedule 1A is inserted by Mental Health Act 2007, Sched.8 and will be brought into force by s.50(6) of that Act at a time to be appointed by Secretary of State in a statutory instrument.

SCHEDULE 2   PROPERTY AND AFFAIRS: SUPPLEMENTARY PROVISIONS

Section 18(4)

Wills: general

1   Paragraphs 2 to 4 apply in relation to the execution of a will, by virtue of section 18, on behalf of P.

Provision that may be made in will

2   The will may make any provision (whether by disposing of property or exercising a power or otherwise) which could be made by a will executed by P if he had capacity to make it.

Wills: requirements relating to execution

3   (1)   Sub-paragraph (2) applies if under section 16 the court makes an order or gives directions requiring or authorising a person ('the authorised person') to execute a will on behalf of P.

(2)   Any will executed in pursuance of the order or direction –

(a)   must state that it is signed by P acting by the authorised person,

(b)   must be signed by the authorised person with the name of P and his own name, in the presence of two or more witnesses present at the same time,

(c)   must be attested and subscribed by those witnesses in the presence of the authorised person, and

(d)   must be sealed with the official seal of the court.

Wills: effect of execution

4   (1)   This paragraph applies where a will is executed in accordance with paragraph 3.

(2)   The Wills Act 1837 (c. 26) has effect in relation to the will as if it were signed by P by his own hand, except that –

(a)   section 9 of the 1837 Act (requirements as to signing and attestation) does not apply, and

(b)   in the subsequent provisions of the 1837 Act any reference to execution in the manner required by the previous provisions is to be read as a reference to execution in accordance with paragraph 3.

(3)   The will has the same effect for all purposes as if –

(a)   P had had the capacity to make a valid will, and

(b)   the will had been executed by him in the manner required by the 1837 Act.

(4)   But sub-paragraph (3) does not have effect in relation to the will –

(a)   in so far as it disposes of immovable property outside England and Wales, or

(b)   in so far as it relates to any other property or matter if, when the will is executed –

(i)   P is domiciled outside England and Wales, and

(ii)   the condition in sub-paragraph (5) is met.

(5)   The condition is that, under the law of P's domicile, any question of his testamentary capacity would fall to be determined in accordance with the law of a place outside England and Wales.

Vesting orders ancillary to settlement etc.

5   (1)   If provision is made by virtue of section 18 for –

(a)   the settlement of any property of P, or

(b)   the exercise of a power vested in him of appointing trustees or retiring from a trust,

the court may also make as respects the property settled or the trust property such consequential vesting or other orders as the case may require.

(2)   The power under sub-paragraph (1) includes, in the case of the exercise of such a power, any order which could have been made in such a case under Part 4 of the Trustee Act 1925 (c. 19).

Variation of settlements

6   (1)   If a settlement has been made by virtue of section 18, the court may by order vary or revoke the settlement if –

(a)   the settlement makes provision for its variation or revocation,

(b)   the court is satisfied that a material fact was not disclosed when the settlement was made, or

(c)   the court is satisfied that there has been a substantial change of circumstances.

(2)   Any such order may give such consequential directions as the court thinks fit.

Vesting of stock in curator appointed outside England and Wales

7   (1)   Sub-paragraph (2) applies if the court is satisfied –

(a)   that under the law prevailing in a place outside England and Wales a person ('M') has been appointed to exercise powers in respect of the property or affairs of P on the ground (however formulated) that P lacks capacity to make decisions with respect to the management and administration of his property and affairs, and

(b)   that, having regard to the nature of the appointment and to the circumstances of the case, it is expedient that the court should exercise its powers under this paragraph.

(2)   The court may direct –

(a)   any stocks standing in the name of P, or

(b)   the right to receive dividends from the stocks,

to be transferred into M's name or otherwise dealt with as required by M, and may give such directions as the court thinks fit for dealing with accrued dividends from the stocks.

(3)   'Stocks' includes –

(a)   shares, and

(b)   any funds, annuity or security transferable in the books kept by any body corporate or unincorporated company or society or by an instrument of transfer either alone or accompanied by other formalities,

and 'dividends' is to be construed accordingly.

Preservation of interests in property disposed of on behalf of person lacking capacity

8   (1)   Sub-paragraphs (2) and (3) apply if –

    (a)   P's property has been disposed of by virtue of section 18,

    (b)   under P's will or intestacy, or by a gift perfected or nomination taking effect on his death, any other person would have taken an interest in the property but for the disposal, and

    (c)   on P's death, any property belonging to P's estate represents the property disposed of.

    (2)   The person takes the same interest, if and so far as circumstances allow, in the property representing the property disposed of.

    (3)   If the property disposed of was real property, any property representing it is to be treated, so long as it remains part of P's estate, as if it were real property.

    (4)   The court may direct that, on a disposal of P's property –

    (a)   which is made by virtue of section 18, and

    (b)   which would apart from this paragraph result in the conversion of personal property into real property,

property representing the property disposed of is to be treated, so long as it remains P's property or forms part of P's estate, as if it were personal property.

    (5)   References in sub-paragraphs (1) to (4) to the disposal of property are to –

    (a)   the sale, exchange, charging of or other dealing (otherwise than by will) with property other than money;

    (b)   the removal of property from one place to another;

    (c)   the application of money in acquiring property;

    (d)   the transfer of money from one account to another;

and references to property representing property disposed of are to be construed accordingly and as including the result of successive disposals.

    (6)   The court may give such directions as appear to it necessary or expedient for the purpose of facilitating the operation of sub-paragraphs (1) to (3), including the carrying of money to a separate account and the transfer of property other than money.

9   (1)   Sub-paragraph (2) applies if the court has ordered or directed the expenditure of money –

    (a)   for carrying out permanent improvements on any of P's property, or

    (b)   otherwise for the permanent benefit of any of P's property.

    (2)   The court may order that –

    (a)   the whole of the money expended or to be expended, or

    (b)   any part of it,

is to be a charge on the property either without interest or with interest at a specified rate.

    (3)   An order under sub-paragraph (2) may provide for excluding or restricting the operation of paragraph 8(1) to (3).

    (4)   A charge under sub-paragraph (2) may be made in favour of such person as may be just and, in particular, where the money charged is paid out of P's general estate, may be made in favour of a person as trustee for P.

    (5)   No charge under sub-paragraph (2) may confer any right of sale or foreclosure during P's lifetime.

Powers as patron of benefice

10 (1) Any functions which P has as patron of a benefice may be discharged only by a person ('R') appointed by the court.

(2) R must be an individual capable of appointment under section 8(1)(b) of the 1986 Measure (which provides for an individual able to make a declaration of communicant status, a clerk in Holy Orders, etc. to be appointed to discharge a registered patron's functions).

(3) The 1986 Measure applies to R as it applies to an individual appointed by the registered patron of the benefice under section 8(1)(b) or (3) of that Measure to discharge his functions as patron.

(4) 'The 1986 Measure' means the Patronage (Benefices) Measure 1986 (No. 3).

SCHEDULE 3   INTERNATIONAL PROTECTION OF ADULTS

Section 63

PART 1   PRELIMINARY

Introduction

1   This Part applies for the purposes of this Schedule.

The Convention

2   (1) 'Convention' means the Convention referred to in section 63.

(2) 'Convention country' means a country in which the Convention is in force.

(3) A reference to an Article or Chapter is to an Article or Chapter of the Convention.

(4) An expression which appears in this Schedule and in the Convention is to be construed in accordance with the Convention.

Countries, territories and nationals

3   (1) 'Country' includes a territory which has its own system of law.

(2) Where a country has more than one territory with its own system of law, a reference to the country, in relation to one of its nationals, is to the territory with which the national has the closer, or the closest, connection.

Adults with incapacity

4   'Adult' means a person who –

(a) as a result of an impairment or insufficiency of his personal faculties, cannot protect his interests, and

(b) has reached 16.

Protective measures

5   (1) 'Protective measure' means a measure directed to the protection of the person or property of an adult; and it may deal in particular with any of the following –

(a) the determination of incapacity and the institution of a protective regime,

(b) placing the adult under the protection of an appropriate authority,

(c) guardianship, curatorship or any corresponding system,

(d) the designation and functions of a person having charge of the adult's person or property, or representing or otherwise helping him,

(e) placing the adult in a place where protection can be provided,

(f) administering, conserving or disposing of the adult's property,

(g) authorising a specific intervention for the protection of the person or property of the adult.

(2) Where a measure of like effect to a protective measure has been taken in relation to a person before he reaches 16, this Schedule applies to the measure in so far as it has effect in relation to him once he has reached 16.

Central Authority

6   (1) Any function under the Convention of a Central Authority is exercisable in England and Wales by the Lord Chancellor.

(2) A communication may be sent to the Central Authority in relation to England and Wales by sending it to the Lord Chancellor.

PART 2   JURISDICTION OF COMPETENT AUTHORITY

Scope of jurisdiction

7   (1) The court may exercise its functions under this Act (in so far as it cannot otherwise do so) in relation to –

(a) an adult habitually resident in England and Wales,

(b) an adult's property in England and Wales,

(c) an adult present in England and Wales or who has property there, if the matter is urgent, or

(d) an adult present in England and Wales, if a protective measure which is temporary and limited in its effect to England and Wales is proposed in relation to him.

(2) An adult present in England and Wales is to be treated for the purposes of this paragraph as habitually resident there if –

(a) his habitual residence cannot be ascertained,

(b) he is a refugee, or

(c) he has been displaced as a result of disturbance in the country of his habitual residence.

8   (1) The court may also exercise its functions under this Act (in so far as it cannot otherwise do so) in relation to an adult if sub-paragraph (2) or (3) applies in relation to him.

(2) This sub-paragraph applies in relation to an adult if –

(a) he is a British citizen,

(b) he has a closer connection with England and Wales than with Scotland or Northern Ireland, and

(c) Article 7 has, in relation to the matter concerned, been complied with.

(3) This sub-paragraph applies in relation to an adult if the Lord Chancellor, having consulted such persons as he considers appropriate, agrees to a request under Article 8 in relation to the adult.

Exercise of jurisdiction

9 (1) This paragraph applies where jurisdiction is exercisable under this Schedule in connection with a matter which involves a Convention country other than England and Wales.

   (2) Any Article on which the jurisdiction is based applies in relation to the matter in so far as it involves the other country (and the court must, accordingly, comply with any duty conferred on it as a result).

   (3) Article 12 also applies, so far as its provisions allow, in relation to the matter in so far as it involves the other country.

10 A reference in this Schedule to the exercise of jurisdiction under this Schedule is to the exercise of functions under this Act as a result of this Part of this Schedule.

PART 3 APPLICABLE LAW

Applicable law

11 In exercising jurisdiction under this Schedule, the court may, if it thinks that the matter has a substantial connection with a country other than England and Wales, apply the law of that other country.

12 Where a protective measure is taken in one country but implemented in another, the conditions of implementation are governed by the law of the other country.

Lasting powers of attorney, etc.

13 (1) If the donor of a lasting power is habitually resident in England and Wales at the time of granting the power, the law applicable to the existence, extent, modification or extinction of the power is –

   (a) the law of England and Wales, or
   (b) if he specifies in writing the law of a connected country for the purpose, that law.

   (2) If he is habitually resident in another country at that time, but England and Wales is a connected country, the law applicable in that respect is –

   (a) the law of the other country, or
   (b) if he specifies in writing the law of England and Wales for the purpose, that law.

   (3) A country is connected, in relation to the donor, if it is a country –

   (a) of which he is a national,
   (b) in which he was habitually resident, or
   (c) in which he has property.

   (4) Where this paragraph applies as a result of sub-paragraph (3)(c), it applies only in relation to the property which the donor has in the connected country.

   (5) The law applicable to the manner of the exercise of a lasting power is the law of the country where it is exercised.

   (6) In this Part of this Schedule, 'lasting power' means –

   (a) a lasting power of attorney (see section 9),
   (b) an enduring power of attorney within the meaning of Schedule 4, or
   (c) any other power of like effect.

14 (1) Where a lasting power is not exercised in a manner sufficient to guarantee the protection of the person or property of the donor, the court, in exercising jurisdiction under this Schedule, may disapply or modify the power.

(2) Where, in accordance with this Part of this Schedule, the law applicable to the power is, in one or more respects, that of a country other than England and Wales, the court must, so far as possible, have regard to the law of the other country in that respect (or those respects).

15 Regulations may provide for Schedule 1 (lasting powers of attorney: formalities) to apply with modifications in relation to a lasting power which comes within paragraph 13(6)(c) above.

Protection of third parties

16 (1) This paragraph applies where a person (a 'representative') in purported exercise of an authority to act on behalf of an adult enters into a transaction with a third party.

(2) The validity of the transaction may not be questioned in proceedings, nor may the third party be held liable, merely because –

(a) where the representative and third party are in England and Wales when entering into the transaction, sub-paragraph (3) applies;

(b) where they are in another country at that time, sub-paragraph (4) applies.

(3) This sub-paragraph applies if –

(a) the law applicable to the authority in one or more respects is, as a result of this Schedule, the law of a country other than England and Wales, and

(b) the representative is not entitled to exercise the authority in that respect (or those respects) under the law of that other country.

(4) This sub-paragraph applies if –

(a) the law applicable to the authority in one or more respects is, as a result of this Part of this Schedule, the law of England and Wales, and

(b) the representative is not entitled to exercise the authority in that respect (or those respects) under that law.

(5) This paragraph does not apply if the third party knew or ought to have known that the applicable law was –

(a) in a case within sub-paragraph (3), the law of the other country;

(b) in a case within sub-paragraph (4), the law of England and Wales.

Mandatory rules

17 Where the court is entitled to exercise jurisdiction under this Schedule, the mandatory provisions of the law of England and Wales apply, regardless of any system of law which would otherwise apply in relation to the matter.

Public policy

18 Nothing in this Part of this Schedule requires or enables the application in England and Wales of a provision of the law of another country if its application would be manifestly contrary to public policy.

PART 4   RECOGNITION AND ENFORCEMENT

Recognition

19 (1) A protective measure taken in relation to an adult under the law of a country other than England and Wales is to be recognised in England and Wales if it was taken on the ground that the adult is habitually resident in the other country.

(2) A protective measure taken in relation to an adult under the law of a Convention country other than England and Wales is to be recognised in England and Wales if it was taken on a ground mentioned in Chapter 2 (jurisdiction).

(3) But the court may disapply this paragraph in relation to a measure if it thinks that –

(a) the case in which the measure was taken was not urgent,

(b) the adult was not given an opportunity to be heard, and

(c) that omission amounted to a breach of natural justice.

(4) It may also disapply this paragraph in relation to a measure if it thinks that –

(a) recognition of the measure would be manifestly contrary to public policy,

(b) the measure would be inconsistent with a mandatory provision of the law of England and Wales, or

(c) the measure is inconsistent with one subsequently taken, or recognised, in England and Wales in relation to the adult.

(5) And the court may disapply this paragraph in relation to a measure taken under the law of a Convention country in a matter to which Article 33 applies, if the court thinks that that Article has not been complied with in connection with that matter.

20 (1) An interested person may apply to the court for a declaration as to whether a protective measure taken under the law of a country other than England and Wales is to be recognised in England and Wales.

(2) No permission is required for an application to the court under this paragraph.

21 For the purposes of paragraphs 19 and 20, any finding of fact relied on when the measure was taken is conclusive.

Enforcement

22 (1) An interested person may apply to the court for a declaration as to whether a protective measure taken under the law of, and enforceable in, a country other than England and Wales is enforceable, or to be registered, in England and Wales in accordance with Court of Protection Rules.

(2) The court must make the declaration if –

(a) the measure comes within sub-paragraph (1) or (2) of paragraph 19, and

(b) the paragraph is not disapplied in relation to it as a result of sub-paragraph (3), (4) or (5).

(3) A measure to which a declaration under this paragraph relates is enforceable in England and Wales as if it were a measure of like effect taken by the court.

Measures taken in relation to those aged under 16

23 (1) This paragraph applies where –

(a) provision giving effect to, or otherwise deriving from, the Convention in a country other than England and Wales applies in relation to a person who has not reached 16, and

(b)   a measure is taken in relation to that person in reliance on that provision.

(2)   This Part of this Schedule applies in relation to that measure as it applies in relation to a protective measure taken in relation to an adult under the law of a Convention country other than England and Wales.

Supplementary

24   The court may not review the merits of a measure taken outside England and Wales except to establish whether the measure complies with this Schedule in so far as it is, as a result of this Schedule, required to do so.

25   Court of Protection Rules may make provision about an application under paragraph 20 or 22.

PART 5   CO-OPERATION

Proposal for cross-border placement

26   (1)   This paragraph applies where a public authority proposes to place an adult in an establishment in a Convention country other than England and Wales.

   (2)   The public authority must consult an appropriate authority in that other country about the proposed placement and, for that purpose, must send it –

   (a)   a report on the adult, and

   (b)   a statement of its reasons for the proposed placement.

   (3)   If the appropriate authority in the other country opposes the proposed placement within a reasonable time, the public authority may not proceed with it.

27   A proposal received by a public authority under Article 33 in relation to an adult is to proceed unless the authority opposes it within a reasonable time.

Adult in danger etc.

28   (1)   This paragraph applies if a public authority is told that an adult –

   (a)   who is in serious danger, and

   (b)   in relation to whom the public authority has taken, or is considering taking, protective measures,

   is, or has become resident, in a Convention country other than England and Wales.

   (2)   The public authority must tell an appropriate authority in that other country about –

   (a)   the danger, and

   (b)   the measures taken or under consideration.

29   A public authority may not request from, or send to, an appropriate authority in a Convention country information in accordance with Chapter 5 (co-operation) in relation to an adult if it thinks that doing so –

   (a)   would be likely to endanger the adult or his property, or

   (b)   would amount to a serious threat to the liberty or life of a member of the adult's family.

PART 6   GENERAL

Certificates

30   A certificate given under Article 38 by an authority in a Convention country other than England and Wales is, unless the contrary is shown, proof of the matters contained in it.

Powers to make further provision as to private international law

31   Her Majesty may by Order in Council confer on the Lord Chancellor, the court or another public authority functions for enabling the Convention to be given effect in England and Wales.

32   (1)   Regulations may make provision –

      (a)   giving further effect to the Convention, or

      (b)   otherwise about the private international law of England and Wales in relation to the protection of adults.

    (2)   The regulations may –

      (a)   confer functions on the court or another public authority;

      (b)   amend this Schedule;

      (c)   provide for this Schedule to apply with specified modifications;

      (d)   make provision about countries other than Convention countries.

Exceptions

33   Nothing in this Schedule applies, and no provision made under paragraph 32 is to apply, to any matter to which the Convention, as a result of Article 4, does not apply.

Regulations and orders

34   A reference in this Schedule to regulations or an order (other than an Order in Council) is to regulations or an order made for the purposes of this Schedule by the Lord Chancellor.

Commencement

35   The following provisions of this Schedule have effect only if the Convention is in force in accordance with Article 57 –

    (a)   paragraph 8,

    (b)   paragraph 9,

    (c)   paragraph 19(2) and (5),

    (d)   Part 5,

    (e)   paragraph 30.

SCHEDULE 4   PROVISIONS APPLYING TO EXISTING ENDURING POWERS OF ATTORNEY

Section 66(3)

PART 1   ENDURING POWERS OF ATTORNEY

Enduring power of attorney to survive mental incapacity of donor

1   (1)   Where an individual has created a power of attorney which is an enduring power within the meaning of this Schedule –

    (a)   the power is not revoked by any subsequent mental incapacity of his,

    (b)   upon such incapacity supervening, the donee of the power may not do anything under the authority of the power except as provided by sub-paragraph (2) unless or until the instrument creating the power is registered under paragraph 13, and

    (c)   if and so long as paragraph (b) operates to suspend the donee's authority to act under the power, section 5 of the Powers of Attorney Act 1971 (c. 27) (protection of donee and third persons), so far as applicable, applies as if the power had been revoked by the donor's mental incapacity,

and, accordingly, section 1 of this Act does not apply.

(2)   Despite sub-paragraph (1)(b), where the attorney has made an application for registration of the instrument then, until it is registered, the attorney may take action under the power –

    (a)   to maintain the donor or prevent loss to his estate, or

    (b)   to maintain himself or other persons in so far as paragraph 3(2) permits him to do so.

(3)   Where the attorney purports to act as provided by sub-paragraph (2) then, in favour of a person who deals with him without knowledge that the attorney is acting otherwise than in accordance with sub-paragraph (2)(a) or (b), the transaction between them is as valid as if the attorney were acting in accordance with sub-paragraph (2)(a) or (b).

Characteristics of an enduring power of attorney

2   (1)   Subject to sub-paragraphs (5) and (6) and paragraph 20, a power of attorney is an enduring power within the meaning of this Schedule if the instrument which creates the power –

    (a)   is in the prescribed form,

    (b)   was executed in the prescribed manner by the donor and the attorney, and

    (c)   incorporated at the time of execution by the donor the prescribed explanatory information.

(2)   In this paragraph, 'prescribed' means prescribed by such of the following regulations as applied when the instrument was executed –

    (a)   the Enduring Powers of Attorney (Prescribed Form) Regulations 1986 (SI 1986/126),

    (b)   the Enduring Powers of Attorney (Prescribed Form) Regulations 1987 (SI 1987/1612),

    (c)   the Enduring Powers of Attorney (Prescribed Form) Regulations 1990 (SI 1990/1376),

    (d)   the Enduring Powers of Attorney (Welsh Language Prescribed Form) Regulations 2000 (SI 2000/289).

(3) An instrument in the prescribed form purporting to have been executed in the prescribed manner is to be taken, in the absence of evidence to the contrary, to be a document which incorporated at the time of execution by the donor the prescribed explanatory information.

(4) If an instrument differs in an immaterial respect in form or mode of expression from the prescribed form it is to be treated as sufficient in point of form and expression.

(5) A power of attorney cannot be an enduring power unless, when he executes the instrument creating it, the attorney is –

(a)   an individual who has reached 18 and is not bankrupt, or
(b)   a trust corporation.

(6) A power of attorney which gives the attorney a right to appoint a substitute or successor cannot be an enduring power.

(7) An enduring power is revoked by the bankruptcy of the donor or attorney.

(8) But where the donor or attorney is bankrupt merely because an interim bankruptcy restrictions order has effect in respect of him, the power is suspended for so long as the order has effect.

(9) An enduring power is revoked if the court –

(a)   exercises a power under sections 16 to 20 in relation to the donor, and
(b)   directs that the enduring power is to be revoked.

(10) No disclaimer of an enduring power, whether by deed or otherwise, is valid unless and until the attorney gives notice of it to the donor or, where paragraph 4(6) or 15(1) applies, to the Public Guardian.

Scope of authority etc. of attorney under enduring power

3   (1) If the instrument which creates an enduring power of attorney is expressed to confer general authority on the attorney, the instrument operates to confer, subject to –

(a)   the restriction imposed by sub-paragraph (3), and
(b)   any conditions or restrictions contained in the instrument,

authority to do on behalf of the donor anything which the donor could lawfully do by an attorney at the time when the donor executed the instrument.

(2) Subject to any conditions or restrictions contained in the instrument, an attorney under an enduring power, whether general or limited, may (without obtaining any consent) act under the power so as to benefit himself or other persons than the donor to the following extent but no further –

(a)   he may so act in relation to himself or in relation to any other person if the donor might be expected to provide for his or that person's needs respectively, and
(b)   he may do whatever the donor might be expected to do to meet those needs.

(3) Without prejudice to sub-paragraph (2) but subject to any conditions or restrictions contained in the instrument, an attorney under an enduring power, whether general or limited, may (without obtaining any consent) dispose of the property of the donor by way of gift to the following extent but no further –

(a)   he may make gifts of a seasonal nature or at a time, or on an anniversary, of a birth, a marriage or the formation of a civil partnership, to persons (including himself) who are related to or connected with the donor, and
(b)   he may make gifts to any charity to whom the donor made or might be expected to make gifts,

provided that the value of each such gift is not unreasonable having regard to all the circumstances and in particular the size of the donor's estate.

PART 2   ACTION ON ACTUAL OR IMPENDING INCAPACITY OF DONOR

Duties of attorney in event of actual or impending incapacity of donor

4   (1)   Sub-paragraphs (2) to (6) apply if the attorney under an enduring power has reason to believe that the donor is or is becoming mentally incapable.

(2)   The attorney must, as soon as practicable, make an application to the Public Guardian for the registration of the instrument creating the power.

(3)   Before making an application for registration the attorney must comply with the provisions as to notice set out in Part 3 of this Schedule.

(4)   An application for registration –

(a)   must be made in the prescribed form, and

(b)   must contain such statements as may be prescribed.

(5)   The attorney –

(a)   may, before making an application for the registration of the instrument, refer to the court for its determination any question as to the validity of the power, and

(b)   must comply with any direction given to him by the court on that determination.

(6)   No disclaimer of the power is valid unless and until the attorney gives notice of it to the Public Guardian; and the Public Guardian must notify the donor if he receives a notice under this sub-paragraph.

(7)   A person who, in an application for registration, makes a statement which he knows to be false in a material particular is guilty of an offence and is liable –

(a)   on summary conviction, to imprisonment for a term not exceeding 12 months or a fine not exceeding the statutory maximum or both;

(b)   on conviction on indictment, to imprisonment for a term not exceeding 2 years or a fine or both.

(8)   In this paragraph, 'prescribed' means prescribed by regulations made for the purposes of this Schedule by the Lord Chancellor.

PART 3   NOTIFICATION PRIOR TO REGISTRATION

Duty to give notice to relatives

5   Subject to paragraph 7, before making an application for registration the attorney must give notice of his intention to do so to all those persons (if any) who are entitled to receive notice by virtue of paragraph 6.

6   (1)   Subject to sub-paragraphs (2) to (4), persons of the following classes ('relatives') are entitled to receive notice under paragraph 5 –

(a)   the donor's spouse or civil partner,

(b)   the donor's children,

(c)   the donor's parents,

(d)   the donor's brothers and sisters, whether of the whole or half blood,

(e)   the widow, widower or surviving civil partner of a child of the donor,

(f)   the donor's grandchildren,

(g)   the children of the donor's brothers and sisters of the whole blood,
(h)   the children of the donor's brothers and sisters of the half blood,
(i)   the donor's uncles and aunts of the whole blood,
(j)   the children of the donor's uncles and aunts of the whole blood.

(2)   A person is not entitled to receive notice under paragraph 5 if –

(a)   his name or address is not known to the attorney and cannot be reasonably ascertained by him, or
(b)   the attorney has reason to believe that he has not reached 18 or is mentally incapable.

(3)   Except where sub-paragraph (4) applies –

(a)   no more than 3 persons are entitled to receive notice under paragraph 5, and
(b)   in determining the persons who are so entitled, persons falling within the class in sub-paragraph (1)(a) are to be preferred to persons falling within the class in sub-paragraph (1)(b), those falling within the class in sub-paragraph (1)(b) are to be preferred to those falling within the class in sub-paragraph (1)(c), and so on.

(4)   Despite the limit of 3 specified in sub-paragraph (3), where –

(a)   there is more than one person falling within any of classes (a) to (j) of sub-paragraph (1), and
(b)   at least one of those persons would be entitled to receive notice under paragraph 5,

then, subject to sub-paragraph (2), all the persons falling within that class are entitled to receive notice under paragraph 5.

7   (1)   An attorney is not required to give notice under paragraph 5 –

(a)   to himself, or
(b)   to any other attorney under the power who is joining in making the application,

even though he or, as the case may be, the other attorney is entitled to receive notice by virtue of paragraph 6.

(2)   In the case of any person who is entitled to receive notice by virtue of paragraph 6, the attorney, before applying for registration, may make an application to the court to be dispensed from the requirement to give him notice; and the court must grant the application if it is satisfied –

(a)   that it would be undesirable or impracticable for the attorney to give him notice, or
(b)   that no useful purpose is likely to be served by giving him notice.

Duty to give notice to donor

8   (1)   Subject to sub-paragraph (2), before making an application for registration the attorney must give notice of his intention to do so to the donor.

(2)   Paragraph 7(2) applies in relation to the donor as it applies in relation to a person who is entitled to receive notice under paragraph 5.

Contents of notices

9   A notice to relatives under this Part of this Schedule must –

(a)   be in the prescribed form,

(b) state that the att rney proposes to make an application to the Public Guardian for the registrati n of the instrument creating the enduring power in question,

(c) inform the persc a to whom it is given of his right to object to the registration under paragraph 13(4), and

(d) specify, as the grounds on which an objection to registration may be made, the grounds set out in paragraph 13(9).

10   A notice to the donor under this Part of this Schedule –

(a) must be in the prescribed form,

(b) must contain the statement mentioned in paragraph 9(b), and

(c) must inform the donor that, while the instrument remains registered, any revocation of the power by him will be ineffective unless and until the revocation is confirmed by the court.

Duty to give notice to other attorneys

11 (1) Subject to sub-paragraph (2), before making an application for registration an attorney under a joint and several power must give notice of his intention to do so to any other attorney under the power who is not joining in making the application; and paragraphs 7(2) and 9 apply in relation to attorneys entitled to receive notice by virtue of this paragraph as they apply in relation to persons entitled to receive notice by virtue of paragraph 6.

(2) An attorney is not entitled to receive notice by virtue of this paragraph if –

(a) his address is not known to the applying attorney and cannot reasonably be ascertained by him, or

(b) the applying attorney has reason to believe that he has not reached 18 or is mentally incapable.

Supplementary

12   Despite section 7 of the Interpretation Act 1978 (c. 30) (construction of references to service by post), for the purposes of this Part of this Schedule a notice given by post is to be regarded as given on the date on which it was posted.

PART 4   REGISTRATION

Registration of instrument creating power

13 (1) If an application is made in accordance with paragraph 4(3) and (4) the Public Guardian must, subject to the provisions of this paragraph, register the instrument to which the application relates.

(2) If it appears to the Public Guardian that –

(a) there is a deputy appointed for the donor of the power created by the instrument, and

(b) the powers conferred on the deputy would, if the instrument were registered, to any extent conflict with the powers conferred on the attorney,

the Public Guardian must not register the instrument except in accordance with the court's directions.

(3) The court may, on the application of the attorney, direct the Public Guardian to register an instrument even though notice has not been given as required by paragraph 4(3) and Part 3 of this Schedule to a person entitled to receive it, if the court is satisfied –

(a) that it was undesirable or impracticable for the attorney to give notice to that person, or

(b) that no useful purpose is likely to be served by giving him notice.

(4) Sub-paragraph (5) applies if, before the end of the period of 5 weeks beginning with the date (or the latest date) on which the attorney gave notice under paragraph 5 of an application for registration, the Public Guardian receives a valid notice of objection to the registration from a person entitled to notice of the application.

(5) The Public Guardian must not register the instrument except in accordance with the court's directions.

(6) Sub-paragraph (7) applies if, in the case of an application for registration –

(a) it appears from the application that there is no one to whom notice has been given under paragraph 5, or

(b) the Public Guardian has reason to believe that appropriate inquiries might bring to light evidence on which he could be satisfied that one of the grounds of objection set out in sub-paragraph (9) was established.

(7) The Public Guardian –

(a) must not register the instrument, and

(b) must undertake such inquiries as he thinks appropriate in all the circumstances.

(8) If, having complied with sub-paragraph (7)(b), the Public Guardian is satisfied that one of the grounds of objection set out in sub-paragraph (9) is established –

(a) the attorney may apply to the court for directions, and

(b) the Public Guardian must not register the instrument except in accordance with the court's directions.

(9) A notice of objection under this paragraph is valid if made on one or more of the following grounds –

(a) that the power purported to have been created by the instrument was not valid as an enduring power of attorney,

(b) that the power created by the instrument no longer subsists,

(c) that the application is premature because the donor is not yet becoming mentally incapable,

(d) that fraud or undue pressure was used to induce the donor to create the power,

(e) that, having regard to all the circumstances and in particular the attorney's relationship to or connection with the donor, the attorney is unsuitable to be the donor's attorney.

(10) If any of those grounds is established to the satisfaction of the court it must direct the Public Guardian not to register the instrument, but if not so satisfied it must direct its registration.

(11) If the court directs the Public Guardian not to register an instrument because it is satisfied that the ground in sub-paragraph (9)(d) or (e) is established, it must by order revoke the power created by the instrument.

(12) If the court directs the Public Guardian not to register an instrument because it is satisfied that any ground in sub-paragraph (9) except that in paragraph (c) is established, the instrument must be delivered up to be cancelled unless the court otherwise directs.

Register of enduring powers

14 The Public Guardian has the function of establishing and maintaining a register of enduring powers for the purposes of this Schedule.

PART 5   LEGAL POSITION AFTER REGISTRATION

Effect and proof of registration

15 (1) The effect of the registration of an instrument under paragraph 13 is that –

(a) no revocation of the power by the donor is valid unless and until the court confirms the revocation under paragraph 16(3);

(b) no disclaimer of the power is valid unless and until the attorney gives notice of it to the Public Guardian;

(c) the donor may not extend or restrict the scope of the authority conferred by the instrument and no instruction or consent given by him after registration, in the case of a consent, confers any right and, in the case of an instruction, imposes or confers any obligation or right on or creates any liability of the attorney or other persons having notice of the instruction or consent.

(2) Sub-paragraph (1) applies for so long as the instrument is registered under paragraph 13 whether or not the donor is for the time being mentally incapable.

(3) A document purporting to be an office copy of an instrument registered under this Schedule is, in any part of the United Kingdom, evidence of –

(a) the contents of the instrument, and

(b) the fact that it has been so registered.

(4) Sub-paragraph (3) is without prejudice to section 3 of the Powers of Attorney Act 1971 (c. 27) (proof by certified copies) and to any other method of proof authorised by law.

Functions of court with regard to registered power

16 (1) Where an instrument has been registered under paragraph 13, the court has the following functions with respect to the power and the donor of and the attorney appointed to act under the power.

(2) The court may –

(a) determine any question as to the meaning or effect of the instrument;

(b) give directions with respect to –

(i) the management or disposal by the attorney of the property and affairs of the donor;

(ii) the rendering of accounts by the attorney and the production of the records kept by him for the purpose;

(iii) the remuneration or expenses of the attorney whether or not in default of or in accordance with any provision made by the instrument, including directions for the repayment of excessive or the payment of additional remuneration;

(c) require the attorney to supply information or produce documents or things in his possession as attorney;

(d) give any consent or authorisation to act which the attorney would have to obtain from a mentally capable donor;

(e) authorise the attorney to act so as to benefit himself or other persons than the donor otherwise than in accordance with paragraph 3(2) and (3) (but subject to any conditions or restrictions contained in the instrument);

(f) relieve the attorney wholly or partly from any liability which he has or may have incurred on account of a breach of his duties as attorney.

(3) On application made for the purpose by or on behalf of the donor, the court must confirm the revocation of the power if satisfied that the donor –

(a) has done whatever is necessary in law to effect an express revocation of the power, and

(b) was mentally capable of revoking a power of attorney when he did so (whether or not he is so when the court considers the application).

(4) The court must direct the Public Guardian to cancel the registration of an instrument registered under paragraph 13 in any of the following circumstances –

(a) on confirming the revocation of the power under sub-paragraph (3),

(b) on directing under paragraph 2(9)(b) that the power is to be revoked,

(c) on being satisfied that the donor is and is likely to remain mentally capable,

(d) on being satisfied that the power has expired or has been revoked by the mental incapacity of the attorney,

(e) on being satisfied that the power was not a valid and subsisting enduring power when registration was effected,

(f) on being satisfied that fraud or undue pressure was used to induce the donor to create the power,

(g) on being satisfied that, having regard to all the circumstances and in particular the attorney's relationship to or connection with the donor, the attorney is unsuitable to be the donor's attorney.

(5) If the court directs the Public Guardian to cancel the registration of an instrument on being satisfied of the matters specified in sub-paragraph (4)(f) or (g) it must by order revoke the power created by the instrument.

(6) If the court directs the cancellation of the registration of an instrument under sub-paragraph (4) except paragraph (c) the instrument must be delivered up to the Public Guardian to be cancelled, unless the court otherwise directs.

Cancellation of registration by Public Guardian

17   The Public Guardian must cancel the registration of an instrument creating an enduring power of attorney –

(a) on receipt of a disclaimer signed by the attorney;

(b) if satisfied that the power has been revoked by the death or bankruptcy of the donor or attorney or, if the attorney is a body corporate, by its winding up or dissolution;

(c) on receipt of notification from the court that the court has revoked the power;

(d) on confirmation from the court that the donor has revoked the power.

PART 6   PROTECTION OF ATTORNEY AND THIRD PARTIES

Protection of attorney and third persons where power is invalid or revoked

18   (1) Sub-paragraphs (2) and (3) apply where an instrument which did not create a valid power of attorney has been registered under paragraph 13 (whether or not the registration has been cancelled at the time of the act or transaction in question).

(2) An attorney who acts in pursuance of the power does not incur any liability (either to the donor or to any other person) because of the non-existence of the power unless at the time of acting he knows –

(a) that the instrument did not create a valid enduring power,

(b) that an event has occurred which, if the instrument had created a valid enduring power, would have had the effect of revoking the power, or

(c) that, if the instrument had created a valid enduring power, the power would have expired before that time.

(3) Any transaction between the attorney and another person is, in favour of that person, as valid as if the power had then been in existence, unless at the time of the transaction that person has knowledge of any of the matters mentioned in sub-paragraph (2).

(4) If the interest of a purchaser depends on whether a transaction between the attorney and another person was valid by virtue of sub-paragraph (3), it is conclusively presumed in favour of the purchaser that the transaction was valid if –

(a) the transaction between that person and the attorney was completed within 12 months of the date on which the instrument was registered, or

(b) that person makes a statutory declaration, before or within 3 months after the completion of the purchase, that he had no reason at the time of the transaction to doubt that the attorney had authority to dispose of the property which was the subject of the transaction.

(5) For the purposes of section 5 of the Powers of Attorney Act 1971 (c. 27) (protection where power is revoked) in its application to an enduring power the revocation of which by the donor is by virtue of paragraph 15 invalid unless and until confirmed by the court under paragraph 16 –

(a) knowledge of the confirmation of the revocation is knowledge of the revocation of the power, but

(b) knowledge of the unconfirmed revocation is not.

Further protection of attorney and third persons

19 (1) If –

(a) an instrument framed in a form prescribed as mentioned in paragraph 2(2) creates a power which is not a valid enduring power, and

(b) the power is revoked by the mental incapacity of the donor,

sub-paragraphs (2) and (3) apply, whether or not the instrument has been registered.

(2) An attorney who acts in pursuance of the power does not, by reason of the revocation, incur any liability (either to the donor or to any other person) unless at the time of acting he knows –

(a) that the instrument did not create a valid enduring power, and

(b) that the donor has become mentally incapable.

(3) Any transaction between the attorney and another person is, in favour of that person, as valid as if the power had then been in existence, unless at the time of the transaction that person knows –

(a) that the instrument did not create a valid enduring power, and

(b) that the donor has become mentally incapable.

(4) Paragraph 18(4) applies for the purpose of determining whether a transaction was valid by virtue of sub-paragraph (3) as it applies for the purpose or determining whether a transaction was valid by virtue of paragraph 18(3).

PART 7   JOINT AND JOINT AND SEVERAL ATTORNEYS

Application to joint and joint and several attorneys

20 (1) An instrument which appoints more than one person to be an attorney cannot create an enduring power unless the attorneys are appointed to act –

    (a) jointly, or
    (b) jointly and severally.

  (2) This Schedule, in its application to joint attorneys, applies to them collectively as it applies to a single attorney but subject to the modifications specified in paragraph 21.

  (3) This Schedule, in its application to joint and several attorneys, applies with the modifications specified in sub-paragraphs (4) to (7) and in paragraph 22.

  (4) A failure, as respects any one attorney, to comply with the requirements for the creation of enduring powers –

    (a) prevents the instrument from creating such a power in his case, but
    (b) does not affect its efficacy for that purpose as respects the other or others or its efficacy in his case for the purpose of creating a power of attorney which is not an enduring power.

  (5) If one or more but not both or all the attorneys makes or joins in making an application for registration of the instrument –

    (a) an attorney who is not an applicant as well as one who is may act pending the registration of the instrument as provided in paragraph 1(2),
    (b) notice of the application must also be given under Part 3 of this Schedule to the other attorney or attorneys, and
    (c) objection may validly be taken to the registration on a ground relating to an attorney or to the power of an attorney who is not an applicant as well as to one or the power of one who is an applicant.

  (6) The Public Guardian is not precluded by paragraph 13(5) or (8) from registering an instrument and the court must not direct him not to do so under paragraph 13(10) if an enduring power subsists as respects some attorney who is not affected by the ground or grounds of the objection in question; and where the Public Guardian registers an instrument in that case, he must make against the registration an entry in the prescribed form.

  (7) Sub-paragraph (6) does not preclude the court from revoking a power in so far as it confers a power on any other attorney in respect of whom the ground in paragraph 13(9)(d) or (e) is established; and where any ground in paragraph 13(9) affecting any other attorney is established the court must direct the Public Guardian to make against the registration an entry in the prescribed form.

  (8) In sub-paragraph (4), 'the requirements for the creation of enduring powers' means the provisions of –

    (a) paragraph 2 other than sub-paragraphs (8) and (9), and
    (b) the regulations mentioned in paragraph 2.

Joint attorneys

21 (1) In paragraph 2(5), the reference to the time when the attorney executes the instrument is to be read as a reference to the time when the second or last attorney executes the instrument.

  (2) In paragraph 2(6) to (8), the reference to the attorney is to be read as a reference to any attorney under the power.

(3) Paragraph 13 has effect as if the ground of objection to the registration of the instrument specified in sub-paragraph (9)(e) applied to any attorney under the power.

(4) In paragraph 16(2), references to the attorney are to be read as including references to any attorney under the power.

(5) In paragraph 16(4), references to the attorney are to be read as including references to any attorney under the power.

(6) In paragraph 17, references to the attorney are to be read as including references to any attorney under the power.

Joint and several attorneys

22 (1) In paragraph 2(7), the reference to the bankruptcy of the attorney is to be read as a reference to the bankruptcy of the last remaining attorney under the power; and the bankruptcy of any other attorney under the power causes that person to cease to be an attorney under the power.

(2) In paragraph 2(8), the reference to the suspension of the power is to be read as a reference to its suspension in so far as it relates to the attorney in respect of whom the interim bankruptcy restrictions order has effect.

(3) The restriction upon disclaimer imposed by paragraph 4(6) applies only to those attorneys who have reason to believe that the donor is or is becoming mentally incapable.

PART 8   INTERPRETATION

23 (1) In this Schedule –

'enduring power' is to be construed in accordance with paragraph 2,

'mentally incapable' or 'mental incapacity', except where it refers to revocation at common law, means in relation to any person, that he is incapable by reason of mental disorder [(*within the meaning of the Mental Health Act*)] of managing and administering his property and affairs and 'mentally capable' and 'mental capacity' are to be construed accordingly,

'notice' means notice in writing, and

'prescribed', except for the purposes of paragraph 2, means prescribed by regulations made for the purposes of this Schedule by the Lord Chancellor.

[(1A) In sub-paragraph (1), 'mental disorder' has the same meaning as in the Mental Health Act but disregarding the amendments made to that Act by the Mental Health Act 2007.]

(2) Any question arising under or for the purposes of this Schedule as to what the donor of the power might at any time be expected to do is to be determined by assuming that he had full mental capacity at the time but otherwise by reference to the circumstances existing at that time.

Notes:
The words '(within the meaning of the Mental Health Act)' in Sched.4, para.23(1) are omitted by the Mental Health Act 2007, Sched.1, para.23(2) at a time to be appointed by the Secretary of State in a statutory instrument.
Schedule 4, para.23(1A) is inserted by the Mental Health Act 2007, Sched.1, para.23(3) at a time to be appointed by the Secretary of State in a statutory instrument.

SCHEDULE 5   TRANSITIONAL PROVISIONS AND SAVINGS

Section 66(4)

PART 1   REPEAL OF PART 7 OF THE MENTAL HEALTH ACT 1983

Existing receivers

1   (1)   This paragraph applies where, immediately before the commencement day, there is a receiver ('R') for a person ('P') appointed under section 99 of the Mental Health Act.

(2)   On and after that day –

(a)   this Act applies as if R were a deputy appointed for P by the court, but with the functions that R had as receiver immediately before that day, and

(b)   a reference in any other enactment to a deputy appointed by the court includes a person appointed as a deputy as a result of paragraph (a).

(3)   On any application to it by R, the court may end R's appointment as P's deputy.

(4)   Where, as a result of section 20(1), R may not make a decision on behalf of P in relation to a relevant matter, R must apply to the court.

(5)   If, on the application, the court is satisfied that P is capable of managing his property and affairs in relation to the relevant matter –

(a)   it must make an order ending R's appointment as P's deputy in relation to that matter, but

(b)   it may, in relation to any other matter, exercise in relation to P any of the powers which it has under sections 15 to 19.

(6)   If it is not satisfied, the court may exercise in relation to P any of the powers which it has under sections 15 to 19.

(7)   R's appointment as P's deputy ceases to have effect if P dies.

(8)   'Relevant matter' means a matter in relation to which, immediately before the commencement day, R was authorised to act as P's receiver.

(9)   In sub-paragraph (1), the reference to a receiver appointed under section 99 of the Mental Health Act includes a reference to a person who by virtue of Schedule 5 to that Act was deemed to be a receiver appointed under that section.

Orders, appointments etc.

2   (1)   Any order or appointment made, direction or authority given or other thing done which has, or by virtue of Schedule 5 to the Mental Health Act was deemed to have, effect under Part 7 of the Act immediately before the commencement day is to continue to have effect despite the repeal of Part 7.

(2)   In so far as any such order, appointment, direction, authority or thing could have been made, given or done under sections 15 to 20 if those sections had then been in force –

(a)   it is to be treated as made, given or done under those sections, and

(b)   the powers of variation and discharge conferred by section 16(7) apply accordingly.

(3)   Sub-paragraph (1) –

(a)   does not apply to nominations under section 93(1) or (4) of the Mental Health Act, and

(b)   as respects receivers, has effect subject to paragraph 1.

(4) This Act does not affect the operation of section 109 of the Mental Health Act (effect and proof of orders etc.) in relation to orders made and directions given under Part 7 of that Act.

(5) This paragraph is without prejudice to section 16 of the Interpretation Act 1978 (c. 30) (general savings on repeal).

Pending proceedings

3   (1) Any application for the exercise of a power under Part 7 of the Mental Health Act which is pending immediately before the commencement day is to be treated, in so far as a corresponding power is exercisable under sections 16 to 20, as an application for the exercise of that power.

(2) For the purposes of sub-paragraph (1) an application for the appointment of a receiver is to be treated as an application for the appointment of a deputy.

Appeals

4   (1) Part 7 of the Mental Health Act and the rules made under it are to continue to apply to any appeal brought by virtue of section 105 of that Act which has not been determined before the commencement day.

(2) If in the case of an appeal brought by virtue of section 105(1) (appeal to nominated judge) the judge nominated under section 93 of the Mental Health Act has begun to hear the appeal, he is to continue to do so but otherwise it is to be heard by a puisne judge of the High Court nominated under section 46.

Fees

5   All fees and other payments which, having become due, have not been paid to the former Court of Protection before the commencement day, are to be paid to the new Court of Protection.

Court records

6   (1) The records of the former Court of Protection are to be treated, on and after the commencement day, as records of the new Court of Protection and are to be dealt with accordingly under the Public Records Act 1958 (c. 51).

(2) On and after the commencement day, the Public Guardian is, for the purpose of exercising any of his functions, to be given such access as he may require to such of the records mentioned in sub-paragraph (1) as relate to the appointment of receivers under section 99 of the Mental Health Act.

Existing charges

7   This Act does not affect the operation in relation to a charge created before the commencement day of –

(a) so much of section 101(6) of the Mental Health Act as precludes a charge created under section 101(5) from conferring a right of sale or foreclosure during the lifetime of the patient, or

(b) section 106(6) of the Mental Health Act (charge created by virtue of section 106(5) not to cause interest to fail etc.).

Preservation of interests on disposal of property

8   Paragraph 8(1) of Schedule 2 applies in relation to any disposal of property (within the meaning of that provision) by a person living on 1st November 1960, being a disposal effected under the Lunacy Act 1890 (c. 5) as it applies in relation to the disposal of property effected under sections 16 to 20.

Accounts

9   Court of Protection Rules may provide that, in a case where paragraph 1 applies, R is to have a duty to render accounts –

(a)   while he is receiver;
(b)   after he is discharged.

Interpretation

10   In this Part of this Schedule –

(a)   'the commencement day' means the day on which section 66(1)(a) (repeal of Part 7 of the Mental Health Act) comes into force,
(b)   'the former Court of Protection' means the office abolished by section 45, and
(c)   'the new Court of Protection' means the court established by that section.

PART 2   REPEAL OF THE ENDURING POWERS OF ATTORNEY ACT 1985

Orders, determinations, etc.

11   (1)   Any order or determination made, or other thing done, under the 1985 Act which has effect immediately before the commencement day continues to have effect despite the repeal of that Act.

(2)   In so far as any such order, determination or thing could have been made or done under Schedule 4 if it had then been in force –

(a)   it is to be treated as made or done under that Schedule, and
(b)   the powers of variation and discharge exercisable by the court apply accordingly.

(3)   Any instrument registered under the 1985 Act is to be treated as having been registered by the Public Guardian under Schedule 4.

(4)   This paragraph is without prejudice to section 16 of the Interpretation Act 1978 (c. 30) (general savings on repeal).

Pending proceedings

12   (1)   An application for the exercise of a power under the 1985 Act which is pending immediately before the commencement day is to be treated, in so far as a corresponding power is exercisable under Schedule 4, as an application for the exercise of that power.

(2)   For the purposes of sub-paragraph (1) –

(a)   a pending application under section 4(2) of the 1985 Act for the registration of an instrument is to be treated as an application to the Public Guardian under paragraph 4 of Schedule 4 and any notice given in connection with that application under Schedule 1 to the 1985 Act is to be treated as given under Part 3 of Schedule 4,

(b) a notice of objection to the registration of an instrument is to be treated as a notice of objection under paragraph 13 of Schedule 4, and

(c) pending proceedings under section 5 of the 1985 Act are to be treated as proceedings on an application for the exercise by the court of a power which would become exercisable in relation to an instrument under paragraph 16(2) of Schedule 4 on its registration.

Appeals

13 (1) The 1985 Act and, so far as relevant, the provisions of Part 7 of the Mental Health Act and the rules made under it as applied by section 10 of the 1985 Act are to continue to have effect in relation to any appeal brought by virtue of section 10(1)(c) of the 1985 Act which has not been determined before the commencement day.

(2) If, in the case of an appeal brought by virtue of section 105(1) of the Mental Health Act as applied by section 10(1)(c) of the 1985 Act (appeal to nominated judge), the judge nominated under section 93 of the Mental Health Act has begun to hear the appeal, he is to continue to do so but otherwise the appeal is to be heard by a puisne judge of the High Court nominated under section 46.

Exercise of powers of donor as trustee

14 (1) Section 2(8) of the 1985 Act (which prevents a power of attorney under section 25 of the Trustee Act 1925 (c. 19) as enacted from being an enduring power) is to continue to apply to any enduring power –

(a) created before 1st March 2000, and

(b) having effect immediately before the commencement day.

(2) Section 3(3) of the 1985 Act (which entitles the donee of an enduring power to exercise the donor's powers as trustee) is to continue to apply to any enduring power to which, as a result of the provision mentioned in sub-paragraph (3), it applies immediately before the commencement day.

(3) The provision is section 4(3)(a) of the Trustee Delegation Act 1999 (c. 15) (which provides for section 3(3) of the 1985 Act to cease to apply to an enduring power when its registration is cancelled, if it was registered in response to an application made before 1st March 2001).

(4) Even though section 4 of the 1999 Act is repealed by this Act, that section is to continue to apply in relation to an enduring power –

(a) to which section 3(3) of the 1985 Act applies as a result of sub-paragraph (2), or

(b) to which, immediately before the repeal of section 4 of the 1999 Act, section 1 of that Act applies as a result of section 4 of it.

(5) The reference in section 1(9) of the 1999 Act to section 4(6) of that Act is to be read with sub-paragraphs (2) to (4).

Interpretation

15 In this Part of this Schedule, 'the commencement day' means the day on which section 66(1)(b) (repeal of the 1985 Act) comes into force.

SCHEDULE 6   MINOR AND CONSEQUENTIAL AMENDMENTS

Section 67(1)

Fines and Recoveries Act 1833 (c. 74)

1   (1)   The Fines and Recoveries Act 1833 (c. 74) is amended as follows.
    (2)   In section 33 (case where protector of settlement lacks capacity to act), for the words from 'shall be incapable' to 'is incapable as aforesaid' substitute 'lacks capacity (within the meaning of the Mental Capacity Act 2005) to manage his property and affairs, the Court of Protection is to take his place as protector of the settlement while he lacks capacity'.
    (3)   In sections 48 and 49 (mental health jurisdiction), for each reference to the judge having jurisdiction under Part 7 of the Mental Health Act substitute a reference to the Court of Protection.

Improvement of Land Act 1864 (c. 114)

2   In section 68 of the Improvement of Land Act 1864 (c. 114) (apportionment of rentcharges) –
    (a)   for ', curator, or receiver of' substitute 'or curator of, or a deputy with powers in relation to property and affairs appointed by the Court of Protection for,', and
    (b)   for 'or patient within the meaning of Part VII of the Mental Health Act 1983' substitute 'person who lacks capacity (within the meaning of the Mental Capacity Act 2005) to receive the notice'.

Trustee Act 1925 (c. 19)

3   (1)   The Trustee Act 1925 (c. 19) is amended as follows.
    (2)   In section 36 (appointment of new trustee) –
        (a)   in subsection (6C), for the words from 'a power of attorney' to the end, substitute 'an enduring power of attorney or lasting power of attorney registered under the Mental Capacity Act 2005', and
        (b)   in subsection (9) –
            (i)   for the words from 'is incapable' to 'exercising' substitute 'lacks capacity to exercise', and
            (ii)   for the words from 'the authority' to the end substitute 'the Court of Protection'.
    (3)   In section 41(1) (power of court to appoint new trustee) for the words from 'is incapable' to 'exercising' substitute 'lacks capacity to exercise'.
    (4)   In section 54 (mental health jurisdiction) –
        (a)   for subsection (1) substitute –
            '(1)   Subject to subsection (2), the Court of Protection may not make an order, or give a direction or authority, in relation to a person who lacks capacity to exercise his functions as trustee, if the High Court may make an order to that effect under this Act.',
        (b)   in subsection (2) –
            (i)   for the words from the beginning to 'of a receiver' substitute 'Where a person lacks capacity to exercise his functions as a trustee and a deputy is appointed for him by the Court of Protection or an application for the appointment of a deputy',
            (ii)   for 'the said authority', in each place, substitute 'the Court of Protection', and

(iii) for 'the patient', in each place, substitute 'the person concerned', and

(c) omit subsection (3).

(5) In section 55 (order made on particular allegation to be conclusive evidence of it) –

(a) for the words from 'Part VII' to 'Northern Ireland' substitute 'sections 15 to 20 of the Mental Capacity Act 2005 or any corresponding provisions having effect in Northern Ireland', and

(b) for paragraph (a) substitute –

'(a) that a trustee or mortgagee lacks capacity in relation to the matter in question;'.

(6) In section 68 (definitions), at the end add –

'(3) Any reference in this Act to a person who lacks capacity in relation to a matter is to a person –

(a) who lacks capacity within the meaning of the Mental Capacity Act 2005 in relation to that matter, or

(b) in respect of whom the powers conferred by section 48 of that Act are exercisable and have been exercised in relation to that matter.'.

Law of Property Act 1925 (c. 20)

4   (1) The Law of Property Act 1925 (c. 20) is amended as follows.

(2) In section 22 (conveyances on behalf of persons who lack capacity) –

(a) in subsection (1) –

(i) for the words from 'in a person suffering' to 'is acting' substitute ', either solely or jointly with any other person or persons, in a person lacking capacity (within the meaning of the Mental Capacity Act 2005) to convey or create a legal estate, a deputy appointed for him by the Court of Protection or (if no deputy is appointed', and

(ii) for 'the authority having jurisdiction under Part VII of the Mental Health Act 1983' substitute 'the Court of Protection',

(b) in subsection (2), for 'is incapable, by reason of mental disorder, of exercising' substitute 'lacks capacity (within the meaning of that Act) to exercise', and

(c) in subsection (3), for the words from 'an enduring power' to the end substitute 'an enduring power of attorney or lasting power of attorney (within the meaning of the 2005 Act) is entitled to act for the trustee who lacks capacity in relation to the dealing.'.

(3) In section 205(1) (interpretation), omit paragraph (xiii).

Administration of Estates Act 1925 (c. 23)

5   (1) The Administration of Estates Act 1925 (c. 23) is amended as follows.

(2) In section 41(1) (powers of personal representatives to appropriate), in the proviso –

(a) in paragraph (ii) –

(i) for the words from 'is incapable' to 'the consent' substitute 'lacks capacity (within the meaning of the Mental Capacity Act 2005) to give the consent, it', and

(ii) for 'or receiver' substitute 'or a person appointed as deputy for him by the Court of Protection', and

(b)   in paragraph (iv), for 'no receiver is acting for a person suffering from mental disorder' substitute 'no deputy is appointed for a person who lacks capacity to consent'.

(3)   Omit section 55(1)(viii) (definitions of 'person of unsound mind' and 'defective').

National Assistance Act 1948 (c. 29)

6   In section 49 of the National Assistance Act 1948 (c. 29) (expenses of council officers acting for persons who lack capacity) –

(a)   for the words from 'applies' to 'affairs of a patient' substitute 'applies for appointment by the Court of Protection as a deputy', and
(b)   for 'such functions' substitute 'his functions as deputy'.

U.S.A. Veterans' Pensions (Administration) Act 1949 (c. 45)

7   In section 1 of the U.S.A. Veterans' Pensions (Administration) Act 1949 (c. 45) (administration of pensions) –

(a)   in subsection (4), omit the words from 'or for whom' to '1983', and
(b)   after subsection (4), insert –

'(4A) An agreement under subsection (1) is not to be made in relation to a person who lacks capacity (within the meaning of the Mental Capacity Act 2005) for the purposes of this Act if –

(a)   there is a donee of an enduring power of attorney or lasting power of attorney (within the meaning of the 2005 Act), or a deputy appointed for the person by the Court of Protection, and
(b)   the donee or deputy has power in relation to the person for the purposes of this Act.

(4B) The proviso at the end of subsection (4) also applies in relation to subsection (4A).'.

Intestates' Estates Act 1952 (c. 64)

8   In Schedule 2 to the Intestates' Estates Act 1952 (c. 64) (rights of surviving spouse or civil partner in relation to home), for paragraph 6(1) substitute –

'(1) Where the surviving spouse or civil partner lacks capacity (within the meaning of the Mental Capacity Act 2005) to make a requirement or give a consent under this Schedule, the requirement or consent may be made or given by a deputy appointed by the Court of Protection with power in that respect or, if no deputy has that power, by that court.'.

Variation of Trusts Act 1958 (c. 53)

9   In section 1 of the Variation of Trusts Act 1958 (c. 53) (jurisdiction of courts to vary trusts) –

(a)   in subsection (3), for the words from 'shall be determined' to the end substitute 'who lacks capacity (within the meaning of the Mental Capacity Act 2005) to give his assent is to be determined by the Court of Protection', and
(b)   in subsection (6), for the words from 'the powers' to the end substitute 'the powers of the Court of Protection'.

Administration of Justice Act 1960 (c. 65)

10   In section 12(1)(b) of the Administration of Justice Act 1960 (c. 65) (contempt of court to publish information about proceedings in private relating to persons with incapacity) for the words from 'under Part VIII' to 'that Act' substitute 'under the Mental Capacity Act 2005, or under any provision of the Mental Health Act 1983'.

Industrial and Provident Societies Act 1965 (c. 12)

11   In section 26 of the Industrial and Provident Societies Act 1965 (c. 12) (payments for mentally incapable people), for subsection (2) substitute –

'(2)   Subsection (1) does not apply where the member or person concerned lacks capacity (within the meaning of the Mental Capacity Act 2005) for the purposes of this Act and –

(a)   there is a donee of an enduring power of attorney or lasting power of attorney (within the meaning of the 2005 Act), or a deputy appointed for the member or person by the Court of Protection, and

(b)   the donee or deputy has power in relation to the member or person for the purposes of this Act.'.

Compulsory Purchase Act 1965 (c. 56)

12   In Schedule 1 to the Compulsory Purchase Act 1965 (c. 56) (persons without power to sell their interests), for paragraph 1(2)(b) substitute –

'(b)   do not have effect in relation to a person who lacks capacity (within the meaning of the Mental Capacity Act 2005) for the purposes of this Act if –

(i)   there is a donee of an enduring power of attorney or lasting power of attorney (within the meaning of the 2005 Act), or a deputy appointed for the person by the Court of Protection, and

(ii)   the donee or deputy has power in relation to the person for the purposes of this Act.'.

Leasehold Reform Act 1967 (c. 88)

13   (1)   For section 26(2) of the Leasehold Reform Act 1967 (c. 88) (landlord lacking capacity) substitute –

'(2)   Where a landlord lacks capacity (within the meaning of the Mental Capacity Act 2005) to exercise his functions as a landlord, those functions are to be exercised –

(a)   by a donee of an enduring power of attorney or lasting power of attorney (within the meaning of the 2005 Act), or a deputy appointed for him by the Court of Protection, with power to exercise those functions, or

(b)   if no donee or deputy has that power, by a person authorised in that respect by that court.'.

(2)   That amendment does not affect any proceedings pending at the commencement of this paragraph in which a receiver or a person authorised under Part 7 of the Mental Health Act is acting on behalf of the landlord.

Medicines Act 1968 (c. 67)

14   In section 72 of the Medicines Act 1968 (c. 67) (pharmacist lacking capacity) –

(a)   in subsection (1)(c), for the words from 'a receiver' to '1959' substitute 'he becomes a person who lacks capacity (within the meaning of the Mental Capacity Act 2005) to carry on the business',

(b)   after subsection (1) insert –

'(1A) In subsection (1)(c), the reference to a person who lacks capacity to carry on the business is to a person –

(a)   in respect of whom there is a donee of an enduring power of attorney or lasting power of attorney (within the meaning of the Mental Capacity Act 2005), or

(b)   for whom a deputy is appointed by the Court of Protection,

and in relation to whom the donee or deputy has power for the purposes of this Act.',

(c)   in subsection (3)(d) –

(i)   for 'receiver' substitute 'deputy', and

(ii)   after 'guardian' insert 'or from the date of registration of the instrument appointing the donee', and

(d)   in subsection (4)(c), for 'receiver' substitute 'donee, deputy'.

Family Law Reform Act 1969 (c. 46)

15   For section 21(4) of the Family Law Reform Act 1969 (c. 46) (consent required for taking of bodily sample from person lacking capacity), substitute –

'(4) A bodily sample may be taken from a person who lacks capacity (within the meaning of the Mental Capacity Act 2005) to give his consent, if consent is given by the court giving the direction under section 20 or by –

(a)   a donee of an enduring power of attorney or lasting power of attorney (within the meaning of that Act), or

(b)   a deputy appointed, or any other person authorised, by the Court of Protection,

with power in that respect.'.

Local Authority Social Services Act 1970 (c. 42)

16   (1)   Schedule 1 to the Local Authority Social Services Act 1970 (c. 42) (enactments conferring functions assigned to social services committee) is amended as follows.

(2)   In the entry for section 49 of the National Assistance Act 1948 (expenses of local authority officer appointed for person who lacks capacity) for 'receiver' substitute 'deputy'.

(3)   At the end, insert –

'Mental Capacity Act 2005

Section 39   Instructing independent mental capacity advocate before providing accommodation for person lacking capacity.

Section 49   Reports in proceedings.'.

Courts Act 1971 (c. 23)

17   In Part 1A of Schedule 2 to the Courts Act 1971 (c. 23) (office-holders eligible for appointment as circuit judges), omit the reference to a Master of the Court of Protection.

Local Government Act 1972 (c. 70)

18   (1)   Omit section 118 of the Local Government Act 1972 (c. 70) (payment of pension etc. where recipient lacks capacity).

(2)   Sub-paragraph (3) applies where, before the commencement of this paragraph, a local authority has, in respect of a person referred to in that section as 'the patient', made payments under that section –

(a)   to an institution or person having the care of the patient, or

(b)   in accordance with subsection (1)(a) or (b) of that section.

(3)   The local authority may, in respect of the patient, continue to make payments under that section to that institution or person, or in accordance with subsection (1)(a) or (b) of that section, despite the repeal made by sub-paragraph (1).

Matrimonial Causes Act 1973 (c. 18)

19   In section 40 of the Matrimonial Causes Act 1973 (c. 18) (payments to person who lacks capacity) (which becomes subsection (1)) –

(a)   for the words from 'is incapable' to 'affairs' substitute '('P') lacks capacity (within the meaning of the Mental Capacity Act 2005) in relation to the provisions of the order',

(b)   for 'that person under Part VIII of that Act' substitute 'P under that Act',

(c)   for the words from 'such persons' to the end substitute 'such person ('D') as it may direct', and

(d)   at the end insert –

'(2)   In carrying out any functions of his in relation to an order made under subsection (1), D must act in P's best interests (within the meaning of that Act).'.

Juries Act 1974 (c. 23)

20   In Schedule 1 to the Juries Act 1974 (c. 23) (disqualification for jury service), for paragraph 3 substitute –

'3   A person who lacks capacity, within the meaning of the Mental Capacity Act 2005, to serve as a juror.'.

Consumer Credit Act 1974 (c. 39)

21   For section 37(1)(c) of the Consumer Credit Act 1974 (c. 39) (termination of consumer credit licence if holder lacks capacity) substitute –

'(c)   becomes a person who lacks capacity (within the meaning of the Mental Capacity Act 2005) to carry on the activities covered by the licence.'.

Solicitors Act 1974 (c. 47)

22 (1) The Solicitors Act 1974 (c. 47) is amended as follows.

(2) [*For section 12(1)(j) (application for practising certificate by solicitor lacking capacity) substitute –*

'(j) *while he lacks capacity (within the meaning of the Mental Capacity Act 2005) to act as a solicitor and powers under sections 15 to 20 or section 48 of that Act are exercisable in relation to him;'.*]

(3) In section 62(4) (contentious business agreements made by clients) for paragraphs (c) and (d) substitute –

'(c) as a deputy for him appointed by the Court of Protection with powers in relation to his property and affairs, or

(d) as another person authorised under that Act to act on his behalf.'.

(4) In paragraph 1(1) of Schedule 1 (circumstances in which Law Society may intervene in solicitor's practice), for paragraph (f) substitute –

'(f) a solicitor lacks capacity (within the meaning of the Mental Capacity Act 2005) to act as a solicitor and powers under sections 15 to 20 or section 48 of that Act are exercisable in relation to him;'.

Note:
Schedule 6, para.22(2) is omitted by the Legal Services Act 2007, Sched.23 at a time to be appointed by the Secretary of State in a statutory instrument.

Local Government (Miscellaneous Provisions) Act 1976 (c. 57)

23 In section 31 of the Local Government (Miscellaneous Provisions) Act 1976 (c. 57) (the title to which becomes 'Indemnities for local authority officers appointed as deputies or administrators'), for the words from 'as a receiver' to '1959' substitute 'as a deputy for a person by the Court of Protection'.

Sale of Goods Act 1979 (c. 54)

24 In section 3(2) of the Sale of Goods Act 1979 (c. 54) (capacity to buy and sell) the words 'mental incapacity or' cease to have effect in England and Wales.

Limitation Act 1980 (c. 58)

25 In section 38 of the Limitation Act 1980 (c. 58) (interpretation) substitute –

(a) in subsection (2) for 'of unsound mind' substitute 'lacks capacity (within the meaning of the Mental Capacity Act 2005) to conduct legal proceedings', and

(b) omit subsections (3) and (4).

Public Passenger Vehicles Act 1981 (c. 14)

26 In section 57(2)(c) of the Public Passenger Vehicles Act 1981 (c. 14) (termination of public service vehicle licence if holder lacks capacity) for the words from 'becomes a patient' to 'or' substitute 'becomes a person who lacks capacity (within the meaning of the Mental Capacity Act 2005) to use a vehicle under the licence, or'.

Judicial Pensions Act 1981 (c. 20)

27   In Schedule 1 to the Judicial Pensions Act 1981 (c. 20) (pensions of Supreme Court officers, etc.), in paragraph 1, omit the reference to a Master of the Court of Protection except in the case of a person holding that office immediately before the commencement of this paragraph or who had previously retired from that office or died.

[Supreme Court Act 1981] [Senior Courts Act 1981] (c. 54)

28   In Schedule 2 to the [*Supreme Court Act 1981*] [*Senior Courts Act 1981*] (c. 54) (qualifications for appointment to office in Supreme Court), omit paragraph 11 (Master of the Court of Protection).

Note:
In Sched.6, para.28, the words 'Supreme Court Act 1981' are substituted with 'Senior Courts Act 1981' by Constitutional Reform Act 2005, Sched.11, para.1(2) at a time to be appointed by the Secretary of State in a statutory instrument.

Mental Health Act 1983 (c. 20)

29   (1)   The Mental Health Act is amended as follows.

(2)   In section 134(3) (cases where correspondence of detained patients may not be withheld) for paragraph (b) substitute –

'(b)   any judge or officer of the Court of Protection, any of the Court of Protection Visitors or any person asked by that Court for a report under section 49 of the Mental Capacity Act 2005 concerning the patient;'.

(3)   In section 139 (protection for acts done in pursuance of 1983 Act), in subsection (1), omit from 'or in, or in pursuance' to 'Part VII of this Act,'.

(4)   Section 142 (payment of pension etc. where recipient lacks capacity) ceases to have effect in England and Wales.

(5)   Sub-paragraph (6) applies where, before the commencement of sub-paragraph (4), an authority has, in respect of a person referred to in that section as 'the patient', made payments under that section –

(a)   to an institution or person having the care of the patient, or

(b)   in accordance with subsection (2)(a) or (b) of that section.

(6)   The authority may, in respect of the patient, continue to make payments under that section to that institution or person, or in accordance with subsection (2)(a) or (b) of that section, despite the amendment made by sub-paragraph (4).

(7)   In section 145(1) (interpretation), in the definition of 'patient', omit '(except in Part VII of this Act)'.

(8)   In section 146 (provisions having effect in Scotland), omit from '104(4)' to 'section),'.

(9)   In section 147 (provisions having effect in Northern Ireland), omit from '104(4)' to 'section),'.

Administration of Justice Act 1985 (c. 61)

30   In section 18(3) of the Administration of Justice Act 1985 (c. 61) (licensed conveyancer who lacks capacity), for the words from 'that person' to the end substitute 'he becomes a person who lacks capacity (within the meaning of the Mental Capacity Act 2005) to practise as a licensed conveyancer.'.

Insolvency Act 1986 (c. 45)

31 (1) The Insolvency Act 1986 (c. 45) is amended as follows.
    (2) In section 389A (people not authorised to act as nominee or supervisor in voluntary arrangement), in subsection (3) –

     (a) omit the 'or' immediately after paragraph (b),
     (b) in paragraph (c), omit 'Part VII of the Mental Health Act 1983 or', and
     (c) after that paragraph, insert ', or
     (d) he lacks capacity (within the meaning of the Mental Capacity Act 2005) to act as nominee or supervisor'.

    (3) In section 390 (people not qualified to be insolvency practitioners), in subsection (4) –

     (a) omit the 'or' immediately after paragraph (b),
     (b) in paragraph (c), omit 'Part VII of the Mental Health Act 1983 or', and
     (c) after that paragraph, insert ', or
     (d) he lacks capacity (within the meaning of the Mental Capacity Act 2005) to act as an insolvency practitioner.'.

Building Societies Act 1986 (c. 53)

32 In section 102D(9) of the Building Societies Act 1986 (c. 53) (references to a person holding an account on trust for another) –

     (a) in paragraph (a), for 'Part VII of the Mental Health Act 1983' substitute 'the Mental Capacity Act 2005', and
     (b) for paragraph (b) substitute –

     '(b) to an attorney holding an account for another person under –

       (i) an enduring power of attorney or lasting power of attorney registered under the Mental Capacity Act 2005, or
       (ii) an enduring power registered under the Enduring Powers of Attorney (Northern Ireland) Order 1987;'.

Public Trustee and Administration of Funds Act 1986 (c. 57)

33 In section 3 of the Public Trustee and Administration of Funds Act 1986 (c. 57) (functions of the Public Trustee) –

     (a) for subsections (1) to (5) substitute –

     '(1) The Public Trustee may exercise the functions of a deputy appointed by the Court of Protection.',

     (b) in subsection (6), for 'the 1906 Act' substitute 'the Public Trustee Act 1906', and
     (c) omit subsection (7).

Patronage (Benefices) Measure 1986 (No.3)

34 (1) The Patronage (Benefices) Measure 1986 (No. 3) is amended as follows.
    (2) In section 5 (rights of patronage exercisable otherwise than by registered patron), after subsection (3) insert –

     '(3A) The reference in subsection (3) to a power of attorney does not include an enduring power of attorney or lasting power of attorney (within the meaning of the Mental Capacity Act 2005).'

(3) In section 9 (information to be sent to designated officer when benefice becomes vacant), after subsection (5) insert –

'(5A) Subsections (5B) and (5C) apply where the functions of a registered patron are, as a result of paragraph 10 of Schedule 2 to the Mental Capacity Act 2005 (patron's loss of capacity to discharge functions), to be discharged by an individual appointed by the Court of Protection.

(5B) If the individual is a clerk in Holy Orders, subsection (5) applies to him as it applies to the registered patron.

(5C) If the individual is not a clerk in Holy Orders, subsection (1) (other than paragraph (b)) applies to him as it applies to the registered patron.'

Courts and Legal Services Act 1990 (c. 41)

35 (1) The Courts and Legal Services Act 1990 (c. 41) is amended as follows.

(2) In Schedule 11 (judges etc. barred from legal practice), for the reference to a Master of the Court of Protection substitute a reference to each of the following –

(a) Senior Judge of the Court of Protection,

(b) President of the Court of Protection,

(c) Vice-President of the Court of Protection.

(3) In paragraph 5(3) of Schedule 14 (exercise of powers of intervention in registered foreign lawyer's practice), for paragraph (f) substitute –

'(f) he lacks capacity (within the meaning of the Mental Capacity Act 2005) to act as a registered foreign lawyer and powers under sections 15 to 20 or section 48 are exercisable in relation to him;'.

Child Support Act 1991 (c. 48)

36 In section 50 of the Child Support Act 1991 (c. 48) (unauthorised disclosure of information) –

(a) in subsection (8) –

(i) immediately after paragraph (a), insert 'or',

(ii) omit paragraphs (b) and (d) and the 'or' immediately after paragraph (c), and

(iii) for ', receiver, custodian or appointee' substitute 'or custodian', and

(b) after that subsection, insert –

'(9) Where the person to whom the information relates lacks capacity (within the meaning of the Mental Capacity Act 2005) to consent to its disclosure, the appropriate person is –

(a) a donee of an enduring power of attorney or lasting power of attorney (within the meaning of that Act), or

(b) a deputy appointed for him, or any other person authorised, by the Court of Protection,

with power in that respect.'.

Social Security Administration Act 1992 (c. 5)

37 In section 123 of the Social Security Administration Act 1992 (c. 5) (unauthorised disclosure of information) –

(a) in subsection (10), omit –

(i)   in paragraph (b), 'a receiver appointed under section 99 of the Mental Health Act 1983 or',

(ii)   in paragraph (d)(i), 'sub-paragraph (a) of rule 41(1) of the Court of Protection Rules 1984 or',

(iii) in paragraph (d)(ii), 'a receiver ad interim appointed under sub-paragraph (b) of the said rule 41(1) or', and

(iv)   'receiver,', and

(b) after that subsection, insert –

'(11) Where the person to whom the information relates lacks capacity (within the meaning of the Mental Capacity Act 2005) to consent to its disclosure, the appropriate person is –

(a)   a donee of an enduring power of attorney or lasting power of attorney (within the meaning of that Act), or

(b)   a deputy appointed for him, or any other person authorised, by the Court of Protection,

with power in that respect.'.

Judicial Pensions and Retirement Act 1993 (c. 8)

38 (1) The Judicial Pensions and Retirement Act 1993 (c. 8) is amended as follows.

(2) In Schedule 1 (qualifying judicial offices), in Part 2, under the cross-heading 'Court officers', omit the reference to a Master of the Court of Protection except in the case of a person holding that office immediately before the commencement of this sub-paragraph or who had previously retired from that office or died.

(3) In Schedule 5 (retirement: the relevant offices), omit the entries relating to the Master and Deputy or temporary Master of the Court of Protection, except in the case of a person holding any of those offices immediately before the commencement of this sub-paragraph.

(4) In Schedule 7 (retirement: transitional provisions), omit paragraph 5(5)(i)(g) except in the case of a person holding office as a deputy or temporary Master of the Court of Protection immediately before the commencement of this sub-paragraph.

Leasehold Reform, Housing and Urban Development Act 1993 (c. 28)

39 (1) For paragraph 4 of Schedule 2 to the Leasehold Reform, Housing and Urban Development Act 1993 (c. 28) (landlord under a disability), substitute –

'4(1) This paragraph applies where a Chapter I or Chapter II landlord lacks capacity (within the meaning of the Mental Capacity Act 2005) to exercise his functions as a landlord.

(2) For the purposes of the Chapter concerned, the landlord's place is to be taken –

(a)   by a donee of an enduring power of attorney or lasting power of attorney (within the meaning of the 2005 Act), or a deputy appointed for him by the Court of Protection, with power to exercise those functions, or

(b)   if no deputy or donee has that power, by a person authorised in that respect by that court.'.

(2) That amendment does not affect any proceedings pending at the commencement of this paragraph in which a receiver or a person authorised under Part 7 of the Mental Health Act 1983 (c. 20) is acting on behalf of the landlord.

Goods Vehicles (Licensing of Operators) Act 1995 (c. 23)

40   (1)   The Goods Vehicles (Licensing of Operators) Act 1995 (c. 23) is amended as follows.

 (2)   In section 16(5) (termination of licence), for 'he becomes a patient within the meaning of Part VII of the Mental Health Act 1983' substitute 'he becomes a person who lacks capacity (within the meaning of the Mental Capacity Act 2005) to use a vehicle under the licence'.

 (3)   In section 48 (licence not to be transferable, etc.) –

 (a)   in subsection (2) –

 (i)   for 'or become a patient within the meaning of Part VII of the Mental Health Act 1983' substitute ', or become a person who lacks capacity (within the meaning of the Mental Capacity Act 2005) to use a vehicle under the licence,', and

 (ii)   in paragraph (a), for 'became a patient' substitute 'became a person who lacked capacity in that respect', and

 (b)   in subsection (5), for 'a patient within the meaning of Part VII of the Mental Health Act 1983' substitute 'a person lacking capacity'.

Disability Discrimination Act 1995 (c. 50)

41   In section 20(7) of the Disability Discrimination Act 1995 (c. 50) (regulations to disapply provisions about incapacity), in paragraph (b), for 'Part VII of the Mental Health Act 1983' substitute 'the Mental Capacity Act 2005'.

Trusts of Land and Appointment of Trustees Act 1996 (c. 47)

42   (1)   The Trusts of Land and Appointment of Trustees Act 1996 (c. 47) is amended as follows.

 (2)   In section 9 (delegation by trustees), in subsection (6), for the words from 'an enduring power' to the end substitute 'an enduring power of attorney or lasting power of attorney within the meaning of the Mental Capacity Act 2005'.

 (3)   In section 20 (the title to which becomes 'Appointment of substitute for trustee who lacks capacity') –

 (a)   in subsection (1)(a), for 'is incapable by reason of mental disorder of exercising' substitute 'lacks capacity (within the meaning of the Mental Capacity Act 2005) to exercise', and

 (b)   in subsection (2) –

 (i)   for paragraph (a) substitute –

 '(a)   a deputy appointed for the trustee by the Court of Protection,',

 (ii)   in paragraph (b), for the words from 'a power of attorney' to the end substitute 'an enduring power of attorney or lasting power of attorney registered under the Mental Capacity Act 2005', and

 (iii)   in paragraph (c), for the words from 'the authority' to the end substitute 'the Court of Protection'.

Human Rights Act 1998 (c. 42)

43   In section 4(5) of the Human Rights Act 1998 (c. 42) (courts which may make declarations of incompatibility), after paragraph (e) insert –

'(f)   the Court of Protection, in any matter being dealt with by the President of the Family Division, the Vice-Chancellor or a puisne judge of the High Court.'

Access to Justice Act 1999 (c. 22)

44   In paragraph 1 of Schedule 2 to the Access to Justice Act 1999 (c. 22) (services excluded from the Community Legal Service), after paragraph (e) insert –

'(ea) the creation of lasting powers of attorney under the Mental Capacity Act 2005, (eb) the making of advance decisions under that Act,'.

Adoption and Children Act 2002 (c. 38)

45   In section 52(1)(a) of the Adoption and Children Act 2002 (c. 38) (parental consent to adoption), for 'is incapable of giving consent' substitute 'lacks capacity (within the meaning of the Mental Capacity Act 2005) to give consent'.

Licensing Act 2003 (c. 17)

46   (1)   The Licensing Act 2003 (c.17) is amended as follows.
     (2)   In section 27(1) (lapse of premises licence), for paragraph (b) substitute –

'(b)   becomes a person who lacks capacity (within the meaning of the Mental Capacity Act 2005) to hold the licence,'.

     (3)   In section 47 (interim authority notice in relation to premises licence) –

(a)   in subsection (5), for paragraph (b) substitute –

'(b)   the former holder lacks capacity (within the meaning of the Mental Capacity Act 2005) to hold the licence and that person acts for him under an enduring power of attorney or lasting power of attorney registered under that Act,', and

(b)   in subsection (10), omit the definition of 'mentally incapable'.

Courts Act 2003 (c. 39)

47   (1)   The Courts Act 2003 (c. 39) is amended as follows.
     (2)   In section 1(1) (the courts in relation to which the Lord Chancellor must discharge his general duty), after paragraph (a) insert –

'(aa) the Court of Protection,'.

     (3)   In section 64(2) (judicial titles which the Lord Chancellor may by order alter) –

(a)   omit the reference to a Master of the Court of Protection, and
(b)   at the appropriate place insert a reference to each of the following –

(i)   Senior Judge of the Court of Protection,
(ii)   President of the Court of Protection,
(iii) Vice-president of the Court of Protection.

SCHEDULE 7   REPEALS

Section 67(2)

Short title and chapter	Extent of repeal
Trustee Act 1925 (c. 19)	Section 54(3).
Law of Property Act 1925 (c. 20)	Section 205(1)(xiii).
Administration of Estates Act 1925 (c. 23)	Section 55(1)(viii)
U.S.A. Veterans' Pensions (Administration) Act 1949 (c. 45)	In section 1(4), the words from 'or for whom' to '1983'.
Mental Health Act 1959 (c. 72)	In Schedule 7, in Part 1, the entries relating to – section 33 of the Fines and Recoveries Act 1833, section 68 of the Improvement of Land Act 1864, section 55 of the Trustee Act 1925, section 205(1) of the Law of Property Act 1925, section 49 of the National Assistance Act 1948, and section 1 of the Variation of Trusts Act 1958.
Courts Act 1971 (c. 23)	In Schedule 2, in Part 1A, the words 'Master of the Court of Protection'.
Local Government Act 1972 (c. 70)	Section 118.
Limitation Act 1980 (c. 58)	Section 38(3) and (4).
[Supreme Court Act 1981] [Senior Courts Act 1981] (c. 54)	In Schedule 2, in Part 2, paragraph 11.
Mental Health Act 1983 (c. 20)	Part 7. In section 139(1) the words from 'or in, or in pursuance' to 'Part VII of this Act,'. In section 145(1), in the definition of 'patient' the words '(except in Part VII of this Act)'. In sections 146 and 147 the words from '104(4)' to 'section),'. Schedule 3 In Schedule 4, paragraphs 1, 2, 4, 5, 7, 9, 14, 20, 22, 25, 32, 38, 55 and 56. In Schedule 5, paragraphs 26, 43, 44 and 45.
Enduring Powers of Attorney Act 1985 (c. 29)	The whole Act.
Insolvency Act 1986 (c. 45)	In section 389A(3) – the 'or' immediately after paragraph (b), and in paragraph (c), the words 'Part VII of the Mental Health Act 1983 or'. In section 390(4) –

	the 'or' immediately after paragraph (b), and in paragraph (c), the words 'Part VII of the Mental Health Act 1983 or'.
Public Trustee and Administration of Funds Act 1986 (c. 57)	Section 2. Section 3(7).
Child Support Act 1991 (c. 48)	In section 50(8) – paragraphs (b) and (d), and the 'or' immediately after paragraph (c).
Social Security Administration Act 1992 (c. 5)	In section 123(10) – in paragraph (b), 'a receiver appointed under section 99 of the Mental Health Act 1983 or', in paragraph (d)(i), 'sub-paragraph (a) of rule 41(1) of the Court of Protection Rules Act 1984 or', in paragraph (d)(ii), 'a receiver ad interim appointed under sub-paragraph (b) of the said rule 41(1) or', and 'receiver,'.
Trustee Delegation Act 1999 (c. 15)	Section 4. Section 6. In section 7(3), the words 'in accordance with section 4 above'.
Care Standards Act 2000 (c. 14)	In Schedule 4, paragraph 8.
Licensing Act 2003 (c. 17)	In section 47(10), the definition of 'mentally incapable'.
Courts Act 2003 (c. 64)	In section 64(2), the words 'Master of the Court of Protection'.

Note:
In Sched.7 the words 'Supreme Court Act 1981' are substituted with 'Senior Courts Act 1981' by Constitutional Reform Act 2005, Sched.11, para.1(2) at a time to be appointed by the Secretary of State in a statutory instrument.

Appendix B
MENTAL CAPACITY ACT 2005 (COMMENCEMENT NO.2) ORDER 2007

MENTAL CAPACITY ACT 2005 (COMMENCEMENT NO. 2) ORDER 2007, SI 2007/1897 (C. 72)

Made   *22nd June 2007*

The Lord Chancellor makes the following Order, in exercise of the powers conferred upon him by section 68(1) and (3) of the Mental Capacity Act 2005.

1 Citation, application and interpretation

(1) This Order may be cited as the Mental Capacity Act 2005 (Commencement No. 2) Order 2007.

(2) In this Order, "the Act" means the Mental Capacity Act 2005.

2 Appointed day

(1) The following provisions of the Act come into force on 1 October 2007 –

    (a) sections 5 to 29;
    (b) sections 45 to 63;
    (c) sections 65 to 69; and
    (d) Schedules 1 to 7.

(2) The following provisions of the Act, which have already been commenced for limited purposes, come into force on 1 October 2007 for all purposes –

    (a) section 1 (principles);
    (b) section 2 (people who lack capacity);
    (c) section 3 (inability to make decisions);
    (d) section 4 (best interests);
    (e) sections 42(4) and (5) (codes of practice); and
    (f) section 64 (interpretation).

Signed by authority of the Lord Chancellor

Catherine Ashton
Parliamentary Under-Secretary of State
Ministry of Justice

22nd June 2007

EXPLANATORY NOTE

(This note is not part of the Order)

This Order is the fourth commencement order under the Mental Capacity Act 2005.

The Mental Capacity Act 2005 (Commencement No. 1) Order (2006/2814) (as amended by S.I. 2006/3473), the Mental Capacity Act 2005 (Commencement No. 1) (England and Wales) Order (2007/563) and the Mental Capacity Act 2005 (Commencement) (Wales) Order (2007/856) brought or will bring provisions of the Act into force as follows –

	Provision	Date of commencement	Application
(a)	Sections 30 to 34 (in respect of any research carried out as part of a project begun on or after 1 October 2007).	01.10.2007	England
(b)	Sections 30 to 34 (for the purpose of enabling research applications to be made to, and determined by, an appropriate body).	01.07.2007	England
(c)	Sections 30 to 34 (where a research project has begun before 1 October 2007 and was approved before that date).	01.10.2008	England
(d)	Sections 35 to 41 (to enable the Secretary of State for Health to make arrangements to make independent mental capacity advocates available and to enable local authorities to approve independent mental capacity advocates).	01.11.2006	England
(e)	Sections 35 to 41 (fully into force).	01.04.2007	England
(f)	Sections 42(1), (2), (3), (6) and (7), 43 and 44 (fully into force).	01.04.2007	England and Wales
(g)	Sections 1 to 4, 42(4) and 42(5) (for purposes relating to the independent mental capacity advocate service).	01.04.2007	England
(h)	Sections 1 to 4, 42(4) and 42(5) (for the purposes of section 44).	01.04.2007	England and Wales
(i)	Section 64 (for the purposes of sections 1 to 4, 42, 43 and 44).	01.04.2007	England (g), England and Wales (f) and (h).
(j)	Sections 30 to 34 (in respect of any research carried out as part of a project begun on or after 1 October 2007).	01.10.2007	Wales
(k)	Sections 30 to 34 (for the purpose of enabling research applications to be made to, and determined by, an appropriate body).	01.07.2007	Wales
(l)	Sections 30 to 34 (where a research project has begun before 1 October 2007 and was approved before that date).	01.10.2008	Wales
(m)	Section 35 to 41 (fully into force).	01.10.2007	Wales

This Order brings into force on 1 October 2007 those provisions of the Mental Capacity Act 2005 (sections 5 to 29, 45 to 63, 65 to 69 and Schedules 1 to 7) which are not already in force.

This Order also brings into force on 1 October 2007 for all purposes those sections of the Mental Capacity Act 2005 (sections 1 to 4, 42(4), 42(5) and 64) which have already been commenced for limited purposes only.

Appendix C
LASTING POWERS OF ATTORNEY, ENDURING POWERS OF ATTORNEY AND PUBLIC GUARDIAN REGULATIONS 2007 (SI 2007/1253)

[The Lasting Powers of Attorney, Enduring Powers of Attorney and Public Regulations (SI 2007/1253) is reproduced here without Schedules 1–8 which contain the LPA forms and notices. The forms can be downloaded from the Office of the Public Guardian website, **www.publicguardian.gov.uk**.]

LASTING POWERS OF ATTORNEY, ENDURING POWERS OF ATTORNEY AND PUBLIC GUARDIAN REGULATIONS, SI 2007/1253

Made	*16th April 2007*
Laid before Parliament	*17th April 2007*
Coming into force	*1st October 2007*

CONTENTS

SCHEDULE 3 – Application to Register a Lasting Power of Attorney: LPA 002
SCHEDULE 4 – Notice of Receipt of an Application to Register a Lasting Power of Attorney: LPA 003A and LPA 003B
SCHEDULE 5 – Notice of Registration of a Lasting Power of Attorney: LPA 004
SCHEDULE 6 – Disclaimer by Donee of a Lasting Power of Attorney: LPA 005
SCHEDULE 7 – Notice of Intention to Apply for Registration of an Enduring Power of Attorney
SCHEDULE 8 – Application to Register an Enduring Power of Attorney

The Lord Chancellor makes the following Regulations in exercise of the powers conferred by sections 13(6)(a), 58(3) and 64(1) of, and Schedules 1 and 4 to, the Mental Capacity Act 2005 (**a**).

PART 1   PRELIMINARY

1 Citation and commencement

(1) These Regulations may be cited as the Lasting Powers of Attorney, Enduring Powers of Attorney and Public Guardian Regulations 2007.
(2) These Regulations shall come into force on 1 October 2007.

2 Interpretation

(1) In these Regulations –

'the Act' means the Mental Capacity Act 2005;
'court' means the Court of Protection;
'LPA certificate', in relation to an instrument made with a view to creating a lasting power of attorney, means the certificate which is required to be included in the instrument by virtue of paragraph 2(1)(e) of Schedule 1 to the Act;
'named person', in relation to an instrument made with a view to creating a lasting power of attorney, means a person who is named in the instrument as being a person to be notified of any application for the registration of the instrument;
'prescribed information', in relation to any instrument intended to create a lasting power of attorney, means the information contained in the form used for the instrument which appears under the heading 'prescribed information'.

3 Minimal differences from forms prescribed in these Regulations

(1) In these Regulations, any reference to a form –

(a) in the case of a form set out in Schedules 1 to 7 to these Regulations, is to be regarded as including a Welsh version of that form; and
(b) in the case of a form set out in Schedules 2 to 7 to these Regulations, is to be regarded as also including –

(i) a form to the same effect but which differs in an immaterial respect in form or mode of expression;
(ii) a form to the same effect but with such variations as the circumstances may require or the court or the Public Guardian may approve; or
(iii) a Welsh version of a form within (i) or (ii).

4 Computation of time

(1) This regulation shows how to calculate any period of time which is specified in these Regulations.
(2) A period of time expressed as a number of days must be computed as clear days.
(3) Where the specified period is 7 days or less, and would include a day which is not a business day, that day does not count.

(4) When the specified period for doing any act at the office of the Public Guardian ends on a day on which the office is closed, that act will be done in time if done on the next day on which the office is open.

(5) In this regulation –

'business day' means a day other than –

    (a) a Saturday, Sunday, Christmas Day or Good Friday; or

    (b) a bank holiday under the Banking and Financial Dealings Act 1971, in England and Wales; and

'clear days' means that in computing the number of days –

    (a) the day on which the period begins, and

    (b) if the end of the period is defined by reference to an event, the day on which that event occurs, are not included.

PART 2   LASTING POWERS OF ATTORNEY

Instruments intended to create a lasting power of attorney

5 Forms for lasting powers of attorney

The forms set out in Parts 1 and 2 of Schedule 1 to these Regulations are the forms which, in the circumstances to which they apply, are to be used for instruments intended to create a lasting power of attorney.

6 Maximum number of named persons

The maximum number of named persons that the donor of a lasting power of attorney may specify in the instrument intended to create the power is 5.

7 Requirement for two LPA certificates where instrument has no named persons

Where an instrument intended to create a lasting power of attorney includes a statement by the donor that there are no persons whom he wishes to be notified of any application for the registration of the instrument –

(a) the instrument must include two LPA certificates; and

(b) each certificate must be completed and signed by a different person.

8 Persons who may provide an LPA certificate

(1) Subject to paragraph (3), the following persons may give an LPA certificate –

    (a) a person chosen by the donor as being someone who has known him personally for the period of at least two years which ends immediately before the date on which that person signs the LPA certificate;

    (b) a person chosen by the donor who, on account of his professional skills and expertise, reasonably considers that he is competent to make the judgments necessary to certify the matters set out in paragraph (2)(1)(e) of Schedule 1 to the Act.

(2) The following are examples of persons within paragraph (1)(b) –

    (a) a registered health care professional;

    (b) a barrister, solicitor or advocate called or admitted in any part of the United Kingdom;

    (c) a registered social worker; or

    (d) an independent mental capacity advocate.

(3) A person is disqualified from giving an LPA certificate in respect of any instrument intended to create a lasting power of attorney if that person is –

(a)   a family member of the donor;
(b)   a donee of that power;
(c)   a donee of –

    (i)   any other lasting power of attorney, or
    (ii)   an enduring power of attorney,

which has been executed by the donor (whether or not it has been revoked);
(d)   a family member of a donee within sub-paragraph (b);
(e)   a director or employee of a trust corporation acting as a donee within sub-paragraph (b);
(f)   a business partner or employee of –

    (i)   the donor, or
    (ii)   a donee within sub-paragraph (b);

(g)   an owner, director, manager or employee of any care home in which the donor is living when the instrument is executed; or
(h)   a family member of a person within sub-paragraph (g).

(4)   In this regulation –

'care home' has the meaning given in section 3 of the Care Standards Act 2000;
'registered health care professional' means a person who is a member of a profession regulated by a body mentioned in section 25(3) of the National Health Service Reform and Health Care Professions Act 2002; and
'registered social worker' means a person registered as a social worker in a register maintained by –

    (a)   the General Social Care Council;
    (b)   the Care Council for Wales;
    (c)   the Scottish Social Services Council; or
    (d)   the Northern Ireland Social Care Council.

9   Execution of instrument

(1)   An instrument intended to create a lasting power of attorney must be executed in accordance with this regulation.
(2)   The donor must read (or have read to him) all the prescribed information.
(3)   As soon as reasonably practicable after the steps required by paragraph (2) have been taken, the donor must –

    (a)   complete the provisions of Part A of the instrument that apply to him (or direct another person to do so); and
    (b)   subject to paragraph (7), sign Part A of the instrument in the presence of a witness.

(4)   As soon as reasonably practicable after the steps required by paragraph (3) have been taken –

    (a)   the person giving an LPA certificate, or
    (b)   if regulation 7 applies (two LPA certificates required), each of the persons giving a certificate,

must complete the LPA certificate at Part B of the instrument and sign it.
(5)   As soon as reasonably practicable after the steps required by paragraph (4) have been taken –

    (a)   the donee, or
    (b)   if more than one, each of the donees,

must read (or have read to him) all the prescribed information.
(6)   As soon as reasonably practicable after the steps required by paragraph (5) have been taken, the donee or, if more than one, each of them –

    (a)   must complete the provisions of Part C of the instrument that apply to him (or direct another person to do so); and

(b)   subject to paragraph (7), must sign Part C of the instrument in the presence of a witness.

(7)   If the instrument is to be signed by any person at the direction of the donor, or at the direction of any donee, the signature must be done in the presence of two witnesses.

(8)   For the purposes of this regulation –

(a)   the donor may not witness any signature required for the power;

(b)   a donee may not witness any signature required for the power apart from that of another donee.

(9)   A person witnessing a signature must –

(a)   sign the instrument; and

(b)   give his full name and address.

(10) Any reference in this regulation to a person signing an instrument (however expressed) includes his signing it by means of a mark made on the instrument at the appropriate place.

Registering the instrument

10 Notice to be given by a person about to apply for registration of lasting power of attorney

Schedule 2 to these Regulations sets out the form of notice ('LPA 001') which must be given by a donor or donee who is about to make an application for the registration of an instrument intended to create a lasting power of attorney.

11 Application for registration

(1)   Schedule 3 to these Regulations sets out the form ('LPA 002') which must be used for making an application to the Public Guardian for the registration of an instrument intended to create a lasting power of attorney.

(2)   Where the instrument to be registered which is sent with the application is neither –

(a)   the original instrument intended to create the power, nor

(b)   a certified copy of it,

the Public Guardian must not register the instrument unless the court directs him to do so.

(3)   In paragraph (2) 'a certified copy' means a photographic or other facsimile copy which is certified as an accurate copy by –

(a)   the donor; or

(b)   a solicitor or notary.

12 Period to elapse before registration in cases not involving objection or defect

The period at the end of which the Public Guardian must register an instrument in accordance with paragraph 5 of Schedule 1 to the Act is the period of 6 weeks beginning with –

(a)   the date on which the Public Guardian gave the notice or notices under paragraph 7 or 8 of Schedule 1 to the Act of receipt of an application for registration; or

(b)   if notices were given on more than one date, the latest of those dates.

13 Notice of receipt of application for registration

(1)   Part 1 of Schedule 4 to these Regulations sets out the form of notice ('LPA 003A') which the Public Guardian must give to the donee (or donees) when the Public Guardian receives an application for the registration of a lasting power of attorney.

(2) Part 2 of Schedule 4 sets out the form of notice ('LPA 003B') which the Public Guardian must give to the donor when the Public Guardian receives such an application.

(3) Where it appears to the Public Guardian that there is good reason to do so, the Public Guardian must also provide (or arrange for the provision of) an explanation to the donor of –

(a) the notice referred to in paragraph (2) and what the effect of it is; and
(b) why it is being brought to his attention.

(4) Any information provided under paragraph (3) must be provided –

(a) to the donor personally; and
(b) in a way that is appropriate to the donor's circumstances (for example using simple language, visual aids or other appropriate means).

14 Objection to registration: notice to Public Guardian

(1) This regulation deals with any objection to the registration of an instrument as a lasting power of attorney which is to be made to the Public Guardian.

(2) Where any person –

(a) is entitled to receive notice under paragraph 6, 7 or 8 of Schedule 1 to the Act of an application for the registration of the instrument, and
(b) wishes to object to registration on a ground set out in paragraph 13(1) of Schedule 1 to the Act,

he must do so before the end of the period of 5 weeks beginning with the date on which the notice is given.

(3) A notice of objection must be given in writing, setting out –

(a) the name and address of the objector;
(b) if different, the name and address of the donor of the power;
(c) if known, the name and address of the donee (or donees); and
(d) the ground for making the objection.

(4) The Public Guardian must notify the objector as to whether he is satisfied that the ground of the objection is established.

(5) At any time after receiving the notice of objection and before giving the notice required by paragraph (4), the Public Guardian may require the objector to provide such further information, or produce such documents, as the Public Guardian reasonably considers necessary to enable him to determine whether the ground for making the objection is established.

(6) Where –

(a) the Public Guardian is satisfied that the ground of the objection is established, but
(b) by virtue of section 13(7) of the Act, the instrument is not revoked,

the notice under paragraph (4) must contain a statement to that effect.

(7) Nothing in this regulation prevents an objector from making a further objection under paragraph 13 of Schedule 1 to the Act where –

(a) the notice under paragraph (4) indicates that the Public Guardian is not satisfied that the particular ground of objection to which that notice relates is established; and
(b) the period specified in paragraph (2) has not expired.

15 Objection to registration: application to the court

(1) This regulation deals with any objection to the registration of an instrument as a lasting power of attorney which is to be made to the court.

(2) The grounds for making an application to the court are –

    (a) that one or more of the requirements for the creation of a lasting power of attorney have not been met;

    (b) that the power has been revoked, or has otherwise come to an end, on a ground other than the grounds set out in paragraph 13(1) of Schedule 1 to the Act;

    (c) any of the grounds set out in paragraph (a) or (b) of section 22(3) of the Act.

(3) Where any person –

    (a) is entitled to receive notice under paragraph 6, 7 or 8 of Schedule 1 to the Act of an application for the registration of the instrument, and

    (b) wishes to object to registration on one or more of the grounds set out in paragraph (2),

he must make an application to the court before the end of the period of 5 weeks beginning with the date on which the notice is given.

(4) The notice of an application to the court, which a person making an objection to the court is required to give to the Public Guardian under paragraph 13(3)(b)(ii) of Schedule 1 to the Act, must be in writing.

16 Notifying applicants of non-registration of lasting power of attorney

Where the Public Guardian is prevented from registering an instrument as a lasting power of attorney by virtue of –

(a) paragraph 11(1) of Schedule 1 to the Act (instrument not made in accordance with Schedule),

(b) paragraph 12(2) of that Schedule (deputy already appointed),

(c) paragraph 13(2) of that Schedule (objection by donee or named person on grounds of bankruptcy, disclaimer, death etc),

(d) paragraph 14(2) of that Schedule (objection by donor), or

(e) regulation 11(2) of these Regulations (application for registration not accompanied by original instrument or certified copy),

he must notify the person (or persons) who applied for registration of that fact.

17 Notice to be given on registration of lasting power of attorney

(1) Where the Public Guardian registers an instrument as a lasting power of attorney, he must –

    (a) retain a copy of the instrument; and

    (b) return to the person (or persons) who applied for registration the original instrument, or the certified copy of it, which accompanied the application for registration.

(2) Schedule 5 to these Regulations sets out the form of notice ('LPA 004') which the Public Guardian must give to the donor and donee (or donees) when the Public Guardian registers an instrument.

(3) Where it appears to the Public Guardian that there is good reason to do so, the Public Guardian must also provide (or arrange for the provision of) an explanation to the donor of –

    (a) the notice referred to in paragraph (2) and what the effect of it is; and

    (b) why it is being brought to his attention.

(4) Any information provided under paragraph (3) must be provided –

    (a) to the donor personally; and

    (b) in a way that is appropriate to the donor's circumstances (for example using simple language, visual aids or other appropriate means).

(5) 'Certified copy' is to be construed in accordance with regulation 11(3).

Post-registration

18 Changes to instrument registered as lasting power of attorney

(1) This regulation applies in any case where any of paragraphs 21 to 24 of Schedule 1 to the Act requires the Public Guardian to attach a note to an instrument registered as a lasting power of attorney.

(2) The Public Guardian must give a notice to the donor and the donee (or, if more than one, each of them) requiring him to deliver to the Public Guardian –

    (a)   the original of instrument which was sent to the Public Guardian for registration;

    (b)   any office copy of that registered instrument; and

    (c)   any certified copy of that registered instrument.

(3) On receipt of the document, the Public Guardian must –

    (a)   attach the required note; and

    (b)   return the document to the person from whom it was obtained.

19 Loss or destruction of instrument registered as lasting power of attorney

(1) This regulation applies where –

    (a)   a person is required by or under the Act to deliver up to the Public Guardian any of the following documents –

        (i)   an instrument registered as a lasting power of attorney;

        (ii)   an office copy of that registered instrument;

        (iii) a certified copy of that registered instrument; and

    (b)   the document has been lost or destroyed.

(2) The person required to deliver up the document must provide to the Public Guardian in writing –

    (a)   if known, the date of the loss or destruction and the circumstances in which it occurred;

    (b)   otherwise, a statement of when he last had the document in his possession.

20 Disclaimer of appointment by a donee of lasting power of attorney

(1) Schedule 6 to these Regulations sets out the form ('LPA 005') which a donee of an instrument registered as a lasting power of attorney must use to disclaim his appointment as donee.

(2) The donee must send –

    (a)   the completed form to the donor; and

    (b)   a copy of it to –

        (i)   the Public Guardian; and

        (ii)   any other donee who, for the time being, is appointed under the power.

21 Revocation by donor of lasting power of attorney

(1) A donor who revokes a lasting power to attorney must –

    (a)   notify the Public Guardian that he has done so; and

    (b)   notify the donee (or, if more than one, each of them) of the revocation.

(2) Where the Public Guardian receives a notice under paragraph (1)(a), he must cancel the registration of the instrument creating the power if he is satisfied that the donor has taken such steps as are necessary in law to revoke it.

(3) The Public Guardian may require the donor to provide such further information, or produce such documents, as the Public Guardian reasonably considers necessary to enable him to determine whether the steps necessary for revocation have been taken.

(4) Where the Public Guardian cancels the registration of the instrument he must notify –

  (a) the donor; and

  (b) the donee or, if more than one, each of them.

22 Revocation of a lasting power of attorney on death of donor

(1) The Public Guardian must cancel the registration of an instrument as a lasting power of attorney if he is satisfied that the power has been revoked as a result of the donor's death.

(2) Where the Public Guardian cancels the registration of an instrument he must notify the donee or, if more than one, each of them.

PART 3   ENDURING POWERS OF ATTORNEY

23 Notice of intention to apply for registration of enduring power of attorney

(1) Schedule 7 to these Regulations sets out the form of notice ('EP1PG') which an attorney (or attorneys) under an enduring power of attorney must give of his intention to make an application for the registration of the instrument creating the power.

(2) In the case of the notice to be given to the donor, the attorney must also provide (or arrange for the provision of) an explanation to the donor of –

  (a) the notice and what the effect of it is; and

  (b) why it is being brought to his attention.

(3) The information provided under paragraph (2) must be provided –

  (a) to the donor personally; and

  (b) in a way that is appropriate to the donor's circumstances (for example using simple language, visual aids or other appropriate means).

24 Application for registration

(1) Schedule 8 to these Regulations sets out the form ('EP2PG') which must be used for making an application to the Public Guardian for the registration of an instrument creating an enduring power of attorney.

(2) Where the instrument to be registered which is sent with the application is neither –

  (a) the original instrument creating the power, nor

  (b) a certified copy of it,

  the Public Guardian must not register the instrument unless the court directs him to do so.

(3) 'Certified copy', in relation to an enduring power of attorney, means a copy certified in accordance with section 3 of the Powers of Attorney Act 1971.

25 Notice of objection to registration

(1) This regulation deals with any objection to the registration of an instrument creating an enduring power of attorney which is to be made to the Public Guardian under paragraph 13(4) of Schedule 4 to the Act.

(2) A notice of objection must be given in writing, setting out –

  (a) the name and address of the objector;

  (b) if different, the name and address of the donor of the power;

  (c) if known, the name and address of the attorney (or attorneys); and

  (d) the ground for making the objection.

26 Notifying applicants of non-registration of enduring power of attorney

Where the Public Guardian is prevented from registering an instrument creating an enduring power of attorney by virtue of –

(a) paragraph 13(2) of Schedule 4 to the Act (deputy already appointed),
(b) paragraph 13(5) of that Schedule (receipt by Public Guardian of valid notice of objection from person entitled to notice of application to register),
(c) paragraph 13(7) of that Schedule (Public Guardian required to undertake appropriate enquiries in certain circumstances), or
(d) regulation 24(2) of these Regulations (application for registration not accompanied by original instrument or certified copy),

he must notify the person (or persons) who applied for registration of that fact.

27 Registration of instrument creating an enduring power of attorney

(1) Where the Public Guardian registers an instrument creating an enduring power of attorney, he must –
    (a) retain a copy of the instrument; and
    (b) return to the person (or persons) who applied for registration the original instrument, or the certified copy of it, which accompanied the application.

(2) 'Certified copy' has the same meaning as in regulation 24(3).

28 Objection or revocation not applying to all joint and several attorneys

In a case within paragraph 20(6) or (7) of Schedule 4 to the Act, the form of the entry to be made in the register in respect of an instrument creating the enduring power of attorney is a stamp bearing the following words (inserting the information indicated, as appropriate) –

'THE REGISTRATION OF THIS ENDURING POWER OF ATTORNEY IS QUALIFIED AND EXTENDS TO THE APPOINTMENT OF .... (insert name of attorney(s) not affected by ground(s) of objection or revocation) ONLY AS THE ATTORNEY(S) OF .... (insert name of donor)'.

29 Loss or destruction of instrument registered as enduring power of attorney

(1) This regulation applies where –
    (a) a person is required by or under the Act to deliver up to the Public Guardian any of the following documents –
        (i) an instrument registered as an enduring power of attorney;
        (ii) an office copy of that registered instrument; or
        (iii) a certified copy of that registered instrument; and
    (b) the document has been lost or destroyed.

(2) The person who is required to deliver up the document must provide to the Public Guardian in writing –
    (a) if known, the date of the loss or destruction and the circumstances in which it occurred;
    (b) otherwise, a statement of when he last had the document in his possession.

PART 4   FUNCTIONS OF THE PUBLIC GUARDIAN

The registers

30 Establishing and maintaining the registers

(1) In this Part 'the registers' means –

   (a) the register of lasting powers of attorney,
   (b) the register of enduring powers of attorney, and
   (c) the register of court orders appointing deputies,

   which the Public Guardian must establish and maintain.

(2) On each register the Public Guardian may include –

   (a) such descriptions of information about a registered instrument or a registered order as the Public Guardian considers appropriate; and
   (b) entries which relate to an instrument or order for which registration has been cancelled.

31 Disclosure of information on a register: search by the Public Guardian

(1) Any person may, by an application made under paragraph (2), request the Public Guardian to carry out a search of one or more of the registers.

(2) An application must –

   (a) state –

      (i)   the register or registers to be searched;
      (ii)   the name of the person to whom the application relates; and
      (iii) such other details about that person as the Public Guardian may require for the purpose of carrying out the search; and

   (b) be accompanied by any fee provided for under section 58(4)(b) of the Act.

(3) The Public Guardian may require the applicant to provide such further information, or produce such documents, as the Public Guardian reasonably considers necessary to enable him to carry out the search.

(4) As soon as reasonably practicable after receiving the application –

   (a) the Public Guardian must notify the applicant of the result of the search; and
   (b) in the event that it reveals one or more entries on the register, the Public Guardian must disclose to the applicant all the information appearing on the register in respect of each entry.

32 Disclosure of additional information held by the Public Guardian

(1) This regulation applies in any case where, as a result of a search made under regulation 31, a person has obtained information relating to a registered instrument or a registered order which confers authority to make decisions about matters concerning a person ('P').

(2) On receipt of an application made in accordance with paragraph (4), the Public Guardian may, if he considers that there is good reason to do so, disclose to the applicant such additional information as he considers appropriate.

(3) 'Additional information' means any information relating to P –

   (a) which the Public Guardian has obtained in exercising the functions conferred on him under the Act; but
   (b) which does not appear on the register.

(4) An application must state –

   (a) the name of P;
   (b) the reasons for making the application; and
   (c) what steps, if any, the applicant has taken to obtain the information from P.

(5) The Public Guardian may require the applicant to provide such further information, or produce such documents, as the Public Guardian reasonably considers necessary to enable him to determine the application.

(6) In determining whether to disclose any additional information to P, the Public Guardian must, in particular, have regard to –

    (a)   the connection between P and the applicant;

    (b)   the reasons for requesting the information (in particular, why the information cannot or should not be obtained directly from P);

    (c)   the benefit to P, or any detriment he may suffer, if a disclosure is made; and

    (d)   any detriment that another person may suffer if a disclosure is made.

Security for discharge of functions

33 Persons required to give security for the discharge of their functions

(1) This regulation applies in any case where the court orders a person ('S') to give to the Public Guardian security for the discharge of his functions.

(2) The security must be given by S –

    (a)   by means of a bond which is entered into in accordance with regulation 34; or

    (b)   in such other manner as the court may direct.

(3) For the purposes of paragraph (2)(a), S complies with the requirement to give the security only if –

    (a)   the endorsement required by regulation 34(2) has been provided; and

    (b)   the person who provided it has notified the Public Guardian of that fact.

(4) For the purposes of paragraph (2)(b), S complies with the requirement to give the security –

    (a)   in any case where the court directs that any other endorsement must be provided, only if –

        (i)   that endorsement has been provided; and

        (ii)   the person who provided it has notified the Public Guardian of that fact;

    (b)   in any case where the court directs that any other requirements must be met in relation to the giving of the security, only if the Public Guardian is satisfied that those other requirements have been met.

34 Security given under regulation 33(2)(a): requirement for endorsement

(1) This regulation has effect for the purposes of regulation 33(2)(a).

(2) A bond is entered into in accordance with this regulation only if it is endorsed by –

    (a)   an authorised insurance company; or

    (b)   an authorised deposit-taker.

(3) A person may enter into the bond under –

    (a)   arrangements made by the Public Guardian; or

    (b)   other arrangements which are made by the person entering into the bond or on his behalf.

(4) The Public Guardian may make arrangements with any person specified in paragraph (2) with a view to facilitating the provision by them of bonds which persons required to give security to the Public Guardian may enter into.

(5) In this regulation –

    'authorised insurance company' means –

        (a)   a person who has permission under Part 4 of the Financial Services and Markets Act 2000 to effect or carry out contracts of insurance;

(b)   an EEA firm of the kind mentioned in paragraph 5(d) of Schedule 3 to that Act, which has permission under paragraph 15 of that Schedule to effect or carry out contracts of insurance;

(c)   a person who carries on insurance market activity (within the meaning given in section 316(3) of that Act); and

'authorised deposit-taker' means –

(a)   a person who has permission under Part 4 of the Financial Services and Markets Act 2000 to accept deposits;

(b)   an EEA firm of the kind mentioned in paragraph 5(d) of Schedule 3 to that Act, which has permission under paragraph 15 of that Schedule to accept deposits.

(6)   The definitions of 'authorised insurance company' and 'authorised deposit-taker' must be read with –

(a)   section 22 of the Financial Services and Markets Act 2000;

(b)   any relevant order under that section; and

(c)   Schedule 2 to that Act.

35 Security given under regulation 33(2)(a): maintenance or replacement

(1)   This regulation applies to any security given under regulation 33(2)(a).

(2)   At such times or at such intervals as the Public Guardian may direct by notice in writing, any person ('S') who has given the security must satisfy the Public Guardian that any premiums payable in respect of it have been paid.

(3)   Where S proposes to replace a security already given by him, the new security is not to be regarded as having been given until the Public Guardian is satisfied that –

(a)   the requirements set out in sub-paragraphs (a) and (b) of regulation 33(3) have been met in relation to it; and

(b)   no payment is due from S in connection with the discharge of his functions.

36 Enforcement following court order of any endorsed security

(1)   This regulation applies to any security given to the Public Guardian in respect of which an endorsement has been provided.

(2)   Where the court orders the enforcement of the security, the Public Guardian must –

(a)   notify any person who endorsed the security of the contents of the order; and

(b)   notify the court when payment has been made of the amount secured.

37 Discharge of any endorsed security

(1)   This regulation applies to any security given by a person ('S') to the Public Guardian in respect of which an endorsement has been provided.

(2)   The security may be discharged if the court makes an order discharging it.

(3)   In any other case, the security may not be discharged until the end of the period of 7 years commencing with whichever of the following dates first occurs –

(a)   if the person on whose behalf S was appointed to act dies, the date of his death;

(b)   if S dies, the date of his death;

(c)   if the court makes an order which discharges S but which does not also discharge the security under paragraph (2), the date of the order;

(d)   the date when S otherwise ceases to be under a duty to discharge the functions in respect of which he was ordered to give security.

(4)   For the purposes of paragraph (3), if a person takes any step with a view to discharging the security before the end of the period specified in that paragraph, the security is to be treated for all purposes as if it were still in place.

Deputies

38 Application for additional time to submit a report

(1) This regulation applies where the court requires a deputy to submit a report to the Public Guardian and specifies a time or interval for it to be submitted.·

(2) A deputy may apply to the Public Guardian requesting more time for submitting a particular report.

(3) An application must –

(a) state the reason for requesting more time; and

(b) contain or be accompanied by such information as the Public Guardian may reasonably require to determine the application.

(4) In response to an application, the Public Guardian may, if he considers it appropriate to do so, undertake that he will not take steps to secure performance of the deputy's duty to submit the report at the relevant time on the condition that the report is submitted on or before such later date as he may specify.

39 Content of reports

(1) Any report which the court requires a deputy to submit to the Public Guardian must include such material as the court may direct.

(2) The report must also contain or be accompanied by –

(a) specified information or information of a specified description; or

(b) specified documents or documents of a specified description.

(3) But paragraph (2) –

(a) extends only to information or documents which are reasonably required in connection with the exercise by the Public Guardian of functions conferred on him under the Act; and

(b) is subject to paragraph (1) and to any other directions given by the court.

(4) Where powers as respects a person's property and affairs are conferred on a deputy under section 16 of the Act, the information specified by the Public Guardian under paragraph (2) may include accounts which –

(a) deal with specified matters; and

(b) are provided in a specified form.

(5) The Public Guardian may require –

(a) any information provided to be verified in such manner, or

(b) any document produced to be authenticated in such manner,

as he may reasonably require.

(6) 'Specified' means specified in a notice in writing given to the deputy by the Public Guardian.

40 Power to require final report on termination of appointment

(1) This regulation applies where –

(a) the person on whose behalf a deputy was appointed to act has died;

(b) the deputy has died;

(c) the court has made an order discharging the deputy; or

(d) the deputy otherwise ceases to be under a duty to discharge the functions to which his appointment relates.

(2) The Public Guardian may require the deputy (or, in the case of the deputy's death, his personal representatives) to submit a final report on the discharge of his functions.

(3) A final report must be submitted –

(a) before the end of such reasonable period as may be specified; and

(b) at such place as may be specified.

(4) The Public Guardian must consider the final report, together with any other information that he may have relating to the discharge by the deputy of his functions.

(5) Where the Public Guardian is dissatisfied with any aspect of the final report he may apply to the court for an appropriate remedy (including enforcement of security given by the deputy).

(6) 'Specified' means specified in a notice in writing given to the deputy or his personal representatives by the Public Guardian.

41 Power to require information from deputies

(1) This regulation applies in any case where –

(a) the Public Guardian has received representations (including complaints) about –

(i) the way in which a deputy is exercising his powers; or

(ii) any failure to exercise them; or

(b) it appears to the Public Guardian that there are other circumstances which –

(i) give rise to concerns about, or dissatisfaction with, the conduct of the deputy (including any failure to act); or

(ii) otherwise constitute good reason to seek information about the deputy's discharge of his functions.

(2) The Public Guardian may require the deputy –

(a) to provide specified information or information of a specified description; or

(b) to produce specified documents or documents of a specified description.

(3) The information or documents must be provided or produced –

(a) before the end of such reasonable period as may be specified; and

(b) at such place as may be specified.

(4) The Public Guardian may require –

(a) any information provided to be verified in such manner, or

(b) any document produced to be authenticated in such manner,

as he may reasonably require.

(5) 'Specified' means specified in a notice in writing given to the deputy by the Public Guardian.

42 Right of deputy to require review of decisions made by the Public Guardian

(1) A deputy may require the Public Guardian to reconsider any decision he has made in relation to the deputy.

(2) The right under paragraph (1) is exercisable by giving notice of exercise of the right to the Public Guardian before the end of the period of 14 days beginning with the date on which notice of the decision is given to the deputy.

(3) The notice of exercise of the right must –

(a) state the grounds on which reconsideration is required; and

(b) contain or be accompanied by any relevant information or documents.

(4) At any time after receiving the notice and before reconsidering the decision to which it relates, the Public Guardian may require the deputy to provide him with such further information, or to produce such documents, as he reasonably considers necessary to enable him to reconsider the matter.

(5) The Public Guardian must give to the deputy –

(a) written notice of his decision on reconsideration, and

(b) if he upholds the previous decision, a statement of his reasons.

Miscellaneous functions

43 Applications to the Court of Protection

The Public Guardian has the function of making applications to the court in connection with his functions under the Act in such circumstances as he considers it necessary or appropriate to do so.

44 Visits by the Public Guardian or by Court of Protection Visitors at his direction

(1) This regulation applies where the Public Guardian visits, or directs a Court of Protection Visitor to visit, any person under any provision of the Act or these Regulations.

(2) The Public Guardian must notify (or make arrangements to notify) the person to be visited of –

    (a) the date or dates on which it is proposed that the visit will take place;

    (b) to the extent that it is practicable to do so, any specific matters likely to be covered in the course of the visit; and

    (c) any proposal to inform any other person that the visit is to take place.

(3) Where the visit is to be carried out by a Court of Protection Visitor –

    (a) the Public Guardian may –

        (i)   give such directions to the Visitor, and

        (ii) provide him with such information concerning the person to be visited,

        as the Public Guardian considers necessary for the purposes of enabling the visit to take place and the Visitor to prepare any report the Public Guardian may require; and

    (b) the Visitor must seek to carry out the visit and take all reasonable steps to obtain such other information as he considers necessary for the purpose of preparing a report.

(4) A Court of Protection Visitor must submit any report requested by the Public Guardian in accordance with any timetable specified by the Public Guardian.

(5) If he considers it appropriate to do so, the Public Guardian may, in relation to any person interviewed in the course of preparing a report –

    (a) disclose the report to him; and

    (b) invite him to comment on it.

45 Functions in relation to persons carrying out specific transactions

(1) This regulation applies where, in accordance with an order made under section 16(2)(a) of the Act, a person ('T') has been authorised to carry out any transaction for a person who lacks capacity.

(2) The Public Guardian has the functions of –

    (a) receiving any reports from T which the court may require;

    (b) dealing with representations (including complaints) about –

        (i)   the way in which the transaction has been or is being carried out; or

        (ii) any failure to carry it out.

(3) Regulations 38 to 41 have effect in relation to T as they have effect in relation a deputy.

46 Power to require information from donees of lasting power of attorney

(1) This regulation applies where it appears to the Public Guardian that there are circumstances suggesting that the donee of a lasting power of attorney may –

    (a) have behaved, or may be behaving, in a way that contravenes his authority or is not in the best interests of the donor of the power,

    (b) be proposing to behave in a way that would contravene that authority or would not be in the donor's best interests, or

    (c) have failed to comply with the requirements of an order made, or directions given, by the court.

(2) The Public Guardian may require the donee –

    (a) to provide specified information or information of a specified description; or

    (b) to produce specified documents or documents of a specified description.

(3) The information or documents must be provided or produced –

    (a) before the end of such reasonable period as may be specified; and

    (b) at such place as may be specified.

(4) The Public Guardian may require –

    (a) any information provided to be verified in such manner, or

    (b) any document produced to be authenticated in such manner,

as he may reasonably require.

(5) 'Specified' means specified in a notice in writing given to the donee by the Public Guardian.

47 Power to require information from attorneys under enduring power of attorney

(1) This regulation applies where it appears to the Public Guardian that there are circumstances suggesting that, having regard to all the circumstances (and in particular the attorney's relationship to or connection with the donor) the attorney under a registered enduring power of attorney may be unsuitable to be the donor's attorney.

(2) The Public Guardian may require the attorney –

    (a) to provide specified information or information of a specified description; or

    (b) to produce specified documents or documents of a specified description.

(3) The information or documents must be provided or produced –

    (a) before the end of such reasonable period as may be specified; and

    (b) at such place as may be specified.

(4) The Public Guardian may require –

    (a) any information provided to be verified in such manner, or

    (b) any document produced to be authenticated in such manner,

as he may reasonably require.

(5) 'Specified' means specified in a notice in writing given to the attorney by the Public Guardian.

48 Other functions in relation to enduring powers of attorney

The Public Guardian has the following functions –

    (a) directing a Court of Protection Visitor –

        (i) to visit an attorney under a registered enduring power of attorney, or

        (ii) to visit the donor of a registered enduring power of attorney,

        and to make a report to the Public Guardian on such matters as he may direct;

(b)   dealing with representations (including complaints) about the way in which an attorney under a registered enduring power of attorney is exercising his powers.

Signed by authority of the Lord Chancellor.

Cathy Ashton,
Parliamentary Under-Secretary of State,
Department for Constitutional Affairs

16th April 2007

[Schedules 1–8 are not reproduced here. The forms and notices can be downloaded from **www.publicguardian.gov.uk**.]

Appendix D
MENTAL CAPACITY ACT 2005 CODE OF PRACTICE

[The Mental Capacity Act 2005 Code of Practice was issued by the Lord Chancellor on 23 April 2007 in accordance with ss.42 and 43 of the Mental Capacity Act 2005.

It is © Crown copyright 2007 and published online by The Stationery Office at **www.publicguardian.gov.uk**.

The Code of Practice is reproduced here with some minor omissions: the preliminary pages, introduction, key words and phrases, and Annex A (contacts). Due to the limitations of space in this book, the scenarios which illustrate the Code of Practice have also been removed. However, the titles of each scenario have been retained to indicate where a scenario exists.]

CONTENTS

1   WHAT IS THE MENTAL CAPACITY ACT 2005?

1.1   The Mental Capacity Act 2005 (the Act) provides the legal framework for acting and making decisions on behalf of individuals who lack the mental capacity to make particular decisions for themselves. Everyone working with and/or caring for an adult who may lack capacity to make specific decisions must comply with this Act when making decisions or acting for that person, when the person lacks the capacity to make a particular decision for themselves. The same rules apply whether the decisions are life-changing events or everyday matters.

1.2   The Act's starting point is to confirm in legislation that it should be assumed that an adult (aged 16 or over) has full legal capacity to make decisions for themselves (the right to autonomy) unless it can be shown that they lack capacity to make a decision for themselves at the time the decision needs to be made. This is known as the presumption of capacity. The Act also states that people must be given all appropriate help and support to enable them to make their own decisions or to maximise their participation in any decision-making process.

1.3   The underlying philosophy of the Act is to ensure that any decision made, or action taken, on behalf of someone who lacks the capacity to make the decision or act for themselves is made in their best interests.

1.4   The Act is intended to assist and support people who may lack capacity and to discourage anyone who is involved in caring for someone who lacks capacity from being overly restrictive or controlling. But the Act also aims to balance an individual's right to make decisions for themselves with their right to be protected from harm if they lack capacity to make decisions to protect themselves.

1.5   The Act sets out a legal framework of how to act and make decisions on behalf of people who lack capacity to make specific decisions for themselves. It sets out some core principles and methods for making decisions and carrying out actions in relation to personal welfare, healthcare and financial matters affecting people who may lack capacity to make specific decisions about these issues for themselves.

1.6   Many of the provisions in the Act are based upon existing common law principles (i.e. principles that have been established through decisions made by courts in individual cases). The Act clarifies and improves upon these principles and builds on current good practice which is based on the principles.

1.7   The Act introduces several new roles, bodies and powers, all of which will support the Act's provisions. These include:

- Attorneys appointed under Lasting Powers of Attorney (see chapter 7)
- The new Court of Protection, and court-appointed deputies (see chapter 8)
- Independent Mental Capacity Advocates (see chapter 10).

The roles, bodies and powers are all explained in more depth in the specific chapters of the Code highlighted above.

What decisions are covered by the Act, and what decisions are excluded?

1.8   The Act covers a wide range of decisions made, or actions taken, on behalf of people who may lack capacity to make specific decisions for themselves. These can be decisions about day-to-day matters – like what to wear, or what to buy when doing the weekly shopping – or decisions about major life-changing events, such as whether the person should move into a care home or undergo a major surgical operation.

1.9   There are certain decisions which can never be made on behalf of a person who lacks capacity to make those specific decisions. This is because they are either so personal to the individual concerned, or governed by other legislation.

1.10   Sections 27–29 and 62 of the Act set out the specific decisions which can never be made or actions which can never be carried out under the Act, whether by family members, carers, professionals, attorneys or the Court of Protection. These are summarised below.

Decisions concerning family relationships (section 27)

Nothing in the Act permits a decision to be made on someone else's behalf on any of the following matters:

- consenting to marriage or a civil partnership
- consenting to have sexual relations
- consenting to a decree of divorce on the basis of two years' separation
- consenting to the dissolution of a civil partnership
- consenting to a child being placed for adoption or the making of an adoption order
- discharging parental responsibility for a child in matters not relating to the child's property, or
- giving consent under the Human Fertilisation and Embryology Act 1990.

Mental Health Act matters (section 28)

Where a person who lacks capacity to consent is currently detained and being treated under Part 4 of the Mental Health Act 1983, nothing in the Act authorises anyone to:

- give the person treatment for mental disorder, or
- consent to the person being given treatment for mental disorder.

Further guidance is given in chapter 13 of the Code.

Voting rights (section 29)

Nothing in the Act permits a decision on voting, at an election for any public office or at a referendum, to be made on behalf of a person who lacks capacity to vote.

Unlawful killing or assisting suicide (section 62)

For the avoidance of doubt, nothing in the Act is to be taken to affect the law relating to murder, manslaughter or assisting suicide.

1.11   Although the Act does not allow anyone to make a decision about these matters on behalf of someone who lacks capacity to make such a decision for themselves (for example, consenting to have sexual relations), this does not prevent action being taken to protect a vulnerable person from abuse or exploitation.

How does the Act relate to other legislation?

1.12   The Mental Capacity Act 2005 will apply in conjunction with other legislation affecting people who may lack capacity in relation to specific matters. This means that healthcare and social care staff acting under the Act should also be aware of their obligations under other legislation, including (but not limited to) the:

- Care Standards Act 2000
- Data Protection Act 1998
- Disability Discrimination Act 1995
- Human Rights Act 1998
- Mental Health Act 1983

- National Health Service and Community Care Act 1990
- Human Tissue Act 2004.

What does the Act say about the Code of Practice?

1.13   Section 42 of the Act sets out the purpose of the Code of Practice, which is to provide guidance for specific people in specific circumstances. Section 43 explains the procedures that had to be followed in preparing the Code and consulting on its contents, and for its consideration by Parliament.

Section 42, subsections (4) and (5), set out the categories of people who are placed under a legal duty to 'have regard to' the Code and gives further information about the status of the Code. More details can be found in the Introduction, which explains the legal status of the Code.

2   WHAT ARE THE STATUTORY PRINCIPLES AND HOW SHOULD THEY BE APPLIED?

Section 1 of the Act sets out the five 'statutory principles' – the values that underpin the legal requirements in the Act. The Act is intended to be enabling and supportive of people who lack capacity, not restricting or controlling of their lives. It aims to protect people who lack capacity to make particular decisions, but also to maximise their ability to make decisions, or to participate in decision-making, as far as they are able to do so.

The five statutory principles are:

1. A person must be assumed to have capacity unless it is established that they lack capacity.
2. A person is not to be treated as unable to make a decision unless all practicable steps to help him to do so have been taken without success.
3. A person is not to be treated as unable to make a decision merely because he makes an unwise decision.
4. An act done, or decision made, under this Act for or on behalf of a person who lacks capacity must be done, or made, in his best interests.
5. Before the act is done, or the decision is made, regard must be had to whether the purpose for which it is needed can be as effectively achieved in a way that is less restrictive of the person's rights and freedom of action.

This chapter provides guidance on how people should interpret and apply the statutory principles when using the Act. Following the principles and applying them to the Act's framework for decision-making will help to ensure not only that appropriate action is taken in individual cases, but also to point the way to solutions in difficult or uncertain situations.

In this chapter, as throughout the Code, a person's capacity (or lack of capacity) refers specifically to their capacity to make a particular decision at the time it needs to be made.

Quick summary

- Every adult has the right to make their own decisions if they have the capacity to do so. Family carers and healthcare or social care staff must assume that a person has the capacity to make decisions, unless it can be established that the person does not have capacity.

■ People should receive support to help them make their own decisions. Before concluding that individuals lack capacity to make a particular decision, it is important to take all possible steps to try to help them reach a decision themselves.

■ People have the right to make decisions that others might think are unwise. A person who makes a decision that others think is unwise should not automatically be labelled as lacking the capacity to make a decision.

■ Any act done for, or any decision made on behalf of, someone who lacks capacity must be in their best interests.

■ Any act done for, or any decision made on behalf of, someone who lacks capacity should be an option that is less restrictive of their basic rights and freedoms – as long as it is still in their best interests.

What is the role of the statutory principles?

2.1   The statutory principles aim to:

■ protect people who lack capacity and
■ help them take part, as much as possible, in decisions that affect them.

They aim to assist and support people who may lack capacity to make particular decisions, not to restrict or control their lives.

2.2   The statutory principles apply to any act done or decision made under the Act. When followed and applied to the Act's decision-making framework, they will help people take appropriate action in individual cases. They will also help people find solutions in difficult or uncertain situations.

How should the statutory principles be applied?

Principle 1: '*A person must be assumed to have capacity unless it is established that he lacks capacity.*' (*section1(2)*)

2.3   This principle states that every adult has the right to make their own decisions – unless there is proof that they lack the capacity to make a particular decision when it needs to be made. This has been a fundamental principle of the common law for many years and it is now set out in the Act.

2.4   It is important to balance people's right to make a decision with their right to safety and protection when they can't make decisions to protect themselves. But the starting assumption must always be that an individual has the capacity, until there is proof that they do not. Chapter 4 explains the Act's definition of 'lack of capacity' and the processes involved in assessing capacity.

[*Scenario: Assessing a person's capacity to make decisions*]

2.5   Some people may need help to be able to make a decision or to communicate their decision. However, this does not necessarily mean that they cannot make that decision – unless there is proof that they do lack capacity to do so. Anyone who believes that a person lacks capacity should be able to prove their case. Chapter 4 explains the standard of proof required.

Principle 2: '*A person is not to be treated as unable to make a decision unless all practicable steps to help him to do so have been taken without success.*' (*section1(3)*)

2.6   It is important to do everything practical (the Act uses the term 'practicable') to help a person make a decision for themselves before concluding that they lack capacity to do so. People with an illness or disability affecting their ability to make a decision should receive support to help them make as many decisions as they can. This principle aims to stop people being automatically labelled as lacking capacity to make particular decisions. Because it encourages individuals to play as big a role as possible in decision-making, it also helps prevent unnecessary interventions in their lives.

2.7   The kind of support people might need to help them make a decision varies. It depends on personal circumstances, the kind of decision that has to be made and the time available to make the decision. It might include:

- using a different form of communication (for example, non-verbal communication)
- providing information in a more accessible form (for example, photographs, drawings, or tapes)
- treating a medical condition which may be affecting the person's capacity or
- having a structured programme to improve a person's capacity to make particular decisions (for example, helping a person with learning disabilities to learn new skills).

Chapter 3 gives more information on ways to help people make decisions for themselves.

[Scenario: Taking steps to help people make decisions for themselves]

2.8   Anyone supporting a person who may lack capacity should not use excessive persuasion or 'undue pressure'.[1] This might include behaving in a manner which is overbearing or dominating, or seeking to influence the person's decision, and could push a person into making a decision they might not otherwise have made. However, it is important to provide appropriate advice and information.

[Scenario: Giving appropriate advice and support]

2.9   In some situations treatment cannot be delayed while a person gets support to make a decision. This can happen in emergency situations or when an urgent decision is required (for example, immediate medical treatment). In these situations, the only practical and appropriate steps might be to keep a person informed of what is happening and why.

Principle 3: *'A person is not to be treated as unable to make a decision merely because he makes an unwise decision.' (section 1(4))*

2.10   Everybody has their own values, beliefs, preferences and attitudes. A person should not be assumed to lack the capacity to make a decision just because other people think their decision is unwise. This applies even if family members, friends or healthcare or social care staff are unhappy with a decision.

[Scenario: Allowing people to make decisions that others think are unwise]

2.11   There may be cause for concern if somebody:

- repeatedly makes unwise decisions that put them at significant risk of harm or exploitation or
- makes a particular unwise decision that is obviously irrational or out of character.

These things do not necessarily mean that somebody lacks capacity. But there might be need for further investigation, taking into account the person's past decisions and choices. For example, have they developed a medical condition or dis-

---

[1] Undue influence in relation to consent to medical treatment was considered in *Re T (Adult: Refusal of Treatment)* [1992] 4 All E R 649, 662 and in financial matters in *Royal Bank of Scotland* v. *Etridge* [2001] UKHL 44.

order that is affecting their capacity to make particular decisions? Are they easily influenced by undue pressure? Or do they need more information to help them understand the consequences of the decision they are making?

[*Scenario: Decisions that cause concern*]

Principle 4: '*An act done, or decision made, under this Act for or on behalf of a person who lacks capacity must be done, or made, in his best interests.' (section 1(5))*

2.12   The principle of acting or making a decision in the best interests of a person who lacks capacity to make the decision in question is a well-established principle in the common law.[2] This principle is now set out in the Act, so that a person's best interests must be the basis for all decisions made and actions carried out on their behalf in situations where they lack capacity to make those particular decisions for themselves. The only exceptions to this are around research (see chapter 11) and advance decisions to refuse treatment (see chapter 9) where other safeguards apply.

2.13   It is impossible to give a single description of what 'best interests' are, because they depend on individual circumstances. However, section 4 of the Act sets out a checklist of steps to follow in order to determine what is in the best interests of a person who lacks capacity to make the decision in question each time someone acts or makes a decision on that person's behalf. See chapter 5 for detailed guidance and examples.

Principle 5: '*Before the act is done, or the decision is made, regard must be had to whether the purpose for which it is needed can be as effectively achieved in a way that is less restrictive of the person's rights and freedom of action.' (section 1(6))*

2.14   Before somebody makes a decision or acts on behalf of a person who lacks capacity to make that decision or consent to the act, they must always question if they can do something else that would interfere less with the person's basic rights and freedoms. This is called finding the 'less restrictive alternative'. It includes considering whether there is a need to act or make a decision at all.

2.15   Where there is more than one option, it is important to explore ways that would be less restrictive or allow the most freedom for a person who lacks capacity to make the decision in question. However, the final decision must always allow the original purpose of the decision or act to be achieved.

2.16   Any decision or action must still be in the best interests of the person who lacks capacity. So sometimes it may be necessary to choose an option that is not the least restrictive alternative if that option is in the person's best interests. In practice, the process of choosing a less restrictive option and deciding what is in the person's best interests will be combined. But both principles must be applied each time a decision or action may be taken on behalf of a person who lacks capacity to make the relevant decision.

[*Scenario: Finding a less restrictive option*]

3   HOW SHOULD PEOPLE BE HELPED TO MAKE THEIR OWN DECISIONS?

Before deciding that someone lacks capacity to make a particular decision, it is important to take all practical and appropriate steps to enable them to make that decision themselves

---

[2]   See for example *Re MB (Medical Treatment)* [1997] 2 FLR 426, CA; *Re A (Male Sterilisation)* [2000] 1 FLR 549; *Re S (Sterilisation: Patient's Best Interests)* [2000] 2 FLR 389; *Re F (Adult Patient: Sterilisation)* [2001] Fam 15.

(statutory principle 2, see chapter 2). In addition, as section 3(2) of the Act underlines, these steps (such as helping individuals to communicate) must be taken in a way which reflects the person's individual circumstances and meets their particular needs. This chapter provides practical guidance on how to support people to make decisions for themselves, or play as big a role as possible in decision-making.

> In this chapter, as throughout the Code, a person's capacity (or lack of capacity) refers specifically to their capacity to make a particular decision at the time it needs to be made.

Quick summary

To help someone make a decision for themselves, check the following points:

Providing relevant information

- Does the person have all the relevant information they need to make a particular decision?
- If they have a choice, have they been given information on all the alternatives?

Communicating in an appropriate way

- Could information be explained or presented in a way that is easier for the person to understand (for example, by using simple language or visual aids)?
- Have different methods of communication been explored if required, including non-verbal communication?
- Could anyone else help with communication (for example, a family member, support worker, interpreter, speech and language therapist or advocate)?

Making the person feel at ease

- Are there particular times of day when the person's understanding is better?
- Are there particular locations where they may feel more at ease?
- Could the decision be put off to see whether the person can make the decision at a later time when circumstances are right for them?

Supporting the person

- Can anyone else help or support the person to make choices or express a view?

How can someone be helped to make a decision?

3.1   There are several ways in which people can be helped and supported to enable them to make a decision for themselves. These will vary depending on the decision to be made, the time-scale for making the decision and the individual circumstances of the person making it.

3.2   The Act applies to a wide range of people with different conditions that may affect their capacity to make particular decisions. So, the appropriate steps to take will depend on:

- a person's individual circumstances (for example, somebody with learning difficulties may need a different approach to somebody with dementia)
- the decision the person has to make and
- the length of time they have to make it.

3.3   Significant, one-off decisions (such as moving house) will require different consid-
        erations from day-to-day decisions about a person's care and welfare. However, the
        same general processes should apply to each decision.

3.4   In most cases, only some of the steps described in this chapter will be relevant or
        appropriate, and the list included here is not exhaustive. It is up to the people
        (whether family carers, paid carers, healthcare staff or anyone else) caring for or
        supporting an individual to consider what is possible and appropriate in individual
        cases. In all cases it is extremely important to find the most effective way of com-
        municating with the person concerned. Good communication is essential for
        explaining relevant information in an appropriate way and for ensuring that the
        steps being taken meet an individual's needs.

3.5   Providing appropriate help with decision-making should form part of care plan-
        ning processes for people receiving health or social care services. Examples
        include:

        ■ Person Centred Planning for people with learning disabilities
        ■ the Care Programme Approach for people with mental disorders
        ■ the Single Assessment Process for older people in England, and
        ■ the Unified Assessment Process in Wales.

What happens in emergency situations?

3.6   Clearly, in emergency medical situations (for example, where a person collapses
        with a heart attack or for some unknown reason and is brought unconscious into
        a hospital), urgent decisions will have to be made and immediate action taken in
        the person's best interests. In these situations, it may not be practical or appropri-
        ate to delay the treatment while trying to help the person make their own decisions,
        or to consult with any known attorneys or deputies. However, even in emergency
        situations, healthcare staff should try to communicate with the person and keep
        them informed of what is happening.

What information should be provided to people and how should it be provided?

3.7   Providing relevant information is essential in all decision-making. For example, to
        make a choice about what they want for breakfast, people need to know what food
        is available. If the decision concerns medical treatment, the doctor must explain the
        purpose and effect of the course of treatment and the likely consequences of
        accepting or refusing treatment.

3.8   All practical and appropriate steps must be taken to help people to make a decision
        for themselves. Information must be tailored to an individual's needs and abilities
        It must also be in the easiest and most appropriate form of communication for the
        person concerned.

What information is relevant?

3.9   The Act cannot state exactly what information will be relevant in each case.
        Anyone helping someone to make a decision for themselves should therefore fol-
        low these steps.

        ■ Take time to explain anything that might help the person make a decision. It is
          important that they have access to all the information they need to make an
          informed decision.

- Try not to give more detail than the person needs – this might confuse them. In some cases, a simple, broad explanation will be enough. But it must not miss out important information.
- What are the risks and benefits? Describe any foreseeable consequences of making the decision, and of not making any decision at all.
- Explain the effects the decision might have on the person and those close to them – including the people involved in their care.
- If they have a choice, give them the same information in a balanced way for all the options.
- For some types of decisions, it may be important to give access to advice from elsewhere. This may be independent or specialist advice (for example, from a medical practitioner or a financial or legal adviser). But it might simply be advice from trusted friends or relatives.

Communication – general guidance

3.10   To help someone make a decision for themselves, all possible and appropriate means of communication should be tried.

- Ask people who know the person well about the best form of communication (try speaking to family members, carers, day centre staff or support workers). They may also know somebody the person can communicate with easily, or the time when it is best to communicate with them.
- Use simple language. Where appropriate, use pictures, objects or illustrations to demonstrate ideas.
- Speak at the right volume and speed, with appropriate words and sentence structure. It may be helpful to pause to check understanding or show that a choice is available.
- Break down difficult information into smaller points that are easy to understand. Allow the person time to consider and understand each point before continuing.
- It may be necessary to repeat information or go back over a point several times.
- Is help available from people the person trusts (relatives, friends, GP, social worker, religious or community leaders)? If so, make sure the person's right to confidentiality is respected.
- Be aware of cultural, ethnic or religious factors that shape a person's way of thinking, behaviour or communication. For example, in some cultures it is important to involve the community in decision-making. Some religious beliefs (for example, those of Jehovah's Witnesses or Christian Scientists) may influence the person's approach to medical treatment and information about treatment decisions.
- If necessary, consider using a professional language interpreter. Even if a person communicated in English or Welsh in the past, they may have lost some verbal skills (for example, because of dementia). They may now prefer to communicate in their first language. It is often more appropriate to use a professional interpreter rather than to use family members.
- If using pictures to help communication, make sure they are relevant and the person can understand them easily. For example, a red bus may represent a form of transport to one person but a day trip to another.
- Would an advocate (someone who can support and represent the person) improve communication in the current situation? (See chapters 10 and 15 for more information about advocates.)

[*Scenario: Providing relevant information*]

Helping people with specific communication or cognitive problems

3.11   Where people have specific communication or cognitive problems, the following steps can help:

- Find out how the person is used to communicating. Do they use picture boards or Makaton (signs and symbols for people with communication or learning difficulties)? Or do they have a way of communicating that is only known to those close to them?
- If the person has hearing difficulties, use their preferred method of communication (for example, visual aids, written messages or sign language). Where possible, use a qualified interpreter.
- Are mechanical devices such as voice synthesisers, keyboards or other computer equipment available to help?
- If the person does not use verbal communication skills, allow more time to learn how to communicate effectively.
- For people who use non-verbal methods of communication, their behaviour (in particular, changes in behaviour) can provide indications of their feelings.
- Some people may prefer to use non-verbal means of communication and can communicate most effectively in written form using computers or other communication technologies. This is particularly true for those with autistic spectrum disorders.
- For people with specific communication difficulties, consider other types of professional help (for example, a speech and language therapist or an expert in clinical neuropsychology).

[*Scenario: Helping people with specific communication difficulties*]

What steps should be taken to put a person at ease?

3.12   To help put someone at ease and so improve their ability to make a decision, careful consideration should be given to both location and timing.

Location

3.13   In terms of location, consider the following:

- Where possible, choose a location where the person feels most at ease. For example, people are usually more comfortable in their own home than at a doctor's surgery.
- Would the person find it easier to make their decision in a relevant location? For example, could you help them decide about medical treatment by taking them to hospital to see what is involved?
- Choose a quiet location where the discussion can't be easily interrupted.
- Try to eliminate any background noise or distractions (for example, the television or radio, or people talking).
- Choose a location where the person's privacy and dignity can be properly respected.

Timing

3.14   In terms of timing, consider the following:

- Try to choose the time of day when the person is most alert – some people are better in the mornings, others are more lively in the afternoon or early evening. It may be necessary to try several times before a decision can be made.

- If the person's capacity is likely to improve in the foreseeable future, wait until it has done so – if practical and appropriate. For example, this might be the case after treatment for depression or a psychotic episode. Obviously, this may not be practical and appropriate if the decision is urgent.
- Some medication could affect a person's capacity (for example, medication which causes drowsiness or affects memory). Can the decision be delayed until side effects have subsided?
- Take one decision at a time – be careful to avoid making the person tired or confused.
- Don't rush – allow the person time to think things over or ask for clarification, where that is possible and appropriate.
- Avoid or challenge time limits that are unnecessary if the decision is not urgent. Delaying the decision may enable further steps to be taken to assist people to make the decision for themselves.

[*Scenario: Getting the location and timing right*]

Support from other people

3.15   In some circumstances, individuals will be more comfortable making decisions when someone else is there to support them.

- Might the person benefit from having another person present? Sometimes having a relative or friend nearby can provide helpful support and reduce anxiety. However, some people might find this intrusive, and it could increase their anxiety or affect their ability to make a free choice. Find ways of getting the person's views on this, for example, by watching their behaviour towards other people.
- Always respect a person's right to confidentiality.

[*Scenario: Getting help from other people*]

What other ways are there to enable decision-making?

3.16   There are other ways to help someone make a decision for themselves.

- Many people find it helpful to talk things over with people they trust – or people who have been in a similar situation or faced similar dilemmas. For example, people with learning difficulties may benefit from the help of a designated support worker or being part of a support network.
- If someone is very distressed (for example, following a death of someone close) or where there are long-standing problems that affect someone's ability to understand an issue, it may be possible to delay a decision so that the person can have psychological therapy, if needed.
- Some organisations have produced materials to help people who need support to make decisions and for those who support them. Some of this material is designed to help people with specific conditions, such as Alzheimer's disease or profound learning disability.
- It may be important to provide access to technology. For example, some people who appear not to communicate well verbally can do so very well using computers.

[*Scenario: Making the most of technology*]

4   HOW DOES THE ACT DEFINE A PERSON'S CAPACITY TO MAKE A DECISION AND HOW SHOULD CAPACITY BE ASSESSED?

This chapter explains what the Act means by 'capacity' and 'lack of capacity'. It provides guidance on how to assess whether someone has the capacity to make a decision, and suggests when professionals should be involved in the assessment.

> In this chapter, as throughout the Code, a person's capacity (or lack of capacity) refers specifically to their capacity to make a particular decision at the time it needs to be made.

Quick summary

This checklist is a summary of points to consider when assessing a person's capacity to make a specific decision. Readers should also refer to the more detailed guidance in this chapter and chapters 2 and 3.

Presuming someone has capacity

■ The starting assumption must always be that a person has the capacity to make a decision, unless it can be established that they lack capacity.

Understanding what is meant by capacity and lack of capacity

■ A person's capacity must be assessed specifically in terms of their capacity to make a particular decision at the time it needs to be made.

Treating everyone equally

■ A person's capacity must not be judged simply on the basis of their age, appearance, condition or an aspect of their behaviour.

Supporting the person to make the decision for themselves

■ It is important to take all possible steps to try to help people make a decision for themselves (see chapter 2, principle 2, and chapter 3).

Assessing capacity

Anyone assessing someone's capacity to make a decision for themselves should use the two-stage test of capacity.

■ Does the person have an impairment of the mind or brain, or is there some sort of disturbance affecting the way their mind or brain works? (It doesn't matter whether the impairment or disturbance is temporary or permanent.)

■ If so, does that impairment or disturbance mean that the person is unable to make the decision in question at the time it needs to be made?

Assessing ability to make a decision

■ Does the person have a general understanding of what decision they need to make and why they need to make it?

■ Does the person have a general understanding of the likely consequences of making, or not making, this decision?

- Is the person able to understand, retain, use and weigh up the information relevant to this decision?
- Can the person communicate their decision (by talking, using sign language or any other means)? Would the services of a professional (such as a speech and language therapist) be helpful?

Assessing capacity to make more complex or serious decisions

- Is there a need for a more thorough assessment (perhaps by involving a doctor or other professional expert)?

What is mental capacity?

4.1   Mental capacity is the ability to make a decision.

  - This includes the ability to make a decision that affects daily life – such as when to get up, what to wear or whether to go to the doctor when feeling ill – as well as more serious or significant decisions.
  - It also refers to a person's ability to make a decision that may have legal consequences – for them or others. Examples include agreeing to have medical treatment, buying goods or making a will.

4.2   The starting point must always be to assume that a person has the capacity to make a specific decision (see chapter 2, principle 1). Some people may need help to be able to make or communicate a decision (see chapter 3). But this does not necessarily mean that they lack capacity to do so. What matters is their ability to carry out the processes involved in making the decision – and not the outcome.

What does the Act mean by 'lack of capacity'?

4.3   Section 2(1) of the Act states:

'For the purposes of this Act, a person lacks capacity in relation to a matter if at the material time he is unable to make a decision for himself in relation to the matter because of an impairment of, or a disturbance in the functioning of, the mind or brain.'

This means that a person lacks capacity if:

  - they have an impairment or disturbance (for example, a disability, condition or trauma) that affects the way their mind or brain works, and
  - the impairment or disturbance means that they are unable to make a specific decision at the time it needs to be made.

4.4   An assessment of a person's capacity must be based on their ability to make a specific decision at the time it needs to be made, and not their ability to make decisions in general. Section 3 of the Act defines what it means to be unable to make a decision (this is explained in paragraph 4.14 below).

4.5   Section 2(2) states that the impairment or disturbance does not have to be permanent. A person can lack capacity to make a decision at the time it needs to be made even if:

  - the loss of capacity is partial
  - the loss of capacity is temporary
  - their capacity changes over time.

A person may also lack capacity to make a decision about one issue but not about others.

4.6   The Act generally applies to people who are aged 16 or older. Chapter 12 explains how the Act affects children and young people – in particular those aged 16 and 17 years.

What safeguards does the Act provide around assessing someone's capacity?

4.7   An assessment that a person lacks capacity to make a decision must never be based simply on:

- their age
- their appearance
- assumptions about their condition, or
- any aspect of their behaviour. (section 2(3))

4.8   The Act deliberately uses the word 'appearance', because it covers all aspects of the way people look. So for example, it includes the physical characteristics of certain conditions (for example, scars, features linked to Down's syndrome or muscle spasms caused by cerebral palsy) as well as aspects of appearance like skin colour, tattoos and body piercings, or the way people dress (including religious dress).

4.9   The word 'condition' is also wide-ranging. It includes physical disabilities, learning difficulties and disabilities, illness related to age, and temporary conditions (for example, drunkenness or unconsciousness). Aspects of behaviour might include extrovert (for example, shouting or gesticulating) and withdrawn behaviour (for example, talking to yourself or avoiding eye contact).

[*Scenario: Treating everybody equally*]

What proof of lack of capacity does the Act require?

4.10   Anybody who claims that an individual lacks capacity should be able to provide proof. They need to be able to show, on the balance of probabilities, that the individual lacks capacity to make a particular decision, at the time it needs to be made (section 2(4)). This means being able to show that it is more likely than not that the person lacks capacity to make the decision in question.

What is the test of capacity?

To help determine if a person lacks capacity to make particular decisions, the Act sets out a two-stage test of capacity.

Stage 1: Does the person have an impairment of, or a disturbance in the functioning of, their mind or brain?

4.11   Stage 1 requires proof that the person has an impairment of the mind or brain, or some sort of or disturbance that affects the way their mind or brain works. If a person does not have such an impairment or disturbance of the mind or brain, they will not lack capacity under the Act.

4.12   Examples of an impairment or disturbance in the functioning of the mind or brain may include the following:

- conditions associated with some forms of mental illness
- dementia
- significant learning disabilities
- the long-term effects of brain damage

- physical or medical conditions that cause confusion, drowsiness or loss of consciousness
- delirium
- concussion following a head injury, and
- the symptoms of alcohol or drug use.

[*Scenario: Assessing whether an impairment or disturbance is affecting someone's ability to make a decision*]

Stage 2: Does the impairment or disturbance mean that the person is unable to make a specific decision when they need to?

4.13   For a person to lack capacity to make a decision, the Act says their impairment or disturbance must affect their ability to make the specific decision when they need to. But first people must be given all practical and appropriate support to help them make the decision for themselves (see chapter 2, principle 2). Stage 2 can only apply if all practical and appropriate support to help the person make the decision has failed. See chapter 3 for guidance on ways of helping people to make their own decisions.

What does the Act mean by 'inability to make a decision'?

4.14   A person is unable to make a decision if they cannot:

1. understand information about the decision to be made (the Act calls this 'relevant information')
2. retain that information in their mind
3. use or weigh that information as part of the decision-making process, or
4. communicate their decision (by talking, using sign language or any other means). See section 3(1).

4.15   These four points are explained in more detail below. The first three should be applied together. If a person cannot do any of these three things, they will be treated as unable to make the decision. The fourth only applies in situations where people cannot communicate their decision in any way.

Understanding information about the decision to be made

4.16   It is important not to assess someone's understanding before they have been given relevant information about a decision. Every effort must be made to provide information in a way that is most appropriate to help the person to understand. Quick or inadequate explanations are not acceptable unless the situation is urgent (see chapter 3 for some practical steps). Relevant information includes:

- the nature of the decision
- the reason why the decision is needed, and
- the likely effects of deciding one way or another, or making no decision at all.

4.17   Section 3(2) outlines the need to present information in a way that is appropriate to meet the individual's needs and circumstances. It also stresses the importance of explaining information using the most effective form of communication for that person (such as simple language, sign language, visual representations, computer support or any other means).

4.18   For example:

- a person with a learning disability may need somebody to read information to them. They might also need illustrations to help them to understand what is happening. Or they might stop the reader to ask what things mean. It might also be helpful for them to discuss information with an advocate.

- a person with anxiety or depression may find it difficult to reach a decision about treatment in a group meeting with professionals. They may prefer to read the relevant documents in private. This way they can come to a conclusion alone, and ask for help if necessary.
- someone who has a brain injury might need to be given information several times. It will be necessary to check that the person understands the information. If they have difficulty understanding, it might be useful to present information in a different way (for example, different forms of words, pictures or diagrams). Written information, audiotapes, videos and posters can help people remember important facts.

[Scenario: Providing relevant information in an appropriate format]

4.19   Relevant information must include what the likely consequences of a decision would be (the possible effects of deciding one way or another) – and also the likely consequences of making no decision at all (section 3(4)). In some cases, it may be enough to give a broad explanation using simple language. But a person might need more detailed information or access to advice, depending on the decision that needs to be made. If a decision could have serious or grave consequences, it is even more important that a person understands the information relevant to that decision.

Retaining information

4.20   The person must be able to hold the information in their mind long enough to use it to make an effective decision. But section 3(3) states that people who can only retain information for a short while must not automatically be assumed to lack the capacity to decide – it depends on what is necessary for the decision in question. Items such as notebooks, photographs, posters, videos and voice recorders can help people record and retain information.

[Scenario: Assessing a person's ability to retain information]

Using or weighing information as part of the decision-making process

4.21   For someone to have capacity, they must have the ability to weigh up information and use it to arrive at a decision. Sometimes people can understand information but an impairment or disturbance stops them using it. In other cases, the impairment or disturbance leads to a person making a specific decision without understanding or using the information they have been given.[3]

4.22   For example, a person with the eating disorder anorexia nervosa may understand information about the consequences of not eating. But their compulsion not to eat might be too strong for them to ignore. Some people who have serious brain damage might make impulsive decisions regardless of information they have been given or their understanding of it.

Inability to communicate a decision in any way

4.23   Sometimes there is no way for a person to communicate. This will apply to very few people, but it does include:

- people who are unconscious or in a coma, or
- those with the very rare condition sometimes known as 'locked-in syndrome', who are conscious but cannot speak or move at all.

[3] This issue has been considered in a number of court cases, including *Re MB* [1997] 2 FLR 426; *R v Collins and Ashworth Hospital Authority ex parte Brady* [2001] 58 BMLR 173

If a person cannot communicate their decision in any way at all, the Act says they should be treated as if they are unable to make that decision.

4.24   Before deciding that someone falls into this category, it is important to make all practical and appropriate efforts to help them communicate. This might call for the involvement of speech and language therapists, specialists in non-verbal communication or other professionals. Chapter 3 gives advice for communicating with people who have specific disabilities or cognitive problems.

4.25   Communication by simple muscle movements can show that somebody can communicate and may have capacity to make a decision.[4] For example, a person might blink an eye or squeeze a hand to say 'yes' or 'no'. In these cases, assessment must use the first three points listed in paragraph 4.14, which are explained in more depth in paragraphs 4.16–4.22.

What other issues might affect capacity?

People with fluctuating or temporary capacity

4.26   Some people have fluctuating capacity – they have a problem or condition that gets worse occasionally and affects their ability to make decisions. For example, someone who has manic depression may have a temporary manic phase which causes them to lack capacity to make financial decisions, leading them to get into debt even though at other times they are perfectly able to manage their money. A person with a psychotic illness may have delusions that affect their capacity to make decisions at certain times but disappear at others. Temporary factors may also affect someone's ability to make decisions. Examples include acute illness, severe pain, the effect of medication, or distress after a death or shock. More guidance on how to support someone with fluctuating or temporary capacity to make a decision can be found in chapter 3, particularly paragraphs 3.12–3.16. More information about factors that may indicate that a person may regain or develop capacity in the future can be found at paragraph 5.28.

4.27   As in any other situation, an assessment must only examine a person's capacity to make a particular decision when it needs to be made. It may be possible to put off the decision until the person has the capacity to make it (see also guidance on best interests in chapter 5).

Ongoing conditions that may affect capacity

4.28   Generally, capacity assessments should be related to a specific decision. But there may be people with an ongoing condition that affects their ability to make certain decisions or that may affect other decisions in their life. One decision on its own may make sense, but may give cause for concern when considered alongside others.

4.29   Again, it is important to review capacity from time to time, as people can improve their decision-making capabilities. In particular, someone with an ongoing condition may become able to make some, if not all, decisions. Some people (for example, people with learning disabilities) will learn new skills throughout their life, improving their capacity to make certain decisions. So assessments should be reviewed from time to time. Capacity should always be reviewed:

- whenever a care plan is being developed or reviewed
- at other relevant stages of the care planning process, and
- as particular decisions need to be made.

4.30   It is important to acknowledge the difference between:

- unwise decisions, which a person has the right to make (chapter 2, principle 3), and

---

[4] This was demonstrated in the case *Re AK (Adult Patient) (Medical Treatment: Consent)* [2001] 1 FLR 129

■ decisions based on a lack of understanding of risks or inability to weigh up the information about a decision.

Information about decisions the person has made based on a lack of understanding of risks or inability to weigh up the information can form part of a capacity assessment – particularly if someone repeatedly makes decisions that put them at risk or result in harm to them or someone else.

[*Scenario: Ongoing conditions*]

What other legal tests of capacity are there?

4.31   The Act makes clear that the definition of 'lack of capacity' and the two-stage test for capacity set out in the Act are 'for the purposes of this Act'. This means that the definition and test are to be used in situations covered by this Act. Schedule 6 of the Act also amends existing laws to ensure that the definition and test are used in other areas of law not covered directly by this Act.

For example, Schedule 6, paragraph 20 allows a person to be disqualified from jury service if they lack the capacity (using this Act's definition) to carry out a juror's tasks.

4.32   There are several tests of capacity that have been produced following judgments in court cases (known as common law tests).[5] These cover:

■ capacity to make a will[6]
■ capacity to make a gift[7]
■ capacity to enter into a contract[8]
■ capacity to litigate (take part in legal cases),[9] and
■ capacity to enter into marriage.[10]

4.33   The Act's new definition of capacity is in line with the existing common law tests, and the Act does not replace them. When cases come before the court on the above issues, judges can adopt the new definition if they think it is appropriate. The Act will apply to all other cases relating to financial, healthcare or welfare decisions.

When should capacity be assessed?

4.34   Assessing capacity correctly is vitally important to everyone affected by the Act. Someone who is assessed as lacking capacity may be denied their right to make a specific decision – particularly if others think that the decision would not be in their best interests or could cause harm. Also, if a person lacks capacity to make specific decisions, that person might make decisions they do not really understand. Again, this could cause harm or put the person at risk. So it is important to carry out an assessment when a person's capacity is in doubt. It is also important that the person who does an assessment can justify their conclusions. Many organisations will provide specific professional guidance for members of their profession.[11]

[5] For details, see British Medical Association & Law Society, *Assessment of Mental Capacity: Guidance for Doctors and Lawyers* (Second edition) (London: BMJ Books, 2004)
[6] *Banks v. Goodfellow* (1870) LR 5 QB 549
[7] *Re Beaney (deceased)* [1978] 2 All ER 595
[8] *Boughton v. Knight* (1873) LR 3 PD 64
[9] *Masterman-Lister v. Brutton & Co and Jewell & Home Counties Dairies* [2003] 3 All ER 162 (CA)
[10] *Sheffield City Council v. E & S* [2005] 1 FLR 965
[11] See for example, British Medical Association & Law Society, *Assessment of Mental Capacity: Guidance for Doctors and Lawyers* (Second edition) (London: BMJ Books, 2004); the Joint Royal Colleges Ambulance Service Liaison Committee Clinical Practice Guidelines (JRCALC, available online at www2.warwick.ac.uk/fac/med/research/hsri/emergencycare/jrcalc_2006/clinical_guidelines_2006.pdf) and British Psychological Society, *Guidelines on assessing capacity* (BPS, 2006 available online at www.bps.org.uk)

4.35   There are a number of reasons why people may question a person's capacity to make a specific decision:

- the person's behaviour or circumstances cause doubt as to whether they have the capacity to make a decision
- somebody else says they are concerned about the person's capacity, or
- the person has previously been diagnosed with an impairment or disturbance that affects the way their mind or brain works (see paragraphs 4.11–4.12 above), and it has already been shown they lack capacity to make other decisions in their life.

4.36   The starting assumption must be that the person has the capacity to make the specific decision. If, however, anyone thinks a person lacks capacity, it is important to then ask the following questions:

- Does the person have all the relevant information they need to make the decision?
- If they are making a decision that involves choosing between alternatives, do they have information on all the different options?
- Would the person have a better understanding if information was explained or presented in another way?
- Are there times of day when the person's understanding is better?
- Are there locations where they may feel more at ease?
- Can the decision be put off until the circumstances are different and the person concerned may be able to make the decision?
- Can anyone else help the person to make choices or express a view (for example, a family member or carer, an advocate or someone to help with communication)?

4.37   Chapter 3 describes ways to deal with these questions and suggest steps which may help people make their own decisions. If all practical and appropriate steps fail, an assessment will then be needed of the person's capacity to make the decision that now needs to be made.

Who should assess capacity?

4.38   The person who assesses an individual's capacity to make a decision will usually be the person who is directly concerned with the individual at the time the decision needs to be made. This means that different people will be involved in assessing someone's capacity to make different decisions at different times.

For most day-to-day decisions, this will be the person caring for them at the time a decision must be made. For example, a care worker might need to assess if the person can agree to being bathed. Then a district nurse might assess if the person can consent to have a dressing changed.

4.39   For acts of care or treatment (see chapter 6), the assessor must have a 'reasonable belief' that the person lacks capacity to agree to the action or decision to be taken (see paragraphs 4.44–4.45 for a description of reasonable belief).

4.40   If a doctor or healthcare professional proposes treatment or an examination, they must assess the person's capacity to consent. In settings such as a hospital, this can involve the multi-disciplinary team (a team of people from different professional backgrounds who share responsibility for a patient). But ultimately, it is up to the professional responsible for the person's treatment to make sure that capacity has been assessed.

4.41   For a legal transaction (for example, making a will), a solicitor or legal practitioner must assess the client's capacity to instruct them. They must assess whether the client has the capacity to satisfy any relevant legal test. In cases of doubt, they should get an opinion from a doctor or other professional expert.

4.42   More complex decisions are likely to need more formal assessments (see paragraph 4.54 below). A professional opinion on the person's capacity might be necessary. This could be, for example, from a psychiatrist, psychologist, a speech and language therapist, occupational therapist or social worker. But the final decision about a person's capacity must be made by the person intending to make the decision or carry out the action on behalf of the person who lacks capacity – not the professional, who is there to advise.

4.43   Any assessor should have the skills and ability to communicate effectively with the person (see chapter 3). If necessary, they should get professional help to communicate with the person.

[*Scenario: Getting help with assessing capacity*]

What is 'reasonable belief' of lack of capacity?

4.44   Carers (whether family carers or other carers) and care workers do not have to be experts in assessing capacity. But to have protection from liability when providing care or treatment (see chapter 6), they must have a 'reasonable belief' that the person they care for lacks capacity to make relevant decisions about their care or treatment (section 5 (1)). To have this reasonable belief, they must have taken 'reasonable' steps to establish that that the person lacks capacity to make a decision or consent to an act at the time the decision or consent is needed. They must also establish that the act or decision is in the person's best interests (see chapter 5).

They do not usually need to follow formal processes, such as involving a professional to make an assessment. However, if somebody challenges their assessment (see paragraph 4.63 below), they must be able to describe the steps they have taken. They must also have objective reasons for believing the person lacks capacity to make the decision in question.

4.45   The steps that are accepted as 'reasonable' will depend on individual circumstances and the urgency of the decision. Professionals, who are qualified in their particular field, are normally expected to undertake a fuller assessment, reflecting their higher degree of knowledge and experience, than family members or other carers who have no formal qualifications. See paragraph 4.36 for a list of points to consider when assessing someone's capacity. The following may also be helpful:

- Start by assuming the person has capacity to make the specific decision. Is there anything to prove otherwise?
- Does the person have a previous diagnosis of disability or mental disorder? Does that condition now affect their capacity to make this decision? If there has been no previous diagnosis, it may be best to get a medical opinion.
- Make every effort to communicate with the person to explain what is happening.
- Make every effort to try to help the person make the decision in question.
- See if there is a way to explain or present information about the decision in a way that makes it easier to understand. If the person has a choice, do they have information about all the options?
- Can the decision be delayed to take time to help the person make the decision, or to give the person time to regain the capacity to make the decision for themselves?
- Does the person understand what decision they need to make and why they need to make it?
- Can they understand information about the decision? Can they retain it, use it and weigh it to make the decision?
- Be aware that the fact that a person agrees with you or assents to what is proposed does not necessarily mean that they have capacity to make the decision.

What other factors might affect an assessment of capacity?

4.46   It is important to assess people when they are in the best state to make the decision, if possible. Whether this is possible will depend on the nature and urgency of the decision to be made. Many of the practical steps suggested in chapter 3 will help to create the best environment for assessing capacity. The assessor must then carry out the two stages of the test of capacity (see paragraphs 4.11–4.25 above).

4.47   In many cases, it may be clear that the person has an impairment or disturbance in the functioning of their mind or brain which could affect their ability to make a decision. For example, there might be a past diagnosis of a disability or mental disorder, or there may be signs that an illness is returning. Old assumptions about an illness or condition should be reviewed. Sometimes an illness develops gradually (for example, dementia), and it is hard to know when it starts to affect capacity. Anyone assessing someone's capacity may need to ask for a medical opinion as to whether a person has an illness or condition that could affect their capacity to make a decision in this specific case.

[*Scenario: Getting a professional opinion*]

4.48   Anyone assessing someone's capacity must not assume that a person lacks capacity simply because they have a particular diagnosis or condition. There must be proof that the diagnosed illness or condition affects the ability to make a decision when it needs to be made. The person assessing capacity should ask the following questions:

- Does the person have a general understanding of what decision they need to make and why they need to make it?
- Do they understand the likely consequences of making, or not making, this decision?
- Can they understand and process information about the decision? And can they use it to help them make a decision?

In borderline cases, or where there is doubt, the assessor must be able to show that it is more likely than not that the answer to these questions is 'no'.

4.49   Anyone assessing someone's capacity will need to decide which of these steps are relevant to their situation.

- They should make sure that they understand the nature and effect of the decision to be made themselves. They may need access to relevant documents and background information (for example, details of the person's finances if assessing capacity to manage affairs). See chapter 16 for details on access to information.
- They may need other relevant information to support the assessment (for example, healthcare records or the views of staff involved in the person's care).
- Family members and close friends may be able to provide valuable background information (for example, the person's past behaviour and abilities and the types of decisions they can currently make). But their personal views and wishes about what they would want for the person must not influence the assessment.
- They should again explain to the person all the information relevant to the decision. The explanation must be in the most appropriate and effective form of communication for that person.
- Check the person's understanding after a few minutes. The person should be able to give a rough explanation of the information that was explained. There are different methods for people who use non-verbal means of communication (for example, observing behaviour or their ability to recognise objects or pictures).
- Avoid questions that need only a 'yes' or 'no' answer (for example, did you understand what I just said?). They are not enough to assess the person's capacity to make a decision. But there may be no alternative in cases where there are

major communication difficulties. In these cases, check the response by asking questions again in a different way.

- Skills and behaviour do not necessarily reflect the person's capacity to make specific decisions. The fact that someone has good social or language skills, polite behaviour or good manners doesn't necessarily mean they understand the information or are able to weigh it up.
- Repeating these steps can help confirm the result.

4.50   For certain kinds of complex decisions (for example, making a will), there are specific legal tests (see paragraph 4.32 above) in addition to the two-stage test for capacity. In some cases, medical or psychometric tests may also be helpful tools (for example, for assessing cognitive skills) in assessing a person's capacity to make particular decisions, but the relevant legal test of capacity must still be fulfilled.

When should professionals be involved?

4.51   Anyone assessing someone's capacity may need to get a professional opinion when assessing a person's capacity to make complex or major decisions. In some cases this will simply involve contacting the person's general practitioner (GP) or family doctor. If the person has a particular condition or disorder, it may be appropriate to contact a specialist (for example, consultant psychiatrist, psychologist or other professional with experience of caring for patients with that condition). A speech and language therapist might be able to help if there are communication difficulties. In some cases, a multi-disciplinary approach is best. This means combining the skills and expertise of different professionals.

4.52   Professionals should never express an opinion without carrying out a proper examination and assessment of the person's capacity to make the decision. They must apply the appropriate test of capacity. In some cases, they will need to meet the person more than once – particularly if the person has communication difficulties. Professionals can get background information from a person's family and carers. But the personal views of these people about what they want for the person who lacks capacity must not influence the outcome of that assessment.

4.53   Professional involvement might be needed if:

- the decision that needs to be made is complicated or has serious consequences
- an assessor concludes a person lacks capacity, and the person challenges the finding
- family members, carers and/or professionals disagree about a person's capacity
- there is a conflict of interest between the assessor and the person being assessed
- the person being assessed is expressing different views to different people – they may be trying to please everyone or telling people what they think they want to hear
- somebody might challenge the person's capacity to make the decision – either at the time of the decision or later (for example, a family member might challenge a will after a person has died on the basis that the person lacked capacity when they made the will)
- somebody has been accused of abusing a vulnerable adult who may lack capacity to make decisions that protect them
- a person repeatedly makes decisions that put them at risk or could result in suffering or damage.

[*Scenario: Involving professional opinion*]

4.54   In some cases, it may be a legal requirement, or good professional practice, to undertake a formal assessment of capacity. These cases include:

- where a person's capacity to sign a legal document (for example, a will), could later be challenged, in which case an expert should be asked for an opinion[12]
- to establish whether a person who might be involved in a legal case needs the assistance of the Official Solicitor or other litigation friend (somebody to represent their views to a court and give instructions to their legal representative) and there is doubt about the person's capacity to instruct a solicitor or take part in the case[13]
- whenever the Court of Protection has to decide if a person lacks capacity in a certain matter
- if the courts are required to make a decision about a person's capacity in other legal proceedings[14]
- if there may be legal consequences of a finding of capacity (for example, deciding on financial compensation following a claim for personal injury).

Are assessment processes confidential?

4.55   People involved in assessing capacity will need to share information about a person's circumstances. But there are ethical codes and laws that require professionals to keep personal information confidential. As a general rule, professionals must ask their patients or clients if they can reveal information to somebody else – even close relatives. But sometimes information may be disclosed without the consent of the person who the information concerns (for example, to protect the person or prevent harm to other people).[15]

4.56   Anyone assessing someone's capacity needs accurate information concerning the person being assessed that is relevant to the decision the person has to make. So professionals should, where possible, make relevant information available. They should make every effort to get the person's permission to reveal relevant information. They should give a full explanation of why this is necessary, and they should tell the person about the risks and consequences of revealing, and not revealing information. If the person is unable to give permission, the professional might still be allowed to provide information that will help make an accurate assessment of the person's capacity to make the specific decision. Chapter 16 has more detail on how to access information.

What if someone refuses to be assessed?

4.57   There may be circumstances in which a person whose capacity is in doubt refuses to undergo an assessment of capacity or refuses to be examined by a doctor or other professional. In these circumstances, it might help to explain to someone refusing an assessment why it is needed and what the consequences of refusal are. But threats or attempts to force the person to agree to an assessment are not acceptable.

4.58   If the person lacks capacity to agree or refuse, the assessment can normally go ahead, as long as the person does not object to the assessment, and it is in their best interests (see chapter 5).

4.59   Nobody can be forced to undergo an assessment of capacity. If someone refuses to open the door to their home, it cannot be forced. If there are serious worries about the person's mental health, it may be possible to get a warrant to force entry and assess the person for treatment in hospital – but the situation must meet the

---

[12] *Kenward v. Adams*, The Times, 29 November 1975
[13] Civil Procedure Rules 1998, r 21.1
[14] *Masterman-Lister v. Brutton & Co and Jewell & Home Counties Dairies* [2002] EWCA Civ 1889, CA at 54
[15] For example, in the circumstances discussed in *W v. Egdell and others* [1990] 1 All ER 835 at 848; *S v. Plymouth City Council and C* [2002] EWCA Civ 388) at 49

requirements of the Mental Health Act 1983 (section 135). But simply refusing an assessment of capacity is in no way sufficient grounds for an assessment under the Mental Health Act 1983 (see chapter 13).

Who should keep a record of assessments?

4.60 Assessments of capacity to take day-to-day decisions or consent to care require no formal assessment procedures or recorded documentation. Paragraphs 4.44–4.45 above explain the steps to take to reach a 'reasonable belief' that someone lacks capacity to make a particular decision. It is good practice for paid care workers to keep a record of the steps they take when caring for the person concerned.

Professional records

4.61 It is good practice for professionals to carry out a proper assessment of a person's capacity to make particular decisions and to record the findings in the relevant professional records.

- A doctor or healthcare professional proposing treatment should carry out an assessment of the person's capacity to consent (with a multi-disciplinary team, if appropriate) and record it in the patient's clinical notes.
- Solicitors should assess a client's capacity to give instructions or carry out a legal transaction (obtaining a medical or other professional opinion, if necessary) and record it on the client's file.
- An assessment of a person's capacity to consent or agree to the provision of services will be part of the care planning processes for health and social care needs, and should be recorded in the relevant documentation. This includes:
  - Person Centred Planning for people with learning disabilities
  - the Care Programme Approach for people with mental illness
  - the Single Assessment Process for older people in England, and
  - the Unified Assessment Process in Wales.

Formal reports or certificates of capacity

4.62 In some cases, a more detailed report or certificate of capacity may be required, for example,

- for use in court or other legal processes
- as required by Regulations, Rules or Orders made under the Act.

How can someone challenge a finding of lack of capacity?

4.63 There are likely to be occasions when someone may wish to challenge the results of an assessment of capacity. The first step is to raise the matter with the person who carried out the assessment. If the challenge comes from the individual who is said to lack capacity, they might need support from family, friends or an advocate. Ask the assessor to:

- give reasons why they believe the person lacks capacity to make the decision, and
- provide objective evidence to support that belief.

4.64 The assessor must show they have applied the principles of the Mental Capacity Act (see chapter 2). Attorneys, deputies and professionals will need to show that they have also followed guidance in this chapter.

4.65 It might be possible to get a second opinion from an independent professional or another expert in assessing capacity. Chapter 15 has other suggestions for dealing with disagreements. But if a disagreement cannot be resolved, the person who is challenging the assessment may be able to apply to the Court of Protection. The Court of Protection can rule on whether a person has capacity to make the decision covered by the assessment (see chapter 8).

5 WHAT DOES THE ACT MEAN WHEN IT TALKS ABOUT 'BEST INTERESTS'?

One of the key principles of the Act is that any act done for, or any decision made on behalf of a person who lacks capacity must be done, or made, in that person's *best interests*. That is the same whether the person making the decision or acting is a family carer, a paid care worker, an attorney, a court-appointed deputy, or a healthcare professional, and whether the decision is a minor issue – like what to wear – or a major issue, like whether to provide particular healthcare.

As long as these acts or decisions are in the best interests of the person who lacks capacity to make the decision for themselves, or to consent to acts concerned with their care or treatment, then the decision-maker or carer will be protected from liability.

There are exceptions to this, including circumstances where a person has made an advance decision to refuse treatment (see chapter 9) and, in specific circumstances, the involvement of a person who lacks capacity in research (see chapter 11). But otherwise the underpinning principle of the Act is that all acts and decisions should be made in the best interests of the person without capacity.

Working out what is in someone else's best interests may be difficult, and the Act requires people to follow certain steps to help them work out whether a particular act or decision is in a person's best interests. In some cases, there may be disagreement about what someone's best interests really are. As long as the person who acts or makes the decision has followed the steps to establish whether a person has capacity, and done everything they reasonably can to work out what someone's best interests are, the law should protect them.

This chapter explains what the Act means by 'best interests' and what things should be considered when trying to work out what is in someone's best interests. It also highlights some of the difficulties that might come up in working out what the best interests of a person who lacks capacity to make the decision actually are.

> In this chapter, as throughout the Code, a person's capacity (or lack of capacity) refers specifically to their capacity to make a particular decision at the time it needs to be made.

Quick summary

A person trying to work out the best interests of a person who lacks capacity to make a particular decision ('lacks capacity') should:

Encourage participation

- do whatever is possible to permit and encourage the person to take part, or to improve their ability to take part, in making the decision

Identify all relevant circumstances

■ try to identify all the things that the person who lacks capacity would take into account if they were making the decision or acting for themselves

Find out the person's views

■ try to find out the views of the person who lacks capacity, including:

– the person's past and present wishes and feelings – these may have been expressed verbally, in writing or through behaviour or habits.
– any beliefs and values (e.g. religious, cultural, moral or political) that would be likely to influence the decision in question.
– any other factors the person themselves would be likely to consider if they were making the decision or acting for themselves.

Avoid discrimination

■ not make assumptions about someone's best interests simply on the basis of the person's age, appearance, condition or behaviour.

Assess whether the person might regain capacity

■ consider whether the person is likely to regain capacity (e.g. after receiving medical treatment). If so, can the decision wait until then?

If the decision concerns life-sustaining treatment

■ not be motivated in any way by a desire to bring about the person's death. They should not make assumptions about the person's quality of life.

Consult others

■ if it is practical and appropriate to do so, consult other people for their views about the person's best interests and to see if they have any information about the person's wishes and feelings, beliefs and values. In particular, try to consult:

– anyone previously named by the person as someone to be consulted on either the decision in question or on similar issues
– anyone engaged in caring for the person
– close relatives, friends or others who take an interest in the person's welfare
– any attorney appointed under a Lasting Power of Attorney or Enduring Power of Attorney made by the person
– any deputy appointed by the Court of Protection to make decisions for the person.

■ For decisions about major medical treatment or where the person should live and where there is no-one who fits into any of the above categories, an Independent Mental Capacity Advocate (IMCA) must be consulted. (See chapter 10 for more information about IMCAs.)

■ When consulting, remember that the person who lacks the capacity to make the decision or act for themselves still has a right to keep their affairs private – so it would not be right to share every piece of information with everyone.

Avoid restricting the person's rights

■ see if there are other options that may be less restrictive of the person's rights.

Take all of this into account

■ weigh up all of these factors in order to work out what is in the person's best interests.

What is the best interests principle and who does it apply to?

5.1   The best interests principle underpins the Mental Capacity Act. It is set out in section 1(5) of the Act.

'An act done, or decision made, under this Act for or on behalf of a person who lacks capacity must be done, or made, in his best interests.'

The concept has been developed by the courts in cases relating to people who lack capacity to make specific decisions for themselves, mainly decisions concerned with the provision of medical treatment or social care.

5.2   This principle covers all aspects of financial, personal welfare and healthcare decision-making and actions. It applies to anyone making decisions or acting under the provisions of the Act, including:

- family carers, other carers and care workers
- healthcare and social care staff
- attorneys appointed under a Lasting Power of Attorney or registered Enduring Power of Attorney
- deputies appointed by the court to make decisions on behalf of someone who lacks capacity, and
- the Court of Protection.

5.3   However, as chapter 2 explained, the Act's first key principle is that people must be assumed to have capacity to make a decision or act for themselves unless it is established that they lack it. That means that working out a person's best interests is only relevant when that person has been assessed as lacking, or is reasonably believed to lack, capacity to make the decision in question or give consent to an act being done.

People with capacity are able to decide for themselves what they want to do. When they do this, they might choose an option that other people don't think is in their best interests. That is their choice and does not, in itself, mean that they lack capacity to make those decisions.

Exceptions to the best interests principle

5.4   There are two circumstances when the best interests principle will not apply. The first is where someone has previously made an advance decision to refuse medical treatment while they had the capacity to do so. Their advance decision should be respected when they lack capacity, even if others think that the decision to refuse treatment is not in their best interests (guidance on advance decisions is given in chapter 9).

The second concerns the involvement in research, in certain circumstances, of someone lacking capacity to consent (see chapter 11).

What does the Act mean by best interests?

5.5   The term 'best interests' is not actually defined in the Act. This is because so many different types of decisions and actions are covered by the Act, and so many different people and circumstances are affected by it.

5.6   Section 4 of the Act explains how to work out the best interests of a person who lacks capacity to make a decision at the time it needs to be made. This section sets out a checklist of common factors that must always be considered by anyone who needs to decide what is in the best interests of a person who lacks capacity in any particular situation. This checklist is only the starting point: in many cases, extra factors will need to be considered.

5.7   When working out what is in the best interests of the person who lacks capacity to
make a decision or act for themselves, decision-makers must take into account all
relevant factors that it would be reasonable to consider, not just those that they
think are important. They must not act or make a decision based on what they
would want to do if they were the person who lacked capacity.

[*Scenario: Whose best interests?*]

Who can be a decision-maker?

5.8   Under the Act, many different people may be required to make decisions or act on
behalf of someone who lacks capacity to make decisions for themselves. The person making the decision is referred to throughout this chapter, and in other parts
of the Code, as the 'decision-maker', and it is the decision-maker's responsibility to
work out what would be in the best interests of the person who lacks capacity.

5.9   What this means is that a range of different decision-makers may be involved with
a person who lacks capacity to make different decisions.

5.10   In some cases, the same person may make different types of decision for someone
who lacks capacity to make decisions for themselves. For instance, a family carer
may carry out certain acts in caring for the person on a day-to-day basis, but if they
are also an attorney, appointed under a Lasting Power of Attorney (LPA), they may
also make specific decisions concerning the person's property and affairs or their
personal welfare (depending on what decisions the LPA has been set up to cover).

5.11   There are also times when a joint decision might be made by a number of people.
For example, when a care plan for a person who lacks capacity to make relevant
decisions is being put together, different healthcare or social care staff might be
involved in making decisions or recommendations about the person's care package.
Sometimes these decisions will be made by a team of healthcare or social care staff
as a whole. At other times, the decision will be made by a specific individual within
the team. A different member of the team may then implement that decision, based
on what the team has worked out to be the person's best interests.

5.12   No matter who is making the decision, the most important thing is that the
decision-maker tries to work out what would be in the best interests of the person
who lacks capacity.

[*Scenario: Coming to a joint decision*]

What must be taken into account when trying to work out someone's best interests?

5.13   Because every case – and every decision – is different, the law can't set out all the
factors that will need to be taken into account in working out someone's best interests. But section 4 of the Act sets out some common factors that must always be
considered when trying to work out someone's best interests. These factors are
summarised in the checklist here:

- Working out what is in someone's best interests cannot be based simply on
someone's age, appearance, condition or behaviour. (see paragraphs 5.16–5.17).
- All relevant circumstances should be considered when working out someone's
best interests (paragraphs 5.18–5.20).
- Every effort should be made to encourage and enable the person who lacks
capacity to take part in making the decision (paragraphs 5.21–5.24).
- If there is a chance that the person will regain the capacity to make a particular
decision, then it may be possible to put off the decision until later if it is not
urgent (paragraphs 5.25–5.28).

- Special considerations apply to decisions about life-sustaining treatment (paragraphs 5.29–5.36).
- The person's past and present wishes and feelings, beliefs and values should be taken into account (paragraphs 5.37–5.48).
- The views of other people who are close to the person who lacks capacity should be considered, as well as the views of an attorney or deputy (paragraphs 5.49–5.55).

It's important not to take shortcuts in working out best interests, and a proper and objective assessment must be carried out on every occasion. If the decision is urgent, there may not be time to examine all possible factors, but the decision must still be made in the best interests of the person who lacks capacity. Not all the factors in the checklist will be relevant to all types of decisions or actions, and in many cases other factors will have to be considered as well, even though some of them may then not be found to be relevant.

5.14   What is in a person's best interests may well change over time. This means that even where similar actions need to be taken repeatedly in connection with the person's care or treatment, the person's best interests should be regularly reviewed.

5.15   Any staff involved in the care of a person who lacks capacity should make sure a record is kept of the process of working out the best interests of that person for each relevant decision, setting out:

- how the decision about the person's best interests was reached
- what the reasons for reaching the decision were
- who was consulted to help work out best interests, and
- what particular factors were taken into account.

This record should remain on the person's file.

For major decisions based on the best interests of a person who lacks capacity, it may also be useful for family and other carers to keep a similar kind of record.

What safeguards does the Act provide around working out someone's best interests?

5.16   Section 4(1) states that anyone working out someone's best interests must not make unjustified assumptions about what their best interests might be simply on the basis of the person's age, appearance, condition or any aspect of their behaviour. In this way, the Act ensures that people who lack capacity to make decisions for themselves are not subject to discrimination or treated any less favourably than anyone else.

5.17   'Appearance' is a broad term and refers to all aspects of physical appearance, including skin colour, mode of dress and any visible medical problems, disfiguring scars or other disabilities. A person's 'condition' also covers a range of factors including physical disabilities, learning difficulties or disabilities, age-related illness or temporary conditions (such as drunkenness or unconsciousness). 'Behaviour' refers to behaviour that might seem unusual to others, such as talking too loudly or laughing inappropriately.

[*Scenario: Following the checklist*]

How does a decision-maker work out what 'all relevant circumstances' are?

5.18   When trying to work out someone's best interests, the decision-maker should try to identify all the issues that would be most relevant to the individual who lacks capacity and to the particular decision, as well as those in the 'checklist'. Clearly, it is not always possible or practical to investigate in depth every issue which may have some relevance to the person who lacks capacity or the decision in question. So relevant circumstances are defined in section 4(11) of the Act as those:

'(a) of which the person making the determination is aware, and
(b) which it would be reasonable to regard as relevant.'

5.19   The relevant circumstances will of course vary from case to case. For example, when making a decision about major medical treatment, a doctor would need to consider the clinical needs of the patient, the potential benefits and burdens of the treatment on the person's health and life expectancy and any other factors relevant to making a professional judgement.[16] But it would not be reasonable to consider issues such as life expectancy when working out whether it would be in someone's best interests to be given medication for a minor problem.

5.20   Financial decisions are another area where the relevant circumstances will vary. For example, if a person had received a substantial sum of money as compensation for an accident resulting in brain injury, the decision-maker would have to consider a wide range of circumstances when making decisions about how the money is spent or invested, such as:

■ whether the person's condition is likely to change
■ whether the person needs professional care, and
■ whether the person needs to live somewhere else to make it easier for them.

These kinds of issues can only be decided on a case-by-case basis.

How should the person who lacks capacity be involved in working out their best interests?

5.21   Wherever possible, the person who lacks capacity to make a decision should still be involved in the decision-making process (section 4(4)).

5.22   Even if the person lacks capacity to make the decision, they may have views on matters affecting the decision, and on what outcome would be preferred. Their involvement can help work out what would be in their best interests.

5.23   The decision-maker should make sure that all practical means are used to enable and encourage the person to participate as fully as possible in the decision-making process and any action taken as a result, or to help the person improve their ability to participate.

5.24   Consulting the person who lacks capacity will involve taking time to explain what is happening and why a decision needs to be made. Chapter 3 includes a number of practical steps to assist and enable decision-making which may be also be helpful in encouraging greater participation. These include:

■ using simple language and/or illustrations or photographs to help the person understand the options
■ asking them about the decision at a time and location where the person feels most relaxed and at ease
■ breaking the information down into easy-to-understand points
■ using specialist interpreters or signers to communicate with the person.

This may mean that other people are required to communicate with the person to establish their views. For example, a trusted relative or friend, a full-time carer or

---

[16] *An Hospital NHS Trust v. S* [2003] EWHC 365 (Fam), paragraph 47

an advocate may be able to help the person to express wishes or aspirations or to indicate a preference between different options.

More information on all of these steps can be found in chapter 3.

[Scenario: Involving someone in working out their best interests]

How do the chances of someone regaining and developing capacity affect working out what is in their best interests?

5.25   There are some situations where decisions may be deferred, if someone who currently lacks capacity may regain the capacity to make the decision for themselves. Section 4(3) of the Act requires the decision-maker to consider:

- whether the individual concerned is likely to regain the capacity to make that particular decision in the future, and
- if so, when that is likely to be.

It may then be possible to put off the decision until the person can make it for themselves.

5.26   In emergency situations – such as when urgent medical treatment is needed – it may *not* be possible to wait to see if the person may regain capacity so they can decide for themselves whether or not to have the urgent treatment.

5.27   Where a person currently lacks capacity to make a decision relating to their day-to-day care, the person may – over time and with the right support – be able to develop the skills to do so. Though others may need to make the decision on the person's behalf at the moment, all possible support should be given to that person to enable them to develop the skills so that they can make the decision for themselves in the future.

[Scenario: Taking a short-term decision for someone who may regain capacity]

5.28   Some factors which may indicate that a person may regain or develop capacity in the future are:

- the cause of the lack of capacity can be treated, either by medication or some other form of treatment or therapy
- the lack of capacity is likely to decrease in time (for example, where it is caused by the effects of medication or alcohol, or following a sudden shock)
- a person with learning disabilities may learn new skills or be subject to new experiences which increase their understanding and ability to make certain decisions
- the person may have a condition which causes capacity to come and go at various times (such as some forms of mental illness) so it may be possible to arrange for the decision to be made during a time when they do have capacity
- a person previously unable to communicate may learn a new form of communication (see chapter 3).

How should someone's best interests be worked out when making decisions about life-sustaining treatment?

5.29   A special factor in the checklist applies to decisions about treatment which is necessary to keep the person alive ('life-sustaining treatment') and this is set out in section 4(5) of the Act. The fundamental rule is that anyone who is deciding whether or not life-sustaining treatment is in the best interests of someone who lacks capacity to consent to or refuse such treatment must not be motivated by a desire to bring about the person's death.

5.30   Whether a treatment is 'life-sustaining' depends not only on the type of treatment, but also on the particular circumstances in which it may be prescribed. For example, in some situations giving antibiotics may be life-sustaining, whereas in other circumstances antibiotics are used to treat a non-life-threatening condition. It is up to the doctor or healthcare professional providing treatment to assess whether the treatment is life-sustaining in each particular situation.

5.31   All reasonable steps which are in the person's best interests should be taken to prolong their life. There will be a limited number of cases where treatment is futile, overly burdensome to the patient or where there is no prospect of recovery. In circumstances such as these, it may be that an assessment of best interests leads to the conclusion that it would be in the best interests of the patient to withdraw or withhold life-sustaining treatment, even if this may result in the person's death. The decision-maker must make a decision based on the best interests of the person who lacks capacity. They must not be motivated by a desire to bring about the person's death for whatever reason, even if this is from a sense of compassion. Healthcare and social care staff should also refer to relevant professional guidance when making decisions regarding life-sustaining treatment.

5.32   As with all decisions, before deciding to withdraw or withhold life-sustaining treatment, the decision-maker must consider the range of treatment options available to work out what would be in the person's best interests. All the factors in the best interests checklist should be considered, and in particular, the decision-maker should consider any statements that the person has previously made about their wishes and feelings about life-sustaining treatment.

5.33   Importantly, section 4(5) cannot be interpreted to mean that doctors are under an obligation to provide, or to continue to provide, life-sustaining treatment where that treatment is not in the best interests of the person, even where the person's death is foreseen. Doctors must apply the best interests' checklist and use their professional skills to decide whether life-sustaining treatment is in the person's best interests. If the doctor's assessment is disputed, and there is no other way of resolving the dispute, ultimately the Court of Protection may be asked to decide what is in the person's best interests.

5.34   Where a person has made a written statement in advance that requests particular medical treatments, such as artificial nutrition and hydration (ANH), these requests should be taken into account by the treating doctor in the same way as requests made by a patient who has the capacity to make such decisions. Like anyone else involved in making this decision, the doctor must weigh written statements alongside all other relevant factors to decide whether it is in the best interests of the patient to provide or continue life-sustaining treatment.

5.35   If someone has made an advance decision to refuse life-sustaining treatment, specific rules apply. More information about these can be found in chapter 9 and in paragraph 5.45 below.

5.36   As mentioned in paragraph 5.33 above, where there is any doubt about the patient's best interests, an application should be made to the Court of Protection for a decision as to whether withholding or withdrawing life-sustaining treatment is in the patient's best interests.

How do a person's wishes and feelings, beliefs and values affect working out what is in their best interests?

5.37   Section 4(6) of the Act requires the decision-maker to consider, as far as they are 'reasonably ascertainable':

   '(a) the person's past and present wishes and feelings (and in particular, any relevant written statements made by him when he had capacity),

(b) the beliefs and values that would be likely to influence his decision if he had capacity, and

(c) the other factors that he would be likely to consider if he were able to do so.'

Paragraphs 5.38–5.48 below give further guidance on each of these factors.

5.38   In setting out the requirements for working out a person's 'best interests', section 4 of the Act puts the person who lacks capacity at the centre of the decision to be made. Even if they cannot make the decision, their wishes and feelings, beliefs and values should be taken fully into account – whether expressed in the past or now. But their wishes and feelings, beliefs and values will not necessarily be the deciding factor in working out their best interests. Any such assessment must consider past and current wishes and feelings, beliefs and values alongside all other factors, but the final decision must be based entirely on what is in the person's best interests.

[*Scenario: Considering wishes and feelings as part of best interests*]

What is 'reasonably ascertainable'?

5.39   How much someone can learn about a person's past and present views will depend on circumstances and the time available. 'Reasonably ascertainable' means considering all possible information in the time available. What is available in an emergency will be different to what is available in a non-emergency. But even in an emergency, there may still be an opportunity to try to communicate with the person or his friends, family or carers (see chapter 3 for guidance on helping communication).

What role do a person's past and present wishes and feelings play?

5.40   People who cannot express their current wishes and feelings in words may express themselves through their behaviour. Expressions of pleasure or distress and emotional responses will also be relevant in working out what is in their best interests. It is also important to be sure that other people have not influenced a person's views. An advocate could help the person make choices and express their views.

5.41   The person may have held strong views in the past which could have a bearing on the decision now to be made. All reasonable efforts must be made to find out whether the person has expressed views in the past that will shape the decision to be made. This could have been through verbal communication, writing, behaviour or habits, or recorded in any other way (for example, home videos or audiotapes).

5.42   Section 4(6)(a) places special emphasis on written statements the person might have made before losing capacity. These could provide a lot of information about a person's wishes. For example, these statements could include information about the type of medical treatment they would want in the case of future illness, where they would prefer to live, or how they wish to be cared for.

5.43   The decision-maker should consider written statements carefully. If their decision does not follow something a person has put in writing, they must record the reasons why. They should be able to justify their reasons if someone challenges their decision.

5.44   A doctor should take written statements made by a person before losing capacity which request specific treatments as seriously as those made by people who currently have capacity to make treatment decisions. But they would not have to follow a written request if they think the specific treatment would be clinically unnecessary or not appropriate for the person's condition, so not in the person's best interests.

5.45   It is important to note the distinction between a written statement expressing treatment preferences and a statement which constitutes an advance decision to refuse treatment. This is covered by section 24 of the Act, and it has a different status in law. Doctors cannot ignore a written statement that is a valid advance decision to refuse treatment. An advance decision to refuse treatment must be followed if it meets the Act's requirements and applies to the person's circumstances. In these cases, the treatment must not be given (see chapter 9 for more information). If there is not a valid and applicable advance decision, treatment should be provided based on the person's best interests.

What role do beliefs and values play?

5.46 Everybody's values and beliefs influence the decisions they make. They may become especially important for someone who lacks capacity to make a decision because of a progressive illness such as dementia, for example. Evidence of a person's beliefs and values can be found in things like their:

- cultural background
- religious beliefs
- political convictions, or
- past behaviour or habits.

Some people set out their values and beliefs in a written statement while they still have capacity.

[*Scenario: Considering beliefs and values*]

What other factors should a decision-maker consider?

5.47 Section 4(6)(c) of the Act requires decision-makers to consider any other factors the person who lacks capacity would consider if they were able to do so. This might include the effect of the decision on other people, obligations to dependants or the duties of a responsible citizen.

5.48 The Act allows actions that benefit other people, as long as they are in the best interests of the person who lacks capacity to make the decision. For example, having considered all the circumstances of the particular case, a decision might be made to take a blood sample from a person who lacks capacity to consent, to check for a genetic link to cancer within the family, because this might benefit someone else in the family. But it might still be in the best interests of the person who lacks capacity. 'Best interests' goes beyond the person's medical interests.

For example, courts have previously ruled that possible wider benefits to a person who lacks capacity to consent, such as providing or gaining emotional support from close relationships, are important factors in working out the person's own best interests.[17] If it is likely that the person who lacks capacity would have considered these factors themselves, they can be seen as part of the person's best interests.

Who should be consulted when working out someone's best interests?

5.49 The Act places a duty on the decision-maker to consult other people close to a person who lacks capacity, where practical and appropriate, on decisions affecting the person and what might be in the person's best interests. This also applies to those involved in caring for the person and interested in the person's welfare. Under section 4(7), the decision-maker has a duty to take into account the views of the following people, where it is practical and appropriate to do so:

---

[17] See for example *Re Y (Mental Incapacity: Bone marrow transplant)* [1996] 2 FLR 787; *Re A (Male Sterilisation)* [2000] 1 FLR 549.

- anyone the person has previously named as someone they want to be consulted
- anyone involved in caring for the person
- anyone interested in their welfare (for example, family carers, other close relatives, or an advocate already working with the person)
- an attorney appointed by the person under a Lasting Power of Attorney, and
- a deputy appointed for that person by the Court of Protection.

5.50   If there is no-one to speak to about the person's best interests, in some circumstances the person may qualify for an Independent Mental Capacity Advocate (IMCA). For more information on IMCAs, see chapter 10.

5.51   Decision-makers must show they have thought carefully about who to speak to. If it is practical and appropriate to speak to the above people, they must do so and must take their views into account. They must be able to explain why they did not speak to a particular person – it is good practice to have a clear record of their reasons. It is also good practice to give careful consideration to the views of family carers, if it is possible to do so.

5.52   It is also good practice for healthcare and social care staff to record at the end of the process why they think a specific decision is in the person's best interests. This is particularly important if healthcare and social care staff go against the views of somebody who has been consulted while working out the person's best interests.

5.53   The decision-maker should try to find out:

- what the people consulted think is in the person's best interests in this matter, and
- if they can give information on the person's wishes and feelings, beliefs and values.

5.54   This information may be available from somebody the person named before they lost capacity as someone they wish to be consulted. People who are close to the person who lacks capacity, such as close family members, are likely to know them best. They may also be able to help with communication or interpret signs that show the person's present wishes and feelings. Everybody's views are equally important – even if they do not agree with each other. They must be considered alongside the views of the person who lacks capacity and other factors. See paragraphs 5.62–5.69 below for guidance on dealing with conflicting views.

[*Scenario: Considering other people's views*]

5.55   Where an attorney has been appointed under a Lasting Power of Attorney or Enduring Power of Attorney, or a deputy has been appointed by a court, they must make the decisions on any matters they have been appointed to deal with. Attorneys and deputies should also be consulted, if practical and appropriate, on other issues affecting the person who lacks capacity.

For instance, an attorney who is appointed only to look after the person's property and affairs may have information about the person's beliefs and values, wishes and feelings, that could help work out what would be in the person's best interests regarding healthcare or treatment decisions. (See chapters 7 and 8 for more information about the roles of attorneys and deputies.)

How can decision-makers respect confidentiality?

5.56   Decision-makers must balance the duty to consult other people with the right to confidentiality of the person who lacks capacity. So if confidential information is to be discussed, they should only seek the views of people who it is appropriate to consult, where their views are relevant to the decision to be made and the particular circumstances.

5.57   There may be occasions where it is in the person's best interests for personal information (for example, about their medical condition, if the decision concerns the provision of medical treatment) to be revealed to the people consulted as part of the process of working out their best interests (further guidance on this is given in chapter 16). Healthcare and social care staff who are trying to determine a person's best interests must follow their professional guidance, as well as other relevant guidance, about confidentiality.

When does the best interests principle apply?

5.58   Section 1(5) of the Act confirms that the principle applies to any act done, or any decision made, on behalf of someone where there is reasonable belief that the person lacks capacity under the Act. This covers informal day-to-day decisions and actions as well as decisions made by the courts.

Reasonable belief about a person's best interests

5.59   Section 4(9) confirms that if someone acts or makes a decision in the reasonable belief that what they are doing is in the best interests of the person who lacks capacity, then – provided they have followed the checklist in section 4 – they will have complied with the best interests principle set out in the Act. Coming to an incorrect conclusion about a person's capacity or best interests does not necessarily mean that the decision-maker would not get protection from liability (this is explained in chapter 6). But they must be able to show that it was reasonable for them to think that the person lacked capacity and that they were acting in the person's best interests at the time they made their decision or took action.

5.60   Where there is a need for a court decision, the court is likely to require formal evidence of what might be in the person's best interests. This will include evidence from relevant professionals (for example, psychiatrists or social workers). But in most day-to-day situations, there is no need for such formality. In emergency situations, it may not be practical or possible to gather formal evidence.

5.61   Where the court is not involved, people are still expected to have reasonable grounds for believing that they are acting in somebody's best interests. This does not mean that decision-makers can simply impose their own views. They must have objective reasons for their decisions – and they must be able to demonstrate them. They must be able to show they have considered all relevant circumstances and applied all elements of the best interests checklist.

[*Scenario: Demonstrating reasonable belief*]

What problems could arise when working out someone's best interests?

5.62   It is important that the best interests principle and the statutory checklist are flexible. Without flexibility, it would be impossible to prioritise factors in different cases – and it would be difficult to ensure that the outcome is the best possible for the person who lacks capacity to make the particular decision. Some cases will be straightforward. Others will require decision-makers to balance the pros and cons of all relevant factors.[18] But this flexibility could lead to problems in reaching a conclusion about a person's best interests.

---

[18] *Re A (Male Sterilisation)* [2000] 1 FLR 549.

What happens when there are conflicting concerns?

5.63   A decision-maker may be faced with people who disagree about a person's best interests. Family members, partners and carers may disagree between themselves. Or they might have different memories about what views the person expressed in the past. Carers and family might disagree with a professional's view about the person's care or treatment needs.

5.64   The decision-maker will need to find a way of balancing these concerns or deciding between them. The first approach should be to review all elements of the best interests checklist with everyone involved. They should include the person who lacks capacity (as much as they are able to take part) and anyone who has been involved in earlier discussions. It may be possible to reach an agreement at a meeting to air everyone's concerns. But an agreement in itself might not be in the person's best interests. Ultimate responsibility for working out best interests lies with the decision-maker.

[*Scenario: Dealing with disagreement*]

Family, partners and carers who are consulted

5.65,   If disagreement continues, the decision-maker will need to weigh up the views of different parties. This will depend entirely upon the circumstances of each case, the people involved and their relationship with the person who lacks capacity. Sometimes the decision-maker will find that carers have an insight into how to interpret a person's wishes and feelings that can help them reach a decision.

5.66   At the same time, paid care workers and voluntary sector support workers may have specialist knowledge about up-to-date care options or treatments. Some may also have known the person for many years.

5.67   People with conflicting interests should not be cut out of the process (for example, those who stand to inherit from the person's will may still have a right to be consulted about the person's care or medical treatment). But decision-makers must always ensure that the interests of those consulted do not overly influence the process of working out a person's best interests. In weighing up different contributions, the decision-maker should consider:

- how long an individual has known the person who lacks capacity, and
- what their relationship is.

[*Scenario: Settling disagreements*]

Settling disputes about best interests

5.68   If someone wants to challenge a decision-maker's conclusions, there are several options:

- Involve an advocate to act on behalf of the person who lacks capacity to make the decision (see paragraph 5.69 below).
- Get a second opinion.
- Hold a formal or informal 'best interests' case conference.
- Attempt some form of mediation (see chapter 15).
- Pursue a complaint through the organisation's formal procedures.

Ultimately, if all other attempts to resolve the dispute have failed, the court might need to decide what is in the person's best interests. Chapter 8 provides more information about the Court of Protection.

Advocacy

5.69 An advocate might be useful in providing support for the person who lacks capacity to make a decision in the process of working out their best interests, if:

- the person who lacks capacity has no close family or friends to take an interest in their welfare, and they do not qualify for an Independent Mental Capacity Advocate (see chapter 10)
- family members disagree about the person's best interests
- family members and professionals disagree about the person's best interests
- there is a conflict of interest for people who have been consulted in the best interests assessment (for example, the sale of a family property where the person lives)
- the person who lacks capacity is already in contact with an advocate
- the proposed course of action may lead to the use of restraint or other restrictions on the person who lacks capacity
- there is a concern about the protection of a vulnerable adult.

6 WHAT PROTECTION DOES THE ACT OFFER FOR PEOPLE PROVIDING CARE OR TREATMENT?

Section 5 of the Act allows carers, healthcare and social care staff to carry out certain tasks without fear of liability. These tasks involve the personal care, healthcare or treatment of people who lack capacity to consent to them. The aim is to give legal backing for acts that need to be carried out in the best interests of the person who lacks capacity to consent.[19]

This chapter explains:

- how the Act provides protection from liability
- how that protection works in practice
- where protection is restricted or limited, and
- when a carer can use a person's money to buy goods or services without formal permission.

> In this chapter, as throughout the Code, a person's capacity (or lack of capacity) refers specifically to their capacity to make a particular decision at the time it needs to be made.

Quick summary

The following steps list all the things that people providing care or treatment should bear in mind to ensure they are protected by the Act.

Acting in connection with the care or treatment of someone who lacks capacity to consent

- Is the action to be carried out in connection with the care or treatment of a person who lacks capacity to give consent to that act?
- Does it involve major life changes for the person concerned? If so, it will need special consideration.

---

[19] The provisions of section 5 are based on the common law 'doctrine of necessity' as set out in *Re F (Mental Patient: Sterilisation)* [1990] 2 AC 1.

- Who is carrying out the action? Is it appropriate for that person to do so at the relevant time?

Checking whether the person has capacity to consent

- Have all possible steps been taken to try to help the person make a decision for themselves about the action?
- Has the two-stage test of capacity been applied?
- Are there reasonable grounds for believing the person lacks capacity to give permission?

Acting in the person's best interests

- Has the best interests checklist been applied and all relevant circumstances considered?
- Is a less restrictive option available?
- Is it reasonable to believe that the proposed act is in the person's best interests?

Understanding possible limitations on protection from liability

- If restraint is being considered, is it necessary to prevent harm to the person who lacks capacity, and is it a proportionate response to the likelihood of the person suffering harm – and to the seriousness of that harm?
- Could the restraint be classed as a 'deprivation of the person's liberty'?
- Does the action conflict with a decision that has been made by an attorney or deputy under their powers?

Paying for necessary goods and services

- If someone wishes to use the person's money to buy goods or pay for services for someone who lacks capacity to do so themselves, are those goods or services necessary and in the person's best interests?
- Is it necessary to take money from the person's bank or building society account or to sell the person's property to pay for goods or services? If so, formal authority will be required.

What protection do people have when caring for those who lack capacity to consent?

6.1   Every day, millions of acts are done to and for people who lack capacity either to:

- take decisions about their own care or treatment, or
- consent to someone else caring for them.

Such acts range from everyday tasks of caring (for example, helping someone to wash) to life-changing events (for example, serious medical treatment or arranging for someone to go into a care home).

In theory, many of these actions could be against the law. Legally, people have the right to stop others from interfering with their body or property unless they give permission. But what happens if someone lacks capacity to give permission? Carers who dress people who cannot dress themselves are potentially interfering with someone's body without their consent, so could theoretically be prosecuted for assault. A neighbour who enters and cleans the house of a person who lacks capacity could be trespassing on the person's property.

6.2   Section 5 of the Act provides 'protection from liability'. In other words, it protects people who carry out these actions. It stops them being prosecuted for acts that could otherwise be classed as civil wrongs or crimes. By protecting family and other carers from liability, the Act allows necessary caring acts or treatment to take place as if a person who lacks capacity to consent had consented to them.

People providing care of this sort do not therefore need to get formal authority to act.

6.3   Importantly, section 5 does not give people caring for or treating someone the power to make any other decisions on behalf of those who lack capacity to make their own decisions. Instead, it offers protection from liability so that they can act in connection with the person's care or treatment. The power to make decisions on behalf of someone who lacks capacity can be granted through other parts of the Act (such as the powers granted to attorneys and deputies, which are explained in chapters 7 and 8).

What type of actions might have protection from liability?

6.4   Section 5(1) provides possible protection for actions carried out *in connection with care or treatment*. The action may be carried out on behalf of someone who is believed to lack capacity to give permission for the action, so long as it is in that person's best interests (see chapter 5). The Act does not define 'care' or 'treatment'. They should be given their normal meaning. However, section 64(1) makes clear that treatment includes diagnostic or other procedures.

6.5   Actions that might be covered by section 5 include:

Personal care

- helping with washing, dressing or personal hygiene
- helping with eating and drinking
- helping with communication
- helping with mobility (moving around)
- helping someone take part in education, social or leisure activities
- going into a person's home to drop off shopping or to see if they are alright
- doing the shopping or buying necessary goods with the person's money
- arranging household services (for example, arranging repairs or maintenance for gas and electricity supplies)
- providing services that help around the home (such as homecare or meals on wheels)
- undertaking actions related to community care services (for example, day care, residential accommodation or nursing care) – but see also paragraphs 6.7–6.14 below
- helping someone to move home (including moving property and clearing the former home).

Healthcare and treatment

- carrying out diagnostic examinations and tests (to identify an illness, condition or other problem)
- providing professional medical, dental and similar treatment
- giving medication
- taking someone to hospital for assessment or treatment
- providing nursing care (whether in hospital or in the community)
- carrying out any other necessary medical procedures (for example, taking a blood sample) or therapies (for example, physiotherapy or chiropody)
- providing care in an emergency.

6.6   These actions only receive protection from liability if the person is reasonably believed to lack capacity to give permission for the action. The action must also be in the person's best interests and follow the Act's principles (see paragraph 6.26 onwards).

6.7   Some acts in connection with care or treatment may cause major life changes with significant consequences for the person concerned. Those requiring particularly careful consideration include a change of residence, perhaps into a care home or nursing home, or major decisions about healthcare and medical treatment. These are described in the following paragraphs.

A CHANGE OF RESIDENCE

6.8   Sometimes a person cannot get sufficient or appropriate care in their own home, and they may have to move – perhaps to live with relatives or to go into a care home or nursing home. If the person lacks capacity to consent to a move, the decision-maker(s) must consider whether the move is in the person's best interests (by referring to the best interests checklist in chapter 5 and in particular the person's past and present wishes and feelings, as well as the views of other relevant people). The decision-maker(s) must also consider whether there is a less restrictive option (see chapter 2, principle 5).

This may involve speaking to:

- anyone currently involved in the person's care
- family carers and other family members close to the person and interested in their welfare
- others who have an interest in the person's welfare
- anyone the person has previously named as someone to be consulted, and
- an attorney or deputy who has been legally appointed to make particular decisions on their behalf.

6.9   Some cases will require an Independent Mental Capacity Advocate (IMCA). The IMCA represents and supports the person who lacks capacity and they will provide information to make sure the final decision is in the person's best interests (see chapter 10). An IMCA is needed when there is no-one close to the person who lacks capacity to give an opinion about what is best for them, and:

- an NHS body is proposing to provide serious medical treatment or
- an NHS body or local authority is proposing to arrange accommodation in hospital or a care home or other longer-term accommodation and

    – the person will stay in hospital longer than 28 days, or
    – they will stay in a care home for more than eight weeks.

There are also some circumstances where an IMCA may be appointed on a discretionary basis. More guidance is available in chapter 10.

6.10   Sometimes the final outcome may not be what the person who lacks capacity wanted. For example, they might want to stay at home, but those caring for them might decide a move is in their best interests. In all cases, those making the decision must first consider other options that might restrict the person's rights and freedom of action less (see chapter 2, principle 5).

6.11   In some cases, there may be no alternative but to move the person. Such a move would normally require the person's formal consent if they had capacity to give, or refuse, it. In cases where a person lacks capacity to consent, section 5 of the Act allows carers to carry out actions relating to the move – as long as the Act's principles and the requirements for working out best interests have been followed. This applies even if the person continues to object to the move.

However, section 6 places clear limits on the use of force or restraint by only permitting restraint to be used (for example, to transport the person to their new home) where this is necessary to protect the person from harm and is a proportionate response to the risk of harm (see paragraphs 6.40–6.53). Any action taken to move the person concerned or their property could incur liability unless protected under section 5.

6.12   If there is a serious disagreement about the need to move the person that cannot be settled in any other way, the Court of Protection can be asked to decide what the person's best interests are and where they should live. For example, this could happen if members of a family disagree over what is best for a relative who lacks capacity to give or deny permission for a move.

6.13   In some circumstances, being placed in a hospital or care home may deprive the person of their liberty (see paragraphs 6.49–6.53). If this is the case, there is no protection from liability – even if the placement was considered to be in the best interests of the person (section 6(5)). It is up to the decision-maker to first look at a range of alternative and less restrictive options to see if there is any way of avoiding taking away the person's liberty.

6.14   If there is no alternative way of caring for the person, specific authority will be required to keep the person in a situation which deprives them of their liberty. For instance, sometimes the Court of Protection might be prepared to grant an order of which a consequence is the deprivation of a person's liberty – if it is satisfied that this is in the person's best interests. In other cases, if the person needs treatment for a mental disorder and meets the criteria for detention under the Mental Health Act 1983, this may be used to admit or keep the person in hospital (see chapter 13).

HEALTHCARE AND TREATMENT DECISIONS

6.15   Section 5 also allows actions to be taken to ensure a person who lacks capacity to consent receives necessary medical treatment. This could involve taking the person to hospital for out-patient treatment or arranging for admission to hospital. Even if a person who lacks capacity to consent objects to the proposed treatment or admission to hospital, the action might still be allowed under section 5 (but see paragraphs 6.20 and 6.22 below). But there are limits about whether force or restraint can be used to impose treatment (see paragraphs 6.40–6.53).

6.16   Major healthcare and treatment decisions – for example, major surgery or a decision that no attempt is to be made to resuscitate the patient (known as 'DNR' decisions) – will also need special consideration. Unless there is a valid and applicable advance decision to refuse the specific treatment, healthcare staff must carefully work out what would be in the person's best interests (see chapter 5). As part of the process of working this out, they will need to consider (where practical and appropriate):

■ the past and present wishes and feelings, beliefs and values of the person who lacks capacity to make the treatment decision, including any advance statement the person wrote setting out their wishes when they had capacity

■ the views of anyone previously named by the person as someone to be consulted

■ the views of anyone engaged in caring for the person

■ the views of anyone interested in their welfare, and

■ the views of any attorney or deputy appointed for the person.

In specific cases where there is no-one else available to consult about the person's best interests, an IMCA must be appointed to support and represent the person (see paragraph 6.9 above and chapter 10).

Healthcare staff must also consider whether there are alternative treatment options that might be less intrusive or restrictive (see chapter 2, principle 5). When deciding about the provision or withdrawal of life-sustaining treatment, anyone working out what is in the best interests of a person who lacks capacity must not be motivated by a desire to bring about the person's death (see chapter 5).

6.17   Multi-disciplinary meetings are often the best way to decide on a person's best interests. They bring together healthcare and social care staff with different skills to discuss the person's options and may involve those who are closest to the person concerned. But final responsibility for deciding what is in a person's best interest lies with the member of healthcare staff responsible for the person's treatment. They should record their decision, how they reached it and the reasons for it in the person's clinical notes. As long as they have recorded objective reasons to show that the decision is in the person's best interests, and the other requirements of section 5 of the Act are met, all healthcare staff taking actions in connection with the particular treatment will be protected from liability.

6.18   Some treatment decisions are so serious that the court has to make them – unless the person has previously made a Lasting Power of Attorney appointing an attorney to make such healthcare decisions for them (see chapter 7) or they have made a valid advance decision to refuse the proposed treatment (see chapter 9). The Court of Protection must be asked to make decisions relating to:[20]

- the proposed withholding or withdrawal of artificial nutrition and hydration (ANH) from a patient in a permanent vegetative state (PVS)
- cases where it is proposed that a person who lacks capacity to consent should donate an organ or bone marrow to another person
- the proposed non-therapeutic sterilisation of a person who lacks capacity to consent (for example, for contraceptive purposes)
- cases where there is a dispute about whether a particular treatment will be in a person's best interests.

See paragraphs 8.18–8.24 for more details on these types of cases.

6.19   This last category may include cases that introduce ethical dilemmas concerning untested or innovative treatments (for example, new treatments for variant Creutzfeldt-Jakob Disease (CDJ)) where it is not known if the treatment will be effective, or certain cases involving a termination of pregnancy. It may also include cases where there is conflict between professionals or between professionals and family members which cannot be resolved in any other way.

Where there is conflict, it is advisable for parties to get legal advice, though they may not necessarily be able to get legal aid to pay for this advice. Chapter 8 gives more information about the need to refer cases to court for a decision.

Who is protected from liability by section 5?

6.20   Section 5 of the Act is most likely to affect:

- family carers and other kinds of carers
- care workers
- healthcare and social care staff, and
- others who may occasionally be involved in the care or treatment of a person who lacks capacity to consent (for example, ambulance staff, housing workers, police officers and volunteer support workers).

6.21   At any time, it is likely that several people will be carrying out tasks that are covered by section 5 of the Act. Section 5 does not:

- give one person more rights than another to carry out tasks
- specify who has the authority to act in a specific instance

[20] The procedures resulting from those court judgments are set out in a Practice Note from the Official Solicitor (available at **www.officialsolicitor.gov.uk**) and will be set out in a Practice Direction from the new Court of Protection.

- allow somebody to make decisions relating to subjects other than the care or treatment of the person who lacks capacity, or
- allow somebody to give consent on behalf of a person who lacks capacity to do so.

6.22   To receive protection from liability under section 5, all actions must be related to the care or treatment of the person who lacks capacity to consent. Before taking action, carers must first reasonably believe that:

- the person lacks the capacity to make that particular decision at the time it needs to be made, and
- the action is in the person's best interests.

This is explained further in paragraphs 6.26–6.34 below.

[Scenario: Protecting multiple carers]

6.23   Section 5 may also protect carers who need to use the person's money to pay for goods or services that the person needs but lacks the capacity to purchase for themselves. However, there are strict controls over who may have access to another person's money. See paragraphs 6.56–6.66 for more information.

6.24   Carers who provide personal care services must not carry out specialist procedures that are normally done by trained healthcare staff. If the action involves medical treatment, the doctor or other member of healthcare staff with responsibility for the patient will be the decision-maker who has to decide whether the proposed treatment is in the person's best interests (see chapter 5). A doctor can delegate responsibility for giving the treatment to other people in the clinical team who have the appropriate skills or expertise. People who do more than their experience or qualifications allow may not be protected from liability.

Care planning

6.25   Decisions about a person's care or treatment are often made by a multi-disciplinary team (a team of professionals with different skills that contribute to a person's care), by drawing up a care plan for the person. The preparation of a care plan should always include an assessment of the person's capacity to consent to the actions covered by the care plan, and confirm that those actions are agreed to be in the person's best interests. Healthcare and social care staff may then be able to assume that any actions they take under the care plan are in the person's best interests, and therefore receive protection from liability under section 5. But a person's capacity and best interests must still be reviewed regularly.

What steps should people take to be protected from liability?

6.26   As well as taking the following steps, somebody who wants to be protected from liability should bear in mind the statutory principles set out in section 1 of the Act (see chapter 2).

6.27   First, reasonable steps must be taken to find out whether a person has the capacity to make a decision about the proposed action (section 5(1)(a)). If the person has capacity, they must give their consent for anyone to take an action on their behalf, so that the person taking the action is protected from liability. For guidance on what is classed as 'reasonable steps', see paragraphs 6.29–6.34. But reasonable steps must always include:

- taking all practical and appropriate steps to help people to make a decision about an action themselves, and
- applying the two-stage test of capacity (see chapter 4).

The person who is going to take the action must have a 'reasonable belief' that the individual lacks capacity to give consent for the action at the time it needs to be taken.

6.28   Secondly, the person proposing to take action must have reasonable grounds for believing that the action is in the best interests of the person who lacks capacity. They should apply all elements of the best interests checklist (see chapter 5), and in particular

- consider whether the person is likely to regain capacity to make this decision in the future. Can the action wait until then?
- consider whether a less restrictive option is available (chapter 2, principle 5), and
- have objective reasons for thinking an action is in the best interests of the person who lacks capacity to consent to it.

What is 'reasonable'?

6.29   As explained in chapter 4, anyone assessing a person's capacity to make decisions for themselves or give consent must focus wholly on whether the person has capacity to make a specific decision at the time it needs to be made and not the person's capacity to make decisions generally. For example, a carer helping a person to dress can assess a person's capacity to agree to their help by explaining the different options (getting dressed or staying in nightclothes), and the consequences (being able to go out, or staying in all day).

6.30   Carers do not have to be experts in assessing capacity. But they must be able to show that they have taken reasonable steps to find out if the person has the capacity to make the specific decision. Only then will they have reasonable grounds for believing the person lacks capacity in relation to that particular matter. See paragraphs 4.44–4.45 for guidance on what is classed as 'reasonable' – although this will vary, depending on circumstances.

6.31   For the majority of decisions, formal assessment processes are unlikely to be required. But in some circumstances, professional practice requires some formal procedures to be carried out (for example, where consent to medical treatment is required, the doctor will need to assess – and record the person's capacity to consent). Under section 5, carers and professionals will be protected from liability as long as they are able to provide some objective reasons that explain why they believe that the person lacks capacity to consent to the action. If somebody challenges their belief, both carers and professionals will be protected from liability as long as they can show that they took steps to find out whether the person has capacity and that they have a reasonable belief that the person lacks capacity.

6.32   Similarly, carers, relatives and others involved in caring for someone who lacks capacity must have reasonable grounds for believing that their action is in the person's best interests. They must not simply impose their own views. They must be able to show that they considered all relevant circumstances and applied the best interests checklist. This includes showing that they have tried to involve the person who lacks capacity, and find out their wishes and feelings, beliefs and values. They must also have asked other people's opinions, where practical and appropriate. If somebody challenges their decision, they will be protected from liability if they can show that it was reasonable for them to believe that their action was in the person's best interests – in all the circumstances of that particular case.

6.33   If healthcare and social care staff are involved, their skills and knowledge will affect what is classed as 'reasonable'. For example, a doctor assessing somebody's capacity to consent to treatment must demonstrate more skill than someone without medical training. They should also record in the person's healthcare record the steps they took and the reasons for the finding. Healthcare and social care staff should apply normal clinical and professional standards when deciding what treatments to offer. They must then decide whether the proposed treatment is in the best interests of the person who lacks capacity to consent. This includes considering all relevant circumstances and applying the best interests checklist (see chapter 5).

6.34 Healthcare and social care staff can be said to have 'reasonable grounds for believing' that a person lacks capacity if:

■ they are working to a person's care plan, and
■ the care planning process involved an assessment of the person's capacity to make a decision about actions in the care plan.

It is also reasonable for them to assume that the care planning process assessed a person's best interests. But they should still make every effort to communicate with the person to find out if they still lack capacity and the action is still in their best interests.

[*Scenario: Working with a care plan*]

What happens in emergency situations?

6.35 Sometimes people who lack capacity to consent will require emergency medical treatment to save their life or prevent them from serious harm. In these situations, what steps are 'reasonable' will differ to those in non-urgent cases. In emergencies, it will almost always be in the person's best interests to give urgent treatment without delay. One exception to this is when the healthcare staff giving treatment are satisfied that an advance decision to refuse treatment exists (see paragraph 6.37).

What happens in cases of negligence?

6.36 Section 5 does not provide a defence in cases of negligence – either in carrying out a particular act or by failing to act where necessary. For example, a doctor may be protected against a claim of battery for carrying out an operation that is in a person's best interests. But if they perform the operation negligently, they are not protected from a charge of negligence. So the person who lacks capacity has the same rights in cases of negligence as someone who has consented to the operation.

What is the effect of an advance decision to refuse treatment?

6.37 Sometimes people will make an advance decision to refuse treatment while they still have capacity to do so and before they need that particular treatment. Healthcare staff must respect this decision if it is valid and applies to the proposed treatment.

6.38 If healthcare staff are satisfied that an advance decision is valid and applies to the proposed treatment, they are not protected from liability if they give any treatment that goes against it. But they are protected from liability if they did not know about an advance decision or they are not satisfied that the advance decision is valid and applies in the current circumstances (section 26(2)). See chapter 9 for further guidance.

What limits are there on protection from liability?

6.39 Section 6 imposes some important limitations on acts which can be carried out with protection from liability under section 5 (as described in the first part of this chapter). The key areas where acts might not be protected from liability are where there is inappropriate use of restraint or where a person who lacks capacity is deprived of their liberty.

Using restraint

6.40   Section 6(4) of the Act states that someone is using restraint if they:

- use force – or threaten to use force – to make someone do something that they are resisting, or
- restrict a person's freedom of movement, whether they are resisting or not.

6.41   Any action intended to restrain a person who lacks capacity will not attract protection from liability unless the following two conditions are met:

- the person taking action must reasonably believe that restraint is necessary to prevent harm to the person who lacks capacity, and
- the amount or type of restraint used and the amount of time it lasts must be a proportionate response to the likelihood and seriousness of harm.

See paragraphs 6.44–6.48 for more explanation of the terms *necessary*, *harm* and a *proportionate response*.

6.42   Healthcare and social care staff should also refer to:

- professional and other guidance on restraint or physical intervention, such as that issued by the Department of Health[21] or Welsh Assembly Government,[22] and
- limitations imposed by regulations and standards, such as the national minimum standards for care services (see chapter 14).

6.43   In addition to the requirements of the Act, the common law imposes a duty of care on healthcare and social care staff in respect of all people to whom they provide services. Therefore if a person who lacks capacity to consent has challenging behaviour, or is in the acute stages of illness causing them to act in way which may cause harm to others, staff may, under the common law, take appropriate and necessary action to restrain or remove the person, in order to prevent harm, both to the person concerned and to anyone else.

However, within this context, the common law would not provide sufficient grounds for an action that would have the effect of depriving someone of their liberty (see paragraphs 6.49–6.53).

When might restraint be 'necessary'?

6.44   Anybody considering using restraint must have objective reasons to justify that restraint is necessary. They must be able to show that the person being cared for is likely to suffer harm unless proportionate restraint is used. A carer or professional must not use restraint just so that they can do something more easily. If restraint is necessary to prevent harm to the person who lacks capacity, it must be the minimum amount of force for the shortest time possible.

[*Scenario: Appropriate use of restraint*]

6.45   The Act does not define 'harm', because it will vary depending on the situation. For example,

---

[21] For guidance on using restraint with people with learning disabilities and autistic spectrum disorder, see Guidance for restrictive physical interventions (published by the Department of Health and Department for Education and Skills and available at **www.dh.gov.uk/assetRoot/04/06/84/61/04068461.pdf**).

[22] In Wales, the relevant guidance is the Welsh Assembly Government's Framework for restrictive physical intervention policy and practice (available at **www.childrenfirst.wales.gov.uk/content/framework/phys-int-e.pdf**).

- a person with learning disabilities might run into a busy road without warning, if they do not understand the dangers of cars
- a person with dementia may wander away from home and get lost, if they cannot remember where they live
- a person with manic depression might engage in excessive spending during a manic phase, causing them to get into debt
- a person may also be at risk of harm if they behave in a way that encourages others to assault or exploit them (for example, by behaving in a dangerously provocative way).

6.46   Common sense measures can often help remove the risk of harm (for example, by locking away poisonous chemicals or removing obstacles). Also, care planning should include risk assessments and set out appropriate actions to try to prevent possible risks. But it is impossible to remove all risk, and a proportionate response is needed when the risk of harm does arise.

What is a 'proportionate response'?

6.47   A 'proportionate response' means using the least intrusive type and minimum amount of restraint to achieve a specific outcome in the best interests of the person who lacks capacity. On occasions when the use of force may be necessary, carers and healthcare and social care staff should use the minimum amount of force for the shortest possible time.

For example, a carer may need to hold a person's arm while they cross the road, if the person does not understand the dangers of roads. But it would not be a proportionate response to stop the person going outdoors at all. It may be appropriate to have a secure lock on a door that faces a busy road, but it would not be a proportionate response to lock someone in a bedroom all the time to prevent them from attempting to cross the road.

6.48   Carers and healthcare and social care staff should consider less restrictive options before using restraint. Where possible, they should ask other people involved in the person's care what action they think is necessary to protect the person from harm. For example, it may be appropriate to get an advocate to work with the person to see if they can avoid or minimise the need for restraint to be used.

When are acts seen as depriving a person of their liberty?

6.49   Although section 5 of the Act permits the use of restraint where it is necessary under the above conditions, section 6(5) confirms that there is no protection under the Act for actions that result in someone being deprived of their liberty (as defined by Article 5(1) of the European Convention on Human Rights). This applies not only to public authorities covered by the Human Rights Act 1998 but to everyone who might otherwise get protection under section 5 of the Act. It also applies to attorneys or deputies – they cannot give permission for an action that takes away a person's liberty.

6.50   Sometimes there is no alternative way to provide care or treatment other than depriving the person of their liberty. In this situation, some people may be detained in hospital under the Mental Health Act 1983 – but this only applies to people who require hospital treatment for a mental disorder (see chapter 13). Otherwise, actions that amount to a deprivation of liberty will not be lawful unless formal authorisation is obtained.

6.51   In some cases, the Court of Protection might grant an order that permits the deprivation of a person's liberty, if it is satisfied that this is in a person's best interests.

6.52   It is difficult to define the difference between actions that amount to a restriction of someone's liberty and those that result in a deprivation of liberty. In recent legal cases, the European Court of Human Rights said that the difference was 'one of degree or intensity, not one of nature or substance'.[23] There must therefore be particular factors in the specific situation of the person concerned which provide the 'degree' or 'intensity' to result in a deprivation of liberty. In practice, this can relate to:

- the type of care being provided
- how long the situation lasts
- its effects, or
- the way in a particular situation came about.[24]

The European Court of Human Rights has identified the following as factors contributing to deprivation of liberty in its judgments on cases to date:

- restraint was used, including sedation, to admit a person who is resisting
- professionals exercised complete and effective control over care and movement for a significant period
- professionals exercised control over assessments, treatment, contacts and residence
- the person would be prevented from leaving if they made a meaningful attempt to do so
- a request by carers for the person to be discharged to their care was refused
- the person was unable to maintain social contacts because of restrictions placed on access to other people
- the person lost autonomy because they were under continuous supervision and control.[25]

6.53   The Government has announced that it intends to amend the Act to introduce new procedures and provisions for people who lack capacity to make relevant decisions but who need to be deprived of their liberty, in their best interests, otherwise than under the Mental Health Act 1983 (the so-called 'Bournewood provisions'). This chapter will be fully revised in due course to reflect those changes. Information about the Government's current proposals in respect of the Bournewood safeguards is available on the Department of Health website. This information includes draft illustrative Code of Practice guidance about the proposed safeguards. See paragraphs 13.52–13.55 for more details.

How does section 5 apply to attorneys and deputies?

6.54   Section 5 does not provide protection for actions that go against the decision of someone who has been authorised to make decisions for a person who lacks capacity to make such decision for themselves. For instance, if someone goes against the decision of an attorney acting under a Lasting Power of Attorney (LPA) (see chapter 7) or a deputy appointed by the Court of Protection (see chapter 8), they will not be protected under section 5.

6.55   Attorneys and deputies must only make decisions within the scope of the authority of the LPA or court order. Sometimes carers or healthcare and social care staff might feel that an attorney or deputy is making decisions they should not be making, or that are not in a person's best interests. If this is the case, and the disagree-

---

[23] *HL v. The United Kingdom (Application no. 45508/99)*. Judgment 5 October 2004, paragraph 89.

[24] In *HL v. UK* (also known as the 'Bournewood' case), the European Court said that 'the key factor in the present case [is] that the health care professionals treating and managing the applicant exercised complete and effective control over his care and movements'. They found 'the concrete situation was that the applicant was under continuous supervision and control and was not free to leave'.

[25] These are listed in the Department of Health's draft illustrative Code of Practice guidance about the proposed safeguards, **www.dh.gov.uk/assetRoot/04/14/17/64/04141764.pdf**

ment cannot be settled any other way, either the carers, the staff or the attorney or deputy can apply to the Court of Protection. If the dispute concerns the provision of medical treatment, medical staff can still give life-sustaining treatment, or treatment which stops a person's condition getting seriously worse, while the court is coming to a decision (section 6(6)).

Who can pay for goods or services?

6.56   Carers may have to spend money on behalf of someone who lacks capacity to purchase necessary goods or services. For example, they may need to pay for a milk delivery or for a chiropodist to provide a service at the person's home. In some cases, they might have to pay for more costly arrangements such as house repairs or organising a holiday. Carers are likely to be protected from liability if their actions are properly taken under section 5, and in the best interests of the person who lacks capacity.

6.57   In general, a contract entered into by a person who lacks capacity to make the contract cannot be enforced if the other person knows, or must be taken to have known, of the lack of capacity. Section 7 of the Act modifies this rule and states that where the contract is for 'necessary' goods or services for a person who lacks capacity to make the arrangements for themselves, that person must pay a reasonable price for them.

What are necessary goods and services?

6.58   'Necessary' means something that is suitable to the person's condition in life (their place in society, rather than any mental or physical condition) and their actual requirements when the goods or services are provided (section 7(2)). The aim is to make sure that people can enjoy a similar standard of living and way of life to those they had before lacking capacity. For example, if a person who now lacks capacity previously chose to buy expensive designer clothes, these are still necessary goods – as long as they can still afford them. But they would not be necessary for a person who always wore cheap clothes, no matter how wealthy they were.

6.59   Goods are not necessary if the person already has a sufficient supply of them. For example, buying one or two new pairs of shoes for a person who lacks capacity could be necessary. But a dozen pairs would probably not be necessary.

How should payments be arranged?

6.60   If a person lacks capacity to arrange for payment for necessary goods and services, sections 5 and 8 allow a carer to arrange payment on their behalf.

6.61   The carer must first take reasonable steps to check whether a person can arrange for payment themselves, or has the capacity to consent to the carer doing it for them. If the person lacks the capacity to consent or pay themselves, the carer must decide what goods or services would be necessary for the person and in their best interests. The carer can then lawfully deal with payment for those goods and services in one of three ways:

■ If neither the carer nor the person who lacks capacity can produce the necessary funds, the carer may promise that the person who lacks capacity will pay. A supplier may not be happy with this, or the carer may be worried that they will be held responsible for any debt. In such cases, the carer must follow the formal steps in paragraphs 6.62–6.66 below.

■ If the person who lacks capacity has cash, the carer may use that money to pay for goods or services (for example, to pay the milkman or the hairdresser).

■ The carer may choose to pay for the goods or services with their own money. The person who lacks capacity must pay them back. This may involve using cash in the person's possession or running up an IOU. (This is not appropriate for paid care workers, whose contracts might stop them handling their clients' money.) The carer must follow formal steps to get money held in a bank or building society account (see paragraphs 6.63–6.66 below).

6.62   Carers should keep bills, receipts and other proof of payment when paying for goods and services. They will need these documents when asking to get money back. Keeping appropriate financial records and documentation is a requirement of the national minimum standards for care homes or domiciliary care agencies.

Access to a person's assets

6.63   The Act does not give a carer or care worker access to a person's income or assets. Nor does it allow them to sell the person's property.

6.64   Anyone wanting access to money in a person's bank or building society will need formal legal authority. They will also need legal authority to sell a person's property. Such authority could be given in a Lasting Power of Attorney (LPA) appointing an attorney to deal with property and affairs, or in an order of the Court of Protection (either a single decision of the court or an order appointing a deputy to make financial decisions for the person who lacks capacity to make such decisions).

[*Scenario: Being granted access to a person's assets*]

6.65   Sometimes another person will already have legal control of the finances and property of a person who lacks capacity to manage their own affairs. This could be an attorney acting under a registered EPA or an appropriate LPA (see chapter 7) or a deputy appointed by the Court of Protection (see chapter 8). Or it could be someone (usually a carer) that has the right to act as an 'appointee' (under Social Security Regulations) and claim benefits for a person who lacks capacity to make their own claim and use the money on the person's behalf. But an appointee cannot deal with other assets or savings from sources other than benefits.

6.66   Section 6(6) makes clear that a family carer or other carer cannot make arrangements for goods or services to be supplied to a person who lacks capacity if this conflicts with a decision made by someone who has formal powers over the person's money and property, such as an attorney or deputy acting within the scope of their authority. Where there is no conflict and the carer has paid for necessary goods and services the carer may ask for money back from an attorney, a deputy or where relevant, an appointee.

7 WHAT DOES THE ACT SAY ABOUT LASTING POWERS OF ATTORNEY?

This chapter explains what Lasting Powers of Attorney (LPAs) are and how they should be used. It also sets out:

- how LPAs differ from Enduring Powers of Attorney (EPAs)
- the types of decisions that people can appoint attorneys to make (attorneys are also called 'donees' in the Act)
- situations in which an LPA can and cannot be used
- the duties and responsibilities of attorneys
- the standards required of attorneys, and
- measures for dealing with attorneys who don't meet appropriate standards.

This chapter also explains what should happen to EPAs that were made before the Act comes into force.

In this chapter, as throughout the Code, a person's capacity (or lack of capacity) refers specifically to their capacity to make a particular decision at the time it needs to be made.

Quick summary

Anyone asked to be an attorney should:

- consider whether they have the skills and ability to act as an attorney (especially if it is for a property and affairs LPA)
- ask themselves whether they actually want to be an attorney and take on the duties and responsibilities of the role.

Before acting under an LPA, attorneys must:

- make sure the LPA has been registered with the Public Guardian
- take all practical and appropriate steps to help the donor make the particular decision for themselves.

When acting under an LPA:

- make sure that the Act's statutory principles are followed
- check whether the person has the capacity to make that particular decision for themselves. If they do:
  - a personal welfare LPA cannot be used – the person must make the decision
  - a property and affairs LPA can be used even if the person has capacity to make the decision, unless they have stated in the LPA that they should make decisions for themselves when they have capacity to do so.

At all times, remember:

- anything done under the authority of the LPA must be in the person's best interests
- anyone acting as an attorney must have regard to guidance in this Code of Practice that is relevant to the decision that is to be made
- attorneys must fulfil their responsibilities and duties to the person who lacks capacity.

What is a Lasting Power of Attorney (LPA)?

7.1   Sometimes one person will want to give another person authority to make a decision on their behalf. A power of attorney is a legal document that allows them to do so. Under a power of attorney, the chosen person (the attorney or donee) can make decisions that are as valid as one made by the person (the donor).

7.2   Before the Enduring Powers of Attorney Act 1985, every power of attorney automatically became invalid as soon as the donor lacked the capacity to make their own decision. But that Act introduced the Enduring Power of Attorney (EPA). An EPA allows an attorney to make decisions about property and financial affairs even if the donor lacks capacity to manage their own affairs.

7.3   The Mental Capacity Act replaces the EPA with the Lasting Power of Attorney (LPA). It also increases the range of different types of decisions that people can authorise others to make on their behalf. As well as property and affairs (including financial matters), LPAs can also cover personal welfare (including healthcare and consent to medical treatment) for people who lack capacity to make such decisions for themselves.

7.4   The donor can choose one person or several to make different kinds of decisions. See paragraphs 7.21–7.31 for more information about personal welfare LPAs. See paragraphs 7.32–7.42 for more information about LPAs on property and affairs.

How do LPAs compare to EPAs?

7.5   There are a number of differences between LPAs and EPAs. These are summarised as follows:

- EPAs only cover property and affairs. LPAs can also cover personal welfare.
- Donors must use the relevant specific form (prescribed in regulations) to make EPAs and LPAs. There are different forms for EPAs, personal welfare LPAs and property and affairs LPAs.
- EPAs must be registered with the Public Guardian when the donor can no longer manage their own affairs (or when they start to lose capacity). But LPAs can be registered at any time before they are used – before or after the donor lacks capacity to make particular decisions that the LPA covers. If the LPA is not registered, it can't be used.
- EPAs can be used while the donor still has capacity to manage their own property and affairs, as can property and affairs LPAs, so long as the donor does not say otherwise in the LPA. But personal welfare LPAs can only be used once the donor lacks capacity to make the welfare decision in question.
- Once the Act comes into force, only LPAs can be made but existing EPAs will continue to be valid. There will be different laws and procedures for EPAs and LPAs.
- Attorneys making decisions under a registered EPA or LPA must follow the Act's principles and act in the best interests of the donor.
- The duties under the law of agency apply to attorneys of both EPAs and LPAs (see paragraphs 7.58–7.68 below).
- Decisions that the courts have made about EPAs may also affect how people use LPAs.
- Attorneys acting under an LPA have a legal duty to have regard to the guidance in this Code of Practice. EPA attorneys do not. But the Code's guidance will still be helpful to them.

How does a donor create an LPA?

7.6   The donor must also follow the right procedures for creating and registering an LPA, as set out below. Otherwise the LPA might not be valid. It is not always necessary to get legal advice. But it is a good idea for certain cases (for example, if the donor's circumstances are complicated).

7.7   Only adults aged 18 or over can make an LPA, and they can only make an LPA if they have the capacity to do so. For an LPA to be valid:

- the LPA must be a written document set out in the statutory form prescribed by regulations[26]
- the document must include prescribed information about the nature and effect of the LPA (as set out in the regulations)
- the donor must sign a statement saying that they have read the prescribed information (or somebody has read it to them) and that they want the LPA to apply when they no longer have capacity

[26] The prescribed forms will be available from the Office of the Public Guardian (OPG) or from legal stationers.

- the document must name people (not any of the attorneys) who should be told about an application to register the LPA, or it should say that there is no-one they wish to be told
- the attorneys must sign a statement saying that they have read the prescribed information and that they understand their duties – in particular the duty to act in the donor's best interests
- the document must include a certificate completed by an independent third party,[27] confirming that:
  - in their opinion, the donor understands the LPA's purpose
  - nobody used fraud or undue pressure to trick or force the donor into making the LPA and
  - there is nothing to stop the LPA being created.

Who can be an attorney?

7.8   A donor should think carefully before choosing someone to be their attorney. An attorney should be someone who is trustworthy, competent and reliable. They should have the skills and ability to carry out the necessary tasks.

7.9   Attorneys must be at least 18 years of age. For property and affairs LPAs, the attorney could be either:

- an individual (as long as they are not bankrupt at the time the LPA is made), or
- a trust corporation (often parts of banks or other financial institutions).

If an attorney nominated under a property and affairs LPA becomes bankrupt at any point, they will no longer be allowed to act as an attorney for property and affairs. People who are bankrupt can still act as an attorney for personal welfare LPAs.

7.10   The donor must name an individual rather than a job title in a company or organisation, (for example, 'The Director of Adult Services' or 'my solicitor' would not be sufficient). A paid care worker (such as a care home manager) should not agree to act as an attorney, apart from in unusual circumstances (for example, if they are the only close relative of the donor).

7.11   Section 10(4) of the Act allows the donor to appoint two or more attorneys and to specify whether they should act 'jointly', 'jointly and severally', or 'jointly in respect of some matters and jointly and severally in respect of others'.

- Joint attorneys must always act together. All attorneys must agree decisions and sign any relevant documents.
- Joint and several attorneys can act together but may also act independently if they wish. Any action taken by any attorney alone is as valid as if they were the only attorney.

7.12   The donor may want to appoint attorneys to act jointly in some matters but jointly and severally in others. For example, a donor could choose to appoint two or more financial attorneys jointly and severally. But they might say then when selling the donor's house, the attorneys must act jointly. The donor may appoint welfare attorneys to act jointly and severally but specify that they must act jointly in relation to giving consent to surgery. If a donor who has appointed two or more attorneys does not specify how they should act, they must always act jointly (section 10(5)).

7.13   Section 10(8) says that donors may choose to name replacement attorneys to take over the duties in certain circumstances (for example, in the event of an attorney's death). The donor may name a specific attorney to be replaced, or the replacements

---

[27] Details of who may and who may not be a certificate provider will be available in regulations. The OPG will produce guidance for certificate providers on their role.

can take over from any attorney, if necessary. Donors cannot give their attorneys the right to appoint a substitute or successor.

How should somebody register and use an LPA?

7.14   An LPA must be registered with the Office of the Public Guardian (OPG) before it can be used. An unregistered LPA will not give the attorney any legal powers to make a decision for the donor. The donor can register the LPA while they are still capable, or the attorney can apply to register the LPA at any time.

7.15   There are advantages in registering the LPA soon after the donor makes it (for example, to ensure that there is no delay when the LPA needs to be used). But if this has not been done, an LPA can be registered after the donor lacks the capacity to make a decision covered by the LPA.

7.16   If an LPA is unregistered, attorneys must register it before making any decisions under the LPA. If the LPA has been registered but not used for some time, the attorney should tell the OPG when they begin to act under it – so that the attorney can be sent relevant, up-to-date information about the rules governing LPAs.

7.17   While they still have capacity, donors should let the OPG know of permanent changes of address for the donor or the attorney or any other changes in circumstances. If the donor no longer has capacity to do this, attorneys should report any such changes to the OPG. Examples include an attorney of a property and affairs LPA becoming bankrupt or the ending of a marriage between the donor and their attorney. This will help keep OPG records up to date, and will make sure that attorneys do not make decisions that they no longer have the authority to make.

What guidance should an attorney follow?

7.18   Section 9(4) states that attorneys must meet the requirements set out in the Act. Most importantly, they have to follow the statutory principles (section 1) and make decisions in the best interests of the person who lacks capacity (section 4). They must also respect any conditions or restrictions that the LPA document contains. See chapter 2 for guidance on how to apply the Act's principles.

7.19   Chapter 3 gives suggestions of ways to help people make their own decisions in accordance with the Act's second principle . Attorneys should also refer to the guidance in chapter 4 when assessing the donor's capacity to make particular decisions, and in particular, should follow the steps suggested for establishing a 'reasonable belief' that the donor lacks capacity (see paragraphs 4.44–4.45). Assessments of capacity or best interests must not be based merely on:

- a donor's age or appearance, or
- unjustified assumptions about any condition they might have or their behaviour.

7.20   When deciding what is in the donor's best interests, attorneys should refer to the guidance in chapter 5. In particular, they must consider the donor's past and present wishes and feelings, beliefs and values. Where practical and appropriate, they should consult with:

- anyone involved in caring for the donor
- close relatives and anyone else with an interest in their welfare
- other attorneys appointed by the donor.

See paragraphs 7.52–7.68 for a description of an attorney's duties.

[*Scenario: Making decisions in a donor's best interests*]

What decisions can an LPA attorney make?

Personal welfare LPAs

7.21   LPAs can be used to appoint attorneys to make decisions about personal welfare, which can include healthcare and medical treatment decisions. Personal welfare LPAs might include decisions about:

- where the donor should live and who they should live with
- the donor's day-to-day care, including diet and dress
- who the donor may have contact with
- consenting to or refusing medical examination and treatment on the donor's behalf
- arrangements needed for the donor to be given medical, dental or optical treatment
- assessments for and provision of community care services
- whether the donor should take part in social activities, leisure activities, education or training
- the donor's personal correspondence and papers
- rights of access to personal information about the donor, or
- complaints about the donor's care or treatment.

7.22   The standard form for personal welfare LPAs allows attorneys to make decisions about anything that relates to the donor's personal welfare. But donors can add restrictions or conditions to areas where they would not wish the attorney to have the power to act. For example, a donor might only want an attorney to make decisions about their social care and not their healthcare. There are particular rules for LPAs authorising an attorney to make decisions about life-sustaining treatment (see paragraphs 7.30–7.31 below).

7.23   A general personal welfare LPA gives the attorney the right to make all of the decisions set out above although this is not a full list of the actions they can take or decisions they can make. However, a personal welfare LPA can only be used at a time when the donor lacks capacity to make a specific welfare decision.

[Scenario: Denying attorneys the right to make certain decisions]

7.24   Before making a decision under a personal welfare LPA, the attorney must be sure that:

- the LPA has been registered with the OPG
- the donor lacks the capacity to make the particular decision or the attorney reasonably believes that the donor lacks capacity to take the decisions covered by the LPA (having applied the Act's principles), and
- they are making the decision in the donor's best interests.

7.25   When healthcare or social care staff are involved in preparing a care plan for someone who has appointed a personal welfare attorney, they must first assess whether the donor has capacity to agree to the care plan or to parts of it. If the donor lacks capacity, professionals must then consult the attorney and get their agreement to the care plan. They will also need to consult the attorney when considering what action is in the person's best interests.

Personal welfare LPAs that authorise an attorney to make healthcare decisions

7.26   A personal welfare LPA allows attorneys to make decisions to accept or refuse healthcare or treatment unless the donor has stated clearly in the LPA that they do not want the attorney to make these decisions.

7.27   Even where the LPA includes healthcare decisions, attorneys do not have the right to consent to or refuse treatment in situations where:

- **the donor has capacity to make the particular healthcare decision (section 11(7)(a))**

  An attorney has no decision-making power if the donor can make their own treatment decisions.

- **the donor has made an advance decision to refuse the proposed treatment (section 11(7)(b))**

  An attorney cannot consent to treatment if the donor has made a valid and applicable advance decision to refuse a specific treatment (see chapter 9). But if the donor made an LPA after the advance decision, and gave the attorney the right to consent to or refuse the treatment, the attorney can choose not to follow the advance decision.

- **a decision relates to life-sustaining treatment (section 11(7)(c))**

  An attorney has no power to consent to or refuse life-sustaining treatment, unless the LPA document expressly authorises this (see paragraphs 7.30–7.31 below).

- **the donor is detained under the Mental Health Act (section 28)**

  An attorney cannot consent to or refuse treatment for a mental disorder for a patient detained under the Mental Health Act 1983 (see also chapter 13).

7.28 LPAs cannot give attorneys the power to demand specific forms of medical treatment that healthcare staff do not believe are necessary or appropriate for the donor's particular condition.

7.29 Attorneys must always follow the Act's principles and make decisions in the donor's best interests. If healthcare staff disagree with the attorney's assessment of best interests, they should discuss the case with other medical experts and/or get a formal second opinion. Then they should discuss the matter further with the attorney. If they cannot settle the disagreement, they can apply to the Court of Protection (see paragraphs 7.45–7.49 below). While the court is coming to a decision, healthcare staff can give life-sustaining treatment to prolong the donor's life or stop their condition getting worse.

Personal welfare LPAs that authorise an attorney to make decisions about life-sustaining treatment

7.30 An attorney can only consent to or refuse life-sustaining treatment on behalf of the donor if, when making the LPA, the donor has specifically stated in the LPA document that they want the attorney to have this authority.

7.31 As with all decisions, an attorney must act in the donor's best interests when making decisions about such treatment. This will involve applying the best interests checklist (see chapter 5) and consulting with carers, family members and others interested in the donor's welfare. In particular, the attorney must not be motivated in any way by the desire to bring about the donor's death (see paragraphs 5.29–5.36). Anyone who doubts that the attorney is acting in the donor's best interests can apply to the Court of Protection for a decision.

[Scenario: Making decisions about life-sustaining treatment]

Property and affairs LPAs

7.32 A donor can make an LPA giving an attorney the right to make decisions about property and affairs (including financial matters). Unless the donor states otherwise, once the LPA is registered, the attorney is allowed to make all decisions about the donor's property and affairs even if the donor still has capacity to make the decisions for themselves. In this situation, the LPA will continue to apply when the donor no longer has capacity.

7.33   Alternatively a donor can state in the LPA document that the LPA should only apply when they lack capacity to make a relevant decision. It is the donor's responsibility to decide how their capacity should then be assessed. For example, the donor may trust the attorney to carry out an assessment, or they may say that the LPA only applies if their GP or another doctor confirms in writing that they lack capacity to make specific decisions about property or finances. Financial institutions may wish to see the written confirmation before recognising the attorney's authority to act under the LPA.

7.34   The fact that someone has made a property and affairs LPA does not mean that they cannot continue to carry out financial transactions for themselves. The donor may have full capacity, but perhaps anticipates that they may lack capacity at some future time. Or they may have fluctuating or partial capacity and therefore be able to make some decisions (or at some times), but need an attorney to make others (or at other times). The attorney should allow and encourage the donor to do as much as possible, and should only act when the donor asks them to or to make those decisions the donor lacks capacity to make. However, in other cases, the donor may wish to hand over responsibility for all decisions to the attorney, even those they still have capacity to make.

7.35   If the donor restricts the decisions an attorney can make, banks may ask the attorney to sign a declaration that protects the bank from liability if the attorney misuses the account.[28]

7.36   If a donor does not restrict decisions the attorney can make, the attorney will be able to decide on any or all of the person's property and financial affairs. This might include:

- buying or selling property
- opening, closing or operating any bank, building society or other account
- giving access to the donor's financial information
- claiming, receiving and using (on the donor's behalf) all benefits, pensions, allowances and rebates (unless the Department for Work and Pensions has already appointed someone and everyone is happy for this to continue)
- receiving any income, inheritance or other entitlement on behalf of the donor
- dealing with the donor's tax affairs
- paying the donor's mortgage, rent and household expenses
- insuring, maintaining and repairing the donor's property
- investing the donor's savings
- making limited gifts on the donor's behalf (but see paragraphs 7.40–7.42 below)
- paying for private medical care and residential care or nursing home fees
- applying for any entitlement to funding for NHS care, social care or adaptations
- using the donor's money to buy a vehicle or any equipment or other help they need
- repaying interest and capital on any loan taken out by the donor.

7.37   A general property and affairs LPA will allow the attorney to carry out any or all of the actions above (although this is not a full list of the actions they can take). However, the donor may want to specify the types of powers they wish the attorney to have, or to exclude particular types of decisions. If the donor holds any assets as trustee, they should get legal advice about how the LPA may affect this.

7.38   The attorney must make these decisions personally and cannot generally give someone else authority to carry out their duties (see paragraphs 7.61–7.62 below).

---

[28] See British Banking Association's guidance for bank staff on 'Banking for mentally incapacitated and learning disabled customers'.

But if the donor wants the attorney to be able to give authority to a specialist to make specific decisions, they need to state this clearly in the LPA document (for example, appointing an investment manager to make particular investment decisions).

7.39   Donors may like to appoint someone (perhaps a family member or a professional) to go through their accounts with the attorney from time to time. This might help to reassure donors that somebody will check their financial affairs when they lack capacity to do so. It may also be helpful for attorneys to arrange a regular check that everything is being done properly. The donor should ensure that the person is willing to carry out this role and is prepared to ask for the accounts if the attorney does not provide them. They should include this arrangement in the signed LPA document. The LPA should also say whether the person can charge a fee for this service.

What gifts can an attorney make under a property and affairs LPA?

7.40   An attorney can only make gifts of the donor's money or belongings to people who are related to or connected with the donor (including the attorney) on specific occasions, including:

- births or birthdays
- weddings or wedding anniversaries
- civil partnership ceremonies or anniversaries, or
- any other occasion when families, friends or associates usually give presents (section 12(3)(b)).

7.41   If the donor previously made donations to any charity regularly or from time to time, the attorney can make donations from the person's funds. This also applies if the donor could have been expected to make such payments (section 12(2)(b)). But the value of any gift or donation must be reasonable and take into account the size of the donor's estate. For example, it would not be reasonable to buy expensive gifts at Christmas if the donor was living on modest means and had to do without essential items in order to pay for them.

7.42   The donor cannot use the LPA to make more extensive gifts than those allowed under section 12 of the Act. But they can impose stricter conditions or restrictions on the attorney's powers to make gifts. They should state these restrictions clearly in the LPA document when they are creating it. When deciding on appropriate gifts, the attorney should consider the donor's wishes and feelings to work out what would be in the donor's best interests. The attorney can apply to the Court of Protection for permission to make gifts that are not included in the LPA (for example, for tax planning purposes).

Are there any other restrictions on attorneys' powers?

7.43   Attorneys are not protected from liability if they do something that is intended to restrain the donor, unless:

- the attorney reasonably believes that the donor lacks capacity to make the decision in question, and
- the attorney reasonably believes that restraint is necessary to prevent harm to the donor, and
- the type of restraint used is in proportion to the likelihood and the seriousness of the harm.

If an attorney needs to make a decision or take action which may involve the use of restraint, they should take account of the guidance set out in chapter 6.

7.44   Attorneys have no authority to take actions that result in the donor being deprived of their liberty. Any deprivation of liberty will only be lawful if this has been properly authorised and there is other protection available for the person who lacks capacity. An example would be the protection around detention under the Mental Health Act 1983 (see chapter 13) or a court ruling. Chapter 6 gives more guidance on working out whether an action is restraint or a deprivation of liberty.

What powers does the Court of Protection have over LPAs?

7.45   The Court of Protection has a range of powers to:

- determine whether an LPA is valid
- give directions about using the LPA, and
- to remove an attorney (for example, if the attorney does not act in the best interests of the donor).

Chapter 8 gives more information about the Court of Protection's powers.

7.46   If somebody has doubts over whether an LPA is valid, they can ask the court to decide whether the LPA:

- meets the Act's requirements
- has been revoked (cancelled) by the donor, or
- has come to an end for any other reason.

7.47   The court can also stop somebody registering an LPA or rule that an LPA is invalid if:

- the donor made the LPA as a result of undue pressure or fraud, or
- the attorney behaves, has behaved or is planning to behave in a way that goes against their duties or is not in the donor's best interests.

7.48   The court can also clarify an LPA's meaning, if it is not clear, and it can tell attorneys how they should use an LPA. If an attorney thinks that an LPA does not give them enough powers, they can ask the court to extend their powers – if the donor no longer has capacity to authorise this. The court can also authorise an attorney to give a gift that the Act does not normally allow (section 12(2)), if it is in the donor's best interests.

7.49   All attorneys should keep records of their dealings with the donor's affairs (see also paragraph 7.67 below). The court can order attorneys to produce records (for example, financial accounts) and to provide specific reports, information or documentation. If somebody has concerns about an attorney's payment or expenses, the court could resolve the matter.

What responsibilities do attorneys have?

7.50   A donor cannot insist on somebody agreeing to become an attorney. It is down to the proposed attorney to decide whether to take on this responsibility. When an attorney accepts the role by signing the LPA document, this is confirmation that they are willing to act under the LPA once it is registered. An attorney can withdraw from the appointment if they ever become unable or unwilling to act, but if the LPA has been registered they must follow the correct procedures for withdrawing (see paragraph 7.66 below).

7.51   Once the attorney starts to act under an LPA, they must meet certain standards. If they don't carry out the duties below, they could be removed from the role. In some circumstances they could face charges of fraud or negligence.

What duties does the Act impose?

7.52   Attorneys acting under an LPA have a duty to:

- follow the Act's statutory principles (see chapter 2)
- make decisions in the donor's best interests
- have regard to the guidance in the Code of Practice
- only make those decisions the LPA gives them authority to make.

Principles and best interests

7.53   Attorneys must act in accordance with the Act's statutory principles (section 1) and in the best interests of the donor (the steps for working out best interests are set out in section 4). In particular, attorneys must consider whether the donor has capacity to make the decision for themselves. If not, they should consider whether the donor is likely to regain capacity to make the decision in the future. If so, it may be possible to delay the decision until the donor can make it.

The Code of Practice

7.54   As well as this chapter, attorneys should pay special attention to the following guidance set out in the Code:

- chapter 2, which sets out how the Act's principles should be applied
- chapter 3, which describes the steps which can be taken to try to help the person make decisions for themselves
- chapter 4, which describes the Act's definition of lack of capacity and gives guidance on assessing capacity, and
- chapter 5, which gives guidance on working out the donor's best interests.

7.55   In some circumstances, attorneys might also find it useful to refer to guidance in:

- chapter 6, which explains when attorneys who have caring responsibilities may have protection from liability and gives guidance on the few circumstances when the Act allows restraint in connection with care and treatment
- chapter 8, which gives a summary of the Court of Protection's powers relating to LPAs
- chapter 9, which explains how LPAs may be affected if the donor has made an advance decision to refuse treatment, and
- chapter 15, which describes ways to settle disagreements.

Only making decisions covered by an LPA

7.56   A personal welfare attorney has no authority to make decisions about a donor's property and affairs (such as their finances). A property and affairs attorney has no authority in decisions about a donor's personal care. (But the same person could be appointed in separate LPAs to carry out both these roles.) Under any LPA, the attorney will have authority in a wide range of decisions. But if a donor includes restrictions in the LPA document, this will limit the attorney's authority (section 9(4)(b)). If the attorney thinks that they need greater powers, they can apply to the Court of Protection which may decide to give the attorney the authority required or alternatively to appoint the attorney as a deputy with the necessary powers (see chapter 8).

7.57   It is good practice for decision-makers to consult attorneys about any decision or action, whether or not it is covered by the LPA. This is because an attorney is likely to have known the donor for some time and may have important information about their wishes and feelings. Researchers can also consult attorneys if they are thinking about involving the donor in research (see chapter 11).

[*Scenario: Consulting attorneys*]

What are an attorney's other duties?

7.58 An attorney appointed under an LPA is acting as the chosen agent of the donor and therefore, under the law of agency, the attorney has certain duties towards the donor. An attorney takes on a role which carries a great deal of power, which they must use carefully and responsibly. They have a duty to:

- apply certain standards of care and skill (duty of care) when making decisions
- carry out the donor's instructions
- not take advantage of their position and not benefit themselves,
- but benefit the donor (fiduciary duty)
- not delegate decisions, unless authorised to do so
- act in good faith
- respect confidentiality
- comply with the directions of the Court of Protection
- not give up the role without telling the donor and the court.

In relation to property and affairs LPAs, they have a duty to:

- keep accounts
- keep the donor's money and property separate from their own.

Duty of care

7.59 'Duty of care' means applying a certain standard of care and skill – depending on whether the attorney is paid for their services or holds relevant professional qualifications.

- Attorneys who are not being paid must apply the same care, skill and diligence they would use to make decisions about their own life. An attorney who claims to have particular skills or qualifications must show greater skill in those particular areas than someone who does not make such claims.
- If attorneys are being paid for their services, they should demonstrate a higher degree of care and skill.
- Attorneys who undertake their duties in the course of their professional work (such as solicitors or corporate trustees) must display professional competence and follow their profession's rules and standards.

Fiduciary duty

7.60 A fiduciary duty means attorneys must not take advantage of their position. Nor should they put themselves in a position where their personal interests conflict with their duties. They also must not allow any other influences to affect the way in which they act as an attorney. Decisions should always benefit the donor, and not the attorney. Attorneys must not profit or get any personal benefit from their position, apart from receiving gifts where the Act allows it, whether or not it is at the donor's expense.

Duty not to delegate

7.61 Attorneys cannot usually delegate their authority to someone else. They must carry out their duties personally. The attorney may seek professional or expert advice (for example, investment advice from a financial adviser or advice on medical treatment from a doctor). But they cannot, as a general rule, allow someone else to make a decision that they have been appointed to make, unless this has been specifically authorised by the donor in the LPA.

7.62   In certain circumstances, attorneys may have limited powers to delegate (for example, through necessity or unforeseen circumstances, or for specific tasks which the donor would not have expected the attorney to attend to personally). But attorneys cannot usually delegate any decisions that rely on their discretion.

Duty of good faith

7.63   Acting in good faith means acting with honesty and integrity. For example, an attorney must try to make sure that their decisions do not go against a decision the donor made while they still had capacity (unless it would be in the donor's best interests to do so).

Duty of confidentiality

7.64   Attorneys have a duty to keep the donor's affairs confidential, unless:

- before they lost capacity to do so, the donor agreed that some personal or financial information may be revealed for a particular purpose (for example, they have named someone they want to check their financial accounts), or
- there is some other good reason to release it (for example, it is in the public interest or the best interests of the person who lacks capacity, or there is a risk of harm to the donor or others).

In the latter circumstances, it may be advisable for the attorney to get legal advice. Chapter 16 gives more information about confidentiality.

Duty to comply with the directions of the Court of Protection

7.65   Under sections 22 and 23 of the Act, the Court of Protection has wide-ranging powers to decide on issues relating to the operation or validity of an LPA. It can also:

- give extra authority to attorneys
- order them to produce records (for example, financial accounts), or
- order them to provide specific information or documentation to the court.

Attorneys must comply with any decision or order that the court makes.

Duty not to disclaim without notifying the donor and the OPG

7.66   Once someone becomes an attorney, they cannot give up that role without notifying the donor and the OPG. If they decide to give up their role, they must follow the relevant guidance available from the OPG.

Duty to keep accounts

7.67   Property and affairs attorneys must keep accounts of transactions carried out on the donor's behalf. Sometimes the Court of Protection will ask to see accounts. If the attorney is not a financial expert and the donor's affairs are relatively straightforward, a record of the donor's income and expenditure (for example, through bank statements) may be enough. The more complicated the donor's affairs, the more detailed the accounts may need to be.

Duty to keep the donor's money and property separate

7.68   Property and affairs attorneys should usually keep the donor's money and property separate from their own or anyone else's. There may be occasions where donors and attorneys have agreed in the past to keep their money in a joint bank account (for example, if a husband is acting as his wife's attorney). It might be possible to continue this under the LPA. But in most circumstances, attorneys must keep finances separate to avoid any possibility of mistakes or confusion.

How does the Act protect donors from abuse?

What should someone do if they think an attorney is abusing their position?

7.69   Attorneys are in a position of trust, so there is always a risk of them abusing their position. Donors can help prevent abuse by carefully choosing a suitable and trustworthy attorney. But others have a role to play in looking out for possible signs of abuse or exploitation, and reporting any concerns to the OPG. The OPG will then follow this up in co-operation with relevant agencies.

7.70   Signs that an attorney may be exploiting the donor (or failing to act in the donor's best interests) include:

- stopping relatives or friends contacting the donor – for example, the attorney may prevent contact or the donor may suddenly refuse visits or telephone calls from family and friends for no reason
- sudden unexplained changes in living arrangements (for example, someone moves in to care for a donor they've had little contact with)
- not allowing healthcare or social care staff to see the donor
- taking the donor out of hospital against medical advice, while the donor is having necessary medical treatment
- unpaid bills (for example, residential care or nursing home fees)
- an attorney opening a credit card account for the donor
- spending money on things that are not obviously related to the donor's needs
- the attorney spending money in an unusual or extravagant way
- transferring financial assets to another country.

7.71   Somebody who suspects abuse should contact the OPG immediately. The OPG may direct a Court of Protection Visitor to visit an attorney to investigate. In cases of suspected physical or sexual abuse, theft or serious fraud, the person should contact the police. They might also be able to refer the matter to the relevant local adult protection authorities.

7.72   In serious cases, the OPG will refer the matter to the Court of Protection. The court may revoke (cancel) the LPA or (through the OPG) prevent it being registered, if it decides that:

- the LPA does not meet the legal requirements for creating an LPA
- the LPA has been revoked or come to an end for any other reason
- somebody used fraud or undue pressure to get the donor to make the LPA
- the attorney has done something that they do not have authority to do, or
- the attorney has behaved or is planning to behave in a way that is not in the donor's best interests.

The court might then consider whether the authority previously given to an attorney can be managed by:

- the court making a single decision, or
- appointing a deputy.

What should an attorney do if they think someone else is abusing the donor?

7.73   An attorney who thinks someone else is abusing or exploiting the donor should report it to the OPG and ask for advice on what action they should take. They should contact the police if they suspect physical or sexual abuse, theft or serious fraud. They might also be able to refer the matter to local adult protection authorities.

7.74   Chapter 13 gives more information about protecting vulnerable people from abuse, ill treatment or neglect. It also discusses the duties and responsibilities of the various agencies involved, including the OPG and local authorities. In particular, it is a criminal offence (with a maximum penalty of five years' imprisonment, a fine, or both) for anyone (including attorneys) to wilfully neglect or ill-treat a person in their care who lacks capacity to make decisions for themselves (section 44).

What happens to existing EPAs once the Act comes into force?

7.75   Once the Act comes into force, it will not be possible to make new EPAs. Only LPAs can then be made.

7.76   Some donors will have created EPAs before the Act came into force with the expectation that their chosen attorneys will manage their property and affairs in the future, whether or not they have capacity to do so themselves.

7.77   If donors still have capacity after the Act comes into force, they can cancel the EPA and make an LPA covering their property and affairs. They should also notify attorneys and anyone else aware of the EPA (for example, a bank) that they have cancelled it.

7.78   Some donors will choose not to cancel their EPA or they may already lack the capacity to do so. In such cases, the Act allows existing EPAs, whether registered or not, to continue to be valid so that attorneys can meet the donor's expectations (Schedule 4). An EPA must be registered with the OPG when the attorney thinks the donor lacks capacity to manage their own affairs, or is beginning to lack capacity to do so.

7.79   EPA attorneys may find guidance in this chapter helpful. In particular, all attorneys must comply with the duties described in paragraphs 7.58–7.68 above. EPA attorneys can also be found liable under section 44 of the new Act, which sets out the new criminal offences of ill treatment and wilful neglect. The OPG has produced guidance on EPAs (see Annex A for details of publications and contact information).

8   WHAT IS THE ROLE OF THE COURT OF PROTECTION AND COURT-APPOINTED DEPUTIES?

This chapter describes the role of the Court of Protection and the role of court-appointed deputies. It explains the powers that the court has and how to make an application to the court. It also looks at how the court appoints a deputy to act and make decisions on behalf of someone who lacks capacity to make those decisions. In particular, it gives guidance on a deputy's duties and the consequences of not carrying them out responsibly.

The Office of the Public Guardian (OPG) produces detailed guidance for deputies. See the Annex for more details of the publications and how to get them. Further details on the court's procedures are given in the Court of Protection Rules and Practice Directions issued by the court.

In this chapter, as throughout the Code, a person's capacity (or lack of capacity) refers specifically to their capacity to make a particular decision at the time it needs to be made.

Quick summary

The Court of Protection has powers to:

- decide whether a person has capacity to make a particular decision for themselves
- make declarations, decisions or orders on financial or welfare matters affecting people who lack capacity to make such decisions
- appoint deputies to make decisions for people lacking capacity to make those decisions
- decide whether an LPA or EPA is valid, and
- remove deputies or attorneys who fail to carry out their duties.

Before accepting an appointment as a deputy, a person the court nominates should consider whether:

- they have the skills and ability to carry out a deputy's duties (especially in relation to property and affairs)
- they actually want to take on the duties and responsibilities.

Anyone acting as a deputy must:

- make sure that they only make those decisions that they are authorised to make by the order of the court
- make sure that they follow the Act's statutory principles, including:
  - considering whether the person has capacity to make a particular decision for themselves. If they do, the deputy should allow them to do so unless the person agrees that the deputy should make the decision
  - taking all possible steps to try to help a person make the particular decision
- always make decisions in the person's best interests
- have regard to guidance in the Code of Practice that is relevant to the situation
- fulfil their duties towards the person concerned (in particular the duty of care and fiduciary duties to respect the degree of trust placed in them by the court).

What is the Court of Protection?

8.1   Section 45 of the Act sets up a specialist court, the Court of Protection, to deal with decision-making for adults (and children in a few cases) who may lack capacity to make specific decisions for themselves. The new Court of Protection replaces the old court of the same name, which only dealt with decisions about the property and financial affairs of people lacking capacity to manage their own affairs. As well as property and affairs, the new court also deals with serious decisions affecting healthcare and personal welfare matters. These were previously dealt with by the High Court under its inherent jurisdiction.

8.2   The new Court of Protection is a superior court of record and is able to establish precedent (it can set examples for future cases) and build up expertise in all issues related to lack of capacity. It has the same powers, rights, privileges and authority as the High Court. When reaching any decision, the court must apply all the statutory principles set out in section 1 of the Act. In particular, it must make a decision in the best interests of the person who lacks capacity to make the specific decision. There will usually be a fee for applications to the court.[29]

How can somebody make an application to the Court of Protection?

8.3   In most cases concerning personal welfare matters, the core principles of the Act and the processes set out in chapters 5 and 6 will be enough to:

- help people take action or make decisions in the best interests of someone who lacks capacity to make decisions about their own care or treatment, or
- find ways of settling disagreements about such actions or decisions.

But an application to the Court of Protection may be necessary for:

- particularly difficult decisions
- disagreements that cannot be resolved in any other way (see chapter 15), or
- situations where ongoing decisions may need to be made about the personal welfare of a person who lacks capacity to make decisions for themselves.

8.4   An order of the court will usually be necessary for matters relating to the property and affairs (including financial matters) of people who lack capacity to make specific financial decisions for themselves, unless:

- their only income is state benefits (see paragraph 8.36 below), or
- they have previously made an Enduring Power of Attorney (EPA) or a Lasting Power of Attorney (LPA) to give somebody authority to manage their property and affairs (see chapter 7).

8.5   Receivers appointed by the court before the Act commences will be treated as deputies. But they will keep their existing powers and duties. They must meet the requirements set out in the Act and, in particular, follow the statutory principles and act in the best interests of the person for whom they have been appointed. They must also have regard to guidance in this chapter and other parts of the Code of Practice. Further guidance for receivers is available from the OPG.

Cases involving young people aged 16 or 17

8.6   Either a court dealing with family proceedings or the Court of Protection can hear cases involving people aged 16 or 17 who lack capacity. In some cases, the Court of Protection can hear cases involving people younger than 16 (for example, when somebody needs to be appointed to make longer-term decisions about their financial affairs). Under section 21 of the Mental Capacity Act, the Court of Protection can transfer cases concerning children to a court that has powers under the Children Act 1989. Such a court can also transfer cases to the Court of Protection, if necessary. Chapter 12 gives more detail on cases where this might apply.

Who should make the application?

8.7   The person making the application will vary, depending on the circumstances. For example, a person wishing to challenge a finding that they lack capacity may apply to the court, supported by others where necessary. Where there is a disagreement among family members, for example, a family member may wish to apply to the court to settle the disagreement – bearing in mind the need, in most cases, to get permission beforehand (see paragraphs 8.11–8.12 below).

---

[29] Details of the fees charged by the court, and the circumstances in which the fees may be waived or remitted, are available from the Office of the Public Guardian (OPG).

8.8   For cases about serious or major decisions concerning medical treatment (see paragraphs 8.18–8.24 below), the NHS Trust or other organisation responsible for the patient's care will usually make the application. If social care staff are concerned about a decision that affects the welfare of a person who lacks capacity, the relevant local authority should make the application.

8.9   For decisions about the property and affairs of someone who lacks capacity to manage their own affairs, the applicant will usually be the person (for example, family carer) who needs specific authority from the court to deal with the individual's money or property.

8.10   If the applicant is the person who is alleged to lack capacity, they will always be a party to the court proceedings. In all other cases, the court will decide whether the person who lacks, or is alleged to lack, capacity should be involved as a party to the case. Where the person is a party to the case, the court may appoint the Official Solicitor to act for them.

Who must ask the court for permission to make an application?

8.11   As a general rule, potential applicants must get the permission of the Court of Protection before making an application (section 50). People who the Act says do not need to ask for permission include:

- a person who lacks, or is alleged to lack, capacity in relation to a specific decision or action (or anyone with parental responsibility, if the person is under 18 years)
- the donor of the LPA an application relates to – or their attorney
- a deputy who has been appointed by the court to act for the person concerned, and
- a person named in an existing court order relating to the application.

The Court of Protection Rules also set out specific types of cases where permission is not required.

8.12   When deciding whether to give permission for an application, the court must consider:

- the applicant's connection to the person the application is about
- the reasons for the application
- whether a proposed order or direction of the court will benefit the person the application is about, and
- whether it is possible to get that benefit another way.

[*Scenario: Considering whether to give permission for an application*]

What powers does the Court of Protection have?

8.13   The Court of Protection may:

- make declarations, decisions and orders on financial and welfare matters affecting people who lack, or are alleged to lack, capacity (the lack of capacity must relate to the particular issue being presented to the court)
- appoint deputies to make decisions for people who lack capacity to make those decisions
- remove deputies or attorneys who act inappropriately.

The Court can also hear cases about LPAs and EPAs. The court's powers concerning EPAs are set out in Schedule 4 of the Act.

8.14   The court must always follow the statutory principles set out in section 1 of the Act (see chapter 2) and make the decision in the best interests of the person concerned (see chapter 5).

What declarations can the court make?

8.15   Section 15 of the Act provides the court with powers to make a declaration (a ruling) on specific issues. For example, it can make a declaration as to whether a person has capacity to make a particular decision or give consent for or take a particular action. The court will require evidence of any assessment of the person's capacity and may wish to see relevant written evidence (for example, a diary, letters or other papers). If the court decides the person has capacity to make that decision, they will not take the case further. The person can now make the decision for themselves.

8.16   Applications concerning a person's capacity are likely to be rare – people can usually settle doubts and disagreements informally (see chapters 4 and 15). But an application may be relevant if:

- a person wants to challenge a decision that they lack capacity
- professionals disagree about a person's capacity to make a specific (usually serious) decision
- there is a dispute over whether the person has capacity (for example, between family members).

8.17   The court can also make a declaration as to whether a specific act relating to a person's care or treatment is lawful (either where somebody has carried out the action or is proposing to). Under section 15, this can include an omission or failure to provide care or treatment that the person needs.

This power to decide on the lawfulness of an act is particularly relevant for major medical treatment cases where there is doubt or disagreement over whether the treatment would be in the person's best interests. Healthcare staff can still give life-sustaining treatment, or treatment which stops a person's condition getting seriously worse, while the court is coming to a decision.

Serious healthcare and treatment decisions

8.18   Prior to the Act coming into force, the courts decided that some decisions relating to the provision of medical treatment were so serious that in each case, an application should be made to the court for a declaration that the proposed action was lawful before that action was taken. Cases involving any of the following decisions should therefore be brought before a court:

- decisions about the proposed withholding or withdrawal of artificial nutrition and hydration (ANH) from patients in a permanent vegetative state (PVS)
- cases involving organ or bone marrow donation by a person who lacks capacity to consent
- cases involving the proposed non-therapeutic sterilisation of a person who lacks capacity to consent to this (e.g. for contraceptive purposes) and
- all other cases where there is a doubt or dispute about whether a particular treatment will be in a person's best interests.

8.19   The case law requirement to seek a declaration in cases involving the withholding or withdrawing of artificial nutrition and hydration to people in a permanent vegetative state is unaffected by the Act[30] and as a matter of practice, these cases should be put to the Court of Protection for approval.

8.20   Cases involving organ or bone marrow donation by a person who lacks capacity to consent should also be referred to the Court of Protection. Such cases involve medical procedures being performed on a person who lacks capacity to consent but which would benefit a third party (though would not necessarily directly or phys-

[30]   *Airedale NHS Trust v. Bland* [1993] AC 789.

ically benefit the person who lacks capacity). However, sometimes such procedures may be in the person's overall best interests (see chapter 5). For example, the person might receive emotional, social and psychological benefits as a result of the help they have given, and in some cases the person may experience only minimal physical discomfort.

8.21   A prime example of this is the case of Re Y[31] where it was found to be in Y's best interests for her to donate bone marrow to her sister. The court decided that it was in Y's best interests to continue to receive strong emotional support from her mother, which might be diminished if her sister's health were to deteriorate further, or she were to die.

Further details on this area are available in Department of Health or Welsh Assembly guidance.[32]

8.22   Non-therapeutic sterilisation is the sterilisation for contraceptive purposes of a person who cannot consent. Such cases will require a careful assessment of whether such sterilisation would be in the best interests of the person who lacks capacity and such cases should continue to be referred to the court.[33] The court has also given guidance on when certain termination of pregnancy cases should be brought before the court.[34]

8.23   Other cases likely to be referred to the court include those involving ethical dilemmas in untested areas (such as innovative treatments for variant CJD), or where there are otherwise irresolvable conflicts between healthcare staff, or between staff and family members.

8.24   There are also a few types of cases that should generally be dealt with by the court, since other dispute resolution methods are unlikely to be appropriate (see chapter 15). This includes, for example, cases where it is unclear whether proposed serious and/or invasive medical treatment is likely to be in the best interests of the person who lacks capacity to consent.

What powers does the court have to make decisions and appoint deputies?

8.25   In cases of serious dispute, where there is no other way of finding a solution or when the authority of the court is needed in order to make a particular decision or take a particular action, the court can be asked to make a decision to settle the matter using its powers under section 16. However, if there is a need for ongoing decision-making powers and there is no relevant EPA or LPA, the court may appoint a deputy to make future decisions. It will also state what decisions the deputy has the authority to make on the person's behalf.

8.26   In deciding what type of order to make, the court must apply the Act's principles and the best interests checklist. In addition, it must follow two further principles, intended to make any intervention as limited as possible:

■ Where possible, the court should make the decision itself in preference to appointing a deputy.
■ If a deputy needs to be appointed, their appointment should be as limited in scope and for as short a time as possible.

---

[31]   *Re Y (Mental incapacity: Bone marrow transplant)* [1996] 2 FLR 787.
[32]   Reference Guide to Consent for Examination or Treatment, Department of Health, March 2001 www.dh.gov.uk/PublicationsAndStatistics/Publications/PublicationsPolicyAndGuidance/ PublicationsPolicyAndGuidanceArticle/fs/en?CONTENT_ID=4006757&chk=snmdw8
[33]   See e.g. *Re A (medical treatment: male sterilisation)* (1999) 53 BMLR 66 where a mother applied for a declaration that a vasectomy was in the best interests of A, her son (who had Down's syndrome and was borderline between significant and severe impairment of intelligence), in the absence of his consent. After balancing the burdens and benefits of the proposed vasectomy to A, the Court of Appeal held that the vasectomy would not be in A's best interests.
[34]   *D v. An NHS Trust (Medical Treatment: Consent: Termination)* [2004] 1 FLR 1110.

What decisions can the court make?

8.27   In some cases, the court must make a decision, because someone needs specific authority to act and there is no other route for getting it. These include cases where:

■ there is no EPA or property and affairs LPA in place and someone needs to make a financial decision for a person who lacks capacity to make that decision (for example, the decision to terminate a tenancy agreement), or

■ it is necessary to make a will, or to amend an existing will, on behalf of a person who lacks capacity to do so.

8.28   Examples of other types of cases where a court decision might be appropriate include cases where:

■ there is genuine doubt or disagreement about the existence, validity or applicability of an advance decision to refuse treatment (see chapter 9)

■ there is a major disagreement regarding a serious decision (for example, about where a person who lacks capacity to decide for themselves should live)

■ a family carer or a solicitor asks for personal information about someone who lacks capacity to consent to that information being revealed (for example, where there have been allegations of abuse of a person living in a care home)

■ someone suspects that a person who lacks capacity to make decisions to protect themselves is at risk of harm or abuse from a named individual (the court could stop that individual contacting the person who lacks capacity).

8.29   Anyone carrying out actions under a decision or order of the court must still also follow the Act's principles.

[*Scenario: Making a decision to settle disagreements*]

What powers does the court have in relation to LPAs?

8.30   The Court of Protection can determine the validity of an LPA or EPA and can give directions as to how an attorney should use their powers under an LPA (see chapter 7). In particular, the court can cancel an LPA and end the attorney's appointment. The court might do this if the attorney was not carrying out their duties properly or acting in the best interests of the donor. The court must then decide whether it is necessary to appoint a deputy to take over the attorney's role.

What are the rules for appointing deputies?

8.31   Sometimes it is not practical or appropriate for the court to make a single declaration or decision. In such cases, if the court thinks that somebody needs to make future or ongoing decisions for someone whose condition makes it likely they will lack capacity to make some further decisions in the future, it can appoint a deputy to act for and make decisions for that person. A deputy's authority should be as limited in scope and duration as possible (see paragraphs 8.35–8.39 below).

How does the court appoint deputies?

8.32   It is for the court to decide who to appoint as a deputy. Different skills may be required depending on whether the deputy's decisions will be about a person's welfare (including healthcare), their finances or both. The court will decide whether the proposed deputy is reliable and trustworthy and has an appropriate level of skill and competence to carry out the necessary tasks.

8.33   In the majority of cases, the deputy is likely to be a family member or someone who knows the person well. But in some cases the court may decide to appoint a deputy who is independent of the family (for example, where the person's affairs or care needs are particularly complicated). This could be, for example, the Director of Adult Services in the relevant local authority (but see paragraph 8.60 below) or a professional deputy. The OPG has a panel of professional deputies (mainly solicitors who specialise in this area of law) who may be appointed to deal with property and affairs if the court decides that would be in the person's best interests.

When might a deputy need to be appointed?

8.34   Whether a person who lacks capacity to make specific decisions needs a deputy will depend on:

- the individual circumstances of the person concerned
- whether future or ongoing decisions are likely to be necessary, and
- whether the appointment is for decisions about property and affairs or personal welfare.

Property and affairs

8.35   The court will appoint a deputy to manage a person's property and affairs (including financial matters) in similar circumstances to those in which they would have appointed a receiver in the past. If a person who lacks capacity to make decisions about property and affairs has not made an EPA or LPA, applications to the court are necessary:

- for dealing with cash assets over a specified amount that remain after any debts have been paid
- for selling a person's property, or
- where the person has a level of income or capital that the court thinks a deputy needs to manage.

8.36   If the only income of a person who lacks capacity is social security benefits and they have no property or savings, there will usually be no need for a deputy to be appointed. This is because the person's benefits can be managed by an appointee, appointed by the Department for Work and Pensions to receive and deal with the benefits of a person who lacks capacity to do this for themselves. Although appointees are not covered by the Act, they will be expected to act in the person's best interests and must do so if they are involved in caring for the person. If the court does appoint a property and affairs deputy for someone who has an appointee, it is likely that the deputy would take over the appointee's role.

8.37   Anybody considered for appointment as a property and affairs deputy will need to sign a declaration giving details of their circumstances and ability to manage financial affairs. The declaration will include details of the tasks and duties the deputy must carry out. The deputy must assure the court that they have the skills, knowledge and commitment to carry them out.

Personal welfare (including healthcare)

8.38   Deputies for personal welfare decisions will only be required in the most difficult cases where:

- important and necessary actions cannot be carried out without the court's authority, or
- there is no other way of settling the matter in the best interests of the person who lacks capacity to make particular welfare decisions.

8.39   Examples include when:

- someone needs to make a series of linked welfare decisions over time and it would not be beneficial or appropriate to require all of those decisions to be made by the court. For example, someone (such as a family carer) who is close to a person with profound and multiple learning disabilities might apply to be appointed as a deputy with authority to make such decisions
- the most appropriate way to act in the person's best interests is to have a deputy, who will consult relevant people but have the final authority to make decisions
- there is a history of serious family disputes that could have a detrimental effect on the person's future care unless a deputy is appointed to make necessary decisions
- the person who lacks capacity is felt to be at risk of serious harm if left in the care of family members. In these rare cases, welfare decisions may need to be made by someone independent of the family, such as a local authority officer. There may even be a need for an additional court order prohibiting those family members from having contact with the person.

Who can be a deputy?

8.40   Section 19(1) states that deputies must be at least 18 years of age. Deputies with responsibility for property and affairs can be either an individual or a trust corporation (often parts of banks or other financial institutions). No-one can be appointed as a deputy without their consent.

8.41   Paid care workers (for example, care home managers) should not agree to act as a deputy because of the possible conflict of interest – unless there are exceptional circumstances (for example, if the care worker is the only close relative of the person who lacks capacity). But the court can appoint someone who is an office-holder or in a specified position (for example, the Director of Adult Services of the relevant local authority). In this situation, the court will need to be satisfied that there is no conflict of interest before making such an appointment (see paragraphs 8.58–8.60).

8.42   The court can appoint two or more deputies and state whether they should act 'jointly', 'jointly and severally' or 'jointly in respect of some matters and jointly and severally in respect of others' (section 19(4)(c)).

- Joint deputies must always act together. They must all agree decisions or actions, and all sign any relevant documents.
- Joint and several deputies can act together, but they may also act independently if they wish. Any action taken by any deputy alone is as valid as if that person were the only deputy.

8.43   Deputies may be appointed jointly for some issues and jointly and severally for others. For example, two deputies could be appointed jointly and severally for most decisions, but the court might rule that they act jointly when selling property.

[*Scenario: Acting jointly and severally*]

What happens if a deputy can no longer carry out their duties?

8.44   When appointing a deputy, the court can also appoint someone to be a successor deputy (someone who can take over the deputy's duties in certain situations). The court will state the circumstances under which this could occur. In some cases it will also state a period of time in which the successor deputy can act. Appointment of a successor deputy might be useful if the person appointed as deputy is already elderly and wants to be sure that somebody will take over their duties in the future, if necessary.

[*Scenario: Appointing a successor deputy*]

Can the court protect people lacking capacity from financial loss?

8.45   Under section 19(9)(a) of the Act the court can ask a property and affairs deputy to provide some form of security (for example, a guarantee bond) to the Public Guardian to cover any loss as a result of the deputy's behaviour in carrying out their role. The court can also ask a deputy to provide reports and accounts to the Public Guardian, as it sees fit.

Are there any restrictions on a deputy's powers?

8.46   Section 20 sets out some specific restrictions on a deputy's powers. In particular, a deputy has no authority to make decisions or take action:

- if they do something that is intended to restrain the person who lacks capacity – apart from under certain circumstances (guidance on the circumstances when restraint might be permitted is given in chapter 6)[35]
- if they think that the person concerned has capacity to make the particular decision for themselves
- if their decision goes against a decision made by an attorney acting under a Lasting Power of Attorney granted by the person before they lost capacity, or
- to refuse the provision or continuation of life-sustaining treatment for a person who lacks capacity to consent – such decisions must be taken by the court.

If a deputy thinks their powers are not enough for them to carry out their duties effectively, they can apply to the court to change their powers. See paragraph 8.54 below.

What responsibilities do deputies have?

8.47   Once a deputy has been appointed by the court, the order of appointment will set out their specific powers and the scope of their authority. On taking up the appointment, the deputy will assume a number of duties and responsibilities and will be required to act in accordance with certain standards. Failure to comply with the duties set out below could result in the Court of Protection revoking the order appointing the deputy and, in some circumstances, the deputy could be personally liable to claims for negligence or criminal charges of fraud.

8.48   Deputies should always inform any third party they are dealing with that the court has appointed them as deputy. The court will give the deputy official documents to prove their appointment and the extent of their authority.

8.49   A deputy must act whenever a decision or action is needed and it falls within their duties as set out in the court order appointing them. A deputy who fails to act at all in such situations could be in breach of duty.

---

[35] It is worth noting that there is a drafting error in section 20 of the Act. The word 'or' in section 20(11)(a) should have been 'and' in order to be consistent with sections 6(3)(a) and 11(4)(a). The Government will make the necessary amendment to correct this error at the earliest available legislative opportunity.

What duties does the Act impose?

8.50   Deputies must:

- follow the Act's statutory principles (see chapter 2)
- make decisions or act in the best interests of the person who lacks capacity
- have regard to the guidance in this Code of Practice
- only make decisions the Court has given them authority to make.

Principles and best interests

8.51   Deputies must act in accordance with the Act's statutory principles (section 1) and in particular the best interests of the person who lacks capacity (the steps for working out best interests are set out in section 4). In particular, deputies must consider whether the person has capacity to make the decision for themselves. If not, they should consider whether the person is likely to regain capacity to make the decision in the future. If so, it may be possible to delay the decision until the person can make it.

The Code of Practice

8.52   As well as this chapter, deputies should pay special attention to the following guidance set out in the Code:

- chapter 2, which sets out how the Act's principles should be applied
- chapter 3, which describes the steps which can be taken to try to help the person make decisions for themselves
- chapter 4, which describes the Act's definition of lack of capacity and gives guidance on assessing capacity, and
- chapter 5, which gives guidance on working out someone's best interests.

8.53   In some situations, deputies might also find it useful to refer to guidance in:

- chapter 6, which explains when deputies who have caring responsibilities may have protection from liability and gives guidance on the few circumstances when the Act allows restraint in connection with care and treatment, and
- chapter 15, which describes ways to settle disagreements.

Only making decisions the court authorises a deputy to make

8.54   A deputy has a duty to act only within the scope of the actual powers given by the court, which are set out in the order of appointment. It is possible that a deputy will think their powers are not enough for them to carry out their duties effectively. In this situation, they must apply to the court either to:

- ask the court to make the decision in question, or
- ask the court to change the deputy's powers.

What are a deputy's other duties?

8.55   Section 19(6) states that a deputy is to be treated as 'the agent' of the person who lacks capacity when they act on their behalf. Being an agent means that the deputy has legal duties (under the law of agency) to the person they are representing. It also means that when they carry out tasks within their powers, they are not personally liable to third parties.

8.56   Deputies must carry out their duties carefully and responsibly. They have a duty to:

- act with due care and skill (duty of care)
- not take advantage of their situation (fiduciary duty)

- indemnify the person against liability to third parties caused by the deputy's negligence
- not delegate duties unless authorised to do so
- act in good faith
- respect the person's confidentiality, and
- comply with the directions of the Court of Protection.

Property and affairs deputies also have a duty to:

- keep accounts, and
- keep the person's money and property separate from own finances.

Duty of care

8.57 'Duty of care' means applying a certain standard of care and skill – depending on whether the deputy is paid for their services or holds relevant professional qualifications.

- Deputies who are not being paid must use the same care, skill and diligence they would use when making decisions for themselves or managing their own affairs. If they do not, they could be held liable for acting negligently. A deputy who claims to have particular skills or qualifications must show greater skill in those particular areas than a person who does not make such claims.
- If deputies are being paid for their services, they are expected to demonstrate a higher degree of care or skill when carrying out their duties.
- Deputies whose duties form part of their professional work (for example, solicitors or accountants) must display normal professional competence and follow their profession's rules and standards.

Fiduciary duty

8.58 A fiduciary duty means deputies must not take advantage of their position. Nor should they put themselves in a position where their personal interests conflict with their duties. For example, deputies should not buy property that they are selling for the person they have been appointed to represent. They should also not accept a third party commission in any transactions. Deputies must not allow anything else to influence their duties. They cannot use their position for any personal benefit, whether or not it is at the person's expense.

8.59 In many cases, the deputy will be a family member. In rare situations, this could lead to potential conflicts of interests. When making decisions, deputies should follow the Act's statutory principles and apply the best interests checklist and not allow their own personal interests to influence the decision.

8.60 Sometimes the court will consider appointing the Director of Adult Services in England or Director of Social Services in Wales of the relevant local authority as a deputy. The court will need to be satisfied that the authority has arrangements to avoid possible conflicts of interest. For example where the person for whom a financial deputy is required receives community care services from the local authority, the court will wish to be satisfied that decisions about the person's finances will be made in the best interests of that person, regardless of any implications for the services provided.

Duty not to delegate

8.61 A deputy may seek professional or expert advice (for example, investment advice from a financial adviser or a second medical opinion from a doctor). But they cannot give their decision-making responsibilities to someone else. In certain circumstances, the court will authorise the delegation of specific tasks (for example, appointing a discretionary investment manager for the conduct of investment business).

8.62   In certain circumstances, deputies may have limited powers to delegate (for example, through necessity or unforeseen circumstances, or for specific tasks which the court would not have expected the deputy to attend to personally). But deputies cannot usually delegate any decisions that rely on their discretion. If the deputy is the Director of Adult Services in England or Director of Social Services in Wales, or a solicitor, they can delegate specific tasks to other staff. But the deputy is still responsible for any actions or decisions taken, and can therefore be held accountable for any errors that are made.

Duty of good faith

8.63   Acting in good faith means acting with honesty and integrity. For example, a deputy must try to make sure that their decisions do not go against a decision the person made while they still had capacity (unless it would be in the person's best interests to do so).

Duty of confidentiality

8.64   Deputies have a duty to keep the person's affairs confidential, unless:

- before they lost capacity to do so, the person agreed that information could be revealed where necessary
- there is some other good reason to release information (for example, it is in the public interest or in the best interests of the person who lacks capacity, or where there is a risk of harm to the person concerned or to other people).

In the latter circumstances, it is advisable for the deputy to contact the OPG for guidance or get legal advice. See chapter 16 for more information about revealing personal information.

Duty to comply with the directions of the Court of Protection

8.65   The Court of Protection may give specific directions to deputies about how they should use their powers. It can also order deputies to provide reports (for example, financial accounts or reports on the welfare of the person who lacks capacity) to the Public Guardian at any time or at such intervals as the court directs. Deputies must comply with any direction of the court or request from the Public Guardian.

Duty to keep accounts

8.66   A deputy appointed to manage property and affairs is expected to keep, and periodically submit to the Public Guardian, correct accounts of all their dealings and transactions on the person's behalf.

Duty to keep the person's money and property separate

8.67   Property and affairs deputies should usually keep the person's money and property separate from their own or anyone else's. This is to avoid any possibility of mistakes or confusion in handling the person's affairs. Sometimes there may be good reason not to do so (for example, a husband might be his wife's deputy and they might have had a joint account for many years).

Changes of contact details

8.68   A deputy should inform the OPG of any changes of contact details or circumstances (for the deputy or the person they are acting for). This will help make sure that the OPG has up-to-date records. It will also allow the court to discharge people who are no longer eligible to act as deputies.

Who is responsible for supervising deputies?

8.69 Deputies are accountable to the Court of Protection. The court can cancel a deputy's appointment at any time if it decides the appointment is no longer in the best interests of the person who lacks capacity.

8.70 The OPG is responsible for supervising and supporting deputies. But it must also protect people lacking capacity from possible abuse or exploitation. Anybody who suspects that a deputy is abusing their position should contact the OPG immediately. The OPG may instruct a Court of Protection Visitor to visit a deputy to investigate any matter of concern. It can also apply to the court to cancel a deputy's appointment.

8.71 The OPG will consider carefully any concerns or complaints against deputies. But if somebody suspects physical or sexual abuse or serious fraud, they should contact the police and/or social services immediately, as well as informing the OPG. Chapter 14 gives more information about the role of the OPG. It also discusses the protection of vulnerable people from abuse, ill treatment or wilful neglect and the responsibilities of various relevant agencies.

9 WHAT DOES THE ACT SAY ABOUT ADVANCE DECISIONS TO REFUSE

This chapter explains what to do when somebody has made an advance decision to refuse treatment. It sets out:

- what the Act means by an 'advance decision'
- guidance on making, updating and cancelling advance decisions
- how to check whether an advance decision exists
- how to check that an advance decision is valid and that it applies to current circumstances
- the responsibilities of healthcare professionals when an advance decision exists
- how to handle disagreements about advance decisions.

In this chapter, as throughout the Code, a person's capacity (or lack of capacity) refers specifically to their capacity to make a particular decision at the time it needs to be made.

Quick summary

- An advance decision enables someone aged 18 and over, while still capable, to refuse specified medical treatment for a time in the future when they may lack the capacity to consent to or refuse that treatment.
- An advance decision to refuse treatment must be valid and applicable to current circumstances. If it is, it has the same effect as a decision that is made by a person with capacity: healthcare professionals must follow the decision.
- Healthcare professionals will be protected from liability if they:

  - stop or withhold treatment because they reasonably believe that an advance decision exists, and that it is valid and applicable

- treat a person because, having taken all practical and appropriate steps to find out if the person has made an advance decision to refuse treatment, they do not know or are not satisfied that a valid and applicable advance decision exists.

- People can only make an advance decision under the Act if they are 18 or over and have the capacity to make the decision. They must say what treatment they want to refuse, and they can cancel their decision – or part of it – at any time.
- If the advance decision refuses life-sustaining treatment, it must:

  - be in writing (it can be written by a someone else or recorded in healthcare notes)
  - be signed and witnessed, and
  - state clearly that the decision applies even if life is at risk.

- To establish whether an advance decision is valid and applicable, healthcare professionals must try to find out if the person:

  - has done anything that clearly goes against their advance decision
  - has withdrawn their decision
  - has subsequently conferred the power to make that decision on an attorney, or
  - would have changed their decision if they had known more about the current circumstances.

- Sometimes healthcare professionals will conclude that an advance decision does not exist, is not valid and/or applicable – but that it is an expression of the person's wishes. The healthcare professional must then consider what is set out in the advance decision as an expression of previous wishes when working out the person's best interests (see chapter 5).
- Some healthcare professionals may disagree in principle with patients' decisions to refuse life-sustaining treatment. They do not have to act against their beliefs. But they must not simply abandon patients or act in a way that that affects their care.
- Advance decisions to refuse treatment for mental disorder may not apply if the person who made the advance decision is or is liable to be detained under the Mental Health Act 1983.

How can someone make an advance decision to refuse treatment?

What is an advance decision to refuse treatment?

9.1   It is a general principle of law and medical practice that people have a right to consent to or refuse treatment. The courts have recognised that adults have the right to say in advance that they want to refuse treatment if they lose capacity in the future – even if this results in their death. A valid and applicable advance decision to refuse treatment has the same force as a contemporaneous decision. This has been a fundamental principle of the common law for many years and it is now set out in the Act. Sections 24–26 of the Act set out the when a person can make an advance decision to refuse treatment. This applies if:

- the person is 18 or older, and
- they have the capacity to make an advance decision about treatment.

Information on advance decisions to refuse treatment made by young people (under the age of 18) will be available at www.dh.gov.uk/consent

9.2   Healthcare professionals must follow an advance decision if it is valid and applies to the particular circumstances. If they do not, they could face criminal prosecution (they could be charged for committing a crime) or civil liability (somebody could sue them).

9.3   Advance decisions can have serious consequences for the people who make them. They can also have an important impact on family and friends, and professionals involved in their care. Before healthcare professionals can apply an advance decision, there must be proof that the decision:

- exists
- is valid, and
- is applicable in the current circumstances.

These tests are legal requirements under section 25(1). Paragraphs 9.38–9.44 explain the standard of proof the Act requires.

Who can make an advance decision to refuse treatment?

9.4   It is up to individuals to decide whether they want to refuse treatment in advance. They are entitled to do so if they want, but there is no obligation to do so. Some people choose to make advance decisions while they are still healthy, even if there is no prospect of illness. This might be because they want to keep some control over what might happen to them in the future. Others may think of an advance decision as part of their preparations for growing older (similar to making a will). Or they might make an advance decision after they have been told they have a specific disease or condition.

Many people prefer not to make an advance decision, and instead leave healthcare professionals to make decisions in their best interests at the time a decision needs to be made. Another option is to make a Lasting Power of Attorney. This allows a trusted family member or friend to make personal welfare decisions, such as those around treatment, on someone's behalf, and in their best interests if they ever lose capacity to make those decisions themselves (see paragraph 9.33 below and chapter 7).

9.5   People can only make advance decisions to refuse treatment. Nobody has the legal right to demand specific treatment, either at the time or in advance. So no-one can insist (either at the time or in advance) on being given treatments that healthcare professionals consider to be clinically unnecessary, futile or inappropriate. But people can make a request or state their wishes and preferences in advance. Healthcare professionals should then consider the request when deciding what is in a patient's best interests (see chapter 5) if the patient lacks capacity.

9.6   Nobody can ask for and receive procedures that are against the law (for example, help with committing suicide). As section 62 sets out, the Act does not change any of the laws relating to murder, manslaughter or helping someone to commit suicide.

Capacity to make an advance decision

9.7   For most people, there will be no doubt about their capacity to make an advance decision. Even those who lack capacity to make some decisions may have the capacity to make an advance decision. In some cases it may be helpful to get evidence of a person's capacity to make the advance decision (for example, if there is a possibility that the advance decision may be challenged in the future). It is also important to remember that capacity can change over time, and a person who lacks capacity to make a decision now might be able to make it in the future.

Chapter 3 explains how to assess a person's capacity to make a decision.

[Scenario: Respecting capacity to make an advance decision]

9.8   In line with principle 1 of the Act, that 'a person must be assumed to have capacity unless it is established that he lacks capacity', healthcare professionals should always start from the assumption that a person who has made an advance decision had capacity to make it, unless they are aware of reasonable grounds to doubt the person had the capacity to make the advance decision at the time they made it.

If a healthcare professional is not satisfied that the person had capacity at the time they made the advance decision, or if there are doubts about its existence, validity or applicability, they can treat the person without fear of liability. It is good practice to record their decisions and the reasons for them. The Act does not require them to record their assessment of the person's capacity at the time the decision was made, but it would be good practice to do so.

9.9   Healthcare professionals may have particular concerns about the capacity of someone with a history of suicide attempts or suicidal thoughts who has made an advance decision. It is important to remember that making an advance decision which, if followed, may result in death does not necessarily mean a person is or feels suicidal. Nor does it necessarily mean the person lacks capacity to make the advance decision. If the person is clearly suicidal, this may raise questions about their capacity to make an advance decision at the time they made it.

What should people include in an advance decision?

9.10   There are no particular formalities about the format of an advance decision. It can be written or verbal, unless it deals with life-sustaining treatment, in which case it must be written and specific rules apply (see paragraphs 9.24–9.28 below).

9.11   An advance decision to refuse treatment:

- must state precisely what treatment is to be refused – a statement giving a general desire not to be treated is not enough
- may set out the circumstances when the refusal should apply – it is helpful to include as much detail as possible
- will only apply at a time when the person lacks capacity to consent to or refuse the specific treatment.

Specific rules apply to life-sustaining treatment.

9.12   People can use medical language or everyday language in their advance decision. But they must make clear what their wishes are and what treatment they would like to refuse.

9.13   An advance decision refusing all treatment in any situation (for example, where a person explains that their decision is based on their religion or personal beliefs) may be valid and applicable.

9.14   It is recommended that people who are thinking about making an advance decision get advice from:

- healthcare professionals (for example, their GP or the person most closely involved with current healthcare or treatment), or
- an organisation that can provide advice on specific conditions or situations (they might have their own format for recording an advance decision).

But it is up to the person whether they want to do this or not. Healthcare professionals should record details of any discussion on healthcare records.

9.15   Some people may also want to get legal advice. This will help them make sure that they express their decision clearly and accurately. It will also help to make sure that people understand their advance decision in the future.

9.16   It is a good idea to try to include possible future circumstances in the advance decision. For example, a woman may want to state in the advance decision whether or not it should still apply if she later becomes pregnant. If the document does not anticipate a change in circumstance, healthcare professionals may decide that it is not applicable if those particular circumstances arise.

9.17   If an advance decision is recorded on a patient's healthcare records, it is confidential. Some patients will tell others about their advance decision (for example, they might tell healthcare professionals, friends or family). Others will not. People who do not ask for their advance decision to be recorded on their healthcare record will need to think about where it should be kept and how they are going to let people know about their decision.

Written advance decisions

9.18 A written document can be evidence of an advance decision. It is helpful to tell others that the document exists and where it is. A person may want to carry it with them in case of emergency, or carry a card, bracelet or other indication that they have made an advance decision and explaining where it is kept.

9.19 There is no set form for written advance decisions, because contents will vary depending on a person's wishes and situation. But it is helpful to include the following information:

- full details of the person making the advance decision, including date of birth, home address and any distinguishing features (in case healthcare professionals need to identify an unconscious person, for example)
- the name and address of the person's GP and whether they have a copy of the document
- a statement that the document should be used if the person ever lacks capacity to make treatment decisions
- a clear statement of the decision, the treatment to be refused and the circumstances in which the decision will apply
- the date the document was written (or reviewed)
- the person's signature (or the signature of someone the person has asked to sign on their behalf and in their presence)
- the signature of the person witnessing the signature, if there is one (or a statement directing somebody to sign on the person's behalf).

See paragraphs 9.24–9.28 below if the advance decision deals with life-sustaining treatment.

9.20 Witnessing the person's signature is not essential, except in cases where the person is making an advance decision to refuse life-sustaining treatment. But if there is a witness, they are witnessing the signature and the fact that it confirms the wishes set out in the advance decision. It may be helpful to give a description of the relationship between the witness and person making the advance decision. The role of the witness is to witness the person's signature, it is not to certify that the person has the capacity to make the advance decision – even if the witness is a healthcare professional or knows the person.

9.21 It is possible that a professional acting as a witness will also be the person who assesses the person's capacity. If so, the professional should also make a record of the assessment, because acting as a witness does not prove that there has been an assessment.

Verbal advance decisions

9.22 There is no set format for verbal advance decisions. This is because they will vary depending on a person's wishes and situation. Healthcare professionals will need to consider whether a verbal advance decision exists and whether it is valid and applicable (see paragraphs 9.38–9.44).

9.23 Where possible, healthcare professionals should record a verbal advance decision to refuse treatment in a person's healthcare record. This will produce a written record that could prevent confusion about the decision in the future. The record should include:

- a note that the decision should apply if the person lacks capacity to make treatment decisions in the future

- a clear note of the decision, the treatment to be refused and the circumstances in which the decision will apply
- details of someone who was present when the oral advance decision was recorded and the role in which they were present (for example, healthcare professional or family member), and
- whether they heard the decision, took part in it or are just aware that it exists.

What rules apply to advance decisions to refuse life-sustaining treatment?

9.24   The Act imposes particular legal requirements and safeguards on the making of advance decisions to refuse life-sustaining treatment. Advance decisions to refuse life-sustaining treatment must meet specific requirements:

- They must be put in writing. If the person is unable to write, someone else should write it down for them. For example, a family member can write down the decision on their behalf, or a healthcare professional can record it in the person's healthcare notes.
- The person must sign the advance decision. If they are unable to sign, they can direct someone to sign on their behalf in their presence.
- The person making the decision must sign in the presence of a witness to the signature. The witness must then sign the document in the presence of the person making the advance decision. If the person making the advance decision is unable to sign, the witness can witness them directing someone else to sign on their behalf. The witness must then sign to indicate that they have witnessed the nominated person signing the document in front of the person making the advance decision.
- The advance decision must include a clear, specific written statement from the person making the advance decision that the advance decision is to apply to the specific treatment even if life is at risk.
- If this statement is made at a different time or in a separate document to the advance decision, the person making the advance decision (or someone they have directed to sign) must sign it in the presence of a witness, who must also sign it.

9.25   Section 4(10) states that life-sustaining treatment is treatment which a healthcare professional who is providing care to the person regards as necessary to sustain life. This decision will not just depend on the type of treatment. It will also depend on the circumstances in which the healthcare professional is giving it. For example, in some situations antibiotics may be life-sustaining, but in others they can be used to treat conditions that do not threaten life.

9.26   Artificial nutrition and hydration (ANH) has been recognised as a form of medical treatment. ANH involves using tubes to provide nutrition and fluids to someone who cannot take them by mouth. It bypasses the natural mechanisms that control hunger and thirst and requires clinical monitoring. An advance decision can refuse ANH. Refusing ANH in an advance decision is likely to result in the person's death, if the advance decision is followed.

9.27   It is very important to discuss advance decisions to refuse life-sustaining treatment with a healthcare professional. But it is not compulsory. A healthcare professional will be able to explain:

- what types of treatment may be life-sustaining treatment, and in what circumstances
- the implications and consequences of refusing such treatment (see also paragraph 9.14).

9.28   An advance decision cannot refuse actions that are needed to keep a person comfortable (sometimes called basic or essential care). Examples include warmth, shel-
ter, actions to keep a person clean and the offer of food and water by mouth.
Section 5 of the Act allows healthcare professionals to carry out these actions in the
best interests of a person who lacks capacity to consent (see chapter 6). An advance
decision can refuse artificial nutrition and hydration.

When should someone review or update an advance decision?

9.29   Anyone who has made an advance decision is advised to regularly review and
update it as necessary. Decisions made a long time in advance are not automatically
invalid or inapplicable, but they may raise doubts when deciding whether they are
valid and applicable. A written decision that is regularly reviewed is more likely to
be valid and applicable to current circumstances – particularly for progressive illnesses. This is because it is more likely to have taken on board changes that have
occurred in a person's life since they made their decision.

9.30   Views and circumstances may change over time. A new stage in a person's illness,
the development of new treatments or a major change in personal circumstances
may be appropriate times to review and update an advance decision.

How can someone withdraw an advance decision?

9.31   Section 24(3) allows people to cancel or alter an advance decision at any time while
they still have capacity to do so. There are no formal processes to follow. People can
cancel their decision verbally or in writing, and they can destroy any original written document. Where possible, the person who made the advance decision should
tell anybody who knew about their advance decision that it has been cancelled.
They can do this at any time. For example, they can do this on their way to the
operating theatre or immediately before being given an anaesthetic. Healthcare professionals should record a verbal cancellation in healthcare records. This then
forms a written record for future reference.

How can someone make changes to an advance decision?

9.32   People can makes changes to an advance decision verbally or in writing (section
24(3)) whether or not the advance decision was made in writing. It is good practice for healthcare professionals to record a change of decision in the person's
healthcare notes. But if the person wants to change an advance decision to include
a refusal of life-sustaining treatment, they must follow the procedures described in
paragraphs 9.24–9.28.

How do advance decisions relate to other rules about decision-making?

9.33   A valid and applicable advance decision to refuse treatment is as effective as a
refusal made when a person has capacity. Therefore, an advance decision overrules:

- the decision of any personal welfare Lasting Power of Attorney (LPA) made
  before the advance decision was made. So an attorney cannot give consent to
  treatment that has been refused in an advance decision made after the LPA was
  signed
- the decision of any court-appointed deputy (so a deputy cannot give consent
  to treatment that has been refused in an advance decision which is valid and
  applicable)

- the provisions of section 5 of the Act, which would otherwise allow healthcare professionals to give treatment that they believe is in a person's best interests.

9.34   An LPA made after an advance decision will make the advance decision invalid, if the LPA gives the attorney the authority to make decisions about the same treatment (see paragraph 9.40).

9.35   The Court of Protection may make declarations as to the existence, validity and applicability of an advance decision, but it has no power to overrule a valid and applicable advance decision to refuse treatment.

9.36   Where an advance decision is being followed, the best interests principle (see chapter 5) does not apply. This is because an advance decision reflects the decision of an adult with capacity who has made the decision for themselves. Healthcare professionals must follow a valid and applicable advance decision, even if they think it goes against a person's best interests.

Advance decisions regarding treatment for mental disorder

9.37   Advance decisions can refuse any kind of treatment, whether for a physical or mental disorder. But generally an advance decision to refuse treatment for mental disorder can be overruled if the person is detained in hospital under the Mental Health Act 1983, when treatment could be given compulsorily under Part 4 of that Act. Advance decisions to refuse treatment for other illnesses or conditions are not affected by the fact that the person is detained in hospital under the Mental Health Act. For further information see chapter 13.

How can somebody decide on the existence, validity and applicability of advance decisions?

Deciding whether an advance decision exists

9.38   It is the responsibility of the person making the advance decision to make sure their decision will be drawn to the attention of healthcare professionals when it is needed. Some people will want their decision to be recorded on their healthcare records. Those who do not will need to find other ways of alerting people that they have made an advance decision and where somebody will find any written document and supporting evidence. Some people carry a card or wear a bracelet. It is also useful to share this information with family and friends, who may alert healthcare professionals to the existence of an advance decision. But it is not compulsory. Providing their GP with a copy of the written document will allow them to record the decision in the person's healthcare records.

9.39   It is important to be able to establish that the person making the advance decision was 18 or over when they made their decision, and that they had the capacity to make that decision when they made it, in line with the two-stage test for capacity set out in chapter 3. But as explained in paragraphs 9.7–9.9 above, healthcare professionals should always start from the assumption that the person had the capacity to make the advance decision.

Deciding whether an advance decision is valid

9.40   An existing advance decision must still be valid at the time it needs to be put into effect. Healthcare professionals must consider the factors in section 25 of the Act before concluding that an advance decision is valid. Events that would make an advance decision invalid include those where:

- the person withdrew the decision while they still had capacity to do so

- after making the advance decision, the person made a Lasting Power of Attorney (LPA) giving an attorney authority to make treatment decisions that are the same as those covered by the advance decision (see also paragraph 9.33)
- the person has done something that clearly goes against the advance decision which suggests that they have changed their mind.

[*Scenario: Assessing whether an advance decision is valid*]

Deciding whether an advance decision is applicable

9.41 To be applicable, an advance decision must apply to the situation in question and in the current circumstances. Healthcare professionals must first determine if the person still has capacity to accept or refuse treatment at the relevant time (section 25(3)). If the person has capacity, they can refuse treatment there and then. Or they can change their decision and accept treatment. The advance decision is not applicable in such situations.

9.42 The advance decision must also apply to the proposed treatment. It is not applicable to the treatment in question if (section 25(4)):

- the proposed treatment is not the treatment specified in the advance decision
- the circumstances are different from those that may have been set out in the advance decision, or
- there are reasonable grounds for believing that there have been changes in circumstance, which would have affected the decision if the person had known about them at the time they made the advance decision.

9.43 So when deciding whether an advance decision applies to the proposed treatment, healthcare professionals must consider:

- how long ago the advance decision was made, and
- whether there have been changes in the patient's personal life (for example, the person is pregnant, and this was not anticipated when they made the advance decision) that might affect the validity of the advance decision, and
- whether there have been developments in medical treatment that the person did not foresee (for example, new medications, treatment or therapies).

9.44 For an advance decision to apply to life-sustaining treatment, it must meet the requirements set out in paragraphs 9.24–9.28.

[*Scenario: Assessing if an advance decision is applicable*]

What should healthcare professionals do if an advance decision is not valid or applicable?

9.45 If an advance decision is not valid or applicable to current circumstances.

- healthcare professionals must consider the advance decision as part of their assessment of the person's best interests (see chapter 5) if they have reasonable grounds to think it is a true expression of the person's wishes, and
- they must not assume that because an advance decision is either invalid or not applicable, they should always provide the specified treatment (including life-sustaining treatment) – they must base this decision on what is in the person's best interests.

What happens to decisions made before the Act comes into force?

9.46 Advance decisions made before the Act comes into force may still be valid and applicable. Healthcare professionals should apply the rules in the Act to advance decisions made before the Act comes into force, subject to the transitional protections that will apply to advance decisions that refuse life-sustaining treatment. Further guidance will be available at www.dh.gov.uk/consent.

What implications do advance decisions have for healthcare professionals?

What are healthcare professionals' responsibilities?

9.47   Healthcare professionals should be aware that:

- a patient they propose to treat may have refused treatment in advance, and
- valid and applicable advance decisions to refuse treatment have the same legal status as decisions made by people with capacity at the time of treatment.

9.48   Where appropriate, when discussing treatment options with people who have capacity, healthcare professionals should ask if there are any specific types of treatment they do not wish to receive if they ever lack capacity to consent in the future.

9.49   If somebody tells a healthcare professional that an advance decision exists for a patient who now lacks capacity to consent, they should make reasonable efforts to find out what the decision is. Reasonable efforts might include having discussions with relatives of the patient, looking in the patient's clinical notes held in the hospital or contacting the patient's GP.

9.50   Once they know a verbal or written advance decision exists, healthcare professionals must determine whether:

- it is valid (see paragraph 9.40), and
- it is applicable to the proposed treatment (see paragraphs 9.41–9.44).

9.51   When establishing whether an advance decision applies to current circumstances, healthcare professionals should take special care if the decision does not seem to have been reviewed or updated for some time. If the person's current circumstances are significantly different from those when the decision was made, the advance decision may not be applicable. People close to the person concerned, or anyone named in the advance decision, may be able to help explain the person's prior wishes.

9.52   If healthcare professionals are satisfied that an advance decision to refuse treatment exists, is valid and is applicable, they must follow it and not provide the treatment refused in the advance decision.

9.53   If healthcare professionals are not satisfied that an advance decision exists that is both valid and applicable, they can treat the person without fear of liability. But treatment must be in the person's best interests (see chapter 5). They should make clear notes explaining why they have not followed an advance decision which they consider to be invalid or not applicable.

9.54   Sometimes professionals can give or continue treatment while they resolve doubts over an advance decision. It may be useful to get information from someone who can provide information about the person's capacity when they made the advance decision. The Court of Protection can settle disagreements about the existence, validity or applicability of an advance decision. Section 26 of the Act allows healthcare professionals to give necessary treatment, including life-sustaining treatment, to stop a person's condition getting seriously worse while the court decides.

Do advance decisions apply in emergencies?

9.55   A healthcare professional must provide treatment in the patient's best interests, unless they are satisfied that there is a advance decision that is:

- valid, and
- applicable in the circumstances.

9.56   Healthcare professionals should not delay emergency treatment to look for an advance decision if there is no clear indication that one exists. But if it is clear that a person has made an advance decision that is likely to be relevant, healthcare professionals should assess its validity and applicability as soon as possible. Sometimes the urgency of treatment decisions will make this difficult.

When can healthcare professionals be found liable?

9.57   Healthcare professionals must follow an advance decision if they are satisfied that it exists, is valid and is applicable to their circumstances. Failure to follow an advance decision in this situation could lead to a claim for damages for battery or a criminal charge of assault.

9.58   But they are protected from liability if they are not:

■ aware of an advance decision, or
■ satisfied that an advance decision exists, is valid and is applicable to the particular treatment and the current circumstances (section 26(2)).

If healthcare professionals have genuine doubts, and are therefore not 'satisfied', about the existence, validity or applicability of the advance decision, treatment can be provided without incurring liability.

9.59   Healthcare professionals will be protected from liability for failing to provide treatment if they 'reasonably believe' that a valid and applicable advance decision to refuse that treatment exists. But they must be able to demonstrate that their belief was reasonable (section 26(3)) and point to reasonable grounds showing why they believe this. Healthcare professionals can only base their decision on the evidence that is available at the time they need consider an advance decision.

9.60   Some situations might be enough in themselves to raise concern about the existence, validity or applicability of an advance decision to refuse treatment. These could include situations when:

■ a disagreement between relatives and healthcare professionals about whether verbal comments were really an advance decision
■ evidence about the person's state of mind raises questions about their capacity at the time they made the decision (see paragraphs 9.7–9.9)
■ evidence of important changes in the person's behaviour before they lost capacity that might suggest a change of mind.

In cases where serious doubt remains and cannot be resolved in any other way, it will be possible to seek a declaration from the court.

What if a healthcare professional has a conscientious objection to stopping or providing life-sustaining treatment?

9.61   Home healthcare professionals may disagree in principle with patients' rights to refuse life-sustaining treatment. The Act does not change the current legal situation. They do not have to do something that goes against their beliefs. But they must not simply abandon patients or cause their care to suffer.

9.62   Healthcare professionals should make their views clear to the patient and the healthcare team as soon as someone raises the subject of withholding, stopping or providing life-sustaining treatment. Patients who still have capacity should then have the option of transferring their care to another healthcare professional, if it is possible to do this without affecting their care.

9.63   In cases where the patient now lacks capacity but has made a valid and applicable advance decision to refuse treatment which a doctor or health professional cannot, for reasons of conscience, comply with, arrangements should be made for the management of the patient's care to be transferred to another healthcare professional.[36] Where a transfer cannot be agreed, the Court of Protection can direct those responsible for the person's healthcare (for example, a Trust, doctor or other health professional) to make arrangements to take over responsibility for the person's healthcare (section 17(1)(e)).

What happens if there is a disagreement about an advance decision?

9.64   It is ultimately the responsibility of the healthcare professional who is in charge of the person's care when the treatment is required to decide whether there is an advance decision which is valid and applicable in the circumstances. In the event of disagreement about an advance decision between healthcare professionals, or between healthcare professionals and family members or others close to the person, the senior clinician must consider all the available evidence. This is likely to be a hospital consultant or the GP where the person is being treated in the community.

9.65   The senior clinician may need to consult with relevant colleagues and others who are close to or familiar with the patient. All staff involved in the person's care should be given the opportunity to express their views. If the person is in hospital, their GP may also have relevant information.

9.66   The point of such discussions should not be to try to overrule the person's advance decision but rather to seek evidence concerning its validity and to confirm its scope and its applicability to the current circumstances. Details of these discussions should be recorded in the person's healthcare records. Where the senior clinician has a reasonable belief that an advance decision to refuse medical treatment is both valid and applicable, the person's advance decision should be complied with.

When can somebody apply to the Court of Protection?

9.67   The Court of Protection can make a decision where there is genuine doubt or disagreement about an advance decision's existence, validity or applicability. But the court does not have the power to overturn a valid and applicable advance decision.

9.68   The court has a range of powers (sections 16–17) to resolve disputes concerning the personal care and medical treatment of a person who lacks capacity (see chapter 8). It can decide whether:

- a person has capacity to accept or refuse treatment at the time it is proposed
- an advance decision to refuse treatment is valid
- an advance decision is applicable to the proposed treatment in the current circumstances.

9.69   While the court decides, healthcare professionals can provide life-sustaining treatment or treatment to stop a serious deterioration in their condition. The court has emergency procedures which operate 24 hours a day to deal with urgent cases quickly. See chapter 8 for guidance on applying to the court.

10   WHAT IS THE NEW INDEPENDENT MENTAL CAPACITY ADVOCATE SERVICE AND HOW DOES IT WORK?

This chapter describes the new Independent Mental Capacity Advocate (IMCA) service created under the Act. The purpose of the IMCA service is to help particularly vulnerable people who lack the capacity to make important decisions about serious medical treatment and changes of accommodation, and who have no family or friends that it would be appro-

---

[36] *Re B (Adult: Refusal of Medical Treatment)* [2002] EWHC 429 (Fam) at paragraph 100(viii).

priate to consult about those decisions. IMCAs will work with and support people who lack capacity, and represent their views to those who are working out their best interests.

The chapter provides guidance both for IMCAs and for everyone who may need to instruct an IMCA. It explains how IMCAs should be appointed. It also explains the IMCA's duties and the situations when an IMCA should be instructed. Both IMCAs and decision-makers are required to have regard to the Code of Practice.

> In this chapter, as throughout the Code, a person's capacity (or lack of capacity) refers specifically to their capacity to make a particular decision at the time it needs to be made.

Quick summary

Understanding the role of the IMCA service

- The aim of the IMCA service is to provide independent safeguards for people who lack capacity to make certain important decisions and, at the time such decisions need to be made, have no-one else (other than paid staff) to support or represent them or be consulted.
- IMCAs must be independent.

Instructing and consulting an IMCA

- An IMCA must be instructed, and then consulted, for people lacking capacity who have no-one else to support them (other than paid staff), whenever:
  - an NHS body is proposing to provide serious medical treatment, or
  - an NHS body or local authority is proposing to arrange accommodation (or a change of accommodation) in hospital or a care home, and
  - the person will stay in hospital longer than 28 days, or
  - they will stay in the care home for more than eight weeks.
- An IMCA may be instructed to support someone who lacks capacity to make decisions concerning:
  - care reviews, where no-one else is available to be consulted
  - adult protection cases, whether or not family, friends or others are involved

Ensuring an IMCA's views are taken into consideration

- The IMCA's role is to support and represent the person who lacks capacity. Because of this, IMCAs have the right to see relevant healthcare and social care records.
- Any information or reports provided by an IMCA must be taken into account as part of the process of working out whether a proposed decision is in the person's best interests.

What is the IMCA service?

10.1   Sections 35–41 of the Act set up a new IMCA service that provides safeguards for people who:

- lack capacity to make a specified decision at the time it needs to be made
- are facing a decision on a long-term move or about serious medical treatment and
- have nobody else who is willing and able to represent them or be consulted in the process of working out their best interests.

10.2   Regulations made under the Act also state that IMCAs may be involved in other decisions, concerning:

- a care review, or
- an adult protection case.

In adult protection cases, an IMCA may be appointed even where family members or others are available to be consulted.

10.3   Most people who lack capacity to make a specific decision will have people to support them (for example, family members or friends who take an interest in their welfare). Anybody working out a person's best interests must consult these people, where possible, and take their views into account (see chapter 5). But if a person who lacks capacity has nobody to represent them or no-one who it is appropriate to consult, an IMCA must be instructed in prescribed circumstances. The prescribed circumstances are:

- providing, withholding or stopping serious medical treatment
- moving a person into long-term care in hospital or a care home (see 10.11 for definition), or
- moving the person to a different hospital or care home.

The only exception to this can be in situations where an urgent decision is needed. Further details on the situations where there is a duty to instruct an IMCA are given in paragraphs 10.40–10.58.

In other circumstances, an IMCA may be appointed for the person (see paragraphs 10.59–10.68). These include:

- care reviews or
- adult protection cases.

10.4   The IMCA will:

- be independent of the person making the decision
- provide support for the person who lacks capacity
- represent the person without capacity in discussions to work out whether he proposed decision is in the person's best interests
- provide information to help work out what is in the person's best interests (see chapter 5), and
- raise questions or challenge decisions which appear not to be in the best interests of the person.

The information the IMCA provides must be taken into account by decision-makers whenever they are working out what is in a person's best interests. See paragraphs 10.20–10.39 for more information on an IMCA's role. For more information on who is a decision-maker, see chapter 5.

10.5   The IMCA service will build on good practice in the independent advocacy sector. But IMCAs have a different role from many other advocates. They:

- provide statutory advocacy
- are instructed to support and represent people who lack capacity to make decisions on specific issues
- have a right to meet in private the person they are supporting
- are allowed access to relevant healthcare records and social care records
- provide support and representation specifically while the decision is being made, and
- act quickly so their report can form part of decision-making.

Who is responsible for delivering the service?

10.6   The IMCA service is available in England and Wales. Both countries have regulations for setting up and managing the service.

- England's regulations[37] are available at www.opsi.gov.uk/si/si200618.htm and www.opsi.gov.uk/si/dsis2006.htm.
- The regulations for Wales[38] are available at www.new.wales.gov.uk/consultations/closed/healandsoccarecloscons/.

Guidance has been issued to local health boards and local authorities involved in commissioning IMCA services for their area.

10.7   In England the Secretary of State for Health delivers the service through local authorities, who work in partnership with NHS organisations. Local authorities have financial responsibility for the service. In Wales the National Assembly for Wales delivers the service through local health boards, who have financial responsibility for the service and work in partnership with local authority social services departments and other NHS organisations. The service is commissioned from independent organisations, usually advocacy organisations.

10.8   Local authorities or NHS organisations are responsible for instructing an IMCA to represent a person who lacks capacity. In these circumstances they are called the 'responsible body'.

10.9   For decisions about serious medical treatment, the responsible body will be the NHS organisation providing the person's healthcare or treatment. But if the person is in an independent or voluntary sector hospital, the responsible body will be the NHS organisation arranging and funding the person's care, which should have arrangements in place with the independent or voluntary sector hospital to ensure an IMCA is appointed promptly.

10.10   For decisions about admission to accommodation in hospital for 28 days or more, the responsible body will be the NHS body that manages the hospital. For admission to an independent or voluntary sector hospital for 28 days or more, the responsible body will be the NHS organisation arranging and funding the person's care. The independent or voluntary hospital must have arrangements in place with the NHS organisation to ensure that an IMCA can be appointed without delay.

10.11   For decisions about moves into long-term accommodation[39] (for eight weeks or longer), or about a change of accommodation, the responsible body will be either:

- the NHS body that proposes the move or change of accommodation (e.g. a nursing home), or

---

[37] The Mental Capacity Act 2005 (Independent Mental Capacity Advocate) (General) Regulations 2006 SI: 2006 /No 1832. The 'General Regulations'. These regulations set out the details on how the IMCA will be appointed, the functions of the IMCA, including their role in challenging the decision-maker and include definitions of 'serious medical treatment' and 'NHS body'. The Mental Capacity Act 2005 (Independent Mental Capacity Advocate) (Expansion of Role) Regulations 2006 SI: 2883. The 'Expansion Regulations'. These regulations specify the circumstances in which local authorities and NHS bodies may provide the IMCA service on a discretionary basis. These include involving the IMCA in a care review and in adult protection cases.

[38] The Mental Capacity Act 2005 (Independent Mental Capacity Advocate) (Wales) Regulations 2007 SI: /No (W.). These regulations will remain in draft form until they are made by the National Assembly for Wales. The target coming into force date is 1 October 2007. Unlike the two sets of English regulations there will be one set only for Wales. Although the Welsh regulations will remain in draft form until the coming into force date, these have been drafted to give effect to similar and corresponding provisions to the regulations in England.

[39] This may be accommodation in a care home, nursing home, ordinary and sheltered housing, housing association or other registered social housing or in private sector housing provided by a local authority or in hostel accommodation.

- the local authority that has carried out an assessment of the person under the NHS and Community Care Act 1990 and decided the move may be necessary.

10.12 Sometimes NHS organisations and local authorities will make decisions together about moving a person into long-term care. In these cases, the organisation that must instruct the IMCA is the one that is ultimately responsible for the decision to move the person. The IMCA to be instructed is the one who works wherever the person is at the time that the person needs support and representation.

What are the responsible body's duties?

10.13 The responsible body:

- *must* instruct an IMCA to support and represent a person in the situations set out in paragraphs 10.40–10.58
- *may* decide to instruct an IMCA in situations described in paragraphs 10.59–10.68
- *must*, in all circumstances when an IMCA is instructed, take properly into account the information that the IMCA provides when working out whether the particular decision (such as giving, withholding or stopping treatment, changing a person's accommodation, or carrying out a recommendation following a care review or an allegation requiring adult protection) is in the best interests of the person who lacks capacity.

10.14 The responsible body should also have procedures, training and awareness programmes to make sure that:

- all relevant staff know when they need to instruct an IMCA and are able to do so promptly
- all relevant staff know how to get in touch with the IMCA service and know the procedure for instructing an IMCA
- they record an IMCA's involvement in a case and any information the IMCA provides to help decision-making
- they also record how a decision-maker has taken into account the IMCA's report and information as part of the process of working out the person's best interests (this should include reasons for disagreeing with that advice, if relevant)
- they give access to relevant records when requested by an IMCA under section 35(6)(b) of the Act
- the IMCA gets information about changes that may affect the support and representation the IMCA provides
- decision-makers let all relevant people know when an IMCA is working on a person's case, and
- decision-makers inform the IMCA of the final decision taken and the reason for it.

10.15 Sometimes an IMCA and staff working for the responsible body might disagree. If this happens, they should try to settle the disagreement through discussion and negotiation as soon as possible. If they cannot do this, they should then follow the responsible body's formal procedures for settling disputes or complaints (see paragraphs 10.34 to 10.39 below).

10.16 In some situations the IMCA may challenge a responsible body's decision, or they may help somebody who is challenging a decision. The General Regulations in England and the Regulations in Wales set out when this may happen (see also chapter 15). If there is no other way of resolving the disagreement, the decision may be challenged in the Court of Protection.

Who can be an IMCA?

10.17   In England, a person can only be an IMCA if the local authority approves their appointment. In Wales, the local health board will provide approval. Qualified employees of an approved organisation can act as IMCAs. Local authorities and health boards will usually commission independent advocacy organisations to provide the IMCA service. These organisations will work to appropriate organisational standards set through the contracting/commissioning process.

10.18   Individual IMCAs must:

- have specific experience
- have IMCA training
- have integrity and a good character, and
- be able to act independently.

All IMCAs must complete the IMCA training in order that they can work as an independent mental capacity advocate. A national advocacy qualification is also being developed, which will include the IMCA training.

Before a local authority or health board appoints an IMCA, they must carry out checks with the Criminal Records Bureau (CRB) to get a criminal record certificate or enhanced criminal record certificate for that individual.[40]

10.19   IMCAs must be independent. People cannot act as IMCAs if they:

- care for or treat (in a paid or professional capacity) the person they will be representing (this does not apply if they are an existing advocate acting for that person), or
- have links to the person instructing them, to the decision-maker or to other individuals involved in the person's care or treatment that may affect their independence.

What is an IMCA's role?

10.20   An IMCA must decide how best to represent and support the person who lacks capacity that they are helping. They:

- must confirm that the person instructing them has the authority to do so
- should interview or meet in private the person who lacks capacity, if possible
- must act in accordance with the principles of the Act (as set out in section 1 of the Act and chapter 2 of the Code) and take account of relevant guidance in the Code
- may examine any relevant records that section 35(6) of the Act gives them access to
- should get the views of professionals and paid workers providing care or treatment for the person who lacks capacity
- should get the views of anybody else who can give information about the wishes and feelings, beliefs or values of the person who lacks capacity
- should get hold of any other information they think will be necessary
- must find out what support a person who lacks capacity has had to help them make the specific decision
- must try to find out what the person's wishes and feelings, beliefs and values would be likely to be if the person had capacity
- should find out what alternative options there are

---

[40] IMCAs were named as a group that is subject to mandatory checking under the new vetting and barring system in the Safeguarding Vulnerable Groups Act 2006. Roll-out of the bulk of the scheme will take place in 2008.

- should consider whether getting another medical opinion would help the person who lacks capacity, and
- must write a report on their findings for the local authority or NHS body.

10.21 Where possible, decision-makers should make decisions based on a full under-standing of a person's past and present wishes. The IMCA should provide the decision-maker with as much of this information as possible – and anything else they think is relevant. The report they give the decision-maker may include questions about the proposed action or may include suggested alternatives, if they think that these would be better suited to the person's wishes and feelings.

10.22 Another important part of the IMCA's role is communicating their findings. Decision-makers should find the most effective way to enable them to do this. In some of the IMCA pilot areas,[41] hospital discharge teams added a 'Need to instruct an IMCA?' question on their patient or service user forms. This allowed staff to identify the need for an IMCA as early as possible, and to discuss the timetable for the decision to be made. Some decisions need a very quick IMCA response, others will allow more time. In the pilot areas, IMCA involvement led to better informed discharge planning, with a clearer focus on the best interests of a person who lacked capacity. It did not cause additional delays in the hospital discharge.

Representing and supporting the person who lacks capacity

10.23 IMCAs should take account of the guidance in chapter 5.

- IMCAs should find out whether the decision-maker has given all practical and appropriate support to help the person who lacks capacity to be involved as much as possible in decision-making. If the person has communication difficulties, the IMCA should also find out if the decision-maker has obtained any specialist help (for example, from a speech and language therapist).
- Sometimes an IMCA may find information to suggest a person might regain capacity in the future, either so they can make the decision themselves or be more involved in decision-making. In such a situation, the IMCA can ask the decision-maker to delay the decision, if it is not urgent.
- The IMCA will need to get as much information as possible about the person's wishes, feelings, beliefs and values – both past and present. They should also consider the person's religion and any cultural factors that may influence the decision.

10.24 Sometimes a responsible body will not have time to instruct an IMCA (for example in an emergency or if a decision is urgent). If this is the case, this should be recorded, with the reason an IMCA has not been instructed. Where the decision concerns a move of accommodation, the local authority must appoint an IMCA as soon as possible afterwards. Sometimes the IMCA will not have time to carry out full investigations. In these situations, the IMCA must make a judgement about what they can achieve in the time available to support and represent the person who lacks capacity.

10.25 Sometimes an IMCA might not be able to get a good picture of what the person might want. They should still try to make sure the decision-maker considers all relevant information by:

- raising relevant issues and questions, and
- providing additional, relevant information to help the final decision.

---

[41] For further information see www.dh.gov.uk/imca

Finding and evaluating information

10.26 Section 35(6) provides IMCAs with certain powers to enable them to carry out their duties. These include:

- the right to have an interview in private with the person who lacks capacity, and
- the right to examine, and take copies of, any records that the person holding the record thinks are relevant to the investigation (for example, clinical records, care plans, social care assessment documents or care home records).

10.27 The IMCA may also need to meet professionals or paid carers providing care or treatment for the person who lacks capacity. These people can help assess the information in case records or other sources. They can also comment on possible alternative courses of action. Ultimately, it is the decision-maker's responsibility to decide whether a proposed course of action is in the person's best interests. However, the Act requires the decision-maker to take account of the reports made and information given by the IMCA. In most cases a decision on the person's best interests will be made through discussion involving all the relevant people who are providing care or treatment, as well as the IMCA.

Finding out the person's wishes and feelings, beliefs and values

10.28 The IMCA needs to try and find out what the person's wishes and feelings might be, and what their underlying beliefs and values might also be. The IMCA should try to communicate both verbally and non-verbally with the person who may lack capacity, as appropriate. For example, this might mean using pictures or photographs. But there will be cases where the person cannot communicate at all (for example, if they are unconscious). The IMCA may also talk to other professionals or paid carers directly involved in providing present or past care or treatment. The IMCA might also need to examine health and social care records and any written statements of preferences the person may have made while they still had capacity to do so.

Chapter 5 contains further guidance on finding out the views of people who lack capacity. Chapter 3 contains further guidance on helping someone to make their own decision.

Considering alternative courses of action

10.29 The IMCA will need to check whether the decision-maker has considered all possible options. They should also ask whether the proposed option is less restrictive of the person's rights or future choices or would allow them more freedom (chapter 2, principle 5).

10.30 The IMCA may wish to discuss possible options with other professionals or paid carers directly involved in providing care or treatment for the person. But they must respect the confidentiality of the person they are representing.

[*Scenario: Using an IMCA*]

Getting a second medical opinion

10.31 For decisions about serious medical treatment, the IMCA may consider seeking a second medical opinion from a doctor with appropriate expertise. This puts a person who lacks the capacity to make a specific decision in the same position as a person who has capacity, who has the right to request a second opinion.

What happens if the IMCA disagrees with the decision-maker?

10.32   The IMCA's role is to support and represent their client. They may do this through asking questions, raising issues, offering information and writing a report. They will often take part in a meeting involving different healthcare and social care staff to work out what is in the person's best interests. There may sometimes be cases when an IMCA thinks that a decision-maker has not paid enough attention to their report and other relevant information and is particularly concerned about the decision made. They may then need to challenge the decision.

10.33   An IMCA has the same rights to challenge a decision as any other person caring for the person or interested in his welfare. The right of challenge applies both to decisions about lack of capacity and a person's best interests.

10.34   Chapter 15 sets out how disagreements can be settled. The approach will vary, depending on the type and urgency of the disagreement. It could be a formal or informal approach.

Disagreements about health care or treatment

- Consult the Patient Advice and Liaison Service (England)
- Consult the Community Health Council (Wales)
- Use the NHS Complaints Procedure
- Refer the matter to the local continuing care review panel
- Engage the services of the Independent Complaints Advocacy Service (England) or another advocate.

Disagreements about social care

- Use the care home's complaints procedure (if the person is in a care home)
- Use the local authority complaints procedure.

10.35   Before using these formal methods, the IMCA and the decision-maker should discuss the areas they disagree about – particularly those that might have a serious impact on the person the IMCA is representing. The IMCA and decision-maker should make time to listen to each other's views and to understand the reason for the differences. Sometimes these discussions can help settle a disagreement.

10.36   Sometimes an IMCA service will have a steering group, with representatives from the local NHS organisations and the local authority. These representatives can sometimes negotiate between two differing views. Or they can clarify policy on a certain issue. They should also be involved if an IMCA believes they have discovered poor practice on an important issue.

10.37   IMCAs may use complaints procedures as necessary to try to settle a disagreement – and they can pursue a complaint as far as the relevant ombudsman if needed. In particularly serious or urgent cases, an IMCA may seek permission to refer a case to the Court of Protection for a decision. The Court will make a decision in the best interests of the person who lacks capacity.

10.38   The first step in making a formal challenge is to approach the Official Solicitor (OS) with the facts of the case. The OS can decide to apply to the court as a litigation friend (acting on behalf of the person the IMCA is representing). If the OS decides not to apply himself, the IMCA can ask for permission to apply to the Court of Protection. The OS can still be asked to act as a litigation friend for the person who lacks capacity.

10.39   In extremely serious cases, the IMCA might want to consider an application for judicial review in the High Court. This might happen if the IMCA thinks there are very serious consequences to a decision that has been made by a public authority. There are time limits for making an application, and the IMCA would have to instruct solicitors – and may be liable for the costs of the case going to court. So

IMCAs should get legal advice before choosing this approach. The IMCA can also ask the OS to consider making the claim.

What decisions require an IMCA?

10.40   There are three types of decisions which require an IMCA to be instructed for people who lack capacity. These are:

- decisions about providing, withholding or stopping serious medical treatment
- decisions about whether to place people into accommodation (for example a care home or a long stay hospital), and
- decisions about whether to move people to different long stay accommodation.

For these decisions all local authorities and all health bodies must refer the same kinds of decisions to an IMCA for anyone who lacks capacity and qualifies for the IMCA service.

10.41   There are two further types of decisions where the responsible body has the power to instruct an IMCA for a person who lacks capacity. These are decisions relating to:

- care reviews and
- adult protection cases.

In such cases, the relevant local authority or NHS body must decide in each individual case whether it would be of particular benefit to the person who lacks capacity to have an IMCA to support them. The factors which should be considered are explained in paragraphs 10.59–10.68.[42]

Decisions about serious medical treatment

10.42   Where a serious medical treatment decision is being considered for a person who lacks the capacity to consent, and who qualifies for additional safeguards, section 37 of the Act imposes a duty on the NHS body to instruct an IMCA. NHS bodies must instruct an IMCA whenever they are proposing to take a decision about 'serious medical treatment', or proposing that another organisation (such as a private hospital) carry out the treatment on their behalf, if:

- the person concerned does not have the capacity to make a decision about the treatment, and
- there is no-one appropriate to consult about whether the decision is in the person's best interests, other than paid care staff.

10.43   Regulations for England and Wales set out the definition of 'serious medical treatment' for decisions that require an IMCA. It includes treatments for both mental and physical conditions.

Serious medical treatment is defined as treatment which involves giving new treatment, stopping treatment that has already started or withholding treatment that could be offered in circumstances where:

- if a single treatment is proposed there is a fine balance between the likely benefits and the burdens to the patient and the risks involved
- a decision between a choice of treatments is finely balanced, or
- what is proposed is likely to have serious consequences for the patient.

---

[42] See chapter 11 for information about the role of 'consultees' when research is proposed involving a person who lacks capacity to make a decision about whether to agree to take part in research. In certain situations IMCAs may be involved as consultees for research purposes

10.44 'Serious consequences' are those which could have a serious impact on the patient, either from the effects of the treatment itself or its wider implications. This may include treatments which:

- cause serious and prolonged pain, distress or side effects
- have potentially major consequences for the patient (for example, stopping life-sustaining treatment or having major surgery such as heart surgery), or
- have a serious impact on the patient's future life choices (for example, interventions for ovarian cancer).

10.45 It is impossible to set out all types of procedures that may amount to 'serious medical treatment', although some examples of medical treatments that might be considered serious include:

- chemotherapy and surgery for cancer
- electro-convulsive therapy
- therapeutic sterilisation
- major surgery (such as open-heart surgery or brain/neuro-surgery)
- major amputations (for example, loss of an arm or leg)
- treatments which will result in permanent loss of hearing or sight
- withholding or stopping artificial nutrition and hydration, and
- termination of pregnancy.

These are illustrative examples only, and whether these or other procedures are considered serious medical treatment in any given case, will depend on the circumstances and the consequences for the patient. There are also many more treatments which will be defined as serious medical treatments under the Act's regulations. Decision-makers who are not sure whether they need to instruct an IMCA should consult their colleagues.

10.46 The only situation in which the duty to instruct an IMCA need not be followed, is when an urgent decision is needed (for example, to save the person's life). This decision must be recorded with the reason for the non-referral. Responsible bodies will however still need to instruct an IMCA for any serious treatment that follows the emergency treatment.

10.47 While a decision-maker is waiting for the IMCA's report, they must still act in the person's best interests (for example, to give treatment that stops the person's condition getting worse).

[*Scenario: Using an IMCA for serious medical treatment*]

10.48 Some decisions about medical treatment are so serious that the courts need to make them (see chapter 8). But responsible bodies should still instruct an IMCA in these cases. The OS may be involved as a litigation friend of the person who lacks capacity.

10.49 Responsible bodies do not have to instruct an IMCA for patients detained under the Mental Health Act 1983, if:

- the treatment is for mental disorder, and
- they can give it without the patient's consent under that Act.

10.50 If serious medical treatment proposed for the detained patient is not for their mental disorder, the patient then has a right to an IMCA – as long as they meet the Mental Capacity Act's requirements. So a detained patient without capacity to consent to cancer treatment, for example, should qualify for an IMCA if there are no family or friends whom it would be appropriate to consult.

Decisions about accommodation or changes of residence

10.51 The Act imposes similar duties on NHS bodies and local authorities who are responsible for long-term accommodation decisions for a person who lacks the capacity to agree to the placement and who qualifies for the additional safeguard of an IMCA. The right to an IMCA applies to decisions about long-term accommodation in a hospital or care home if it is:

- provided or arranged by the NHS, or
- residential care that is provided or arranged by the local authority or provided under section 117 of the Mental Health Act 1983, or
- a move between such accommodation.

10.52 Responsible bodies have a duty to instruct an IMCA if:

- an NHS organisation proposes to place a person who lacks capacity in a hospital – or to move them to another hospital – for longer than 28 days, or
- an NHS organisation proposes to place a person who lacks capacity in a care home – or to move them to a different care home – for what is likely to be longer than eight weeks.

In either situation the other qualifying conditions apply. So, if the accommodation is for less than 28 days in a hospital or less than 8 weeks in a care home, then an IMCA need not be appointed.

10.53 The duty also applies if a local authority carries out an assessment under section 47 of the NHS and Community Care Act 1990, and it decides to:

- provide care services for a person who lacks capacity in the form of residential accommodation in a care home or its equivalent (see paragraph 10.11) which is likely to be longer than eight weeks, or
- move a person who lacks capacity to another care home or its equivalent for a period likely to exceed eight weeks.

10.54 In some cases, a care home may decide to de-register so that they can provide accommodation and care in a different way. If a local authority makes the new arrangements, then an IMCA should still be instructed if a patient lacks capacity and meets the other qualifying conditions.

10.55 Sometimes a person's placement will be longer than expected. The responsible body should involve an IMCA as soon as they realise the stay will be longer than 28 days or eight weeks, as appropriate.

10.56 People who fund themselves in long-term accommodation have the same rights to an IMCA as others, if the local authority:

- carries out an assessment under section 47 of the NHS and Community Care Act 1990, and
- decides it has a duty to the person (under either section 21 or 29 of the National Assistance Act 1947 or section 117 of the Mental Health Act 1983).

10.57 Responsible bodies can only put aside the duty to involve an IMCA if the placement or move is urgent (for example, an emergency admission to hospital or possible homelessness). The decision-maker must involve an IMCA as soon as possible after making an emergency decision, if:

- the person is likely to stay in hospital for longer than 28 days, or
- they will stay in other accommodation for longer than eight weeks.

10.58 Responsible bodies do not have to involve IMCAs if the person in question is going to be required to stay in the accommodation under the Mental Health Act 1983. But if a person is discharged from detention, they have a right to an IMCA in future accommodation decisions (if they meet the usual conditions set out in the Act).

When can a local authority or NHS body decide to instruct an IMCA?

10.59   The Expansion Regulations have given local authorities and NHS bodies the power to apply the IMCA role to two further types of decisions:

- a care review, and
- adult protection cases that involve vulnerable people.

10.60   In these situations, the responsible body must consider in each individual case whether to instruct an IMCA. Where an IMCA is instructed:

- the decision-maker must be satisfied that having an IMCA will be of particular benefit to the person who lacks capacity
- the decision-maker must also follow the best interests checklist, including getting the views of anyone engaged in caring for a person when assessing their best interests, and
- the decision-maker must consider the IMCA's report and related information when making a decision.

10.61   Responsible bodies are expected to take a strategic approach in deciding when they will use IMCAs in these two additional situations. They should establish a policy locally for determining these decisions, setting out the criteria for appointing an IMCA including the issues to be taken into account when deciding if an IMCA will be of particular benefit to the person concerned. However, decision-makers will need to consider each case separately to see if the criteria are met. Local authorities or NHS bodies may want to publish their approach for ease of access, setting out the ways they intend to use these additional powers and review it periodically.

Involving an IMCA in care reviews

10.62   A responsible body can instruct an IMCA to support and represent a person who lacks capacity when:

- they have arranged accommodation for that person
- they aim to review the arrangements (as part of a care plan or otherwise), and
- there are no family or friends who it would be appropriate to consult.

10.63   Section 7 of the Local Authority Social Services Act 1970 sets out current requirements for care reviews. It states that there should be a review 'within three months of help being provided or major changes made to services'. There should then be a review every year – or more often, if needed.

10.64   Reviews should relate to decisions about accommodation:

- for someone who lacks capacity to make a decision about accommodation
- that will be provided for a continuous period of more than 12 weeks
- that are not the result of an obligation under the Mental Health Act 1983, and
- that do not relate to circumstances where sections 37 to 39 of the Act would apply.

10.65   Where the person is to be detained or required to live in accommodation under the Mental Health Act 1983, an IMCA will not be needed since the safeguards available under that Act will apply.

Involving IMCAs in adult protection cases

10.66   Responsible bodies have powers to instruct an IMCA to support and represent a person who lacks capacity where it is alleged that:

- the person is or has been abused or neglected by another person, or
- the person is abusing or has abused another person.

The responsible bodies can only instruct an IMCA if they propose to take, or have already taken, protective measures. This is in accordance with adult protection procedures set up under statutory guidance.[43]

10.67 In adult protection cases (and no other cases), access to IMCAs is not restricted to people who have no-one else to support or represent them. People who lack capacity who have family and friends can still have an IMCA to support them in the adult protection procedures.

10.68 In some situations, a case may start out as an adult protection case where a local authority may consider whether or not to involve an IMCA under the criteria they have set – but may then become a case where the allegations or evidence give rise to the question of whether the person should be moved in their best interests. In these situations the case has become one where an IMCA must be involved if there is no-one else appropriate to support and represent the person in this decision.

Who qualifies for an IMCA?

10.69 Apart from the adult protection cases discussed above, IMCAs are only available to people who:

- lack capacity to make a specific decision about serious medical treatment or long-term accommodation, and
- have no family or friends who are available and appropriate to support or represent them apart from professionals or paid workers providing care or treatment, and
- have not previously named someone who could help with a decision, and
- have not made a Lasting Power of Attorney or Enduring Power of Attorney (see paragraph 10.70 below).

10.70 The Act says that IMCAs cannot be instructed if:

- a person who now lacks capacity previously named a person that should be consulted about decisions that affect them, and that person is available and willing to help
- the person who lacks capacity has appointed an attorney, either under a Lasting Power of Attorney or an Enduring Power of Attorney, and the attorney continues to manage the person's affairs
- the Court of Protection has appointed a deputy, who continues to act on the person's behalf.

10.71 However, where a person has no family or friends to represent them, but does have an attorney or deputy who has been appointed solely to deal with their property and affairs, they should not be denied access to an IMCA. The Government is seeking to amend the Act at the earliest opportunity to ensure that, in such circumstances, an IMCA should always be appointed to represent the person's views when they lack the capacity to make decisions relating to serious medical treatment or long-term accommodation moves.

---

[43] Published guidance: *No secrets: Guidance on developing and implementing multi-agency policies and procedures to protect vulnerable adults from abuse* for England (on the Department of Health website) and *In safe hands* in Wales. No secrets applies to adults aged 18 or over. The Children Act 1989 applies to 16 and 17 year olds who may be facing abuse. Part V of the Act covers the Protection of Children, which includes at section 47 the duty to investigate by a local authority in order to decide whether they should take any action to safeguard or promote a child's welfare where he or she requires protection or may suffer harm. See also chapter 12 of this Code.

10.72 A responsible body can still instruct an IMCA if the Court of Protection is deciding on a deputy, but none is in place when a decision needs to be made.

[*Scenario: Qualifying for an IMCA*]

Will IMCAs be available to people in prisons?

10.73 IMCAs should be available to people who are in prison and lack capacity to make decisions about serious medical treatment or long-term accommodation.

Who is it 'appropriate to consult'?

10.74 The IMCA is a safeguard for those people who lack capacity, who have no-one close to them who 'it would be appropriate to consult'. (This is apart from adult protection cases where this criterion does not apply.) The safeguard is intended to apply to those people who have little or no network of support, such as close family or friends, who take an interest in their welfare or no-one willing or able to be formally consulted in decision-making processes.

10.75 The Act does not define those 'whom it would be appropriate to consult' and the evaluation of the IMCA pilots reported that decision-makers in the local authority and in the NHS, whose decision it is to determine this, sometimes found it difficult to establish when an IMCA was required.[44] Section 4(7) provides that consultation about a person's best interests shall include among others, anyone:

- named by the person as someone to be consulted on a relevant decision
- engaged in caring for them, or
- interested in their welfare (see chapter 4).

10.76 The decision-maker must determine if it is possible and practical to speak to these people, and those described in paragraph 10.70 when working out whether the proposed decision is in the person's best interests. If it is not possible, practical and appropriate to consult anyone, an IMCA should be instructed.

10.77 There may be situations where a person who lacks capacity has family or friends, but it is not practical or appropriate to consult them. For example, an elderly person with dementia may have an adult child who now lives in Australia, or an older person may have relatives who very rarely visit. Or, a family member may simply refuse to be consulted. In such cases, decision-makers must instruct an IMCA – for serious medical treatment and care moves and record the reason for the decision.

10.78 The person who lacks capacity may have friends or neighbours who know their wishes and feelings but are not willing or able to help with the specific decision to be made. They may think it is too much of a responsibility. If they are elderly and frail themselves, it may be too difficult for them to attend case conferences and participate formally. In this situation, the responsible body should instruct an IMCA, and the IMCA may visit them and enable them to be involved more informally.

10.79 If a family disagrees with a decision-maker's proposed action, this is not grounds for concluding that there is nobody whose views are relevant to the decision.

10.80 A person who lacks capacity and already has an advocate may still be entitled to an IMCA. The IMCA would consult with the advocate. Where that advocate meets the appointment criteria for the IMCA service, they may be appointed to fulfil the IMCA role for this person in addition to their other duties.

---

[44] See www.dh.gov.uk/PolicyAndGuidance/HealthAndSocialCareTopics/SocialCare/IMCA/fs/en

11 HOW DOES THE ACT AFFECT RESEARCH PROJECTS INVOLVING A PERSON WHO LACKS CAPACITY?

It is important that research involving people who lack capacity can be carried out, and that is carried out properly. Without it, we would not improve our knowledge of what causes a person to lack or lose capacity, and the diagnosis, treatment, care and needs of people who lack capacity.

This chapter gives guidance on involving people who lack capacity to consent to take part in research. It sets out:

- what the Act means by 'research'
- the requirements that people must meet if their research project involves somebody who lacks capacity
- the specific responsibilities of researchers, and
- how the Act applies to research that started before the Act came into force.

This chapter only deals with research in relation to adults. Further guidance will be provided on how the Act applies in relation to research involving those under the age of 18.

> In this chapter, as throughout the Code, a person's capacity (or lack of capacity) refers specifically to their capacity to make a particular decision at the time it needs to be made.

Quick summary

The Act's rules for research that includes people who lack capacity to consent to their involvement cover:

- when research can be carried out
- the ethical approval process
- respecting the wishes and feelings of people who lack capacity
- other safeguards to protect people who lack capacity
- how to engage with a person who lacks capacity
- how to engage with carers and other relevant people.

This chapter also explains:

- the specific rules that apply to research involving human tissue and
- what to do if research projects have already been given the go-ahead.

The Act applies to all research that is intrusive. 'Intrusive' means research that would be unlawful if it involved a person who had capacity but had not consented to take part. The Act does not apply to research involving clinical trials (testing new drugs).

Why does the Act cover research?

11.1   Because the Act is intended to assist and support people who may lack capacity, the Act protects people who take part in research projects but lack capacity to make decisions about their involvement. It makes sure that researchers respect their wishes and feelings. The Act does not apply to research that involves clinical trials of medicines – because these are covered by other rules.[45]

---

[45] The Medicines for Human Use (Clinical Trials) Regulations 2004.

How can research involving people who lack capacity help?

A high percentage of patients with Down's syndrome lack capacity to agree or refuse to take part in research. Research involving patients with Down's syndrome has shown that they are more likely than other people to get pre-senile dementia. Research has also shown that when this happens the pathological changes that occur in a person with Down's syndrome (changes affecting their body and brain) are similar to those that occur in someone with Alzheimer's disease. This means that we now know that treatment similar to that used for memory disorders in patients with Alzheimer's is appropriate to treat dementia in those with Down's syndrome.

What is 'research'?

11.2   The Act does not have a specific definition for 'research'. The Department of Health and National Assembly for Wales publications Research governance framework for health and social care both state:

'research can be defined as the attempt to derive generalisable new knowledge by addressing clearly defined questions with systematic and rigorous methods.'[46]

Research may:

- provide information that can be applied generally to an illness, disorder or condition
- demonstrate how effective and safe a new treatment is
- add to evidence that one form of treatment works better than another
- add to evidence that one form of treatment is safer than another, or
- examine wider issues (for example, the factors that affect someone's capacity to make a decision).

11.3   Researchers must state clearly if an activity is part of someone's care and not part of the research. Sometimes experimental medicine or treatment may be performed for the person's benefit and be the best option for their care. But in these cases, it may be difficult to decide whether treatment is research or care. Where there is doubt, the researcher should seek legal advice.

What assumptions can a researcher make about capacity?

11.4   Researchers should assume that a person has capacity, unless there is proof that they lack capacity to make a specific decision (see chapter 3). The person must also receive support to try to help them make their own decision (see chapter 2). The person whose capacity is in question has the right to make decisions that others might not agree with, and they have the right not to take part in research.

What research does the Act cover?

11.5   It is expected that most of the researchers who ask for their research to be approved under the Act will be medical or social care researchers. However, the Act can cover more than just medical and social care research. Intrusive research which does not

---

[46] www.dh.gov.uk/PublicationsAndStatistics/Publications/PublicationsPolicyAndGuidance/ PublicationsPolicyAndGuidanceArticle/fs/en?CONTENT_ID=4008777&chk=dMRd/5 and www.word.wales.gov.uk/content/governance/governance-e.htm

meet the requirements of the Act cannot be carried out lawfully in relation to people who lack capacity.

11.6   The Act applies to research that:

- is 'intrusive' (if a person taking part had capacity, the researcher would need to get their consent to involve them)
- involves people who have an impairment of, or a disturbance in the functioning of, their mind or brain which makes them unable to decide whether or not to agree to take part in the research (i.e. they lack capacity to consent), and
- is not a clinical trial covered under the Medicines for Human Use (Clinical Trials) Regulations 2004.

11.7   There are circumstances where no consent is needed to lawfully involve a person in research. These apply to all persons, whether they have capacity or not:

- Sometimes research only involves data that has been anonymised (it cannot be traced back to individuals). Confidentiality and data protection laws do not apply in this case.
- Under the Human Tissue Act 2004, research that deals only with human tissue that has been anonymised does not require consent (see paragraphs 11.37–11.40). This applies to both those who have capacity and those who do not. But the research must have ethical approval, and the tissue must come from a living person.[47]
- If researchers collected human tissue samples before 31 August 2006, they do not need a person's consent to work on them. But they will normally have to get ethical approval.
- Regulations[48] made under section 251 of the NHS Act 2006 (formerly known as section 60 of the Health and Social Care Act 2001[49]) allow people to use confidential patient information without breaking the law on confidentiality by applying to the Patient Information Advisory Group for approval on behalf of the Secretary of State.[50]

Who is responsible for making sure research meets the Act's requirements?

11.8   Responsibility for meeting the Act's requirements lies with:

- the 'appropriate body', as defined in regulations made by the Secretary of State (for regulations applying in England) or the National Assembly for Wales (for regulations applying in Wales) (see paragraph 11.10), and
- the researchers carrying out the research (see paragraphs 11.20–11.40).

How can research get approval?

11.9   Research covered by the Act cannot include people who lack capacity to consent to the research unless:

- it has the approval of 'the appropriate body', and
- it follows other requirements in the Act to:

---

[47] Human Tissue Act 2004 section 1(9).
[48] Health Service (Control of Patient Information) Regulations 2002 Section I. 2002/1438.
[49] Section 60 of the Health and Social Care Act 2001 was included in the NHS Act 2006 which consolidated all the previous health legislation still in force
[50] The Patient Information Advisory Group considers applications on behalf of the Secretary of State to allow the common law duty of confidentiality to be aside. It was established under section 61of the Health and Social Care Act 2006 (now known as section 252 of the NHS Act 2006). Further information can be found at www.advisorybodies.doh.gov.uk/PIAG.

  - consider the views of carers and other relevant people
  - treat the person's interests as more important than those of science and society, and
  - respect any objections a person who lacks capacity makes during research.

11.10 An 'appropriate body' is an organisation that can approve research projects. In England, the 'appropriate body' must be a research ethics committee recognised by the Secretary of State.[51] In Wales, the 'appropriate body' must be a research ethics committee recognised by the Welsh Assembly Government.

11.11 The appropriate body can only approve a research project if the research is linked to:

  - an impairing condition that affects the person who lacks capacity, or
  - the treatment of that condition (see paragraph 11.17)

and:

  - there are reasonable grounds for believing that the research would be less effective if only people with capacity are involved, and
  - the research project has made arrangements to consult carers and to follow the other requirements of the Act.

11.12 Research must also meet one of two requirements:

  1. The research must have some chance of benefiting the person who lacks capacity, as set out in paragraph 11.14 below. The benefit must be in proportion to any burden caused by taking part, or
  2. The aim of the research must be to provide knowledge about the cause of, or treatment or care of people with, the same impairing condition – or a similar condition.

If researchers are relying on the second requirement, the Act sets out further requirements that must be met:

  - the risk to the person who lacks capacity must be negligible
  - there must be no significant interference with the freedom of action or privacy of the person who lacks capacity, and
  - nothing must be done to or in relation to the person who lacks capacity which is unduly invasive or restrictive (see paragraphs 11.16–11.19 below).

11.13 An impairing condition:

  - is caused by (or may be caused by) an impairment of, or disturbance in the functioning of, the person's mind or brain
  - causes (or may cause) an impairment or disturbance of the mind or brain, or
  - contributes to (or may contribute to) an impairment or disturbance of the mind or brain.

Balancing the benefit and burden of research

11.14 Potential benefits of research for a person who lacks capacity could include:

  - developing more effective ways of treating a person or managing their condition
  - improving the quality of healthcare, social care or other services that they have access to
  - discovering the cause of their condition, if they would benefit from that knowledge, or
  - reducing the risk of the person being harmed, excluded or disadvantaged.

---

[51] Mental Capacity Act 2005 (Appropriate Body) (England) Regulations 2006.

11.15 Benefits may be direct or indirect (for example, the person might benefit at a later date if policies or care packages affecting them are changed because of the research). It might be that participation in the research itself will be of benefit to the person in particular circumstances. For example, if the research involves interviews and the person has the opportunity to express their views, this could be considered of real benefit to a particular individual.

Providing knowledge about causes, treatment or care of people with the same impairing condition or a similar condition

11.16 It is possible for research to be carried out which doesn't actually benefit the person taking part, as long as it aims to provide knowledge about the causes, treatment or care of people with the same impairing condition, or a similar condition. 'Care' and 'treatment' are not limited to medical care and treatment. For example, research could examine how day-to-day life in prison affects prisoners with mental health conditions.

11.17 It is the person's actual condition that must be the same or similar in research, not the underlying cause. A 'similar condition' may therefore have a different cause to that suffered by the participant. For example, research into ways of supporting people with learning disabilities to live more independently might involve a person with a learning disability caused by a head trauma. But its findings might help people with similar learning disabilities that have different causes.

[*Scenario: Research that helps find a cause or treatment*]

11.18 Any risk to people involved in this category of research must be 'negligible' (minimal). This means that a person should suffer no harm or distress by taking part. Researchers must consider risks to psychological wellbeing as well as physical wellbeing. This is particularly relevant for research related to observations or interviews.

11.19 Research in this category also must not affect a person's freedom of action or privacy in a significant way, and it should not be unduly invasive or restrictive. What will be considered as unduly invasive will be different for different people and different types of research. For example, in psychological research some people may think a specific question is intrusive, but others would not. Actions will not usually be classed as unduly invasive if they do not go beyond the experience of daily life, a routine medical examination or a psychological examination.

[*Scenario: Assessing the risk to research participants*]

What responsibilities do researchers have?

11.20 Before starting the research, the research team must make arrangements to:

- obtain approval for the research from the 'appropriate body'
- get the views of any carers and other relevant people before involving a person who lacks capacity in research (see paragraphs 11.22–11.28). There is an exception to this consultation requirement in situations where urgent treatment needs to be given or is about to be given
- respect the objections, wishes and feelings of the person, and
- place more importance on the person's interests than on those of science and society.

11.21 The research proposal must give enough information about what the team will do if a person who lacks capacity needs urgent treatment during research and it is not possible to speak to the person's carer or someone else who acts or makes decisions on behalf of the person (see paragraphs 11.32–11.36).

Consulting carers

11.22 Once it has been established that a person lacks capacity to agree to participate, then before they are included in research the researcher must consult with specified people in accordance with section 32 of the Act to determine whether the person should be included in the research.

Who can researchers consult?

11.23 The researcher should as a matter of good practice take reasonable steps to identify someone to consult. That person (the consultee) must be involved in the person's care, interested in their welfare and must be willing to help. They must not be a professional or paid care worker. They will probably be a family member, but could be another person.

11.24 The researcher must take into account previous wishes and feelings that the person might have expressed about who they would, or would not, like involved in future decisions.

11.25 A person is not prevented from being consulted if they are an attorney authorised under a registered Lasting Power of Attorney or are a deputy appointed by the Court of Protection. But that person must not be acting in a professional or paid capacity (for example, person's solicitor).

11.26 Where there is no-one who meets the conditions mentioned at paragraphs 11.23 and 11.25, the researcher must nominate a person to be the consulted. In this situation, they must follow guidance from the Secretary of State for Health in England or the National Assembly for Wales (the guidance will be available from mid-2007). The person who is nominated must have no connection with the research project.

11.27 The researcher must provide the consultee with information about the research project and ask them:

- for advice about whether the person who lacks capacity should take part in the project, and
- what they think the person's feelings and wishes would be, if they had capacity to decide whether to take part.

11.28 Sometimes the consultee will say that the person would probably not take part in the project or that they would ask to be withdrawn. In this situation, the researcher must not include the person in the project, or they should withdraw them from it. But if the project has started, and the person is getting treatment as part of the research, the researcher may decide that the person should not be withdrawn if the researcher reasonably believes that this would cause a significant risk to the person's health. The researcher may decide that the person should continue with the research while the risk exists. But they should stop any parts of the study that are not related to the risk to the person's health.

What other safeguards does the Act require?

11.29 Even when a consultee agrees that a person can take part in research, the researcher must still consider the person's wishes and feelings.

11.30 Researchers must not do anything the person who lacks capacity objects to. They must not do anything to go against any advance decision to refuse treatment or other statement the person has previously made expressing preferences about their care or treatment. They must assume that the person's interests in this matter are more important than those of science and society.

11.31 A researcher must withdraw someone from a project if:

- they indicate in any way that they want to be withdrawn from the project (for example, if they become upset or distressed), or
- any of the Act's requirements are no longer met.

What happens if urgent decisions are required during the research project?

11.32 Anyone responsible for caring for a person must give them urgent treatment if they need it. In some circumstances, it may not be possible to separate the research from the urgent treatment.

11.33 A research proposal should explain to the appropriate body how researchers will deal with urgent decisions which may occur during the project, when there may not be time to carry out the consultations required under the Act. For example, after a patient has arrived in intensive care, the doctor may want to chart the course of an injury by taking samples or measurements immediately and then taking further samples after some type of treatment to compare with the first set.

11.34 Special rules apply where a person who lacks capacity is getting, or about to get, urgent treatment and researchers want to include them in a research project. If in these circumstances a researcher thinks that it is necessary to take urgent action for the purposes of the research, and they think it is not practical to consult someone about it, the researcher can take that action if:

- they get agreement from a registered medical practitioner not involved with the research, or
- they follow a procedure that the appropriate body agreed to at approval stage.

11.35 The medical practitioner may have a connection to the person who lacks capacity (for example, they might be their doctor). But they must not be involved in the research project in any way. This is to avoid conflicts of interest.

11.36 This exception to the duty to consult only applies:

- for as long as the person needs urgent treatment, and
- when the researcher needs to take action urgently for research to be valid.

It is likely to be limited to research into procedures or treatments used in emergencies. It does not apply where the researcher simply wants to act quickly.

What happens for research involving human tissue?

11.37 A person with capacity has to give their permission for someone to remove tissue from their body (for example, taking a biopsy (a sample) for diagnosis or removal of tissue in surgery). The Act allows the removal of tissue from the body of a person who lacks capacity, if it is in their best interests (see chapter 5).

11.38 People with capacity must also give permission for the storage or use of tissue for certain purposes, set out in the Human Tissue Act 2004, (for example, transplants and research). But there are situations in which permission is not required by law:

- research where the samples are anonymised and the research has ethical approval[52]
- clinical audit
- education or training relating to human health
- performance assessment

[52] Section 1(9) of the Human Tissue Act 2004.

- public health monitoring, and
- quality assurance.

11.39   If an adult lacks capacity to consent, the Human Tissue Act 2004 says that tissue can be stored or used without seeking permission if the storage or use is:

- to get information relevant to the health of another individual (for example, before conducting a transplant), as long as the researcher or healthcare professional storing or using the human tissue believes they are doing it in the best interests of the person who lacks capacity to consent
- for a clinical trial approved and carried out under the Medicines for Human Use (Clinical Trials) Regulations 2004, or
- for intrusive research:
  - after the Mental Capacity Act comes into force
  - that meets the Act's requirements, and
  - that has ethical approval.

11.40   Tissue samples that were obtained before 31 August 2006 are existing holdings under the Human Tissue Act. Researchers can work with these tissues without seeking permission. But they will still need to get ethical approval. Guidance is available in the Human Tissue Authority Code of Practice on consent.[53]

What should happen to research that started before the Act came into force?

What if a person has capacity when research starts but loses capacity?

11.41   Some people with capacity will agree to take part in research but may then lose capacity before the end of the project. In this situation, researchers will be able to continue research as long as they comply with the conditions set out in the Mental Capacity Act 2005 (Loss of Capacity During Research Project) (England) Regulations 2007 or equivalent Welsh regulations.

The regulations only apply to tissue and data collected before the loss of capacity from a person who gave consent before 31 March 2008 to join a project that starts before 1 October 2007.

11.42   The regulations do not cover research involving direct intervention (for example, taking of further blood pressure readings) or the taking of further tissue after loss of capacity. Such research must comply with sections 30 to 33 of the Act to be lawful.

11.43   Where the regulations do apply, research can only continue if the project already has procedures to deal with people who lose capacity during the project. An appropriate body must have approved the procedures. The researcher must follow the procedures that have been approved.

11.44   The researcher must also:

- seek out the views of someone involved in the person's care or interested in their welfare and if a carer can't be found they must nominate a consultee (see paragraphs 11.22–11.28)
- respect advance decisions and expressed preferences, wishes or objections that the person has made in the past, and
- treat the person's interests as more important than those of science and society.

The appropriate body must be satisfied that the research project has reasonable arrangements to meet these requirements.

---

[53] www.hta.gov.uk

11.45 If at any time the researcher believes that procedures are no longer in place or the appropriate body no longer approves the research, they must stop research on the person immediately.

11.46 Where regulations do apply, research does not have to:

- be linked to an impairing condition of the person
- have the potential to benefit that person, or
- aim to provide knowledge relevant to others with the same or a similar condition.

What happens to existing projects that a person never had capacity to agree to?

11.47 There are no regulations for projects that:

- started before the Act comes into force, and
- a person never had the capacity to agree to.

Projects that already have ethical approval will need to obtain approval from an appropriate body under sections 30 and 31 of the Mental Capacity Act and to comply with the requirements of sections 32 and 33 of that Act by 1 October 2008. Research that does not have ethical approval must get approval from an appropriate body by 1 October 2007 to continue lawfully. This is the case in England and it is expected that similar arrangements will apply in Wales.

12 HOW DOES THE ACT APPLY TO CHILDREN AND YOUNG PEOPLE?

This chapter looks at the few parts of the Act that may affect children under 16 years of age. It also explains the position of young people aged 16 and 17 years and the overlapping laws that affect them.

This chapter does not deal with research. Further guidance will be provided on how the Act applies in relation to research involving those under the age of 18.

Within this Code of Practice, 'children' refers to people aged below 16. 'Young people' refers to people aged 16–17. This differs from the Children Act 1989 and the law more generally, where the term 'child' is used to refer to people aged under 18.

In this chapter, as throughout the Code, a person's capacity (or lack of capacity) refers specifically to their capacity to make a particular decision at the time it needs to be made.

Quick summary

Children under 16

- The Act does not generally apply to people under the age of 16.
- There are two exceptions:
  - The Court of Protection can make decisions about a child's property or finances (or appoint a deputy to make these decisions) if the child lacks capacity to make such decisions within section 2(1) of the Act and is likely to still lack capacity to make financial decisions when they reach the age of 18 (section 18(3)).
  - Offences of ill treatment or wilful neglect of a person who lacks capacity within section 2(1) can also apply to victims younger than 16 (section 44).

Young people aged 16–17 years

- Most of the Act applies to young people aged 16–17 years, who may lack capacity within section 2(1) to make specific decisions.
- There are three exceptions:
  - Only people aged 18 and over can make a Lasting Power of Attorney (LPA).
  - Only people aged 18 and over can make an advance decision to refuse medical treatment.

  The Court of Protection may only make a statutory will for a person aged 18 and over.

Care or treatment for young people aged 16–17

- People carrying out acts in connection with the care or treatment of a young person aged 16–17 who lacks capacity to consent within section 2(1) will generally have protection from liability (section 5), as long as the person carrying out the act:
  - has taken reasonable steps to establish that the young person lacks capacity
  - reasonably believes that the young person lacks capacity and that the act is in the young person's best interests, and
  - follows the Act's principles.
- When assessing the young person's best interests (see chapter 5), the person providing care or treatment must consult those involved in the young person's care and anyone interested in their welfare – if it is practical and appropriate to do so. This may include the young person's parents. Care should be taken not to unlawfully breach the young person's right to confidentiality (see chapter 16).
- Nothing in section 5 excludes a person's civil liability for loss or damage, or his criminal liability, resulting from his negligence in carrying out the act.

Legal proceedings involving young people aged 16–17

- Sometimes there will be disagreements about the care, treatment or welfare of a young person aged 16 or 17 who lacks capacity to make relevant decisions. Depending on the circumstances, the case may be heard in the family courts or the Court of Protection.
- The Court of Protection may transfer a case to the family courts, and vice versa.

Does the Act apply to children?

12.1   Section 2(5) of the Act states that, with the exception of section 2(6), as explained below, no powers under the Act may be exercised in relation to a child under 16.

12.2   Care and treatment of children under the age of 16 is generally governed by common law principles. Further information is provided at www.dh.gov.uk/consent.

Can the Act help with decisions about a child's property or finances?

12.3   Section 2(6) makes an exception for some decisions about a child's property and financial affairs. The Court of Protection can make decisions about property and affairs of those under 16 in cases where the person is likely to still lack capacity to make financial decisions after reaching the age of 18. The court's ruling will still apply when the person reaches the age of 18, which means there will not be a need for further court proceedings once the person reaches the age of 18.

12.4   The Court of Protection can:

  - make an order (for example, concerning the investment of an award of compensation for the child), and/or
  - appoint a deputy to manage the child's property and affairs and to make ongoing financial decisions on the child's behalf.

In making a decision, the court must follow the Act's principles and decide in the child's best interests as set out in chapter 5 of the Code.

[*Scenario: Applying the Act to children*]

What if somebody mistreats or neglects a child who lacks capacity?

12.5   Section 44 covers the offences of ill treatment or wilful neglect of a person who lacks capacity to make relevant decisions (see chapter 14). This section also applies to children under 16 and young people aged 16 or 17. But it only applies if the child's lack of capacity to make a decision for themselves is caused by an impairment or disturbance that affects how their mind or brain works (see chapter 4). If the lack of capacity is solely the result of the child's youth or immaturity, then the ill treatment or wilful neglect would be dealt with under the separate offences of child cruelty or neglect.

Does the Act apply to young people aged 16–17?

12.6   Most of the Act applies to people aged 16 years and over. There is an overlap with the Children Act 1989. For the Act to apply to a young person, they must lack capacity to make a particular decision (in line with the Act's definition of lack of capacity described in chapter 4). In such situations either this Act or the Children Act 1989 may apply, depending upon the particular circumstances.

However, there may also be situations where neither of these Acts provides an appropriate solution. In such cases, it may be necessary to look to the powers available under the Mental Health Act 1983 or the High Court's inherent powers to deal with cases involving young people.

12.7   There are currently no specific rules for deciding when to use either the Children Act 1989 or the Mental Capacity Act 2005 or when to apply to the High Court. But, the examples below show circumstances where this Act may be the most appropriate (see also paragraphs 12.21–12.23 below).

- In unusual circumstances it might be in a young person's best interests for the Court of Protection to make an order and/or appoint a property and affairs deputy. For example, this might occur when a young person receives financial compensation and the court appoints a parent or a solicitor as a property and affairs deputy.
- It may be appropriate for the Court of Protection to make a welfare decision concerning a young person who lacks capacity to decide for themselves (for example, about where the young person should live) if the court decides that the parents are not acting in the young person's best interests.
- It might be appropriate to refer a case to the Court of Protection where there is disagreement between a person interested in the care and welfare of a young person and the young person's medical team about the young person's best interests or capacity.

Do any parts of the Act not apply to young people aged 16 or 17?

LPAs

12.8   Only people aged 18 or over can make a Lasting Power of Attorney (LPA) (section 9(2)(c)).

Advance decisions to refuse treatment

12.9   Information on decisions to refuse treatment made in advance by young people under the age of 18 will be available at www.dh.gov.uk/consent.

Making a will

12.10   The law generally does not allow anyone below the age of 18 to make a will. So section 18(2) confirms that the Court of Protection can only make a statutory will on behalf of those aged 18 and over.

What does the Act say about care or treatment of young people aged 16 or 17?

Background information concerning competent young people

12.11   The Family Law Reform Act 1969 presumes that young people have the legal capacity to agree to surgical, medical or dental treatment.[54] This also applies to any associated procedures (for example, investigations, anaesthesia or nursing care).

12.12   It does not apply to some rarer types of procedure (for example, organ donation or other procedures which are not therapeutic for the young person) or research. In those cases, anyone under 18 is presumed to lack legal capacity, subject to the test of 'Gillick competence' (testing whether they are mature and intelligent enough to understand a proposed treatment or procedure).[55]

12.13   Even where a young person is presumed to have legal capacity to consent to treatment, they may not necessarily be able to make the relevant decision. As with adults, decision-makers should assess the young person's capacity to consent to the proposed care or treatment (see chapter 4). If a young person lacks capacity to consent within section 2(1) of the Act because of an impairment of, or a disturbance in the functioning of, the mind or brain then the Mental Capacity Act will apply in the same way as it does to those who are 18 and over. If however they are unable to make the decision for some other reason, for example because they are overwhelmed by the implications of the decision, the Act will not apply to them and the legality of any treatment should be assessed under common law principles.

12.14   If a young person has capacity to agree to treatment, their decision to consent must be respected. Difficult issues can arise if a young person has legal and mental capacity and refuses consent – especially if a person with parental responsibility wishes to give consent on the young person's behalf. The Family Division of the High Court can hear cases where there is disagreement. The Court of Protection has no power to settle a dispute about a young person who is said to have the mental capacity to make the specific decision.

12.15   It may be unclear whether a young person lacks capacity within section 2(1) of the Act. In those circumstances, it would be prudent for the person providing care or treatment for the young person to seek a declaration from the court. If the young person lacks capacity to make care or treatment decisions

12.16   Under the common law, a person with parental responsibility for a young person is generally able to consent to the young person receiving care or medical treatment

---

[54] Family Law Reform Act 1969, section 8(1)

[55] In the case of *Gillick v. West Norfolk and Wisbech Area Health Authority* [1986] 1 AC 112 the court found that a child below 16 years of age will be competent to consent to medical treatment if they have sufficient intelligence and understanding to understand what is proposed. This test applies in relation to all people under 18 where there is no presumption of competence in relation to the procedure – for example where the procedure is not one referred to in section 8 of the Family Law Reform Act 1969, e.g. organ donation.

where they lack capacity under section 2(1) of the Act. They should act in the young person's best interests.

12.17 However if a young person lacks the mental capacity to make a specific care or treatment decision within section 2(1) of the Act, healthcare staff providing treatment, or a person providing care to the young person, can carry out treatment or care with protection from liability (section 5) whether or not a person with parental responsibility consents.[56] They must follow the Act's principles and make sure that the actions they carry out are in the young person's best interests. They must make every effort to work out and consider the young person's wishes, feelings, beliefs and values – both past and present – and consider all other factors in the best interests checklist (see chapter 5).

12.18 When assessing a young person's best interests, healthcare staff must take into account the views of anyone involved in caring for the young person and anyone interested in their welfare, where it is practical and appropriate to do so. This may include the young person's parents and others with parental responsibility for the young person. Care should be taken not to unlawfully breach the young person's right to confidentiality (see chapter 16).

12.19 If a young person has said they do not want their parents to be consulted, it may not be appropriate to involve them (for example, where there have been allegations of abuse).

12.20 If there is a disagreement about whether the proposed care or treatment is in the best interests of a young person, or there is disagreement about whether the young person lacks capacity and there is no other way of resolving the matter, it would be prudent for those in disagreement to seek a declaration or other order from the appropriate court (see paragraphs 12.23–12.25 below).

[Scenario: Working out a young person's best interests]

12.21 There may be particular difficulties where young people with mental health problems require in-patient psychiatric treatment, and are treated informally rather than detained under the Mental Health Act 1983. The Mental Capacity Act and its principles apply to decisions related to the care and treatment of young people who lack mental capacity to consent, including treatment for mental disorder. As with any other form of treatment, somebody assessing a young person's best interests should consult anyone involved in caring for the young person or anyone interested in their welfare, as far as is practical and appropriate. This may include the young person's parents or those with parental responsibility for the young person.

But the Act does not allow any actions that result in a young person being deprived of their liberty (see chapter 6). In such circumstances, detention under the Mental Health Act 1983 and the safeguards provided under that Act might be appropriate (see also chapter 13).

12.22 People may disagree about a young person's capacity to make the specific decision or about their best interests, or it may not be clear whether they lack capacity within section 2(1) or for some other reason. In this situation, legal proceedings may be necessary if there is no other way of settling the disagreement (see chapters 8 and 15). If those involved in caring for the young person or who are interested in the young person's welfare do not agree with the proposed treatment, it may be necessary for an interested party to make an application to the appropriate court.

---

[56] Nothing in section 5 excludes a person's civil liability for loss or damage, or his criminal liability, resulting from his negligence in doing the Act.

What powers do the courts have in cases involving young people?

12.23 A case involving a young person who lacks mental capacity to make a specific decision could be heard in the family courts (probably in the Family Division of the High Court) or in the Court of Protection.

12.24 If a case might require an ongoing order (because the young person is likely to still lack capacity when they are 18), it may be more appropriate for the Court of Protection to hear the case. For one-off cases not involving property or finances, the Family Division may be more appropriate.

12.25 So that the appropriate court hears a case, the Court of Protection can transfer cases to the family courts, and vice versa (section 21).

[*Scenario: Hearing cases in the appropriate court*]

13 WHAT IS THE RELATIONSHIP BETWEEN THE MENTAL CAPACITY ACT AND THE MENTAL HEALTH ACT 1983?

This chapter explains the relationship between the Mental Capacity Act 2005 (MCA) and the Mental Health Act 1983 (MHA). It:

- sets out when it may be appropriate to detain someone under the MHA rather than to rely on the MCA
- describes how the MCA affects people lacking capacity who are also subject to the MHA
- explains when doctors cannot give certain treatments for a mental disorder (in particular, psychosurgery) to someone who lacks capacity to consent to it, and
- sets out changes that the Government is planning to make to both Acts.

It does not provide a full description of the MHA. The MHA has its own Memorandum to explain the Act and its own Code of Practice to guide people about how to use it.[57]

> In this chapter, as throughout the Code, a person's capacity (or lack of capacity) refers specifically to their capacity to make a particular decision at the time it needs to be made.

Quick summary

- Professionals may need to think about using the MHA to detain and treat somebody who lacks capacity to consent to treatment (rather than use the MCA), if:
  - it is not possible to give the person the care or treatment they need without doing something that might deprive them of their liberty
  - the person needs treatment that cannot be given under the MCA (for example, because the person has made a valid and applicable advance decision to refuse an essential part of treatment)
  - the person may need to be restrained in a way that is not allowed under the MCA
  - it is not possible to assess or treat the person safely or effectively without treatment being compulsory (perhaps because the person is expected to regain capacity to consent, but might then refuse to give consent)
  - the person lacks capacity to decide on some elements of the treatment but has capacity to refuse a vital part of it – and they have done so, or

---

[57] Department of Health & Welsh Office, *Mental Health Act 1983 Code of Practice* (TSO, 1999), www.dh.gov.uk/assetRoot/04/07/49/61/04074961.pdf

- there is some other reason why the person might not get treatment, and they or somebody else might suffer harm as a result.

■ Before making an application under the MHA, decision-makers should consider whether they could achieve their aims safely and effectively by using the MCA instead.

■ Compulsory treatment under the MHA is not an option if:

- the patient's mental disorder does not justify detention in hospital, or
- the patient needs treatment only for a physical illness or disability.

■ The MCA applies to people subject to the MHA in the same way as it applies to anyone else, with four exceptions:

- if someone is detained under the MHA, decision-makers cannot normally rely on the MCA to give treatment for mental disorder or make decisions about that treatment on that person's behalf
- if somebody can be treated for their mental disorder without their consent because they are detained under the MHA, healthcare staff can treat them even if it goes against an advance decision to refuse that treatment
- if a person is subject to guardianship, the guardian has the exclusive right to take certain decisions, including where the person is to live, and
- Independent Mental Capacity Advocates do not have to be involved in decisions about serious medical treatment or accommodation, if those decisions are made under the MHA.

■ Healthcare staff cannot give psychosurgery (i.e. neurosurgery for mental disorder) to a person who lacks capacity to agree to it. This applies whether or not the person is otherwise subject to the MHA.

Who does the MHA apply to?

13.1   The MHA provides ways of assessing, treating and caring for people who have a serious mental disorder that puts them or other people at risk. It sets out when:

■ people with mental disorders can be detained in hospital for assessment or treatment

■ people who are detained can be given treatment for their mental disorder without their consent (it also sets out the safeguards people must get in this situation), and

■ people with mental disorders can be made subject to guardianship or after-care under supervision to protect them or other people.

13.2   Most of the MHA does not distinguish between people who have the capacity to make decisions and those who do not. Many people covered by the MHA have the capacity to make decisions for themselves. Most people who lack capacity to make decisions about their treatment will never be affected by the MHA, even if they need treatment for a mental disorder.

13.3   But there are cases where decision-makers will need to decide whether to use the MHA or MCA, or both, to meet the needs of people with mental health problems who lack capacity to make decisions about their own treatment.

What are the MCA's limits?

13.4   Section 5 of the MCA provides legal protection for people who care for or treat someone who lacks capacity (see chapter 6). But they must follow the Act's principles and may only take action that is in a person's best interests (see chapter 5). This applies to care or treatment for physical and mental conditions. So it can apply to treatment for people with mental disorders, however serious those disorders are.

13.5   But section 5 does have its limits. For example, somebody using restraint only has protection if the restraint is:

- necessary to protect the person who lacks capacity from harm, and
- in proportion to the likelihood and seriousness of that harm.

13.6   There is no protection under section 5 for actions that deprive a person of their liberty (see chapter 6 for guidance). Similarly, the MCA does not allow giving treatment that goes against a valid and applicable advance decision to refuse treatment (see chapter 9).

13.7   None of these restrictions apply to treatment for mental disorder given under the MHA – but other restrictions do.

When can a person be detained under the MHA?

13.8   A person may be taken into hospital and detained for assessment under section 2 of the MHA for up to 28 days if:

- they have a mental disorder that is serious enough for them to be detained in a hospital for assessment (or for assessment followed by treatment) for at least a limited period, and
- they need to be detained to protect their health or safety, or to protect others.

13.9   A patient may be admitted to hospital and detained for treatment under section 3 of the MHA if:

- they have a mental illness, severe mental impairment, psychopathic disorder or mental impairment (the MHA sets out definitions for these last three terms)
- their mental disorder is serious enough to need treatment in hospital
- treatment is needed for the person's health or safety, or for the protection of other people – and it cannot be provided without detention under this section, and
- (if the person has a mental impairment or psychopathic disorder) treatment is likely to improve their condition or stop it getting worse.

13.10   Decision-makers should consider using the MHA if, in their professional judgment, they are not sure it will be possible, or sufficient, to rely on the MCA. They do not have to ask the Court of Protection to rule that the MCA does not apply before using the MHA.

13.11   If a clinician believes that they can safely assess or treat a person under the MCA, they do not need to consider using the MHA. In this situation, it would be difficult to meet the requirements of the MHA anyway.

13.12   It might be necessary to consider using the MHA rather than the MCA if:

- it is not possible to give the person the care or treatment they need without carrying out an action that might deprive them of their liberty
- the person needs treatment that cannot be given under the MCA (for example, because the person has made a valid and applicable advance decision to refuse all or part of that treatment)
- the person may need to be restrained in a way that is not allowed under the MCA
- it is not possible to assess or treat the person safely or effectively without treatment being compulsory (perhaps because the person is expected to regain capacity to consent, but might then refuse to give consent)
- the person lacks capacity to decide on some elements of the treatment but has capacity to refuse a vital part of it – and they have done so, or
- there is some other reason why the person might not get the treatment they need, and they or somebody else might suffer harm as a result.

13.13   But it is important to remember that a person cannot be treated under the MHA unless they meet the relevant criteria for being detained. Unless they are sent to hospital under Part 3 of the MHA in connection with a criminal offence, people can only be detained where:

- the conditions summarised in paragraph 13.8 or 13.9 are met
- the relevant people agree that an application is necessary (normally two doctors and an approved social worker), and
- (in the case of section 3) the patient's nearest relative has not objected to the application.

'Nearest relative' is defined in section 26 of the MHA. It is usually, but not always, a family member.

[*Scenario: Using the MHA*]

13.14 Compulsory treatment under the MHA is not an option if:

- the patient's mental disorder does not justify detention in hospital, or
- the patient needs treatment only for a physical illness or disability.

13.15 There will be some cases where a person who lacks capacity cannot be treated either under the MHA or the MCA – even if the treatment is for mental disorder.

[*Scenario: Deciding whether to use the MHA or MCA*]

How does the MCA apply to a patient subject to guardianship under the MHA?

13.16 Guardianship gives someone (usually a local authority social services department) the exclusive right to decide where a person should live – but in doing this they cannot deprive the person of their liberty. The guardian can also require the person to attend for treatment, work, training or education at specific times and places, and they can demand that a doctor, approved social worker or another relevant person have access to the person wherever they live. Guardianship can apply whether or not the person has the capacity to make decisions about care and treatment. It does not give anyone the right to treat the person without their permission or to consent to treatment on their behalf.

13.17 An application can be made for a person who has a mental disorder to be received into guardianship under section 7 of the MHA when:

- the situation meets the conditions summarised in paragraph 13.18
- the relevant people agree an application for guardianship should be made (normally two doctors and an approved social worker), and
- the person's nearest relative does not object.

13.18 An application can be made in relation to any person who is 16 years or over if:

- they have a mental illness, severe mental impairment, psychopathic disorder or mental impairment that is serious enough to justify guardianship (see paragraph 13.20 below), and
- guardianship is necessary in the interests of the welfare of the patient or to protect other people.

13.19 Applicants (usually approved social workers) and doctors supporting the application will need to determine whether they could achieve their aims without guardianship. For patients who lack capacity, the obvious alternative will be action under the MCA.

13.20 But the fact that the person lacks capacity to make relevant decision is not the only factor that applicants need to consider. They need to consider all the circumstances of the case. They may conclude that guardianship is the best option for a person with a mental disorder who lacks capacity to make those decisions if, for example:

- they think it is important that one person or authority should be in charge of making decisions about where the person should live (for example, where there have been long-running or difficult disagreements about where the person should live)
- they think the person will probably respond well to the authority and attention of a guardian, and so be more prepared to accept treatment for the mental disorder (whether they are able to consent to it or it is being provided for them under the MCA), or
- they need authority to return the person to the place they are to live (for example, a care home) if they were to go absent.

Decision-makers must never consider guardianship as a way to avoid applying the MCA.

13.21   A guardian has the exclusive right to decide where a person lives, so nobody else can use the MCA to arrange for the person to live elsewhere. Somebody who knowingly helps a person leave the place a guardian requires them to stay may be committing a criminal offence under the MHA. A guardian also has the exclusive power to require the person to attend set times and places for treatment, occupation, education or training. This does not stop other people using the MCA to make similar arrangements or to treat the person in their best interests. But people cannot use the MCA in any way that conflicts with decisions which a guardian has a legal right to make under the MHA. See paragraph 13.16 above for general information about a guardian's powers.

How does the MCA apply to a patient subject to after-care under supervision under the MHA?

13.22   When people are discharged from detention for medical treatment under the MHA, their responsible medical officer may decide to place them on after-care under supervision. The responsible medical officer is usually the person's consultant psychiatrist. Another doctor and an approved social worker must support their application.

13.23   After-care under supervision means:

- the person can be required to live at a specified place (where they can be taken to and returned, if necessary)
- the person can be required to attend for treatment, occupation, education or training at a specific time and place (where they can be taken, if necessary), and
- their supervisor, any doctor or approved social worker or any other relevant person must be given access to them wherever they live.

13.24   Responsible medical officers can apply for after-care under supervision under section 25A of the MHA if:

- the person is 16 or older and is liable to be detained in a hospital for treatment under section 3 (and certain other sections) of the MHA
- the person has a mental illness, severe mental impairment, psychopathic disorder or mental impairment
- without after-care under supervision the person's health or safety would be at risk of serious harm, they would be at risk of serious exploitation, or other people's safety would be at risk of serious harm, and
- after-care under supervision is likely to help make sure the person gets the after-care services they need.

'Liable to be detained' means that a hospital is allowed to detain them. Patients who are liable to be detained are not always actually in hospital, because they may have been given permission to leave hospital for a time.

13.25 After-care under supervision can be used whether or not the person lacks capacity to make relevant decisions. But if a person lacks capacity, decision-makers will need to decide whether action under the MCA could achieve their aims before making an application. The kinds of cases in which after-care under supervision might be considered for patients who lack capacity to take decisions about their own care and treatment are similar to those for guardianship.

How does the Mental Capacity Act affect people covered by the Mental Health Act?

13.26 There is no reason to assume a person lacks capacity to make their own decisions just because they are subject (under the MHA) to:

- detention
- guardianship, or
- after-care under supervision.

13.27 People who lack capacity to make specific decisions are still protected by the MCA even if they are subject to the MHA (this includes people who are subject to the MHA as a result of court proceedings). But there are four important exceptions:

- if someone is liable to be detained under the MHA, decision-makers cannot normally rely on the MCA to give mental health treatment or make decisions about that treatment on someone's behalf
- if somebody can be given mental health treatment without their consent because they are liable to be detained under the MHA, they can also be given mental health treatment that goes against an advance decision to refuse treatment
- if a person is subject to guardianship, the guardian has the exclusive right to take certain decisions, including where the person is to live, and
- Independent Mental Capacity Advocates do not have to be involved in decisions about serious medical treatment or accommodation, if those decisions are made under the MHA.

What are the implications for people who need treatment for a mental disorder?

13.28 Subject to certain conditions, Part 4 of the MHA allows doctors to give patients who are liable to be detained treatment for mental disorders without their consent – whether or not they have the capacity to give that consent. Paragraph 13.31 below lists a few important exceptions.

13.29 Where Part 4 of the MHA applies, the MCA cannot be used to give medical treatment for a mental disorder to patients who lack capacity to consent. Nor can anyone else, like an attorney or a deputy, use the MCA to give consent for that treatment. This is because Part 4 of the MHA already allows clinicians, if they comply with the relevant rules, to give patients medical treatment for mental disorder even though they lack the capacity to consent. In this context, medical treatment includes nursing and care, habilitation and rehabilitation under medical supervision.

13.30 But clinicians treating people for mental disorder under the MHA cannot simply ignore a person's capacity to consent to treatment. As a matter of good practice (and in some cases in order to comply with the MHA) they will always need to assess and record:

- whether patients have capacity to consent to treatment, and
- if so, whether they have consented to or refused that treatment.

For more information, see the MHA Code of Practice.

13.31   Part 4 of the MHA does not apply to patients:

- admitted in an emergency under section 4(4)(a) of the MHA, following a single medical recommendation and awaiting a second recommendation
- temporarily detained (held in hospital) under section 5 of the MHA while awaiting an application for detention under section 2 or section 3
- remanded by a court to hospital for a report on their medical condition under section 35 of the MHA
- detained under section 37(4), 135 or 136 of the MHA in a place of safety, or
- who have been conditionally discharged by the Mental Health Review Tribunal (and not recalled to hospital).

13.32   Since the MHA does not allow treatment for these patients without their consent, the MCA applies in the normal way, even if the treatment is for mental disorder.

13.33   Even when the MHA allows patients to be treated for mental disorders, the MCA applies in the normal way to treatment for physical disorders. But sometimes healthcare staff may decide to focus first on treating a detained patient's mental disorder in the hope that they will get back the capacity to make a decision about treatment for the physical disorder.

13.34   Where people are subject to guardianship or after-care under supervision under the MHA, the MCA applies as normal to all treatment. Guardianship and after-care under supervision do not give people the right to treat patients without consent.

[*Scenario: Using the MCA to treat a patient who is detained under the MHA*]

How does the Mental Health Act affect advance decisions to refuse treatment?

13.35   The MHA does not affect a person's advance decision to refuse treatment, unless Part 4 of the MHA means the person can be treated for mental disorder without their consent. In this situation healthcare staff can treat patients for their mental disorder, even if they have made an advance decision to refuse such treatment.

13.36   But even then healthcare staff must treat a valid and applicable advance decision as they would a decision made by a person with capacity at the time they are asked to consent to treatment. For example, they should consider whether they could use a different type of treatment which the patient has not refused in advance. If healthcare staff do not follow an advance decision, they should record in the patient's notes why they have chosen not to follow it.

13.37   Even if a patient is being treated without their consent under Part 4 of the MHA, an advance decision to refuse other forms of treatment is still valid. Being subject to guardianship or after-care under supervision does not affect an advance decision in any way. See chapter 9 for further guidance on advance decisions to refuse treatment.

[*Scenario: Deciding on whether to follow an advance decision to refuse treatment*]

Does the MHA affect the duties of attorneys and deputies?

13.38   In general, the MHA does not affect the powers of attorneys and deputies. But there are two exceptions:

- they will not be able to give consent on a patient's behalf for treatment under Part 4 of the MHA, where the patient is liable to be detained under the MHA (see 13.28–13.34 above), and
- they will not be able to take decisions:

     – about where a person subject to guardianship should live, or

     – that conflict with decisions that a guardian has a legal right to make.

13.39 Being subject to the MHA does not stop patients creating new Lasting Powers of Attorney (if they have the capacity to do so). Nor does it stop the Court of Protection from appointing a deputy for them.

13.40 In certain cases, people subject to the MHA may be required to meet specific conditions relating to:

- leave of absence from hospital
- after-care under supervision, or
- conditional discharge.

Conditions vary from case to case, but could include a requirement to:

- live in a particular place
- maintain contact with health services, or
- avoid a particular area.

13.41 If an attorney or deputy takes a decision that goes against one of these conditions, the patient will be taken to have gone against the condition. The MHA sets out the actions that could be taken in such circumstances. In the case of leave of absence or conditional discharge, this might involve the patient being recalled to hospital.

13.42 Attorneys and deputies are able to exercise patients' rights under the MHA on their behalf, if they have the relevant authority. In particular, some personal welfare attorneys and deputies may be able to apply to the Mental Health Review Tribunal (MHRT) for the patient's discharge from detention, guardianship or after-care under supervision.

13.43 The MHA also gives various rights to a patient's nearest relative. These include the right to:

- insist that a local authority social services department instructs an approved social worker to consider whether the patient should be made subject to the MHA
- apply for the patient to be admitted to hospital or guardianship
- object to an application for admission for treatment
- order the patient's discharge from hospital (subject to certain conditions) and
- order the patient's discharge from guardianship.

13.44 Attorneys and deputies may not exercise these rights, unless they are themselves the nearest relative. If the nearest relative and an attorney or deputy disagree, it may be helpful for them to discuss the issue, perhaps with the assistance of the patient's clinicians or social worker. But ultimately they have different roles and both must act as they think best. An attorney or deputy must act in the patient's best interests.

13.45 It is good practice for clinicians and others involved in the assessment or treatment of patients under the MHA to try to find out if the person has an attorney or deputy. But this may not always be possible. So attorneys and deputies should contact either:

- the healthcare professional responsible for the patient's treatment (generally known as the patient's RMO)
- the managers of the hospital where the patient is detained
- the person's guardian (normally the local authority social services department), or
- the person's supervisor (if the patient is subject to after-care under supervision).

Hospitals that treat detained patients normally have a Mental Health Act Administrator's office, which may be a useful first point of contact.

Does the MHA affect when Independent Mental Capacity Advocates must be instructed?

13.46   As explained in chapter 10, there is no duty to instruct an Independent Mental Capacity Advocate (IMCA) for decisions about serious medical treatment which is to be given under Part 4 of the MHA. Nor is there a duty to do so in respect of a move into accommodation, or a change of accommodation, if the person in question is to be required to live in it because of an obligation under the MHA. That obligation might be a condition of leave of absence or conditional discharge from hospital or a requirement imposed by a guardian or a supervisor.

13.47   However, the rules for instructing an IMCA for patients subject to the MHA who might undergo serious medical treatment not related to their mental disorder are the same as for any other patient.

13.48   The duty to instruct an IMCA would also apply as normal if accommodation is being planned as part of the after-care under section 117 of the MHA following the person's discharge from detention (and the person is not going to be required to live in it as a condition of after-care under supervision). This is because the person does not have to accept that accommodation.

What is the effect of section 57 of the Mental Health Act on the MCA?

13.49   Section 57 of the MHA states that psychosurgery (neurosurgery for mental disorder) requires:

- the consent of the patient, and
- the approval of an independent doctor and two other people appointed by the Mental Health Act Commission.

Psychosurgery is any surgical operation that destroys brain tissue or the function of brain tissue.

13.50   The same rules apply to other treatments specified in regulations under section 57. Currently, the only treatment included in regulations is the surgical implantation of hormones to reduce a man's sex drive.

13.51   The combined effect of section 57 of the MHA and section 28 of the MCA is, effectively, that a person who lacks the capacity to consent to one of these treatments for mental disorder may never be given it. Healthcare staff cannot use the MCA as an alternative way of giving these kinds of treatment. Nor can an attorney or deputy give permission for them on a person's behalf.

What changes does the Government plan to make to the MHA and the MCA?

13.52   The Government has introduced a Mental Health Bill into Parliament in order to modernise the MHA. Among the changes it proposes to make are:

- some amendments to the criteria for detention, including a new requirement that appropriate medical treatment be available for patients before they can be detained for treatment,
- the introduction of supervised treatment in the community for suitable patients following a period of detention and treatment in hospital. This will help make sure that patients get the treatment they need and help stop them relapsing and returning to hospital,
- the replacement of the approved social worker with the approved mental health professional. This will open up the possibility of approved mental healthcare professionals being drawn from other disciplines as well as social work. Other changes will open up the possibility of clinicians who are not doctors being

approved to take on the role of the responsible medical officer. This role will be renamed the responsible clinician,

- provisions to make it possible for patients to apply to the county court for an unsuitable nearest relative to be replaced, and
- the abolition of after-care under supervision.

13.53 The Bill will also amend the MCA to introduce new procedures and provisions to make relevant decisions but who need to be deprived of their liberty, in their best interests, otherwise than under the Mental Health Act 1983 (the so-called 'Bournewood provisions').[58]

13.54 This chapter, as well as chapter 6, will be fully revised in due course to reflect those changes. Information about the Government's current proposals in respect of the Bournewood safeguards is available on the Department of Health website. This information includes draft illustrative Code of Practice guidance about the proposed safeguards.[59]

13.55 In the meantime, people taking decisions under both the MCA and the MHA must base those decisions on the Acts as they stand now.

14 WHAT MEANS OF PROTECTION EXIST FOR PEOPLE WHO LACK CAPACITY TO MAKE DECISIONS FOR THEMSELVES?

This chapter describes the different agencies that exist to help make sure that adults who lack capacity to make decisions for themselves are protected from abuse. It also explains the services those agencies provide and how they supervise people who provide care for or make decisions on behalf of people who lack capacity. Finally, it explains what somebody should do if they suspect that somebody is abusing a vulnerable adult who lacks capacity.

In this chapter, as throughout the Code, a person's capacity (or lack of capacity) refers specifically to their capacity to make a particular decision at the time it needs to be made.

Quick summary

- Always report suspicions of abuse of a person who lacks capacity to the relevant agency.

Concerns about an appointee

- When someone is concerned about the collection or use of social security benefits by an appointee on behalf a person who lacks capacity, they should contact the local Jobcentre Plus. If the appointee is for someone who is over the age of 60, contact The Pension Service.

Concerns about an attorney or deputy

- If someone is concerned about the actions of an attorney or deputy, they should contact the Office of the Public Guardian.

---

[58] This refers to the European Court of Human Rights judgment (5 October 2004) in the case of *HL v. The United Kingdom* (Application no. 45508/99).

[59] See   www.dh.gov.uk/PublicationsAndStatistics/Publications/PublicationsPolicyAndGuidance/ PublicationsPolicyAndGuidanceArticle/fs/en?CONTENT_ID=4141656&chk=jlw07L

Concerns about a possible criminal offence

- If there is a good reason to suspect that someone has committed a crime against a vulnerable person, such as theft or physical or sexual assault, contact the police.
- In addition, social services should also be contacted, so that they can support the vulnerable person during the investigation.

Concerns about possible ill treatment or wilful neglect

- The Act introduces new criminal offences of ill treatment or wilful neglect of a person who lacks capacity to make relevant decisions (section 44).
- If someone is not being looked after properly, contact social services.
- In serious cases, contact the police.

Concerns about care standards

- In cases of concern about the standard of care in a care home or an adult placement scheme, or about the care provided by a home care worker, contact social services.
- It may also be appropriate to contact the Commission for Social Care Inspection (in England) or the Care and Social Services Inspectorate for Wales.

Concerns about healthcare or treatment

- If someone is concerned about the care or treatment given to the person in any NHS setting (such as an NHS hospital or clinic) contact the managers of the service.
- It may also be appropriate to make a formal complaint through the NHS complaints procedure (see chapter 15).

What is abuse?

14.1   The word 'abuse' covers a wide range of actions. In some cases, abuse is clearly deliberate and intentionally unkind. But sometimes abuse happens because somebody does not know how to act correctly – or they haven't got appropriate help and support. It is important to prevent abuse, wherever possible. If somebody is abused, it is important to investigate the abuse and take steps to stop it happening.

14.2   Abuse is anything that goes against a person's human and civil rights. This includes sexual, physical, verbal, financial and emotional abuse. Abuse can be:

- a single act
- a series of repeated acts
- a failure to provide necessary care, or
- neglect.

Abuse can take place anywhere (for example, in a person's own home, a care home or a hospital).

14.3   The main types of abuse are:

Type of abuse	Examples
Financial	■ theft
	■ fraud
	■ undue pressure
	■ misuse of property, possessions or benefits
	■ dishonest gain of property, possessions or benefits.

Physical	■ slapping, pushing, kicking or other forms of violence
	■ misuse of medication (for example, increasing dosage to make someone drowsy)
	■ inappropriate punishments (for example, not giving someone a meal because they have been 'bad').
Sexual	■ rape
	■ sexual assault
	■ sexual acts without consent (this includes if a person is not able to give consent or the abuser used pressure).
Psychological	■ emotional abuse
	■ threats of harm, restraint or abandonment
	■ refusing contact with other people
	■ intimidation
	■ threats to restrict someone's liberty.
Neglect and acts of omission	■ ignoring the person's medical or physical care needs
	■ failing to get healthcare or social care
	■ withholding medication, food or heating.

14.4   The Department of Health and the National Assembly for Wales have produced separate guidance on protecting vulnerable adults from abuse. No secrets[60] (England) and In safe hands[61] (Wales) both define vulnerable adults as people aged 18 and over who:

■ need community care services due to a mental disability, other disability, age or illness, and
■ may be unable to take care of themselves or protect themselves against serious harm or exploitation.

This description applies to many people who lack capacity to make decisions for themselves.

14.5   Anyone who thinks that someone might be abusing a vulnerable adult who lacks capacity should:

■ contact the local social services (see paragraphs 14.27–14.28 below)
■ contact the Office of the Public Guardian (see paragraph 14.8 below), or
■ seek advice from a relevant telephone helpline[62] or through the Community Legal Service.[63]

Full contact details are provided in Annex A.

14.6   In most cases, local adult protection procedures will say who should take action (see paragraphs 14.28–14.29 below). But some abuse will be a criminal offence, such as physical assault, sexual assault or rape, theft, fraud and some other forms of financial exploitation. In these cases, the person who suspects abuse should contact the police urgently. The criminal investigation may take priority over all other

---

[60] Department of Health and Home Office, No secrets: Guidance on developing and implementing multi-agency policies and procedures to protect vulnerable adults from abuse, (2000) www.dh.gov.uk/assetRoot/04/07/45/40/04074540.pdf.

[61] National Assembly for Wales, In safe hands: Implementing adult protection procedures in Wales (2000), http://new.wales.gov.uk.about.departments/dhss/publications/social_services_publications/reports/insafehands?lang=en.

[62] For example, the Action on Elder Abuse (0808 808 8141), Age Concern (0800 009966) or CarersLine (0808 808 7777).

[63] Community Legal Service Direct www.clsdirect.org.uk.

forms of investigation. So all agencies will have to work together to plan the best way to investigate possible abuse.

14.7   The Fraud Act 2006 (due to come into force in 2007) creates a new offence of 'fraud by abuse of position'. This new offence may apply to a range of people, including:

- attorneys under a Lasting Power of Attorney (LPA) or an Enduring Power of Attorney (EPA), or
- deputies appointed by the Court of Protection to make financial decisions on behalf of a person who lacks capacity.

Attorneys and deputies may be guilty of fraud if they dishonestly abuse their position, intend to benefit themselves or others, and cause loss or expose a person to the risk of loss. People who suspect fraud should report the case to the police.

How does the Act protect people from abuse?

The Office of the Public Guardian

14.8   Section 57 of the Act creates a new Public Guardian, supported by staff of the Office of the Public Guardian (OPG). The Public Guardian helps protect people who lack capacity by:

- setting up and managing a register of LPAs
- setting up and managing a register of EPAs
- setting up and managing a register of court orders that appoint deputies
- supervising deputies, working with other relevant organisations (for example, social services, if the person who lacks capacity is receiving social care)
- sending Court of Protection Visitors to visit people who may lack capacity to make particular decisions and those who have formal powers to act on their behalf (see paragraphs 14.10–14.11 below)
- receiving reports from attorneys acting under LPAs and from deputies
- providing reports to the Court of Protection, as requested, and
- dealing with representations (including complaints) about the way in which attorneys or deputies carry out their duties.

14.9   Section 59 of the Act creates a Public Guardian Board to oversee and review how the Public Guardian carries out these duties.

Court of Protection Visitors

14.10   The role of a Court of Protection Visitor is to provide independent advice to the court and the Public Guardian. They advise on how anyone given power under the Act should be, and is, carrying out their duties and responsibilities. There are two types of visitor: General Visitors and Special Visitors. Special visitors are registered medical practitioners with relevant expertise. The court or Public Guardian can send whichever type of visitor is most appropriate to visit and interview a person who may lack capacity. Visitors can also interview attorneys or deputies and inspect any relevant healthcare or social care records. Attorneys and deputies must co-operate with the visitors and provide them with all relevant information. If attorneys or deputies do not co-operate, the court can cancel their appointment, where it thinks that they have not acted in the person's best interests.

[Scenario: Using a General Visitor]

14.11   Court of Protection Visitors have an important part to play in investigating possible abuse. But their role is much wider than this. They can also check on the general wellbeing of the person who lacks capacity, and they can give support to attorneys and deputies who need help to carry out their duties.

How does the Public Guardian oversee LPAs?

14.12 An LPA is a private arrangement between the donor and the attorney (see chapter 7). Donors should only choose attorneys that they can trust. The OPG provides information to help potential donors understand:

- the impact of making an LPA
- what they can give an attorney authority to do
- what to consider when choosing an attorney.

14.13 The Public Guardian must make sure that an LPA meets the Act's requirements. Before registering an LPA, the OPG will check documentation. For property and affairs LPAs, it will check whether an attorney appointed under the LPA is bankrupt since this would revoke the authority.

14.14 The Public Guardian will not usually get involved once somebody has registered an LPA – unless someone is worried about how an attorney is carrying out their duties. If concerns are raised about an attorney, the OPG works closely with organisations such as local authorities and NHS Trusts to carry out investigations.

How does the Public Guardian supervise deputies?

14.15 Individuals do not choose who will act as a deputy for them. The court will make the decision. There are measures to make sure that the court appoints an appropriate deputy. The OPG will then supervise deputies and support them in carrying out their duties, while also making sure they do not abuse their position.

14.16 When a case comes before the Court of Protection, the Act states that the court should make a decision to settle the matter rather than appoint a deputy, if possible. Deputies are most likely to be needed for financial matters where someone needs continued authority to make decisions about the person's money or other assets. It will be easier for the courts to make decisions in cases where a one-off decision is needed about a person's welfare, so there are likely to be fewer personal welfare deputies. But there will be occasions where ongoing decisions about a person's welfare will be required, and so the court will appoint a personal welfare deputy (see chapter 8).

[Scenario: Appointing deputies]

14.17 The OPG may run checks on potential deputies if requested to by the court. It will carry out a risk assessment to determine what kind of supervision a deputy will need once they are appointed.

14.18 Deputies are accountable to the court. The OPG supervises the deputy's actions on the court's behalf, and the court may want the deputy to provide financial accounts or other reports to the OPG. The Public Guardian deals with complaints about the way deputies carry out their duties. It works with other relevant agencies to investigate them. Chapter 8 gives detailed information about the responsibilities of deputies.

What happens if someone says they are worried about an attorney or deputy?

14.19 Many people who lack capacity are likely to get care or support from a range of agencies. Even when an attorney or deputy is acting on behalf of a person who lacks capacity, the other carers still have a responsibility to the person to provide care and act in the person's best interests. Anybody who is caring for a person who lacks capacity, whether in a paid or unpaid role, who is worried about how attorneys or deputies carry out their duties should contact the Public Guardian.

14.20   The OPG will not always be the most appropriate organisation to investigate all complaints. It may investigate a case jointly with:

- healthcare or social care professionals
- social services
- NHS bodies
- the Commission for Social Care Inspection in England or the Care and Social Services Inspectorate for Wales (CSSIW)[64]
- the Healthcare Commission in England or the Healthcare Inspectorate for Wales, and
- in some cases, the police.

14.21   The OPG will usually refer concerns about personal welfare LPAs or personal welfare deputies to the relevant agency. In certain circumstances it will alert the police about a case. When it makes a referral, the OPG will make sure that the relevant agency keeps it informed of the action it takes. It will also make sure that the court has all the information it needs to take possible action against the attorney or deputy.

14.22   Examples of situations in which a referral might be necessary include where:

- someone has complained that a welfare attorney is physically abusing a donor – the OPG would refer this case to the relevant local authority adult protection procedures and possibly the police
- the OPG has found that a solicitor appointed as a financial deputy for an elderly woman has defrauded her estate – the OPG would refer this case to the police and the Law Society Consumer Complaints Service.

How does the Act deal with ill treatment and wilful neglect?

14.23   The Act introduces two new criminal offences: ill treatment and wilful neglect of a person who lacks capacity to make relevant decisions (section 44). The offences may apply to:

- anyone caring for a person who lacks capacity – this includes family carers, healthcare and social care staff in hospital or care homes and those providing care in a person's home
- an attorney appointed under an LPA or an EPA, or
- a deputy appointed for the person by the court.

14.24   These people may be guilty of an offence if they ill-treat or wilfully neglect the person they care for or represent. Penalties will range from a fine to a sentence of imprisonment of up to five years – or both.

14.25   Ill treatment and neglect are separate offences.[65] For a person to be found guilty of ill treatment, they must either:

- have deliberately ill-treated the person, or
- be reckless in the way they were ill-treating the person or not.

It does not matter whether the behaviour was likely to cause, or actually caused, harm or damage to the victim's health.

---

[64] In April 2007, the Care Standards Inspectorate for Wales (CSIW) and the Social Services Inspectorate for Wales (SSIW) came together to form the Care and Social Services Inspectorate for Wales.

[65] *R v. Newington* (1990) 91 Cr App R 247, CA.

14.26 The meaning of 'wilful neglect' varies depending on the circumstances. But it usually means that a person has deliberately failed to carry out an act they knew they had a duty to do.

[*Scenario: Reporting abuse*]

What other measures protect people from abuse?

14.27 Local agencies have procedures that allow them to work together (called multi-agency working) to protect vulnerable adults – in care settings and elsewhere. Most areas have Adult Protection Committees. These committees:

- create policy (including reporting procedures)
- oversee investigations and other activity between agencies
- carry out joint training, and
- monitor and review progress.

Other local authorities have developed multi-agency Adult Protection Procedures, which are managed by a dedicated Adult Protection Co-ordinator.

14.28 Adult Protection Committees and Procedures (APCP) involve representatives from the NHS, social services, housing, the police and other relevant agencies. In England, they are essential points of contact for anyone who suspects abuse or ill treatment of a vulnerable adult. They can also give advice to the OPG if it is uncertain whether an intervention is necessary in a case of suspected abuse. In Wales, APCPs are not necessarily points of contact themselves, but they publish details of points of contact.

Who should check that staff are safe to work with vulnerable adults?

14.29 Under the Safeguarding Vulnerable Groups Act 2006, criminal record checks are now compulsory for staff who:

- have contact with service users in registered care homes
- provide personal care services in someone's home, and
- are involved in providing adult placement schemes.

14.30 Potential employers must carry out a pre-employment criminal record check with the Criminal Records Bureau (CRB) for all potential new healthcare and social care staff. This includes nursing agency staff and home care agency staff.

See Annex A for sources of more detailed information.

14.31 The Protection of Vulnerable Adults (POVA) list has the names of people who have been barred from working with vulnerable adults (in England and Wales). Employers providing care in a residential setting or a person's own home must check whether potential employees are on the list.[66] If they are on the list, they must:

- refuse to employ them, or
- employ them in a position that does not give them regular contact with vulnerable adults.

It is an offence for anyone on the list to apply for a care position. In such cases, the employer should report the person making the application.

---

[66] www.dh.gov.uk/PublicationsAndStatistics/Publications/PublicationsPolicyAndGuidance/PublicationsPolicyAndGuidanceArticle/fs/en?CONTENT_ID=4085855&chk=p0kQeS

Who is responsible for monitoring the standard of care providers?

14.32 All care providers covered by the Care Standards Act 2000 must register with the Commission for Social Care Inspection in England (CSCI) or the Care and Social Services Inspectorate for Wales (CSSIW).[67] These agencies make sure that care providers meet certain standards. They require care providers to have procedures to protect people from harm or abuse. These agencies can take action if they discover dangerous or unsafe practices that could place people at risk.

14.33 Care providers must also have effective complaints procedures. If providers cannot settle complaints, CSCI or CSSIW can look into them.

14.34 CSCI or CSSIW assesses the effectiveness of local adult protection procedures. They will also monitor the arrangements local councils make in response to the Care Standards Act.

What is an appointee, and who monitors them?

14.35 The Department for Work and Pensions (DWP) can appoint someone (an appointee) to claim and spend benefits on a person's behalf[68] if that person:

- gets social security benefits or pensions
- lacks the capacity to act for themselves
- has not made a property and affairs LPA or an EPA, and
- the court has not appointed a property and affairs deputy.

14.36 The DWP checks that an appointee is trustworthy. It also investigates any allegations that an appointee is not acting appropriately or in the person's interests. It can remove an appointee who abuses their position. Concerns about appointees should be raised with the relevant DWP agency (the local Jobcentre Plus, or if the person is aged 60 or over, The Pension Service).

Are there any other means of protection that people should be aware of?

14.37 There are a number of additional means that exist to protect people who lack capacity to make decisions for themselves. Healthcare and social care staff, attorneys and deputies should be aware of:

- National Minimum Standards (for example, for healthcare, care homes, and home care agencies) which apply to both England and Wales (see paragraph 14.38)
- National Service Frameworks, which set out national standards for specific health and care services for particular groups (for example, for mental health services[69] or services for older people[70])
- complaints procedures for all NHS bodies and local councils (see chapter 15)
- Stop Now Orders (also known as Enforcement Orders) that allow consumer protection bodies to apply for court orders to stop poor trading practices (for example, unfair door-step selling or rogue traders).[71]

---

[67] See note 64 above regarding the merger of the Care Standards Inspectorate for Wales and the Social Services Inspectorate for Wales.

[68] www.dwp.gov.uk/publications/dwp/2005/gl21_apr.pdf

[69] www.dh.gov.uk/assetRoot/04/07/72/09/04077209.pdf and
www.wales.nhs.uk/sites3/page.cfm?orgid=438&pid=11071

[70] www.dh.gov.uk/assetRoot/04/07/12/83/04071283.pdf and
www.wales.nhs.uk/sites3/home.cfm?orgid=439&redirect=yes&CFID=298511&CFTOKEN=6985382

[71] www.oft.gov.uk/Business/Legal/Stop+Now+Regulations.htm

- The Public Interest Disclosure Act 1998, which encourages people to report malpractice in the workplace and protects people who report malpractice from being sacked or victimised.

14.38 Information about all national minimum standards are available on the CSCI[72] and Healthcare Commission websites[73] and the Welsh Assembly Government website. Chapter 15 gives guidance on complaints procedures. Individual local authorities will have their own complaints system in place.

15 WHAT ARE THE BEST WAYS TO SETTLE DISAGREEMENTS AND DISPUTES ABOUT ISSUES COVERED IN THE ACT?

Sometimes people will disagree about:

- a person's capacity to make a decision
- their best interests
- a decision someone is making on their behalf, or
- an action someone is taking on their behalf.

It is in everybody's interests to settle disagreements and disputes quickly and effectively, with minimal stress and cost. This chapter sets out the different options available for settling disagreements. It also suggests ways to avoid letting a disagreement become a serious dispute. Finally, it sets out when it might be necessary to apply to the Court of Protection and when somebody can get legal funding.

> In this chapter, as throughout the Code, a person's capacity (or lack of capacity) refers specifically to their capacity to make a particular decision at the time it needs to be made.

Quick summary

- When disagreements occur about issues that are covered in the Act, it is usually best to try and settle them before they become serious.
- Advocates can help someone who finds it difficult to communicate their point of view. (This may be someone who has been assessed as lacking capacity.)
- Some disagreements can be effectively resolved by mediation.
- Where there is a concern about healthcare or social care provided to a person who lacks capacity, there are formal and informal ways of complaining about the care or treatment.
- The Health Service Ombudsman or the Local Government Ombudsman (in England) or the Public Services Ombudsman (in Wales) can be asked to investigate some problems that have not been resolved through formal complaints procedures.
- Disputes about the finances of a person who lacks capacity should usually be referred to the Office of the Public Guardian (OPG).
- When other methods of resolving disagreements are not appropriate, the matter can be referred to the Court of Protection.
- There are some decisions that are so serious that the Court of Protection should always make them.

---

[72] www.csci.org.uk/information_for_service_providers/national_minimum_standards/default.htm
[73] www.healthcarecommission.org.uk/_db/_documents/The_annual_health_check_in_2006_2007_assessing_and_rating_the_NHS_200609225143.pdf

What options are there for settling disagreements?

15.1   Disagreements about healthcare, social or other welfare services may be between:

- people who have assessed a person as lacking capacity to make a decision and the person they have assessed (see chapter 4 for how to challenge an assessment of lack of capacity)
- family members or other people concerned with the care and welfare of a person who lacks capacity
- family members and healthcare or social care staff involved in providing care or treatment
- healthcare and social care staff who have different views about what is in the best interests of a person who lacks capacity.

15.2   In general, disagreements can be resolved by either formal or informal procedures, and there is more information on both in this chapter. However, there are some disagreements and some subjects that are so serious they can only be resolved by the Court of Protection.

15.3   It is usually best to try and settle disagreements before they become serious disputes. Many people settle them by communicating effectively and taking the time to listen and to address worries. Disagreements between family members are often best settled informally, or sometimes through mediation. When professionals are in disagreement with a person's family, it is a good idea to start by:

- setting out the different options in a way that is easy to understand
- inviting a colleague to talk to the family and offer a second opinion
- offering to get independent expert advice
- using an advocate to support and represent the person who lacks capacity
- arranging a case conference or meeting to discuss matters in detail
- listening to, acknowledging and addressing worries, and
- where the situation is not urgent, allowing the family time to think it over.

Further guidance on how to deal with problems without going to court may also be found in the Community Legal Services Information Leaflet 'Alternatives to Court'.[74]

When is an advocate useful?

15.4   An advocate helps communicate the feelings and views of someone who has communication difficulties. The definition of advocacy set out in the Advocacy Charter adopted by most advocacy schemes is as follows: 'Advocacy is taking action to help people say what they want, secure their rights, represent their interests and obtain services they need. Advocates and advocacy schemes work in partnership with the people they support and take their side. Advocacy promotes social inclusion, equality and social justice.'[75]

An advocate may be able to help settle a disagreement simply by presenting a person's feelings to their family, carers or professionals. Most advocacy services are provided by the voluntary sector and are arranged at a local level. They have no link to any agency involved with the person.

15.5   Using advocates can help people who find it difficult to communicate (including those who have been assessed as lacking capacity) to:

---

[74] CLS (Community Legal Services) Direct Information Leaflet Number 23, www.clsdirect.org.uk/legalhelp/leaflet23.jsp?lang=en

[75] Advocacy across London, Advocacy Charter (2002)

- say what they want
- claim their rights
- represent their interests, and
- get the services they need.

15.6   Advocates may also be involved in supporting the person during mediation (see paragraphs 15.7–15.13 below) or helping with complaints procedures. Sometimes people who lack capacity or have been assessed as lacking capacity have a legal right to an advocate, for example:

- when making a formal complaint against the NHS (see paragraph 15.18), and
- where the Act requires the involvement of an Independent Mental Capacity Advocate (IMCA) (see chapter 10).

When is mediation useful?

15.7   A mediator helps people to come to an agreement that is acceptable to all parties. Mediation can help solve a problem at an early stage. It offers a wider range of solutions than the court can – and it may be less stressful for all parties, more cost-effective and quicker. People who come to an agreement through mediation are more likely to keep to it, because they have taken part in decision-making.

15.8   Mediators are independent. They have no personal interest in the outcome of a case. They do not make decisions or impose solutions. The mediator will decide whether the case is suitable for mediation. They will consider the likely chances of success and the need to protect the interests of the person who lacks capacity.

15.9   Any case that can be settled through negotiation is likely to benefit from mediation. It is most suitable when people are not communicating well or not understanding each other's point of view. It can improve relationships and stop future disputes, so it is a good option when it is in the person's interests for people to have a good relationship in the future.

[*Scenario: Using mediation*]

15.10   In mediation, everybody needs to take part as equally as possible so that a mediator can help everyone involved to focus on the person's best interests. It might also be appropriate to involve an advocate to help communicate the wishes of the person who lacks capacity.

15.11   The National Mediation Helpline[76] helps callers to identify an effective means of resolving their difficulty without going to court. It will arrange an appointment with a trained and accredited mediator. The Family Mediation Helpline[77] can provide information on family mediation and referrals to local family mediation services. Family mediators are trained to deal with the emotional, practical and financial needs of those going through relationship breakdown.

15.12   Healthcare and social care staff may also take part in mediation processes. But it may be more appropriate to follow the relevant healthcare or social care complaints procedures (see paragraphs 15.14–15.32).

15.13   In certain situations (mainly family mediation), legal aid may be available to fund mediation for people who meet the qualifying criteria (see paragraphs 15.38–15.44).

---

[76] National Mediation Helpline, Tel: 0845 60 30 809, www.nationalmediationhelpline.com
[77] Family Mediation Helpline, Tel: 0845 60 26 627, www.familymediationhelpline.co.uk

How can someone complain about healthcare?

15.14 There are formal and informal ways of complaining about a patient's healthcare or treatment. Healthcare staff and others need to know which methods are suitable in which situations.

15.15 In England, the Patient Advice and Liaison Service (PALS) provides an informal way of dealing with problems before they reach the complaints stage. PALS operate in every NHS and Primary Care Trust in England. They provide advice and information to patients (or their relatives or carers) to try to solve problems quickly. They can direct people to specialist support services (for example, advocates, mental health support teams, social services or interpreting services). PALS do not investigate complaints. Their role is to explain complaints procedures and direct people to the formal NHS complaints process, if necessary. NHS complaints procedures deal with complaints about something that happened in the past that requires an apology or explanation. A court cannot help in this situation, but court proceedings may be necessary in some clinical negligence cases (see paragraph 15.22).

15.16 In Wales, complaints advocates based at Community Health Councils provide advice and support to anyone with concerns about treatment they have had.

Disagreements about proposed treatments

15.17 If a case is not urgent, the supportive atmosphere of the PALS may help settle it. In Wales, the local Community Health Council may be able to help. But urgent cases about proposed serious treatment may need to go to the Court of Protection (see paragraphs 15.35–15.36).

[Scenario: Disagreeing about treatment or an assessment]

The formal NHS complaints procedure

15.18 The formal NHS complaints procedure deals with complaints about NHS services provided by NHS organisations or primary care practitioners. As a first step, people should try to settle a disagreement through an informal discussion between:

- the healthcare staff involved
- the person who may lack capacity to make the decision in question (with support if necessary)
- their carers, and
- any appropriate relatives.

If the person who is complaining is not satisfied, the Independent Complaints Advocacy Service (ICAS) may help. In Wales, the complaints advocates based at Community Health Councils will support and advise anyone who wants to make a complaint.

15.19 In England, if the person is still unhappy after a local investigation, they can ask for an independent review by the Healthcare Commission. If the patient involved in the complaint was or is detained under the Mental Health Act 1983, the Mental Health Act Commission can be asked to look into the complaint. If people are still unhappy after this stage, they can go to the Health Service Ombudsman. More information on how to make a complaint in England is available from the Department of Health.

15.20 In Wales, if patients are still unhappy after a local investigation, they can ask for an independent review of their complaint by independent lay reviewers. After this, they can take their case to the Public Services Ombudsman for Wales. People can take their complaint direct to the Ombudsman if:

- the complaint is about care or treatment that took place after 1 April 2006, and
- they have tried to settle the problem locally first.

The Mental Health Act Commission may also investigate complaints about the care or treatment of detained patients in Wales, if attempts have been made to settle the complaint locally without success.

15.21   Regulations about first trying to settle complaints locally do not apply to NHS Foundation Trusts. But these Trusts are covered by the independent review stage operated by the Healthcare Commission and by the Health Service Ombudsman. People who have a complaint about an NHS Foundation Trust should contact the Trust for advice on how to make a complaint.

Cases of clinical negligence

15.22   The NHS Litigation Authority oversees all clinical negligence cases brought against the NHS in England. It actively encourages people to try other forms of settling complaints before going to court. The National Assembly for Wales also encourages people to try other forms of settling complaints before going to court.

How can somebody complain about social care?

15.23   The social services complaints procedure has been reformed. The reformed procedure came into effect on 1 September 2006 in England and on 1 April 2006 in Wales.

15.24   A service provider's own complaints procedure should deal with complaints about:

- the way in which care services are delivered
- the type of services provided, or
- a failure to provide services.

15.25   Care agencies contracted by local authorities or registered with the Commission for Social Care Inspection (CSCI) in England or Care and Social Services Inspectorate for Wales (CSSIW) are legally obliged to have their own written complaints procedures. This includes residential homes, agencies providing care in people's homes, nursing agencies and adult placement schemes. The procedures should set out how to make a complaint and what to do with a complaint that cannot be settled locally.

Local authority complaints procedures

15.26   For services contracted by a local authority, it may be more appropriate to use the local authority's complaints procedure. A simple example would be a situation where a local authority places a person in a care home and the person's family are not happy with the placement. If their complaint is not about the services the home provides (for example, it might be about the local authority's assessment of the person's needs), it might be more appropriate to use the local authority's complaints procedure.

15.27   As a first step, people should try to settle a disagreement through an informal discussion, involving:

- the professionals involved
- the person who may lack capacity to make the decision in question (with support if necessary)
- their carers, and
- any appropriate relatives.

15.28   If the person making the complaint is not satisfied, the local authority will carry out a formal investigation using its complaints procedure. In England, after this stage, a social service Complaints Review Panel can hear the case. In Wales complaints can be referred to the National Assembly for Wales for hearing by an independent panel.

Other complaints about social care

15.29   People can take their complaint to the CSCI in England or the CSSIW in Wales, if:

- the complaint is about regulations or national minimum standards not being met, and
- the complainants are not happy with the provider's own complaints procedure or the response to their complaint.

15.30   If a complaint is about a local authority's administration, it may be referred to the Commission for Local Administration in England (the Local Government Ombudsman) or the Public Services Ombudsman for Wales.

What if a complaint covers healthcare and social care?

15.31   Taking a complaint through NHS or local authority complaints procedures can be a complicated process – especially if the complaint covers a number of service providers or both healthcare and social care. In such situations, local authorities and the NHS must work together and agree which organisation will lead in handling the complaint. If a person is not happy with the outcome, they can take their case to the Health Service Ombudsman or to the Local Government Ombudsman (in England). There is guidance which sets out how organisations should work together to handle complaints that cover healthcare and social care (in England Learning from Complaints and in Wales Listening and learning). The Public Services Ombudsman for Wales handles complaints that cover both healthcare and social care.

Who can handle complaints about other welfare issues?

15.32   The Independent Housing Ombudsman deals with complaints about registered social landlords in England. This applies mostly to housing associations. But it also applies to many landlords who manage homes that were formerly run by local authorities and some private landlords. In Wales, the Public Services Ombudsman for Wales deals with complaints about registered social landlords. Complaints about local authorities may be referred to the Local Government Ombudsman in England or the Public Services Ombudsman for Wales. They look at complaints about decisions on council housing, social services, Housing Benefit and planning applications. More information about complaints to an Ombudsman is available on the relevant websites (see Annex A).

What is the best way to handle disagreement about a person's finances?

15.33   Some examples of disagreements about a person's finances are:

- disputes over the amount of money a person who lacks capacity should pay their carer
- disputes over whether a person who lacks capacity should sell their house
- somebody questioning the actions of a carer, who may be using the money of a person who lacks capacity inappropriately or without proper authority
- somebody questioning the actions of an attorney appointed under a Lasting Power of Attorney or an Enduring Power of Attorney or a deputy appointed by the court.

15.34   In all of the above circumstances, the most appropriate action would usually be to contact the Office of the Public Guardian (OPG) for guidance and advice. See chapter 14 for further details on the role of the OPG.

How can the Court of Protection help?

15.35   The Court of Protection deals with all areas of decision-making for adults who lack capacity to make particular decisions for themselves (see chapter 8 for more information about its roles and responsibilities). But the court is not always the right place to settle problems involving people who lack capacity. Other forms of settling disagreements may be more appropriate and less distressing.

15.36   There are some decisions that are so serious that the court should always make them. There are also other types of cases that the court should deal with when another method would generally not be suitable. See chapter 8 for more information about both kinds of cases.

Right of Appeal

15.37   Section 53 of the Act describes the rights of appeal against any decision taken by the Court of Protection. There are further details in the Court of Protection Rules. It may be advisable for anyone who wishes to appeal a decision made by the court to seek legal advice.

Will public legal funding be available?

15.38   Depending on their financial situation, once the Act comes into force people may be entitled to:

- publicly funded legal advice from accredited solicitors or advice agencies
- legal representation before the new Court of Protection (in the most serious cases).

Information about solicitors and organisations who give advice on different areas of law is available from Community Legal Services Direct (CLS Direct).[78] Further information about legal aid and public funding can be obtained from the Legal Services Commission.[79] See Annex A for full contact details.

15.39   People who lack capacity to instruct a solicitor or conduct their own case will need a litigation friend. This person could be a relative, friend, attorney or the Official Solicitor (when no-one else is available). The litigation friend is able to instruct the solicitor and conduct the case on behalf of a person who lacks capacity to give instructions. If the person qualifies for public legal funding, the litigation friend can claim funding on their behalf.

When can someone get legal help?

15.40   Legal help is a type of legal aid (public funding) that pays for advice and assistance on legal issues, including those affecting a person who lacks capacity. But it does not provide representation for a full court hearing, although there is a related form of funding called 'help at court' under which a legal representative can speak in court on a client's behalf on an informal basis. To qualify for legal help, applicants must show that:

- they get specific social security benefits, or they earn less than a specific amount and do not have savings or other financial assets in excess of a specific amount
- they would benefit sufficiently from legal advice to justify the amount it costs, and
- they cannot get another form of funding.

---

[78]   CLS Direct, Tel: 0845 345 4 345, www.clsdirect.org.uk
[79]   www.legalservices.gov.uk

15.41 Legal help can include:

- help from a solicitor or other representative in writing letters
- in exceptional circumstances, getting a barrister's opinion, and
- assistance in preparing for Court of Protection hearings.

15.42 People cannot get legal help for making a Lasting Power of Attorney or an advance decision to refuse treatment. But they can get general help and information from the OPG. The OPG cannot give legal or specialist advice. For example, they will not be able to advise someone on what powers they should delegate to their attorney under an LPA.

When can someone get legal representation?

15.43 Public funding for legal representation in the Court of Protection will be available from solicitors with a relevant contract – but only for the most serious cases. To qualify, applicants will normally face the same test as for legal help to qualify financially (paragraph 15.40). They will generally have to satisfy more detailed criteria than applicants for legal help, relating, for instance, to their prospects of being successful, to whether legal representation is necessary and to the cost benefit of being represented. They will also have to establish that the case could not be brought or funded in another way and that there are not alternatives to court proceedings that should be explored first.

15.44 Serious personal welfare cases that were previously heard by the High Court will continue to have public funding for legal representation when they are transferred to the Court of Protection. These cases will normally be related to personal liberty, serious welfare decisions or medical treatment for a person who lacks capacity. But legal representation may also be available in other types of cases, depending on the particular circumstances.

16 WHAT RULES GOVERN ACCESS TO INFORMATION ABOUT A PERSON WHO LACKS CAPACITY?

This chapter gives guidance on:

- what personal information about someone who lacks capacity people involved in their care have the right to see, and
- how they can get hold of that information.

This chapter is only a general guide. It does not give detailed information about the law. Nor does it replace professional guidance or the guidance of the Information Commissioner's Office on the Data Protection Act 1998 (this guidance is available on its website, see Annex A). Where necessary, people should take legal advice.

This chapter is mainly for people such as family carers and other carers, deputies and attorneys, who care for or represent someone who lacks capacity to make specific decisions and in particular, lacks capacity to allow information about them to be disclosed. Professionals have their own codes of conduct, and they may have the support of experts in their organisations.

In this chapter, as throughout the Code, a person's capacity (or lack of capacity) refers specifically to their capacity to make a particular decision at the time it needs to be made.

Quick summary

Questions to ask when requesting personal information about someone who may lack capacity

- Am I acting under a Lasting Power of Attorney or as a deputy with specific authority?
- Does the person have capacity to agree that information can be disclosed? Have they previously agreed to disclose the information?
- What information do I need?
- Why do I need it?
- Who has the information?
- Can I show that:
  - I need the information to make a decision that is in the best interests of the person I am acting for, and
  - the person does not have the capacity to act for themselves?

- Do I need to share the information with anyone else to make a decision that is in the best interests of the person who lacks capacity?
- Should I keep a record of my decision or action?
- How long should I keep the information for?
- Do I have the right to request the information under section 7 of the Data Protection Act 1998?

Questions to ask when considering whether to disclose information

- Is the request covered by section 7 of the Data Protection Act 1998? Is the request being made by a formally authorised representative?

If not:

- Is the disclosure legal?
- Is the disclosure justified, having balanced the person's best interests and the public interest against the person's right to privacy?

Questions to ask to decide whether the disclosure is legal or justified

- Do I (or does my organisation) have the information?
- Am I satisfied that the person concerned lacks capacity to agree to disclosure?
- Does the person requesting the information have any formal authority to act on behalf of the person who lacks capacity?
- Am I satisfied that the person making the request:
  - is acting in the best interests of the person concerned?
  - needs the information to act properly?
  - will respect confidentiality?
  - will keep the information for no longer than necessary?

- Should I get written confirmation of these things?

16.1 People caring for, or managing the finances of, someone who lacks capacity may need information to:

   - assess the person's capacity to make a specific decision
   - determine the person's best interests, and
   - make appropriate decisions on the person's behalf.

16.2 The information they need varies depending on the circumstances. For example:

   - a daughter providing full-time care for an elderly parent will make decisions based on her own experience and knowledge of her parent

- a deputy may need information from other people. For instance, if they were deciding whether a person needs to move into a care home or whether they should sell the person's home, they might need information from family members, the family doctor, the person's bank and their solicitor to make sure they are making the decision in the person's best interests.

16.3 Much of the information needed to make decisions under the Act is sensitive or confidential. It is regulated by:

- the Data Protection Act 1998
- the common law duty of confidentiality
- professional codes of conduct on confidentiality, and
- the Human Rights Act 1998 and European Convention on Human Rights, in particular Article 8 (the right to respect for private and family life), which means that it is only lawful to reveal someone's personal information if:

  - there is a legitimate aim in doing so
  - a democratic society would think it necessary to do so, and
  - the kind and amount of information disclosed is in relation to the need.

16.4 Section 7 of the Data Protection Act 1998 gives everyone the right to see personal information that an organisation holds about them. They may also authorise someone else to access their information on their behalf. The person holding the information has a legal duty to release it. So, where possible, it is important to try to get a person's consent before requesting to see information about them.

16.5 A person may have the capacity to agree to someone seeing their personal information, even if they do not have the capacity to make other decisions. In some situations, a person may have previously given consent (while they still had capacity) for someone to see their personal information in the future.

16.6 Doctors and lawyers cannot share information about their clients, or that clients have given them, without the client's consent. Sometimes it is fair to assume that a doctor or lawyer already has someone's consent (for example, patients do not usually expect healthcare staff or legal professionals to get consent every time they share information with a colleague – but staff may choose to get clients' consent in writing when they begin treating or acting for that person). But in other circumstances, doctors and lawyers must get specific consent to 'disclose' information (share it with someone else).

16.7 If someone's capacity changes from time to time, the person needing the information may want to wait until that person can give their consent. Or they may decide that it is not necessary to get access to information at all, if the person will be able to make a decision on their own in the future.

16.8 If someone lacks the capacity to give consent, someone else might still be able to see their personal information. This will depend on:

- whether the person requesting the information is acting as an agent (a representative recognised by the law, such as a deputy or attorney) for the person who lacks capacity
- whether disclosure is in the best interests of the person who lacks capacity, and
- what type of information has been requested.

When can attorneys and deputies ask to see personal information?

16.9 An attorney acting under a valid LPA or EPA (and sometimes a deputy) can ask to see information concerning the person they are representing, as long as the information applies to decisions the attorney has the legal right to make.

16.10 In practice, an attorney or deputy may only require limited information and may not need to make a formal request. In such circumstances, they can approach the information holder informally. Once satisfied that the request comes from an attorney or deputy (having seen appropriate authority), the person holding information should be able to release it. The attorney or deputy can still make a formal request for information in the future.

16.11 The attorney or deputy must treat the information confidentially. They should be extremely careful to protect it. If they fail to do so, the court can cancel the LPA or deputyship.

16.12 Before the Act came into effect, only a few receivers were appointed with the general authority to manage a person's property and affairs. So they needed specific authority from the Court of Protection to ask for access to the person's personal information. Similarly, a deputy who only has authority to act in specific areas only has the right to ask for information relating to decisions in those specific areas. For information relating to other areas, the deputy will need to apply to the Court of Protection.

16.13 Requests for personal information must be in writing, and there might be a fee. Information holders should release it promptly (always within 40 calendar days). Fees may be particularly high for getting copies of healthcare records – particularly where information may be in unusual formats (for example, x-rays). The maximum fee is currently £50. Complaints about a failure to comply with the Data Protection Act 1998 should be directed to the Information Commissioner's Office (see Annex A for contact details).

What limitations are there?

16.14 Attorneys and deputies should only ask for information that will help them make a decision they need to make on behalf of the person who lacks capacity. For example, if the attorney needs to know when the person should take medication, they should not ask to see the entire healthcare record. The person who releases information must make sure that an attorney or deputy has official authority (they may ask for proof of identity and appointment). When asking to see personal information, attorneys and deputies should bear in mind that their decision must always be in the best interests of the person who lacks capacity to make that decision.

16.15 The attorney or deputy may not know the kind of information that someone holds about the person they are representing. So sometimes it might be difficult for them to make a specific request. They might even need to see all the information to make a decision. But again, the 'best interests' principle applies.

[Scenario: Giving attorneys access to personal information]

16.16 The deputy or attorney may find that some information is held back (for example, when this contains references to people other than the person who lacks capacity). This might be to protect another person's privacy, if that person is mentioned in the records. It is unlikely that information relating to another person would help an attorney make a decision on behalf of the person who lacks capacity. The information holder might also be obliged to keep information about the other person confidential. There might be another reason why the person does not want information about them to be released. Under these circumstances, the attorney does not have the right to see that information.

16.17 An information holder should not release information if doing so would cause serious physical or mental harm to anyone – including the person the information is about. This applies to information on health, social care and education records.

16.18 The Information Commissioner's Office can give further details on:

- how to request personal information
- restrictions on accessing information, and
- how to appeal against a decision not to release information.

When can someone see information about healthcare or social care?

16.19 Healthcare and social care staff may disclose information about somebody who lacks capacity only when it is in the best interests of the person concerned to do so, or when there is some other, lawful reason for them to do so.

16.20 The Act's requirement to consult relevant people when working out the best interests of a person who lacks capacity will encourage people to share the information that makes a consultation meaningful. But people who release information should be sure that they are acting lawfully and that they can justify releasing the information. They need to balance the person's right to privacy with what is in their best interests or the wider public interest (see paragraphs 16.24–16.25 below).

16.21 Sometimes it will be fairly obvious that staff should disclose information. For example, a doctor would need to tell a new care worker about what drugs a person needs or what allergies the person has. This is clearly in the person's best interests.

16.22 Other information may need to be disclosed as part of the process of working out someone's best interests. A social worker might decide to reveal information about someone's past when discussing their best interests with a close family member. But staff should always bear in mind that the Act requires them to consider the wishes and feelings of the person who lacks capacity.

16.23 In both these cases, staff should only disclose as much information as is relevant to the decision to be made.

[*Scenario: Sharing appropriate information*]

16.24 Sometimes a person's right to confidentiality will conflict with broader public concerns. Information can be released if it is in the public interest, even if it is not in the best interests of the person who lacks capacity. It can be difficult to decide in these cases, and information holders should consider each case on its merits. The NHS Code on Confidentiality gives examples of when disclosure is in the public interest. These include situations where disclosing information could prevent, or aid investigation of, serious crimes, or to prevent serious harm, such as spread of an infectious disease. It is then necessary to judge whether the public good that would be achieved by the disclosure outweighs both the obligation of confidentiality to the individual concerned and the broader public interest in the provision of a confidential service.

16.25 For disclosure to be in the public interest, it must be proportionate and limited to the relevant details. Healthcare or social care staff faced with this decision should seek advice from their legal advisers. It is not just things for 'the public's benefit' that are in the public interest – disclosure for the benefit of the person who lacks capacity can also be in the public interest (for example, to stop a person who lacks capacity suffering physical or mental harm).

What financial information can carers ask to see?

16.26 It is often more difficult to get financial information than it is to get information on a person's welfare. A bank manager, for example, is less likely to:

- know the individual concerned
- be able to make an assessment of the person's capacity to consent to disclosure, and
- be aware of the carer's relationship to the person.

So they are less likely than a doctor or social worker to be able to judge what is in a person's best interests and are bound by duties to keep clients' affairs confidential. It is likely that someone wanting financial information will need to apply to the Court of Protection for access to that information. This clearly does not apply to an attorney or a deputy appointed to manage the person's property and affairs, who will generally have the authority (because of their appointment) to obtain all relevant information about the person's property and affairs.

Is information still confidential after someone shares it?

16.27 Whenever a carer gets information, they should treat the information in confidence, and they should not share it with anyone else (unless there is a lawful basis for doing so). In some circumstances, the information holder might ask the carer to give a formal confirmation that they will keep information confidential.

16.28 Where the information is in written form, carers should store it carefully and not keep it for longer than necessary. In many cases, the need to keep the information will be temporary. So the carer should be able to reassure the information holder that they will not keep a permanent record of the information.

What is the best way to settle a disagreement about personal information?

16.29 A carer should always start by trying to get consent from the person whose information they are trying to access. If the person lacks capacity to consent, the carer should ask the information holder for the relevant information and explain why they need it. They may need to remind the information holder that they have to make a decision in the person's best interests and cannot do so without the relevant information.

16.30 This can be a sensitive area and disputes will inevitably arise. Healthcare and social care staff have a difficult judgement to make. They might feel strongly that disclosing the information would not be in the best interests of the person who lacks capacity and would amount to an invasion of their privacy. This may be upsetting for the carer who will probably have good motives for wanting the information. In all cases, an assessment of the interests and needs of the person who lacks capacity should determine whether staff should disclose information.

16.31 If a discussion fails to settle the matter, and the carer still is not happy, there are other ways to settle the disagreement (see chapter 15). The carer may need to use the appropriate complaints procedure. Since the complaint involves elements of data protection and confidentiality, as well as best interests, relevant experts should help deal with the complaint.

16.32 In cases where carers and staff cannot settle their disagreement, the carer can apply to the Court of Protection for the right to access to the specific information. The court would then need to decide if this was in the best interests of the person who lacks capacity to consent. In urgent cases, it might be necessary for the carer to apply directly to the court without going through the earlier stages.

Appendix E
MENTAL CAPACITY ACT 2005 DEPRIVATION OF LIBERTY SAFEGUARDS CODE OF PRACTICE

[The Mental Capacity Act 2005 Deprivation of Liberty Safeguards Code of Practice was issued by the Lord Chancellor in accordance with ss.42 and 43 of the Mental Capacity Act 2005. It adds to the guidance in the main Mental Capacity Act 2005 Code of Practice and should be used in conjunction with the main Code.

It is © Crown copyright 2008 and published online by The Stationery Office at **www.publicguardian.gov.uk.**

The Code of Practice is reproduced here with some minor omissions: the preliminary pages, introduction, key words and phrases, and Annexes. Due to the limitations of space in this book, the scenarios which illustrate the Code of Practice have also been removed. However, the titles of each scenario have been retained to indicate where a scenario exists.]

CONTENTS

1 WHAT ARE THE DEPRIVATION OF LIBERTY SAFEGUARDS AND WHY WERE THEY INTRODUCED?

The deprivation of liberty safeguards were introduced to provide a legal framework around the deprivation of liberty. Specifically, they were introduced to prevent breaches of the European Convention on Human Rights (ECHR) such as the one identified by the judgment of the European Court of Human Rights (ECtHR) in the case of *HL v the United Kingdom*[1] (commonly referred to as the 'Bournewood' judgment). The case concerned an

---

[1] (2004) Application No: 00045508/99.

autistic man (HL) with a learning disability, who lacked the capacity to decide whether he should be admitted to hospital for specific treatment. He was admitted on an informal basis under common law in his best interests, but this decision was challenged by HL's carers. In its judgment, the ECtHR held that this admission constituted a deprivation of HL's liberty and, further, that:

- the deprivation of liberty had not been in accordance with 'a procedure prescribed by law' and was, therefore, in breach of Article 5(1) of the ECHR, and
- there had been a contravention of Article 5(4) of the ECHR because HL had no means of applying quickly to a court to see if the deprivation of liberty was lawful.

To prevent further similar breaches of the ECHR, the Mental Capacity Act 2005 has been amended to provide safeguards for people who lack capacity specifically to consent to treatment or care in either a hospital or a care home[2] that, in their own best interests, can only be provided in circumstances that amount to a deprivation of liberty, and where detention under the Mental Health Act 1983 is not appropriate for the person at that time. These safeguards are referred to in this Code of Practice as 'deprivation of liberty safeguards'.

What are the deprivation of liberty safeguards?

1.1   The deprivation of liberty safeguards provide legal protection for those vulnerable people who are, or may become, deprived of their liberty within the meaning of Article 5 of the ECHR in a hospital or care home, whether placed under public or private arrangements. They do not apply to people detained under the Mental Health Act 1983. The safeguards exist to provide a proper legal process and suitable protection in those circumstances where deprivation of liberty appears to be unavoidable, in a person's own best interests.

1.2   Every effort should be made, in both commissioning and providing care or treatment, to prevent deprivation of liberty. If deprivation of liberty cannot be avoided, it should be for no longer than is necessary.

1.3   The safeguards provide for deprivation of liberty to be made lawful through 'standard' or 'urgent' authorisation processes. These processes are designed to prevent arbitrary decisions to deprive a person of liberty and give a right to challenge deprivation of liberty authorisations.

1.4   The deprivation of liberty safeguards mean that a 'managing authority' (i.e. the relevant hospital or care home – see paragraph 3.1) must seek authorisation from a 'supervisory body' in order to be able lawfully to deprive someone of their liberty. Before giving such an authorisation, the supervisory body must be satisfied that the person has a mental disorder[3] and lacks capacity to decide about their residence or treatment. The supervisory body could be a primary care trust, a local authority, Welsh Ministers or a local health board (LHB) (see paragraph 3.3).

1.5   A decision as to whether or not deprivation of liberty arises will depend on all the circumstances of the case (as explained more fully in chapter 2). It is neither necessary nor appropriate to apply for a deprivation of liberty authorisation for everyone who is in hospital or a care home simply because the person concerned lacks capacity to decide whether or not they should be there. In deciding whether or not an application is necessary, a managing authority should carefully consider whether

---

[2] Throughout this document, the term 'care home' means a care home registered under the Care Standards Act 2000.

[3] As defined in section 1 of the Mental Health Act 1983, a mental disorder is any disorder or disability of the mind, apart from dependence on alcohol and drugs. This includes all learning disabilities. The distinction in the Mental Health Act 1983 between learning disabilities depending on whether or not they are associated with abnormally aggressive or seriously irresponsible behaviour is not relevant.

any restrictions that are, or will be, needed to provide ongoing care or treatment amount to a deprivation of liberty when looked at together.

1.6   The deprivation of liberty safeguards cover:

- how an application for authorisation should be applied for
- how an application for authorisation should be assessed
- the requirements that must be fulfilled for an authorisation to be given
- how an authorisation should be reviewed
- what support and representation must be provided for people who are subject to an authorisation, and
- how people can challenge authorisations.

Who is covered by these safeguards?

1.7   The safeguards apply to people in England and Wales who have a mental disorder and lack capacity to consent to the arrangements made for their care or treatment, but for whom receiving care or treatment in circumstances that amount to a deprivation of liberty may be necessary to protect them from harm and appears to be in their best interests. A large number of these people will be those with significant learning disabilities, or older people who have dementia or some similar disability, but they can also include those who have certain other neurological conditions (for example as a result of a brain injury).

1.8   In order to come within the scope of a deprivation of liberty authorisation, a person must be detained in a hospital or care home, for the purpose of being given care or treatment in circumstances that amount to a deprivation of liberty. The authorisation must relate to the individual concerned and to the hospital or care home in which they are detained.

1.9   For the purposes of Article 5 of the ECHR, there is no distinction in principle between depriving a person who lacks capacity of their liberty for the purpose of treating them for a physical condition, and depriving them of their liberty for treatment of a mental disorder. There will therefore be occasions when people who lack capacity to consent to admission are taken to hospital for treatment of physical illnesses or injuries, and then need to be cared for in circumstances that amount to a deprivation of liberty. In these circumstances, a deprivation of liberty authorisation must be applied for. Consequently, this Code of Practice must be followed and applied in acute hospital settings as well as care homes and mental health units.

1.10   It is important to bear in mind that, while the deprivation of liberty might be for the purpose of giving a person treatment, a deprivation of liberty authorisation does not itself authorise treatment. Treatment that is proposed following authorisation of deprivation of liberty may only be given with the person's consent (if they have capacity to make the decision) or in accordance with the wider provisions of the Mental Capacity Act 2005. More details of this are contained in paragraphs 5.10 to 5.13 of this Code.

1.11   The safeguards cannot apply to people while they are detained in hospital under the Mental Health Act 1983. The safeguards can, however, apply to a person who has previously been detained in hospital under the Mental Health Act 1983. There are other cases in which people who are – or could be – subject to the Mental Health Act 1983 will not meet the eligibility requirement for the safeguards. Chapter 13 of the main Code contains guidance on the relationship between the Mental Capacity Act 2005 and the Mental Health Act 1983 generally, as does the Code of Practice to the Mental HealthAct 1983 itself. Paragraphs 4.40 to 4.57 of the present Code explain the relationship of the deprivation of liberty safeguards to the Mental Health Act 1983, and in particular how to assess if a person is eligible to be deprived of their liberty under the safeguards.

1.12   The safeguards relate only to people aged 18 and over. If the issue of depriving a person under the age of 18 of their liberty arises, other safeguards must be considered – such as the existing powers of the court, particularly those under section 25 of the Children Act 1989, or use of the Mental Health Act 1983.

When can someone be deprived of their liberty?

1.13   Depriving someone who lacks the capacity to consent to the arrangements made for their care or treatment of their liberty is a serious matter, and the decision to do so should not be taken lightly. The deprivation of liberty safeguards make it clear that a person may only be deprived of their liberty:

- in their own best interests to protect them from harm
- if it is a proportionate response to the likelihood and seriousness of the harm, and
- if there is no less restrictive alternative.

1.14   Under no circumstances must deprivation of liberty be used as a form of punishment, or for the convenience of professionals, carers or anyone else. Deprivation of liberty should not be extended due to delays in moving people between care or treatment settings, for example when somebody awaits discharge after completing a period of hospital treatment.

Are there any cultural considerations in implementing the safeguards?

1.15   The deprivation of liberty safeguards should not impact in any different way on different racial or ethnic groups, and care should be taken to ensure that the provisions are not operated in a manner that discriminates against particular racial or ethnic groups. It is up to managing authorities and supervisory bodies to ensure that their staff are aware of their responsibilities in this regard and of the need to ensure that the safeguards are operated fairly and equitably.

1.16   Assessors who carry out deprivation of liberty assessments to help decide whether a person should be deprived of their liberty (seechapter 4) should have the necessary skills and experience to take account of people's diverse backgrounds. Accordingly, they will need to have an understanding of, and respect for, the background of the relevant person. Supervisory bodies must take these factors into account when appointing assessors and must seek to appoint the most suitable available person for each case.

1.17   Interpreters should be available, where necessary, to help assessors to communicate not only with the relevant person but also with people with an interest in their care and treatment. An interpreter should be suitably qualified and experienced to enable them to provide effective language and communication support in the particular case concerned, and to offer appropriate assistance to the assessors involved. Information should be made available in other languages where relevant.

1.18   Any decision about the instruction of Independent Mental Capacity Advocates (see paragraphs 3.22 to 3.28) or relevant person's representatives (see chapter 7) should take account of the cultural, national, racial or ethnic background of the relevant person.

Where do the safeguards apply?

1.19   Although the Bournewood judgment was specifically about a patient who lacked capacity to consent to admission to hospital for mental health treatment, the judgment has wider implications that extend to people who lack capacity and who might be deprived of their liberty either in a hospital or in a care home.

1.20   It will only be lawful to deprive somebody of their liberty elsewhere (for example, in their own home, in supported living arrangements other than in a care home, or in a day centre) when following an order of the Court of Protection on a personal welfare matter. In such a case, the Court of Protection order itself provides a legal basis for the deprivation of liberty. This means that a separate deprivation of liberty authorisation under the processes set out in this Code of Practice is not required. More information about applying to the Court of Protection regarding personal welfare matters is given in chapter 10.

How do the safeguards apply to privately arranged care or treatment?

1.21   Under the Human Rights Act 1998, the duty to act in accordance with the ECHR applies only to public authorities. However, all states that have signed up to the ECHR are obliged to make sure that the rights set out in the ECHR apply to all of their citizens. The Mental Capacity Act 2005 therefore makes it clear that the deprivation of liberty safeguards apply to both publicly and privately arranged care or treatment.

How do the safeguards relate to the rest of the Mental Capacity Act 2005?

1.22   The deprivation of liberty safeguards are in addition to, and do not replace, other safeguards in the Mental Capacity Act 2005. This means that decisions made, and actions taken, for a person who is subject to a deprivation of liberty authorisation must fulfil the requirements of the Act in the same way as for any other person. In particular, any action taken under the deprivation of liberty safeguards must be in line with the principles of the Act:

- A person must be assumed to have capacity to make a decision unless it is established that they lack the capacity to make that decision.
- A person is not to be treated as unable to make a decision unless all practicable steps to help them to do so have been taken without success.
- A person is not to be treated as unable to make a decision merely because they make an unwise decision.
- An act done, or decision made, under the Act for or on behalf of a person who lacks capacity must be done, or made, in their best interests.
- Before the act is done, or the decision is made, regard must be had to whether the purpose for which it is needed can be as effectively achieved in a way that is less restrictive of the person's rights and freedom of action.

These principles are set out in chapter 2 of the main Code and explained in more detail in chapters 3 to 6 of the same document. Paragraph 5.13 of the main Code contains a checklist of factors that need to be taken into account in determining a person's best interests.

2.   WHAT IS DEPRIVATION OF LIBERTY?

There is no simple definition of deprivation of liberty. The question of whether the steps taken by staff or institutions in relation to a person amount to a deprivation of that person's liberty is ultimately a legal question, and only the courts can determine the law. This guidance seeks to assist staff and institutions in considering whether or not the steps they are taking, or proposing to take, amount to a deprivation of a person's liberty. The deprivation of liberty safeguards give best interests assessors the authority to make recommendations about proposed deprivations of liberty, and supervisory bodies the power to give authorisations that deprive people of their liberty.

This chapter provides guidance for staff and institutions on how to assess whether particular steps they are taking, or proposing to take, might amount to a deprivation of liberty, based on existing case law. It also considers what other factors may be taken into account when considering the issue of deprivation of liberty, including, importantly, what is permissible under the Mental Capacity Act 2005 in relation to restraint or restriction. Finally, it provides a summary of some of the most important cases to date.

Further legal developments may occur after this guidance has been issued, and healthcare and social care staff need to keep themselves informed of legal developments that may have a bearing on their practice.

What does case law say to date?

2.1   The European Court of Human Rights (ECtHR) has drawn a distinction between the deprivation of liberty of an individual (which is unlawful, unless authorised) and restrictions on the liberty of movement of an individual.

2.2   The ECtHR made it clear that the question of whether someone has been deprived of liberty depends on the particular circumstances of the case. Specifically, the ECtHR said in its October 2004 judgment in *HL v the United Kingdom*:

> 'to determine whether there has been a deprivation of liberty, the starting-point must be the specific situation of the individual concerned and account must be taken of a whole range of factors arising in a particular case such as the type, duration, effects and manner of implementation of the measure in question. The distinction between a deprivation of, and restriction upon, liberty is merely one of degree or intensity and not one of nature or substance.'

2.3   The difference between deprivation of liberty and restriction upon liberty is one of degree or intensity. It may therefore be helpful to envisage a scale, which moves from 'restraint' or 'restriction' to 'deprivation of liberty'. Where an individual is on the scale will depend on the concrete circumstances of the individual and may change over time. For more information on how the Act defines restraint, see paragraphs 2.8–2.12.

2.4   Although the guidance in this chapter includes descriptions of past decisions of the courts, which should be used to help evaluate whether deprivation of liberty may be occurring, each individual case must be assessed on its own circumstances. No two cases are likely to be identical, so it is important to be aware of previous court judgments and the factors that the courts have identified as important.

2.5   The ECtHR and UK courts have determined a number of cases about deprivation of liberty. Their judgments indicate that the following factors can be relevant to identifying whether steps taken involve more than restraint and amount to a deprivation of liberty. It is important to remember that this list is not exclusive; other factors may arise in future in particular cases.

- Restraint is used, including sedation, to admit a person to an institution where that person is resisting admission.
- Staff exercise complete and effective control over the care and movement of a person for a significant period.
- Staff exercise control over assessments, treatment, contacts and residence.
- A decision has been taken by the institution that the person will not be released into the care of others, or permitted to live elsewhere, unless the staff in the institution consider it appropriate.
- A request by carers for a person to be discharged to their care is refused.

- The person is unable to maintain social contacts because of restrictions placed on their access to other people.
- The person loses autonomy because they are under continuous supervision and control.

There is more information on some relevant cases at the end of this chapter (paragraphs 2.17–2.23).

How can deprivation of liberty be identified?

2.6   In determining whether deprivation of liberty has occurred, or is likely to occur, decision-makers need to consider all the facts in a particular case. There is unlikely to be any simple definition that can be applied in every case, and it is probable that no single factor will, in itself, determine whether the overall set of steps being taken in relation to the relevant person amount to a deprivation of liberty. In general, the decision-maker should always consider the following:

- All the circumstances of each and every case
- What measures are being taken in relation to the individual? When are they required? For what period do they endure? What are the effects of any restraints or restrictions on the individual? Why are they necessary? What aim do they seek to meet?
- What are the views of the relevant person, their family or carers? Do any of them object to the measures?
- How are any restraints or restrictions implemented? Do any of the constraints on the individual's personal freedom go beyond 'restraint' or 'restriction' to the extent that they constitute a deprivation of liberty?
- Are there any less restrictive options for delivering care or treatment that avoid deprivation of liberty altogether?
- Does the cumulative effect of all the restrictions imposed on the person amount to a deprivation of liberty, even if individually they would not?

What practical steps can be taken to reduce the risk of deprivation of liberty occurring?

2.7   There are many ways in which providers and commissioners of care can reduce the risk of taking steps that amount to a deprivation of liberty, by minimising the restrictions imposed and ensuring that decisions are taken with the involvement of the relevant person and their family, friends and carers. The processes for staff to follow are:

- Make sure that all decisions are taken (and reviewed) in a structured way, and reasons for decisions recorded.
- Follow established good practice for care planning.
- Make a proper assessment of whether the person lacks capacity to decide whether or not to accept the care or treatment proposed, in line with the principles of the Act (see chapter 3 of the main Code for further guidance).
- Before admitting a person to hospital or residential care in circumstances that may amount to a deprivation of liberty, consider whether the person's needs could be met in a less restrictive way. Any restrictions placed on the person while in hospital or in a care home must be kept to the minimum necessary, and should be in place for the shortest possible period.
- Take proper steps to help the relevant person retain contact with family, friends and carers. Where local advocacy services are available, their involvement should be encouraged to support the person and their family, friends and carers.

- Review the care plan on an ongoing basis. It may well be helpful to include an independent element, possibly via an advocacy service, in the review.

What does the Act mean by 'restraint'?

2.8   Section 6(4) of the Act states that someone is using restraint if they:

- use force – or threaten to use force – to make someone do something that they are resisting, or
- restrict a person's freedom of movement, whether they are resisting or not.

2.9   Paragraphs 6.40 to 6.48 of the main Code contain guidance about the appropriate use of restraint. Restraint is appropriate when it is used to prevent harm to the person who lacks capacity and it is a proportionate response to the likelihood and seriousness of harm. Appropriate use of restraint falls short of deprivation of liberty.

2.10   Preventing a person from leaving a care home or hospital unaccompanied because there is a risk that they would try to cross a road in a dangerous way, for example, is likely to be seen as a proportionate restriction or restraint to prevent the person from coming to harm. That would be unlikely, in itself, to constitute a deprivation of liberty. Similarly, locking a door to guard against immediate harm is unlikely, in itself, to amount to a deprivation of liberty.

2.11   The ECtHR has also indicated that the duration of any restrictions is a relevant factor when considering whether or not a person is deprived of their liberty. This suggests that actions that are immediately necessary to prevent harm may not, in themselves, constitute a deprivation of liberty.

2.12   However, where the restriction or restraint is frequent, cumulative and ongoing, or if there are other factors present, then care providers should consider whether this has gone beyond permissible restraint, as defined in the Act. If so, then they must either apply for authorisation under the deprivation of liberty safeguards (as explained in chapter 3) or change their care provision to reduce the level of restraint.

How does the use of restraint apply within a hospital or when taking someone to a hospital or a care home?

Within a hospital

2.13   If a person in hospital for mental health treatment, or being considered for admission to a hospital for mental health treatment, needs to be restrained, this is likely to indicate that they are objecting to treatment or to being in hospital. The care providers should consider whether the need for restraint means the person is objecting (see paragraph 4.46 of this Code for guidance on how to decide whether a person is objecting for this purpose). A person who objects to mental health treatment, and who meets the criteria for detention under the Mental Health Act 1983, is normally ineligible for an authorisation under the deprivation of liberty safeguards. If the care providers believe it is necessary to detain the person, they may wish to consider use of the Mental Health Act 1983.

Taking someone to a hospital or a care home

2.14   Transporting a person who lacks capacity from their home, or another location, to a hospital or care home will not usually amount to a deprivation of liberty (for example, to take them to hospital by ambulance in an emergency.) Even where there is an expectation that the person will be deprived of liberty within the care home or hospital, it is unlikely that the journey itself will constitute a deprivation of liberty so that an authorisation is needed before the journey commences. In almost all cases, it is likely that a person can be lawfully taken to a hospital or a care home under the wider provisions of the Act, as long as it is considered that being in the hospital or care home will be in their best interests.

2.15 In a very few cases, there may be exceptional circumstances where taking a person to a hospital or a care home amounts to a deprivation of liberty, for example where it is necessary to do more than persuade or restrain the person for the purpose of transportation, or where the journey is exceptionally long. In such cases, it may be necessary to seek an order from the Court of Protection to ensure that the journey is taken on a lawful basis.

How should managing authorities avoid unnecessary applications for standard authorisations?

2.16 While it is unlawful to deprive a person of their liberty without authorisation, managing authorities should take into consideration that unnecessary applications for standard authorisations in cases that do not in fact involve depriving a person of liberty may place undue stress upon the person being assessed and on their families or carers. Moreover, consideration must always be given to the possibility of less restrictive options for delivering care or treatment that avoid deprivation of liberty altogether.

Examples of case law

2.17 To provide further guidance, the following paragraphs contain short descriptions of what appear to be the significant features of recent or important cases in England and Wales and the ECtHR dealing with deprivation of liberty. Remember that:

- these descriptions are for guidance only
- only the courts can authoritatively determine the law; and
- the courts are likely to give judgments in cases after this guidance is issued. Staff will need to keep up to date and take account of further relevant legal developments.

Cases where the courts found that the steps taken did not involve a deprivation of liberty

2.18 *LLBC v TG* (judgment of High Court of 14 November 2007)

TG was a 78-year-old man with dementia and cognitive impairment. TG was resident in a care home, but was admitted to hospital with pneumonia and septicaemia. While he was in hospital, there was a dispute between the local authority and TG's daughter and granddaughter about TG's future. The daughter and granddaughter wanted TG to live with them, but the local authority believed that TG needed 24-hour care in a residential care home.

The council obtained an order from the court, directing that TG be delivered to the care home identified as appropriate by the council. Neither the daughter nor granddaughter was informed that a court hearing was taking place. That order was subsequently changed and TG was able to live with his daughter and granddaughter.

TG's daughter and granddaughter claimed that the period of time he had spent at the care home amounted to a deprivation of his liberty.

The judge considered that there was no deprivation of liberty, but the case was borderline. The key factors in his decision included:

- The care home was an ordinary care home where only ordinary restrictions of liberty applied.

- The family were able to visit TG on a largely unrestricted basis and were entitled to take him out from the home for outings.
- TG was personally compliant and expressed himself as happy in the care home. He had lived in a local authority care home for over three years and was objectively content with his situation there.
- There was no occasion where TG was objectively deprived of his liberty.

The judge said:

'Whilst I agree that the circumstances of the present case may be near the borderline between mere restrictions of liberty and Article 5 detention, I have come to the conclusion that, looked at as a whole and having regard to all the relevant circumstances, the placement of TG in Towerbridge falls short of engaging Article 5.'

2.19   *Nielsen v Denmark* (ECtHR; (1988) 11 EHRR 175)

The mother of a 12-year-old boy arranged for his admission to the state hospital's psychiatric ward. The boy had a nervous disorder and required treatment in the form of regular talks and environmental therapy. The treatment given, and the conditions under which it was administered, was appropriate. The duration of treatment was 5½ months. The boy, however, applied to the ECtHR, feeling that he had been deprived of his liberty.

The restrictions placed on the applicant's freedom of movement and contacts with the outside world were not much different from restrictions that might be imposed on a child in an ordinary hospital. The door of the ward was locked to prevent children exposing themselves to danger or running around disturbing other patients. The applicant was free to leave the ward with permission and to go out if accompanied by a member of staff. He was able to visit his family and friends, and towards the end of his stay to go to school.

The Court held:

'The restrictions imposed on the applicant were not of a nature or degree similar to the cases of deprivation of liberty specified in paragraph (1) of Article 5. In particular, he was not detained as a person of unsound mind ... Indeed, the restrictions to which the applicant was subject were no more than the normal requirements for the care of a child of 12 years of age receiving treatment in hospital. The conditions in which the applicant stayed thus did not, in principle, differ from those obtaining in many hospital wards where children with physical disorders are treated.'

It concluded:

'the hospitalisation of the applicant did not amount to a deprivation of liberty within the meaning of Article 5, but was a responsible exercise by his mother of her custodial rights in the interests of the child.'

2.20   *HM v Switzerland* (ECtHR; (2002) 38 EHRR 314)

An 84-year-old woman was placed indefinitely in a nursing home by state authorities. She had had the possibility of staying at home and being cared for there, but she and her son had refused to co-operate with the relevant care association, and her living conditions had subsequently deteriorated. The state authorities placed her in the home in order to provide her with necessary medical care and satisfactory living conditions and hygiene.

The woman was not placed in the secure ward of the home but was free to move within the home and to have social contacts with the outside world. She was initially undecided as to what solution she preferred and, after moving into the home, the applicant had agreed to stay there. However, she subsequently applied to the courts saying that she had been deprived of her liberty.

The Court held that she had not been deprived of her liberty:

'Bearing these elements in mind, in particular the fact that [the authorities] had ordered the applicant's placement in the nursing home in her own interests in order to provide her with the necessary medical care and satisfactory living conditions and standards of hygiene, and also taking into consideration the comparable circumstances of *Nielsen* v *Denmark* [see case summary above], the Court concludes that in the circumstances of the present case the applicant's placement in the nursing home did not amount to a deprivation of liberty within the meaning of Article 5(1), but was a responsible measure taken by the competent authorities in the applicant's best interests.'

Cases where the courts have found that the steps taken involve a deprivation of liberty

2.21   *DE and JE* v *Surrey County Council (SCC)* (High Court judgment of 29 December 2006)

DE was a 76-year-old man who, following a major stroke, had become blind and had significant short-term memory impairment. He also had dementia and lacked capacity to decide where he should live, but was still often able to express his wishes with some clarity and force.

DE was married to JE. In August 2003, DE was living at home with JE. There was an occasion when JE felt that she could not care for DE, and placed him on a chair on the pavement in front of the house and called the police. The local authority then placed him in two care homes, referred to in the judgment of the court as the X home and the Y home.

Within the care homes, DE had a very substantial degree of freedom and lots of contact with the outside world. He was never subject to physical or chemical restraint.

DE repeatedly expressed the wish to live with JE, and JE also wanted DE to live with her. SCC would not agree to DE returning to live with, or visit, JE and made it clear that if JE were to persist in an attempt to remove DE, SCC would contact the police. DE and JE applied to the courts that this was a deprivation of his liberty.

In his judgment, Justice Munby said:

'The fundamental issue in this case . . . is whether DE has been and is deprived of his liberty to leave the X home and whether DE has been and is deprived of his liberty to leave the Y home. And when I refer to leaving the X home and the Y home, I do not mean leaving for the purpose of some trip or outing approved by SCC or by those managing the institution; I mean leaving in the sense of removing himself permanently in order to live where and with whom he chooses, specifically removing himself to live at home with JE.'

He then said:

'DE was not and is not "free to leave", and was and is, in that sense, completely under the control of [the local authority], because, as [counsel for DE] put it, it was and is [the local authority] who decides the essential matters of where DE can live, whether he can leave and whether he can be with JE.'

He concluded:

'The simple reality is that DE will be permitted to leave the institution in which [the local authority] has placed him and be released to the care of JE only as and when, – if ever; probably never, – [the local authority] considers it appropriate. [The local authority's] motives may be the purest, but in my judgment, [it] has been and is continuing to deprive DE of his liberty.'

2.22   *HL v United Kingdom* (ECtHR; (2004) 40 EHRR 761)

A 48-year-old man who had had autism since birth was unable to speak and his level of understanding was limited. He was frequently agitated and had a history of self-harming behaviour. He lacked the capacity to consent to treatment.

For over 30 years, he was cared for in Bournewood Hospital. In 1994, he was entrusted to carers and for three years he lived successfully with his carers. Following an incident of self-harm at a day centre on 22 July 1997, the applicant was taken to Bournewood Hospital where he was re-admitted informally (not under the Mental Health Act 1983).

The carers wished to have the applicant released to their care, which the hospital refused. The carers were unable to visit him.

In its judgment in *HL v the United Kingdom*, the ECtHR said that:

'the key factor in the present case [is] that the health care professionals treating and managing the applicant exercised complete and effective control over his care and movements from the moment he presented acute behavioural problems on July 22, 1997 to the date when he was compulsorily detained on October 29, 1997.

'His responsible medical officer (Dr M) was clear that, had the applicant resisted admission or tried to leave thereafter, she would have prevented him from doing so and would have considered his involuntary committal under s. 3 of the 1983 Act; indeed, as soon as the Court of Appeal indicated that his appeal would be allowed, he was compulsorily detained under the 1983 Act. The correspondence between the applicant's carers and Dr M reflects both the carer's wish to have the applicant immediately released to their care and, equally, the clear intention of Dr M and the other relevant health care professionals to exercise strict control over his assessment, treatment, contacts and, notably, movement and residence; the applicant would only be released from hospital to the care of Mr and Mrs E as and when those professionals considered it appropriate. . . . it was clear from the above noted correspondence that the applicant's contact with his carers was directed and controlled by the hospital, his carers visiting him for the first time after his admission on 2 November 1997.

'Accordingly, the concrete situation was that the applicant was under continuous supervision and control and was not free to leave.'

2.23   *Storck v Germany* (ECtHR; (2005) 43 EHRR 96)

A young woman was placed by her father in a psychiatric institution on occasions in 1974 and 1975. In July 1977, at the age of 18, she was placed again in a psychiatric institution. She was kept in a locked ward and was under the continuous supervision and control of the clinic personnel and was not free to leave the clinic during her entire stay of 20 months. When she attempted to flee, she was shackled. When she succeeded one time, she was brought back by the police. She was unable to maintain regular contact with the outside world.

She applied to the courts on the basis that she had been deprived of her liberty. There was a dispute about whether she consented to her confinement.

The Court noted:

'the applicant, on several occasions, had tried to flee from the clinic. She had to be shackled in order to prevent her from absconding and had to be brought back to the clinic by the police when she managed to escape on one occasion. Under these circumstances, the Court is unable to discern any factual basis for the assumption that the applicant – presuming that she had the capacity to consent – agreed to her continued stay in the clinic. In the alternative, assuming that the applicant was no longer capable of consenting following her treatment with strong medication, she cannot, in any event, be considered to have validly agreed to her stay in the clinic.'

2.24   These cases reinforce the need to carefully consider all the specific circumstances of the relevant individual before deciding whether or not a person is being deprived of their liberty. They also underline the vital importance of involving family, friends and carers in this decision-making process: a significant feature of a number of the cases that have come before the courts is a difference of opinion or communication issue between the commissioners or providers of care and family members and carers.

3.   HOW AND WHEN CAN DEPRIVATION OF LIBERTY BE APPLIED FOR AND AUTHORISED?

There are some circumstances in which depriving a person, who lacks capacity to consent to the arrangements made for their care or treatment, of their liberty is necessary to protect them from harm, and is in their best interests.

Deprivation of liberty can be authorised by supervisory bodies (primary care trusts (PCTs), local authorities, Welsh Ministers or local health boards (LHBs). To obtain authorisation to deprive someone of their liberty, managing authorities have to apply for an authorisation following the processes set out in this chapter.[4] Once an application has been received, the supervisory body must then follow the assessment processes set out in chapter 4 before it can authorise deprivation of liberty. It should be borne in mind that a deprivation of liberty authorisation does not, in itself, give authority to treat someone. This issue is covered in paragraphs 5.10 to 5.13.

In the vast majority of cases, it should be possible to plan in advance so that a standard authorisation can be obtained before the deprivation of liberty begins. There may, however, be some exceptional cases where the need for the deprivation of liberty is so urgent that it is in the best interests of the person for it to begin while the application is being considered. In that case, the care home or hospital may give an urgent authorisation for up to seven days (see chapter 6).

How, in summary, can deprivation of liberty be authorised?

3.1   A managing authority has responsibility for applying for authorisation of deprivation of liberty for any person who may come within the scope of the deprivation of liberty safeguards:

---

[4] If a person is lawfully deprived of liberty in a care home or hospital as a consequence of an order of the Court of Protection, there is no need to apply for an authorisation. However, once the order of the Court of Protection has expired, for lawful deprivation of liberty to continue authorisation must be obtained by following the processes set out in this chapter.

- In the case of an NHS hospital, the managing authority is the NHS body responsible for the running of the hospital in which the relevant person is, or is to be, a resident.
- In the case of a care home or a private hospital, the managing authority will be the person registered, or required to be registered, under part 2 of the Care Standards Act 2000 in respect of the hospital or care home.

3.2   If a healthcare or social care professional thinks that an authorisation is needed, they should inform the managing authority. This might be as a result of a care review or needs assessment but could happen at any other time too. (See chapter 9 for guidance on action to take if there is a concern that a person is already being deprived of their liberty, without authorisation.)

3.3   A **supervisory body** is responsible for considering requests for authorisations, commissioning the required assessments (see chapter 4) and, where all the assessments agree, authorising the deprivation of liberty:

- Where the deprivation of liberty safeguards are applied to a person in a hospital situated in England, the supervisory body will be:

  - if a PCT commissions[5] the relevant care or treatment (or it is commissioned on the PCT's behalf), that PCT
  - if the Welsh Ministers or an LHB commissions the relevant care and treatment in England, the Welsh Ministers, or
  - in any other case, the PCT for the area in which the hospital is situated.

- Where the deprivation of liberty safeguards are applied to a person in a hospital situated in Wales, the supervisory body will be the Welsh Ministers or an LHB **unless** a PCT commissions the relevant care and treatment in Wales, in which case the PCT will be the supervisory body.
- Where the deprivation of liberty safeguards are applied to a person in a care home, whether situated in England or Wales, the supervisory body will be the local authority for the area in which the person is ordinarily resident. However, if the person is not ordinarily resident in the area of any local authority (for example a person of no fixed abode), the supervisory body will be the local authority for the area in which the care home is situated.[6]

3.4   There are two types of authorisation: standard and urgent. A managing authority must request a standard authorisation when it appears likely that, at some time during the next 28 days, someone will be accommodated in its hospital or care home in circumstances that amount to a deprivation of liberty within the meaning of Article 5 of the European Convention on Human Rights. The request must be made to the supervisory body. Whenever possible, authorisation should be obtained in advance. Where this is not possible, and the managing authority believes it is necessary to deprive someone of their liberty in their best interests

---

[5] Guidance on establishing the responsible commissioner can be found at http://www.dh.gov.uk/en/Publicationsandstatistics/Publiscations/PublicationsPolicyandGuidance/DH_078466

[6] To work out the place of ordinary residence, the usual mechanisms under the National Assistance Act 1948 apply (see http://www.dh.gov.uk/en/SocialCare/Deliveringadultsocialcare/Ordinaryresidence/ DH_079346). Any unresolved questions about the ordinary residence of a person will be handled by the Secretary of State or by the Welsh Ministers. Until a decision is made, the local authority that received the application must act as the supervisory body. After the decision is made, the local authority of ordinary residence must become the supervisory body. Regulations 17 to 19 of the Mental Capacity (Deprivation of Liberty: Standard Authorisations, Assessments and Ordinary Residence) Regulations 2008 set out, for England, arrangements that are to have effect while any question as to the ordinary residence of a person is determined in a case in which a local authority has received a request for a standard authorisation or a request to decide whether there is an unauthorised deprivation of liberty.

before the standard authorisation process can be completed, the managing authority must itself give an urgent authorisation and then obtain standard authorisation within seven calendar days (see chapter 6).

3.5   The flowchart at Annex 1 gives an overview of how the deprivation of liberty safeguards process should operate.

How should managing authorities decide whether to apply for an authorisation?

3.6   Managing authorities should have a procedure in place that identifies:

- whether deprivation of liberty is or may be necessary in a particular case
- what steps they should take to assess whether to seek authorization
- whether they have taken all practical and reasonable steps to avoid a deprivation of liberty
- what action they should take if they do need to request an authorisation
- how they should review cases where authorisation is or may be necessary, and
- who should take the necessary action.

A flowchart that can be used to help develop such a procedure is at Annex 2.

What is the application process?

3.7   A managing authority must apply for a standard authorisation. The application should be made in writing to the supervisory body. A standard form is available for this purpose.

3.8   In England, the request from a managing authority for a standard authorisation must include:

- the name and gender of the relevant person
- the age of the relevant person or, where this is not known, whether the managing authority reasonably believes that the relevant person is aged 18 years or older
- the address at which the relevant person is currently located, and the telephone number at the address
- the name, address and telephone number of the managing authority and the name of the person within the managing authority who is dealing with the request
- the purpose for which the authorisation is requested
- the date from which the authorisation is sought, and
- whether the managing authority has given an urgent authorization and, if so, the date on which it expires.

3.9   A request for a standard authorisation must also include, if it is available or could reasonably be obtained by the managing authority:

- any medical information relating to the relevant person's health that the managing authority reasonably considers to be relevant to the proposed restrictions to their liberty
- the diagnosis of the mental disorder (within the meaning of the Mental Health Act 1983 but disregarding any exclusion for persons with learning disability) from which the relevant person is suffering
- any relevant care plans and needs assessments
- the racial, ethnic or national origins of the relevant person
- whether the relevant person has any special communication needs
- details of the proposed restrictions on the relevant person's liberty
- whether it is necessary for an Independent Mental Capacity Advocate (IMCA) to be instructed

- where the purpose of the proposed restrictions to the relevant person's liberty is to give treatment, whether the relevant person has made an advance decision that may be valid and applicable to some or all of that treatment
- whether there is an existing standard authorisation in relation to the detention of the relevant person and, if so, the date of the expiry of that authorisation
- whether the relevant person is subject to any requirements of the Mental Health Act 1983, and
- the name, address and telephone number of:

  - anyone named by the relevant person as someone to be consulted about their welfare
  - anyone engaged in caring for the person or interested in their welfare
  - any donee of a Lasting Power of Attorney ('donee') granted by the person
  - any deputy appointed for the person by the court, and
  - any IMCA who has already been instructed.

If there is an existing authorisation, information that has not changed does not have to be resupplied.

3.10   In Wales, the request from a managing authority for a standard authorisation must include:

- the name of the relevant person
- the name, address and telephone number of the managing authority
- the reasons why the managing authority considers that the relevant person is being or will be detained in circumstances which amount to a deprivation of liberty
- the reasons why the managing authority considers that the relevant person satisfies the qualifying requirements
- details of any urgent authorisation
- information or documents in support of why the relevant person satisfies the qualifying requirements
- the name, address and telephone number of any person who has an interest in the welfare of the relevant person, and
- details of any relevant valid and applicable advance decision.

Where should applications be sent?

3.11   If the application is being made by a care home, the application must be sent to the local authority for the area in which the relevant person is ordinarily resident. If the relevant person is not ordinarily resident in the area of any local authority (for example, is of no fixed abode), if the care home does not know where the person currently lives, or if the person does not live in England or Wales, the application should be sent to the local authority in whose area the care home is located.

3.12   When the application is being made by a hospital.

- if the care is commissioned by a PCT, the application should be sent to that PCT
- if the care is commissioned by the Welsh Ministers, the application should be sent to the LHB for the area in which the relevant person is ordinarily resident
- if the care is commissioned by an LHB, the application should be sent to that LHB, and
- in any other case (for example, care that is commissioned privately), the application should be sent to the PCT for the area in which the relevant hospital is situated.

3.13   An application sent to the wrong supervisory body can be passed on to the correct supervisory body without the managing authority needing to reapply. But the managing authority should make every effort to establish which is the correct supervisory body to minimise delays in handling the application. (Footnote 6 explains how place of ordinary residence is determined and how disputes about the place of ordinary residence will be resolved.)

3.14   The managing authority must keep a written record of each request made for a standard authorisation and the reasons for making the request.

Who should be informed that an application has been made?

3.15   The managing authority should tell the relevant person's family, friends and carers, and any IMCA already involved in the relevant person's case, that it has applied for an authorisation of deprivation of liberty, unless it is impractical or impossible to do so, or undesirable in terms of the interests of the relevant person's health or safety. Anyone who is engaged in caring for the relevant person or interested in their welfare, or who has been named by them as a person to consult, must be given the opportunity to input their views on whether deprivation of liberty is in the best interests of the relevant person, as part of the best interests assessment (see paragraphs 4.58 to 4.76), as far as is practical and appropriate. The views of the relevant person about who to inform and consult should be taken into account.

3.16   The managing authority must notify the supervisory body if it is satisfied that there is no one who should be consulted in determining the relevant person's best interests, except those providing care and treatment for the relevant person in a professional capacity or for remuneration. In such a case, the supervisory body must instruct an IMCA to represent and support the relevant person before any assessments take place (see paragraphs 3.22 to 3.27 regarding the rights and role of an IMCA instructed in these circumstances).

What action does the supervisory body need to take when it receives an application for authorisation?

3.17   When it receives an application for authorisation of deprivation of liberty, the supervisory body must, as soon as is practical and possible:

- consider whether the request is appropriate and should be pursued, and
- seek any further information that it requires from the managing authority to help it with the decision.

If the supervisory body has any doubts about proceeding with the request, it should seek to resolve them with the managing authority.

3.18   Supervisory bodies should have a procedure in place that identifies the action they should take, who should take it and within what timescale. As far as practical and possible, they should communicate the procedure to managing authorities and give them the relevant contact details for making an application. The flowchart at Annex 3 summarises the process that a supervisory body should follow on receipt of a request from a managing authority for a standard deprivation of liberty authorisation.

Can an application for authorisation be made in advance?

3.19   A standard authorisation comes into force when it is given, or at any later time specified in the authorisation. Paragraph 3.4 refers to the timescales for initially applying for authorisations: 28 days are allowed so that authorisations can usually be sought as part of care planning (such as planning of discharge from hospital). There is no statutory limit on how far in advance of the expiry of one authorisation a fresh authorisation can be sought. Clearly, however, an authorisation should not be applied for too far in advance as this may prevent an assessor from making an accurate assessment of what the person's circumstances will be at the time the authorisation will come into force.

3.20   If a supervisory body considers that an application for an authorisation has been made too far in advance, it should raise the matter with the managing authority. The outcome may be an agreement with the managing authority that the application should be withdrawn, to be resubmitted at a more appropriate time.

What happens when the managing authority and the supervisory body are the same organisation?

3.21   In some cases, a single organisation will be both supervisory body and managing authority – for example, where a local authority itself provides a residential care home, rather than purchasing the service from another organisation. This does not prevent it from acting in both capacities. However, in England the regulations specify that in such a situation the best interests assessor cannot be an employee of the supervisory body/managing authority, or providing services to it. For example, in a case involving a local authority care home, the best interests assessor could be an NHS employee or an independent practitioner. (See paragraphs 4.13 and 4.60 for full details of who can be a best interests assessor.) There are similar provisions for Wales.

When should an IMCA be instructed?

3.22   If there is nobody appropriate to consult, other than people engaged in providing care or treatment for the relevant person in a professional capacity[7] or for remuneration, the managing authority must notify the supervisory body when it submits the application for the deprivation of liberty authorisation. The supervisory body must then instruct an IMCA straight away to represent the person. It is particularly important that the IMCA is instructed quickly if an urgent authorisation has been given, so that they can make a meaningful input at a very early stage in the process. (See paragraph 3.28 for other stages in the deprivation of liberty safeguards process when an IMCA must or may be instructed.)

3.23   Chapter 10 of the main Code ('What is the new Independent Mental Capacity Advocate service and how does it work?') describes the wider rights and role of an IMCA. Supervisory bodies should follow the guidance in that chapter in identifying an IMCA who is suitably qualified to represent the relevant person. However, it is also important to note that an IMCA instructed at this initial stage of the deprivation of liberty safeguards process has additional rights and responsibilities compared to an IMCA more generally instructed under the Mental Capacity Act 2005. IMCAs in this context have the right to:

-   as they consider appropriate, give information or make submissions to assessors, which assessors must take into account in carrying out their assessments
-   receive copies of any assessments from the supervisory body
-   receive a copy of any standard authorisation given by the supervisory body
-   be notified by the supervisory body if they are unable to give a standard authorisation because one or more of the deprivation of liberty assessments did not meet the qualifying requirements
-   receive a copy of any urgent authorisation from the managing authority
-   receive from the managing authority a copy of any notice declining to extend the duration of an urgent authorisation

[7] A friend or family member is **not** considered to be acting in a professional capacity simply because they have been appointed as the person's representative for a previous authorisation.

- receive from the supervisory body a copy of any notice that an urgent authorisation has ceased to be in force, and
- apply to the Court of Protection for permission to take the relevant person's case to the Court in connection with a matter relating to the giving or refusal of a standard or urgent authorisation (in the same way as any other third party can).

The assessment and authorisation processes are described in chapters 4 and 5.

3.24   IMCAs will need to familiarise themselves with the relevant person's circumstances and to consider what they may need to tell any of the assessors during the course of the assessment process. They will also need to consider whether they have any concerns about the outcome of the assessment process.

3.25   Differences of opinion between an IMCA and an assessor should ideally be resolved while the assessment is still in progress. Where there are significant disagreements between an IMCA and one or more of the assessors that cannot be resolved between them, the supervisory body should be informed before the assessment is finalised. The supervisory body should then consider what action might be appropriate, including perhaps convening a meeting to discuss the matter. Wherever possible, differences of opinion should be resolved informally in order to minimise the need for an IMCA to make an application to the Court of Protection. However, an IMCA should not be discouraged from making an application to the Court of Protection should they consider it necessary. (Chapter 15 of the main Code ('What are the best ways to settle disagreements and disputes about issues covered in the Act?') contains general guidance about the resolution of disputes arising under the Act.)

3.26   An IMCA will also need to consider whether they have any concerns about the giving of an urgent authorisation (see chapter 6), and whether it would be appropriate to challenge the giving of such an authorisation via the Court of Protection.

3.27   Once a relevant person's representative is appointed (see chapter 7), the duties imposed on the IMCA cease to apply. The IMCA may, however, still apply to the Court of Protection for permission to take the relevant person's case to the Court in connection with the giving of a standard authorisation; but, in doing so, the IMCA must take account of the views of the relevant person's representative.

Other circumstances in which an IMCA must or may be instructed

3.28   An IMCA must also be instructed during gaps in the appointment of a relevant person's representative (for instance, if a new representative is being sought – see paragraphs 7.34 to 7.36). In addition, an IMCA may be instructed at any time where:

- the relevant person does not have a paid 'professional' representative
- the relevant person or their representative requests that an IMCA is instructed to help them, or
- a supervisory body believes that instructing an IMCA will help to ensure that the person's rights are protected (see paragraphs 7.37 to 7.41).

4.   WHAT IS THE ASSESSMENT PROCESS FOR A STANDARD AUTHORISATION OF DEPRIVATION OF LIBERTY?

When a supervisory body gives a standard authorisation of deprivation of liberty, the managing authority may lawfully deprive the relevant person of their liberty in the hospital or care home named in the authorisation.

This chapter describes the assessments that have to be undertaken in order for a standard authorisation to be given. It also sets out who is eligible to undertake the assessments.

What assessments are required before giving a standard authorisation?

4.1   As soon as the supervisory body has confirmed that the request for a standard authorisation should be pursued, it must obtain the relevant assessments to ascertain whether the qualifying requirements of the deprivation of liberty safeguards are met. The supervisory body has a legal responsibility to select assessors who are both suitable and eligible. Assessments must be completed within 21 days for a standard deprivation of liberty authorisation, or, where an urgent authorisation has been given, before the urgent authorisation expires.

4.2   The assessments (described in paragraphs 4.23 to 4.76) are:

- age assessment (paragraphs 4.23 and 4.24)
- no refusals assessment (paragraphs 4.25 to 4.28).
- mental capacity assessment (paragraphs 4.29 to 4.32)
- mental health assessment (paragraphs 4.33 to 4.39)
- eligibility assessment (paragraphs 4.40 to 4.57), and
- best interests assessment (paragraphs 4.58 to 4.76).

Standard forms are available for completion by each of the assessors.

4.3   If the person being assessed is not currently in the supervisory body's area, the supervisory body should seek, as far as is practical and possible, to arrange to use assessors based near where the person currently is.

Using equivalent assessments

4.4   The Act states that where an 'equivalent assessment' to any of these assessments has already been obtained, it may be relied upon instead of obtaining a fresh assessment.

4.5   An equivalent assessment is an assessment:

- that has been carried out in the last 12 months, not necessarily for the purpose of a deprivation of liberty authorisation (where the required assessment is an age assessment, there is no time limit on the use of an equivalent assessment)
- that meets all the requirements of the deprivation of liberty assessment,
- of which the supervisory body is satisfied that there is no reason to believe that it is no longer accurate, and
- of which the supervisory body has a written copy.

An example would be a recent assessment carried out for the purposes of the Mental Health Act 1983, which could serve as an equivalent to a mental health assessment.

4.6   Great care should be taken in deciding to use an equivalent assessment and this should not be done routinely. The older the assessment is, even if it took place within the last 12 months, the less likely it is to represent a valid equivalent assessment (unless it is an age assessment). For example, only a very recent mental capacity assessment would be appropriate where capacity is known to fluctuate, since one of the principles of the Act is that a person must be assumed to have capacity unless it is established that they lack capacity.

4.7   If an equivalent best interests assessment is used, the supervisory body must also take into account any information given, or submissions made, by the relevant person's representative or an Independent Mental Capacity Advocate (IMCA) instructed under the deprivation of liberty safeguards.

4.8   Supervisory bodies should record the reasons why they have used any equivalent assessment. A standard form is available for this purpose.

When must assessments take place?

4.9   The regulations for England[8] specify that all assessments required for a standard authorisation must be completed within 21 calendar days from the date on which the supervisory body receives a request from a managing authority. The regulations for Wales specify that all assessments required for a standard authorisation must be completed within 21 days from the date the assessors were instructed by the supervisory body.

4.10   However, if an urgent authorisation is already in force, the assessments must be completed before the urgent authorisation expires. The regulations for Wales specify that, where the managing authority has given itself an urgent authorisation and applies for a standard authorisation, the assessors must complete the assessments within five days of the date of instruction.

4.11   Urgent authorisations may be given by managing authorities for an initial period not exceeding seven days. If there are exceptional reasons why it has not been possible to deal with the request for a standard authorisation within the period of the urgent authorisation, they may be extended **by the supervisory body** for up to a further seven days. It is for the supervisory body to decide what constitutes an 'exceptional reason', taking into account all the circumstances of an individual case.

4.12   Supervisory bodies must keep a record of all requests for standard authorisations that they receive and should acknowledge the receipt of requests from managing authorities for standard authorisations.

How should assessors be selected?

4.13   The six assessments do not have to be completed by different assessors. In fact, it is highly unlikely that there will be six separate assessors – not least because it is desirable to minimise the burden on the person being assessed. However, each assessor must make their own decisions, and to ensure that an appropriate degree of objectivity is brought to the assessment process:

- there **must** be a minimum of two assessors
- the mental health and best interests assessors **must** be different people
- the best interests assessor can be an employee of the supervisory body or managing authority, but **must not** be involved in the care or treatment of the person they are assessing nor in decisions about their care
- a potential best interests assessor should not be used if they are in a line management relationship with the professional proposing the deprivation of liberty or the mental health assessor
- none of the assessors may have a financial interest in the case of the person they are assessing (a person is considered to have a financial interest in a case where that person is a partner, director, other office-holder or major shareholder of the managing authority that has made the application for a standard authorisation)
- an assessor **must not** be a relative of the person being assessed, nor of a person with a financial interest in the person's care. For this purpose, a 'relative' is:

    a. a spouse, ex-spouse, civil partner or ex-civil partner
    b. a person living with the relevant person as if they were a spouse or a civil partner
    c. a parent or child
    d. a brother or sister
    e. a child of a person falling within definitions a, b or d

[8] The Mental Capacity (Deprivation of Liberty: Standard Authorisations, Assessments and Ordinary Residence) Regulations 2008.

    f. a grandparent or grandchild

    g. a grandparent-in-law or grandchild-in-law

    h. an aunt or uncle

    i. a sister-in-law or brother-in-law

    j. a son-in-law or daughter-in-law

    k. a first cousin, or

    l. a half-brother or half-sister.

These relationships include step-relationships

- where the managing authority and supervisory body are both the same body (see paragraph 3.21), the supervisory body may not select to carry out a best interests assessment a person who is employed by the body, or providing services to it, and
- the supervisory body should seek to avoid appointing assessors in any other possible conflict of interests situations that might bring into question the objectivity of an assessment.

4.14 Other relevant factors for supervisory bodies to consider when appointing assessors include:

- the reason for the proposed deprivation of liberty
- whether the potential assessor has experience of working with the service user group from which the person being assessed comes (for example, older people, people with learning disabilities, people with autism, or people with brain injury)
- whether the potential assessor has experience of working with people from the cultural background of the person being assessed, and
- any other specific needs of the person being assessed, for example communication needs.

4.15 Supervisory bodies should ensure that sufficient assessors are available to meet their needs, and must be satisfied in each case that the assessors have the skills, experience, qualifications and training required by regulations to perform the function effectively. The regulations also require supervisory bodies to be satisfied that there is an appropriate criminal record certificate issued in respect of an assessor. It will be useful to keep a record of qualified assessors and their experience and availability. Supervisory bodies should consider making arrangements to ensure that assessors have the necessary opportunities to maintain their skills and knowledge (of legal developments, for example) and share, audit and review their practice.

4.16 Assessors act as individual professionals and are personally accountable for their decisions. Managing authorities and supervisory bodies must not dictate or seek to influence their decisions.

4.17 There is no reason in principle why interviews, examinations and fact-finding required as part of any deprivation of liberty safeguards assessment cannot serve more than one purpose, in order to avoid unnecessary burdens both on the person being assessed and on staff. However, if this does happen, all purposes of the interview or examination should be made clear to the relevant person, and to any family members, friends, carers or advocates supporting them.

Protection against liability

4.18 Nobody can or should carry out an assessment unless they are protected against any liabilities that might arise in connection with carrying out the assessment. Individual assessors will need to satisfy themselves, and any supervisory body that selects them as an assessor, that they are appropriately covered by either employers' or personal insurance.

What is the assessment process?

4.19   As indicated in paragraph 4.2, there are six assessments that must be conducted before a supervisory body can give an authorisation.

4.20   The assessments are set out in the order in which it will normally be most appropriate to complete them. In particular, it is recommended that the best interests assessment, which is likely to be the most timeconsuming, is not started until there is a reasonable expectation that the other five qualifying requirements will be met.

4.21   But, ultimately, it is for the supervisory body to decide on the order in which the assessments should be undertaken and, in the light of the time available to complete the overall assessment process, the extent to which they should be undertaken to separate or simultaneous timescales. The supervisory body's decision about how many assessors will undertake the assessments (see paragraph 4.13) will also be a relevant factor.

4.22   The following paragraphs explain the assessment process.

Age assessment

4.23   The purpose of the age assessment is simply to confirm whether the relevant person is aged 18 or over. This is because, as paragraph 1.12 explains, the deprivation of liberty safeguards apply only to people aged 18 or over. For people under the age of 18, a different safeguards process applies. In most cases, this is likely to be a fairly straightforward assessment. If there is any doubt, age should be established by a birth certificate or other evidence that the assessor considers reliable. Where it is not possible to verify with any certainty whether a person is aged 18 or over, the assessor should base the assessment on the best of their knowledge and belief.

4.24   This assessment can be undertaken by anybody whom the supervisory body is satisfied is eligible to be a best interests assessor.

No refusals assessment

4.25   The purpose of the no refusals assessment is to establish whether an authorisation to deprive the relevant person of their liberty would conflict with other existing authority for decision-making for that person.

4.26   The following are instances of a conflict that would mean that a standard authorisation could not be given:

  ■ If the relevant person has made an **advance decision to refuse treatment** that remains valid and is applicable to some or all of the treatment that is the purpose for which the authorisation is requested, then a standard authorisation cannot be given. See sections 24 to 26 of the Mental Capacity Act 2005 and chapter 9 of the main Code ('What does the Act say about advance decisions to refuse treatment?') for more information about advance decisions and when they are valid and applicable. Remember too that the deprivation of liberty authorisation does not, in itself, provide authority to treat the person (see paragraphs 5.10 to 5.13 of this Code).

  ■ If any part of the proposal to deprive the person of their liberty (including any element of the care plan) would be in conflict with a **valid decision of a donee or a deputy** made within the scope of their authority, then a standard authorisation cannot be given. For example, if a donee or deputy decides that it would not be in the best interests of the relevant person to be in a particular care home, and that decision is within the scope of their authority, then the care plan will need to be reviewed with the donee or deputy.

4.27   If there is any such conflict, the no refusals assessment qualifying requirement will not be met and a standard authorisation for deprivation of liberty cannot be given.

4.28   The no refusals assessment can be undertaken by anybody that the supervisory body is satisfied is eligible to be a best interests assessor.

Mental capacity assessment

4.29   The purpose of the mental capacity assessment is to establish whether the relevant person lacks capacity to decide whether or not they should be accommodated in the relevant hospital or care home to be given care or treatment. The assessment refers specifically to the relevant person's capacity to make this decision at the time it needs to be made. The starting assumption should always be that a person has the capacity to make the decision.

4.30   Sections 1 to 3 of the Act set out how a person's capacity to make decisions should be determined. Chapter 4 of the main Code ('How does the Act define a person's capacity to make a decision and how should capacity be assessed?') gives further guidance on ways to assess capacity. When assessing the capacity of a person being considered for the deprivation of liberty safeguards, these guidelines should be followed.

4.31   The regulations for England specify that the mental capacity assessment can be undertaken by anyone who is eligible to act as a mental health or best interests assessor. In deciding who to appoint for this assessment, the supervisory body should take account of the need for understanding and practical experience of the nature of the person's condition and its impact on decision-making.

4.32   Supervisory bodies may wish to consider using an eligible assessor who already knows the relevant person to undertake this assessment, if they think it would be of benefit. This will primarily arise if somebody involved in the person's care is considered best placed to carry out a reliable assessment, using their knowledge of the person over a period of time. It may also help in reducing any distress that might be caused to the person if they were assessed by somebody they did not know.

Mental health assessment

4.33   The purpose of the mental health assessment is to establish whether the relevant person has a mental disorder within the meaning of the Mental Health Act 1983. That means any disorder or disability of mind, apart from dependence on alcohol or drugs. It includes all learning disabilities. This is not an assessment to determine whether the person requires mental health treatment.

4.34   A distinction can be drawn between the mental health assessment and the mental capacity assessment:

- Although a person must have an impairment or disturbance of the functioning of the mind or brain in order to lack capacity, it does not follow that they automatically have a mental disorder within the meaning of the Mental Health Act 1983.
- The objective of the mental health assessment is to ensure that the person is medically diagnosed as being of 'unsound mind' and so comes within the scope of Article 5 of the European Convention on Human Rights.

4.35   In both England and Wales, the regulations specify that:

- the mental health assessment must be carried out by a doctor, and
- the assessing doctor has to either be approved under section 12 of the Mental Health Act 1983, or be a registered medical practitioner with at least three years' post-registration experience in the diagnosis or treatment of mental disorder, such as a GP with a special interest. This includes doctors who are automatically treated as being section 12 approved because they are approved clinicians under the Mental Health Act 1983.

4.36   To be eligible to undertake assessments, in England a doctor will need to have completed the standard training for deprivation of liberty mental health assessors. Except in the 12 month period beginning with the date the doctor has successfully completed the standard training, the regulations for England also require the supervisory body to be satisfied that the doctor has, in the 12 months prior to selection, completed further training relevant to their role as a mental health assessor. In Wales, a doctor will need to have completed appropriate training and have appropriate skills and experience.

4.37   Supervisory bodies must consider the suitability of the assessor for the particular case (for example, whether they have experience relevant to the person's condition).

4.38   As with the mental capacity assessment, supervisory bodies may wish to consider using an eligible assessor who already knows the relevant person to undertake this assessment, if they think it would be of benefit.

4.39   The mental health assessor is required to consider how the mental health of the person being assessed is likely to be affected by being deprived of their liberty, and to report their conclusions to the best interests assessor. The mental health and best interests assessments cannot be carried out by the same person.

Eligibility assessment

4.40   This assessment relates specifically to the relevant person's status, or potential status, under the Mental Health Act 1983.

4.41   A person is not eligible for a deprivation of liberty authorisation if:

■ they are detained as a hospital in-patient under the Mental Health Act 1983, or
■ the authorisation, if given, would be inconsistent with an obligation placed on them under the Mental Health Act 1983, such as a requirement to live somewhere else. This will only affect people who are on leave of absence from detention under the Mental Health Act 1983 or who are subject to guardianship, supervised community treatment or conditional discharge.

4.42   Where the proposed authorisation relates to a care home, or to deprivation of liberty in a hospital for non-mental health treatment, the eligibility assessment will simply be a matter of checking that authorisation would not be inconsistent with an obligation placed on the person under the Mental Health Act 1983.

4.43   When a person is subject to guardianship under the Mental Health Act 1983, their guardian can decide where they are to live, but cannot authorise deprivation of liberty and cannot require them to live somewhere where they are deprived of liberty unless that deprivation of liberty is authorised.

4.44   Occasionally, a person who is subject to guardianship and who lacks capacity to make the relevant decisions may need specific care or treatment in a care home or hospital that cannot be delivered without deprivation of liberty. This may be in a care home in which they are already living or in which the guardian thinks they ought to live, or it may be in a hospital where they need to be for physical health care. It may also apply if they need to be in hospital for mental health care. The process for obtaining a deprivation of liberty authorisation and the criteria to be applied are the same as for any other person.

4.45   If the proposed authorisation relates to deprivation of liberty in a hospital **wholly or partly for the purpose of treatment of mental disorder**, then the relevant person will not be eligible if:

■ they object to being admitted to hospital, or to some or all the treatment they will receive there for mental disorder, **and**
■ they meet the criteria for an application for admission under section 2 or section 3 of the Mental Health Act 1983 (unless an attorney or deputy, acting within their powers, had consented to the things to which the person is objecting).

4.46   In many cases, the relevant person will be able to state an objection. However, where the person is unable to communicate, or can only communicate to a limited extent, assessors will need to consider the person's behaviour, wishes, feelings, views, beliefs and values, both present and past, so far as they can be ascertained (see paragraphs 5.37 to 5.48 of the main Code for guidance on how to do this). If there is reason to think that a person would object if able to do so, then the person should be assumed to be objecting. Occasionally, it may be that the person's behaviour initially suggests an objection, but that this objection is in fact not directed at the treatment at all. In that case, the person should **not** be taken to be objecting.

4.47   Assessors should always bear in mind that their job is simply to establish whether the person objects to treatment or to being in hospital: whether that objection is reasonable or not is not the issue.

4.48   Even where a person does not object and a deprivation of liberty authorisation is possible, it should not be assumed that such an authorisation is invariably the correct course. There may be other factors that suggest that the Mental Health Act 1983 should be used (for example, where it is thought likely that the person will recover relevant capacity and will then refuse to consent to treatment, or where it is important for the hospital managers to have a formal power to retake a person who goes absent without leave). Further guidance on this is given in the Mental Health Act 1983 Code of Practice.

4.49   The eligibility assessor is not required to decide (or even consider) whether an application under the Mental Health Act 1983 would be in the person's best interests.

4.50   If the proposed authorisation relates to deprivation of liberty in a hospital **wholly or partly for the purpose of treatment of mental disorder**, then the person will also not be eligible if they are:

- currently on leave of absence from detention under the Mental Health Act 1983
- subject to supervised community treatment, or
- subject to conditional discharge, in which case powers of recall under the Mental Health Act 1983 should be used.

4.51   People on leave of absence from detention under the Mental Health Act 1983 or subject to supervised community treatment or conditional discharge are, however, eligible for the deprivation of liberty safeguards if they require treatment in hospital for a physical disorder.

WHO CAN CONDUCT AN ELIGIBILITY ASSESSMENT?

4.52   The regulations for England specify that the eligibility assessment must be completed by:

- a mental health assessor who is also a section 12 doctor, or
- a best interests assessor who is also an approved mental health professional (AMHP).

4.53   The assessment cannot be carried out by a non-section 12 doctor, even if they are qualified to be a mental health assessor, nor by a non-AMHP, even if they are qualified to be a best interests assessor. This will ensure that the eligibility assessor is sufficiently familiar with the Mental Health Act 1983, which will be particularly important in cases in which it appears that the powers available under the Mental Health Act 1983 may be more appropriate than the deprivation of liberty safeguards.

4.54   The eligibility assessment will often be carried out by the best interests assessor but, where this is not the case, the eligibility assessor must request the best interests assessor to provide any relevant eligibility information that the best interests assessor may have, and the best interests assessor must comply with this request.

WHAT HAPPENS WHEN PEOPLE ARE ASSESSED AS INELIGIBLE?

4.55   If the eligibility assessor believes that the relevant person is not eligible, but (on the basis of the report of the best interests assessor) that they should nevertheless be deprived of liberty in their best interests, the eligibility assessor should immediately inform the supervisory body.

4.56   In the case of someone already subject to the Mental Health Act 1983, the eligibility assessor should inform the supervisory body with a view to contact being made with the relevant responsible clinician (i.e. the clinician in overall charge of the person's treatment) or, if the person is subject to guardianship, the relevant local social services authority. Otherwise, the assessor or supervisory body should take steps to arrange for the person to be assessed further with a view to an application being made for admission to hospital under the Mental Health Act 1983. Assessors will need to be familiar with local arrangements for doing this.

4.57   In some cases, even before the eligibility assessment is undertaken, it may be known that there is a chance that the person will have to be assessed with a view to an application under the Mental Health Act 1983 because the eligibility assessment might conclude that they are ineligible for a deprivation of liberty authorisation. In such cases, steps should be taken, where practical and possible, to arrange assessments in a way that minimises the number of separate interviews or examinations the person has to undergo.

Best interests assessment

4.58   The purpose of the best interests assessment is to establish, firstly, whether deprivation of liberty is occurring or is going to occur and, if so, whether:

- it is in the best interests of the relevant person to be deprived of liberty
- it is necessary for them to be deprived of liberty in order to prevent harm to themselves, and
- deprivation of liberty is a proportionate response to the likelihood of the relevant person suffering harm and the seriousness of that harm.

4.59   The best interests assessor is the person who is responsible for assessing what is in the best interests of a relevant person.

4.60   In both England and Wales, the best interests assessment must be undertaken by an AMHP, social worker, nurse, occupational therapist or chartered psychologist with the skills and experience specified in the regulations. In England, this includes at least two years' postregistration experience. In England, the supervisory body must also be satisfied that the assessor:

- is not suspended from the register or list relevant to the person's profession
- has successfully completed training that has been approved[9] by the Secretary of State to be a best interests assessor
- except in the 12 month period beginning with the date the person has successfully completed the approved training, has, in the 12 months prior to selection, completed further training relevant to their role as a best interests assessor, and
- has the skills necessary to obtain, evaluate and analyse complex evidence and differing views and to weigh them appropriately in decision-making.

4.61   Section 4 of the Mental Capacity Act 2005 sets out the best interests principles that apply for the purpose of the Act. Chapter 5 of the main Code ('What does the Act mean when it talks about "best interests"?') explains this in more detail, and, in particular, paragraph 5.13 of the main Code includes a checklist of factors that need to be taken into account in working out what is in a person's best interests.

[9] Approved courses can be found at: http://www.dh.gov.uk/en/SocialCare/Deliveringadultsocialcare/MentalCapacity/MentalCapacityActDeprivationofLibertySafeguards/index.htm

These principles and guidance apply equally to working out a person's best interests for the purpose of the deprivation of liberty safeguards. However, when it comes to best interests around deprivation of liberty, additional factors apply, including:

- whether any harm to the person could arise if the deprivation of liberty does not take place
- what that harm would be
- how likely that harm is to arise (i.e. is the level of risk sufficient to justify a step as serious as depriving a person of liberty?)
- what other care options there are which could avoid deprivation of liberty, and
- if deprivation of liberty is currently unavoidable, what action could be taken to avoid it in future.

ESTABLISHING WHETHER DEPRIVATION OF LIBERTY IS OCCURRING

4.62 The first task of a best interests assessor is to establish whether deprivation of liberty is occurring, or is likely to occur, since there is no point in the assessment process proceeding further if deprivation of liberty is not at issue. If the best interests assessor concludes that deprivation of liberty is **not** occurring and is not likely to occur, they should state in their assessment report to the supervisory body that deprivation of liberty is not in the person's best interests because there is obviously a less restrictive option available. The best interests requirement will therefore not be met in such a case.

4.63 To establish whether deprivation of liberty is occurring, or is likely to occur, the best interests assessor must consult the managing authority of the hospital or care home where the person is, or will be, accommodated and examine any relevant needs assessments and care plans prepared for the person. The best interests assessor must consider whether the care plan and the manner in which it is being, or will be, implemented constitutes a deprivation of liberty. If not, then no deprivation of liberty authorisation is required for that care plan.

4.64 The managing authority and supervisory body must provide the best interests assessor with any needs assessments or care plans that they have undertaken or which have been undertaken on their behalf.

THE BEST INTERESTS ASSESSMENT PROCESS

4.65 If the best interests assessor considers that deprivation of liberty is occurring, or is likely to occur, they should start a full best interests assessment. In line with section 4(7) of the Act this involves seeking the views of a range of people connected to the relevant person to find out whether they believe that depriving the relevant person of their liberty is, or would be, in the person's best interests to protect them from harm or to enable them to follow the care plan proposed. The best interests assessor should, as far as is practical and possible, seek the views of:

- anyone the person has previously named as someone they want to be consulted
- anyone involved in caring for the person
- anyone interested in the person's welfare (for example, family carers, other close relatives, or an advocate already working with the person), and
- any donee or deputy who represents the person.

4.66 This may mean that the best interests assessor needs to explain key aspects of the care plan and what it aims to do to the people being consulted. The best interests assessor should then take the views received into account as far as is practical and appropriate. It is essential that the best interests assessor provides an independent and objective view of whether or not there is a genuine justification for deprivation of liberty, taking account of all the relevant views and factors.

4.67   The best interests assessor must state in their assessment the name and address of every interested person whom they have consulted in carrying out the assessment.

4.68   Family and friends may not be confident about expressing their views: it is the responsibility of the best interests assessor to enable them to do so – using support to meet communication or language needs as necessary.

[*Scenario: Consulting around best interests*]

4.69   The best interests assessor must involve the relevant person in the assessment process as much as is possible and practical, and help them to participate in decision-making. The relevant person should be given the support needed to participate, using non-verbal means of communication where needed (see paragraphs 3.10 and 3.11 of the main Code) or the support of speech and language therapists. It may also help to involve others whom the relevant person already trusts and who are used to communicating with the relevant person.

4.70   The best interests assessor will need to consider the conclusions of the mental health assessor about how the person being assessed is likely to be affected by being deprived of their liberty. If the proposed care would involve the person being moved, then the assessor should consider the impact of the upheaval and of the journey itself on the person.

4.71   If the best interests assessment supports deprivation of liberty in the care home or hospital in question, the assessor must state what the maximum authorisation period should be in the case concerned. This must not exceed 12 months. The assessor should set out the reasons for selecting the period stated. This decision will be based on the information obtained during the consultation process – but should also reflect information from the person's care plan about how long any treatment or care will be required in circumstances that amount to a deprivation of liberty. It should also take into account any available indication of how likely it is that the relevant person's circumstances will change, including the expected progression of the illness or disability. The underlying principle is that deprivation of liberty should be for the minimum period necessary so, for the maximum 12-month period to apply, the assessor will need to be confident that there is unlikely to be a change in the person's circumstances that would affect the authorisation within that timescale.

THE REPORT OF THE BEST INTERESTS ASSESSOR

4.72   The best interests assessor must provide a report that explains their conclusion and their reasons for it. If they do not support deprivation of liberty, then their report should aim to be as useful as possible to the commissioners and providers of care in deciding on future action (for example, recommending an alternative approach to treatment or care in which deprivation of liberty could be avoided). It may be helpful for the best interests assessor to discuss the possibility of any such alternatives with the providers of care **during the assessment process**.

4.73   If the best interests assessor does not support deprivation of liberty, it would be good practice for their report to be included in the relevant person's care plan or case notes, to ensure that any views about how deprivation of liberty can be avoided are made clear to the providers of care and all relevant staff on an ongoing basis.

4.74   The best interests assessor may recommend that conditions should be attached to the authorisation. For example, they may make recommendations around contact issues, issues relevant to the person's culture or other major issues related to the deprivation of liberty, which – if not dealt with – would mean that the deprivation of liberty would cease to be in the person's best interests. The best interests assessor may also recommend conditions in order to work towards avoiding deprivation of liberty in future. But it is not the best interests assessor's role to specify conditions that do not directly relate to the issue of deprivation of liberty.

4.75   Conditions should not be a substitute for a properly constructed care plan (see paragraph 2.7 on good practice for care planning). In recommending conditions, best interests assessors should aim to impose the minimum necessary constraints, so that they do not unnecessarily prevent or inhibit the staff of the hospital or care home from responding appropriately to the person's needs, whether they remain the same or vary over time. It would be good practice for the best interests assessor to discuss any proposed conditions with the relevant personnel at the home or hospital before finalising the assessment, and to make clear in their report whether the rejection or variation of recommended conditions by the supervisory body would significantly affect the other conclusions they have reached.

4.76   Where possible, the best interests assessor should recommend someone to be appointed as the relevant person's representative (see chapter 7). The assessor should be well placed, as a result of the consultation process, to identify whether there is anybody suitable to take on this role. The appointment of the relevant person's representative cannot take place unless and until an authorisation is given. However, by identifying someone to take on this role at an early stage, the best interests assessor can help to ensure that a representative is appointed as soon as possible.

[*Scenario: Application for standard authorisation*]

What guidelines are there relating to the work of assessors?

Access to records

4.77   All assessors may, at any reasonable time, examine and take copies of:

- any health record
- any record of, or held by, a local authority that was compiled in accordance with a social services function, and
- any record held by a care home

which they consider may be relevant to their assessment. Assessors should list in their assessment report what records they examined.

Recording and reporting assessments

4.78   As soon as possible after carrying out their assessments, assessors must keep a written record of the assessment and must give copiesof their assessment report(s) to the supervisory body. The supervisory body must in turn give copies of the assessment report(s) to:

- the managing authority
- the relevant person and their representative, and
- any IMCA instructed

at the same time that it gives them copies of the deprivation of liberty authorisation or notification that an authorisation is not to be given (see paragraphs 5.7 and 5.18 respectively).

5.   WHAT SHOULD HAPPEN ONCE THE ASSESSMENTS ARE COMPLETE?

If all the assessments in the standard authorisation assessment process indicate that the relevant person meets all the qualifying requirements, then the supervisory body will give a deprivation of liberty authorisation. If any of the qualifying requirements are not met, however, different actions will need to be taken, depending on the circumstances of the individual case.

This chapter identifies potential outcomes of the assessment process and offers guidance on what should happen next.

What action should the supervisory body take if the assessments conclude that the person meets the requirements for authorisation?

5.1   If all the assessments conclude that the relevant person meets the requirements for authorisation, and the supervisory body has written copies of all the assessments, it must give a standard authorisation. A standard form is available for this purpose.

5.2   The supervisory body cannot give a standard authorisation if any of the requirements are not fulfilled.

5.3   The supervisory body must set the period of the authorisation, which may not be longer than that recommended by the best interests assessor (see paragraph 4.71).

5.4   When the supervisory body gives a standard authorisation, it must do so in writing and must state the following:

- the name of the relevant person
- the name of the relevant hospital or care home
- the period during which the authorisation is to be in force (which may not exceed the period recommended by the best interests assessor)
- the purpose for which the authorisation is given (i.e. why the person needs to be deprived of their liberty)
- any conditions subject to which the authorisation is given (see paragraph 5.5), and
- the reason why each qualifying requirement is met.

5.5   The supervisory body may attach conditions to the authorisation. Before deciding whether to give the authorisation subject to conditions, the supervisory body must consider any recommendations made by the best interests assessor (see paragraph 4.74). Where the supervisory body does not attach conditions as recommended by the best interests assessor, it should discuss the matter with the best interests assessor in case the rejection or variation of the conditions would significantly affect the other conclusions the best interests assessor reached in their report.

5.6   It is the responsibility of the supervisory body to appoint a representative for the relevant person (see chapter 7).

5.7   As soon as possible after giving the authorisation, the supervisory body must give a copy of the authorisation to:

- the managing authority
- the relevant person
- the relevant person's representative
- any Independent Mental Capacity Advocate (IMCA) involved, and
- every interested person named by the best interests assessor in their report as somebody they have consulted in carrying out their assessment.

The supervisory body must also keep a written record of any standard authorisation that it gives and of the matters referred to in paragraph 5.4.

5.8   The managing authority must take all practical and possible steps to ensure that the relevant person understands the effect of the authorisation and their rights around it. These include their right to challenge the authorisation via the Court of Protection, their right to request a review, and their right to have an IMCA instructed, along with the process for doing so (see paragraphs 7.37 to 7.41). Appropriate information must be given to the relevant person both orally and in writing. Any written information must also be given to the relevant person's representative. This must happen as soon as possible and practical after the authorisation is given.

How long can an authorisation last?

5.9   A deprivation of liberty should last for the shortest period possible. The best inter-ests assessor should only recommend authorisation for as long as the relevant per-son is likely to meet all the qualifying requirements. The authorisation may be for quite a short period. A short period may, for example, be appropriate if:

- the reason that the deprivation of liberty is in the person's best interests is because their usual care arrangements have temporarily broken down, or
- there are likely to be changes in the person's mental disorder in the relatively near future (for example, if the person is in rehabilitation following brain injury).

What restrictions exist on authorisations?

5.10   A deprivation of liberty authorisation – whether urgent or standard – relates solely to the issue of deprivation of liberty. It does not give authority to treat people, nor to do anything else that would normally require their consent. The arrangements for providing care and treatment to people in respect of whom a deprivation of liberty authorisation is in force are subject to the wider provisions of the Mental Capacity Act 2005.

5.11   This means that any treatment can only be given to a person who has not given their consent if:

- it is established that the person lacks capacity to make the decision concerned
- it is agreed that the treatment will be in their best interests, having taken account of the views of the person and of people close to them, and, where relevant in the case of serious medical treatment, of any IMCA involved
- the treatment does not conflict with a valid and applicable advance decision to refuse treatment, and
- the treatment does not conflict with a decision made by a donee of Lasting Power of Attorney or a deputy acting within the scope of their powers.

5.12   In deciding what is in a person's best interests, section 4 of the Act applies in the same way as it would if the person was not deprived of liberty. The guidance in chapter 5 of the main Code on assessing best interests is also relevant.

5.13   Life-sustaining treatment, or treatment to prevent a serious deterioration in the person's condition, may be provided while a decision in respect of any relevant issue is sought from the Court of Protection. The need to act in the best interests of the person concerned will continue to apply in the meantime.

Can a person be moved to a different location under a standard authorisation?

5.14   If a person who is subject to a standard authorisation moves to a different hospital or care home, the managing authority of the new hospital or care home must request a new standard authorisation. The application should be made **before** the move takes place.

5.15   If the move has to take place so urgently that this is impossible, the managing authority of the new hospital or care home will need to give an urgent authorisation (see chapter 6).

5.16   The only exception is if the care regime in the new facility will not involve deprivation of liberty.

5.17   These arrangements are not an alternative to applying the provisions of sections 38 and 39 of the Act regarding change of residence.

What happens if an assessment concludes that one of the requirements is not met?

5.18   If any of the assessments conclude that one of the requirements is not met, then the assessment process should stop immediately and authorisation may not be given. The supervisory body should:

- inform anyone still engaged in carrying out an assessment that they are not required to complete it
- notify the managing authority, the relevant person, any IMCA involved and every interested person consulted by the best interests assessor that authorisation has not been given (a standard form is available for this purpose), and
- provide the managing authority, the relevant person and any IMCA involved with copies of those assessments that have been carried out. This must be done as soon as possible, because in some cases different arrangements will need to be made for the person's care.

5.19   If the reason the standard authorisation cannot be given is because the eligibility requirement is not met, it may be necessary to consider making the person subject to the Mental Health Act 1983. If this is the case, it may be possible to use the same assessors to make that decision, thereby minimising the assessment processes.

What are the responsibilities of the managing authority and the commissioners of care if a request for an authorisation is turned down?

5.20   The managing authority is responsible for ensuring that it does not deprive a person of their liberty without an authorisation. The managing authority must comply with the law in this respect: where a request for an authorisation is turned down, it will need to review the relevant person's actual or proposed care arrangements to ensure that a deprivation of liberty is not allowed to either continue or commence.

5.21   Supervisory bodies and other commissioners of care will need to purchase care packages in a way that makes it possible for managing authorities to comply with the outcome of the deprivation of liberty safeguards assessment process when a request for a standard authorisation is turned down.

5.22   The actions that both managing authorities and commissioners of care should consider if a request for an authorisation is turned down will depend on the reason why the authorisation has not been given:

- If the best interests assessor concluded that the relevant person was not in fact being, or likely to be, deprived of liberty, no action is likely to be necessary.
- If the best interests assessor concluded that the proposed or actual deprivation of liberty was not in the relevant person's best interests, the managing authority, in conjunction with the commissioner of the care, will need to consider how the care plan could be changed to avoid deprivation of liberty. (See, for example, the guidance on practical ways to reduce the risk of deprivation of liberty in paragraph 2.7.) They should examine carefully the reasons given in the best interests assessor's report, and may find it helpful to discuss the matter with the best interests assessor. Where appropriate, they should also discuss the matter with family and carers. If the person is not yet a resident in the care home or hospital, the revised care plan may not involve admission to that facility unless the conditions of care are adapted to be less restrictive and deprivation of liberty will not occur.
- If the mental capacity assessor concluded that the relevant person **has** capacity to make decisions about their care, the care home or hospital will need to consider, in conjunction with the commissioner of the care, how to support the person to make such decisions.
- If the relevant person was identified as not eligible to be subject to deprivation of liberty authorisation, it may be appropriate to assess whether an application should be made to detain the person under the Mental Health Act 1983.
- If the relevant person does not have a mental disorder as defined in the Mental Health Act 1983, the care plan will need to be modified to avoid a deprivation of liberty, since there would be no lawful basis for depriving a person of liberty in those circumstances.
- Where there is a valid refusal by a donee or deputy, or an applicable and valid advance decision (see paragraphs 4.25 to 4.28), alternative care arrangements will need to be made. If there is a question about the refusal, a decision may be sought from the Court of Protection.
- If the person is under 18, use of the Children Act 1989 may be considered.

5.23   Working out what action should be taken where a request for a standard deprivation of liberty authorisation is turned down in respect of a 'self-funder' may present particular problems, because the managing authority may not be able to make alternative care arrangements without discussing them with those controlling the funding, whether relatives of the person concerned or others. The desired outcome should be the provision of a care regime that does not constitute deprivation of liberty.

5.24   Where the best interests assessor comes to the conclusion that the best interests requirement is not met, but it appears to the assessor that the person being assessed is already being deprived of their liberty, the assessor must inform the supervisory body and explain in their report why they have reached that conclusion. The supervisory body must then inform the managing authority to review the relevant person's care plan immediately so that unauthorised deprivation of liberty does not continue. Any necessary changes must be made urgently to stop what would be an unlawful deprivation of liberty. The steps taken to stop the deprivation of liberty should be recorded in the care plan. Where possible, family, friends and carers should be involved in deciding how to prevent the unauthorised deprivation of liberty from continuing. If the supervisory body has any doubts about whether the matter is being satisfactorily resolved within an appropriately urgent timescale, it should alert the inspection body (see chapter 11).

6.   WHEN CAN URGENT AUTHORISATIONS OF DEPRIVATION OF LIBERTY BE GIVEN?

Wherever possible, applications for deprivation of liberty authorisations should be made before the deprivation of liberty commences. However, where deprivation of liberty unavoidably needs to commence before a standard authorisation can be obtained, an urgent authorisation can be given which will make the deprivation of liberty lawful for a short period of time.

This chapter contains guidance on the rules around urgent authorisations.

When can an urgent authorisation be given?

6.1   A managing authority can itself give an urgent authorisation for deprivation of liberty where:

- it is required to make a request to the supervisory body for a standard authorisation, but believes that the need for the person to be deprived of their liberty is so urgent that deprivation needs to begin before the request is made, or
- it has made a request for a standard authorisation, but believes that the need for a person to be deprived of liberty has now become so urgent that deprivation of liberty needs to begin before the request is dealt with by the supervisory body.

This means that an urgent authorisation can never be given without a request for a standard authorisation being made simultaneously. Therefore, before giving an urgent authorisation, a managing authority will need to have a reasonable expectation that the six qualifying requirements for a standard authorisation are likely to be met.

6.2   Urgent authorisations should normally only be used in response to sudden unforeseen needs. However, they can also be used in care planning (for example, to avoid delays in transfer for rehabilitation, where delay would reduce the likely benefit of the rehabilitation).

6.3   However, an urgent authorisation should not be used where there is no expectation that a standard deprivation of liberty authorisation will be needed. Where, for example:

- a person who lacks capacity to make decisions about their care and treatment has developed a mental disorder as a result of a physical illness, and
- the physical illness requires treatment in hospital in circumstances that amount to a deprivation of liberty, and
- the treatment of that physical illness is expected to lead to rapid resolution of the mental disorder such that a standard deprivation of liberty authorisation would not be required,

it would not be appropriate to give an urgent authorisation simply to legitimise the short-term deprivation of liberty.

6.4   Similarly, an urgent deprivation of liberty authorisation should not be given when a person is, for example, in an accident and emergency unit or a care home, and it is anticipated that within a matter of a few hours or a few days the person will no longer be in that environment.

6.5   Any decision to give an urgent authorisation and take action that deprives a person of liberty must be in the person's best interests, as set out in section 4 of the Mental Capacity Act 2005. Where restraint is involved, all actions must comply with the additional conditions in section 6 of the Act (see chapter 6 of the main Code).

6.6   The managing authority must decide the period for which the urgent authorisation is given, but this must not exceed seven days (see paragraphs 6.20 to 6.28 regarding the possible extension of the sevenday period). The authorisation must be in writing and must state:

- the name of the relevant person
- the name of the relevant hospital or care home
- the period for which the authorisation is to be in force, and
- the purpose for which the authorisation is given.

A standard form is available for a managing authority to use to notify a supervisory body that it has given an urgent authorisation.

6.7   Supervisory bodies and managing authorities should have a procedure in place that identifies:

- what actions should be taken when an urgent authorisation needs to be made
- who should take each action, and
- within what timescale.

What records should be kept about urgent authorisations?

6.8   The managing authority must keep a written record of any urgent authorisations given, including details of why it decided to give an urgent authorisation. They must give a copy of the authorisation to the relevant person and any IMCA instructed, and place a copy in the relevant person's records. The managing authority must also seek to ensure that, as far as possible, the relevant person understands the effect of the authorisation and the right to challenge the authorisation via the Court of Protection. Appropriate information must be given both orally and in writing.

6.9   The managing authority should, as far as possible and appropriate, notify the relevant person's family, friends and carers when an urgent authorisation is given in order to enable them to offer informed support to the person.

6.10   The processes surrounding the giving and receiving of urgent authorisations should be clearly recorded, and regularly monitored and audited, as part of a managing authority's or supervisory body's governance structure.

Who should be consulted before giving an urgent authorisation?

6.11   If the managing authority is considering depriving a person of liberty in an emergency and giving an urgent authorisation, they must, as far as is practical and possible, take account of the views of anyone engaged in caring for the relevant person or interested in their welfare. The aim should be to consult carers and family members at as early a stage as possible so that their views can be properly taken into account before a decision to give an urgent authorisation is taken.

6.12   The steps taken to involve family, friends or carers should be recorded in the relevant person's records, along with their views. The views of the carers will be important because their knowledge of the person will put them in a good position to gauge how the person will react to the deprivation of their liberty, and the effect it will have on their mental state. It may also be appropriate to consult any staff who may have some involvement in the person's case.

6.13   The ultimate decision, though, will need to be based on a judgement of what is in the relevant person's best interests. The decision-maker from the managing authority will need to be able to show that they have made a reasonable decision based on their professional judgement and taking account of all the relevant factors. This is an important decision, because it could mean the deprivation of a person's liberty without, at this stage, the full deprivation of liberty safeguards assessment process having taken place. The decision should therefore be taken at a senior level within the managing authority.

[*Scenario: Urgent authorisation followed by short-term standard authorisation*]

Can a person be moved into care under an urgent authorisation?

6.14   There may be cases in which managing authorities are considering giving an urgent authorisation to enable them to move the relevant person to a new type of care. This may occur, for example, when considering whether to admit a person living at home or with relatives into a hospital care regime that would deprive them of their liberty, and when the need for admission appears to be so urgent that there would not be enough time to follow the standard authorisation process.

6.15   For some people, such a change of location may have a detrimental effect on their mental health, which might significantly distort the way they come across during any assessment process. In such a case, managing authorities should consider whether giving the urgent authorisation and admitting the person to hospital would outweigh the benefits of leaving the person in their existing location, where any assessment of their needs might be more accurate. This will involve looking carefully at the existing care arrangements and consulting with any carers involved, to establish whether or not the person could safely and beneficially be cared for in their home environment while the assessment process takes place. Where the relevant person is already known to statutory care providers, for example the community mental health team or social services, it will be important to involve them in this decision-making process. The relevant person's GP may also be an important source of knowledge about the person's situation, and may be able to offer a valuable opinion when the appropriateness of moving the person into a different care setting is under consideration.

What happens at the end of an urgent authorisation period?

6.16   An urgent authorisation will terminate at the end of the period for which it is given. As noted above, this is normally a maximum of seven days, but in exceptional circumstances an urgent authorisation can be extended to a maximum of 14 days **by the supervisory body**, as explained in paragraphs 6.20 to 6.28.

6.17   An urgent authorisation will terminate before this time if the standard authorisation applied for is given.

6.18   An urgent authorisation will also terminate if a managing authority receives notice from the supervisory body that the standard authorisation will not be given. It will not then be lawful to continue to deprive the relevant person of their liberty.

6.19   The supervisory body must inform the relevant person and any IMCA instructed that the urgent authorisation has ended. This notification can be combined with the notification to them of the outcome of the application for standard authorisation.

[*Scenario: Considering an urgent authorisation*]

How and when can an urgent authorisation be extended?

6.20   If there are exceptional reasons why the request for a standard authorisation cannot be dealt with within the period of the original urgent authorisation, the managing authority may ask the supervisory body to extend the duration of the urgent authorisation for a maximum of a further seven days. The managing authority must keep a written record of the reason for making the request and must notify the relevant person, in writing, that they have made the request. Standard forms are available for managing authorities to request the extension of an urgent authorisation from a supervisory body and for supervisory bodies to record their decision in response to such a request.

6.21   Unless the duration of the urgent authorisation is extended by the supervisory body, or a standard authorisation is given before the urgent authorisation expires, the authority to deprive the person of liberty will cease once the urgent authorisation period has expired. It is therefore essential that any request for an extension of an urgent authorisation is made promptly. This will necessitate good communication between the managing authority and the supervisory body regarding the progress of the standard authorisation assessment process. Particular care may need to be taken where an urgent authorisation is due to expire over the weekend or on a bank holiday, when appropriate people at the managing authority and supervisory body may not be immediately available.

6.22   The supervisory body may only extend the duration of the urgent authorisation if:

- the managing authority has made a request for a standard authorisation
- there are exceptional reasons why it has not yet been possible to make a standard authorisation, and
- it is essential for the deprivation of liberty to continue while the supervisory body makes its decision.

6.23   Extensions can only be granted for exceptional reasons. An example of when an extension would be justified might be where:

- it was not possible to contact a person whom the best interests assessor needed to contact
- the assessment could not be relied upon without their input, and
- extension for the specified period would enable them to be contacted.

6.24   It is for the supervisory body to decide what constitutes an 'exceptional reason', but because of the seriousness of the issues involved, the supervisory body's decision must be soundly based and defensible. It would not, for example, be appropriate to use staffing shortages as a reason to extend an urgent authorisation.

6.25   An urgent authorisation can only be extended once.

6.26   The supervisory body must notify the managing authority of the length of any extension granted and must vary the original urgent authorisation so that it states the extended duration. The supervisory body must also keep a written record of the outcome of the request and the period of the extension.

6.27   The managing authority must give a copy of the varied urgent authorisation to the relevant person and any IMCA instructed, and must seek to ensure that, as far as possible, the relevant person understands the effect of the varied authorisation and the right to challenge the authorisation via the Court of Protection. The appropriate information must be given both orally and in writing

6.28   If the supervisory body decides not to extend the urgent authorisation, it must inform the managing authority of its decision and the reasons for it. The managing authority must give a copy of the notice to the relevant person and any IMCA involved.

7.   WHAT IS THE ROLE OF THE RELEVANT PERSON'S REPRESENTATIVE?

Once a standard deprivation of liberty authorisation has been given, supervisory bodies must appoint the relevant person's representative as soon as possible and practical to represent the person who has been deprived of their liberty.

This chapter explains the role of the relevant person's representative and gives guidance on their selection and appointment.

What is the role of the relevant person's representative?

7.1   The supervisory body must appoint a relevant person's representative for every person to whom they give a standard authorisation for deprivation of liberty. It is important that the representative is appointed at the time the authorisation is given or as soon as possible and practical thereafter.

7.2   The role of the relevant person's representative, once appointed, is:

- to maintain contact with the relevant person, and
- to represent and support the relevant person in all matters relating to the deprivation of liberty safeguards, including, if appropriate, triggering a review, using an organisation's complaints procedure on the person's behalf or making an application to the Court of Protection.

This is a crucial role in the deprivation of liberty process, providing the relevant person with representation and support that is independent of the commissioners and providers of the services they are receiving.

7.3   The best interests principle of the Act applies to the relevant person's representative in the same way that it applies to other people acting or making decisions for people who lack capacity.

How should managing authorities work with the relevant person's representative?

7.4   As soon as possible and practical after a standard deprivation of liberty authorisation is given, the managing authority must seek to ensure that the relevant person and their representative understand:

- the effect of the authorisation
- their right to request a review (see chapter 8)
- the formal and informal complaints procedures that are available to them
- their right to make an application to the Court of Protection to seek variation or termination of the authorisation (see chapter 10), and
- their right, where the relevant person does not have a paid 'professional' representative, to request the support of an Independent Mental Capacity Advocate (IMCA) (see paragraphs 7.37 to 7.41).

7.5   When providing information to the person and their representative, the managing authority should take account of the communication and language needs of both the person and their representative. Provision of information should be seen as an ongoing responsibility, rather than a one-off activity.

Who can be the relevant person's representative?[10]

7.6   To be eligible to be the relevant person's representative, a person must be:

- 18 years of age or over
- able to keep in contact with the relevant person, and
- willing to be appointed.

[10] Requirements relating to the eligibility, selection and appointment of relevant person's representatives are covered in regulations. The regulations for England are The Mental Capacity (Deprivation of Liberty: Appointment of Relevant Person's Representative) Regulations 2008. The regulations for Wales are The Mental Capacity (Deprivation of Liberty: Appointment of Relevant Person's Representative) (Wales) Regulations 2008.

The person must not be:

- financially interested in the relevant person's managing authority (a person is considered to be financially interested where that person is a partner, director, other office-holder or major shareholder of the managing authority)
- a relative of a person who has a financial interest in the relevant person's managing authority (paragraph 4.13 explains what is meant by 'relative')
- employed by, or providing services to, the care home in which the person relevant person is residing
- employed by the hospital in a role that is, or could be, related to the treatment or care of the relevant person, or
- employed to work in the relevant person's supervisory body in a role that is, or could be, related to the relevant person's case.

7.7   The appointment of the relevant person's representative is in addition to, and does not affect, any appointment of a donee or deputy. Similarly, the functions of the representative are in addition to, and do not affect, the authority of any donee, the powers of any deputy or any powers of the court. A donee or deputy may themselves be appointed as the relevant person's representative if they meet the eligibility criteria set out in paragraph 7.6.

7.8   There is no presumption that the relevant person's representative should be the same as the person who is their nearest relative for the purposes of the Mental Health Act 1983, even where the relevant person is likely to be subject simultaneously to an authorisation under these safeguards and a provision of the Mental Health Act 1983. This is because the relevant person's representative is not selected in the same way as the nearest relative under the Mental Health Act 1983, nor do they perform the same role. However, there is nothing to stop the relevant person's representative being the same as their nearest relative under the Mental Health Act 1983.

When should the relevant person's representative be identified?

7.9   The process of identifying a representative must begin as soon as possible.

7.10   Normally, this should be when the best interests assessor is appointed – even if one or more of the other assessments has not yet been completed. This is because the best interests assessor must, as part of the assessment process, identify if there is anyone they would recommend to become the relevant person's representative. The best interests assessor should discuss the representative role with the people interviewed as part of the assessment.

7.11   This does leave a risk that the process to identify a representative might begin in cases where authorisation is not given. Nevertheless, it is important that the process begins, so that the representative can be appointed immediately the authorisation is given or as soon as possible and practical thereafter.

How should the relevant person's representative be selected?

7.12   The best interests assessor should first establish whether the relevant person has the capacity to select their own representative and, if so, invite them to do so. If the relevant person has capacity and selects an eligible person (according to the criteria set out in paragraph 7.6), the best interests assessor must recommend that person to the supervisory body for appointment.

7.13   Alternatively, if the relevant person lacks capacity and there is a donee or deputy with the appropriate authority, the donee or deputy may select the person to be recommended as the relevant person's representative, again subject to the criteria set out in paragraph 7.6. If a donee or deputy selects an eligible person, then the best interests assessor must recommend that person to the supervisory body for appointment.

7.14   It is up to the best interests assessor to confirm whether any representative proposed by the relevant person, a donee or a deputy is eligible. If the best interests assessor decides that a proposed representative is not eligible, they must advise the person who made the selection and invite them to make a further selection.

7.15   If neither the relevant person, nor a donee or deputy, selects an eligible person, then the best interests assessor must consider whether they are able to identify someone eligible who could act as the relevant person's representative.

7.16   In making a recommendation, the assessor should consider, and balance, factors such as:

- Does the relevant person have a preference?
- If they do not have the capacity to express a preference now, is there any written statement made by the relevant person when they had capacity that indicates who they may now want to be their representative?
- Will the proposed representative be able to keep in contact with the relevant person?
- Does the relevant person appear to trust and feel comfortable with the proposed representative?
- Would the proposed representative be able to represent the relevant person effectively?
- Is the proposed representative likely to represent the relevant person's best interests?

In most cases, the best interests assessor will be able to check at the same time that the proposed representative is willing to take on the role.

7.17   It should not be assumed that the representative needs to be someone who supports the deprivation of liberty.

7.18   The best interests assessor must not select a representative where the relevant person, if they have the capacity to do so, or a donee or a deputy acting within the scope of their authority, states they are not content with that selection.

7.19   If the best interests assessor is unable to recommend anybody to be the relevant person's representative, they must notify the supervisory body accordingly. The supervisory body must then itself identify an eligible person to be appointed as the representative. In doing so, the supervisory body may select a person who:

- would be performing the role in a professional capacity
- has satisfactory skills and experience to perform the role
- is not a family member, friend or carer of the relevant person
- is not employed by, or providing services to, the relevant person's managing authority, where the relevant person's managing authority is a care home
- is not employed to work in the relevant person's managing authority in a role that is, or could be, related to the relevant person's case, where the relevant person's managing authority is a hospital
- is not employed to work in the supervisory body that is appointing the representative in a role that is, or could be, related to the relevant person's case, and
- the supervisory body is satisfied that an appropriate criminal record certificate has been issued in respect of.

7.20   The supervisory body may pay a person they select to be the relevant person's representative in the circumstances set out in paragraph 7.19. This service could be commissioned, for example, through an advocacy services provider, ensuring that the service provides effective independent representation for the relevant person.

7.21   When selecting a suitable representative for the relevant person, the best interests assessor or supervisory body should pay particular attention to the communication and cultural needs of the relevant person.

How should the relevant person's representative be appointed?

7.22   The supervisory body must invite, in writing, the person recommended by the best interests assessor to become the relevant person's representative. If the best interests assessor does not recommend anyone, then the supervisory body should identify and appoint someone to undertake the role. If the person is willing to become the representative, the supervisory body must formally appoint them. If the person refuses, a further eligible person must be identified and invited to become the representative. This process must continue until an eligible person is appointed.

7.23   The appointment of the relevant person's representative by the supervisory body must be in writing and set out the role and responsibilities of the relevant person's representative. The letter of appointment should also state the name of the appointed person and the date of expiry of the appointment, which must be for the period of the standard authorisation that has been given. The supervisory body must send copies of the written appointment to:

- the appointed person
- the relevant person
- any donee or deputy of the relevant person
- any IMCA involved
- every interested person named by the best interests assessor in their report as somebody they have consulted in carrying out their assessment, and
- the managing authority of the relevant hospital or care home.

7.24   The relevant person's representative must confirm to the supervisory body in writing that they are willing to accept the appointment and have understood their roles and responsibilities in respect of the relevant person.

How should the work of the relevant person's representative be supported and monitored?

7.25   It is important that the representative has sufficient contact with the relevant person to ensure that the relevant person's best interests are being safeguarded. In order to fulfil their role, therefore, the representative will need to be able to have face-to-face contact with the relevant person. That means that the care home or hospital should accommodate visits by the representative at reasonable times. The name of the person's representative should be recorded in the person's health and social care records.

7.26   Managing authorities and supervisory bodies should inform the relevant person's representative about sources of support and information available to help them in the role, including how to access the support of an IMCA (see paragraphs 7.37 to 7.41).

7.27   If the representative has insufficient contact with the relevant person, for whatever reason, the person may effectively be unable to access important review and appeal rights. For this reason, if the representative does not maintain an appropriate level of contact with the person, the managing authority will need to consider informing the supervisory body. When the managing authority is reviewing the person's care plan, it should consider whether the representative is in sufficient contact with the relevant person to offer effective support. Records kept by managing authorities about frequency of contact will support this consideration.

7.28   Because the appropriate levels and methods of contact between a relevant person and their representative will vary from case to case, this is a matter about which the managing authority will need to exercise discretion. If the managing authority has any concerns, it may be best to raise the matter with the representative initially to see whether any perceived problems can be resolved informally. If after this the representative still does not maintain what the managing authority considers to be an appropriate level of contact with the relevant person, then the managing authority should notify the supervisory body.

When can the appointment of the relevant person's representative be terminated?

7.29   The appointment of the relevant person's representative will be terminated in any of the following circumstances:

- The standard authorisation comes to an end and a new authorisation is not applied for or, if applied for, is not given.
- The relevant person, if they have capacity to do so, objects to the representative continuing in their role and a different person is selected to be their representative instead.
- A donee or deputy, if it is within their authority to do so and the relevant person lacks the capacity to decide, objects to the representative continuing in their role and a different person is selected to be the representative instead.
- The supervisory body becomes aware that the representative is no longer willing or eligible to continue in the role.
- The supervisory body becomes aware that the relevant person's representative is not keeping in touch with the person, is not representing and supporting them effectively or is not acting in the person's best interests.
- The relevant person's representative dies.

7.30   If the supervisory body becomes aware that the representative may not be keeping in touch with the person, is not acting in the relevant person's best interests, or is no longer eligible, it should contact the representative to clarify the position before deciding whether to terminate the appointment.

7.31   When the appointment of the relevant person's representative ends, the supervisory body must give notice to all those listed in paragraph 7.23. This notice should be given as soon as possible, stating when the appointment ended and the reason why.

7.32   When the appointment of a relevant person's representative ends but the lawful deprivation of liberty continues, the supervisory body must appoint a suitable replacement to be the relevant person's representative as soon as possible and practical after they become aware of the vacancy. As before, a person qualified to be a best interests assessor should make a recommendation to the supervisory body and the supervisory body should take account of any such recommendations.

7.33   If the reason for the termination of the former representative's appointment is that they are no longer eligible, the views of the former representative on who might replace them should be sought. The person identified as most suitable should then be invited to accept the appointment. This process should continue until an eligible person is willing to accept appointment.

What happens when there is no relevant person's representative available?

7.34   A person who is being deprived of their liberty will be in a particularly vulnerable position during any gaps in the appointment of the relevant person's representative, since there may be nobody to represent their interests or to apply for a review on their behalf. In these circumstances, if there is nobody who can support and represent the person (other than a person engaged in providing care and treatment for the relevant person in a professional capacity or for remuneration), the managing authority must notify the supervisory body, who must instruct an IMCA to represent the relevant person until a new representative is appointed.

7.35   The role of an IMCA instructed in these circumstances is essentially the same as that of the relevant person's representative. The role of the IMCA in this situation ends when the new relevant person's representative is appointed.

7.36   At any time when the relevant person does not have a representative, it will be particularly important for supervisory bodies to consider exercising their discretion to carry out a review if there is any significant change in the person's circumstances.

When should an IMCA be instructed?

7.37   Both the person who is deprived of liberty under a standard authorisation and their representative have a statutory right of access to an IMCA. It is the responsibility of the supervisory body to instruct an IMCA if the relevant person or their representative requests one. The intention is to provide extra support to the relevant person or a family member or friend acting as their representative if they need it, and to help them make use of the review process or access the Court of Protection safeguards. Where the relevant person has a paid 'professional' representative (see paragraphs 7.19 and 7.20), the need for additional advocacy support should not arise and so there is no requirement for an IMCA to be provided in those circumstances.

7.38   The role of the IMCA is to help represent the relevant person and, in particular, to assist the relevant person and their representative to understand the effect of the authorisation, what it means, why it has been given, why the relevant person meets the criteria for authorisation, how long it will last, any conditions to which the authorisation is subject and how to trigger a review or challenge in the Court of Protection. The IMCA can also provide support with a review (see chapter 8) or with an application to the Court of Protection (see chapter 10), for example to help the person to communicate their views.

7.39   The IMCA will have the right to make submissions to the supervisory body on the question of whether a qualifying requirement should be reviewed, or to give information, or make submissions, to any assessor carrying out a review assessment. Both the person and their representative must be told about the IMCA service and how to request an IMCA.

7.40   An IMCA must be instructed whenever requested by the relevant person or their representative. A request may be made more than once during the period of the authorisation. For example, help may be sought at the start of the authorisation and then again later in order to request a review.

7.41   In addition, if the supervisory body has reason to believe that the review and Court of Protection safeguards might not be used without the support of an IMCA, then they must instruct an IMCA. For example, if the supervisory body is aware that the person has selected a representative who needs support with communication, it should consider whether an IMCA is needed.

8.   WHEN SHOULD AN AUTHORISATION BE REVIEWED AND WHAT HAPPENS WHEN IT ENDS?

When a person is deprived of their liberty, the managing authority has a duty to monitor the case on an ongoing basis to see if the person's circumstances change – which may mean they no longer need to be deprived of their liberty.

The managing authority must set out in the care plan clear roles and responsibilities for monitoring and confirm under what circumstances a review is necessary. For example, if a person's condition is changing frequently, then their situation should be reviewed more frequently.

This chapter explains the duties of managing authorities and supervisory bodies in relation to reviewing cases, and what happens when an authorisation ends. The review process is set out in flowchart form at Annex 4.

WHEN SHOULD A STANDARD AUTHORISATION BE REVIEWED?

8.1   A standard authorisation can be reviewed at any time. The review is carried out by the supervisory body.

8.2   There are certain statutory grounds for carrying out a review. If the statutory grounds for a review are met, the supervisory body must carry out a review. If a review is requested by the relevant person, their representative or the managing authority, the supervisory body must carry out a review. Standard letters are available for the relevant person or their representative to request a review. There is also a standard form available for the managing authority to request a review. A supervisory body can also decide to carry out a review at its own discretion.

8.3   The statutory grounds for a review are:

- The relevant person no longer meets the age, no refusals, mental capacity, mental health or best interests requirements.
- The relevant person no longer meets the eligibility requirement because they now object to receiving mental health treatment in hospital and they meet the criteria for an application for admission under section 2 or section 3 of the Mental Health Act 1983 (see paragraphs 4.45 to 4.48).
- There has been a change in the relevant person's situation and, because of the change, it would be appropriate to amend an existing condition to which the authorisation is subject, delete an existing condition or add a new condition.
- The reason(s) the person now meets the qualifying requirement(s) is(are) different from the reason(s) given at the time the standard authorisation was given.

8.4   Different arrangements apply if the person no longer meets the eligibility requirement because they have been detained under the Mental Health Act, or become subject to a requirement under that Act that conflicts with the authorisation. (See paragraphs 8.19 to 8.21 regarding the short-term suspension of a standard authorisation.)

8.5   A managing authority must request a review if it appears to it that one or more of the qualifying requirements is no longer met, or may no longer be met.

What happens when a review is going to take place?

8.6   The supervisory body must tell the relevant person, their representative and the managing authority if they are going to carry out a review. This must be done either before the review begins or as soon as possible and practical after it has begun. A standard form is available for this purpose.

8.7   The relevant person's records must include information about any formal reviews that have been requested, when they were considered, and the outcome. These records must be retained by the supervisory body.

8.8   Deprivation of liberty can be ended before a formal review. An authorisation only **permits** deprivation of liberty: it does not mean that a person **must be** deprived of liberty where circumstances no longer necessitate it. If a care home or hospital decides that deprivation of liberty is no longer necessary then they must end it immediately, by adjusting the care regime or implementing whatever other change is appropriate. The managing authority should then apply to the supervisory body to review and, if appropriate, formally terminate the authorisation.

How should standard authorisations be reviewed?

8.9   When a supervisory body receives a request for a review, it must first decide which, if any, of the qualifying requirements need to be reviewed. A standard form is available for recording this decision.

8.10   If the supervisory body concludes that none of the qualifying requirements need to be reviewed, no further action is necessary. For example, if there has been a very recent assessment or review and no new evidence has been submitted to show that the relevant person does not meet the criteria, or that circumstances have changed, no review is required.

8.11   If it appears that one or more of the qualifying requirements should be reviewed, the supervisory body must arrange for a separate review assessment to be carried out for each of these requirements.

8.12   The supervisory body must record when a review is requested, what it decides to do (whether it decides to carry out a review or not) and the reasons for its decision.

8.13   In general, review processes should follow the standard authorisation processes – so supervisory bodies should conduct the assessments outlined in chapter 4 of this Code of Practice for each of the qualifying requirements that need to be reviewed.

8.14   Where the supervisory body decides that the best interests requirement should be reviewed solely because details of the **conditions** attached to the authorisation need to be changed, and the review request does not include evidence that there is a significant change in the relevant person's overall circumstances, there is no need for a full reassessment of best interests. The supervisory body can simply vary the conditions attached to the authorisation as appropriate. In deciding whether a full reassessment is necessary, the supervisory body should consider whether the grounds for the authorisation, or the nature of the conditions, are being contested by anyone as part of the review request.

8.15   If the review relates to any of the other requirements, or to a significant change in the person's situation under the best interests requirement, the supervisory body must obtain a new assessment.

8.16   If the assessment shows that the requirement is still met, the supervisory body must check whether the reason that it is met has changed from the reason originally stated on the authorisation. If it has, the supervisory body should make any appropriate amendments to the authorisation. In addition, if the review relates to the best interests requirement, the supervisory body must consider whether any conditions should be changed following the new assessment.

[*Scenario: The review process*]

What happens if any of the requirements are not met?

8.17   If any of the requirements are not met, then the authorisation must be terminated immediately.

8.18   The supervisory body must give written notice of the outcome of a review and any changes that have been made to the deprivation of liberty authorisation to:

■ the managing authority and the care home or hospital itself
■ the relevant person
■ the relevant person's representative, and
■ any Independent Mental Capacity Advocate (IMCA) involved.

Short-term suspension of authorisation

8.19   There are separate review arrangements for cases in which the eligibility requirement ceases to be met for a short period of time for reasons other than that the person is objecting to receiving mental health treatment in hospital. For example, if
the relevant person is detained as a hospital in-patient under the Mental Health Act
1983, the managing authority must notify the supervisory body, who will suspend
the authorisation.

8.20   If the relevant person then becomes eligible again within 28 days, the managing
authority must notify the supervisory body who will remove the suspension. If no
such notice is given within 28 days, then the authorisation will be terminated.
Standard forms are available for managing authorities to notify supervisory bodies
about the need for suspension of an authorisation, or that a suspension should be
lifted.

8.21   If the person ceases to meet the eligibility requirement because they begin to object
to receiving mental health treatment in hospital and they meet the criteria for an
application for admission under section 2 or section 3 of the Mental Health Act
1983, a review should be started immediately (see paragraph 8.3).

Is a review necessary when the relevant person's capacity fluctuates?

8.22   Guidance about people with fluctuating or temporary capacity is contained in
paragraphs 4.26 and 4.27 of the main Code. In the context of deprivation of liberty
safeguards, where a relevant person's capacity to make decisions about the arrangements made for their care and treatment fluctuates on a short-term basis, a balance
needs to be struck between:

- the need to review and terminate an authorisation if a person regains capacity,
  and
- spending time and resources constantly reviewing, terminating and then seeking
  fresh deprivation of liberty authorisations as the relevant person's capacity
  changes.

8.23   Each case must be treated on its merits. Managing authorities should keep all cases
under review: where a person subject to an authorisation is deemed to have
regained the capacity to decide about the arrangements made for their care and
treatment, the managing authority must assess whether there is consistent evidence
of the regaining of capacity on a longer-term basis. This is a clinical judgement that
will need to be made by a suitably qualified person.

8.24   Where there is consistent evidence of regaining capacity on this longer-term basis,
deprivation of liberty should be lifted immediately, and a formal review and termination of the authorisation sought. However, it should be borne in mind that a deprivation of liberty authorisation carries with it certain safeguards that the relevant
person will lose if the authorisation is terminated. Where the regaining of capacity
is likely to be temporary, and the authorisation will be required again within a short
period of time, the authorisation should be left in place, but with the situation kept
under ongoing review.

[Scenario: Fluctuating capacity]

What happens when an authorisation ends?

8.25   When an authorisation ends, the managing authority cannot lawfully continue to
deprive a person of their liberty.

8.26   If the managing authority considers that a person will still need to be deprived of
liberty after the authorisation ends, they need to request a further standard
authorisation to begin immediately after the expiry of the existing authorisation.

8.27 There is no statutory time limit on how far in advance of the expiry of one authorisation the managing authority can apply for a renewal authorisation. It will need to be far enough in advance for the renewal authorisation to be given before the existing authorisation ends (but see paragraphs 3.19 and 3.20 about not applying for authorisations too far in advance).

8.28 Once underway, the process for renewing a standard authorisation is the same as that for obtaining an original authorisation, and the same assessment processes must take place. However, the need to instruct an IMCA will not usually arise because the relevant person should at this stage have a representative appointed.

8.29 When the standard authorisation ends, the supervisory body must inform in writing:

- the relevant person
- the relevant person's representative
- the managing authority, and
- every interested person named by the best interests assessor in their report as somebody they have consulted in carrying out their assessment.

9. WHAT HAPPENS IF SOMEONE THINKS A PERSON IS BEING DEPRIVED OF THEIR LIBERTY WITHOUT AUTHORISATION?

It is a serious issue to deprive someone of their liberty without authorisation if they lack the capacity to consent. If anyone believes that a person is being deprived of their liberty without authorisation, they should raise this with the relevant authorities.

If the conclusion is that the person is being deprived of their liberty unlawfully, this will normally result in a change in their care arrangements, or in an application for a deprivation of liberty authorisation being made.

This chapter explains the process for reporting concerns and for assessing whether unauthorised deprivation of liberty is occurring. The flowchart at Annex 3 summarises the process that a supervisory body should follow when it receives a request from somebody other than the managing authority to examine whether or not there is a current unauthorised deprivation of liberty.

What action should someone take if they think a person is being deprived of their liberty without authorisation?

9.1 If the relevant person themselves, any relative, friend or carer or any other third party (such as a person carrying out an inspection visit or a member of an advocacy organisation) believes that a person is being deprived of liberty without the managing authority having applied for an authorisation, they should draw this to the attention of the managing authority. A standard letter is available for this purpose. In the first instance, they should ask the managing authority to apply for an authorisation if it wants to continue with the care regime, or to change the care regime immediately. Given the seriousness of deprivation of liberty, a managing authority must respond within a reasonable time to the request. This would normally mean within 24 hours.

9.2 It may be possible for the managing authority to resolve the matter informally with the concerned person. For example, the managing authority could discuss the case with the concerned person, and perhaps make some adjustment to the care arrangements so that concerns that a deprivation of liberty may be occurring are removed. However, if the managing authority is unable to resolve the issue with the concerned person quickly, they should submit a request for a standard authorisation to the supervisory body.

9.3   If the concerned person has raised the matter with the managing authority, and the managing authority does not apply for an authorisation within a reasonable period, the concerned person can ask the supervisory body to decide whether there is an unauthorised deprivation of liberty. They should:

- tell the supervisory body the name of the person they are concerned about and the name of the hospital or care home, and
- as far as they are able, explain why they think that the person is deprived of their liberty.

A standard letter is available for this purpose.

9.4   In such circumstances, the supervisory body must select and appoint a person who is suitable and eligible to carry out a best interests assessment to consider whether the person is deprived of liberty.

9.5   The supervisory body does not, however, need to arrange such an assessment where it appears to the supervisory body that:

- the request they have received is frivolous or vexatious (for example, where the person is very obviously not deprived of their liberty) or where a very recent assessment has been carried out and repeated requests are received, or
- the question of whether or not there is an unauthorised deprivation of liberty has already been decided, and since that decision, there has been no change of circumstances that would merit the question being considered again.

The supervisory body should record the reasons for their decisions. A standard form is available for this purpose.

9.6   The supervisory body must notify the person who raised the concern, the relevant person, the managing authority of the relevant hospital or care home and any IMCA involved:

- that it has been to asked to assess whether or not there is an unauthorised deprivation of liberty
- whether or not it has decided to commission an assessment, and
- where relevant, who has been appointed as assessor.

What happens if somebody informs the supervisory body directly that they think a person is being deprived of their liberty without authorisation?

9.7   If a person raises concerns about a potential unauthorised deprivation of liberty directly with the supervisory body, the supervisory body should immediately arrange a preliminary assessment to determine whether a deprivation of liberty is occurring. The supervisory body should then immediately notify the managing authority, rather than asking the concerned person to contact the managing authority themselves, to ask them to request a standard authorisation in respect of the person who is possibly deprived of liberty. The supervisory body should agree with the managing authority what is a reasonable period within which a standard authorisation should be requested (unless the managing authority is able to resolve the matter informally with the concerned person as described in paragraph 9.2). If the managing authority does not submit an application within the agreed period, and the matter has not been resolved informally, the supervisory body should follow the process set out in paragraphs 9.3 to 9.6 to assess whether unlawful deprivation of liberty is occurring. Even if the concerned person prefers to deal directly with the managing authority, the supervisory body should monitor what happens very closely to ensure that no unlawful deprivation of liberty may be occurring without proper action being taken.

How will the assessment of unlawful deprivation of liberty be conducted?

9.8   An assessment of whether an unlawful deprivation of liberty is occurring must be carried out within seven calendar days. Although the assessment must be completed by somebody who is suitable and eligible to carry out a best interests assessment, it is not a best interests assessment as such. The purpose of the assessment is simply to establish whether unlawful deprivation of liberty is occurring.

9.9   The person nominated to undertake the assessment must consult the managing authority of the relevant hospital or care home, and examine any relevant needs assessments and care plans to consider whether they constitute a deprivation of liberty. They should also speak to the person who raised the concern about why they believe that the relevant person is being deprived of their liberty and consult, as far as is possible, with the relevant person's family and friends. If there is nobody appropriate to consult among family and friends, they should inform the supervisory body who must arrange for an IMCA to be instructed to support and represent the person. A standard form is available for the assessor to record the outcome of their assessment.

What happens once the assessment has been conducted?

9.10   There are three possible outcomes of this assessment. The assessor may conclude that:

- the person is not being deprived of their liberty
- the person is being lawfully deprived of their liberty because authorisation exists (this, though, is an unlikely outcome since the supervisory body should already be aware if any authorization exists, thus rendering any assessment in response to a third party request unnecessary), or
- the person is being deprived of their liberty unlawfully.

9.11   The supervisory body must notify the following people of the outcome of the assessment:

- the concerned third party who made the request
- the relevant person
- the managing authority of the relevant hospital or care home, and
- any IMCA involved.

A standard form is available for this purpose.

9.12   If the outcome of the assessment is that there is an unauthorised deprivation of liberty, then the full assessment process should be completed as if a standard authorisation for deprivation of liberty had been applied for – unless the managing authority changes the care arrangements so that it is clear that there is no longer any deprivation of liberty.

9.13   If, having considered what could be done to avoid deprivation of liberty, the managing authority decides that the need to continue the deprivation of liberty is so urgent that the care regime should continue while the assessments are carried out, it must give an urgent authorisation and seek a standard authorisation within seven days. The managing authority must supply the supervisory body with the same information it would have had to include in a request for a standard authorisation.

9.14   If the concerned person does not accept the outcome of their request for assessment, they can apply to the Court of Protection to hear their case. See chapter 10 for more details of the role of the Court of Protection.

10.   WHAT IS THE COURT OF PROTECTION AND WHEN CAN PEOPLE APPLY TO IT?

To comply with Article 5(4) of the European Convention on Human Rights, anybody deprived of their liberty in accordance with the safeguards described in this Code of Practice is entitled to the right of speedy access to a court that can review the lawfulness of their deprivation of liberty. The Court of Protection, established by the Mental Capacity Act 2005, is the court for this purpose. Chapter 8 of the main Code provides more details on its role, powers and responsibilities.

When can people apply to the Court of Protection about the deprivation of liberty safeguards and who can apply?

Applying before an authorisation is given

10.1   The relevant person, or someone acting on their behalf, may make an application to the Court of Protection before a decision has been reached on an application for authorisation to deprive a person of their liberty. This might be to ask the court to declare whether the relevant person has capacity, or whether an act done or proposed to be done in relation to that person is lawful (this may include whether or not the act is or would be in the best interests of the relevant person). It is up to the Court of Protection to decide whether or not to consider such an application in advance of the decision on authorisation.

Applying after an authorisation has been given

10.2   Once a standard authorisation has been given, the relevant person ortheir representative has the right to apply to the Court of Protection to determine any question relating to the following matters:

- whether the relevant person meets one or more of the qualifying requirements for deprivation of liberty
- the period for which the standard authorisation is to be in force
- the purpose for which the standard authorisation is given, or
- the conditions subject to which the standard authorisation is given.

10.3   Where an urgent authorisation has been given, the relevant person or certain persons acting on their behalf, such as a donee or deputy, has the right to apply to the Court of Protection to determine any question relating to the following matters:

- whether the urgent authorisation should have been given
- the period for which the urgent authorisation is to be in force, or
- the purpose for which the urgent authorisation has been given.

10.4   Where a standard or urgent authorisation has been given, any other person may also apply to the Court of Protection for permission to take the relevant person's case to court to determine whether an authorisation should have been given. However, the Court of Protection has discretion to decide whether or not to consider an application from these people.

10.5   Wherever possible, concerns about the deprivation of liberty should be resolved informally or through the relevant supervisory body's or managing authority's complaints procedure, rather than through the Court of Protection. Chapter 15 of the main Code ('What are the best ways to settle disagreements and disputes about issues covered in the Act?') contains general guidance on how to settle disputes about issues covered in the Mental Capacity Act 2005. The review processes covered in chapter 8 of this Code also provide a way of resolving disputes or concerns, as explained in that chapter.

10.6   The aim should be to limit applications to the Court of Protection to cases that genuinely need to be referred to the court. However, with deprivation of liberty at stake, people should not be discouraged from making an application to the Court of Protection if it proves impossible to resolve concerns satisfactorily through other routes in a timely manner.

How should people apply to the Court of Protection?

10.7   Guidance on the court's procedures, including how to make an application, is given in the Court of Protection Rules and Practice Directions issued by the court.[11]

10.8   The following people have an automatic right of access to the Court of Protection and do not have to obtain permission from the court to make an application:

- a person who lacks, or is alleged to lack, capacity in relation to a specific decision or action
- the donor of a Lasting Power of Attorney to whom an application relates, or their donee
- a deputy who has been appointed by the court to act for the person concerned
- a person named in an existing court order[12] to which the application relates, and
- the person appointed by the supervisory body as the relevant person's representative.

10.9   All other applicants must obtain the permission of the court before making an application. (See section 50 of the Mental Capacity Act 2005, as amended.) This can be done by completing the appropriate application form.

What orders can the Court of Protection make?

10.10   The court may make an order:

- varying or terminating a standard or urgent authorisation, or
- directing the supervisory body (in the case of a standard authorisation) or the managing authority (in the case of an urgent authorisation) to vary or terminate the authorisation.

What is the role of the Court of Protection in respect of people lacking capacity who are deprived of their liberty in settings other than hospitals or care homes?

10.11   The deprivation of liberty safeguards relate only to circumstances where a person is deprived of their liberty in a hospital or care home. Depriving a person who lacks capacity to consent to the arrangements made for their care or treatment of their liberty in other settings (for example in a person's own home, in supported living arrangements other than in care homes or in a day centre) will only be lawful

---

[11] There will usually be a fee for applications to the court. Details of the fees charged by the court and the circumstances in which fees may be waived or remitted are available from the Office of the Public Guardian (http://www.publicguardian.gov.uk/)

[12] Examples of existing court orders include orders appointing a deputy or declarations made by the court in relation to treatment issues.

following an order of the Court of Protection on a best interests personal welfare matter (see paragraph 6.51 of the main Code).

10.12   In such a case, application to the Court of Protection should be made before deprivation of liberty begins. A Court of Protection order will then itself provide a legal basis for the deprivation of liberty. A separate deprivation of liberty authorisation under the processes set out in this Code will not be required.

Is legal aid available to support applications to the Court of Protection in deprivation of liberty safeguards cases?

10.13   Legal aid will be available both for advice and representation before the Court of Protection.

11.   HOW WILL THE SAFEGUARDS BE MONITORED?

The deprivation of a person's liberty is a significant issue. The deprivation of liberty safeguards are designed to ensure that a person who lacks capacity to consent to the arrangements made for their care or treatment is suitably protected against arbitrary detention. In order to provide reassurance that the safeguards processes are being correctly operated, it is important for there to be an effective mechanism for monitoring the implementation of the safeguards.

Who will monitor the safeguards?

11.1   Regulations[13] will confer the responsibility for the inspection process of the operation of the deprivation of liberty safeguards in England on a new regulator, the Care Quality Commission, bringing together functions from the existing Commission for Social Care Inspection, the Healthcare Commission and the Mental Health Act Commission. The new body will be established during 2008, subject to the passage of the relevant legislation through Parliament, and is expected to be fully operational by 2009/10 in line with the deprivation of liberty safeguards coming into force.

11.2   In Wales, the functions of monitoring the operation of the deprivation of liberty safeguards will fall to Welsh Ministers. These functions will be performed on their behalf by Healthcare Inspectorate Wales and the Care and Social Services Inspectorate Wales.

What will the inspection bodies do and what powers will they have?

11.3   The inspection bodies for care homes and hospitals will be expected to:

- monitor the manner in which the deprivation of liberty safeguards are being operated by:
  - visiting hospitals and care homes in accordance with their existing visiting programme
  - interviewing people accommodated in hospitals and care homes to the extent that they consider it necessary to do so, and
  - requiring the production of, and inspecting, relevant records relating to the care or treatment of people accommodated in hospitals and care homes

---

[13] Draft regulations for England will be consulted upon later. Welsh Ministers are currently considering how they will use their regulation-making powers for Wales.

- report annually, summarising their activity and their findings about the operation of the deprivation of liberty safeguards. In England this report will be made
to the Secretary of State for Health, and in Wales the report will be made to the
Welsh Ministers. It will be for each monitoring body to decide whether there
should be a deprivation of liberty safeguards specific report or whether the report
should form part of a wider report on the monitoring body's activities.

11.4   The inspection bodies will have the power to require supervisory bodies and managing authorities of hospitals or care homes to disclose information to them.

11.5   The inspection process will not cover the revisiting of individual assessments
(other than by way of a limited amount of sampling).

11.6   The inspection process will not constitute an alternative review or appeal process.
However, if the inspection body comes across a case where they believe deprivation
of liberty may be occurring without an authorisation, they should inform the
supervisory body in the same way as any other third party may do.

11.7   The inspection bodies will look at the deprivation of liberty protocols and procedures in place within managing authorities and supervisory bodies. The aim is to
use a small amount of sampling to evaluate the effect of these protocols and procedures on individual cases. Monitoring should take place at a time when the monitoring body is visiting the care home or in-patient setting as part of routine
operations, not as an exception.

11.8   Supervisory bodies and managing authorities should keep their protocols and procedures under review and supervisory bodies should assess the nature of the authorisations they are giving in light of their local population. This information may
be relevant to policy decisions about commissioning care and support services.

CHECKLISTS

Key points for care homes and hospitals (managing authorities)

- Managing authorities need to adapt their care planning processes to incorporate consideration of whether a person has capacity to consent to the services which are to be
provided and whether their actions are likely to result in a deprivation of liberty.
- A managing authority must not, except in an urgent situation, deprive a person of liberty unless a standard authorisation has been given by the supervisory body for that
specific situation, and remains in force.
- It is up to the managing authority to request such authorisation and implement the
outcomes.
- Authorisation should be obtained from the supervisory body in advance of the deprivation of liberty, except in circumstances considered to be so urgent that the deprivation
of liberty needs to begin immediately. In such cases, authorisation must be obtained
within seven calendar days of the start of the deprivation of liberty.
- A managing authority must ensure that they comply with any conditions attached to the
authorisation.
- A managing authority should monitor whether the relevant person's representative
maintains regular contact with the person.
- Authorisation of deprivation of liberty should only be sought if it is genuinely necessary
for a person to be deprived of liberty in their best interests in order to keep them safe.
It is not necessary to apply for authorisations for all admissions to hospitals and care
homes simply because the person concerned lacks capacity to decide whether to be
admitted.

Key points for local authorities and NHS bodies (supervisory bodies)

- Supervisory bodies will receive applications from managing authorities for standard authorisations of deprivation of liberty. Deprivation of liberty cannot lawfully begin until the supervisory body has given authorisation, or the managing authority has itself given an urgent authorisation.
- Before an authorisation for deprivation of liberty may be given, the supervisory body must have obtained written assessments of the relevant person in order to ensure that they meet the qualifying requirements (including that the deprivation of liberty is necessary to protect them from harm and will be in their best interests).
- Supervisory bodies will need to ensure that sufficient assessors are available to meet the needs of their area and that these assessors have the skills, qualifications, experience and training to perform the function.
- Authorisation may not be given unless all the qualifying requirements are met.
- In giving authorisation, the supervisory body must specify its duration, which may not exceed 12 months and may not be for longer than recommended by the best interests assessor. Deprivation of liberty should not continue for longer than is necessary.
- The supervisory body may attach conditions to the authorisation if it considers it appropriate to do so.
- The supervisory body must give notice of its decision in writing to specified people, and notify others.
- The supervisory body must appoint a relevant person's representative to represent the interests of every person for whom they give a standard authorisation for deprivation of liberty.
- When an authorisation is in force, the relevant person, the relevant person's representative and any IMCA representing the individual have a right at any time to request that the supervisory body reviews the authorisation.

Key points for managing authorities and supervisory bodies

In addition to the above, both managing authorities and supervisory bodies should be aware of the following key points:

- An authorisation may last for a maximum period of 12 months.
- Anyone engaged in caring for the person, anyone named by them as a person to consult, and anyone with an interest in the person's welfare must be consulted in decision-making.
- Before the current authorisation expires, the managing authority may seek a fresh authorisation for up to another 12 months, provided it is established, on the basis of further assessment, that the requirements continue to be met.
- The authorisation should be reviewed, and if appropriate revoked, before it expires if there has been a significant change in the person's circumstances. To this end, the managing authority will be required to ensure that the continued deprivation of liberty of a person remains necessary in the best interests of the person.
- A decision to deprive a person of liberty may be challenged by the relevant person, or by the relevant person's representative, by an application to the Court of Protection. However, managing authorities and supervisory bodies should always be prepared to try to resolve disputes locally and informally. No one should be forced to apply to the court because of failure or unwillingness on the part of a managing authority or supervisory body to engage in constructive discussion.
- If the court is asked to decide on a case where there is a question about whether deprivation of liberty is lawful or should continue to be authorised, the managing authority can continue with its current care regime where it is necessary:

- for the purpose of giving the person life-sustaining treatment, or
- to prevent a serious deterioration in their condition while the court makes its decision.

■ The complete process of assessing and authorising deprivation of liberty should be clearly recorded, and regularly monitored and audited, as part of an organisation's governance structure.
■ Management information should be recorded and retained, and used to measure the effectiveness of the deprivation of liberty processes. This information will also need to be shared with the inspection bodies.

LASTING POWERS OF ATTORNEY – PRACTICE NOTE

Legal policy

24 September 2007

Status of this practice note

Practice notes are issued by the Law Society as a professional body for the benefit of its members. They represent the Law Society's view of good practice in a particular area. They are not intended to be the only standard, nor do they necessarily provide a defence to complaints of misconduct or of inadequate professional service. Solicitors are not required to follow them.

They do not constitute legal advice and, while care has been taken to ensure that they are accurate, up to date and useful, the Law Society will not accept any legal liability in relation to them.

1. INTRODUCTION

1.1 The following practice note is intended to assist solicitors in advising clients who wish to draw up a Lasting Power of Attorney (LPA), as well as solicitors who are acting as an attorney under an LPA. It also covers the ongoing arrangements for Enduring Powers of Attorney (EPA).

1.2 LPAs were created by the Mental Capacity Act 2005 (MCA 2005). The MCA 2005 covers England and Wales and provides a statutory framework for adults who lack capacity to make decisions for themselves, or who have capacity and want to make preparations for a time when they may lack capacity in the future. Everyone working with and caring for adults who lack capacity, including solicitors, health and social care professionals, families and other carers, must comply with the MCA 2005.

1.3 The Mental Capacity Act 2005 Code of Practice (the Code of Practice) supports the MCA 2005 and provides guidance and information to all those working under the legislation. Certain categories of people are required to have regard to the relevant guidance in the Code of Practice, including the attorney under an LPA and anyone acting in a professional capacity – such as a solicitor.

1.4 An LPA enables a person aged 18 or over (the donor) to appoint another person or persons (their donee or attorney) to act on their behalf, following the principles of the MCA 2005, if they subsequently lose capacity. This has replaced the EPA as the type of power of attorney that can operate after a person ceases to have capacity. Unlike EPAs, a person can choose to delegate decisions affecting their personal welfare – including healthcare and medical treatment decisions – as well as decisions concerning their property and financial matters to their attorney(s).

1.5 Any solicitor intending to give advice about an LPA or act as an attorney under an LPA must be aware of the provisions in the MCA 2005 and the Code of Practice.

Solicitors should also be familiar with the relevant guidance produced by the Office of the Public Guardian.

1.6   The MCA 2005 repealed the Enduring Powers of Attorney Act 1985 and it is no longer possible to create a new EPA. However, EPAs which were executed before the MCA 2005 came into force on 1 October 2007, whether they have been registered or not, will continue to be valid. The result is that for the foreseeable future there will be two distinct regimes catering for those who lack capacity. EPAs are considered in section 14 of this practice note.

1.7   Ordinary Powers of Attorney can still be created but they will become invalid if the donor loses capacity to make decisions within the scope of the particular power of attorney.

2.   GENERAL OVERVIEW: PROPERTY AND AFFAIRS LPAS AND PERSONAL WELFARE LPAS

2.1   Property and affairs LPAs can be used to appoint attorneys to make a range of decisions – including the buying and selling of property, operating a bank account, dealing with tax affairs, and claiming benefits (see paragraphs 7.32–7.39 of the Code of Practice). A personal welfare LPA might authorise the attorney(s) to make decisions about where the donor should live, consenting to or refusing medical treatment on the donor's behalf, and day-to-day care, including diet and dress (see paragraphs 7.21–7.31 of the Code of Practice).

2.2   There are two separate prescribed forms, one for a property and affairs LPA and one for a personal welfare LPA. Both forms are divided into three parts:

PART A – Donor's statement
This part of the form includes: the donor's details; details of the attorney(s) being appointed and how they are to act; details of the persons to be notified when an application to register the LPA is made; and a number of statements which must be confirmed by the donor.

PART B – Certificate provider's statement
This part must be completed by an independent third party (known as the certificate provider) after he or she has discussed the contents of the LPA with the donor without, if possible, anyone else present. The certificate provider must confirm that in his or her opinion: the donor understands the purpose and scope of the LPA; no undue pressure or fraud is involved in the decision to make the LPA; and there is nothing else to prevent the LPA being created.

Part C – Attorney's statement
Each attorney named in Part A of the LPA must complete a separate statement confirming that he or she understands their duties and obligations as an attorney.

Both LPA forms also include the prescribed information which must be read by the donor, certificate provider and attorney(s).

2.3   The LPA must be registered with the Office of the Public Guardian before it can be used. A property and affairs LPA can be used while the donor still has capacity, unless it specifies that it can't, while a personal welfare LPA can only be used when the donor no longer has capacity to make the particular decision affecting their health or personal welfare.

3.   WHO IS THE CLIENT?: PROPERTY AND AFFAIRS LPAS AND PERSONAL WELFARE LPAS

3.1   Where a solicitor is instructed to prepare an LPA, the donor is the client.

A solicitor should not accept instructions where he or she has reasonable grounds to suspect that those instructions have been given by a client under duress or undue influence – until the solicitor is satisfied that they represent the client's wishes (Solicitors Regulation Authority, Solicitors' Code of Conduct 2007, Rule 2.01).

When asked to prepare an LPA on written instructions alone, a solicitor should always consider carefully whether these instructions are sufficient, or whether he or she should see the client to discuss them.

3.2   A solicitor should be instructed by the client. Where instructions for the prepara-tion of an LPA are given by someone other than the client, a solicitor should not proceed without checking that the client agrees with the instructions given (ibid, Rule 2.01). In any case of doubt the solicitor should attempt the see the client alone or take other appropriate steps, both to confirm the instructions with the donor personally after offering appropriate advice, and also to ensure that the donor has the necessary capacity to make the power (see section 4 below).

3.3   Once the LPA has been registered and the donor lacks the capacity to make the rel-evant decision, instructions may be accepted from the attorney(s) but the solicitor continues to owe his or her duties to the donor. In the case of a property and affairs LPA being used as an Ordinary Power of Attorney, instructions may be accepted from the attorney(s) after the LPA has been registered.

4.   CAPACITY TO MAKE AN LPA: PROPERTY AND AFFAIRS LPAS AND PERSONAL WELFARE LPAS

4.1   The solicitor should be satisfied that, on the balance of probabilities, the donor has the mental capacity to make an LPA. Some LPAs may be made when the donor is already losing capacity and consequently he or she could be unaware of the implications of their actions and more likely to be vulnerable to exploitation.

4.2   A valid LPA must include a certificate completed by an independent third party known as the certificate provider (who can be a solicitor) confirming that

'the donor understands the purpose of the LPA and the scope of the authority under it' and that no fraud or undue pressure is being used (see sections 6.5 and 6.6 below).

4.3   Section 2 of the MCA 2005 provides the core definition of incapacity that applies to decisions made under this Act:

'. . . a person lacks capacity in relation to a matter if at the material time he is unable to make a decision for himself in relation to the matter, because of an impairment of, or a disturbance in the functioning of, the mind or brain.'

4.4   There is however no specific definition or test of what level of capacity is required to make an LPA. It is assumed that a court if asked to make a declaration on this point would use the principles of the MCA 2005 as a starting point – and in particular the following principles:

'A person must be assumed to have capacity unless it is established that he lacks capacity.' (s.1(3))

'A person is not to be treated as unable to make a decision merely because he makes an unwise decision.' (s.1(4))

It is likely that the courts will also consider established case law on EPAs.

4.5   If there is any doubt about the donor's capacity, a medical opinion should be considered. In cases where the LPA is being contested, for example by a family member, it may be necessary for the matter to be decided by the Court of Protection if the dispute cannot be resolved by other means. See chapter 15 of the Code of Practice for guidance on resolving disputes and disagreements.

4.6   Solicitors assessing a client's capacity to create an LPA should refer to sections 2 and 3 of the MCA 2005 and chapters 2–4 of the Code of Practice. Further guidance can be obtained from Assessment of Mental Capacity: Guidance for doctors and lawyers issued by the Law Society and the British Medical Association.

5.   RISK OF ABUSE: PROPERTY AND AFFAIRS LPAS AND PERSONAL WELFARE LPAS

5.1   When advising clients of the benefits of LPAs, the solicitor should also inform them of the risks of abuse, particularly the risk that the attorney(s) could misuse the power. Throughout this practice note, an attempt has been made to identify possible risk areas and to suggest ways of preventing abuse, which the solicitor should discuss with the donor (see for example sections 6.14 and 13 below). Written information for clients on both the benefits and risks of LPAs, whether in a brochure or correspondence, may also be helpful.

5.2   During the initial stages of advising a client, the solicitor should consider that there may be circumstances when an LPA may not be appropriate, and a later application to the Court of Protection for deputyship, with the oversight of the Office of the Public Guardian, may be preferable. This may be advisable, for example:

■ where there are indications of persistent family conflicts suggesting that an LPA may be contested, or
■ where the assets are more substantial or complex than family members are accustomed to handle, or
■ in cases where litigation may lead to a substantial award of damages for personal injury.

6.   TAKING INSTRUCTIONS FOR AN LPA: PROPERTY AND AFFAIRS LPAS AND PERSONAL WELFARE LPAS

The solicitor should take full and careful instructions from the donor, and ensure that the following matters, where applicable, are considered by the donor when giving instructions.

Please note that this section of the practice note covers issues common to both property and affairs LPAs and personal welfare LPAs. For issues specific to property and affairs LPAs see section 7 below. For issues specific to personal welfare LPAs see section 8 below.

6.1   **Choice of attorney(s)**
The choice of attorney(s) is clearly a personal decision for the donor, but it is important for the solicitor to advise the donor of the various options available, and to stress the need for the attorney(s) to be absolutely trustworthy (see section 5 above). The donor should be advised that the appointment of a sole attorney, whether this be for a property and affairs LPA or a personal welfare LPA, may

provide greater opportunity for abuse and exploitation than appointing more than one attorney (see section 6.2 below).

The solicitor should ask questions about the donor's relationship with the proposed attorney(s) including any replacement attorney (see section 6.11 below) and, depending on which type of LPA is being created, whether the attorney(s) has the skills required to manage the donor's property and financial affairs or to make decisions about the donor's personal welfare. The donor should also consider the suitability of appointing a family member or someone independent of the family, or a combination of both.

If the donor wishes to create both a property and affairs LPA and a personal welfare LPA then they should consider whether they wish to appoint different attorneys for each LPA.

6.2   More than one attorney

Where more than one attorney is to be appointed for a property and affairs LPA or for a personal welfare LPA, they must be appointed to act 'jointly', 'jointly and severally', or 'jointly in respect of some matters and jointly and severally in respect of others' (s.10(4), MCA 2005). The LPA forms do not use these legal terms but instead refer to attorneys working 'together', 'together and independently' or 'together in respect of some matters and together and independently in respect of others'.

One of these alternatives must be ticked by the donor in the prescribed form. If more than one attorney has been appointed and it is not stated whether they are appointed jointly or jointly and severally, then when the LPA is registered they will be treated on the basis that they are appointed jointly. This default position however does not extend to EPAs and failure to specify on the prescribed form whether the attorneys should act jointly or jointly and severally invalidates the instrument as an enduring power.

The differences between a 'joint' and 'joint and several' appointment should be explained to the donor.

- In addition to the explanatory information in the prescribed form to the effect that joint attorneys must all act together and cannot act separately, the donor should be advised that an LPA with joint attorneys will terminate if any one of the attorneys: disclaims; dies; becomes bankrupt (this only applies to property and affairs LPAs); or lacks capacity. It will also terminate with the dissolution or annulment of the marriage or civil partnership between the donor and the attorney (unless it specifically states otherwise in the LPA). However, joint appointments may provide a safeguard against possible abuse, since each attorney will be able to oversee the actions of the other(s).
- Similarly, in addition to the explanatory information in the prescribed form to the effect that joint and several attorneys can all act together but can also act independently if they wish, the donor should be advised that, where there is a joint and several appointment, the LPA will not be automatically terminated by the: disclaimer; death; bankruptcy; dissolution/annulment of marriage/civil partnership; or incapacity of one attorney. In these circumstances the LPA would continue and the remaining attorney(s) can continue to act.

See also section 6.11 below regarding replacement attorneys.

(i)   The donor may have to make difficult choices as to which member(s) of the family or others to appoint as his or her attorney. This may partly depend on the type of LPA being created and the different types of decisions that can be taken under a property and affairs LPA and a personal welfare LPA. It is possible to allow some flexibility, for example the donor may wish to appoint:

(ii)   A family member and a professional to act jointly and severally with, perhaps, the family member dealing with day-to-day matters, and the professional dealing with more complex decisions.

However the donor and the attorneys should consider the potential for conflict that could arise from this arrangement. A professional attorney will have a higher duty of care and usually will be remunerated, and this could create tension between the attorneys: for example, if the professional wishes to take a cautious approach and perhaps seek a court declaration or medical opinion – which would result in costs being incurred.

(iii)   His or her spouse or civil partner as attorney, with their adult child(ren) appointed as replacement attorneys (see section 6.11 below) should the spouse or civil partner die or become incapacitated. Alternatively, the donor could appoint everyone to act jointly and severally, with an informal understanding that the children will not act while the spouse or civil partner is able to do so.

(iv)   His or her three adult children as attorneys to act jointly and severally, with a proviso that anything done under the power should be done by at least two of them. This could be achieved by careful wording of the LPA document.

(v)   His or her three adult children to act in respect of some decisions as joint attorneys and as joint and several attorneys in respect of other decisions. However the donor should consider that this arrangement may be confusing for the attorneys and third parties, such as banks and healthcare professionals, and could prove difficult to administer in practice. The prescribed form includes a large text box for the donor to explain how this should work and it is important that this is drafted clearly and precisely to avoid confusion.

Solicitors should be aware that time may be needed to explain the benefits and drawbacks of requiring specific decision to be made jointly, jointly and severally, or jointly in respect of some matters and jointly and severally in respect of others as it may be confusing for the donor and attorneys.

6.3   General or limited authority

The donor must be clear whether the LPA is to be a general power, giving the attorney(s) authority to manage all the donor's property and affairs or to make all personal welfare decisions, or whether any restrictions and/or conditions are to be placed on their power (see also sections 7.1 and 8.1 below). Any restrictions and/or conditions should be carefully drafted and clearly set out in the prescribed form.

In relation to a personal welfare LPA the solicitor should emphasise that a general power will include all healthcare decisions, except: giving or refusing consent to life-sustaining treatment (unless the LPA document expressly authorises this); where the donor has made a valid advance decision; refusing or consenting to medical treatment for mental disorder where the donor is detained under the Mental Health Act 1983; or where the donor is subject to guardianship under the Mental Health Act 1983 (see sections 8.1–8.3 below).

The solicitor should also discuss with the donor what arrangements should be made for the management of those property and financial affairs or personal welfare decisions that are not covered by the LPA. The donor should be advised that if they leave a 'gap' it may be necessary for the Court of Protection to intervene and appoint a deputy – or for other people to make 'best interests' decisions on the donor's behalf under section 4 of the MCA 2005. Where the donor wishes to give discretionary powers to their attorney(s) – such as discretionary investment management powers or authority to disclose the donor's will if necessary, then these should be included in the 'restrictions and/or conditions' section of the prescribed form.

6.4   Guidance

As well as placing restrictions and/or conditions on the attorney(s), the prescribed forms for both property and affairs LPAs and personal welfare LPAs also allows guidance to be provided to the attorney(s) when making decisions in the donor's best interests. Any restrictions or conditions if deemed valid will be binding on the attorney(s) whereas the guidance, although clearly pertinent, is not binding on the attorney(s). It is important that a solicitor advising the client makes clear the distinction and difference between restrictions/conditions and guidance. It will also be important that the drafting of this section of the prescribed form reflects this distinction and that the language used does not suggest that any guidance is binding.

The solicitor could also explain to the donor and the attorney(s) that because guidance is not binding on the attorney(s) a situation could occur where even after taking into account the guidance in the LPA, the attorney(s) might still come to the conclusion that it would be in the overall best interests of the donor – having used the 'best interests checklist' set out in section 4 of the MCA 2005 – to do something different from that suggested in the guidance section of the LPA. However it should also be stressed that the guidance would be relevant in assessing the best interests of the donor.

6.5   The certificate

A valid LPA – whether it be a property LPA and affairs or personal welfare LPA – must include a certificate completed by an independent third party known as the 'certificate provider' confirming that in his or her opinion:

- the donor understands the purpose of the LPA and the scope of the authority under it;
- no fraud or undue pressure is being used to induce the donor to create the LPA; and
- there is nothing else that would prevent the LPA being created.

The donor must be clear that choosing a suitable certificate provider is an important safeguard and without their statement the LPA cannot be registered and used. The choice of certificate provider is clearly a personal decision for the donor, but it is important for the solicitor to advise the donor of the various options available. It may also be important to advise on the quality of the options available – for example where a family dispute may lead to the certificate being challenged, the solicitor may need to advise on the most suitable choice of certificate provider, taking into account the individual circumstances of the case (see also section 6.6 below).

There are two types of certificate provider: a knowledge-based certificate provider who is someone who knows the donor personally and has done so for the previous two years – or a skills-based certificate provider who has the relevant professional skills and expertise to certify the LPA. A skills-based certificate provider must fit into one of the following categories:

- a registered healthcare professional (including GP)
- a registered social worker
- a barrister, solicitor or advocate
- an Independent Mental Capacity Advocate
- someone who considers they have the relevant professional skills and expertise to be a certificate provider

A certificate provider cannot be:

- under 18
- a member of the donor's or attorney's family
- a business partner or paid employee of the donor or attorney(s)
- an attorney appointed in this or another LPA or any EPA made by the donor

- the owner, director, manager or an employee of a care home in which the donor lives or their family member or partner
- an employee of a trust corporation appointed as attorney in this LPA (this only applies to someone certifying a property and affairs LPA)

A person who signs an LPA as a certificate provider will also need to be able to demonstrate:

- they understand what is involved in making an LPA
- they understand the effect of making an LPA
- that they have the skills to assess that the donor understands what an LPA is and what is involved in making an LPA
- that they can assess that the donor also understands the contents of their LPA and what powers they are giving to the attorney(s)
- that they can verify that the donor is under no undue pressure by anyone to make the LPA
- that they have sufficient knowledge and understanding of the donor's affairs to able to be satisfied that no fraud was involved in the creation of the LPA

The donor should also be advised of the benefits of appointing a certificate provider who has the appropriate knowledge or experience of issues relating to mental capacity and in particular the provisions of the MCA 2005 including the core principles.

6.6   Solicitors providing a certificate
6.6.1   A skills-based certificate
Solicitors are one of the professional groups specifically listed in the prescribed form as capable of providing a skills-based certificate. The role of the certificate provider is a vital safeguard against the abuse of vulnerable adults and it is crucial that anyone agreeing to be a certificate provider fully comprehends the significance. A solicitor must ensure that they do not fall into one of the categories of people who cannot provide a certificate (see section 6.5 above). In particular, a solicitor cannot provide a certificate if he or she is:

- a business partner or paid employee of the attorney; or
- an attorney appointed under any LPA or EPA made by the donor. This would mean for example that a solicitor could not provide a certificate if in the past the client executed an EPA in favour of the solicitor, even though the EPA was never used or registered and was perhaps even revoked.

However a solicitor could be the certificate provider if he or she is a business partner or paid employee of the attorney of an EPA or another LPA.

A solicitor signing such a certificate will need to have taken a suitably detailed personal and financial history from the donor, and if necessary insist on seeing them on their own, to satisfy the requirements concerning undue pressure and fraud. This may have both time and costs implications.

The solicitor should also be aware that if, for example, a family member objects to the LPA at the point when it is registered then the certificate provider may be called to the Court of Protection to account for their opinion.

The certificate provider's duty of care is to the donor. In cases where the attorney is a solicitor and another solicitor from a different firm is to act as the certificate provider, then the client will be a client of both solicitors and separate client care letters should be sent by each.

6.6.2   A knowledge-based certificate
A solicitor may be approached by clients, former clients, friends or acquaintances asking them to provide a certificate on the basis that the solicitor has known them

personally over the last two years. It is recommended that a solicitor should exercise caution before providing a certificate on this basis.

According to the LPA notes 'personally' means that that the donor is known to the certificate provider as more than a passing acquaintance. In addition the certificate provider cannot be related to the donor or to any of the attorneys – and must not fall into any of the other categories of people who cannot provide a certificate (see section 6.5 above).

A knowledge-based certificate provider has the same responsibilities as a skills-based certificate provider, for example they must discuss the contents of the LPA with the donor without, if possible, anyone else present. He or she must also confirm that: the donor understands the LPA they are making and that they are not being forced into making it (see section 6.5 above). In order to do this a detailed personal and financial history may need to be taken from the donor – however a fee cannot be charged for providing a knowledge-based certificate.

A knowledge-based certificate provider may also be called to the Court of Protection to account for their opinion if, for example, a family member objects to the LPA. The Court may impose a higher standard of care and skill if the knowledge-based certificate has been provided by a solicitor and the donor is their client or former client.

6.6.3   Referral arrangements

A solicitor may wish to refer a client to another solicitor in order to provide the certificate – or to provide a second certificate where the donor decides not to include anyone to be notified (see section 6.8 below). The solicitor must however ensure that there is no breach of rule 1 of the Solicitor's Code of Conduct or any other applicable provision of these rules.

6.7   **Registration of the LPA**

The donor must understand that the LPA cannot be used until it has been registered with the Office of the Public Guardian. The LPA can be registered anytime after it has been completed and signed by all those who are required to sign (see section 10 below).

It is important that the solicitor clearly explains to the donor the implications of not registering the LPA shortly after it has been made. For example if the donor of an unregistered personal welfare LPA faced a medical emergency their attorney(s) would not be authorised to act on their behalf until the power is registered, which at the very least would take between five and six weeks (see section 11.5 below).

Once registered, a property and affairs LPA can be used while the donor still has capacity, unless it specifies that it can't, while a personal welfare LPA can only be used when the donor no longer has capacity to make the particular decision affecting their healthcare or personal welfare.

6.8   **Notification of intention to register the LPA**

Solicitors should explain to the donor that they can name up to five people to be notified when an application to register the LPA is made. An attorney of the LPA cannot be specified as a named person. If the donor decides not to include anyone to be notified then a second person will be needed to provide an additional certificate (see section 6.5 above). The donor should be clear that including a named person is an important safeguard because if he or she lacks capacity at the time of registration they will be relying on these people to raise concerns.

The donor should be advised to make their named person(s) aware of the LPA, whether it is a property and affairs LPA or personal welfare LPA and what is required of them when an application to register is made, before the LPA is completed. This will ensure that where a person does not wish to take on this role, someone else can be appointed. The donor may also want to tell his or her named person(s) who they have appointed as attorney(s). This will allow them to raise any queries or concerns with the donor and may reduce unfounded objections being made when the application to register the LPA is made, avoiding extra costs and lengthy delays to the process.

6.9 The LPA Register and disclosure of information

The Office of the Public Guardian is responsible for maintaining a register of all LPAs – as well as a register of EPAs and of court appointed deputies. Clients should be aware that once their LPA is registered certain basic information about their LPA will be available to anyone who applies to search the register and pays a fee – such as:

- the donor's name (and previous names) and date of birth;
- whether it is a property and affairs LPA or a personal welfare LPA but not the contents;
- the date the LPA was created and registered;
- the name(s) of the attorney(s);
- the nature of the appointment (joint or joint and several); and
- whether the LPA contains any restrictions, conditions or guidance but not the details of the restrictions, conditions or guidance; and
- whether or not a note has been attached to the LPA, but no details of what the note says.

Clients should also be aware that anyone can also, on application and payment of a fee, undertake a 'second tier search' for further information about their LPA. This will require the applicant to explain in greater detail to the Office of the Public Guardian why they require the information and to demonstrate that the request is in the donor's best interests.

6.10 Delegation by the attorney

It is a basic principle of the law of agency that an attorney cannot delegate his or her authority. Alternatively, this could be expressed as a duty on the part of an agent to perform his or her functions personally. Such a duty is imposed because of the discretion and trust reposed in the attorney(s) by the donor.

There are exceptions to this general rule and, like any other agent, an attorney acting under an LPA has an implied power in certain circumstances to delegate:

- any functions which are of a purely administrative nature and do not involve or require the exercise of discretion;
- any functions which the donor would not expect the attorney to attend to personally; or
- through necessity or unforeseen circumstances;

Any wider power of delegation must be expressly provided for in the LPA itself.

6.11 Substitute appointments

Whilst an LPA cannot provide for an attorney to make a substitute or successor appointment, it can appoint a replacement attorney to act if one or any of the attorneys cannot continue to act.

If the donor of a property and affairs LPA or a personal welfare LPA wants to appoint a replacement attorney he or she can appoint as many replacements as they like. It will be important that the donor sets out clearly how they are to be appointed and how they are to act, for example solely or jointly (see section 6.2 above). If the donor has more than one attorney, he or she can specify who the replacement attorney can replace and who they cannot replace. If no restrictions are put in place by the donor then the first replacement will replace the first attorney who needs replacing. The donor can only appoint a replacement attorney for the original attorneys.

The solicitor should advise that when considering whether a replacement attorney should be appointed, it is important that the donor chooses someone they know well and trust to make decisions in their best interests in the same way as would be the case for their first choice attorney(s).

6.12   Solicitor-attorneys

Where a solicitor is appointed as the attorney of an LPA it is recommended that their current terms and conditions of business (including charging rates and the frequency of billing) are discussed with and approved by the donor at the time of granting the power.

The prescribed forms for both property and affairs LPAs and personal welfare LPAs include a section where the donor can confirm that they have agreed for their attorney to be paid a fee and set out the arrangements which have been agreed. It is recommended that any decisions about payments should be recorded with the appropriate level of detail necessary.

A solicitor acting as an attorney of a property and affairs LPA must be aware of their money laundering compliance requirements (see section 7.7 below).

Further information on making decisions under an LPA and the implications for solicitors is provided in section 12 below.

6.13   Medical evidence

It may be worth asking the donor to give advance consent in writing authorising the solicitor to contact the donor's GP or any other medical practitioner if the need for medical evidence should arise at a later date to assess whether the donor has capacity to make a particular decision.

6.14   Safeguards against abuse

Solicitors should discuss with the donor appropriate measures to safeguard against the power being misused or exploited. This could include notifying other family members or friends (who are not named on the prescribed form as someone to be notified) of the existence of the power, why they have chosen the attorney(s) and how the donor intends it to be used. This may help to guard against the possibility of abuse by an attorney and may also reduce the risk of conflict between family members at a later stage.

The solicitor could also consider offering an auditing service, by inserting a clause into the power requiring the attorney to produce to the solicitor, on a specified date each year, an account of his/her actions as attorney during the last 12 months. If the attorney failed to render a satisfactory account, the solicitor could contact the Office of the Public Guardian (see section 13 below). Again a charging procedure for this auditing service must be agreed with the donor in advance.

7.   TAKING INSTRUCTIONS – PROPERTY AND AFFAIRS LPAS

This section of the practice note covers issues specific to property and affairs LPAs. For issues common to both property and affairs LPAs and personal welfare LPAs see section 6 above. For issues specific to personal welfare LPAs see section 8 below.

7.1   **Scope**
A registered property and affairs LPA can be used whilst the donor retains capacity as an Ordinary Power of Attorney. Alternatively the LPA can specify that it can only be used when the donor no longer has capacity.

The LPA could enable the attorney(s) to take a wide range of actions such as – the buying, selling, or mortgaging of property or dealing with the donor's tax affairs, or claiming benefits on behalf of the donor (paragraph 7.36 of the Code of Practice provides a more extensive list). The donor can limit the power of the LPA by specifying that the LPA only grants authority to the attorney(s) to execute certain specific tasks – or it can include a general authority to act (see section 6.3 above).

7.2   **Gifts**
Section 12 of the MCA 2005 gives the attorney(s) limited authority to make gifts of the donor's money or property:

- The recipient of the gift must be either an individual who is related to or connected with the donor (including the attorney(s)), or a charity to which the donor actually made gifts or might be expected to make gifts if he or she had capacity.
- The timing of the gift must occur within the prescribed parameters. A gift to charity can be made at any time of the year, but a gift to an individual must be of a seasonal nature, or made on the occasion of a birth or marriage/civil partnership, or on the anniversary of a birth or marriage/civil partnership.
- The value of the gift must be not unreasonable having regard to all the circumstances and in particular the size of the donor's estate.

The donor cannot confer wider authority on the attorney than that specified in section 12, but it is open to the donor to restrict or exclude the authority which would otherwise be available to the attorney(s) under that subsection. This should be considered by the donor, since improper gifting in relation to EPAs was a widespread form of abuse in attorneyship. The donor may wish to specify in the power the circumstances in which the attorney(s) may make gifts of money or property.

The Court of Protection can authorise the attorney(s) to act so as to benefit themselves or others, otherwise than in accordance with section 12, provided that there are no restrictions in the LPA itself and the court is satisfied that this would be in the donor's best interests (s.23(4), MCA 2005).

Solicitors must also take account of Rule 3.04 of the Solicitors' Code of Conduct 2007 concerning gifts from clients.

7.3   **Investment business**
Unless the power is restricted to exclude investments as defined by the Financial Services and Markets Act 2000, the attorney(s) may need to consider the investment business implications of his/her appointment. A solicitor who is appointed as the attorney under an LPA is likely to be conducting investment business and if so, will need to be authorised under the Financial Services and Markets Act 2000. In addition, the solicitor will need to consider whether the Solicitors' Financial Services (Scope) Rules 2001 apply.

7.4   **Trusteeships held by the donor**
The solicitor should ask whether the donor holds:

- any trusteeships; and
- any property jointly with others.

Under the Trustee Delegation Act 1999 the general rule is that any trustee functions delegated to an attorney (whether under an ordinary power or an enduring/lasting power) must comply with the provisions of section 25 of the Trustee Act 1925, as amended by the 1999 Act.

However, section 1(1) of the 1999 Act provides an exception to this general rule. An attorney can exercise a trustee function of the donor if it relates to land, or the capital proceeds or income from land, in which the donor has a beneficial interest. This is, of course, subject to any provision to the contrary contained in the trust instrument or the power of attorney itself.

7.5   The donor's property and affairs

It may be helpful for solicitors to record and retain information relating to the donor's property and affairs, even where they are not to be appointed as an attorney themselves. The Law Society's Personal Assets Log, which is sometimes used when taking will-drafting instructions, could be suitably adapted for this purpose. In addition, there are certain requirements under the Solicitors' Financial Services (Conduct of Business) Rules 2001 where solicitors safeguard and administer documents of title to investments e.g. share certificates.

7.6.   Disclosure of the donor's will

Solicitors are under a duty to keep their clients' affairs confidential (Solicitors Regulation Authority, Solicitors' Code of Conduct 2007, Rule 4). However, the attorney(s) may need to know about the contents of the donor's will in order to avoid acting contrary to the testamentary intentions of the donor (for example, by the sale of an asset specifically bequeathed, when other assets that fell into residue could be disposed of instead).

The question of disclosure of the donor's will should be discussed at the time of making the LPA, and instructions should be obtained as to whether disclosure is denied, or the circumstances in which it is permitted – which should be incorporated into the LPA. For example, the donor may agree that the solicitor can disclose the contents of the will to the attorney(s), but only if the solicitor thinks that disclosure of the will is necessary or expedient for the proper performance of the attorney's functions. This type of discretionary power would need to be included in section 6 of the prescribed form under 'restrictions and/or conditions'.

The attorney(s) also has a common law duty to keep the donor's affairs (including the contents of a will) confidential.

7.7   Money laundering

The preparation of an LPA for clients does not itself constitute a 'financial transaction' for the purposes of the Money Laundering Regulations 2007. However, a solicitor acting for an attorney, or as an attorney themselves, is likely to be undertaking 'relevant business'. Guidance is available to help solicitors understand their money laundering compliance requirements (see www.moneylaundering.lawsociety.org.uk) and help may also be obtained from the Law Society's Practice Advice Service.

7.8   Statutory wills

An attorney cannot execute a will on the donor's behalf because the Wills Act 1837 requires a will to be signed by the testator personally or by someone in his or her presence and at his or her direction.

Where a person lacks testamentary capacity, the Court of Protection can order the execution of a statutory will on his or her behalf. The Court's will-making jurisdiction is conferred by section 18 of the MCA 2005.

8.   TAKING INSTRUCTIONS – PERSONAL WELFARE LPAS

This section of the practice note covers issues specific to personal welfare LPAs. For issues common to both property and affairs LPAs and personal welfare LPAs see section 6 above. For issues specific to property and affairs LPAs see section 7 above.

8.1   Scope

Solicitors should make their clients aware that a registered personal welfare LPA only becomes operative once the donor has lost capacity to make the specific personal welfare decision which is required at the material time. Clients should also be informed that, unless the donor adds restrictions or conditions, the attorney(s) of a personal welfare LPA will have authority to make all personal welfare, including healthcare, decisions, except for:

- decisions relating to life sustaining treatment, unless the LPA expressly authorises this (see section 8.2 below);
- where the donor has made a valid advance decision to refuse the proposed treatment (see section 8.3.1 below);
- consent or refusal of medical treatment for a mental disorder where the donor is detained under the Mental Health Act 1983; and
- decisions about where a donor subject to guardianship under the Mental Health Act 1983 is to reside, nor any other decisions which conflict with those of a guardian.

Although the MCA 2005 does not define 'personal welfare', chapter 7 of the Code of Practice gives some guidance and suggests that a personal welfare LPA might include decisions about:

- where the donor should live and who they should live with
- the donor's day-to-day care, including diet and dress
- who the donor may have contact with
- consenting to or refusing medical examination and treatment on the donor's behalf
- arrangements needed for the donor to be given medical, dental or optical treatment
- assessments for and provision of community care services
- whether the donor should take part in social activities, leisure activities, education or training
- the donor's personal correspondence and papers
- rights of access to personal information about the donor
- complaints about the donor's care and treatment

A personal welfare LPA could be a very powerful document because of the wide ranging decisions that could be made on behalf of the donor and therefore clients need to make an informed decision about the scope of the power. Clients should be encouraged to consider this carefully and may want to discuss the scope of authority with their prospective attorney(s) and, where appropriate, their GP or any relevant health or social care professionals.

The personal welfare LPA could of course be limited to specific decisions and it may be helpful to create a checklist of questions and a range of suggested clauses which the client might wish to include when creating a personal welfare LPA. For example, a clause could be included to restrict the power to accommodate the donor at another location without consulting specific members of the family.

Clients can also set out their wishes and preferences for personal care, including healthcare, which are not legally binding but which their attorney(s) will take into account in deciding best interests by completing the guidance for attorney(s) at section 8 of the prescribed form (see also section 6.4 above).

Possible points for the client to consider when deciding whether to make a personal welfare LPA could include:

- do you want your attorney to be able to decide where you will live?
- do you want the attorney to be able to decide whether other members of your family or your friends can visit you?
- do you want your attorney to be able to make all types of health and medical decisions on your behalf including giving consent to have an operation?
- do you want your attorney to decide whether or not you receive life sustaining treatment?
- do you want to limit the scope of the decision-making and leave decisions to the medical team treating you at that time?

Solicitors will need to exercise care in drafting so that the client's instructions are clear to any health or social care professional who inquires as to the scope of the attorney(s) authority under the LPA.

8.2   Life sustaining treatment

Decisions to give or refuse life sustaining treatment can only be made by the attorney(s) if the donor has specifically confirmed this in section 6 of the prescribed form – in the presence of a witness. The witness must be over 18 and cannot be the attorney (see also section 10.2 below).

Life sustaining treatment is defined in section 4(10) of the MCA 2005 as 'treatment which in the view of a person providing healthcare for the person concerned is necessary to sustain life'. Further guidance is provided in paragraphs 5.29–5.36 of the Code of Practice.

8.3   Relationship with advance decisions and advance statements
8.3.1   Advance decisions

Some clients may ask about making a 'living will' – which is described in the MCA 2005 as an 'advance decision' – and whether they should make an advance decision rather than a personal welfare LPA or vice versa.

An advance decision allows a person with capacity to refuse specified medical treatment at a point in the future when he or she lacks the capacity to consent to that treatment. If an advance decision is both valid and applicable in the particular circumstances, it has the same effect as a contemporaneous refusal of treatment by a person with capacity. This means that the treatment specified in the decision cannot lawfully be given. Further information and guidance is provided in chapter 9 of the Code of Practice.

It will be prudent for the solicitor to be prepared with perhaps an information sheet about the differences between a personal welfare LPA and an advance decision together with more detailed clauses which might be included in a personal welfare LPA.

Possible points for the client to consider when choosing between an advance decision and personal welfare LPA include:

- A personal welfare LPA allows a donor to give general authority for the attorney(s) to consent or refuse life sustaining treatment where Option A, section 6, of the prescribed form is completed. Unlike an advance decision it is not necessary to specify a particular treatment. This of course requires a high degree of trust by the donor towards the attorney(s).

- Under a personal welfare LPA the attorney(s) must make decisions in the donor's best interests – and follow the checklist in section 4 of the MCA 2005 which includes consultation with those close to the person who lacks capacity. Where an advance decision is being followed the best interests principle does not apply – and it must be carried out even if the healthcare professionals think it goes against the person's best interests.
- There are stringent requirements for completing and registering an LPA – whereas the MCA 2005 does not impose any particular formalities concerning advance decisions except for decisions relating to life sustaining treatment. This relative informality may be attractive for some clients but it can also lead to uncertainty over whether an advance decision exists or is valid.

Clients should be made aware that where a person makes a personal welfare LPA (regardless of whether it provides authority to consent/refuse life sustaining treatment) and subsequently makes an advance decision, which is valid and applicable in the circumstances, the advance decision takes priority. An LPA made after an advance decision will make the advance decision invalid, if the LPA gives the attorney authority to make decisions about the same treatment.

The solicitor should also advise that the law relating to euthanasia and assisted suicide has not been changed, and the introduction of personal welfare LPAs and statutory advance decisions does not legitimise euthanasia.

8.3.2   Advance statements
The client should also be aware that the MCA 2005 provides for creation of an 'advance statement', which enables a person with capacity to set out their wishes and feelings in writing about the care and treatment they would like to receive should they lose capacity in the future. Advance statements are not legally binding but should be taken into account by decision makers – including attorney(s) – when making best interest decisions under section 4 of the MCA 2005. A client could decide to make an advance statement as a separate exercise to providing guidance for their attorney in section 8 of the prescribed form.

Further information on advance statements is provided in paragraphs 5.37–5.45 of the Code of Practice

9.   DRAWING UP THE LPA – PROPERTY AND AFFAIRS LPAS AND PERSONAL WELFARE LPAS

9.1   The prescribed forms
The LPA must be in the form prescribed by the Lasting Powers of Attorney, Enduring Powers of Attorney and Public Guardian Regulations 2007 (SI 2007 No. 1253) (the regulations)

Solicitors should be aware that new regulations may be issued in the future and ensure that the LPA is in the form prescribed by the regulations in force at the time of execution by the donor.

Where the instrument differs from the prescribed form in an immaterial respect, the Office of the Public Guardian may treat it as sufficient (Schedule 1, Part 1, Para. 3(1) to the MCA 2005).

The Court of Protection has the power to treat an LPA as valid even if it is not in the prescribed form, if it is satisfied 'that the persons executing the instrument intended it to create a lasting power of attorney' (Schedule 1, Part 1, Para. 3(2) to the MCA 2005).

9.2   **Completing the form**

Solicitors should be aware that the prescribed LPA forms are significantly longer than the previous EPA forms – the property and affairs LPA is 25 pages long and the personal welfare LPA is 24 pages long – and this will have implications for both the time spent with clients and the cost.

The donor of the LPA must have read (or have read to him or her) the prescribed information about the LPA and will need to sign a statement in the LPA to that effect. Any solicitor preparing an LPA should consider the time and cost implications of this obligation.

It may take time to provide the client with the appropriate information for him or her to decide whether they want to 'tick the box' to dispense with the provision to notify anyone when the power is registered (see section 6.8 above).

The attorney(s) will have to file a statement confirming that they have read the relevant information, or part of it, and understand the duties imposed on the attorney of an LPA with particular reference to section 1 of the MCA 2005 (the principles) and the duty to have regard to the Code of Practice. This again may have cost implications as explaining these provisions could take time – and simply sending or arranging for the attorney(s) to sign the document is unlikely to be sufficient.

There is space on the prescribed form to provide details of two attorneys. Where it is intended to appoint more than two attorneys, their details may be included on a separate sheet which must be attached securely at the back of the LPA. Where more than two attorneys are to be appointed, details of the first two attorneys should be given in the main document, followed by the words

'and (see additional names on attached sheet)'

and the details given on a sheet to be attached to the main document marked clearly 'Part A, section 3: Names of additional attorneys.' This should be also be signed and dated.

The prescribed form also contains space to appoint a replacement attorney (see section 6.11 above). If the donor wishes to appoint more than one replacement attorney, the above paragraph applies in that the details given on the separate sheet must be attached to the main document and marked clearly.

An LPA may be refused registration because of a defect in the form or the wording of the instrument. In some cases, registration may be possible after the filing of further evidence to overcome the defect. Solicitors who have assisted a donor in drawing up an LPA which is subsequently refused registration because of a defect that is material may be liable for the additional costs of deputyship, since at that point the donor may not have the capacity to execute a new LPA.

10.   EXECUTING THE LPA – PROPERTY AND AFFAIRS LPAS AND PERSONAL WELFARE LPAS

10.1   The regulations require that an LPA must be executed by the donor, the certificate provider and the attorney(s) in the following sequence:

- the donor must read (or have read to him/her) the prescribed information;
- the donor must complete and sign (in the presence of a witness) Part A of the document;
- the certificate provider(s) must complete Part B and sign it;
- the attorney(s) must read (or have read to him/her) the prescribed information;

- the attorney(s) must complete and sign (in the presence of a witness) Part C of the document.

This sequence is necessary because the certificate provider must confirm that they have read Part A and because the attorney(s) cannot accept a power which has not yet been conferred.

Execution by the donor, certificate provider and attorney(s) need not take place simultaneously – however the regulations require that each stage outlined above must take place as soon as reasonably practicable after the previous stage.

(Note, that section 6 of a personal welfare LPA must be signed and witnessed simultaneously, see section 8.2 above.)

10.2   Execution by the donor and the attorney(s) must take place in the presence of a witness (but not necessarily the same witness) who must sign Part A or Part C of the prescribed form, as the case may be, and give his or her full name and address.

There are various restrictions as to who can act as a witness, and in particular:

- the witness must be at least 18
- the donor and attorney must not witness each other's signature;
- it is not advisable for the donor's spouse or civil partner to witness his or her signature – this is because of the rules of evidence relating to compellability; and
- at common law, a blind person cannot witness another person's signature.

10.3   If the donor is physically disabled and unable to sign, he or she may leave a mark. Alternatively, the donor may authorise another person to sign the LPA at his or her direction, in which case it must be signed by that person in the presence of the donor and two witnesses.

Similarly an attorney who is unable to sign can leave a mark or authorise another person to sign at his or her direction in the presence of two witnesses.

A certificate provider can leave a mark but cannot authorise someone to sign at his or her direction.

11.   THE REGISTRATION PROCESS – PROPERTY AND AFFAIRS LPAS AND PERSONAL WELFARE LPAS

11.1   A key difference between LPAs and the old EPA procedure is that an LPA is not created unless the instrument conferring authority has been registered with the Office of the Public Guardian. So even if the LPA has been correctly filled in and properly signed it will have no authority until it is registered.

11.2   There is no time limit for making the application to register the LPA (however see section 6.7 above). The application can be made by the donor, or all the attorneys if the LPA is a joint power, or if a joint and several power by any of the attorneys.

11.3   The donor or the attorney(s) making the application to register must give notice to everyone named by the donor in the LPA as a person who should be notified, of an application to register using the prescribed form of notice (LPA001).

It may be helpful for the donor or attorney(s) to send the notice with an accompanying letter explaining the circumstances because, in the absence of such an explanation, there may be cause for concern. Giving an appropriate explanation and information at this stage may prevent the application from becoming contentious.

Although there is no statutory requirement to do so, a copy of the LPA could also be sent to the named person(s), in view of the fact that one of the grounds on which they can object to registration is that the power purported to have been created by the instrument is not valid as a lasting power.

11.4   When the application to register is made by the attorney(s), the Office of the Public Guardian will notify the donor that the application has been received – using the prescribed form of notice (LPA003B). Where 'it appears there is good reason to do so' the Office of the Public Guardian will inform the donor personally.

When the application is made by the donor, the Office of the Public Guardian will notify the attorney(s) using the prescribed form of notice (LPA003A). The attorney(s) is not obliged to inform the donor of their intention to register the LPA but it is recommended that the donor should be informed either in writing or in person. This should if possible take place at the same time as the named person(s) are notified.

11.5   There is a prescribed period of 5 weeks during which objections can be raised with the Public Guardian. The grounds for objecting include:

- the LPA has been revoked
- the requirements to make an LPA have not been met
- fraud or undue pressure was used to create the LPA
- the attorney has behaved or is behaving in a way that contravenes his or her authority or is not in the best interests of the donor or proposes to behave in a way that would contravene his authority or would not be in the donor's best interests

Where there are no objections or defects, the Office of the Public Guardian must register the power within 6 weeks of the date the notices were sent to the named persons.

11.6   The donor should be told that a fee will be payable for the registration of the LPA. A separate fee will be charged for a property and affairs LPA and for a personal welfare LPA – even if they have been made by the same donor.

11.7   The registered LPA document will be stamped on every page by the Office of the Public Guardian. A copy of the instrument is retained by the Office of the Public Guardian and the original will be returned to the person(s) who applied for registration. A prescribed notice of registration is sent to the donor and the attorney(s) (LPA004).

11.8   Following registration the existence of an LPA can be proved by the original stamped instrument, an office copy or a certified copy. If there is any doubt, a third party may search the register of LPAs which is maintained by the Office of the Public Guardian (see section 6.9 above).

12.   DECISION MAKING UNDER AN LPA – PROPERTY AND AFFAIRS LPAS AND PERSONAL WELFARE LPAS

12.1   **The functional and time-specific test of incapacity and best interests**
Unlike the old EPA regime where registration demonstrates to a third party that the attorney has responsibility and the authority to make financial decisions involving the donor's assets, the MCA 2005 does not have such a readily identifiable point where the attorney(s) takes over.

This is because section 2 of the MCA 2005 sets out a 'functional and time-specific' test of incapacity, which means capacity will vary according to the particular decision to be taken at the particular time. For example, a donor may be able to make decisions about household spending but not about selling his or her home. One month later their capacity to make these decisions may have changed – either improved or become worse. This means that there will not generally be any one point where a person loses capacity to make all decisions and therefore there is no one point when the donor stops acting and the attorney(s) takes over.

Instead, the MCA 2005 sets out a joint approach where the attorney and the donor work together. The starting assumption must always be that a donor has the capacity to make a decision, unless if can be established that they lack capacity (s.1(1), MCA 2005) and a donor should not be treated as unable to make a decision unless all practical steps to help him or her to do so have been taken without success (s.1(3), MCA 2005). Further guidance is provided in chapters 2 and 3 of the Code of Practice.

Where it is established that the donor lacks the capacity to make a particular decision, section 4 of the MCA 2005 requires the attorney to act in the donor's 'best interests'. The MCA 2005 sets out a checklist of factors that should always be considered by a person deciding what is in the best interests of a person who lacks capacity. This includes, amongst other considerations, consulting, where appropriate, with the relatives, carers and others who have an interest in the donor's welfare. It also includes, where reasonably practical, permitting and encouraging the donor to participate as fully as possible or improving their ability to participate in making the decision – which could involve deferring making a decision or setting up further assistance in order to enable the donor to make a decision. This may be particularly relevant in relation to personal welfare LPAs as these will only operate where the person lacks capacity to make the decision. Further guidance on best interests is provided in chapter 5 of the Code of Practice.

The functional and time-specific test of incapacity and determining the donor's best interests under section 4 of the MCA 2005 are likely to prove challenging for solicitors acting as attorneys, and the increased cost implications for the client as well as for firms will need to be considered.

12.2 Duties and responsibilities of attorneys

An attorney has a duty to act within the scope of his or her powers set out in the LPA – but the authority conferred by the LPA is also subject to the provisions of the MCA 2005, in particular section 1 (the principles) and section 4 (best interests). The MCA 2005 also places a specific obligation on attorneys and anyone acting in a professional capacity to have regard to the Code of Practice.

Attorneys also have a duty:

■ of care
■ to carry out the donor's instructions
■ not to take advantage of the position of the attorney
■ not to delegate unless authorised to do so
■ of good faith
■ of confidentiality
■ to comply with directions of the Court of Protection
■ not to disclaim without complying with the relevant guidance

In relation to property and affairs LPA there is also a duty to:

■ keep accounts
■ keep the donor's money and property separate from their own

Solicitors acting as attorneys under an LPA are also required to display a higher standard of care and skill. According to paragraph 7.59 of the Code:

'If attorneys are being paid for their services, they should demonstrate a higher degree of care and skill. Attorneys who undertake their duties in the course of their professional work (such as solicitors or corporate trustees) must display professional competence and abide by their own professional rules and standards.' Further guidance on the duties and responsibilities of attorneys is provided in Chapter 7 of the Code of Practice.

12.3   **Relationship between property and affairs and personal welfare LPAs**
The attorney(s) has a duty to act within the extent of his powers, so a property and affairs LPA does not give the attorney(s) power to make personal welfare decisions – and vice versa. An attorney will however be expected, if practical and appropriate, to consult with the attorney(s) of any other LPA made by the donor, whenever his or her best interests are being considered (s.4(7)(c), MCA 2005 and paragraph 5.55 of the Code of Practice). It is also likely that EPA attorney(s) would also be consulted (see section 14.5 below).

Attorneys should also be aware that the demarcation between decisions made under a property and affairs LPA and a personal welfare LPA may not always be clear. For instance the choice of nursing home may have both welfare and financial implications for the donor. It will be important in these types of cases for the attorneys to consult each other and seek to reach agreement. If there are conflicts then an application could be made to the Court of Protection to resolve the issue but this will in itself have cost implications and should only be considered as a last resort.

12.4   **Disclaiming an appointment**
An attorney or proposed attorney can disclaim his or her appointment by completing the prescribed form (LPA005) which must be sent to the donor and copied to the Office of the Public Guardian and any other attorney(s) appointed under the power.

12.5   **Support for attorneys**
Section 22 of the MCA 2005 provides that the Court of Protection can determine questions about the validity and revocation of LPAs (both registered and unregistered), and can direct that the instrument should not be registered, or where it has been registered and the donor lacks capacity, that it should be revoked.

However, the Court should not be seen as being available to 'hold the hand' of the attorney, who should in normal circumstances be able to act in the best interests of the donor, taking advice where necessary from a solicitor or other professional adviser. It should be noted that, although the Court may interpret the terms of an LPA or give directions as to its exercise, it does not have power to extend or amend the terms of the LPA as granted by the donor.

13.   WHERE ABUSE IS SUSPECTED – PROPERTY AND AFFAIRS LPAS AND PERSONAL WELFARE LPAS

If solicitors suspect that an attorney may be misusing an LPA or acting dishonestly they should contact the Office of the Public Guardian immediately. They should also contact the police if they suspect physical or sexual abuse, theft or serious fraud. It may also be necessary – particularly in cases involving personal welfare LPAs – to refer the matter to local adult protection authorities. Further guidance is provided in paragraphs 7.69–7.74 and Chapter 14 of the Code of Practice.

14.   ENDURING POWERS OF ATTORNEY

14.1   The Enduring Powers of Attorney Act 1985 was repealed by the MCA 2005, but it is reintroduced almost in its entirety, in Schedule 4 to the MCA 2005. The amendments take account of the changes to the Court of Protection and the new role of the Office of the Public Guardian in the registration process. It is not possible to make new EPAs, although the operation of existing EPAs made before 1 October 2007 will fall under Schedule 4 to the MCA 2005.

14.2   Schedule 4 paragraph 1(1) to the MCA 2005 specifically excludes the principles of the MCA 2005 applying to the EPA attorney. However under the law of agency, the EPA attorney has certain duties towards the donor (these are listed in section 12.2 above and further guidance is provided in paragraphs 7.58–7.68 of the Code of Practice).

14.3   According to paragraph 7.5 of the Code of Practice, EPA attorneys do not have a legal duty to have regard to the Code – but the Code's guidance will still be helpful to them.

A solicitor acting as an EPA attorney may still be considered to have a duty to have regard to the Code of Practice since he or she will be acting in a 'professional capacity' for the purposes of section 42(4)(e) of the MCA 2005. However, Schedule 4 of the MCA 2005 retains the EPA concept that there is one point in time when a person is deemed to lack capacity and that the power must be registered with the Office of the Public Guardian when the attorney believes that the donor is becoming or has become incapable of managing his or her financial affairs. This is different to the concept of incapacity used in the rest of the MCA 2005 which is both function and time-specific (see section 12.1 above). It would appear to be the case that the effect of this is that the Code will selectively apply to the professional EPA attorney as there will not be a requirement to assess capacity on each and every decision being made.

14.4   Under an EPA the attorney is under a common law duty to act in the donor's best interests. This does not apply where the client has capacity and the EPA is unregistered and being used as an Ordinary Power of Attorney – although the normal duties under the law of agency apply.

14.5   The attorney of an EPA is not specifically named as a person to be consulted when a decision maker is making a best interests determination under section 4 of the MCA 2005. However it is likely that in the majority of cases any EPA attorney will be considered to be a person who is 'interested in his welfare' for the purposes of section 4(7)(b) of the MCA 2005, and therefore would be consulted. This appears to be confirmed in paragraph 5.55 of the Code of Practice.

14.6   The Office of the Public Guardian is responsible for maintaining a register of EPAs which can be searched by any person on payment of a fee (see section 6.9 above).

15.   FURTHER ADVICE

Solicitors may obtain further help on matters relating to professional ethics from the Solicitors Regulation Authority's Professional Ethics helpline (0870 606 2577) and on practice issues from the Law Society's Practice Advice Service (0870 606 2522).

Information and advice (but not legal advice) can also be obtained from the Office of the Public Guardian (0845 330 2900).

INDEX